Entheogens and the Development of Culture

Also by John A. Rush

Spiritual Tattoo: A Cultural History of Tattooing, Piercing, Scarification, Branding, and Implants

The Twelve Gates: A Spiritual Passage Through the Egyptian Books of the Dead

Failed God: Fractured Myth in a Fragile World

The Mushroom in Christian Art: The Identity of Jesus in the Development of Christianity

Entheogens and the Development of Culture

The Anthropology and Neurobiology of Ecstatic Experience

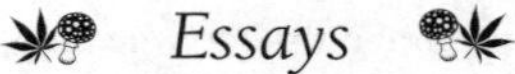

Essays

John A. Rush, PhD, Editor

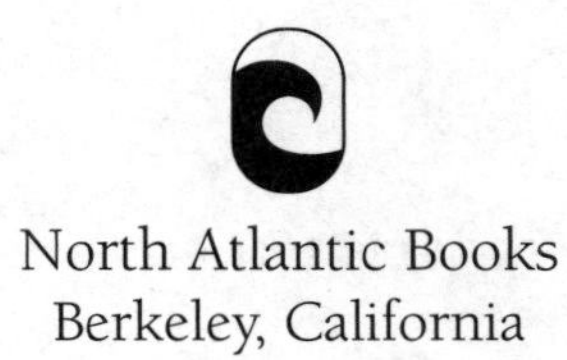

North Atlantic Books
Berkeley, California

Published by

North Atlantic Books
P.O. Box 12327
Berkeley, California 94712

Cover art by Arik Roper
Cover design by Suzanne Albertson
Book design by Aaron Welton

Printed in the United States of America

Entheogens and the Development of Culture: The Anthropology and Neurobiology of Ecstatic Experience is sponsored by the Society for the Study of Native Arts and Sciences, a nonprofit educational corporation whose goals are to develop an educational and cross-cultural perspective linking various scientific, social, and artistic fields; to nurture a holistic view of arts, sciences, humanities, and healing; and to publish and distribute literature on the relationship of mind, body, and nature.

North Atlantic Books' publications are available through most bookstores. For further information, visit our website at www.northatlanticbooks.com or call 800-733-3000.

Library of Congress Cataloging-in-Publication Data

Entheogens and the development of culture : the anthropology and neurobiology of ecstatic experience : Essays / John A. Rush, PhD, editor. pages cm Includes index.

ISBN 978-1-58394-600-8 — ISBN 1-58394-600-4

1. Ecstasy—Social aspects. 2. Ecstasy—Physiological aspects. 3. Hallucinogenic plants—Physiological aspects. 4. Hallucinogenic drugs and religious experience. 5. Hallucinogenic mushrooms—Physiological aspects. 6. Neurobiology. 7. Psychopharmacology. I. Rush, John A.

GN472.4.E67 2013
306.4—dc23

2013016095

1 2 3 4 5 6 7 8 9 United 18 17 16 15 14 13

Printed on recycled paper

Contents

Preface		ix
Chapter 1	***Mind-Altering Substances, Decision Making, and Culture Building*** John A. Rush	1
Chapter 2	***Altered Consciousness and Drugs in Human Evolution*** Michael Winkelman	23
Chapter 3	***Cannabis and the Hebrew Bible*** Chris Bennett and Neil McQueen	51
Chapter 4	***Hildegard of Bingen: Unveiling the Secrets of a Medieval High Priestess and Visionary*** Gerrit J. Keizer	85
Chapter 5	***The Milk of the Goat Heiðrun: An Investigation into the Sacramental Use of Psychoactive Milk and Meat*** Alan Piper	211

Chapter 6 ***The Significance of Pharmacological and Biological Indicators in Identifying Historical Uses of Amanita muscaria***
Kevin Feeney 279

Chapter 7 ***Enter the Jaguar***
Mike Jay 319

Chapter 8 ***Ravens' Bread and Other Manifestations of Fly Agaric in Classical and Biblical Literature***
Edzard Klapp 333

Chapter 9 ***Democracy and the Dionysian Agenda***
Carl A. P. Ruck 343

Chapter 10 ***Virgil's Edible Tables***
Carl A. P. Ruck and Robert Larner 387

Chapter 11 ***The Genesis of a Mushroom/Venus Religion in Mesoamerica***
Carl de Borhegyi with Suzanne de Borhegyi-Forest 451

Chapter 12 ***Sacred Mushrooms and Man: Diversity and Traditions in the World, with Special Reference to Psilocybe***
Gastón Guzmán 485

Chapter 13 ***The Soma Function in Jung's Analytical Psychology***
Dan Merkur 519

Chapter 14 ***R. Gordon Wasson: The Man, the Legend, the Myth: Beginning a New History of Magic Mushrooms, Ethnomycology, and the Psychedelic Revolution***
Jan Irvin 565

Index 617

Preface

Reconstructing our historical past is a difficult task at best, for even when written records are available, interpretations can be challenged and usually are. Prehistory offers artifacts of various types including stone tools, megalithic structures, rock art, burials, and other features that provide a glimpse into a deeper past. But there is always missing information, leading to opinion and speculation, which, when offered in print, sometimes becomes immovable "fact," especially when it enters mainstream academia. For example, Archbishop of the Church of Ireland James Ussher (158–1656), through biblical interpretation and celestial mathematics, tells us the universe was created 4004 BCE (Before Current Era), and this seems to be the approximate date chosen by historians and many archaeologists for the beginnings of what we term "civilization"—despite archaeological finds, available for many, many decades, indicating that elements defining civilization (writing, megalithic architecture, calendars, math, astronomy, etc.) were in place by at least 10,000 BCE (see Schoch 2012 and Coppens 2013 for more-recent discussions of the particular archaeological sites in question). Science is supposed to be self-correcting.

The situation is made even more problematic when information available among, for example, the archaeological remains is overlooked because it seems out of place or "insignificant" according to the bias of the researcher (see Mayor 2011), or because of political correctness, so as not to "offend" a particular group; presenting the data, the evidence is somehow offensive. For example, we find in Well's (2008) publication a compelling case for rethinking conditions in the Dark Ages (fifth through eighth centuries CE). This is a bold position, which essentially questions Church history. He comes close to understanding the significance of specific artifacts (gold bees) connected to important burials, and the story of why Napoleon selected the bee as his symbol of rule rather than the fleur-de-lis of his predecessors. The fleur-de-lis is the mushroom tree, and bees are symbolic of the shaman and mind-altering substances, or their effects (to get a "buzz"; see Ruck et al. 2007). As Pearson (2002) pointed out, burial goods are usually chosen by the individual prior to death or by those left behind, and they tell an incomplete story. When ethnographic data is included, for example the symbol of the bee, it opens to a more complete interpretation as to purpose. Thus, Napoleon chose the bee not simply to be different from his predecessors, but because of its spiritual nature or connection to that ultimate authority legitimizing his rule, as the fleur-de-lis had. The right to rule throughout European history has always been connected to mythical charters, to deities or fairies—for example, Melusina. Thus the question is, How does one connect to that "right to rule," the deity? Entheogens. Wells was possibly unaware of this connection, thus his interpretation is bold but incomplete.

As another recent example, Dhavalikar (2007) questions why phallic stones found at various Indus Valley sites, especially in a more recent Kalibangan excavation, were left out of the analysis, thus obscuring the rituals surrounding these objects. As Dhavalikar states (2007: 126, note 9):

> It is rather surprising that the Kalibangan excavation was done in 1960–1970, and it is only after thirty years that the Siva-linga is reported. How such an object of crucial importance remained unnoticed is an enigma, which will not go unchallenged.

Quality interpretations and decisions for action require as much detail as possible, and when information is left out or distorted, interpretations suffer, and poor decisions are the result. The recent and tragic events at Benghazi, Libya, are a prime example.

Mind-altering substances are usually left out of the culture-building paradigm, either through following incomplete data been tried, and so on. But, with all decisions there are consequences, often negative if a decision for action is ineffective or worse. The laws of thermodynamics apply, for bad decisions represent energy loss for the system, and too many bad decisions can lead to system death through entropy. All one has to do is observe world politics and you see the process in action. Thus consequences must be considered, even unforeseen consequences.

Human survival relies on instinct, experience, continued observation of nature, and making reasonable decisions. Intelligence, by the way, is not necessarily the best indicator of a person's ability to make decisions that do not cause more problems. Age, at least for our ancient ancestors, equaled experience and wisdom, and the reasoning here is simple, that is, if you reached this age you must have done something right. Thus decisions were often left to older members of the group, male and female, and especially ancient ancestors long deceased. These ancestors could be contacted in times of need, when difficult decisions needed to be made, or perhaps just for a reassuring visit. By what means were these visits made, especially when new information or advice was crucial at the moment? Meditation? Sensual deprivation? Dream? Pain? Illness? Fever? All have played their part in reaching the "other side," the ancestors. There is a method, however, that is tried and true, dependable, and available at a moment's notice, and this is the use of mind-altering plants and fungi, of which there is an amazing variety including combinations of plants and fungi.

Surely not all decisions require a consult with ancestors, but the ancestors were there, "on call." Ancestors acted as psychological protection against the hardships of life and the reality of death, and provided plants and fungi so the living could be aided in their survival, through continued contact with wise ancestors. The use of plants and fungi as a conduit to the ancestors, eventually the gods, is an age-old tradition recognized by at least the Upper Paleolithic (c. 33 KYA) and stretching perhaps millions of years into the distant past (see chapter 2). One reason for contacting ancestors and gods through shamans, soothsayers, and priests was for obtaining new information, or at the very least deciding on the best of the options at hand. The use of plants and fungi in the decision-making process was never abandoned and can be followed right up to modern times. Any discussion, then, of the decision-making processes of our ancestors, and thus an understanding of ourselves and how we reached this place in time, cannot be divorced from our emotions, the chemicals that support them, and the use of mind-altering substances. But even as recently as 2008 (see Boyer and Bergstrum 2008) we see little mention in mainstream academia of mind-altering substances in the evolution of religion, let alone the use of these substances to make decisions affecting thousands if not millions of people (see Rush 2008, 2011). However, this is beginning to change as more and more academics and researchers are recognizing the importance of mind-altering substances in the evolution of culture.

Symbols and Social Organization

Humans organize around words or symbols that express shared experiences, things we can talk about and imagine in making decisions now and in the future. Out of these discussions and imagining emerge our stories and our myths, and these direct social action. Sources for information input are, in a way, limited to our senses, the people we talk to, the authors we read, what newscast we listen to, and so on. In former times all one had was his or her senses, and group interpretation of experiences coming through this sensory array. New information might be required, and this meant leaving the bounded territory of the village or countryside and going to another place, the place of the gods. These are hero's journeys, as Joseph Campbell (1949) pointed out many years ago. People make these voyages spontaneously every day, for example, during a near-death experience, during a fever, after intense pain (see Rush 2005, 2007), and so on, but these are rather unpredictable modes of transport to the other side. In my opinion, one of the first sciences for our kind was botany, or the knowledge of plants and fungi. A species that migrates, as we did and do, would continually come across new plants and fungi, and they would be tested (bioassay) at the very least as foodstuffs. But over time our ancestors learned about the metabolic effects of plants and fungi. Specialists would develop around these plants and create stories about how they were encountered, or perhaps about the ancestors providing them. Other plants made you vomit, helped with stomachaches, or even expelled parasites. Some plants and fungi were lethal, but out of this emerged herbal/medical science (see Johns 1999). Our species, early on, perhaps beginning with *Homo erectus* of 1.8 MYA (Million Years Ago), had to collect data on plants just as they would on the nature and behavior of dangerous predators, in particular the leopard and other big felines. The substances, and there are many of them as well as many combinations, would be used in ritual performance, healing ceremonies, or when the chief or shaman had to make a decision and needed new information. This new information, perhaps coming from another dimension, perhaps a visit to our genetic code, or simply a reshuffling of present information, helped the shaman make decisions.

The decisions we make lead us to complex behavioral sets, and what we decide to do can be consciously and unconsciously motivated. The human being, however, is a small-group decision-making animal, a small pack animal, with a will to life, who engages in sex and the food quest to propagate and maintain that life, and who needs acceptance and recognition from group members. Our ancient prehistoric ancestors, living on the edge as they did, required cooperation within the group, at times between groups, and cooperation from nature, if you will, through ritual process and by communing with ancestors. Praying to Jesus to save the car industry, as was the case a few years ago in Detroit, is no different than asking Uncle Bob, deceased now many years, to instruct the animals to return after a long, cold winter.

Behavioral sets surround our daily lives, from how to find a restroom when out shopping to dealing with life-threatening situations, for example, avoiding an oncoming car, or avoiding world catastrophe by appeasing the gods through human sacrifice, as in the Mayan and Aztec traditions. So the decisions we make are wrapped around beliefs about ourselves and the world around us, accumulated over generations during a process anthropologists call "enculturation," which is really a form of brainwashing or setting the individual on the "correct" cultural path. The ancient Greeks paved the way in Western thought by questioning some of this "enculturation," that is, magic and supernatural agencies. It was believed, through a discovery of laws of nature, regularity of nature, and causation in a physical and mechanical sense, that they might then actually know something. This could be accomplished with tools of logical argument and mathematics, used systematically, along with demonstration, and proof. This model includes the practice of rational criticism and debate, along with the presence and encouragement of debates between contrasting schools of thought, and a general climate that tolerates questioning and skepticism.

This process, ideally of course, is designed to rid us of magical thinking and install a filter for recognizing reason and excluding nonsense. We have not been very successful with this, because this process relies heavily on what we know about how the universe "really works," and we cannot be sure; there are always questions, and questions must have answers. The belief in another world full of magical helpers is held by a few billion people on the planet probably because the existence of such a realm cannot be falsified, at least with our current knowledge base. This, then, has led many people past and present to believe that contact with ancestors or magical beings is possible under the right circumstances, some spontaneous, as with illness, fever, dreams, and so on, and purposely through methods of ritual and prayer, deprivation and pain, trance states, dance, and mind-altering substances. The most reliable method of communion is via the latter option, that is, mind-altering substances.

Social and Psychological Models

All problem-solving involves a combination of interconnected conscious and unconscious stored information and motivations for remembering or choosing certain information over other considerations. Archaeologists (see Mithen 1990) have approached this question in the past, and a model has emerged wherein the archaeologist participates in the ancient's mind. The following was offered by Mithen some years ago but is still useful today.

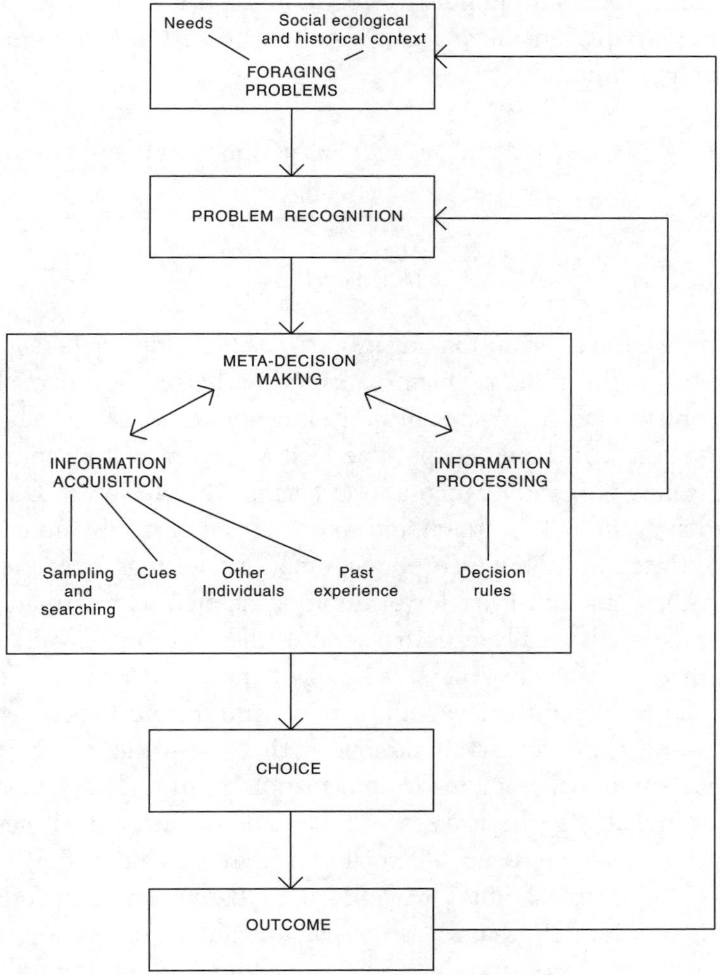

The Mithen Model (1990: 23)

Mithen presents a thoughtful model, which is verifiable using almost any social context, from a local departmental meeting to decisions made by the federal government. Mithen, however, does not reference mind-altering substances, although divination processers are discussed. This model fits well with our small-group nature.

Coming from neurolinguistic programming (see Dilitz et al 1980), we can perhaps generalize about individual decision making in the following manner:

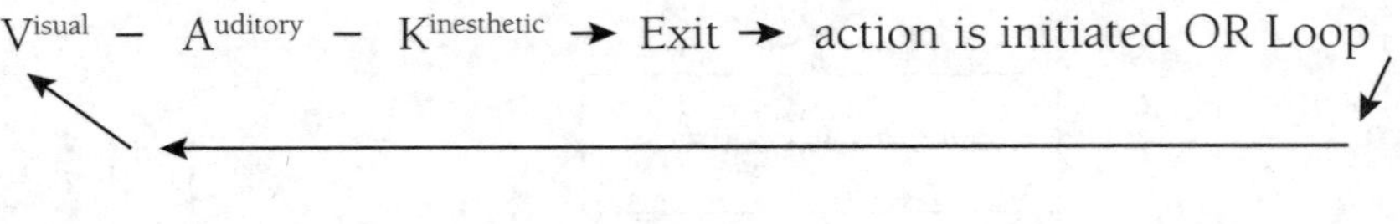

NLP model

Using a basic decision-making process of a digital/visual person, the individual looks at the problem, talks to him/herself or others about the problem, and then generates a feeling about what he or she has seen or heard. If there is a positive feeling, action will be initiated; if the feeling is negative, then a loop begins wherein the situation is looked at again, talked about, and so on. This is certainly more basic than Mithen's model but incorporates emotions, feelings, or sensations within the equation. Fear, for example, generated as information is being processed, usually leads to responses and decisions very different from that of curiosity. The psychologists know the nature of the beast that resides at the level of raw nerve and instinct. These feeling states—anger, joy, fear, contentment, and so on—trigger behaviors, and our emotional reactions to information are not always rational. This irrationality is the necessary "other side of the coin"; it gets us back to the relativity issue, where all things in the field of time come in twos, for sometimes it is the irrational, or that which transcends the bounds of the myth, that saves the day. I heard an old saying many years ago that "art is simply a legitimate expression of insanity," and some of the first artists we can identify were shamans brought to that other side through specific plants and fungi.

In the NLP model above the missing component is content, which Mithen makes clearer in his model. Both would agree that information is drawn from various sources including past experiences, the experiences of others, and so on, but sometimes the information is not available locally and has to be acquired in some other manner from some other place. Humans, as I have noted elsewhere (Rush 1996) are not so much problem-solvers as problem-creators, mainly because we do not always know the consequences of our actions; this is especially true when attempting to predict the behavior of large systems. When you stand back and observe daily rituals, life is one big crisis, experienced as day-to-day problems involving clinging to life, the quest for food and sex to maintain that life, and a continual reassessment of one's position in the group. Human ritual behavior surrounds these three features. For example, we all encounter biological urges, which become ritualized within specific geographies (see Rush 1999) once the individual is enculturated. You experience thirst and a decision is made within the bounds of one's cultural group on how this urge will be satisfied. As an example, you learn not to drink out of the toilet, although your dog, not aware of the germ theory of disease, might. In the food quest a different decision-making process, or perhaps a more elaborate process, is implemented. For example, in the hunt, cooperation and coordination are required, which is usually not necessary when trying to quench one's thirst.

To this process we add data available to the problem-solver through his or her experience or the experiences of others, as well as new data collection, for example in the case of scouts sent ahead to determine dangers or the best route to follow. Along with this we can add divination procedures of various types from dream interpretation, scapulimancy, and so on. "The hero's journey," a trip to the ancestors or gods, a journey to the place of imagination and commingling of thoughts, where all things are possible, is entered with the use of techniques of ecstasy. This is an elite adventure, this trip to the house of the gods, and the faint of heart should not apply.

The following chapters reveal, through art and literature, the importance of mind-altering substances in the cultures from which they are drawn. The art is a representation of these cultures, and what we see in the art must have been important, especially if it is repeated over and over again in diverse cultures of different time periods. These substances and their effects on brain chemistry, coupled with social expectation, aided in the decision-making process, and resulted in decisions that brought people to action during culture-building.

Gods, Aliens, or Amanitas

Before approaching the individual chapters, I must bring forth another consideration, and that is the position that somehow our ancestors were stupid and were given knowledge and technology by the gods. This is an old story told in cultures around the world, and some "researchers" accept the stories as fact. To this end the researchers have transmuted gods into ancient aliens, who apparently taught us everything we know and genetically manipulated *Homo erectus*, one of our ancient ancestors, to produce us, *Homo sapiens*. This is a questionable position at best, as the remains of *Homo erectus* can be traced from one geographical area to the next over a period of 1.75 million years, with this ancestor of ours regionally developing into Neanderthal in Europe, modern *Homo sapiens* in Africa, with *Homo erectus* regionally developing in China and displaced (interbreeding undoubtedly took place) by modern humans sometime after 125 KYA (Thousand Years Ago). In any case, this alleged genetic engineering was designed to produce an intelligent and docile slave who would work in gold mines for precious gold, because this is the only planet in the whole galaxy, the whole universe in fact, with substantial gold deposits (see Sitchin 2007)! So, according to the ancient alien hunters, our ancient ancestors did not have to make decisions—they were slaves. In my opinion, there is a more realistic source for gods and aliens, and that is the experiences our ancestors had with mind-altering substances. This, in my opinion, is the more valid answer to these otherworldly contacts, which fits well with the dream world associated with the ancient myths and art forms, where the laws of physics are ignored and time does not exist. If we could somehow remove the mushrooms and all the other mind-altering substances from the religious art in all its forms (written, pictorial), that very art the ancient alien hunters use to promote the ancient alien scenario, then they might have a case. The ancient alien hunters need to satisfactorily answer this simple question: Why are these mind-altering substances, especially the mushrooms, in the art from Chauvet to San Francisco spanning a time period of 30,000 years? That answer should come from the Vatican, the priests and imams, and especially the art historians; the ancient alien hunters, although challenged, have not spoken to this issue.

The Tree of Life

On the front cover is depicted the Tree of Life (original art by Arik Roper), which can take many configurations as noted from ancient Egypt to China, including the Kabbalistic Tree of Life, which is the path to God. When the Tree of Life is read literally, as directed by the Catholic Church (Tree of Jesse), we see pure genealogy, tracing the authority to rule from David at the bottom, to Jesus at the top, and often emerging from a mushroom, I might add. Through Jesus we pass the baton to Peter and then to the various popes. All, however, is metaphorical of a progression, an evolution, not a physical evolution but a spiritual one, centering on knowledge and the evolution of consciousness. Mind-altering plants and fungi opened the door to ways of seeing, sensing, or combining information, another level of consciousness, when other information was in short supply and could not be obtained locally. These plants and fungi have been shown to be very useful in discovering new information in our own day, by perhaps helping to break down or rearrange our models, our categories of living and experiencing, thus allowing thoughts and images to combine in unique ways.

Chapter Overviews

The contributors to this work come from diverse fields, for example, psychology, anthropology, classical studies, biology, law, and so on. The common denominator is that all have come to similar conclusions regarding the use of mind-altering substances and their importance in culture building. The reader will encounter differences in interpretations as to what substances were used during ritual process and other details often hidden by obscure passages and symbols. But there is one thing we can all agree on, and that is the importance, a neglected importance I might add, of these substances in decision making and culture building.

Chapter 2, by Michael Winkelman, sets the stage for understanding why our kind, *Homo sapiens* (and most likely *Homo erectus* and Neanderthal as well), seeks out methods of altering our consciousness, as evidenced in spiritual traditions around the world, especially the use of plant and fungi chemicals to achieve these altered states. The old model still taught today in sociology, psychology, anthropology, and police science courses at our colleges and universities contains two seemingly interrelated ideas. First, there are people with addictive personalities (genetic predisposition), and second, this predisposition is "turned on," so to speak, by social upbringing, having an alcoholic parent, peer pressure, and so on. This is the medical model, a diagnosis if you will, with the cure wrapped around proper upbringing and eliminating the substance, that is, alcohol, cannabis, and so on, from the individual's environment. Addiction, in the medical model, is a biochemical issue, but psychological as well, for it is the weakness in human will that is the real enemy, an "enemy" to be overcome through AA (Alcoholics Anonymous), belief in Jesus, or better nutrition (also part of the biochemical model). This is also a moralistic position, as well as one designed to instruct people not to go beyond the bounds of the myth, that is to say, don't challenge the prevailing storyline with new ideas using "evil" methods. Keep in mind that in times past prophecy was extremely important and messages from the other side could override prevailing beliefs. People believed in a world full of magical beings (as most people still do), and messages from that side had the weight of truth. This is one reason why the substances were demonized and secretly restricted to the elite in monotheistic traditions—there can be only one celestial truth. This is clearly stated in Islam, for Muhammad is the last prophet, period. Now, individuals can have minor prophecies, but if you have a major prophecy, for example, that Islam will reform, you better keep that to yourself.

The new model is more complicated but suggests there may be a deeper, neurochemical issue, an evolutionary leap away from all the other primates. That is to say, we purposely enhanced receptor sites in the brain, especially dopamine and serotonin, through the use of plants and fungi over a long period of time. The tradeoff for potential drug abuse was more creative thinking, or a leap in consciousness (see McKenna 1992), and the development of primitive medicine wherein certain mind-altering plants and fungi silence fatigue, pain, or depression, while others promote hunger, expel parasites, and so on. Our ancestors selected for our neural hardware, and our propensity for seeking altered forms of consciousness, as a *survival strategy, intimately bound to our decision-making processes,* again going back perhaps a million years or more.

Chimpanzees will consume alcohol, heroin, and so on, but avoid the LSD-type plant/fungus experiences. Why? I'm not sure there is a single answer to this, but I suspect the advent of language or proto-language (see Rush 1996) allowed group members to discuss and formulate theories about their experiences—a chimp cannot do this and is probably left with a frightening or rather terrifying experience of things not there. The human being, as far as I'm aware, is the only animal on the planet that enjoys experiencing fear, at least in the protected environment of a movie theater, and then going back for more. This linguistic ability seems to show up, at least in my opinion, with the advent of the Acheulian hand axe invented by *Homo erectus*–types (our oldest clearly identifiable ancestor) some 1.7 MYA, a major, and I believe symbolic addition to their tool kit—

these hand axes just show up and suggest a leap of consciousness that involves magical thinking (see Rush 1996, 2005). The antiquity of this axe is not surprising, and we see another leap of consciousness beginning 80 KYA with decoration, jewelry, and finely worked bone spear points, and then another shift in consciousness around 50 KYA, leading our kind (*Home sapiens*) out of Africa. One should not be surprised to see the images of these plants and fungi in the various art forms across cultures during the Upper Paleolithic, nor is it unusual that people continue to seek out these experiences.

Winkelman sets the base line for explaining why entheogenic substances are so pervasive throughout history, and, as the genetic data indicates, our association with certain substances, for example, psilocybin, must be longstanding and may go back millions of years. These substances are important to diverse cultures all over the world and are preserved in their art. This then leads us to chapter 3.

In chapter 3, Chris Bennett and Neil McQueen bring us closer to more modern quests for advice, knowledge, and so on. They present convincing evidence that the anointing oil (see Exodus 30: 1-31) used by the Hebrews contained cannabis and was a conduit to God. This is one way the Hebrews made decisions, through the ritual use of cannabis, often resorted to during stressful times. This changes how we view not only Judaism and Christianity, but Islam as well, and it is easy to understand why many scholars are reluctant to bring up the subject. In the Old Testament, the deity Yahweh sets the rules, thus he makes all the decisions. Abraham and the rest were to do what they were told. The major test in the Old Testament is one's loyalty to God (or the king—"as above, below"). In the New Testament, once all the clutter is removed, loyalty is to ideals of living, that is, know thyself, seek knowledge, and be a decent person. To ignore the use of these substances in the development of Judaism, Jewish law, and the Jewish relationship to non-Jews can only be seen as an act of political correctness, withholding important information from those truly attempting to understand the history of our kind, in this case, the part the "conduit to God (entheogens)" and the decisions that evolved from these experiences played in bringing a nation into existence.

In chapter 4, Gerrit Keizer presents a fascinating case study of a nun, recently sainted, Hildegard of Bingen. I gave an overview of Hildegard in a recent publication (see Rush 2011; also see Ruck et al 2001), but here we have a more extensive study of a nun, during a rather liberal time period, that is, before the plague and the Inquisition that ignited from smoldering ashes of popes past. What we are seeing, and we have her art to back the claim, is how an individual renders spiritual philosophy, not necessary as authorized by the bishops and popes, through the use of mind-altering substances. But it is not only Hildegard; she cannot be an isolated case, only the most creative or effective at putting her thoughts to paper or in unusual drawings. This is also an indicator of how the Catholic dogma arose and changes, that is, when a creative mind is able to capture the moment.

In chapter 5, Alan Piper explores the mythic and historical references to the less-well-known mind-altering substances used in initiation, prophecy rendering, poetic inspiration, or for direct contact with supernatural agencies. One often concludes, for example, that because Muhammad outlawed alcohol, there are no mind-altering substances connected to this political tradition called Islam. However, as Piper reveals, there are a wide variety of plants added to or fermented in milk that can take one to the seat of the deity, and Muhammad is no exception. But Piper also reveals that animals that eat psychoactive plants end up with the active ingredients in their flesh. Thus, certainly accidentally, the ancients learned about the connection between specific plants and the effects on the animals, and the effects on themselves when they consumed the flesh and certainly the liver.

There are a number of anecdotal stories suggesting that certain mind-altering substances allow us access to inner knowledge, and perhaps we have the ability to communicate with our DNA. Within this, Kevin Feeney, in chapter 6, offers an interesting suggestion that specific substances, the Mead of Inspiration for example, may have been a trigger to language development or perhaps refinement, with larger metaphors used to express ideas in elaborate form, dividing the universe into small and smaller units. Feeney presents interesting examples, one of which is the Khanty of Siberia, where storytellers will recite heroic poetry for hours on end after consuming *Amanita muscaria* (see Rush 2011 for discussion of inspiration in Christian art). If there is any truth to this, that is, if *Amanita muscaria* (and other substances) helped us to refine language so we could express and achieve more and more complex tasks, cultural elaboration and development was dependent on these substances.

In chapter 7, Mike Jay describes temple structures at Chavín de Huantar, a pilgrimage site in the Peruvian Andes, and the interesting depictions of individuals on mind-altering substances. These substances were mescaline from the San Pedro cactus as well as DMT (Dimethyltryptamine) snuff from *Anadenanthera* species. As Jay comments, "Chavín's architecture, in this sense, can be understood as a visionary technology, designed to externalize and intensify these intoxications and to focus them into a particular inner journey." Jay compares Chavín to that of the Eleusinian mysteries, also a pilgrimage site located in the city of Eleusis, some thirty miles west of Athens. One of the important conclusions drawn from Jay's research is the common practice of using mind-altering substance in diverse areas of the world—not the recreational use of these substances, but, instead, an individual and group spiritual quest and a central component of Chavín beliefs and practices affecting the whole culture.

In chapter 8, Edzard Klapp brings us back to biblical considerations, more specifically the meaning of "raven" and "raven's bread" as connected to the prophet Elias, St. Jerome, and St. Paul, as well as other terms, for example, "tried me with fire" (Psalm 17: 3) and "honey of the rock" (Psalm 81: 16). In chapter 3, Bennett and McQueen presented a compelling case for the use of cannabis especially in the anointing oils. This is a significant issue, for it places contact with God via the anointing oils. Klapp adds to this dimension, that is, contact with God through the use of "raven's bread," an analogue for the Holy Mushroom. It is becoming clear to researchers (see chapters 4, 5, and 6) that a large variety of mind-altering substances were used in rituals, some revealed in the Bible, but going back many thousands of years.

In chapter 9, Carl Ruck gives us the needed detail to understand the connection between the supposed Thespian invention of tragedy and its role in the development of Athenian democracy. I would have great difficulty encapsulating Ruck's paper within a paragraph or two, as with the other chapters. But I can say that in this chapter, as in all of Ruck's works, one sees very clearly the connection between the symbols presented in myth, in the comedies, and in this case the Greek tragedies, the importance of mind-altering substances in these art forms, and, by extension, the development of Greek culture. Following this, it is also clear that the original audiences of the tragedies must have understood the significance of the symbols or these stories would not have acted as tragedies, or comedies for that matter. According to Ruck, it was the use of religion, and the sacraments for communing with the gods, that aided in unifying the diverse classes coming into these Greek city states. Their similar myth was a "framework for interpreting reality."

Virgil's *Aeneid,* the subject of chapter 10, is considered the national epic of ancient Rome. The status of "national epic" means this work is considered to bring together and express the essence or character of a nation. Thus the content points to cultural origins and those features considered essential for national growth and development. Virgil, a Roman poet, whose dates are 70 BCE to 19 BCE, composed the *Aeneid* over a period of many years but died before its completion. Using Homer's *Iliad* and *Odyssey* as a template, the *Aeneid* follows the Trojan exile Aeneas as he strives to fulfill his destiny rendered in prophecy, that is, the founding act of Rome. Virgil's work had a profound influence on Western literature, especially Dante's *Divine Comedy,* wherein Virgil acts as Dante's guide through hell and purgatory.

In chapter 10, Carl Ruck and Robert Larner closely examine Virgil's "edible tables," which are related to a prophecy, that is, the founding of Rome, as mentioned in chapter 9, along with astronomical and other associations. So what are these "edible tables"? Through linguistic analysis it becomes clear that the "edible tables" refer to mushrooms used in the process of revealing the prophecy. Another interesting aspect is the cross, incised on the bread, to "imitate the crossing of the solar elliptic and the celestial equator, symbolically linking the bread astrologically to the cosmos as something similarly 'heaved up' as a 'heaven.'" This incising of the bread, and its intended meaning, is also a common theme in the Mithraic initiation as well as the Christian tradition, wherein the nimbus or halo, an analogue of the mushroom (see Rush 2011) worn by God the Father and Jesus, is incised with a cross, a feature lacking in the nimbus worn by the other saints. In the Christian sense God the Father and Jesus are also symbolic of the mushroom. But through all this we see that the food becomes "inedible" and connected to filth for, as Ruck and Larner report, "It is appropriate for a sacred plant to be taboo and supposedly repulsive, shielding it from profane use." In both chapters 9 and 10, Ruck and Larner explore the connection between prophecy, culture building, and the use of mind-altering substances as expressed in the Greek and Roman myths.

In chapter 11, Carl de Borhegyi and Suzanne de Borhegyi-Forrest give an overview of the descriptions of mushroom cults in Mesoamerica, as evidenced by mushroom stones and other artifacts Stephan de Borhegyi discovered and reported over fifty years ago, as well as more recent findings. Stephan de Borhegyi's conclusions, however, bumped into the prevailing beliefs in the archaeological community, beliefs that excluded mind-altering substances as being in any manner important in religious ritual, let alone cultural development. The authors then go on to explain the many reasons for this bias. By exploring the Aztec, Mayan, as well as Olmec art, however, one can restate Stephan de Borhegyi's conclusions, that is, the importance of entheogens in the building and maintenance of these cultural traditions. As the authors state, in reference to the different and complex variations in the religious traditions over time, they "believe the common denominator that unites them all is the centrality of the hallucinogenic mushroom experience, and the path that it offered for maintaining the daily resurrection of the Sun (and thus metaphorically of humankind) through mediation by the planet Venus."

Gastón Guzman, in chapter 12, presents an extensive review of all the mushrooms with neurotropic properties that have been used in ritual and thus culture building from prehistoric times to the present. He references rock art depicting shamans using *Psilocybe* in ritual context, for example, petroglyphs in Sahara, Africa (Tassili murals), and Spain, illustrating *Psilocybe* species. Rock art in distant Siberia likewise clearly illustrates *Amanita muscaria.* Then there is the case of Eleusis in Greece with the mysteries of the ergot, and several examples of *Amanita muscaria* and *Psilocybe semilanceata* in Europe during the Middle Ages. Finally, Guzman presents the mushrooms in ritual uses in the Americas, that is, *Amanita muscaria* in Canada, the U.S., Mexico, and Guatemala, and then the high traditions in Mexico and all Central and South America using several species of *Psilocybe* (around fifty). From his research in Mexico and the other countries in Latin America, however, Guzman shows a decline in the sacred use of all these mushrooms since the arrival of the Europeans, first through conquest and then outlawing, by the Church, of their use. Moreover, although the ritual use of these mushrooms continued into the 1950s, scientific interest and recreational use has led to a steady decline, and this has drastically altered the beliefs and practices associated with the traditional use of the sacred mushrooms. Nevertheless, we have very interesting artifacts found throughout Latin America that show the important cult use of *Amanita muscaria* and several species of *Psilocybe.*

In chapter 13, Dan Merkur takes a close look at Carl Jung's psychologization of metaphysics, although Jung was warned by colleagues not to put these beliefs in print. Whereas Freud uses a biological language when referring to inner states and one's perceptions of self and others, Jung took a more emotional approach. How academics encapsulate their ideas and opinions in words becomes a political matter wherein important details are left out or dismissed out of political correctness, as mentioned above. Both Jung and especially Freud understood that "soma" or other substances were used to obtain ecstatic experience or communion with deities. Jung saw mind-altering substances as interesting, but not important for obtaining a spiritual life. For Jung one sees the use of substances like LSD as competition to his own dogma and thus rejected as unimportant. However, both Freud and Jung had experiences with mind-altering substances, and these experiences prompted an interest in the connection between neurochemistry and psychosis. This is an important issue that surrounds all academia—what do we teach, what do we withhold, and who should determine this? Just how important is this information on mind-altering substances in terms of understanding human organization and directing people to action? In my opinion, and as contained in the chapters to follow, these substances were paramount in importance and their neglect in mainstream academia robs the research of important insights around the human condition and how we reached this point in history.

A conspiracy can be defined as two individuals plotting against a third (individual or group). All conspiracies have one thing in common and that is controlling information, in the same manner as a conman, or the construction of a reality that will allow the conspiracy to move forward. For those who run across discordant information, or information that produces "red flags," conspiracies emerge. In fact, how governments make decisions can be seen as a conspiracy in action, especially when they are not transparent. How can we say that? Because decision making in all countries, in every place, and at every time, occurs in small groups. This is precisely why civilizations with centralized governments fail—the small groups at the top lose contact with the needs of the small groups below, and these groups eventually rebel, usually violently. For those of you interested in conspiracies, I turn to the final chapter.

In chapter 14, Jan Irvin examines the legend surrounding R. G. Wasson and his connection to various important individuals. By following these connections, Irvin is able to establish "a cover-up of a mind control and propaganda campaign regarding mushrooms and the field of ethnomycology that reaches to the highest levels of the U.S. government, intelligence, and banking, and may tie directly into MK-ULTRA. We've also seen a concerted effort to cover up the origins of one of America's wealthiest banking families—the

in the double-blind study by Griffiths et al (2006) that showed psilocybin produced the characteristic features found in naturally induced mystical experiences. These similarities remind us of the common substrate in the brain and neurotransmitters that underlie all experiences of altered consciousness, irrespective of their origins or interpretations.

The relationships among natural and drug-induced alterations of consciousness must be understood from an evolutionary perspective. This reveals altered consciousness to be related to endogenous mechanisms, which are triggered by both ancient evolutionary adaptations and more recently acquired propensities to use exogenous sources of substances to alter consciousness. Reconceptualizing plant "toxins" as "rewards" in terms of effects on behavior, emotions, and cognition reframes this human attraction as involving adaptations. These adaptations involved an enhanced ability to utilize exogenous sources of important endogenous neurotransmitter substances, as well as more sensitive neurotransmitter receptor systems, for using these chemicals that have such profound effects on human consciousness.

Dopamine and Altered Consciousness

A central feature of the neural transmitter systems involved in altered consciousness is the dopamine system, which is stimulated by an enormous variety of chemicals (Previc 2009). Evolutionary approaches to use of drugs focus on the reward and reinforcement effects they have on the dopamine system; virtually all classes of drugs (including alcohol, nicotine, stimulants, and THC) have effects on dopamine transmission in the limbic system, as well as on serotonergic transmission (Smith and Tasnadi 2007; Mandell 1980). The effects of endogenous opioids on dopaminergic transmission involve similar dynamics for "not only opiates, but also alcohol, nicotine, cocaine, amphetamines, and Δ-9 tetrahydrocannabinol" (Smith and Tasnadi 2003, p. 21). Although they act through a variety of intermediary systems (serotonin, encephalins, GABA), acute exposure to the major categories of drugs of abuse results in increases in dopaminergic activity, specifically in the hippocampus and nucleus accumbens (Smith 1999).

The effects on dopamine receptors are typically characterized as unconditioned pleasurable responses that reinforce behaviors that favor successful adaptation, such as food and sex. In addition to the naturally pleasurable effects, opioids reduce pain avoidance and sexual behavior, and increase eating (Smith and Tasnadi 2007). The mesolimbic dopamine system and its rewarding properties and mediation of pleasures from natural rewards (food, sex) decline when the dopaminergic system is suppressed or impaired (Barbano and Cader 2007). Salamone and Correa (2002) refined this view in proposing that it is the dopamine system that attributes incentive qualities to a reward, potentiating the organism's associated responses. Humans' addictive potential reflects the ability of the same reward systems used to reinforce fitness-enhancing behaviors such as eating and sex to be stimulated by other signals that elicit intrinsic feelings of well-being. They can also produce the powerful experiences that epitomize the importance of altered consciousness in a culture's spiritual traditions found worldwide.

While dopamine is associated with sex and other pleasurable states, it does not appear to have a central role in emotional arousal in general, or social warmth and empathy, which instead depend on serotonin, norepinephrine (NE), opioids, and oxytocin (Previc 2009). In contrast, high levels of dopamine lead to emotional detachment. Endogenous opioid is a general term referring to a class of natural substances in the body that include endorphins, encephalins, dynorphins, and other opiate-like substances (Smith and Tasnadi 2003) that interact with the dopamine system. These substances, particularly B*-endorphin, are functionally identical (analogues) to the opiates found in plants, which have the capacity to interact with the same neurotransmitter sites in our brains. The endorphins are also adaptations for reducing pain and stress and enhancing learning and memory. The uniquely human activities of long-distance running produce enhanced release of endorphins, extending the capacities of such extreme physical activity that was adaptive in flight from predators, with the pain-numbing effects facilitating the ability to continue to flee rather than succumb to pain, muscle cramps, shortness of breath, etc. (Jones 2005). These effects go beyond the endorphins, forming part of the general sympathetic response.

The human dopamine system must be contextualized in broad evolutionary terms as part of our mammalian heritage, with similar effects across mammalian species in social bonding, from mother-infant bonds to broader social groups. The endogenous opioids that stimulate our reward and learning systems also have core functions in the mammalian brain and its emotional, social, and self systems, especially breastfeeding and bonding. Sullivan, Hagen, and Hammerstein (2008) suggest that the central role of these substances in the mesolimbic dopamine system indicates that we should also understand the broader functions of the opioids in regulation of attention, the integration of sensorimotor behavior, and modification of behavioral programs. Previc (2009) reviews evidence that dopamine is also vital for all of the key functions of advanced intelligence and cognition, including: programming and executing motor planning; working memory and capacity for parallel processing; spatial and temporal abstraction; cognitive flexibility/mental set shifting; temporal sequence processing; and creativity/generativity.

Previc notes that all of these higher cognitive functions *are concerned with processing of information in distal space and time*. Dopamine functions are linked to the brain's ability to deal with objects and events distant in space and time. Not only are dopaminergic circuits active during exploration of novelty and reward learning, they result in prolonged effort for delayed gratification and pursuit of goal-directed responses. Dopamine appears central to understanding causal and temporal relationships. The abilities for context-independent cognition are exemplified in the capacities for "off-line thinking" and "mental time travel," the ability to experience and think about things other than those in the here and now. "In essence, ventromedial dopaminergic activation results in the 'triumph' of extrapersonal brain activity over the body systems that anchor our self-concept and our body orientation as well as a triumph over the more 'rational' executive intelligence maintained in the lateral dopaminergic systems" (Previc 2009: 53). The ability for extrapersonal responses or cognition is exemplified in the capacities for "mental time travel." Winkelman (2010) reviews research regarding these abilities for extrapersonal projection and illustrates how these extrapersonal functions of dopamine are key to understanding central aspects of the shamanic soul flight or out-of-body experience, which exemplifies the ability to have a context-independent consciousness of people and places far removed from the physical body.

"The predominance of dopamine in association with cortical areas, in which higher order sensory processing or cross-modal sensory interactions occur indicates that dopamine is especially well-suited to making connections among stimuli and events and organizing them into mental plans. This is beneficial in stimulating creativity and in 'off-line' thinking and strategizing, important components of abstract reasoning" (Previc 2009: 30). Dopamine's central role in the integrative functions of the prefrontal cortex is extended throughout the brain as the nervous system allows the pre-frontal cortex PFC to connect to other cortical regions. The major dopaminergic systems originate in the midbrain area, within the mesolimbic system and its numerous connections to other limbic structures and the frontal cortex. This system is the most important motivational system. These midbrain and brainstem areas contain cell bodies, which produce the neurotransmitters and extend to all of the regions of the cortex.

Human Evolution and Drug Use

The dominant evolutionary approaches to explaining the human propensity for addiction characterizes these desires for consciousness-altering substances and succumbing to their addictive effects as the consequence of a mismatch or discordance between our acquired tendencies and the current environment (e.g., Berridge 1996, Nesse and Berridge 1997; see Lende 2008). According to this view, drug-induced feelings that are linked to adaptive behaviors are the result of our recent exposure to evolutionary novel drug substances. Harmful aspects of addiction result from a mismatch between our innate biological tendencies and the options for meeting those needs provided by the environment. Drugs of abuse are thought to falsely trigger natural reward circuits and their sense of fitness benefits by blocking or short-circuiting the painful feelings that provide the adaptive functions of stimulating avoidance behaviors.

These perspectives have not considered the deeper evolutionary roots of the relationships between our nervous systems and these substances—which are both endogenous to our nervous system and were also found in our ancient environments. The evolutionary approaches to addiction address the genetically based traits that result in behaviors that have effects in increasing fitness (survival and reproduction). Since drugs have generally been conceptualized as causing problematic behaviors that reduce fitness, the idea that their use may confer fitness is initially counterintuitive. But this is the result of a particular paradigmatic perspective.

Drug Use: Mismatch or Adaptation?

Sullivan, Hagen, and Hammerstein (2008) point to a variety of forms of evidence that illustrate problems with the predominant mismatch hypothesis. These substances are not new but were part of ancient environmental exposures that resulted in evolved counter-measures to these plant defenses. A central problem is the paradox of this concept of drugs as sources of hedonistic rewards that stimulate our reward systems because they have their role in ecological relations as toxins that inhibit consumption by poisoning those who consume them. If the presence of these toxins in plants is an evolutionary adaptation to deterring consumption by animals, why is it that these same substances are viewed as producing pleasurable rewards? Since animals do not evolve genetic capacities to reward non-adaptive or fitness-reducing behaviors (rewarding the consumption of dangerous neurotoxins), Sullivan, Hagen, and Hammerstein conclude that humans evolved in order to make use of these exogenous substances.

Several aspects of drug effects suggest an evolved capacity to benefit from these substances. In contrast to the debilitating effects generally attributed to drugs, Smith (1999) illustrates there are a variety of fitness benefits to using these substances. Fitness benefits may have accrued to our ancestors as a consequence of their ability to respond to these psychoactive substances. Across the diverse classes of plant drugs there are effects of enhanced vigilance, the ability to ignore pain in the interest of survival activities, increased access to mating opportunities, reduction of apprehension and stress, feelings of detachment and euphoria, increased endurance and self-confidence, enhanced sensory and mental acuity, reduction of defensiveness, and reduction of depression and self-defeating activities. Clearly many adaptive mechanisms could have been involved in humans' physiological and cultural adaptations to environmental sources of consciousness-altering chemicals.

The effects of these toxins on the brain's reward centers may be an accident of plant-herbivore coevolution but also display hallmark features of natural adaptations (Smith and Tasnadi 2003). A reciprocal relationship between food consumption and taste is provoked by opioids—foods taste better when we are on opioids, and good-tasting food—sugars—cause a release of B-endorphin. Mammals evolved to eat foods with nutritional value, and the rare presence of sugar in the aboriginal environment led to the selection for use of endogenous opioid release, to reinforce additional eating behavior. Gestational nutritional needs may have selected for opioid systems that induce fruit cravings and the many associated nutritional advantages of their consumption.

Defining characteristics of humans, such as abstract, generative, and context-independent cognition and other advanced mental skills, require dopamine as a neurotransmitter (Previc 2009). The use of executive intelligence activates the dopamine system, and dopamine deficiencies are associated with a wide range of cognitive deficits.

Previc shows that dopamine's effects must be related to humans' evolved cognitive capacities, because dopamine is central to advanced intelligence, not only in humans but in other animals as well. All species with advanced intelligence have concentrated dopamine, which may have been the only neurotransmitter that expanded through the evolution of primates and hominids. Furthermore, dopamine is highly concentrated in the prefrontal cortex, which is crucial to humans' higher order reasoning and planning (Previc 2009: 15). The overall expansion of the dopaminergic system in primates and humans led to increased concentrations in most cortical regions, with high concentrations in the prefrontal and frontal regions, especially in sensory processing areas where cross-modal integration occurs. Primates also evidence a greater density of dopamine receptors in Level 1 of the cortex, the layer where coordination of activities underlying cognitive processes takes place. Dopamine and acetylcholine predominate as neurotransmitters in the left hemisphere, which is the brain area managing these skills.

Previc notes that in the overall human evolution of the dopaminergic systems, there was a greater expansion of the prefrontal/striatal dopaminergic system relative to the mesolimbic/ mesocortical pathways. He proposes that this allowed for the sublimation of basic impulsive mesolimbic drives and their control by our rational intellect. Dopamine also plays a central role in goal-directed behavior, and has a role in dampening the physiological aspects of the stress response. This most important dopaminergic function reflects parasympathetic action on the autonomic nervous system ANS, dampening physiological arousal and increasing peripheral vasodilation (which has roles in erectile function and male sexual behavior). Dopamine also mediates pleasant and euphoric states, but appears to have greater importance in inhibiting negative emotional arousal of fear and anxiety, leading to a greater sense of control, an internal locus of control. This ability to use dopamine as a stress-reducer enables highly dopaminergic individuals to function more effectively in extreme environments (Previc 2009: 36), since dopamine helps in managing stress by assisting in active coping.

Drug Use and the Evolution of Consciousness

Sullivan and Hagen (2002) review evidence of a long-term evolutionary relationship between psychotropic plant substances and humans' cognitive capacities that indicates there were selective benefits of substance use. They characterize these benefits in terms of the ability of plants to provide neurotransmitter analogues, which served as substitutes for endogenous transmitters that are rare or otherwise limited by dietary constraints. These are primarily in the monoamine neurotransmitters such as serotonin, as well as acetylcholine, norepinephrine, and dopamine, which are crucial for normal brain function and require dietary precursors. These neurotransmitters are central to managing stress, exerting selective pressures for metabolic systems that utilize these exogenous sources of precursors for these neurotransmitters. Human genetic adaptations to utilize these substances are illustrated in human-chimpanzee differences in neurotransmitter and neurohormone systems and responses, particularly the opioids, dopamine and serotonin.

Human-Chimpanzee Differences in Drug Metabolism and Neurotransmitter Systems

The conservation of aspects of the dopamine and serotonergic neurotransmitter systems across evolution is manifested in their basic similarities across mammalian species; there were also enhancements of these systems in human evolution. Genes that control protein sequences in the brain have evolved much more quickly in humans than chimpanzees (Shi, Bakewell, and Zhang 2006). Since the divergence of hominids from our hominid ancestors, there has been an accelerated evolution of and a positive selection for polypeptide precursors and genes involved in opioid regulation (Wang et al 2005, Rockman et al 2005). The uniquely human pituitary cyclase-activating polypeptide precursor (PACAP) that emerged during human origins and since the time of separation from our common ancestor with chimpanzees underwent accelerated evolution only in the human lineage (Wang et al 2005). The rapid evolution of PACAP precursor genes was a consequence of positive selection, which occurred in the central regions of the gene, sites that have a critical role in enhancing the biological activity of neuropeptides through protecting them from enzymatic degradation and increasing their affinity for receptor binding (Wang et al 2005).

"The Chimpanzee Sequencing and Analysis Consortium" (Wang et al 2005) found significant human and chimpanzee differences that indicate that there was a rapid evolutionary divergence in the human line involving xenobiotic metabolizing genes that provide an ability to metabolize the plant toxins. Some of the most significant differences are in segmental duplication of genes, their repetition in specific areas of the genome. These gene duplications produce changes in the onset and extent of gene expressions, as well as mechanisms for a diversification of genes, which can occur during duplication, providing a basis for novel functions (Wooding and Jorde 2006).

The human CYP2D6 gene illustrates the adaptive functions that can come from segmental duplication and its role in encoding an enzyme (cytochrome P450) involved in the metabolism of drugs. Sullivan et al (2008) point out that the mammalian xenobiotic-metabolizing cytochrome P450 provides evidence of a deep evolutionary history of adaptation to plant toxins. Our ancestors underwent positive selection for CYP2D, an enzyme that enables the body to metabolize opiates, amphetamines, and other drugs, including plant toxins and serotonin reuptake inhibitors.

There have been waves of selective effects in the hominid line for genes associated with opioid cis-regulation (Rockman et al 2005). The prodynorphin gene is found in chimpanzees as well, but it is expressed to a far greater extent in humans. Natural selection resulted in an alteration of human prodynorphin, a significant precursor molecule for a range of endogenous opioids and neuropeptides. The evolution of humans involved natural selection for genetic modifications involving the ability to induce endogenous opioid precursors. This selection for prodynorphin expression contributed in significant ways to the evolution of human perception, emotion, and learning.

Human evolutionary divergence from chimpanzees also involved increases in expression of genes in regions involving regulatory genes that duplicate copies of some genes. Oldham, Horvath, and Geschwind (2006) characterize the chimp-human differences as involving an increased connectivity in the gene co-expression networks in frontal brain networks of humans. Humans have an intensification of expression of genes associated with the CNS and the frontal cortex innervations, particularly circuitry underlying higher cognitive processes.

Highly dopaminergic minds are active, above average in intelligence, achievement-oriented and goal seeking, and confident in their abilities (Previc 2009). This is the positive side of the dopaminergic mind; there is also a dark side. This is illustrated in the numerous pathologies associated with deficiencies of dopamine. There are several different dopamine-mediated personality disorders linked to one of two major dopaminergic systems (i.e., lateral and ventromedial). The ventromedial dopaminergic system provokes intense unconstrained aggressive drives to achieve distant goals, that is, an unleashing of the motivation drives associated with wanting. It also stimulates the creative genius in a search for novel associations among stimuli. The stimulation of the lateral dopaminergic levels that enhances executive control and internal locus of control can at excessive levels lead to delusions of grandeur and invincibility, and magical ideation about abilities to control distant events, and others.

Serotonergic Systems and the Alteration of Consciousness

Another neurotransmitter system involved in altered consciousness is the serotonin system, the primary system that is affected by psychedelics such as LSD and psilocybin. Dopamine and serotonin are the two most important amines, and play a complementary role in balancing the functions of the brain and body. "[T]he serotonergic inhibition of dopamine release is arguably the clinically most important neurochemical interaction in the brain … particularly in the ventromedial and limbic subcortical and cortical areas" (Previc 2009: 21). The right hemisphere and its serotonergic and noradrenergic systems inhibit the left hemisphere and dopamine.

Environmental mechanisms selecting for enhancement of specific neurotransmitter capacities involve the many genres and species of psilocybin-containing mushrooms found worldwide, in frequent association with spiritual traditions. These substances have powerful effects on consciousness through action on the serotonergic neurotransmitter systems, producing alterations of consciousness that typify human concerns with the soul and supernatural. While humans and other animals tend to respond in similar ways to drugs, there are notable human-chimpanzee differences in self-administration of drugs. While laboratory chimps will generally self-administer alcohol, heroin, cocaine, caffeine, nicotine, and other addictive substances, there is a notable class of drugs that they will not continue to self-administer—the psychedelics (McKim 1991). This is specifically true for our closest animal relatives, the chimpanzees. These differences reflect evolved differences in the serotonergic binding properties of humans' hominid ancestors.

Human-Chimpanzee Divergences in Serotonergic Binding

Raghanti et al (2008) review the wide range of evidence that indicates that the role of serotonin (5HT) in support of higher cognitive functions was modified in the course of human evolution and contributed to our cognitive specializations. The central effects of LSD and hallucinogenic drugs on 5-HT receptors indicate that these should be prime candidates for evolution of our capacity for the spiritual experiences produced by these substances. There is significant phylogenetic variation between humans and chimps that appears to have substantial functional implications for our cognitive processing capabilities. Humans do not have, however, quantitative increases in serotonin innervations, in comparison to chimpanzees, although there are species differences in innervations patterns. In many respects chimpanzees and humans are similar in their differences with respect to the serotonergic systems of other primates, including having the serotonergic axons emanating from the median raphe nuclei and unique neuronal cells in cortical areas responsible for processing emotional and cognitive information (Raghanti et al 2008).

Pregenzer et al (1997) report findings that the human and chimpanzee 5-HT_{1D} receptor amino acid sequences do, however, differ. In comparison with chimps, human serotonergic ligands, including several indoles and ergots, have comparable, low nanomolar binding affinities and a remarkable degree of similarity in their binding profiles with other ligands, the agents that bind to receptor sites. Yet while the chimpanzee 5-HT_{1D} receptors show a high degree of similarity to human 5-HT_{1D} receptors, there are chemical template differences that indicate molecular divergences among the 5-HT_{1D} receptors of humans and chimpanzees (Pregenzer et al 1997).

Pregenzer et al (1997) examined the similarity of humans, chimpanzees, other primates, and mammals in the displacement of serotonin by various drugs. In spite of highly analogous responses to indoles and ergots in the binding of a wide variety of subtypes of serotonin and dopamine receptors across primates and mammals, there are notable human differences. Even though humans and chimpanzees do not significantly differ in serotonin dissociation, humans have significantly greater displacement (2.5 to 4 times greater) as compared with chimpanzees on the binding of LSD and the ergots metergoline and dihydroergotamine (Pregenzer et al 1997). This evidence is highly suggestive of the possibility that humans evolved to more efficiently process psychedelic drugs.

Exogenous Neurotransmitters: Psilocybin-Containing Mushrooms

Adaptations to the fungi in their environment, especially the toxic species of mushrooms, was a significant feature affecting hominin evolution. The psychoactive fungi that our foraging ancestors explored as possible food items in their environments exerted a selective influence on hominid evolution. Psychedelic mushrooms would have been invariably encountered in our ancestral past, especially in tropical regions, given their worldwide distribution. Species of mushrooms containing psilocybin have been found around the world (Guzman, Allen, and Gartz 1998). The worldwide distribution of neurotropic fungi used as sacraments in cultures around the world is good evidence that such substances altered consciousness in ways that induced spiritual experiences and contributed directly to the development of religious explanations and activities. The ancient encounter with these substances is manifested in religious and spiritual interpretations associated with mushrooms worldwide (see Schultes and Hofmann, 1979, Ratsch 2005). Hundreds of cultures have been found in which a wide variety of psychoactive substances are used in religions, particularly shamanistic traditions.

The objective ability of the psychedelics to induce mystical and spiritual experiences is attested to in controlled clinical studies. Since the famous "Good Friday" experiment by Pahnke (1966), there has been clinical evidence of the objective ability of psychedelics to produce mystical alterations of consciousness. In this classic experiment, seminary students at Harvard Divinity School took psilocybin or a placebo control. Most of the seminary students who received psilocybin had the most profound spiritual experiences of their lives and remained convinced even decades later that it was the most profound spiritual experience of their very religious lives. This ability of the chemical substrate to produce spiritual experiences was recently confirmed in a study carried out at John Hopkins University by Griffiths et al (2006), which found that when the participants took psilocybin (as opposed to a control substance) they had spiritual and mystical experiences that induced effects on their attitudes, moods, as well as their own experience of spirituality, which persisted for months afterward. Two-thirds of the psilocybin group rated the experience among the most meaningful and spiritual experiences of their entire life. They had significantly higher scores on scales for introvertive mysticism, extravertive mysticism, internal and external unity, sacredness, intuitive knowledge, transcendence of time and space, ineffability, experiences of oceanic boundlessness, and visionary structuralization. In addition, psilocybin participants showed significantly higher levels of peace, harmony, joy, and intense happiness, an enhanced positive attitude and mood about life, and increases in altruistic social behaviors.

These findings indicate that these substances led human ancestors to an enhanced capacity to experience spiritual and transcendental connections, special alterations of consciousness that also had adaptive social significance. These psychedelic-based cognitive experiences constitute a neurotheology, a neurologically based theology derived from properties of the neural system, manifested in a number of similar features associated with the use of psychedelic substances in cultures around the world (Dobkin de Rios 1984; Winkelman 1996, 2000, 2007). These features of psilocybin-induced experiences are also central to shamanism (Winkelman 1992, 2000, 2010). Since shamanism constitutes a primordial worldwide form of religious practice, this suggests that it was the effects of these substances that were responsible for the initial emergence of spirituality and the central alterations of consciousness institutionalized in shamanistic traditions around the world.

A significant aspect of these exogenous neurotransmitter sources, illustrated in the effects of psilocybin-containing mushrooms, is their intrinsic ability to induce an animistic worldview regarding consciousness. This biologically based "neurotheology" presents a mystical view of the world that has been fundamental to the understanding of consciousness for many cultures. This neurotheology reflects an adaptive feature of the ability to use these plant-derived exogenous sources of neurotransmitters. Their effects on the serotonergic nervous system and macro-level processing in the brain produces alterations of consciousness that have been core to consciousness traditions. Their effects subjectively present a model of consciousness as spiritual, multileveled, and transcendent, and consider the typical manifestations of altered consciousness to be the most significant of all forms of consciousness.

Dance as an Adaptation for Altered States

One uniquely human behavior in which both serotonin and opioids were involved is dance. While the uniquely human capacity for dance involves exaptations of capacities provided by bipedalism and mimesis (Donald 1991), it has significant precursors in other mammalian behaviors. The special significance of dance in the alteration of consciousness is reflected in its worldwide association with spiritual, artistic, and collective social practices and its core role in the activities of shamanism.

Bachner-Melman et al (2005) studied specific gene polymorphisms associated with people who are engaged intensively with creative dance performance. This enhanced genotype associated with professional dancers was also associated with serotonin transporters (SLC6A4) and an arginine vasopressin receptor (AVPR1a), which is activated by opioids. Professional dancers had higher levels of both of these gene frequencies than normal controls and professional athletes; furthermore, the higher levels of these genes were significantly associated with a measure of spirituality and altered states of consciousness (the Tellegren Absorption Scale).

Bachner-Melman et al hypothesize that the association of AVPR1a and SLC6A4 with dance reflects a common basis in genes associated with courtship and social communication and mediated by personality factors reflecting the social communication and the spiritual facets of dancing. The association of dance and the AVPR1a gene reflects the central role of communication and social relations in the functions of dance, with the evolutionary linkages of the AVPR1a gene and dance reflected in vasopressin's role in vertebrate courtship behavior, maternal behavior, animal bonding, and romantic attachment in humans. Human dancing is part courtship and part social communication strategies that have a shared evolutionary history with the mating displays and affiliative behaviors of other animals, reflecting a common basis in conservative neurochemical and genetic mechanisms across vertebrates (Bachner-Melman et al 2005).

Adaptive Effects of Altered Consciousness

This coevolution of our capacities for using exogenous neurotransmitter substances and experiencing unusual forms of consciousness involved a variety of adaptive effects. As Sullivan et al (2008) note, these are rare neurotransmitter substances; most require dietary precursors, and the capacity to metabolize and use exogenous sources of these substances provided intrinsic benefits. These psychotropic plants are capable of producing a variety of other adaptive effects as well. The toxic effects of their alkaloids on a wide range of intestinal worms would have contributed to human health, likely contributing to the ubiquitous sense that these plants are in some way "cleansing." There are a range of physiological effects as a function of dose, including increased awareness and attention, enhanced visual acuity and excitement, including erection and sexual arousal (see Winkelman and Schultes, 1996 for review). Psychotropic plants also provided adaptive advantages in their integrative and informational properties associated with the alteration of consciousness (Winkelman 2007, 2010).

Mandell (1980) suggests that the common biological basis of diverse procedures, agents, and conditions involve disinhibiting the temporal lobe structures that result in the emotional flooding experienced as ecstasy and visions from the "inner world." The hippocampal-septal system, whose activation is associated with these effects, has terminal projections from the somatic and autonomic nervous systems that form part of an extensive system of innervations connecting areas of the brain, in particular, linking the frontal cortex with the limbic system. The limbic system (the paleomammalian brain) is that part of the brain where emotions are integrated with memories. Enhancement of these processes with exogenous neurotransmitter analogues such as the DMT in psilocybin mushrooms illustrates their adaptive advantages associated with group bonding.

Although the psychedelics are characterized by a number of different chemical structures and modes of action, they produce a number of common physiological effects through their effects on the serotonergic neurotransmitter system (see Passie et al 2008; also see Aghajanian and Marek 1999). The major naturally occurring psychedelics (such as the mescaline-containing cacti and various genera of psilocybin-containing mushrooms) contain phenylalkylamine and indole alkaloids similar in chemical structure to the neural transmitter serotonin, and have their effects on consciousness and spiritual experiences by their interaction with serotonergic receptors. The role of serotonin as a "neuromodulator," the structural similarity of psychedelics and serotonin, and the specific effects of the psychedelics on serotonergic transmission provide a basis for their recharacterization as "psychointegrators" (Winkelman 1996, 2001, 2007). While there are a number of different substances that produce hallucinogenic reactions in humans, those with a basis in action on serotonin act as psychointegrators, enhancing the integration of information in the brain by releasing the functions of areas central to managing processes related to fundamental aspects of self, emotions, memories, and attachments. This psychointegrative effect is manifested physiologically in the typical effects on brain waves produced by these substances, the stimulation of coherent theta wave synchronization along the neuraxis, the central nerve bundle linking the structural levels of the brain. The effects are manifested psychologically in the experiences of healing, wholeness, interconnectedness, cosmic consciousness, and other transpersonal experiences that these substances regularly produce.

This integration of brain networks as a generic feature underlying ASC is illustrated by Vollenweider's (1998) research on the mechanisms of action of psychedelics on the major cortical loops. The frontal-subcortical circuits provide one of the principal organizational networks of the brain involving neuronal linkages and feedback loops of the cortical areas of the frontal brain with the thalamus of the brain stem region. These loops unite specific regions of the frontal cortex with lower brain regions, providing circuits that are central to brain–behavioral relationships, social actions, motivations, and executive functions. Vollenweider attributes the consciousness-altering properties of psychedelics to their selective effects on the brain's cortico-striato-thalamo-cortical feedback loops that link the information-gating systems of lower levels of the brain with the frontal cortex. These loops are regulated by the thalamus, which limits the ascending information to the frontal cortex from the environment and body. Psychedelics disable this disinhibition process; this increases access to the flow of information that is ordinarily inhibited, overwhelming the frontal cortex and leading to an alteration of experience of self, other, environment, and the internal world of psychological structures and projections.

The effects of these substances upon neural, sensory, emotional, and cognitive processes illustrate the adaptive advantages produced by the inhibition of the serotonergic systems. This involves an enhancement of consciousness provoked by increasing the integrative information-processing, achieved by stimulation of the serotonergic circuitry linking the lower structures of the brain (paleomammalian and reptilian). Psychointegrative effects derive from the disinhibition of emotional and social processes and the stimulation of systemic integration of brain functions, resulting in the integration of limbic system emotional processes with the neocortical processes. This results from the loss of the inhibitory effect of serotonin on the mesolimbic temporal lobe structures, leading to synchronous discharges in the temporal-lobe limbic structures of the visual cortex experienced as visions (Mandel 1980). The psychointegrators have the effect of coupling nonlinguistic behavioral and social-emotional dynamics with rational processes and result in a function integration of the different systems of the brain.

Conclusions

Both dopamine and serotonin are key to understanding the alterations of consciousness found worldwide in shamanistic traditions. Selection for enhanced opioid mechanisms over hominid evolution increased capacities in social, emotional, and cognitive areas, exemplified in group bonding rituals. Species of psilocybin-containing mushrooms found worldwide likely selected for enhanced serotonergic neurotransmitter systems, where the interference effects of these substances produce alterations of consciousness that typify human concerns with the soul and supernatural. These adaptations are manifested in the universality of ritual practices directed at enhancing people's access to these experiences (Winkelman 1992).

Winkelman (2010) describes a variety of adaptive aspects of drugs and the associated conditions of altered consciousness. One feature involves their ability to enhance access to normally unconscious information and to integrate thought processes. These innate propensities produce an integration of different brain systems, enhance learning of information and promote behavioral, emotional, and cognitive integration. Religious altered states of consciousness reflect an adaptive response involving enhanced integration of information from unconscious processes of the mind, integrating the body-level awareness of the prelinguistic mind into consciousness. Religious experiences are encounters with our own unconscious potential in ways that are directly accessible to personal consciousness, enabling normally unconscious information to be used in directing our adaptations to the environment. The functional roles provided by the dream capacity are elicited both by shamanic ritual as well as the exogenous opioid and serotonergic analogues.

The association of serotonin and the opioid system (vasopressin) with alterations of consciousness and mystical experiences, as well as enhanced dance propensities, indicates a coevolution of the capacities of dance and the capacities for altering consciousness. Clearly, dance has that capacity to induce alterations of consciousness through a variety of mechanisms (such as stimulating the release of opioids, producing rhythmic stimulation of the brain, as well as inducing exhaustion and collapse; see Winkelman 2010). Further genetic adaptations involving the serotonergic and opioid systems in dance are linked to the evolution of a set of uniquely human capacities involving the expressive capacity of mimesis, the ability to intentionally represent through imitation. This body-based imagistic system of expression reflects a level of consciousness communicated through a variety of expressive forms—such as play, drama, ritual, music, emotions, shamanic ritual, and ultimately human spirituality and religion.

Previc (2006) contends that there is a common neuroanatomy and neurochemistry underlying phenomena such as dreaming, hallucinations, and extreme religious beliefs. The common neural substrate involves dopamine, particularly elevated levels in the ventromedial cortical areas. This corresponds to the anatomical basis of these phenomena, which he postulated to "be mediated by ventromedial (cortico-limbic) pathways extending from the medial temporal lobe to the anterior cingulate and prefrontal cortex" (2006: 518). Previc notes that there are a number of psychological disorders (i.e., bipolar disorder, obsessive compulsive disorder, and schizophrenia) that are: 1) associated with increased religious activity, experiences, or practices; and 2) involve an overactivation of dopamine, particularly in the left hemisphere. Furthermore, the brain activity typical of disorders associated with hyper-religiosity, as well as dreams, hallucinations, paranormal experience, and paranormal behaviors, involve action in the ventromedial system of extrapersonal functions, which is freed from inhibition by the prefrontal (focal-extrapersonal or executive) dopaminergic system and/or posterior serotonergic (peripersonal) inputs (Previc).

Diverse forms of altering consciousness all involve this enhanced capability to access the output of the unconscious mind and our innate cognitive modules. These capacities are elicited by many mechanisms, particularly in the visual system, where the effects of vision-inducing plants are among the most prominent mechanisms. They enabled an extended exploitation of the visual associational cortex and its ability to manage visual and other information. This expanded associational area improved the brain's capacity to interface with a variety of other neural mechanisms, including those involved in learning, problem-solving, and memory formation.

The role of drugs in the evolution of human consciousness must be understood in relationship to effects on the serotonergic system and its roles in overall brain functioning. The alterations of consciousness enhance paleomammalian brain functions and their coordination and integration with the entire brain. Enhanced serotonergic mechanisms contributed to experiences of altered consciousness in humans, embodied in visionary experiences. The recurrent features of the mystical experiences induced by these substances indicate that they reflect biological bases and neurognostic forms, biologically based aspects of knowing. These experiences reflected an enhanced integration of unconscious processes and potentials into consciousness and the overall integration of brain processes. Human evolution was stimulated by interactions among exogenous neurotransmitter substances, the adaptive potentials of the states of consciousness they produced, and the shamanic ritual practices that supported the engagement with altered states. The worldwide association of psychedelics with spiritual traditions reflects the ability of these substances to produce profound alterations of consciousness. These alterations provide a basic neurophenomenological paradigm for understanding the nature of altered consciousness.

Acknowledgments

I thank Fred Previc for his review of and suggestions on the manuscript.

References

Aghajanian, G., and G. Marek. 1999. "Serotonin and Hallucinogens," *Neuropsychopharmacology* 21: 16S–23S.

Bachner-Melman, Rachel, Christian Dina, Ada H. Zohar, Naama Constantini, Elad Lerer. 2005. "AVPR1a and SLC6A4 Gene Polymorphisms Are Associated with Creative Dance Performance." *PLoS Genetics* 1(3): e42.

Barbano, M. Flavia, and Martine Cader. 2007. "Opioids for Hedonic Experiences and Dopamine to Get Ready for It." *Psychopharmacology* 191:497–506.

Berridge, K. 1996. "Food reward: Brain Substrates of Wanting and Liking," *Neuroscience Biobehavioral Review* 28:309–369.

Dietrich, Arne. 2003. "Functional Neuroanatomy of Altered States of Consciousness: The Transient Hypofrontality Hypothesis." *Consciousness and Cognition* 12: 231–256.

de Rios, Marlene Dobkin. 1984. *Hallucinogens: Cross-Cultural Perspectives*. Albuquerque: University of New Mexico.

Donald, Merlin. 1991. *Origins of the Modern Mind.* Cambridge, MA: Harvard University Press.

Griffiths, R. R., W. A. Richards, U. McCann, and R. Jesse. 2006. "Psilocybin Can Occasion Mystical-Type Experiences Having Substantial, Sustained Personal Meaning and Spiritual Significance." *Psychopharmacology* 187(3): 268–283.

Guzman, G., J. Allen, and J. Gartz. 1998. "A Worldwide Geographical Distribution of the Neurotropic Fungi, an Analysis and Discussion." *Ann. Mus. civ. Rovereto* 14:189–280.

Jones, P. 2005. "Ultrarunners and Chance Encounters with 'Absolute Unitary Being.'" *Anthropology of Consciousness* 15(2): 39–50.

Lende, D. 2008. "Evolution and Modern Behavior Problems: The Case of Addiction." In *Evolutionary Medicine and Health*, edited by W. Trevathan, E. Smith, and J. McKenna. Oxford: Oxford University Press, pp. 277–290.

Mandell, Arnold. 1980. "Toward a Psychobiology of Transcendence: God in the Brain." In *The Psychobiology of Consciousness,* pp. 379–464, edited by Julian Davidson and Richard Davidson. New York: Plenum.

McKim, W. 1991. *Drugs and Behavior An Introduction to Behavioral Pharmacology.* Englewood Cliffs, NJ: Prentice-Hall.

Nesse, R. 1994. "An Evolutionary Perspective on Substance Abuse." *Ethology and Sociobiology* 15: 339–348.

Nesse, R. and K. Berridge. 1997. "Psychoactive Drug Use in Evolutionary Perspective." *Science* 278: 63–66.

Oldham, M., S. Horvath, and D. Geschwind. 2006. "Conservation and Evolution of Gene Coexpression Networks in Human and Chimpanzee Brains." *Proceedings of the National Academy of Sciences of the United States of America.* 103(47): 17973–17978.

Passie, T., Halpern, J., Stichtenoth, D., Emrish, H., and Hintzen, A. 2008. "The Pharmacology of Lysergic Acid Diethylamide: A Review." *CNS Neuroscience & Therapeutics* 14: 295–314.

Pahnke, W. 1966. Drugs and Mysticism, *The International Journal of Parapsychology* 8(2): 295–313.

Pregenzer, J., Alberts, G., Bock, J. Slightom, and W. Im. 1997. "Characterization of Ligand Binding Properties of the 5-HT_{1D} Receptors Cloned from Chimpanzee, Gorilla and Rhesus Monkey in Comparison with Those from the Human and Guinea Pig Receptors." *Neuroscience Letters 3(17) 117–120.*

Previc, F. 2006. "The Role of the Extrapersonal Brain Systems in Religious Activity." *Consciousness and Cognition* 15: 500–539.

Previc, F. 2009. *The Dopaminergic Mind in Human Evolution and History.* Cambridge: Cambridge University Press.

Raghanti, M., C. Stimpson, F. Marcinkiewicz, P. Hof, and C. Sherwood. 2008. "Differences in Cortical Serotonergic Innervation among Humans, Chimpanzees, and Macaque Monkeys: A Comparative Study." *Cerebral Cortex* 18: 584—597.

Rätsch, C. and John R. Baker, trans. (2005). *The Encyclopedia of Psychoactive Plants: Ethnopharmacology and Its Applications.* Rochester, VT: Park Street Press. Originally published as (1998) *Enzyklopädie der psychoaktiven Pflanzen.* Aarau, Switzerland: AT Verlag.

Rockman et al. 2005. "Ancient and Recent Positive Selection Transformed Opioid Cis-Regulation in Humans PLOS," *Biology* 3(12): 2208–2219.

Salamone, J. and Correa, M. 2002. "Motivational Views of Reinforcement: Implications for Understanding the Behavioral Functions of Nucleus Accumbens Dopamine." *Behavioral Brain Research* 137:3–25.

Schultes, R. and Hofmann, A. 1979. *Plants of the Gods: Origins of Hallucinogenic Use.* New York: McGraw Hill. (Reprinted 1992 by Healing Arts Press, Rochester, VT).

Shi, P., M. Bakewell, and J. Zhang. 2006. "Did Brain-Specific Genes Evolve Faster in Humans Than in Chimpanzees?" Trends Genet 22: 608–613.

Smith, E. 1999. "Evolution, Substance Abuse, and Addiction." In *Evolutionary Medicine,* edited by E. Smith and J. McKenna, 375–40. New York: Oxford University Press.

Smith, E. and B. Tasnadi. 2007. "A Theory of Natural Addiction." *Games and Economic Behavior* 59: 316–344.

Sullivan, R., E. Hagen, and P. Hammerstein. 2008. "Revealing the Paradox of Drug Reward in Human Evolution. *Proceedings of the Royal Society B.* 275: 1231–1241.

Sullivan, R. and E. Hagen. 2002. "Psychotrophic Substance-Seeking: Evolutionary pathology or adaptation?" *Addiction* 97: 389–400.

The Chimpanzee Sequencing and Analysis Consortium. 2005. "Initial Sequence of the Chimpanzee Genome and Comparison with the Human Genome." *Nature* 437: 69–87.

Vollenweider, F. 1998. "Recent Advances and Concepts in the Search for Biological Correlates of Hallucinogen-Induced Altered States of Consciousness." *Heffter Review of Psychedelic Research* 1: 21–32.

Wang et al. 2005. "Accelerated Evolution of the Pituitary Adenylate Cyclase-Activating Polypeptide Precursor Gene during Human Origin." *Genetics* 170: 801–806 2005.

Winkelman, M. 1992. "Shamans, Priests, and Witches: A Cross-Cultural Study of Magico-Religious Practitioners." *Anthropological Research Papers #44*. Arizona State University.

Winkelman, M. 1996. "Psychointegrator Plants: Their Roles in Human Culture and Health" In *Sacred Plants, Consciousness and HealingCross-Cultural and Interdisciplinary Perspectives:* Yearbook of Cross-Cultural Medicine and Psychotherapy Volume 6, edited by M. Winkelman and W. Andritzky, pp. 9–53. Berlin: Verlag und Vertrieb.

Winkelman, M. 2000. *Shamanism: The Neural Ecology of Consciousness and Healing.* Westport, CT: Bergin and Garvey.

Winkelman, M. 2001. "Psychointegrators: Multidisciplinary Perspectives on the Therapeutic Effects of Hallucinogens." Complementary Health Practice Review 6(3): 219–237.

Winkelman, M. 2007. "Therapeutic Bases of Psychedelic Medicines: Psychointegrative Effects." In *Psychedelic Medicine,* edited by M. Winkelman and T. Roberts, Vol. 1. Westport, CT: Praeger/Greenwood Perspectives.

Winkelman, M. 2010. *Shamanism: A Biopsychosocial Paradigm of Consciousness and Healing.* Santa Barbara, CA: ABC-CLIO.

Chapter 3

Cannabis and the Hebrew Bible

Chris Bennett and Neil McQueen

Chris Bennett is widely recognized as one of the foremost authorities on the ancient history of cannabis, having written dozens of articles in *High Times, Cannabis Culture,* and other magazines, as well as three books dealing with the subject, *Green Gold the Tree of Life: Marijuana in Magic and Religion* (Access Unlimited 1995), *Sex, Drugs, Violence and the Bible* (www.forbiddenfruitpublishing.com 2001), and *Cannabis and the Soma Solution* (www.trineday.com 2010). Bennett has identified evidence for a religious role for cannabis in a variety of ancient and modern religions, such as Hinduism, Islam, Zoroastrianism, and Taoism, but his work regarding evidence in the Bible for ritual cannabis use by both the ancient Jews and Christians has received the most attention. He lives in Vancouver, British Columbia, Canada, where he runs his entheobotanical shop, The Urban Shaman.

Neil McQueen, a Canadian presently living in New Zealand, is a student of ecstatic religious experience, and received his BA in Humanities/Religious Studies at York University, Toronto in 1985. In the intervening years he has independently continued research in this field, eventually co-authoring with Chris Bennett *Sex, Drugs, Violence and the Bible,* published in 2001. He completed his master's degree at the University of Otago, New Zealand in 2005, and is presently involved in editing *Sex, Drugs, Violence and the Bible* for republication.

Introduction

Sula Benet's article "Early Diffusion and Folk Uses of Hemp," published in *Cannabis and Culture* in 1975, marked a turning point in the study of cannabis references in the Bible. Benet's thesis was that cannabis was known as *kaneh bosm* in the Old Testament and was an ingredient in God's Holy Anointing Oil. Until this point there had been no large-scale publication in English making this information available. Sula Benet has led the authors on an intriguing and fruitful line of inquiry into the validity and implications of this remarkable idea. This article seeks to give a summary of the Biblical references themselves and a history of the scholarship on the subject of cannabis in the Bible.

There are two major problems involved in the investigation of this question. The first problem we come up against is the use of this ancient document as a source of historical truth. Unlike the libraries of cuneiform and hieroglyphic records that have been recovered and translated from antiquity, the Bible is unique. It is a work so heavily edited and rewritten that it cannot be said to accurately depict the times and events it purports to be documenting. Thus, we must lean heavily on other sources of evidence to gain an accurate portrayal of the time in question.

This brings us up against our second difficulty. In dealing with such an immense span of time, and given the perishability of the plant in question, there is a scarcity of archaeological finds. The few cases of preserved identifiable remnants that have come down to us through the intervening millennia, although rare, are enough to maintain the validity of the claim. Given these obstacles, there must be a great deal of care taken in approaching this thorny question, a question that must not, however, be merely discounted or ignored. This is not only a matter of setting the historical record straight—if the many scholars who have taken this particular bull by the horns are correct, there are profound implications for the foundations of Judeo-Christian culture.

Ingredients of the Holy Anointing Oil

In "A Random Walk Through a Cannabis Field," published in *Pharmacology, Biochemistry and Behavior,* the authors remark on the "strange absence" of any reference to cannabis in the Bible (Mechoulam, Devane, Breuer, and Zahalka 1991).

They raise a very good point. Certainly we know that cannabis has an immensely long history of interdependence with humanity, claimed by some to extend back to the late Mesolithic (La Barre 1980). As we shall see, the neighboring cultures surrounding the Levant and the cultural milieu of the entire region were familiar with cannabis. So surely there should be some reference to this highly revered plant within the Bible itself. And yet, apparently, it is silent.

In some respects, this "strange absence" is surprising, considering the long history of scholarship into just this question. The primary reference for cannabis use in the Bible is found in the book of Exodus, which contains a list of ingredients and the proportions to be used in making the sacred anointing oil:

> Then the LORD said to Moses, 'Take the following fine spices: 500 shekels of liquid myrrh, half as much (that is, 250 shekels) of fragrant cinnamon, 250 shekels of aromatic cane, 500 shekels of cassia—all according to the sanctuary shekel—and a hint of olive oil. Make these into a sacred anointing oil, a fragrant blend, the work of a perfumer. It will be the sacred anointing oil (Exodus 30: 22-26).

The ingredients of the sacred anointing oil are all precious. We read in both 2 Kings 20:13 and Isaiah 39:2 that Hezekiah kept spices and "precious oils" in the royal treasury. These goods were highly valued because they were not of local origin and had to be transported great distances into the Levant. In the case of the anointing oil in particular, the proportion of spices used was very large. As we shall see, 500 shekels is a considerable amount.

Myrrh, the resinous accruement of the *Cammiphora myrrha* tree, is native to Arabia, Somalia, and Ethiopia. Fragrant cinnamon is the bark and leaves of the *Cinnamamum zeylanicum* tree indigenous to Sri Lanka (although it was cultivated in various parts of Asia). Cassia is another type of cinnamon, *Cinnamamum cassia,* and native to Southeast Asia. All of these ingredients were therefore imported luxury items.

The final ingredient of the anointing oil is more problematic. The Masoretic Text records the name of this plant as *kaneh bosm* (קנה בשם), literally "sweet" or "fragrant cane." There is difficulty in determining just what this plant was. (For example, see Schoff 1920, Sagarin 1945, Sama 1991.) The English translations of the Bible vary considerably. The King James Version, following the Latin Vulgate, translates the Hebrew term *kaneh bosm* as "calamus." The New King James, however, more accurately renders the word "sweet-smelling cane," as does the New Living Bible. The New Revised Standard translates the term as "aromatic cane," along with the English Standard. The New International, New American Standard, and the Amplified Bible use the similar "fragrant cane." Young's Literal Translation has "spice cane," and the American Standard has "sweet calamus." As we see, only two of the many English translations assert that calamus is the plant in question. Calamus, *Acorus calamus,* also commonly known as sweet flag, is a wetland plant native to South Asia, North America, and Europe. Calamus was used medicinally in Assyria within poultices, but also combined with oils in the treatment of earache, muscle pain, stomachache, and coughs (Jacob 1993). The root of the calamus plant also contains oils whose scent is reminiscent of patchouli, although much fainter, and it has been used in perfumes (Sagarin 1945, Emboden 1972). It is listed by Pliny in his *Natural History,* as an ingredient in various perfumes, including the famous Egyptian Kyphi. Whether it was an item of trade along the ancient spice routes must remain a matter for speculation. Jacob notes that the plant was likely imported from India, where it continues to be used in medicines. This is problematic considering the references to "sweet *kaneh*" in Jeremiah 6:20, as originating from a foreign land: "Of what use to me is frankincense that comes from Sheba, or sweet *kaneh* from a distant land?" (Jeremiah 6: 20) The Hebrew term used in Jeremiah *hatov* (הטב), here translated as "sweet," is literally "good." Likewise in Isaiah 43:24, we read, "you have not bought me sweet *kaneh* with money or satisfied me with the fat of your sacrifices. But you have burdened me with your sins; you have wearied me with your iniquities" (Isaiah 43:24). Clearly *kaneh* was a valuable item of foreign trade and one that was clearly used in public sacrifices. There is further reference to *kaneh* in the Song of Songs, where it is listed as an exotic and fragrant spice along with other "chief spices" (Song of Songs 4:14). Ezekiel states that "Vedan and Uzal entered into trade for your wares; wrought iron, cassia, and sweet *kaneh* were bartered for your merchandise" (Ezekiel 27:19). Although difficult to properly identify, both of these localities are thought to be on Arabian stops of the caravan routes from Central Asia and beyond. That calamus was an item of foreign trade, however, contradicts Pliny, who records that calamus was found in Syria, stating that it grew close to Mt. Lebanon. Polybius (v 46) and Strabo (xvi 4) also maintain that it grew in this region. If *kanehbosm* was available in the local area there would be no need to buy it. This casts doubt on the traditional identification of calamus as *kaneh bosm*. "Fragrant cane," whatever its identity, and like all the other aromatic ingredients of the sacred anointing oil, was clearly imported into Palestine.

The Archeological Record

At present, the earliest archaeological testimony to the use of cannabis in the Fertile Crescent are seeds found in the ruins of ancient Hacilar, close to present-day Ankara, Turkey, and dated to the late sixth-millennium BCE (Mellnick 1962). This puts the cultural use of cannabis in the region into remote antiquity. Unfortunately there is no way of knowing whether it was being used ritually as a psychoactive. Its cultic use as such has been archaeologically established in Western Central Asia. In the late third- and early second-millennium BCE, in the Kara Kum desert in present-day Turkmenistan, there emerged large cities. This culture is known to us as the obscurely named Bactrian-Margiana Archaeological complex (BMAC). Remains of cannabis, ephedra, and poppy have been recovered from these ancient irrigated oasis cities, where they were used in ritual as ingredients in a powerful psychoactive beverage (Sarianidi 1998). Trade with this region and the ancient Near East has long been established. Material remains (principally ceramics) deriving from the BMAC have been recovered from the second-millennium ruins of Elamite Susa (Kohl 1978, Hiebert 1998). It has even been suggested that the Mitanni occupiers of Syria (1500–1380 BCE), known to be Indo-European (or more properly speaking, Proto-Indo-Aryans), had splintered off from the BMAC (Parpola 1998). It has been claimed that cannabis was altogether unknown in the Fertile Crescent. Yet despite there being so few archaeological finds of cannabis in the Near East before the fourth-century CE (see Zias *et al,* 1993), there remains the question of the identity of certain plants holding a central and sacred place throughout the entire region.

There have been several instances of archaeological testimony to the presence of cannabis within ancient Egypt. According to the *Codex of Ancient Egyptian Plant Remains,* cannabis pollen has been identified at Egyptian sites from the Predynastic Period (c. 3500–3100 BCE) and the Twelfth Dynasty (c. 1991–1786 BCE), where not only pollen, but also a hemp "fibre (ball)" was found (de Vartavan and Amoros 1997). Pollen was identified on the Nineteenth Dynasty (c. 1293–1185 BCE) mummy of Ramses II (Manniche 1989), with additional pollen samples from the Ptolemaic period (323–330 BCE) (de Vartavan and Amoros 1997). Furthermore, at El-Amarna pieces of hemp cloth were found in the tomb of Amenhotep IV, also known as Akhenaten (Manniche 1989). From these archaeological finds it is clear that cannabis was not unknown in ancient Egypt. Although this testifies to the presence of *Cannabis sativa* as a source of fiber, it can't establish its use as a psychoactive.

References from ancient Egyptian literature have also been cited (see Reymond 1976). The hieroglyph *shemshemet* (in Egyptian hieroglyphics, *smsm.t*) has been identified by many scholars as cannabis (Dawson 1934a, Nunn 2002, Kabelik 1955, Mathre 1997, Graindorge 1992). There is a good case for it, as it is mentioned in the record as both a medicine and cordage and there are no other candidates that have such characteristics. There have been no references to *shemshemet* being used as a psychoactive, however.

Numerous researchers have seen "nepenthe" as a cannabis concoction—an idea first put forth by the French pharmacist Joseph Virey (1775–1846), who suggested in 1813 that hashish was Homer's nepenthe. Many others have since concurred (see Christen 1822, Watt 1853, Benjamin 1880, Wilkinson & Birch 1878, Walton 1938, Burton 1894, Lewin 1931, Singer and Underwood 1962, Oursler 1968, Wills 1998, Bennett 2001). There is archaeological evidence that confirms this conclusion. As the nepenthe was a wine infusion, it is important to note that ancient amphorae, clay wine vessels from an Egyptian site from the time period in question, revealed evidence of cannabis. In the 2004 paper, "Pollen Analysis of the Contents of Excavated Vessels—Direct Archaeobotanical Evidence of Beverages," Manfred Rosch refers to vessels collected from a site in ˇSaruma/Al-Kom Al-Ahmar, in Middle Egypt on the Nile:

> At this place the Institute of Egyptology of the University of Tubingen is excavating a graveyard, which was used from the 6th Dynasty until the Roman period.... Here some wine amphorae were excavated, from the bottom of which we obtained samples of organic material for pollen analytical investigations.... The useful plants, *Cerealia* and *Humulus/Cannabis,* were present (Rosch 2004).

Unlike in Egypt, there have been no archaeological finds of cannabis from the Tigris-Euphrates valley. This leaves us with the written and iconographic record from this region. In the cuneiform record,

R. Campbell Thompson has identified the Assyrian word *azullu* as cannabis in the ancient Assyrian annals, although this has been contested.

Reginald Campbell Thompson, who spent more than fifty years deciphering cuneiform Assyrian medical texts, summarized his reasoning regarding these translations in *A Dictionary of Assyrian Chemistry and Geology:*

> *Sami nissati,* "a drug for sorrow," coupled with the property of spinning and making a cable, makes "hemp," Cannabis, the Indian *bhang, binj,* certain, which is further borne out by the Persian *gargarinj, Cannabis sativa,* L. (the –nj is a frequent termination). *GAN.ZI.GUN.NU* is one of the most interesting words in cuneiform; we have already seen that *GAN.ZI.SAR* is *kanasu,* a narcotic "like mandragora," presumably opium; *GUN.NU* is the equivalent of some form of *burrumu,* originally apparently "to twist, weave" as well as "to be two-colored." Consequently the word = *GAN.ZI* + "weave," i.e. the weaving narcotic, and there is great philological similarity between this and the Hindustani *ganjha* (cannabis) (Thompson 1936).

Although this translation has been questioned (Farber, 1981; Black, George and Postgate, 2000; Oppenheim et al 1968), as E. Russo has pointed out:

> We have a plant that was considered psychoactive, was used in fabric, was administered as a fumigant, insecticide, orally, cutaneously, and as an enema. It was pounded and strained as hashish, and its seed, stem, leaf and flower were all utilized. An alternative identification beyond cannabis strains credulity (Russo 2005).

In the second quarter of the first millennium BCE, the "word *qunnabu* (*qunapy, qunubu, qunbu*) begins to turn up as for a source of oil, fiber, and medicine" (Barber 1989). There is a more general acceptance of the identification of *qunubu* as cannabis amongst researchers than with *azallu* (Reiner 1995). The Sumerian *šim. Išhara,* "aromatic of the Goddess Ishtar," equated with the Akkadian term *qunnabu*, has likewise been identified as cannabis. In this case, the herb is associated with the goddess of love, Ishara, perhaps indicating an aphrodisiac (Reiner 1995).

In our own time, numerous scholars (Lewin 1931, Meissner 1932-1933, Benetowa 1936, Frisk 1960-72, Thorwald, 1963, Schultes and Hoffman 1979, Abel 1982, Bennett et al 1995, etc.) have come to acknowledge *qunubu* as an early reference to cannabis. Recipes for *qunubu* incense, regarded as copies of much older versions, were found in the cuneiform library of the legendary Assyrian king Assurbanipal (b. 685–c. 627 BC, reigned 669–c. 631 BC). Records from the time of Assurbanipal's father, Esarhaddon (reigned 681–669 BC), give clear evidence of the importance of such substances in Mesopotamia, as *qunubu* is listed as one of the main ingredients of the paramount "Sacred Rites." In a letter written in 680 BCE to the mother of the Assyrian king, Esarhaddon, reference is made to *qunubu*. In response to Esarhaddon's mother's question as to "What is used in the sacred rites?" a high priest named Neralsharrani responded that "the main items … for the rites are fine oil, water, honey, odorous plants (and) hemp [qunubu]" (Waterman 1930). Although this is not as conclusive as the Egyptian finds, it cannot be easily dismissed that cannabis was current among the dwellers of the Tigris-Euphrates. These are not the only cultures familiar with cannabis to have left a presence in the region.

An Assyrian medical tablet from the Louvre collection (AO 7760) (Labat, 1950)(3,10,16) was transliterated as follows … "*ana min sam mastabbariru sam a-zal-la samtar-mus.*"Translating the French [EBR], we obtain, "So that god of man and man should be in good rapport:—with hellebore, cannabis and lupine you will rub him" (Russo 2005).

The Scythian Incursion

In *Le Chanvre les Croyances et les Coutumes Populaires*, first published in 1936, the Polish anthropologist Sara Benetawa proposed an alternate translation of the Hebrew קנה בשם (*kaneh bosm*). She claimed that *kaneh* was the Hebrew name for cannabis. This may be borne out by a reference Benet notes to the use of *kaneh* shirts as a religious requirement for the burial of the dead (Klein 1908). Cannabis is the only plant that is both psychoactive and a fiber source, making its identification as *kaneh* more likely than *Acorus calamus*. Benet goes on to note the similarities between the Hebrew and the Scythian names for cannabis, and suggested a connection between them. There can be no denying the phonetic resemblance the two words bear to each other. That the Scythians were a cannabis-using culture is attested to both by Herodotus and archaeological finds. Herodotus describes the Scythian use of small "tents" in which they would burn cannabis on heated stones. Herodotus also states that the Scythians cultivated cannabis (Herodotus, *History*, II, 4.75). These descriptions have since been borne out by archaeological finds (see Rudenko 1970). That there was a Scythian presence in the Near East is attested to by a number of sources, both textual and archaeological. The Assyrian annals are witness to the threat posed by the Scythians, first appearing in the letters of Esarhaddon (680-669 BCE) and identified by the Assyrians as the Ashguzai or Ishguzai. They represented a substantial threat, putting pressure on the Assyrian northern border. Esarhaddon's letters bear witness to an uneasy alliance forged between the Scythians and the Assyrians through the marriage of Esarhaddon's daughter to one Bartatua, the Scythian king (Phillips 1972). Eventually they fought together against their mutual enemy, the Medes (Johnston 1901).

Herodotus also testifies to the Scythian threat to the regions further west, even recording an incursion through Palestine:

> Thence they marched against Egypt: and when they were in the part of Syria called Palestine, Psammetichos king of Egypt met them and persuaded them with gifts and prayers to come no further. So they turned back, and when they came on their way to the city of Ascalon in Syria, most of the Scythians passed by and did no harm, but a few remained behind and plundered the temple of Heavenly Aphrodite (Herodotus, *History*, I, 1).

The Scythian presence in Palestine is also attested to archaeologically. An excavation conducted in 1886 by W.M. Flinders Petrie in present-day Tel Dafenneh in Egypt revealed hundreds of Scythian-type bronze arrowheads, and a Scythian-style iron dagger (Yamauchi 1983). Flinders Petrie attributed these arrowheads to Ionian and Curian mercenaries. However, Yamauchi notes that "such arrowheads appear only *after* the incursion of the Scythians south of the Caucasus in the late eight and early seventh centuries" (Yamauchi 1983). Tadeusz Sulimirski has presented the collected findings of these Scythian-type arrowheads throughout the Near East, and lists "a number of trilobite arrowheads discovered at Samaria in seventh-century strata. Contemporaneous specimens have been discovered along the Philistine coast at Tell-el-Ajjul and Tell Fara. Sulimirski even reports one three-edged specimen from Jerusalem (1954: 297, 299)." Sulimirski elsewhere cautions regarding the conclusion that Scythian-type arrowheads necessarily points directly to a Scythian presence in an area (Phillips 1972). In the case of Palestine, however, the renaming of Beth-Shan as Scythopolis, at the eastern end of the Jezreel valley and approximately sixty kilometers from Jerusalem, as attested to in Herodotus's writings in the fifth-century BCE, and Flavius Josephus's *Antiquities of the Jews,* serves as testimony that the Scythians had not only passed through Israel, but had settled there. To confirm this, the excavations at Beth-Shan carried out by Clarence Fisher found a seventh-century BCE strata of Scythian remains (Powis Smith 1926).

From this historical and archaeological testimony it cannot be doubted that there was a Scythian presence in Palestine. This, of course, is only circumstantial in regards to the identification of *kaneh bosm* as cannabis, but it raises interesting questions concerning the anointing oil. Perhaps it contained a psychoactive topical compound? The quantity of *kaneh bosm* involved in the recipe found in Exodus 30: 23 would be an extremely large dose of cannabis, and its psychoactive compound, *tetrahydracannabinol* (THC), is oil-soluble. There would certainly be enough THC in the solution to produce a very powerful effect if used topically. Psalm 133 contains reference to the "precious oil on the head, running down the beard ... running down the collar of his robes" (Psalm 133:2); it would seem that quite a quantity of oil was poured in an anointing rite, and not just a mere smudge of the costly unguent. The people who used the holy oil literally drenched themselves in it. Given the quantities of *kaneh bosm* reportedly used, there can be no question as to its effectiveness. As one shekel equals approximately 16.378 grams, this means that the THC of over eighteen pounds of cannabis were extracted into a hind, about 6.5 liters of oil. The effects of such a solution, even when applied topically, would undoubtedly have been intense. Health Canada has done scientific tests that show transdermal absorption of THC can take place. The skin is the largest organ of the body, so of course considerably more cannabis is needed to be effective this way, much more than when ingested or smoked. Based upon a 25 mg/g oil solution, Health Canada found skin penetration of THC to be 33 percent. "The high concentration of THC outside the skin encourages penetration, which is a function of the difference between outside and inside (where the concentration is essentially zero)" (Geiwitz 2001). The accounts of the witch's "flying ointments," compounded and used topically in medieval times and often containing cannabis and hashish as an ingredient, serves as an instance of the viability of cannabis-containing psychoactive topical compounds used as a means of inducing ecstatic states (Rudgley 1998). Additionally Exodus contains prescriptions for the anointing of the incense altar and the altar of burnt offerings (Exodus 30: 27-28), in both cases involving igniting the anointing oil. If the resulting smoke contained cannabis it would have produced a pronounced psychoactive effect upon anyone in attendance. In reference to the anointing of the altar of incense is research done into the psychoactive effects of frankincense, listed as one of the ingredients of the Holy Incense in Exodus 30:34. Reports of altar boys exhibiting addictive behavior toward the burning of frankincense led members of the Academy of Science in Leipzig to test samples. They found that when burned, frankincense produces trahydrocannabinole (Fischer-Rizzi 1990). This compound is psychoactive and related to the cannabinoids produced in cannabis. Additionally, the antidepressant and anti-anxiety effects of frankincense have been exhaustively researched (Moussaieff, Rimmerman, Bregman, Straiker, Felder, Shoham, Kashman, Huang, Lee, Shohami, Mackie, Caterina, Walker, Fride and Mechoulam 2008). Interestingly, the oil of the root of *Acorus calamus* contains asarone and beta-asarone, both of which are reportedly psychoactive. In considerable amounts, the root oils have the potential to induce strong hallucinations, and its effects have been compared to LSD (Evans Schultes and Hofmann 1979). Asarone and beta-asarone seem to be responsible for these effects (Evans Schultes and Hofmann 1973, Ott 1993). Calamus is listed as one of the ingredients used in the abovementioned witch's flying ointments, also raising the possibility that it could have been utilized for its psychoactive effects in God's sacred anointing oil. Thus, whether *cannabis sativa* or *Acorus calamus,* the sacred anointing oil contained a psychoactive botanical compound.

The Persian Conquest

That one of the ingredients of this oil was cannabis, as put forward by Sula Benet, remains a possibility. In addition to the known Scythian presence in Palestine from the seventh-century BCE, it must also be mentioned that the Persians were a cannabis-using culture. Needless to say, Persian cultural influence, concomitant with their complete military and political domination of the region, was pervasive. Central to the Persian cult was the ritual drinking of *haoma,* both by priests and worshippers. The *Zend-Avesta,* in particular *Yasts* 9-11, known as the *Hôm-Yast,* praise this exhilarating beverage. Zoroaster as a reformer didn't innovate the *haoma* rite, it being already current among the Persians (Zaehner 1961). In a legend of his birth, Zoroaster was conceived after his parents drank *haoma* made from his divine essence that had fallen from heaven. The question of whether the Achaemenid dynasty was Zoroastrian is moot as far as the *haoma* rite is concerned, as they were certainly Mazdaist (Jackson and Gray 1900, Cameron 1958). The *haoma* rite is known to have been current at the imperial court of the Achaemenids. At Persepolis great quantities of ritual mortars and pestles were recovered from the Royal Treasury and have been "tentatively identified as ceremonial utensils used for crushing the drug haoma"(Cahill 1985).

It has long been established that the sacred *haoma* was a psychoactive beverage (Stein 1931, Falk 1989, Brough 1971, Rudgley 1998). There has been considerable scholarly debate regarding just what the ingredients of the *haoma* were comprised of, in particular the identification of the psychoactive plant in question. Many candidates for the psychoactive ingredient have been put forward, among them the fly agaric mushroom, (*Amanita muscaria*), cannabis (*Cannabis sativa*), Syrian rue (*Peganum harmala L.*), and ephedra (*Ephedra procera*). *Amanita muscaria* may be discounted, as the *Zend-Avesta* describes the "lofty mountains where the haoma branches spread." Likewise the harmala alkaloid containing Syrian rue, while used in Zoroastrian rites prior to 900 CE, is unlikely as a candidate for the more ancient *haoma,* as it was burnt rather than pressed. As noted, recent archaeological discoveries of the BMAC in the Kara Kum desert have brought to light a Bronze Age temple complex containing not only evidence of fire worship, but more significantly, stone presses for the production of such a beverage, with samples of ephedra, cannabis, and poppy recovered (Sarianidi 1998). Physical remains from this culture have been found as far to the southwest as Elamite Susa, known later as the residence of Darius I, and the setting of the Book of Esther.

Of these three ingredients, cannabishas the most pronounced psychoactive effect; poppy being a depressant and ephedra a stimulant. These discoveries indicate a blend of plants as a likelihood in the production of *haoma,* as does the *Zend-Avesta* itself. *Yasna* 10: 17 states that "all the plants of H(a)oma praise I, on the heights of lofty mountains, in the gorges of the valleys, in the clefts (of the sundered hill-sides) cut for bundles by the women."

There is also testimony to the Persian use of cannabis outside of the *haoma* sacrifice. The *Fravaši-Yašt* refers to a *pouru-bhanga,* a "possessor of cannabis." Ahura Mazda is also described as being "without trance and without hemp," and in the *Vidēvdat* cannabis isvilified. There are also traditions that record that Vishtaspa, one of Zoroaster's early supporters, entered an ecstatic state induced by cannabis.

Vicente Dobroruka, in his thesis "Preparation for Visions in Second Temple Jewish Apocalyptic Literature,"noted a comparison between these Persian techniques of ecstasy and those described in the apocryphal book 4, Ezra. In this text Ezra is described as reciting the entire Bible to scribes after drinking from a fiery cup:

> And on the next day, behold, a voice called me, saying, "Ezra, open your mouth and drink what I give you to drink." Then I opened my mouth, and behold, a full cup was offered to me; it was full of something like water, but its color was like fire. And I took it and drank and when I had drunk of it, my heart uttered understanding, and wisdom grew in my breast, for my spirit strengthened my memory: And my mouth was opened, and shut no more.
>
> The Highest gave understanding unto the five men, and they wrote the wonderful visions of the night that were told, which they knew not: and they sat forty days, and they wrote in the day, and at night they ate bread. As for me. I spake in the day, and I held not my tongue by night. In forty days they wrote two hundred and four books (4 Ezra 14: 38–44).

The inspiration derived from the fiery liquid described in 4 Ezra is a clear use of the Persian *haoma* rite.That Ezra actually drank the fiery beverage and then proceeded to recite the entirety of the Bible to his scribes is clearly a nonhistorical legend as 4 Ezra is accepted to be of a much later date of composition, placed thirty years after the destruction of the Temple by the Romans in 70 CE. However, any ancient readers of 4 Ezra familiar with the *haoma* rite would have immediately recognized it in this work, and that it is influenced by the *haoma* ritual is beyond question.

Dobroruka observes the similarity between this incident and various examples from Persian literature involving similar inspiring psychoactive beverages. He notes *Bhaman Yasht* 3: 7-8. *Dinkard* 7: 4.84-86 and the *Book of Artay Viraz* 2.25-28. In furtherance to this, as Russian anthropologist V. A. Kisel has observed: "The image of a blazing cup was apparently related to ... Zoroastrianism; Zoroastrian texts mention ritual vessels with fire burning inside them" (Kisel 2007). The blazing cup is also found in Scythian mythology. Kisel points to a Scythian legend of a fiery golden cup that fell from the sky and would burst into flames when approached unless the recipient was the future king.

Dobroruka revisited this theme in more detail in his later 2006 article, "Chemically Induced Visions in the Fourth Book of Ezra in Light of Comparative Persian Material," and again draws direct comparisons between Ezra's cup of fire and the haoma of the Persians. Dobroruka expanded on this connection by noting the similar accounts of the flowers eaten by Ezra in 4 Ezra 9, and those used for similar revelation by the Zoroastrian figure "Jamasp."

> But if you will let seven days more pass—do not fast during them, however; but go into a field of flowers where no house has been built, and eat only of the flowers of the field, and taste no meat and drink no wine, but eat only flowers, and pray to the Most High continually—then I will come and talk with you (4 Ezra 9: 23-25).

Dobroruka points to the *Jāmāsp Namag*, a Persian pseudo-epigraphic text that describes Jāmāsp receiving wisdom from Zoroaster by means of a flower. He also refers to a Pahlavi text *Wizirkard i Denig* 19 with the same theme. In the words of Dobroruka:

> All this tends to support the idea that the two mythical themes examined that find way in 4 Ezra (namely, that of the cup and that of the flower, both of which bestow wisdom) were, both by their antiquity and their frequency, primarily Persian ecstatic practices that found themselves echoed in a Jewish apocalypse (Dobroruka 2006).

All of these references point to a currency among the Persians with the sacramental use of cannabis as a psychoactive. Ethnobotanists have suggested that cannabis may have its origins in the foothills of the Himalayas bordering northern Iran, so a close relationship between it and the cultures of the region is not surprising (Evans Schultes and Hofmann 1979). The Achaemenid conquerors may not have necessarily been Zoroastrians, but there is ample testimony that they were Mazdaists. The spread of cannabis through the Persians is also, therefore, a distinct possibility. Of significance is the fact that one of the Persian names for cannabis, *kenab,* like the Scythian "cannabis," closely corresponds to the Hebrew *kaneh bosm.* Although as with the Scythians, a sure identification of the Hebrew *kaneh bosm* with the Persian *kenab* must remain uncertain. Likewise, the Persians as the disseminators of cannabis in this region must remain a possibility only. However, that both the Scythians and the Persians were known cannabis-using cultures, and that both were present within Palestine presents a cultural milieu in which the sacramental use of cannabis was not only accepted, but central.

Although it must presently remain speculative, this points to a relationship between anointing and the deity as being mediated by a psychoactive topical ointment. Cannabis is renowned as a powerful hallucinogen in large doses, and certainly capable of inducing profound ecstatic states. Anyone who doubts this has clearly not experienced its effects. Although a certain identification of *kaneh bosm* as cannabis must remain a possibility until new evidence comes to light, the possibility of the sacred anointing oil described in Exodus being psychoactive cannot be easily discounted. It makes perfect sense that the special reverence expressed for the anointing oil in the Pentateuch and the authority it communicated to its recipients derived from the ecstatic states produced from its use.

The Holy Anointing Oil

The purpose and nature of the Holy Anointing Oil of God is set in Exodus 30: 25-33. The tent of meetings, the Ark of the Covenant, the other contents of the sanctuary, along with the priests are all to be anointed. The nature of the anointing oil is then described, and it is unlike any other substance in the Bible:

> You shall say to the Israelites, "This shall be my holy anointing oil throughout your generations. It shall not be used in any ordinary anointing of the body, and you shall make no other like it in composition; it is holy, and it shall be holy to you" (Exodus 30: 31-32).

The text is explicit; the anointing oil imbues any object or person it touches with holiness. They are made sacred. This is a pivotal point of contact between not just the holy and the mundane, but humanity and God. In the act of anointing the holiness of God is communicated. The power of the oil is underscored by the warning accompanying the instructions in Exodus: "Whoever compounds any like it or whoever puts any of it on an unqualified person shall be cut off from the people" (Exodus 30:33). There are consequences involved with the oil because it had the power to communicate God's holiness and therefore authority. Those anointed were made holy and the oil was reserved strictly for the ordination of priests and kings. The Hebrew term *messiah* (משיח) means "anointed one" and is used only to refer to those who have been consecrated by God's anointing oil.

The text of the Bible relates several noteworthy incidents involving the anointing oil. A look at the descriptions of this rite found within the narrative of the Bible reveals that the first time we see the anointing used is at the coronation rite of the first king of Israel in 1 Samuel 10:1-16. This unlikely incident occurs in secret between Samuel and Saul. Following the impromptu anointing rite:

> …the spirit of Yahweh came mightily upon the new king and he "prophesied among them." The verb "to prophecy" in this context [*nebiim*] meant not to foretell the future but to behave ecstatically, to babble incoherently under the influence of the Spirit. This bizarre conduct associated with prophesying is apparent when in a second burst of such activity, Saul stripped

> off his clothing and lay naked all day and night, causing the people to ask, "Is Saul among the prophets?" (1 Samuel 19: 24) (Cole 1959)

Samuel's anointing of David is also noteworthy for its reference to the Spirit of the Lord apparently being communicated by the anointing: "Then Samuel took the horn of oil and anointed him in the midst of his brothers; and the Spirit of the Lord came mightily upon David from that day forward" (1 Samuel 16:13). Clearly the authors/editors of this passage are emphasizing a direct connection between the anointing rite and the coming of the Spirit of God.

As cautioned in the introductory remarks, care must be taken in interpreting these incidents as actual historical events. There is no evidence, beyond the text itself, that any of these individuals ever existed, and the document has been so thoroughly reworked that to draw conclusions beyond what the editors may have wished to convey is to go out onto very thin ice. It is made abundantly clear from the text that the anointing oil is being emphasized, not only for its holiness and the holiness it can communicate, but for its power. Only those consecrated by the anointing oil could be proclaimed the messiah, the "anointed one," with all the authority this title carries. That this power was infused in the anointing oil by a renowned psychoactive compound is a startling idea, one which casts the Bible in a wholly new light.

Overview of the Scholarship

Due credit must be given to Sula Benet for her groundbreaking work in postulating *kaneh bosm* as a candidate for identifying cannabis in the Bible. This has proven to be a very fruitful avenue of investigation. Although Sula Benet must be acknowledged as the spearhead in the modern diffusion of the identification of cannabis as an ingredient of the holy anointing, there is much testimony to the presence of cannabis in the Bible preceding her.

In *A Cyclopaedia of Biblical Literature,* the nineteenth-century scholar John Kitto put forth two potentially related etymologies for "hashish," through the Hebrew terms *shesh,* which originates in reference to some sort of "fiber plant," and the possibly related word *eshishah* (e-*shesh-ah*?), which holds connotations of "syrup" or "unguent." The term *shesh* occurs thirty-three times in the Bible, where it is used in reference to a fiber-bearing plant or products made of this plant:

> In several passages where we find the word used, we do not obtain any information respecting the plant; but it is clear it was spun by women (Exod. xxx. 25), was used as an article of clothing, also for hangings, and even for the sails of ships, as in Ezekiel xxvii. 7. It is evident from these facts that it must have been a plant known as cultivated in Egypt at the earliest period, and which, or its fiber, the Israelites were able to obtain even when in the desert. As cotton does not appear to have been known at this very early period, we must seek for shesh among the other fiber yielding plants, such as flax and hemp (Kitto 1849).

Kitto goes on to claim that hemp is the most likely candidate for the identity of this plant. How exactly Kitto concludes that *shesh* "must have been a plant known as cultivated in Egypt at the earliest period" he does not say, and goes on to admit that: "We are, indeed, unable at present to prove that it was cultivated in Egypt at an early period, and used for making garments, but there is nothing improbable in its having been so" (Kitto 1849).

Kitto also suggests that e*shishah* may have been a reference to cannabis. *Eshishah* holds a wide variety of somewhat contradictory translations, such as "flagon," "sweet cakes," "syrup," and also, interestingly for our study, "unguent." Kitto bases his claims on the cognate pronunciations of the Persian "duschab [debhash]," which he claims is "but a harsh corruption of the Hebrew eshishah, and is by others called hashish and achicha" (Kitto 1849). Kitto goes on to state that "Hebrew *eshishah* ... is by others called *hashish* ... this substance, in course of time, was converted into a medium of intoxication by means of drugs" (Kitto 1845, 1856). With the cognate pronunciation similarities found between the Hebrew *Shesh* and *Eshishah,* one can only speculate on the possibility of two ancient Hebrew references to one plant that held both fibrous and intoxicating properties.

In a 1903 essay, "Indications of the Hachish-Vice in the Old Testament," a British physician, Dr. C. Creighton, concluded that several references to cannabis can be found in the Old Testament. Creighton felt that "there are some half-dozen passages where cryptic references to hachish may be discovered." His claims focus on "honeycomb" referred to in the Song of Solomon 5:1, and the "honeywood" in I Samuel 14: 25-45. Creighton believed that cannabis dipped in honey was a "secret vice" of the Hebrew temple and palace, and was evidence of a polluting foreign influence.

> Hachish, which is the disreputable intoxicant drug of the East … is of unknown antiquity. It is known that the fiber of hemp-plant, *Cannabis sativa,* was used for cordage in ancient times; and it is therefore probable that the resinous exudation, "honey" or "dew," which is found upon its flowering tops on some soils, or in certain climates (*Cannabis Indica*), was known for its stimulant or intoxicant properties from an equally early date … we may assume it to have been traditional among the Semites from remote antiquity. There are reasons, in the nature of the case, why there should be no clear history. All vices are veiled from view; they are sub rosa; and that is true especially of the vices of the East. Where they are alluded to at all, it is in cryptic, subtle … and allegorical terms. Therefore if we are to discover them, we must be prepared to look below the surface of the text (Creighton 1903).

Creighton pointed to Jonathan's eyes brightening when he ate "honey" off his spear, in 1 Samuel 14: 27, as a reference to this. Another purported instance of cannabis use that Creighton points to is Ezekiel's vision in the temple:

> [I]n the first chapter of Ezekiel a phantasmagoria of composite creatures, of wheels, and of brilliant play of colours, which is strongly suggestive of the subjective visual perceptions of hachish, and is unintelligible from any other point of view, human or divine. This is the chapter of Ezekiel that gave so much trouble to the ancient canonists, and is said to have made them hesitate about including the book. Ezekiel was included in the Canon, but with the instruction that no one in the Synagogue was to attempt to comment upon Chapter I, or, according to another version, that the opening chapter was not to be read by or to persons under a certain age. The subjective sensations stimulated by hachish are those of sight and hearing. It would be easy to quote examples of fantastic composite form, and of wondrous colours, which have been seen by experimenters (Creighton 1903).

Creighton also refers to Nebuchadnezzar's eating of grass in Daniel 4: 25, 32, 33; 5: 21 as an instance of cannabis consumption. He stated that "in the case of Daniel's apologue of Nebuchadnezzar's fall, it arises from the eating of "grass," the Semitic word having both a generic and a colloquial meaning (hachish), as well as from the introduction of the subjective perceptions of hachish intoxication as "gigantic or grotesque objects" (Creighton 1903). Although Crieghton's claims may be considered cryptic, as he himself admits, his article cannot be overlooked in the history of the investigation of cannabis references in the Bible.

Then in 1926, Immanuel Löw, a German researcher, in his *Die Flora Der Juden,* identified a number of ancient Hebrew references to cannabis as an incense, food source, as well as cloth, noting the *kaneh* and *kaneh bosm* references amongst others in this regard. Interestingly, Löw referred to an ancient Jewish Passover recipe that called for wine to be mixed with ground-up saffron and hasisat surur, which he saw as a "a kind of deck name for the resin the Cannabis sativa" (Löw 1924). Löw suggests that this preparation was also made into a burnable and fragrant concoction by being combined with Saffron and Arabic Gum (Löw 1926/1967).

Sula Benet's (as Sara Benetawa) publication in 1936, "*Le Chanvre les Croyances et les Coutumes Populaires,*" which put forth the identification of *kaneh bosm* as cannabis, was followed by an article in English, "Early Diffusion and Folk Uses of Hemp," published in Vera Rubin's *Cannabis and Culture* in 1975. This publication can be acknowledged as the point at which this information was first introduced popularly into the English-speaking world. Any identification of cannabis as *kaneh bosm* following this can be credited to Benet's work as the disseminator of this information. There is ample evidence of this.

In 1980, the anthropologist Weston La Barre referred to the biblical *kaneh* references in an essay on cannabis in which he not only concurs with Benet's earlier hypothesis, but refers directly to her article. In that same year the British Journal *New Scientist* ran a story that referred to the Hebrew Old Testament references: "Linguistic evidence indicates that in the original Hebrew and Aramaic texts of the Old Testament the 'holy oil' which God directed Moses to make (Exodus 30: 23) was composed of myrrh, cinnamon, cannabis and cassia" (Malyon and Henman 1980). Then in 1981, Aryeh Kaplan, a noted American Orthodox rabbi and author, in *The Living Torah,* noted that, "On the basis of cognate pronunciation and a Septuagint reading, some identify Keneh bosem with English and Greek cannabis, the hemp plant" (Kaplan 1981). As well, William McKim noted in *Drugs and Behaviour* that "it is likely that the Hebrews used cannabis.... In the Old Testament (Exodus 30: 23), God tells Moses to make a holy oil of 'myrrh, sweet cinnamon, kaneh bosem and kassia'" (McKim 1986). *A Minister's Handbook of Mental Disorders* records that "some scholars believe that God's command to Moses (Exodus 30: 23) to make a holy oil included cannabis as one of the chosen ingredients" (Ciarrocchi 1993). All of these references may be accredited to Benet's thesis and trace its diffusion through the subsequent academic and popular media.

Independent support for Benet's view of the Semitic origins of the term *kaneh* can be found in *The Word: The Dictionary That Reveals the Hebrew Source of English,* by Isaac E. Mozeson. In reference to Hebrew *kaneh,* Mozeson follows a similar view to Benet's that the "so-called IE root kanna … is admitted to be 'of Semitic origin' … the IE word kannabis (hemp—a late IE word borrowed from an unknown source).… KANBOOS is an early post biblical term for hemp.… The word HEMP is traced to Greek kannabis and Persian kannab.… The ultimate etymon is conceded by Webster's to be "a very early borrowing from a non-IE, possibly Semitic language.… In seeking related words … consider Aramaic … KENABH … and [Hebrew] KANEH" (Mozeson 1989).

Botanist William Emboden wrote that the "shamanistic Ashera priestesses of pre-reformation Jerusalem … anointed their skins with … [a cannabis] mixture as well as burned it" (Emboden 1972). The sources of Emboden's evocative references remain unconfirmed.

Professor Stanley Moore, chairman of the philosophy department at the University of Wisconsin-Olatteville, has stated that biblical references to "aromatic herbs" and "smoke" could mean psychoactive drugs used in religious observances that Moore said are as old as religion itself. "Western Jews and Christians, who shun psychoactive drugs in their faith practices, are the exception, not the norm" (see Moore 1993).

More recently, Raphael Mechoulam and associates at the Hebrew University in Jerusalem have suggested the following etymology for cannabis: Greek *cannabis* < Arabic *kunnab* < Syriac *qunnappa* < Hebrew *pannag* (= *bhanga* in Sanskrit and *bang* in Persian). Mechoulam explains that in Hebrew, only the consonants form the basis of a word and the letters *p* and *b* are frequently interchangeable. The authors think it probable that pannag, which they saw as indicating a preparation of cannabis rather than whole plant, was mentioned in the Bible by the prophet Ezekiel as being an item of trade on an incoming caravan [Ezekiel 27:17] (Mechoulam et al 1991).

Marinus De Waal claimed in 1994 that hemp fabric was used as clothing by the ancient Israelites, later to be replaced by cotton and linen. De Waal went on to state that the hangings and cords used in the sanctuary "in the days of Moses" were hemp (De Waal 1994).

In 1997, George Andrews wrote: "In recent years many eminent scholars have expressed the opinion that, far from being a minor or occasional ingredient, hashish was the main ingredient of the incense burned in temples during the religious ceremonies of antiquity, and was also routinely used in Hebrew ceremonies until the reign of King Josiah in 621 BC, when its use was suddenly suppressed in the Hebrew tradition" (Andrews 1997).

As we can see from this survey of scholarship on the subject, there is a wealth and breadth of inquiry into cannabis in the Bible that spans several centuries. Yet this fascinating and intriguing line of inquiry remains obscure. Given the frequency of psychoactive substances being used in the context of religious ritual throughout history, it shouldn't be surprising to find it once again in the anointing rites of the Hebrews attested to in the Bible.

Conclusion

If Sula Benet is correct and *kaneh bosm* is cannabis, this casts the Bible in a challenging new light. The narrative then attests to the use of a psychoactive anointing oil used in an initiatory rite, which imbued the recipient with the holiness of God. The initiatory rite of all Hebrew priests and kings was carried out using God's Holy Anointing Oil as set out in Exodus 30: 25-33. This most sacred of unctions was reserved for this task, and all who were anointed with it became "messiah," the anointed of God. This points to a ritual complex central to Judaism involving the investiture of individuals with the authority of God, communicated through his holiness imbued within a psychoactive anointing oil. This puts the biblical religions within the context of the worldwide and historical shamanistic use of psychoactive substances as a means of mediation between humanity and sacred reality. In this way the biblical references to cannabis may be as much a threat to fundamental religion as Darwin's theory of evolution was to the myths of Genesis; they reveal the shamanic origins of the religion through the use of cannabis for spiritual revelation. That it is this very relationship with psychoactive plants that believers in the biblical traditions have tried so hard to prohibit around the world in other cultures becomes poignantly ironic. The revelation of this hidden history of cannabis offers the opportunity for a paradigm shift in our understanding of religion and its origins.

References

Primary Sources

Herodotus. 1920. *Herodotus.* Vol. I. Loeb Classic Library. Translated by A. D. Godley. London: William Heinemann.

Herodotus. 1921. *Herodotus.* Vol. II. Loeb Classic Library. Translated by A. D. Godley. London: William Heinemann.

Josephus, Flavius. 1907. *Antiquities of the Jews.* Translated by W. Whiston. London: Ward & Lock.

Polybius. 1889. *The Histories of Polybius.* Vol. I. Translated by Evelyn S. Shuckburgh. London: Macmillan.

Pliny. 1945. *Natural History.* Vol. III. Translated by H. Rackham. London: William Heinemann.

Pliny. 1945. *Natural History.* Vol. IV. Translated by H. Rackham. London: William Heinemann.

Strabo. 1930. *The Geography of Strabo.* Vol. VII. Translated by Horace Leonard Jones. New York: William Heinemann.

The Holy Bible: Containing the Old and New Testaments with the Apocryphal/Deuterocanonical Books. 1995. New Revised Standard Version. Oxford: Oxford UniversityPress.

The Zend-Avesta. Part I. 1965. In *The Vendîdâd (Sacred Books of the East),* edited by F. Max Müller and translated byJames Darmesteter. Delhi: Motilal Banarsidass.

The Zend-Avesta. Part III. 1965. *The Yasna, Visparad, Āfrīnagān, Gāhs and Miscellaneous Fragments (Sacred Books of the East),* edited by F. Max Müller and translated by L. H. Mills. Delhi:Motilal Banarsidass.

Secondary Sources

Andrews, G. 1997. *Drugs and Magic.* Lilburn, GA: Illuminet Press.

Balabanova, S., F. Parsche, and W. Pirsig. 1992. "First Identification of Drugs in Egyptian Mummies." *Naturwissenschaften* 79: 358.

Benet, Sula. 1975. "Early Diffusions and Folk Uses of Hemp." In *Cannabis and Culture,* edited by V. Rubin. The Hague: Moutan.

Benetawa Sara. 1936. *Le chanvre les croyances et les coutumes populaires.* Warsaw: Institute of Anthropological Sciences.

Benetowa, S. (Sula Benet). 1936. "Tracing One Word Through Different Languages." In *Book of Grass: An Anthology on Indian Hemp* edited by G. Andrews and S. Vinkenoog, 16–18.New York: Grove Press 1967.

Bennett, C. and N. McQueen. 2001. *Sex Drugs, Violence and the Bible.* Gibsons, BC: Forbidden Fruit Publishing.

Bennett, C. 2010. *Cannabis and the Soma Solution.* Walterville, OR:TimeDay LLC.

Brough, J. 1971. "Soma and '*Amanita muscaria.*'" *Bulletin of the School of Oriental and African Studies,* University of London, 34: 2.

Buttrick, G. (ed.). 1962. *The Interpreter's Dictionary of the Bible.* Vol. IV. New York: Abingdon.

Dannaway, F. 2007. *Celestial Botany Entheogenic Traces in Islamic Mysticism.* http://www.scribd.com/doc/15744793/Celestial-Botany-Entheogenic-Traces-in-Islamic-Mysticism

Cahill, N. 1985. "The Treasury at Persepolis: Gift-Giving at the City of the Persians." American Journal of Archaeology 89: 3: 373–389.

Cameron, G. 1958. "Persepolis Treasury Tablets Old and New." *Journal of Near Eastern Studies* 17: 3: 161–176.

Campbell, S. and A. Green (eds.). 1995. *The Archaeology of Death in the Ancient Near East.* Oxford: Oxbow Books.

Ciarrocchi, J. 1993. *A Minister's Handbook of Mental Disorders.*New York: Paulist Press.

de Vartavan, C., and V. Amoros. 1997. *Codex of Ancient Egyptian Plant Remains*. London: Triade.

De Waal, M. 1994. *Medicines from the Bible: Roots and Herbs and Woods and Oils*. York Beach, ME: Samuel Weiser.

Dobroruka, V. 2002. *Preparation for Visions in Second Temple Jewish Apocalyptic Literature*. Oxford: University of Oxford Press.

Dobroruka, V. 2006. "Chemically-Induced Visions in the Fourth Book of Ezra in Light of Comparative Persian Material." *Jewish Studies Quarterly*. 13: 1: 1–26.

Eliade, M. 1964. *Shamanism: Archaic Techniques of Ecstasy*. Translated by Willard B. Trask. Bollingen Series LXXVI. New York: Pantheon Books.

Eliade, M. 1978. *A History of Religious Ideas: From the Stone Age to the Eleusinian Mysteries*. Chicago: University of Chicago Press.

Emboden, W. 1972. "Ritual Use of *Cannabis sativa* L.: A Historic-Ethnographic Survey." In *Flesh of the Gods*, edited by P. Furst. New York: Praeger.

Emboden, W. 1972. *Narcotic Plants*. London: Studio Vista.

Falk, H. 1989. "Soma I and II." *Bulletin of the School of Oriental and African Studies*, University of London 52: 1: 77–90.

Fischer-Rizzi, S.1990. *Complete Aromatherapy Handbook*. New York: Sterling Publishing.

Flattery, D. and M. Schwartz. 1989. *Haoma and Harmaline: The Botanical Identity of the Indo-Iranian Sacred Hallucinogen "Soma" and its Legacy in Religion, Language, and Middle Eastern Folklore*. Near Eastern Studies 21. Berkeley: University of California Press.

Geiwitz, J. 2001. *THC in Hemp Foods and Cosmetics: The Appropriate Risk Assessment*, January 15. www.drugpolicy.org/library/pdf_files/HempReport.pdf.

Graindorge, C. 1992. "Les oignons de Sokar." *Revue d'Égyptologie*. 43: 87–105.

Hiebert, F. 1998. "Central Asians on the Iranian Plateau: A Model for Indo-Iranian Expansionism." *The Bronze Age and Early Iron*

Age Peoples of Eastern Central Asia. Journal of Indo-European Studies Monograph 26. Vol. 1. Archeology, Migration and Nomadism,Linguistics edited by V. Mair, 148–161. Philadelphia: The University of Pennsylvania Museum Publications.

Houtman, C. 1992. "On the Function of the Holy Incense (Exodus XXX 34–8) and the Sacred Anointing Oil (Exodus XXX 22–33)." *Vetus Testamentum* 42: 4: 458–465.

Jackson, A., V. Williams, and L. Gray. 1900. "The Religion of the Achaemenian Kings. First Series. The Religion According to the Inscriptions." *Journal of the American Oriental Society* 21. Index to the Journal of the American Oriental Society. Vols. 1–20: 160–184.

Jacob, W. 1993. "Medicinal Plants in the Bible—Another View." In *The Healing Past: Pharmaceuticals in the Biblical and Rabbinic World,* edited by I. and W. Jacobs. *Studies in Ancient Medicine.* Leiden: E. J. Brill.

Johnston, C. 1901. "The Fall of Nineveh." *Journal of the American Oriental Society* 22: 20–22.

Kabelik, J. 1955. "Hemp as a Medicament: History of the Medicinal Use of Hemp." *Acta Universitatis Palackianae Olomucensis Chemica Olomouc,* Czech Republic.

Kaplan, A. 1981. *The Living Torah.* New York: Moznaim Publishing Corporation.

Kisel, V. 2007. "Herodotus' Scythian Logos and Ritual Vessels of the Early Nomads." *Archaeology, Ethnology and Anthropology of Eurasia.* 31: 3: 69–79.

Kitto, J. 1849. *A Cyclopaedia of Biblical Literature.* Edinburgh: Black.

Klein, S. 1908. *Tod und Begrabnis in Palestina.* Berlin: H. Itzkowski.

Kohl, P. 1978. "The Balance of Trade in Southwestern Asia in the Mid-Third Millennium B.C." *Current Anthropology* 19: 3: 463–492.

La Barre,W. 1980. *Culture in Context: Selected Writings of Weston La Barre.* Durham, NC: Duke University Press.

Löw, I. 1967. *Die Flora Der Juden.* Hildesheim: Georg Olmserlagsbuchhandlung.

Manniche, Lisa. 1989. *An Ancient Egyptian Herbal.* Austin, Texas: University of Texas Press.

Mechoulam, R., W. Devane, A. Breuer, and J. Zahalka. 1991. "A Random Walk through a Cannabis Field." *Pharmacology, Biochemistry and Behavior* 40: 461.

Mallory, J. and V. Mair. 2000. *The Tarim Mummies: Ancient China and the Mystery of the Earliest Peoples from the West.* London: Thames and Hudson.

Malyon, T. and A. Henman. 1980. "No Marihuana: Plenty of Hemp." *New Scientist,* November 13, 433–435.

Mathre, M., ed. 1997. *Cannabis in Medical Practice: A Legal, Historical and Pharmacological Overview of the Therapeutic Use of Marijuana.* Jefferson, NC: MacFarland and Company.

McKim, W. 1986. *Drugs and Behavior: An Introduction to Behavioral Pharmacology.* New Jersey: Prentice-Hall.

Mellink, M. 1962. Archaeology in Asia Minor. *American Journal of Archaeology,* 66: 1: 71–85.

Moore, A. 1993. Coptic Priest Claims Church Privilege to Use Marijuana. *Dubuque Telegraph Herald,* Friday, March 26, p. 2A

Moussaieff, A., N. Rimmerman, T. Bregman, A. Straiker, C. Felder, S. Shoham, Y. Kashman, S. Huang, H. Lee, E. Shohami, K. Mackie, M. Caterina, J. Walker, E. Fride, and R. Mechoulam. 2008. "Incensole Acetate, An Incense Component, Elicits Psychoactivity by Activating TRPV3 Channels in the Brain." *The Journal of the Federation of American Societies for Experimental Biology.* August 22(8): 3024–3034.

Mozeson, I. 1989. *The Word: The Dictionary That Reveals the Hebrew Source of English.* New York: Shapolsky Publishers.

Nunn, J. 2002. *Ancient Egyptian Medicine.* Norman, OK: University of Oklahoma Press.

Oppenheim, L. 1967. "Essay on Overland Trade in the First Millennium B.C." *Journal of Cuneiform Studies* 21, Special Volume Honoring Professor Albrecht Goetze.

Ott, J. 1993. *Pharmacotheon: Entheogenic Drugs, Their Plant Sources and History.* Kennewick WA: Natural Products Company.

Parpola, A. 1998. "Aryan Languages, Archaeological Cultures, and Sinkiang: Where Did Proto Iranian Come into Being, and How Did It Spread?" *The Bronze Age and Early Iron Age Peoplesof Eastern Central Asia. Journal of Indo-European Studies.* Monograph 26. Vol.1. Archeology, Migration and Nomadism, Linguistics, edited by V. Mair. Philadelphia: University of Pennsylvania Museum Publications, 114–147.

Phillips, F. 1972. "The Scythian Domination in Western Asia: Its Records in History, Scripture and Archaeology." *World Archaeology* 4: 2: 129–138.

Powis Smith, J. 1922. "Traces of Emperor Worship in the Old Testament." *The American Journal of Semitic Languages and Literature* 39: 1: 32–39.

Reiner, E. 1995. "Astral Magic in Babylonia." *Transactions of the American Philosophical Society* 85: 4: i–150.

Reymond, E. 1976. *From the Contents of the Libraries of the Suchos Temples in the Fayyum,* Part 1, *A Medical Book from Crocodilopolis* D.6257. Translated by P. Vindob. Vienna: Verlag Brüder Hollinek.

Ritner, R. 2000. "Innovations and Adaptations in Ancient Egyptian Medicine." *Journal of Near EasternStudies* 59: 2: 107–117.

Rosch, M. 2005. "Pollen Analysis of the Contents of Excavated Vessels Direct Archaeobotanical Evidence of Beverages." *Vegetation History and Archaeobotany* 14: 3: 179–188.

RudenkoS. 1970. *Frozen Tombs of Siberia: The Pazyryk Burials of Iron Age Horsemen.* Translated by M. W. Thompson. London: Dent.

Rudgley, R.1998. *The Encyclopedia of Psychoactive Substances.* London: Little, Brown and Company.

Russo E. B. 2007. "History of Cannabis and its Preparations in Saga, Science and Sobriquet." *Chemistryand Biodiversity;* 4 (8): 2624–48.

Sagarin, E. 1945. *The Science and Art of Perfumery.* New York: McGraw-Hill.

Sarianidi, V. 1998. *Margiana and Protozoroastrianism.* Translated by Inna Sarianidi. Athens: Kapon Editions.

Sarna, N. 1991. *Exodus: The Traditional Hebrew Text with the New J.P.S. Translation.* The J. P. S. Torah Commentary. New York: The Jewish Publication Society.

Schoff, W. 1920. Cinnamon, Cassia and Somaliland. *Journal of the American Oriental Society* 40: 260–270.

Schultes, R. and A. Hofmann. 1973. *The Botany and Chemistry of Hallucinogens.* Springfield, Ill: Charles C. Thomas.

Schultes, R. and A. Hofmann. 1979. *Plants of the Gods: Origins of Hallucinogenic Use.* New York: Alfred van der Marck Editions.

Stein, A. 1931. "On the Ephedra, the Hum Plant, and the Soma." *Bulletin of the School of Oriental Studies, University of London* 6: 2: 501–514.

Thompson, R. 1924. *Assyrian Herbal.* London: Luzac and Company.

Thompson, R. 1930. Assyrian Prescriptions for Treating Bruises or Swellings. *The American Journal of Semitic Languages and Literatures* 47: 1: 1–25.

Thompson, R. 1937. Assyrian Prescriptions for the Head [Concluded]. *The American Journal of Semitic Languages and Literatures,* 47: 1: 12–40.

Thompson, R. 1949. *Dictionary of Assyrian Botany.* London: The British Academy.

Van Beek, G. 1958. "Frankincense and Myrrh in Ancient South Arabia." *Journal of the American Oriental Society* 78: 3: 141–152.

Waterman, L. 1930. *Royal Correspondence of the Assyrian Empire* Vol. 1. Ann Arbor: University of Michigan Press.

Wills, S. 1998. "Cannabis Use and Abuse by Man: An Historical Perspective." In *Cannabis: The Genus Cannabis,* edited byD. Brown, 1–27. Medicinal and Aromatic Plants Industrial Profiles, Vol.4.Amsterdam: Harwood Academic Publishers.

Yamauchi, E. 1980. "The Archaeological Background of Daniel." *Bibliotheca Sacra* 137: 545: 316.

Zaehner, R. 1961. *The Dawn and Twilight of Zoroastrianism.* London: Weidenfeld and Nicolson.

Zias, J., H. Stark, J. Sellgman., R. Levy, E. Werker, A. Breuer, and R. Mechoulam. 1993.

Early Medical Use of Cannabis. *Nature,* 363: 215.

Chapter 4

Hildegard of Bingen

Unveiling the Secrets of a Medieval High Priestess and Visionary

Gerrit J. Keizer

Gerrit J. Keizer is a clinical and environmental psychologist, mycologist and forest ecologist, author and photographer, and author of the *Illustrated Encyclopedia of Fungi* (1997), published in eight languages, and the CD-ROM *The Interactive Guide to Mushrooms and Other Fungi* (2001/2010). He was employed as a psychotherapist and environmental technologist in Dutch psychiatric hospitals for seventeen years. Beginning in 1996, he worked as a mycological and forest ecological field researcher in several European countries, resulting in the development and publication of the concept of the "Tree Species Specific Ecosystem" (Keizer 2012a). During the past twelve years he has acted as an independent researcher, consultant, and author in various fields of scientific research, including the study of the influence of entheogens and shamanism on pagan traditions and the development of culture and religion.

Synopsis

This chapter deals with the life and works of Hildegard of Bingen, also known as Sybil of the Rhine, the medieval abbess and high priestess of the women's convents of Disibodenberg and Rupertsberg, the latter being founded and rebuilt by her. She wrote the *Liber Scivias* or "*Know the Ways,*" the *Physica* or the "Book of Healing Herbs" (later named "Causae et Curae"), a mystical play, and the lyrics for the church music she composed.

From her works and miniatures, evidence is presented of her reaching a Pentecostal state of "enlightenment" through hallucinatory visions, epiphanies, or revelations, experienced by using entheogen fungi such as the fly agaric, and plants like henbane, Datura, and mandrake, from which she prepared pastes used among others things as witches' ointment. The fungi and plants involved are symbolically represented in the miniatures of her visions by the color and/or shape of the mushrooms and/or the flowers, leaves, or seeds of the plants. Her astro(theo)logical views on the micro- and macrocosmos are also dealt with.

Traumatic experiences during her childhood, and her personality development and psychopathology resulting from it, are discussed. Her close (sexual) relationships with Jutta of Sponheim and Richardis of Stade, her two "sisters" or "daughters," are evaluated. Apart from being Hildegard's intimates in more than one way, both women, together with the Benedictine monk Volmar, Hildegard's secretary at both convents, were Hildegard's confidants and guardians of her secrets, which were partially written in a self-developed secret, still not completely decoded alphabet and language. Her position within the Catholic Church of the twelfth-century and after her death in 1179 is also examined.

Introduction

Always having had a special interest in the role mushrooms play in fairy tales, superstition, religion, and fungilore (Keizer, 1997;

2001/2010), I was intrigued by a picture of one of the miniatures of the visions of Hildegard of Bingen (1098-1176), called "Die Seele und ihr Zelt" (The Golden Tent) [Plate 1], in a recently published book on psychoactive mushrooms and shamanism (Müller-Ebeling, 2010, Keizer 2011d).

In the book, German art historian Müller-Ebeling, in analyzing the hidden symbolism, states that the presence of a dark brown devil spiking a red and white chalice filled with two white "cheeses" with a mushroom she calls "Fäulnispilz" (= fungus, that causes decay)—with a hemispherical to umbilicate dark brown cap and a pale brown stem—is the first evidence of the existence of mycophobia[1] in the early Middle Ages. Even without a Catholic education or background, and although I at that time had not read *The Mushroom in Christian Art* (Rush 2011), I immediately saw that the miniature showed impressive proof of the exact opposite and depicted the worshiping and glorification of the fly agaric (Allegro 1970, Irvin 2008) [Plate 5].

After sharing my findings with John Rush, who was the first not to ignore or deny the obvious and discussed four miniatures of visions of Hildegard of Bingen in his latest book (Rush 2011), suggesting that "her preaching might have been prompted by mind-altering substances" and proposing that "Hildegard was probably seen as someone worthy of knowing the mystery or perhaps figured it out herself. In any case her art is evidence of mind-altering substances. Some of her visions can be read as a knowledgeable person rambling on cannabis, and others seem to be inspired by more potent substances like *Psilocybin* and *Amanita*."[2] Also being shown the miniature of the yoni, "Das Weltall" or "Egg of the Universe" [Plate 2], I decided to study the works of this high priestess of a self-founded sectarian nuns' convent in much greater detail.

In March 2011, I visited the exhibition of Hildegard's works at the Historical Museum Am Strom in Bingen (Germany) and started intensively studying all of the works of the medieval nun, including her book on healing herbs, the *Physica*, and the lyrics of her self-composed religious songs and music.

In my analysis of the symbols and colors used in the miniatures of her "visions," I for the greater part relied on the second edition of *Astrotheology & Shamanism* (Irvin & Rutajit, 2009). For the biography of Hildegard, with permission of the museum, some of the texts were used of the exhibition in Bingen (Dom- und Diözesanmuseum Mainz, 1998).

The quest for Hildegard's "geheimen" or secrets resulted in the book *De geheimen van Hildegard von Bingen* (Keizer, 2012). This chapter reflects the quintessence of the book.

Frame of Reference

Other than the traditional art and church historical or theological approach for the description, analysis, and explanation of Hildegard's writings, miniatures, and lyrics:

> On the one hand a mycological, floristic, biochemical, and psycho-physiological frame of reference was used, with the emphasis on psychoactive plants and fungi or entheogens,
>
> And on the other hand, for an analysis of her personality a developmental and cognitive psychological process, a contextual system and theoretical communication (Watzlawick 1967; Keizer 1991/1994), and a psycho-diagnostic (DSM IV, 2000) frame of reference were used.

The relationship between church and science always has been and still is dominated by ignoring and denying the obvious, even if it stares them right in the face, and concealing and mystification of what displeases church leaders and scribes. In this respect, it is almost comical that in 1927 the Belgian Catholic priest and scholar Georg Le Maitre presented the Cosmic Egg as a model for the primal atom. Because his theory on the big bang was at right angles to the creationistic views of the church, a visit to the Pope was called for, to have his theory legitimized after it had been brought into line with the biblical myth of Creation.

Science, knowledge, and interpretation of "facts" and natural or physical and nuclear or astrophysical phenomenon were until 150 years ago completely determined and dominated by the religious doctrines of the church. Although by then a separation of science and religion was achieved, because the permission of the Pope was no longer needed for the founding of a (Catholic) university, the control of the church of Rome on science and mind control of children through the educational system even today has not ceased to exist.

The finding of a valid and conclusive explanation for the reproduction of mammals (sperm) and the reproduction and dispersion of fungi through spores was not possible until the beginning of the seventeenth-century, when the microscope was invented. The discovery of human semen is attributed to the father of microbiology, Antoni van Leeuwenhoek (1632–1723), who was the first to describe bacteria and sperm he saw through his microscope.

Life of Hildegard of Bingen (1098–1179 CE)

1.0 Childhood

Born September 1098, as the tenth and last child of Count Hildebert of Bermersheim and his wife, Mechthild, Hildegard for eight years lived at the *Herrenhof* of her parents in Bermersheim, a small town close to Alzey in Germany.

From birth on she was frequently ill and bedridden and in need of constant care and nursing. At the age of three, she, for the first time, experienced vivid anxiety-provoking illusions of illuminating objects ("Schau" or "Visio") while being confined to bed because of poor health and serious illness, the hallucinations probably resulting from high fever or maybe (also) from social isolation, as Rush (2011) supposes, and not from cluster headaches or migraines as Sachs (1970/1992) suggests.

The monk Dietrich of Echternach, who was ordered to complete Hildegard's vita (he finished after her death in 1179) using left-behind autobiographic material, and the notes of Wilbert of Gembloux, the monk who was her last secretary from 1177 to 1179, both cite Hildegard stating: "I did not experience many things happening around me because of the often present diseases, I suffered from ever since I was breast-fed, which weakened my body and caused my strength to stay behind." In other words, Hildegard did not have a clue as to what was happening around her.

Hildegard's last biographer, Theodorich of Echternach, who shortly after her death supplemented Hildegard's life history with autobiographic material she left behind, states that Hildegard had asked her nurse whether she also perceived "illusions." After the woman replied that she did not see illuminated objects, Hildegard decided to keep her "secrets" to herself, although contrary to this in looking back on her childhood, Hildegard later claims that "until I was fifteen I saw numerous visions and spoke many things about them in a simple way so that those who heard them were amazed at where they could have come from or who they were from" (Atherton 2001). It was not until after she came under the wing of Jutta of Sponheim, who also experienced visions, that Hildegard's silence ceased and both women shared their "visions" in the period they stayed together in the inclusorium and convent. Jutta was the only person Hildegard trusted. Later on Jutta revealed Hildegard's illusions to Volmar, the Benedictine monk, who educated and supported Hildegard for the greater part of her life, becoming her secretary, teacher, and confidant of her secrets.

Young children have only a limited vocabulary, and adult memories of childhood are not very reliable and often distorted. They are partially made up and/or influenced by the need to make things seem better or worse than they really were. Referring to how she remembers her first "Schau," Hildegard stated: "...and in my third year I saw such a light that my whole soul trembled; but because of my young age I could not put it in words" (Atherton 2001). Mostly these memories came about in retrospect or were supplemented by and based upon stories of events taking place in childhood, told to her at a later age by the child's parents, or directly involving significant others and having the character of false or distorted (pseudo-) memories.

An illustration of this phenomenon of hearsay is found in the testimony Bruno, priest and administrator of Saint Peter in Strasbourg, made under oath before the thirteenth-century committee installed for the canonization of Hildegard. According to the canonization protocol, Bruno declared that from the information that had come to his attention on her reputation and that he had read in the little book on her life published after she died, Hildegard, at the age of five, saw a cow and spoke the following words to her nurse: "Look how beautiful the calf is inside the cow, all white with dark patches on his forehead, feet and back" (Atherton 2001). The bewildered nurse immediately told Hildegard's mother of this incident, after which Hildegard's mother ordered the woman who owned the cow to show her this calf directly after it was born. When the calf conformed to the predictions of Hildegard, her mother realized that her "prophecy" was true. From this incident Hildegard's parents concluded that Hildegard was an extraordinary child and decided to dedicate her as their "tith" to God by bringing her to the monastery at age eight.

According to reports citing her as the source, Hildegard, as a three-year-old child and after her first "Visio," unaware of what was going on in reality because she was bedridden most of the time, decided to keep her terrifying and extremely anxiety-provoking experiences to herself.

Normally, an increase in feelings and expression of aggression toward others takes place between five and eight years, as the child has to stand up for himself because of increased social contacts. Because of a lack of social interactions with children and adults, however, Hildegard became introverted. Moreover, "exceptional" children only start to realize they differ from other children around the age of eight or nine, at the age Hildegard was brought to the monastery. A condition for this realization, of course, is that the child is in contact with other children.

According to Hildegard's recorded history, from ages three to eight years, while she was living at her parents' home, and the following years until she was fifteen, while staying in the monastic enclosure or inclusorium and convent, she did not experience hellish headaches.

For this reason it is not plausible to attribute Hildegard's hallucinations to cluster headaches or migraines. They were more likely caused by delirium brought on by high fever and continued because of a heightened sensitivity and disposition for seeing or hearing hallucinations, without being psychotic.

The "visions" or epiphanies Hildegard had at the age of forty-two and sixty, however, are of such different and nonspontaneous character that they had to have been brought about through the use of entheogens, mainly of the fly agaric—an assumption that will be documented and evidenced later.

Considering the development of consciousness, a child is confronted with primary or basic vital questions such as: who am I, to whom do I belong, why am I here (on Earth), where am I going, what is expected of me, and what will my future life be like? From developmental psychology it is known that, with young children, if there is no "logical" explanation for phenomena such as sickness and death, "magical thinking," an important aspect of cognitive development, becomes prominent if they undergo such dramatic and extreme anxiety-provoking experiences as those of Hildegard at age three.

Growing up in a social environment in which such impressive events were attributed to God's will, Hildegard would not have been able to develop a realistic frame of reference or mindset about what came over her and what happened to her. If little children lack the vocabulary and mastery of a language to facilitate talking about existential fears and feelings of autonomous loss of control (Keizer 1996), and withdraw or shut up and no longer dare to share their experiences with significant others because they fear to be considered insane, fantasy easily runs riot and ideas of being chosen by a higher power or being predestined easily find a foothold.

Children's fantasies, especially at the age of two to five years, can easily lead to problems concerning the quantity and lifelike reality of these fantasies. There can be periods in which the fantasies seem to get the upper hand in the perception and understanding of reality, in the course of which the child lives within his or her own fantasy world and believes in the existence of imaginary persons or other subjects and objects. The assumed effects of a thoroughly limited living environment had a definite impact on Hildegard's identity and personality development.

Until she was put under the tutelage of Jutta von Sponheim at the age of eight, it is reported that Hildegard once again had some "Visio" with—in retrospect—a more prophetic character. If this is true, they must have had an even greater impact on her emotional development as a child, because she had decided to no longer share her experiences with others.

In spite of the illusionary deformation of reality, Hildegard was coherent and in a sane state of mind, and at a later age there are no indications of psychoses associated with hallucinations. Because of the delusional experiences she reports having until the age of fifteen, she becomes more sensible and predisposed for hallucinations, with which the base for her later, more easily triggered, "visions" or epiphanies under the influence of entheogens such as the fly agaric, *Amanita muscaria*, was formed.

Although she was in poor health and often ill during certain periods, caused by her ascetic lifestyle, Hildegard does not seem to have had any hallucinatory experiences from age fifteen until she was forty-three years old. At a later age, and through the influence of Jutta and Richardis, she acquired knowledge of medicinal plants, possibly contributing to the temporary "healing" or bettering of her ailments.

1.1 The Period of Enclosure in the Inclusorium at Disibodenberg

As a child of eight, instead of "giving her in marriage," which probably would have been problematic as Hildegard's visions would have made her unsuitable for finding a nobleman willing to marry her, her parents sent her to the four-hundred-year-old Benedictine monastery of Disibodenberg, which some years later added a section for women. Other than monks, novices and nuns were obliged to donate a dowry or "dote" to the monastery at their entrance into the convent.

At the convent, she was put under tutelage of the six years older, fourteen-year-old anchoress Jutta of Sponheim (1092-1136, [Plate 52]), a daughter from a rich family, who called Hildegard her family's "tithe" to the Lord (Johnson Lewis 2011).

According to Atherton (2001), at first Hildegard spent some years at the house of Jutta, who was already ordained as a novice in 1106, until Jutta, who had a special interest in the spirituality-associated life of a hermit, had found a suitable monastery with an inclusorium or monastic enclosure with a walled garden, separate from the convent, for her and Hildegard to be locked in.

According to the history of Hildegard's life, she already stayed in the monastic enclosure in 1106. However, the annals of the Disibodenberg monastery claim that the first stone for the rebuilt monastery was laid in 1108. On the other hand, Jutta's life history states that on All Saints' Day, November 1, 1112, the day Jutta took her vows as a nun, fourteen-year-old Hildegard and another girl of about the same age were confined to a newly opened inclusorium at the Disibodenberg monastery—where she stayed for about two years. Because of the restricted life circumstances and the imposed intimacy, this must have created a special bond between the two young women.

Being enclosed in an inclusorium as a child, Hildegard again would have experienced another traumatic ritual: Because hermits were considered more or less "dead" to the worldly community, her ceremonial initiation burial was preceded by a funeral Mass. During the Mass, the bier-lying hermit was to be administered the last sacraments by a bishop (Van Elteren 2007).

Regarding the monastic enclosure and the convent from age eight until fourteen, Hildegard stated, while looking back upon her life, that she was "someone, who saw and—in all of her innocence and naivety—even more spoke about many 'things,' so that they who heard of those 'things,' in astonishment wondered where they came from and by whom they were revealed," experiences she until her fourteenth year of age reportedly only shared with Jutta, who during and before that period also had had delusional and prophetic "visions."

Since she took her vows as a nun in 1114 and joined by then as a successor to the nunnery, of which Jutta recently had become the abbess, Hildegard must have spent at least two years in the exclusive company of Jutta (and another young girl).

From an early age on, Jutta was also known to be a visionary, a prophetess, and consultant of the "lower class." Being Hildegard's help during the period preceding (Atherton, 2001), and after becoming a recluse in the monastic enclosure in the first years in the convent, Jutta took Hildegard's education upon herself and taught her to read and write in the old high German language and simple "church" Latin needed to read the bible and other religious documents. Jutta also shared her knowledge of alchemy and the use of healing herbs and "spirits"—possibly including psychoactive plants and fungi such as the fly agaric—with Hildegard.

The monastic enclosure had an open window positioned high up at the side of the church, through which the nuns in the inclusarium could hear the voice of the priest performing the Mass in the monastery's chapel, which made indirect "auditory" participation in the ceremonies possible. The inclusorium was surrounded by a walled garden, where the recluses could do some gardening and produce their own vegetables and herbs. Probably the garden was inhabited and/or surrounded by birch trees, one of the symbiotic partners of the fly agaric, because birches are pioneer trees with tiny and very light seeds that are easily dispersed by wind and germinate in various types of soil. And maybe that is where Hildegard for the first time—pointed out by Jutta—encountered the "Sacred Mushroom," which could have been the reason why Hildegard, after later use of the fly agaric in her *Physica*, called the birch the tree of "happiness and bliss."

The contact between the young women in the inclusorium and the monastery was maintained by the Benedictine monk Volmar of

Disibodenberg (1090–1173), the tutor of both women and a teacher and follower of the Benedictine traditions (tonsure) and rules of convent and spiritual life, who lived at the next-door Benedictine monastery. With the only-eight-years-older Volmar, Hildegard developed such a strong bond that he became her private teacher and secretary, witness of her first epiphany, and—together with her protégée Richardis of Stade—witnessed a later, actively provoked "vision."

1.2 Life of a Benedictine Nun

The first Benedictine monastery, Monte Cassino in Italy, was founded in the sixth-century by Benedict of Nursia (around 480–560), who introduced the Benedictine Rule of Life, which regulates in detail the relationships within the order and between the monastic community and the world outside. The main rules for the "opus Dei" are: stability of residence (*stabilitas loci*), obedience to the abbot and the community (*oboedientia*), commitment to a life in accordance with the Rule (*conversatio morum*), dictate of work (labor) and dictate of prayer (*ora*), personal poverty (*paupertas sancta*), and moderation (*discretio*). According to the Rule there also is the obligation of silence, which has to be strictly observed, as well as abstinence of sexual reproduction and masturbation and repression of erotic feelings. Offending the strict morals and ethics was punished by penance and sometimes even with self-chastisement, as was claimed to be practiced by Jutta in a German docudrama on the life of Hildegard broadcasted by the Zweites Deutsches Fernsehen (2010).

Hildegard lived in an era when, within the Benedictine movement, there was emphasis on the inner experience, personal meditation, a direct relationship with God and visions. In Germany, it also was a time of territorial conflict between papal authority and the ruling power of the Roman Catholic German emperor, and of papal schism. On the one hand, Hildegard preached the superiority of order over change, and the church reforms she forced through included the superiority of ecclesiastical power over secular power and of popes over kings and emperors; on the other hand she did not share the Church's rejection of the human body as a depository of evil desire, a principle the Cathars also adhered to.

It is obvious that Hildegard's different view on sexuality was motivated by her amorous relationship with Richardis of Stade, and presenting it as a pure expression of sisterly "Love" served to justify and legitimize her feelings for Richardis and to escape from feelings of guilt over her sinful behavior, in the eyes of the Church, and over not doing penance for it.

1.3 Hildegard, Nun and Abbess of the Disibodenberg Convent

At age sixteen, Hildegard took her vows as a Benedictine nun in the Disibodenberg monastery and received her veil from bishop Otto of Bamberg. From that moment on it probably was expected that Hildegard obeyed the rules of the Benedictine order.

As a nun, Hildegard initially strictly lived and worked according to the rules and daily routines of the order, including eight hours of sleep, three to four hours of praying, four hour of studying, and eight hours of gardening, illustrating manuscripts, or—as Hildegard did after leaving the inclusorium—nursing the sick. In this period she only wore the prescribed plain habit with hood, making her indistinguishable from other nuns in her uniform display (Keizer 1991).

In the twelfth-century teaching and education in the contemporary theories of science were provided by monasteries and cathedral schools. Natural history including botany, zoology, gemology, and medicine was not taught there, belonging as it does to the canon of subjects taught in the framework of the "Artes Liberales" or Seven Liberal Arts, including the Trivium (grammar, logic, rhetoric), Quadrivium (arithmetic, geometry, music, astronomy), and the Kaballah. As Hildegard only learned to read and write in old high German from Jutta, and simple "church" Latin from Jutta and Volmar, she was not educated in the Seven Liberal Arts, so her mystic experiences cannot be attributed to a profound insight in and practical knowledge of the contemplative methods of influencing the human mind to reach a state of enlightenment.

For the same reason her knowledge of natural history and medicine also has to originate in private study or partially must have come from Jutta. Moral philosophy, metaphysics, and natural philosophy were added to the canon no earlier than the thirteenth-century; thus Hildegard's work could not have been influenced by these scientific theories.

In the Middle Ages, Benedictine monasteries were known to possess well-documented libraries and were oases of science and art, owning extremely rare and valuable manuscripts on witches' brews and ointments, to which only the clergy or the rich and nobles had access (Rush 2011). Hildegard, like many women in convents at that time, after learning Latin and being taught to read and interpret the liturgy and the Psalter, read the scripture and had access to many other books of a religious or philosophical nature. She was a self-learner, an autodidact, and from her writings one can conclude that she must have read extensively, considering the books and manuscripts she seems to have consulted, copied, and used as sources for her later work.

Her general knowledge of church and worldly matters—including the original pagan rites and traditions, and the Greek mythology and display of specific knowledge in the descriptions of her visions—indicates she followed the visio-theory of Augustinus,[3] which, to a great extent, is based on her regular trips to the library.

Although Gerbod and Walter, the provost and dean of the Saint Peter in Mainz, and the church scholar Arnold, declare for the canonization committee that Hildegard herself should have claimed that she who "did not study any writings other than the Psalter, composed and brought many books of great importance to the church to 'light,' that were—in miraculous ways—revealed to her through epiphanies from the Holy Spirit" (Atherton 2001). That is to say, they were beamed down or showered upon her, but in reality Hildegard must have taken note of the contents of numerous medieval and older religious and philosophical writings and miniature books or "evangeliars" and used those for the writing and illustration of her book.

In his overview of important contemporaries of Hildegard, Atherton mentions Ældred of Rievaulx, Ambrosius Autpertus, Hermas or Hermes Trismegistus, and Herrad of Landsberg.

Just as Hildegard conceived her own alphabet and language, she construed her own individual social and physical reality and perception of her environment, while heavily leaning on what she had learned from books on pagan traditions and handed-down rituals from the Levant and antique Greece. And, without revealing her secrets, she presented her (astro-)theological and eclectic views on the world, nature, and mankind in the terms and by means of the symbols the medieval Catholic Church and the secular community accepted, though at a later date often (deliberately) misinterpreted or misunderstood.

Some of her miniatures show colorful and rich ornamental display of Hildegard dressed as high priestess [Plates 3 and 51] and of two of her "sisters." These could have been inspired by or copied from the gown and decorations worn by the Roman Empirical Princess Anicia Juliana (Constantinople 462–527/528), depicted on the frontispiece of her Codex or "Vienna Dioscurides," or from Greek vases portraying the high priestess of the oracle of Delphi.

Maybe the *ephod*, a robe made of sky-blue dyed linen with the main white clothing underneath worn exclusively by Jewish priests, was a source of inspiration too. In the old Jewish culture, the *ephod* was an object of worship and associated with oracles. David was supposed to have worn it while he was dancing in the presence of the arc of the covenant, the central and most holy object in the Jewish tradition. The arc should have contained not only the stone tablets with the Ten Commandments, but also a jar with manna—a dried cap of the fly agaric or the Holy Grail (Rush 2008)—and the flowering staff of Aaron (Irvin 2009).

From her enclosure in the inclusorium on, Hildegard, elaborating on Jutta's knowledge and experience, brought together a great deal of information on the use and application of medicinal herbs and healing metals or gem stones (alchemy). This ultimately resulted in her book on healing plants, the *Physica,* which was finished and published after Richardis of Stade, Hildegard's secondary secretary, died.

Around 1116, after the monastic enclosure had developed into a convent, Jutta became abbess of the Disibodenberg women's convent, and when she died in 1136, thirty-eight-year-old Hildegard was unanimously elected as her successor and became the new abbess or magistrate of the nunnery, which, at that time, still was located within the walls of the Disibodenberg monastery.

Hildegard was not the only member of her family who rose to power within the ranks of the Catholic Church. Her most important and influential brother, Hugo, with whom Hildegard was in contact until the end of her life and who after her death in 1179 temporarily took over the spiritual care at the Rupertsberg convent, was the cathedral cantor of the Dom of Mainz and tutor at the Dom school. Another brother called Rorich was canon in Tholey on the Saar.

From that moment on, Hildegard seemed to feel at liberty to renounce the plain habit with hood and, accompanied by some of her dedicated noble "sisters," dressed up in the luxurious outfit of an antique Greek high priestess in full regalia [Plate 3] while celebrating and performing the rituals of the mass. And apart from this, she also presents herself in her miniatures, and on stage in her "Play of the Virtues," as the Holy Virgin with a golden crown.

One has to take into account that even nowadays the ceremonial vestments worn by the Pope or other important clergymen are meant to demonstrate their superiority over the congregation of "ignorant" believers and lower-hierarchy priests and to emphasize and endorse the supremacy of the church over the worldly community by use of symbolic display (Keizer 1991).

As magistrate, Hildegard succeeded in extricating her convent from the monastery, and because she for obvious reasons did not accept secular supervision, her secretary and confidant Volmar was appointed as provost. In the period between 1141 and 1151, when

Hildegard was writing the *Liber Scivias,* Richardis of Stade joined the Disibodenberg convent and became Hildegard's (secondary) secretary and also her amanuensis, a personal assistant familiar with and/or educated in botany, physics, chemistry, and alchemy.

Although the abbot of the monastery demanded secular supervision, this was probably rejected by Hildegard because she did not tolerate priers into a sectarian community of nuns of nobility developing a convent; only women of noble birth were allowed to join as a novice, because of her opinions on asceticism, penitence, abstinence, and sexuality, which were at right angles to the views of the church of that time.

As an adult, Hildegard is described as being "a physically weak woman, who falls ill with any trial or tribulation that comes her way," who was in poor health throughout her entire life and often more or less seriously ill. The use of potent stimulants such as psychoactive fungi and plants, and living according to the Benedictine rules, including asceticism, probably made her even more vulnerable to the physical effects of using entheogens, as is more often seen with people who are heavy users of or addicted to hallucinogenic substances.

Her personality was set in her early childhood and centered on narcissistic character traits, expressed in ideas of invulnerability and grandeur, and over-identification with the Holy Virgin, martyrs, and saints to compensate for a continuously ambivalence-provoking, deeply rooted inferiority complex.[4]

1.4 The First "Vision" or Epiphany

In 1141, five years after she was elected abbess, Hildegard, as she recalls, received a "vision" or epiphany of purifying fiery flames enclosing her thoughts and soul and clarifying her knowledge of the Psaltery, in which she was summoned by God to "Say and write what you see and hear" [Plate 4].

As is shown in the preface to "Know the Ways," there is a miniature depicting Hildegard in her cell dressed in a plain habit with hood. Hildegard is watched and supported by Volmar, who is looking in through an open window. Because he is wearing a tonsure, according to Allegro (1970/2009), Volmar must have been familiar with and experienced in the use of the "Sacred Mushroom" as an entheogen.

Hildegard experiences her visions fully awake, and devoid of ecstasy: "The visions that I see and hear I do not obtain from dreams, nor during sleep or mental derangement … but awake, calm and collected, with an alert mind … according to God's will." Her visual and auditory hallucinations strikingly resemble the revelations or epiphanies in the Old Testament, of or described by Ezechiel, Job, and Hosea, whom Hildegard quotes in the course of her vision (Atherton 2002), and just like the old Jewish prophets, she was ordered by God to write down her experiences. In this regard, Hildegard falls back upon what is written on Pentecost in the Bible: "Suddenly there came a sound from the sky as if a raging wind was rising that filled the whole house they were in. Then they saw something that looked like tongues of fire: it divided itself and descended upon all of them. They were all fulfilled of the Holy Spirit and started to speak in strange languages" or in tongues (glossolalia). Hildegard's first epiphany seems to be completely derived from the pouring out of the Holy Spirit upon the apostles, the experience that occurred after use of entheogens such as the fly agaric and the event that marks the birth of the Church. In paintings and frescoes, the apostles are either depicted with flames descending upon their heads or "with candle stick flames" arising from the crown of their heads. The Living Light or Holy Ghost is poured out and descends, implicating that the direction of the Pentecost feast is not upward, but downward—from the ceiling of the recluse—as is shown in the miniature of Hildegard's first epiphany.

According to modern liturgy, Pentecost can be compared with a "fire" that warms or with the Living Light, which leads through the darkness and is Jesus the fire, the spark from above. The Dutch "Living Stone" church (philosopher's stone or Cosmic Egg) regards Jesus as the Holy Spirit that "lives inside me" and claims that Jesus was not only baptized with water, but also with the Holy Spirit, ergo with fire the second time around.

Hildegard hesitates to carry out this order, becomes ill, and is confined to bed. But the repeated demands to write eventually convince her to take up the challenge. "Beaten down by many kinds of illnesses, I put hand to writing. Once I did this, a deep and profound exposition of books came over me. I received the strength to rise up from my sickbed, and under that power I continued to carry out the work to the end, using all of ten years to do it" (Fox 2002). And Hildegard continues: "first the soul must be healed, not until then the body can follow … is this out of balance, then the elements can turn against us."

According to Storch (1997), looking back upon her life, Hildegard had the following recorded: "Since my childhood, however, when my bones, nerves and veins were not strengthened until now, I always look forward to this glance into my soul, although I am already seventy years old. In this 'Schau,' my spirit … rises up to the heights of the firmament and elevates itself to the various regions of the sky. And it stretches out over people of a different nature, although they are in environments and places that are far away from me. And because I see this in such a way, I also perceive it consistent with the variability of the clouds and other creatures. This however I do not hear with my physical ears, nor in the fantasy of my heart and also do not receive it through mediation of my five senses, but only in my soul, with open 'exterior' eyes, in such a manner that I never suffer from a state of exhaustion as a result of ecstasy. Much more I see this in a wake state, day and night. And over and over again I am—note from the author: not during, but afterwards—lamed by illness and tormented by such pains, that they threaten me with death. Yet God has saved me up to now.

"The light which I see, is not confined to one place, but it is far, far brighter than a cloud which carries the sun; nor can I gauge its height or length or breadth, and it is known to me by the name of the 'reflection of the living light.' And just as the sun, the moon and the stars appear in the waters, so the scriptures, sermons and virtues and certain works that humans have wrought, shine on me brightly in this light" (Atherton 2001).

"Whatever I see or learn in this vision, I hold in my memory for a long time; so I recall whatever I have once seen or heard; and I simultaneously see and hear and understand and, as it were, learn in this moment what I understand. But what I do not see, I do not understand, because I am unlearned.... And the words in this vision are not like those which sound from the mouth of men, but like a trembling flame, or like a cloud stirred by the clear air" (Atherton 2001). "I cannot recognize the figure of this light at all, as I also cannot behold the ball of the sun in its entirety" (Storch 1997).

With, "I am the fiery life of a divine substance" (Atherton 2001), Hildegard seems to explicitly refer to the potential powers of the Sacred Mushroom. And on the exclusiveness of the use of entheogens by the "happy few," Hildegard writes: "Human beings should not investigate the secrets of God any further than He wishes them to reveal. As is characteristic of men, he desires to know more of the superior plan, but a seal of secrecy will be imposed upon him, because it is not permitted to further investigate God's secrets than the divine majesty wishes to unveil, because of his love for the believers."

Itching with a pencil into small wax plate, in 1141 she starts writing her book *Scivias* or *"Know the Ways."* In the preface to her first theological visionary work she writes: "And it came to pass in the eleven-hundred-and-forty-first year of the incarnation of Jesus Christ, son of God, when I was forty-two years and seven month old, that the heavens opened and a blinding light of exceptional brilliance came down to me. It flowed through my entire brain, kindling my whole heart and breast like a flame, not burning, but warming." Or as Fox (2002) states: "Hildegard was overcome by the experience of intuition, connection-making, and insight and went to bed sick." Hildegard pictures her illumination by the Living Light or Holy Spirit as an experience, which "resurrects and awakens everything that is." "For Hildegard, it is (the 'Living Light' or) the Holy Spirit who illumes. Like the original Pentecost event, which Hildegard draws in her self-portrait ('Die Seherin'), she was awakened by the parted tongues of fire that ... allow deep communication to happen among the peoples" (Fox 2002).

The content of and reaction to Hildegard's first epiphany can simply be linked to present and past experiences of others after oral taking of fresh or dried fly agarics, such as, for instance, seems to be expressed with "purifying fiery flames," the sensation that is also reported by other users of the Sacred Mushroom. After consumption of *Amanita muscaria,* the following effects, experiences, and sensations are documented:

> - Manifestation of hallucinations, an effect that especially is attributed to muscimol, sometimes going together with extreme sweating and tremors;
>
> - Seeing of flames or rays [Plate 4] and the experience of enlightenment through the Living Light or Holy Ghost (Pentecost);
>
> - Contact with "higher" or divine powers and the gods, either or with the reception of messages from "above";
>
> - Macropsy, or the inability to assess proportions of objects correctly;
>
> - Repeated experiences of the phenomenon of "eternal life" by the drinking of "living" water, that is urine saturated with muscimol, from one's own "reservoir," [Plates 7, 33, and 34] symbolized by the ouroborus; [Plate 48]
>
> - Unintentional side effects such as nausea.

It is reported of Amanita species, such as the fly agaric, that they elicit out-of-body experiences that cause the stimulation and the awakening or coming to life of the spirit and senses. In this respect, note that the documented experience issuing from the use of fly agaric "is not only of a blissful experience, but the ups and downs of heaven and hell told in many stories throughout the world. Part of the heaven-like or blissful experience is realizing the totality of your being; the hell-like experiences are the fear- and ego-driven 'bad trips.' These 'bad trips' can be most important, because they can teach the user the most about him or herself. As religion teaches us, all of this symbolism and ritual is about purification and transformation of the soul, to make ourselves better human beings. The purpose is *not* to have a 'blissful experience' … but rather to help you grow spiritually and even mentally" (Irvin and Rutajit 2009).

As was said before, Hildegard's visual and auditory hallucinations show a striking resemblance to the visions as described in the Old Testament. Or as Atherton (2001) states: "Hildegard is a prophet in the Old Testament tradition, touched by 'fire like the burning sun,' rather like Ezekiel, or like Job and Hosea whom she quotes in the course of her vision."

These types of spiritual experiences are also known from other cultures (Beane et al, 1964, Eliade 2004). The phenomenon of cosmic enlightenment has for instance been documented from shamans and the apostle Paul. According to Fox (2002), Eliade draws the following general conclusions: "It is important to stress that whatever the nature and intensity of an experience of the Light, it always evolves into a religious experience. All types of experiences of the Light … have this factor in common: they bring a man out of his worldly Universe or historical situation, and project him into a Universe different in quality, an entirely different world, transcendent and holy. Whatever his previous ideological conditioning, a meeting with the Light produces a break in the subject's existence, revealing to him … the world of the Spirit, of holiness and of freedom; in brief, existence as a divine creation, or the world sanctified by the presence of God."

Hildegard shares her first epiphany and other experiences with her counselor and secretary, Volmar, the Benedictine monk with the tonsure, who understood but hesitated to submit to God's order, and became ill and bedridden for some time. Ultimately the repeated orders to write down her experience, although this is not documented, convinced her to accept the challenge, and Hildegard commenced writing *Scivias* or *"Know the Ways,"* while Volmar assists in correcting her in simple Latin on wax plates, itched scriptures, if you will, which were then transcribed to parchment. The structure of the separate descriptions were under his supervision while Hildegard painted miniatures following the Visio-theory of Aurelius Augustinus (345-430), who distinguishes three steps in the process: The first step is formed by sensory perception or "visio corporalis," the second step by the representation or depiction or "visio spiritualis," followed by the third step, that of the comprehension or "visio intellectualis." If a phenomenon is described in this way, finally recognition and understanding of the meaning of the depiction takes place (Wilhelmy 1998).

And even while writing the *Liber Scivias,* Hildegard is repeatedly filled with doubt. Hence, in 1146–1147, she writes a letter to abbot Bernard of Clervaux for advice and she appears in public for the first time. She describes her uncertainty, but seeks confirmation of her visionary powers and her prophetic call. The abbot congratulates her on her visionary powers, but he cannot dispel her doubts. The epistle to Bernard is the earliest of Hildegard's letters to be handed down. A personal meeting never took place.

Initially, Hildegard's "visions" were treated with suspicion by the Church. Under the chairmanship of the Cistercian Pope Eugene III, members of the clergy and bishops from all over Europe gathered at the synod held in Trier between November 1147 and February 1148. Abbot Bernard of Clervaux (1090–1153) also attended. At the request of abbot Kuno of Disibodenberg, Archbishop Henry of Mainz informs those present of Hildegard and her "epiphanies." Pope Eugene sends an investigative commission to Disibodenberg to examine Hildegard's prophetic powers. When the commission returns with a positive report, the pope "publicly" reads from the completed sections of the *Liber Scivias.* In a letter he orders Hildegard to continue her work, confirming her prophetic powers. The pope encourages her to carry on with his blessing, which must have had quite an impact on the still-insecure Hildegard and would have motivated her to continue her work. The approval of Hildegard's work by the Synod is only documented in her own manuscripts. The minutes of the Synod do not mention nor confirm Hildegard's prophetic powers at all.

On February 18, 1148, Pope Eugene issues a charter of protection to the Disibodenberg convent. Papal and synod approval brings about lasting chances in the life of a Benedictine nun, because Hildegard now has been granted a license and permission to go her own way without exterior supervision.

Hildegard becomes a person of public interest, whose advice and opinion is very much in demand. She engages in active correspondence all over Europe, with spiritual leaders, clergymen or women, members of the middle and upper class including noblemen, and the King and Queen of England. Of her impressive number of letters, in which she gives recommendations and praises, but often scolds the recipient, more than 300 letters written in Latin were preserved, just as some of the replies have survived. And "Sybil of the Rhine" travels three or four times all over Germany to present her lectures and sermons to clergymen and laymen.

In the intermediate period, Hildegard experienced "guided" dreams resembling "visions," in which retrospective and prospective "wishful thinking," yet to come or already realized "self-fulfilling prophecies," and reliving of before-visualized scenes were the central themes. They did not primarily have the character of apocalyptic prophecies or conform to the medieval opinions on the ongoing battle between God and the devil, present were threatening with devils and demons, hell and purgatory and damnation because of Adam's fall, and torturing devices such as the wine press of God's wrath [Plate 5], with which the blood is squeezed from a sinner. However, what draws attention in this respect is that in six of the last ten miniatures in which the building of the Rupertsberg convent [Plate 56] was "foreseen," the miniatures are of a much more restrained, even charming character.

At the age of sixty, Hildegard again hears a voice from heaven, saying: "You, who from childhood on, was not in a physical, but in a spiritual way educated in the true vision by the spirit of the Lord, now proclaim what you see and hear at present. From the start of your visions, you were shown some appearances as if they were from fluid milk; others were offered as if they were refreshing light food; yet others were granted as if they were solid and total nutrition. So now again speak as Me and not as you, write after Me and not after you" (Schipperges 2007). With this Hildegard seems to describe the different solid and liquid substances used as ingredients for eliciting and experiencing her "visions" and portrays herself as a well-informed user (and supplier) of (prescriptions of) psychoactive plants and fungi, who probably, following in the footsteps of Jutta, had mastered all there was to know about recipes, dosage, mixtures, and the effects to be expected of entheogens.

The second "epiphany" was possibly inspired by Hildegard's evaluation of the spirit in a time period twenty years before the conflict over the burial of a deceased nobleman at the churchyard of Rupertsberg (1178–1179), for she felt the tide was turning concerning the tolerance of the church for her religious points of view and practice and sought for a reconfirmation of her "divine orders."

1.5 Hildegard, Abbess of the Rupertsberg Convent

Around the time of the synod of Trier (winter of 1147–1148), against the will of abbot Kuno, Hildegard decided to leave Disibodenberg. Her decision was preceded by an incident that made her realize that she no longer could guarantee the safety of her nuns in the monastery they shared with the monks, as one of the nuns turned out to be pregnant after having intercourse with a monk. Hildegard addressed the abbot, who refused to accept any responsibility, and declared that the monk was not to blame, because the nun must have seduced him (Von Trotta 2009).

After having several visions of her own nunnery, though without witnesses, she planned an independent convent on the Rupertsberg [Plate 56], a hill overlooking the confluence of the rivers Rhine and Nahe, opposite the town of Bingen, approximately thirty kilometers from Disibodenberg. St. Rupertus lived at this site during the early Middle Ages.

When her plan is rejected, because the monastery does not allow its significant source of income to leave and refuses to cofinance her initiative, Hildegard again falls ill, a perfect example of the use of emotional blackmail through submissive coercion (Keizer 1994), and threatens with God's wrath, as a means of pressuring the abbot to give in, if she is not allowed to have her way. After permission is finally granted by the abbot, Hildegard spontaneously recovers, a classic example of secondary profit through manipulation by faking illness.

Strikingly enough, the conflict is about material possessions such as building grounds, valuables, dowries, and money, and not about Hildegard's sectarian religious convictions, which were not brought up for discussion by the monastery.

Despite the protests of the Disibodenberg's monks, reluctant to release their "famous" sister, Hildegard went ahead with the move, accompanied by about twenty fellow sisters. This site, the vita reports, was "revealed" to Hildegard and is depicted in five of her miniatures. Thanks to the financial support of secular patrons [Plate 29], she was able to purchase the land and commenced the construction of an independent convent. The noble ancestry of the nuns would have contributed to the finding of financial backers and support for her initiative by kings and emperors, noblemen and high-ranking clergymen, emperor Barbarossa (1122–1190 CE), and the archbishop of Mainz, whom she had personally met.

Ruck (2007) also suggests she was operating as a "pigmentarius" or "dealer in pigments and ointments," who not only prescribed healing herbs for her high-ranking clientele, but possibly mind-altering substances as well, playing a substantial "healing" role.

The move was completed around 1150 CE. The first few years were characterized by considerable privation, leading to much conflict, which probably arose from the sectarian character of the convent community and the luxurious clothing and ornaments worn during the performance of the rituals and ceremonies of the Mass. Maybe there also was a debate on the secrecy of the use of psychoactives by the members of the circle of trust surrounding Hildegard, who had by then invented her own alphabet and language, to exclude noninitiated others from her secrets. Some of the nuns left the convent. Notwithstanding these initial difficulties, the convent church was completed.

A charter from Archbishop Henry of Mainz dated May 1, 1152 documents the consecration of an altar in the chapel of St. Rupertus, temporarily used for services. A letter from the monk Guibert of Gembloux, Hildegard's secretary from 1177 to 1179, reveals that the convent could accommodate fifty nuns, seven poor women, and the domestics and guests. "This convent was not founded by an emperor or a bishop, but by a poor and weak woman, a newcomer to this region." The nuns who joined the convent were of wealthy backgrounds, and the convent did not discourage them from maintaining some aspects of their previous lifestyle. Hildegard withstood criticism of this practice, claiming that wearing jewelry to worship God was honoring God, not practicing selfishness. In later years the Rupertsberg convent became a popular burial site for the wealthy in the area.

At first the Disibodenberg monks refused to hand over to Rupertsberg the dowry or dote the nuns donated upon their entry in the monastic enclosure and convent. In the next few years Hildegard fought not only for the restitution of these goods, but also for complete independence of her convent from Disibodenberg. Two charters from Archbishop Arnold of Mainz (who was murdered in 1160) dated May 22, 1158, define the legal status of the new convent and confirm all of its properties. The nuns are guaranteed the free election of an abbess and a provost of their choice, placed at their disposal by the Disibodenberg monastery, and the exclusive protectorate of the Archbishop of Mainz. Hildegard successfully refused the institution of a secular overseer. In order to secure the legal status of the convent permanently, Hildegard acquired additional papal and imperial protection for her new convent during the next few years. In the charter issued by Emperor Fredrick Barbarossa at Hildegard's request, she was for the first and only time referred to as the abbess. As the nuns did not accept a secular supervisor, the Benedictine monk Volmar was appointed as provost, who remained Hildegard's secretary and confidant until he died in 1173.

In the newly founded convent only novices and nuns of noble descent were admitted, which paved the way for the protection of the congregation through the influence of the elite of their relatives on the clergymen, who had to consent to and approve of the sectarian way of life and character of the convent.

In this period, Adelheid of Sommerschenburg (c. 1115–1184) entered the convent. Adelheid was a niece of Richardis of Stade and the protégée of Richardis's mother. Adelheid and Richardis grew up together at the house of Richardis's mother's, who had been widowed a year after Richardis was born. Hildegard's older sister Odilia Clementia joined the Rupertsberg convent too.

After the establishment of the convent and the convent's chapel in Rupertsberg, in spite of being criticized by magistrate Tengswich of Andernach, Hildegard withdrew from the influence and evaluation of "outsiders" and could, with informed consent by the church and the emperor, completely have it her way, especially after some, in Hildegard's opinion, "dissident" nuns had left the congregation after a series of conflicts.

After the death of Richardis's mother and the departure of Adelheid in 1115, Richardis's death in 1152, and the death or stepping down of influential high-ranking clergymen such as Bernardus of Clervaux and Pope Eugene III in 1153, problems arose with the outside world. The protection of the exceptional status of Hildegard and her sectarian congregation waned or altogether disappeared because of changing opinions regarding Hildegard and her sisters' way of life that no longer matched the mores of the time.

As was said before, during the celebration ceremonies of the Mass, Hildegard wore the outfit of a Greek high priestess in full regalia [Plate 51], and the nuns were dressed in silk clothing decorated with golden jewelry and gemstones, with their hair hanging loose or worn in a plait.

Hildegard managed a sectarian congregation, of which some members or "brides of Christ," who were probably excluded from participating in the use of entheogens within the circle of intimates and confidants surrounding Hildegard, and/or disagreed with the not particularly ascetic lifestyle within the community, ultimately left. Probably one of them informed or gossipped about the deviation from traditional practices within the sect, which formed the reason for Tengswich of Andernach to write Hildegard a letter, in which she criticized Hildegard for her conduct and for wearing the outfit of a high priestess. Tengswich could not have found out about Hildegard's behavior by herself or by hearing about the performance of the mystical play, as Atherton (2001) claims, because Hildegard was staged in the role of the Holy Mother, who was dressed in a different way and as always wore a golden crown.

Hildegard by then had constructed an encrypted language, the "lingua ignota," and secret code, the "litterae ignotae," which according to the compilers of the exhibition in Bingen (Dom- und Diözesanmuseum Mainz, 1998), was meant to strengthen the bond between Hildegard and her intimates. Probably the meaning of the secret language was only known to her secretary and guardian of her secrets, Volmar, and her amanuensis and confidante Richardis. The secret code was probably constructed as a means of hiding the key to her "secrets" and the entheogen-associated alchemist recipes, even from today's non-initiated.

In 1115, Hildegard won the territorial dispute with Disibodenberg on the ownership of the grounds. In 1158, Archbishop Arnold of Mainz confirmed the financial agreement between Disibodenberg and Rupertsberg. On April 14, 1163, with Archbishop Conrad of Mainz and Bishop Eberhard of Salzburg as witnesses, the protection of the convent of Rupertsberg was obtained by papal and imperial decree.

Because of the numbers of nuns entering the convent, in 1165 Hildegard founded a second convent in Eibingen, near Rüdesheim, by taking over the ruins of and rebuilding the former Augustinian monastery, which was founded by the noblewoman Marka in 1148 CE, and only 17 years later destroyed by imperial troops. It is assumed that at this new convent there was a policy of admitting nuns who were not of noble descent. Until her death in 1179, Hildegard regularly commuted between both convents to manage and govern as their magistrate.

1.6 Hildegard and Richardis of Stade

Preceding the move to the convent of Rupertsberg around 1150, Richardis of Stade (1123–1152) entered the convent of Disibodenberg, of which Hildegard was the abbess, as a novice. Richardis was of rich noble descent and had been educated to such an extent that she was appointed as Hildegard's second secretary and as her amanuensis, acting—as is shown in the miniature "Vom Ursprung des Lebens"—as "mother's little helper" at Hildegard's "experiments" [Plate 6]. According to the Dutch Van Dale dictionary, an amanuensis is "an expert helper or assistant in the field of physics and chemistry in laboratories and schools" (Van Sterkenburg 1990).

It is possible that Hildegard's knowledge and experience of nature, mineralogy, and alchemy, including the philosopher's stone or Cosmic Egg sought by alchemists and magi, was copied or learned from Jutta and Richardis. This knowledge was put down in writing for posterity in 1151 CE, shortly before the death of Richardis, and concealed to outsiders in the secret language; in 1158 CE, Hildegard completed *Physica*. If this was the case, it willIt would certainly not have been in accordance with Hildegard"s personality to cite both women as a source or mention them as co-authors of the *Physica*, which by the way was not consulted or checked for a citation of Jutta or Richardis because neither *Causae* and *Curae*, nor the *Physica*, the original manuscripts, have been preserved.

Hildegard worshipped and adored Richardis [Plate 52] for her beauty, intelligence, and inquisitiveness and adopted her as her prodigal "daughter" and protégée and as a close confidante. In the period of her decision to found Rupertsberg, Hildegard was frustrated in her plans to the point where she fell seriously ill and even temporarily turned blind and became paralyzed. She was nursed by Richardis, the "much loved fellow nun," who according to Bolton Holloway (1992) had colluded with and was involved in a secret (sexual) relationship with Hildegard.

Richardis's mother, the marquise Richardis of Sponheim-Laventtal, was a very influential woman. In 1124, a year after her daughter Richardis was born, she became the widow of the marquis Rudolf I of Stade. She passed on in 1151 CE, about a year before her daughter Richardis died. She maintained very good relations with high clergymen and probably at the instigation of her daughter used her influence to acquire the support of archbishop Heinrich of Mainz for the move to Rupertsberg. Richardis and her mother were also related to Jutta of Sponheim.

In the miniature "Vom Wirken der Liebe," Richardis—together with Jutta and Hildegard—was depicted standing in a well [Plate 52]. Moreover, Richardis was at least once—together with Volmar—depicted as a witness of and amanuensis supporting Hildegard's "vision" in the miniature "Vom Ursprung des Lebens." In the miniature, Richardis has one eye closed, which symbolizes "inner vision" after using entheogens and/or the sharing of a secret, or turning a blind eye to the hoax [Plate 6].

As Rush (2011) already suggested, Richardis developed a more than platonic relationship with and was probably sexually intimate with the twenty-five-years-older Hildegard. Hildegard defines her relationship with Richardis as that of a mother-daughter or sister-sister, or as sisterly love of "blood sisters," where blood stands for the blood of Christ or for the content of the chalice of life or Holy Grail, the fly agaric.

That Hildegard's relationship with Richardis goes beyond that of sisters can be concluded from an analysis of the *Ordo Virtutum* by Bolton Holloway (1992), who writes that: "Yet her writings are full of sexual curiosity and lore, this material granting her writing some of their most powerful images," and "[W]e need to see the mystery play in its contexts, first of monastic obedience, then of flesh and blood reality concerning disobedience behind its morality, the tragedy of Hildegard's companion (and lover), Richardis of Stade."

However, the love affair is confined to a short period. In 1151, Hildegard's "soul mate" and secret lover, against Hildegard's wishes and politically instigated by Richardis's brother, Archbishop Harwich of Bremen, complies with the orders and is transferred to a monastery of the Saxon foundation of Bassum, in the diocese of Bremen, to become the convent's new abbess. In 1151, Adelheid also became abbess of a monastery, after which she also leaves Rupertsberg. According to Bolton Holloway (1992), contrary to her reaction to the departure of Richardis, Hildegard should not have resisted the appointment and departure of Adelheid, which illustrates the completely different character of her relationship with Richardis.

After Richardis's departure, Hildegard, not only out of pangs of love but probably also because of the loss of her private "nurse," emotionally blackmailed Richardis by threatening a recurrence of her earlier symptoms, and Hildegard, once again, fell seriously ill (Atherton 2001).

In order to achieve Richardis's return to Rupertsberg, Hildegard was driven to active correspondence testifying despair and self-pity and addressing admonitory, but also imploring words to the Archbishops of Mainz and Bremen, to Richardis's mother, to Richardis herself, and even to Pope Eugene III. In the letter to the Archbishop of Mainz, Hildegard criticized the assignment of ecclesiastical offices. But beneath the accusation of simony was Hildegard's own selfish motives. To Richardis's mother, the Marchioness of Stade, Hildegard wrote: "I implore and urge you not to confound my soul as to draw out bitter tears from my eyes and pierce my heart with terrible wounds on account of my dearly-loved daughters Richardis and Adelheid. For the newly-one rank that you desired for her of abbess surely, surely, surely, did not come from God."

When even the letters to Richardis's brother Hartwig, Archbishop of Bremen, and to Pope Eugene do not bring about any changes, Hildegard addressed Richardis herself once more and writes a moving, pain-ridden letter: "Hear my daughter, your mother, within the Spirit, says to you: Pain rises within me. Pain destroys the great trust and comfort I once had in mankind. From now on I say: It is better to put trust in the Lord than to put confidence in princes.... And so I transgressed in loving a noble human being.... Woe is me, mother, woe is me, daughter! Why hast thou forsaken me like an orphan? I loved the mobility of your ways, and the wisdom, and the chastity, and your soul, and all of your life...." (Baird 2006).

Hildegard recognizes and regrets her selfish behavior. After she no longer insists on Richardis's return, the whole story takes a tragic turn. Shortly before her appointment as abbess, Richardis loses her mother. Once she decides to rejoin Hildegard, and shortly after receiving permission to return to Rupertsberg, she dies in the year 1152 CE, at the age of 27. Separation anxiety and fear of being abandoned plagued Hildegard all her life and this event surely must have added to her anxiety and fear.

In a letter written by Richardis's brother Hartwig, Hildegard is informed of the sudden death of Richardis. He writes that in her dying hour Richardis had expressed her intention to rejoin Hildegard. Hildegard's amanuensis, Richardis, quite possibly took the only possible way out of the pathological symbiotic relationship, forced upon her by Hildegard, committing suicide by poisoning. She certainly had the knowledge, but this was a secret Richardis took to her grave.

While one would expect Hildegard to enter a period of mourning and depression, there seems to be no indication of an intense or severe reaction to the death of Richardis and the definite departure of Adelheid. Contrary to expectations, Hildegard's stay in Rupertsberg is evaluated as being her most creative and productive period.

Bolton Holloway (1992) states that "Perhaps within that rage is envy of Richardis' freedom. Her headaches and invalidism could indicate suppressed fury. She herself tended to recover from serious illness through being disobedient.... It could well be that had it not been for Richardis' disobedience, first to the concept of women's helplessness, then to the concept of her dependency upon another, and finally Richardis' choice of death as freedom from Hildegard's tyranny, the writings, the music and the illuminations ... could not have come into being."

Hildegard's way of coping with emotional problems can be attributed to her traumatic experiences as a child and the narcissistic personality traits that evolved from these experiences.

Personality Development

From Hildegard's life history one could conclude that frequent illness and the now and then illusory experiences in her early youth had to a great extent determined Hildegard's cognitive, emotional, and sexual development, and the constitution of her personality and identity.

2.0 Cognitive and Emotional Development

As stated before, from the development of consciousness a child is confronted with primary or basic vital questions such as: Who am I? To whom do I belong? Why am I here? Where am I going and what is expected of me? What will my future life be like?

From developmental psychology the phenomenon of "magical thinking" is an important aspect of the cognitive development of a young child. If no "logical" explanation can be given for phenomena such as sickness and death, with very young children "magical thinking" becomes prominent if they undergo such dramatic and extreme anxiety-provoking experiences as those of Hildegard at the age of three.

Growing up in a social environment in which such impressive events were attributed to God's will, Hildegard was not able to develop a realistic frame of reference or mindset about what happened to her. Young children confronted with this loss of autonomous control cannot as yet express themself adequately and seek to find something (transitional objects) or someone (parents) to provide reassurance or confirmation and an explanation for what is bothering or tormenting them.

They tend to either think they are crazy, or very special. Hildegard writes: "[These words] are not like words coming from a human's mouth, but like lightning flames and as a cloud, that passes by in a clear sky. The figure in this light I cannot recognize, just as I also cannot look directly at the sun."

If little children lack the vocabulary and mastery of a language to facilitate talking about existential fears and feelings of loss of control (Keizer 1996) and withdraw or no longer dare to share their experiences with significant others because they fear being considered insane, ideas of being chosen by a higher power or being predestined can easily find a foothold. From a psycho-diagnostic point of view it is apparent that Hildegard's personality traits were characterized by:

- An identity development marked by limited living conditions that predisposed her perception of the social and physical environment surrounding her as a child;

- Few possibilities to identify with something ("transitional objects") or someone such as parents or other children;

- Egocentrism manifesting itself in the feeling of being the center of the universe, the person around whom all things revolve or who should be at the center of attention;

- An inferiority complex at a later age, among others being expressed in false modesty by presenting herself as a "paupercula feminae forma" or poor and weak woman;

- Not daring to and (still) not being able to talk about her existential anxiety-evoking experiences, and still wondering why this happens to her and what the meaning of it is, by which her fantasy easily runs riot and the idea that she possesses magical or healing powers can find a foothold;

- Narcissistic traits, limited self-criticism or introspective abilities, and boundless overestimation of herself associated with extreme powerlessness and a lack of self-control and hold on others on the one hand and having fantasies of omnipotence, grandeur, or being a savior and the idea of having total control and power over others on the other hand;

- Searching for a hold and significance of meaning and of affirmation of her ideas rooted in the traumas she did not deal with, on her position within the church, in the secular world, and the prevailing religious convictions;

- Manipulation through emotional blackmail;

- Being diseased at an early age and being (hysterically) ill as an adult.

Because of her frequently being bedridden for a long time, Hildegard was often left alone as a child. As a result of this, she would have felt abandoned and developed a strong fear of being separated from and experienced difficulties of attachment to significant others.

Fear of separation and abandonment associated with existential anxiety appears from the second year of a child's life, after which the feelings of anxiety from the age of eight to nine years in boys is more strongly developed than in girls. For Hildegard this manifested at a later age, in her near panic and very emotional reaction to the realization that she could not even trust her dearly beloveds, nor rely on them, because they abandoned her by dying or leaving, as happened with Jutta and Richardis.

In puberty, the physical development of girls outpaces their psychological and emotional development. The girl looks like an adult, but her behavior and thinking is not yet that of a woman. In puberty and adolescence, mood swings or sudden mood changes often occur. Gloominess or anger suddenly can show up (premenstrual syndrome), quite often leading to conflicts with parents (although not present in Hildegard's case) and teachers such as Jutta and Volmar. The solidarity and sharing a similar fate as Jutta, as well as the extreme dependence on both her teachers, also strongly influenced Hildegard's emotional development.

Friends are of major importance in puberty. Adolescents want to be part of a group and will adopt the behavior and display of significant others within a reference group; they often overidentify with and mimic or mirror these significant others.

In puberty an important part of consciousness-raising and identity and personality development takes place. The individual feels insecure and looks for someone to hold on to in relationships with significant others, other than parents and those seen as "in authority." "Skewed growth" in the emotional and psychological sense can lead to the development of personality disorders. As a prelude to becoming an adult, adolescents experience their physical growth as "inviting" them to experiment with their bodies (sports, sex) and mind (alcohol, drugs) to explore the boundaries of what they can and dare to do. In this respect, there are great individual differences between girls, ages eleven to fifteen years, and young females of up to twenty-two years.

As an adult, Hildegard quite frequently was illogical and inconsistent in her thinking and behavior and applied a double standard of morality for herself. Bolton Holloway (1996) characterized Hildegard as a woman who—just as in her music—both conformed to and revolted against what was regarded as the regular practice for nuns and monks.

In relationships with significant others on whom she depended and who strongly depended on her, such as Richardis, Hildegard shows claiming and controlling behavior and invests in symbiotic double binds (collusion), which result in smothering or "suffocating" love and pressuring others to give in to her needs and wishes by confronting them with illusions of alternatives and paradoxical intentions (Watzlawick 1967; Keizer 1994). She invests in feigning somatic complaints by falling ill at crucial moments and simulates temporary (hysterical) blindness and paralysis when she does not get things done according to her demands. In this way she tries to be in control of others and to be looked after and nursed (by Richardis) and treated with consideration and compassion. The symptoms disappear miraculously once she has her way through emotional blackmail, with the secondary profits of being "ill" as a reward for her pathological and manipulative behavior.

On top of this, she imposes her will upon others by appealing to self-induced or actually nonexistent messages and orders from "above."

2.1 Visions and Hallucinations

As was stated before, at the age of three Hildegard for the first time experienced vivid illusions of illuminating objects ("Schau" or "Visio"), the hallucinations probably resulting from high fever or maybe (also) from social isolation, as Rush (2011) suggests [Plate 4]. Particularly because Hildegard never mentions the setting in of migraine-associated symptoms such as auras, short light flashes, complex visual and auditory distortions, or very temporary, not feigned or hysterical blindness, the "Visio" would not have been caused by cluster headaches or migraines as Sachs (1970/1992) suggests.

If migraines had been involved, she could have "cured" or diminished the headaches by taking (grinded) ergots or applying ointments to the forehead. Using ergots as a medicine could by itself have triggered hallucinations, caused by the LSD-related component in it. Moreover, she never reported having symptoms of gangrene, common with ergot poisoning, and entheogen-induced "visions" differ greatly from hallucinations caused by migraines.

One of the herbal medicines used in the Middle Ages to counter gravity nausea was cumin (*Cuminum cyminum*). Due to the warning for mixing up cumin seeds with ergots (*Claviceps* spp.), because of the latter's abortive effects, Hildegard must have known of the use of ergots as a medicine against migraines. Keep in mind that the reception of "orders from above" is not associated with migraine, and Hildegard, who at a later age was well informed of all kinds of diseases and in the *Liber compositae medicinae* dealt with "sicknesses of the head" such as migraine, never reported having cluster headaches or migraine attacks herself.

In addition to this, Hildegard's miniatures, when compared with the paintings of contemporary painters suffering from migraine such as Salvador Dali and the Dutch artist Yri Kohl, fundamentally differs from their work in not depicting extremely distorted, contorted, or melting, disproportional and extremely bizarre people, animals, and objects, as is the case in the work of both contemporary artists.

And from a comparison of her writings on her "visions" with the literary work of Lewis Carroll, the author of *Alice in Wonderland,* one can conclude that Hildegard did not suffer from hypnogogia or hypnopompia, as these states of consciousness are characterized by very realistic, dreamlike experiences and by strong sensations of growing, shrinking, or falling, that occur with people sensitive to these phenomena shortly before falling asleep or after awakening.

High fever is often accompanied by convulsions and delirium. Regularly being severely ill, bedridden for a long time, and often being left alone can lead to sensory deprivation and social isolation (Rush 2011), with feelings of fear of being abandoned, at a later age developing problems with attachment to others, and the development of a deviant sense of reality and distortion of reality as a consequence. Besides, as an adult, not adequately socialized children often display egocentric behavior.

In addition to this, because of often being ill, bedridden, and at home—as was customary in medieval times because children did not attend school—Hildegard would not have grown up with other children of the same age.

Moreover, her regular separation from others, or her documented solitary confinement, is associated with sensory deprivation, which can in itself lead to delusions and hallucinations.

2.2 Psycho-Diagnostic Aspects

From the preceding paragraph and the chapter on Hildegard's childhood we see a woman whose personality traits as an adult meet the criteria for a diagnosis of narcissistic personality disorder. According to the definition, individuals suffering from this disorder are described as egocentric, lacking empathy, and being excessively preoccupied with issues of personal adequacy, power, prestige , and vanity. They often demand preferential treatment and if not given it they feel offended and undervalued, which can lead to depression and anger. The consequences of the disorder for entering and supporting relationships with subordinates and superiors are described by Lash (1980).

Most of the foundation for this disorder evolves in childhood. The cause often is found in traumas that have arisen from the behavior of parents or other influential adults during childhood, or of peers at a later age. The narcissistic personality disorder is regarded to be a defensive mechanism based upon feelings of inferiority.

In children, inflated self-views and grandiose feelings, which are characteristics of narcissism, are part of the normal self-development. Children are typically unable to understand the difference between their actual and their ideal self, which causes an unrealistic perception of the self. Although the exact cause of the disorder is unknown, the following factors have been identified as possibly contributing to its development:

- Excessive preoccupation with and admiration of oneself that is never or not enough balanced by realistic feedback by significant others;

- Overindulgence or emotional overinvolvement (smothering) and/or lack of emotional involvement or emotional neglect by parents or caretakers, resulting in over- and/or underestimating or -validating the age-appropriate capabilities of the child by significant others and an imbalance in the relationship between them and the child, characterized by "High Expressed Emotion" (Keizer, 1994);

- Inappropriate valuation by parents as a means to regulate their own lack of self-esteem;

- Excessive praise for good behaviors or excessive criticism for bad behaviors in childhood;

- Unpredictable or unreliable caretaking from parents or significant others.

Some psychotherapists believe that the disorder is, in Freudian terms, the result of fixation to early childhood development.

Following the DSM-IV (2000) classification and diagnosis of a narcissistic personality disorder, for Hildegard at least seven characteristics are documented, while for the diagnosis only five out of nine characteristics need to be manifest. Symptoms of this disorder may include, but are not limited to:

- Having feelings of grandeur and exaggerating his or her own importance, knowledge, achievements, talents, social contacts or personal qualities, demanding acknowledgment of his or her superiority without his or her achievements giving cause to this, and reacting to any slight criticism, real or imagined, or humiliation, with anger, disdain, and/or defiance, shame, or humiliation of others (for example, the letters of Hildegard as a reaction to the departure of Richardis);

- Being controlling, tending to devalue, derogate, and blame others and being self-absorbed or obsessed and preoccupied with oneself and having fantasies of omnipotence, success, glory, genius, beauty (display), sexual performances, or an ideal or idealized love affair (with Richardis);

- Believing he or she is special and unique and that he or she only can be understood by or must get involved with others (or institutions) with high status (noblemen, high clergymen, and the emperor);

- Having an excessive need for admiration, attention, and positive reinforcement (for example, synode of Trier) or wanting to be feared or notorious;

- Claiming privileges, wanting to be treated with special regard or have more rights than others (Rupertsberg convent) and expecting confirmation of his or her unreasonable demands by others;

- Taking advantage of others and manipulating and abusing others to reach his or her own goals;

- Lacking empathy and disregarding the needs of others or being unwilling or incapable of acknowledging and taking their feelings into account (Richardis);

- Often being jealous and easily becoming hurt or feeling rejected, sometimes resulting in anger, and believing that others envy him or her because of his or her superior qualities, which can lead to paranoid delusions;

- Being arrogant, treating others high-handedly and feeling superior and above the law, omnipresent, and reacting with aggression and anger if he or she is contradicted by others he or she regards as inferior to him or her in certain aspects (as examples, correspondence with Tengswich of Echternach, letters to emperor Barbarossa and Christian of Buch).

Starr (2010) writes: "Hildegard of Bingen found herself on the legendary line between genius and insanity. Her inner world was an illuminating web of visions and voices, scientific breakthroughs, artistic divine revelations and emotional obsessions. This is a dance that has always intrigued me: the game between inadequacy and virtuosity, this divine zone where chemical unbalance meets spiritual genius."

Or as Bolton Holloway (1974) characterizes Hildegard: "One admires her work, but not her desire of control" (over others) and "Hildegard ruled her monastery by means of tyrannizing over her nuns with her migraines" (and other psychosomatic and hysterical complaints).

Hildegard's character traits and the behavior resulting from them are readily apparent, just as her megalomania is expressed in the miniatures depicting herself as high priestess in full regalia [Plates 3 and 51] and as Mary with a golden crown [Plates 11 and 17].

Despite reacting with false modesty, as she was no example of humility and submission, by rejecting the status of being "the most holy and pure virgin since the virgin Mary" given to her by her contemporaries, Hildegard sees herself as the chosen one at the center of the events happening in her visions, playing a central role in her mystical play, and as a high priestess in the Mass, projecting and investing in self-fulfilling prophesies or wishful thinking by visualizing events in retrospect or reliving scenes that already happened or "foreseeing" future events she wished to be realized, like founding a sectarian convent at Rupertsberg, financed by secular noblemen and noble women [Plate 56]. She considers herself, and the "happy few" around her, having an unwritten right to privileges from which other nuns and monks were excluded, and being allowed to create an exclusive sectarian refuge for experimenting with entheogens for herself and a small group of her ardent supporters. Because of her status as a visionary and a prophetess, she could have things go her way. She feigned illness, and with her self-induced visions, in which she foresaw events she wanted to happen, or through messages commanding her, she was able to manipulate many others to do things she was "ordered" to do; to do otherwise would bring the wrath of God on their heads.

2.3 Hildegard's Views on Sexuality and Femininity

As mentioned, Hildegard spent several years with Jutta and another anonymous young girl in the inclusorium, and this, to a major extent, influenced her sexual development and identity. Moreover, monastic enclosures were not equipped with running water and included only primitive sanitary conditions. And because of a total lack of privacy, extreme intimacy was forced upon the young women.

Preceding and during the stay in the inclusorium with Jutta from the age of eight until she was fourteen years old, Hildegard would have gone through the hormonally triggered transition of childhood into puberty and adolescence (development of the body: breasts, pubic hair, menstruation). In this period, female sexuality and erotic feelings and physical sensations emerge in social relationships with a more or less explicit sexual character. In discovering her own body and that of the other girls by seeing each other naked (bathing) and experiencing and/or witnessing masturbation and orgasm, Hildegard had no one other than Jutta to turn to for explaining what was happening, implicating that Jutta, who already had "lived through" the phases of puberty and was becoming an adolescent young woman, initiated Hildegard in the mysteries of becoming a woman. In this period experimenting with the erogenous zones of the body and masturbation can begin, sometimes resulting in a first orgasm. In our own time, more than half of all girls and adolescents under the age of twenty have experienced orgasm.

Analyzing the vision "Das Weltall" or "Egg of the Universe" [Plate 2], depicting an (orgasmic) yoni or vagina [Plate 49], one must realize that in the early Middle Ages, mirrors used throughout Europe were simple slightly convex disks of metal, either bronze, tin, or silver, that poorly reflected light off their highly polished surfaces, producing images with lack of detail, and it was not until the end of the twelfth-century that hand mirrors became popular throughout Europe.

The use of glass with a metallic backing commenced in the late twelfth and the beginning of the thirteenth century (Müller-Ebeling 2010). So Hildegard may have had a close look at other women's vaginas, like Jutta's and/or Richardis' and/or that of the anonymous girl in the inclusorium. Besides, if she had used a mirror to study her own vagina, she only would have seen a superficial and distorted upside-down image of her vulva. And she obviously had knowledge of ways of reaching an orgasm by masturbation [Plate 52], copulation, or applying the witches' flying ointment [Plates 2 and 10] to herself, or witnessing and sharing other women's experiences, with whom she had been very intimate for a long time.

Although the Benedictine monk Gottfried, who was provost of the Rupertsberg convent and secretary of Hildegard from 1174 to 1176, and author of the three parts of the *Vita Sanctae Hildegardis,* after Hildegard's death on September 17, 1179, wrote: "Then already in the younger years of her life, she showed an early unawareness of all carnal lust or desires." In his latest book Rush supposes that Hildegard was a sexually experienced woman: "We see, presented in iconic and surrealistic lines and colors, Hildegard, her vulnerability, her sexual experimentation and [same sex] preferences, her fears and desires" (Rush 2011). And adding to this, why should Hildegard depict the God of erotic justice Zealous in "Das Heilsgebaude," if she was not looking for some kind of erotic "justice" or justification herself? Ambivalence? Feeling guilty or demanding the right to engage in erotic or sexual relationships as long as it just happened inside the inclusorium and in the protective environment of her sectarian convent with only one woman?

Hildegard was the first to describe the female (and male) orgasm (ejaculation) and the conception (blood and semen) in great detail. According to her, because of their "open loin" and thighs, women have a more subdued sexuality than men, while men are more easily aroused because they have a narrow and compressed genital region, the scrotum and testicles being necessary to support the penis in erection and keeping it from "falling down." Because of her explicit descriptions, Hildegard must have experienced these sensations herself or, in the manner of a gynecologist, closely witnessed them as experienced by others. She writes, "When a woman makes love to a man, a feeling of heat in her brain, which results in a sensual pleasure, announces the taste of that pleasure during the act and incites the deposition of the man's sperm. And once the semen has fallen into place, this intense heat in her brain attracts the seed and retains it, and soon the female organs [literally: kidneys] contract, and now all parts opening up during menstruation close, in the same way a strong man can lock up an object in his clenched fist."

As was said before, shortly before the move to Rupertsberg, because of hysterical blindness and paralysis, Hildegard was bedridden again. During this period she was cared for and nursed by the younger, sexually inexperienced Richardis, her protégée and the "much loved fellow nun," who according to Bolton Holloway (1992) had colluded with and was involved in a secret (sexual) relationship with Hildegard. Nursing Hildegard would have involved seeing her naked and washing her, including her private parts, which in a more or less "natural" way could have been the start of a more than platonic relationship between the two women. That Hildegard valued personal hygiene and some physical comfort helps to explain why she made a plea that nuns no longer be obliged to wear woolen underwear during their menstrual periods.

Hildegard acted as a midwife, was a marriage counselor for married couples with sexual problems, recommended the use of aphrodisiacs, and advised in matters such as impotence, pregnancy, and infertility.

In her relationships with Jutta and Richardis, Hildegard kept double standards of morality, practicing what she rejected. On the one hand she took vows of asceticism and abstinence, while on the other hand she gave in to her far from purely platonic "sisterly" feelings for both women and the use of stimulants of the erogenous zones such as witch's flying ointment. In "Vom Wirken der Liebe," Hildegard even (posthumously) depicts Jutta with one hand on a breast and the other hand submerged in her groin, while being watched from a "cloud" by saints, who look down with approval and consent on Jutta, Hildegard, and Richardis, while Jutta masturbates [Plate 52].

Contradictory to her own and Jutta's behavior, Hildegard regards masturbation as abuse of carnal pleasures and writes on the sin of engaging in homosexual relationships in the following explicit words: "God united man and woman, thus joining together the weak and the strong, as to each would support the other. But these perverted adulterers change their virile powers in perverse weakness when they reject the female and male role, and in their depravation wickedly follow Satan.... A woman who enacts the practices of the devil and plays the male role in the union with another woman is very despicable in My [God's] vision, and so is she who submits to such a sinful act by someone else. And men who touch and manipulate their genitalia and ejaculate their sperm put their souls in severe danger, as they only incite themselves to their own amusement."

In the Middle Ages the church was somewhat tolerant toward and implicitly accepted loving or lesbian relationships among nuns and regarded not publicly practiced lesbian relationships as more "normal" than homosexual relationships among men or monks, which were forbidden at the counsel of Nabloes in 1120, as well as heterosexual relationships between monks and nuns. The last verdict, however, is somewhat put into perspective by a monk from the Disibodenberg monastery impregnating one of Hildegard's nuns and the discovery of walled-in corpses of newborn babies in a Dutch convent.

Other than giving in to non-reproductive sex in the form of sodomy or masturbation by monks, carnal "sisterly" relationships among nuns and mutual or solo masturbation—with or without using stimulants for the erogenous zones such as witch's flying ointment—were tolerated by the Church because no "seeds" meant for reproduction were lost, a sin that according to the Bible was forbidden.

The Bible tells the story of Onan, who, by spilling his sperm on the ground, did what was evil in the eyes of God in not obeying His order—with the exception of the Catholic clergy—to procreate as much and as often as possible. Even nowadays the Church of Rome fulminates against masturbation and anti-conception because the emphasis still lies on as much as possible increasing the flock of still-pliable children's "souls," to add to the mother church.

Onan's sin, however, was not the result of masturbation, but took place after coitus interruptus, or as we Dutch say, "leaving the church before the singing starts," or pulling out in time to, against God's laws, prevent the childless widow of Onan's older brother from being impregnated by him, while, after his brother's death, being in a compulsory levirate marriage with his sister in law.

Besides, women masturbating or having lesbian relationships were not condemned or execrated, nor mentioned in the Bible. Moreover, for women masturbation would at least not have resulted in "spinal marrow consumption," a "disease" that is continuously threatening the health of masturbating men.

Until Pope Gregory the Great (c. 540-604 CE) introduced celibacy for all clergymen, many priests were married and popes often had more than one concubine or mistress. Because he feared that the offspring of married priests would separate from the mother church and claim land and properties owned by the Church, he ordered celibacy for them as well, which is yet another example of explicit territorial behavior by the Church of Rome.

In Benedictine convents and monasteries, however, there was a high standard of moral and religious rule of law imposed upon the nuns and monks. Regarding sexuality, assuming Hildegard broke her vows on abstinence from hetero- and/or homosexual relationships, her carnal sins normally would have been punished by penance or even self-chastisement, of which she reports no occurrence.

From psychological theory and research, this kind of behavior is known to provoke strong feelings of ambivalence and guilt, resulting in extreme cognitive dissonance, which only can be reduced by ignoring, repressing, or denying the sinful character of the conduct by labeling it as a "pure" expression of sisterly "LOVE." Showing inconsistency in, on the one hand holding a liberal moral on sexuality (marriage counselor, aphrodisiacs), and on the other hand a rigid formal and official position, rejecting what she had practiced or still practiced herself (masturbation, homosexual relationships, nonreproductive sex), Hildegard kept double standards: women enjoying sex versus chastity, and asceticism expected from a Benedictine nun wearing luxury garments and jewelry in sectarian rituals or ceremonies during Mass, versus the nun's habit and hood on regular "working" days. As a consequence, she shows ambivalence (and guilt) toward her own experiences and practices, in seeking tolerance and forgiveness or absolution through her special status within the Catholic Church and her relations with powerful clergymen (bishops, Pope Eugene III) and noblemen, including Emperor Barbarossa, in Germany and other European countries. And she invested in a long-lasting exchange of letters with another exceptionally influential woman of her time, the visionary nun Elisabeth of Schönau (1129–1165), who partially imitated the scenes depicted in the miniatures of the *Scivias* in her "Liber viarum Dei."

In her writings, Hildegard expresses herself in a very positive way on the pleasures of the sexual act, including experiencing an orgasm. She is often regarded as being the first author treating sexual matters from the point of view of a woman, ergo herself and her female intimates. Bolton Holloway (1992) writes that in spite of Hildegard's strong attachment to obedience to her vows, "Her writings are full of expressions of sexual curiosity and [handed down] knowledge from experience, which evoke the most powerful images in her work."

2.4 Hildegard's Healing and Prophetic Powers

As in the twelfth-century, in the opinion of the Catholic Church, accusations of witchcraft had not been instituted, and deluded or confused/hallucinating women were not recognized as possessed or treated as such.

Because of this, Hildegard could present and manifest herself as a "medicine woman" with healing powers, marriage counselor for sexual and reproductive problems, midwife (ergots), alchemist (precious metals, gemstones, philosopher's stone), consultant in spiritual matters, and prophetess without being regarded and prosecuted as a witch, but "after the fourteenth-century—or according to my findings from the beginning of the thirteenth-century on—she would have been burned at the stake" (Rush 2011). Ruck et al (2007) note that "Another term that remains inexplicable outside the pharmaceutical context is [Hildegard's] use of the enigmatic *pigmentarius*, a 'dealer in pigments and unguents' for priests and bishops … and in particular the trusted monk Volmar, who aided her throughout her life in bringing her hidden mysteries to light. She writes of her own intuitive empathy with the plant she calls the philosopher's stone, repeatedly emphasizing that you can feel its powers with your hand—at least if you are what we would call a shaman, in her days a prophetess."

On the philosopher's stone, Hildegard herself writes: "There are three powers in a [philosopher's] stone [or Cosmic Egg]. In a stone there is moist greenness, palpable strength and red-burning fire. Its moist greenness signifies the Father [the grandparents Joachim and Anna or the evergreen spruce], who will never dry out or reach a limit to its [regenerative] power; its palpable strength signifies the Son [a primordium], since he was born of the Virgin [the fly agaric] and could be touched and grasped; its red-burning fire signifies the Spirit [Holy Ghost], who is the fire and illumination of the hearts of the faithful" (Atherton, 2001). According to the Pentacost tradition, Jesus is the fire and illumination, that is, the Holy Spirit.

In the Age of Reason or Enlightenment Hildegard's visions are disqualified as "monk's swindle." In the nineteenth and twentieth centuries, Hildegard is honored as a Holy "prophetissa tutonica," a name that was given to her by Pope Eugene III. Not until 1940 does the Roman Congregation of Rites permit her cult in Germany, perhaps because of her (infamous) flouting of ecclesiastical authority. Although Hildegard, after beatification by Pope Innocent IV in the thirteenth century, was registered in the Roman List of Martyrs in the sixteenth century—which is considered being equal to acceptance as a saint—she never was officially canonized by the Roman Catholic Church. As a consequence of this, in Germany Hildegard only was honored locally as a saint until May 10, 2012, when Hildegard was canonized by the German pope Benedict XVI. In November 2012, Hildegard will also be posthumously appointed as a Doctor of the Church or "Doctor Ecclesiae."

Evidence of the Use of Psychoactives

To keep the reader from needlessly being in the dark about the evidence of Hildegard's use of entheogens, the following overview of the most important indications is presented.

Going back to the earlier chapters and considering the later documented analysis of various parts of Hildegard's heritage, the following strong evidence of her using the fly agaric, Datura, mandrake, and henbane, that is to say, entheogens such as psychoactive mushrooms and plants, can be derived from:

- The descriptions of the characteristics and the content of her first "visionary" and "prophetic" visual and auditory hallucinatory "vision" or "epiphany" at age 42 [Plate 4] and of the second "revelation" at age 60, "epiphanies" in which she was ordered to write down what she heard or saw;

- Saint Catherine of Genoa (1447–1510 CE) having comparable visions probably based on the use of "bitter tasting agarics" like *Amanita muscaria,* inducing ecstatic ruptures and hallucinatory images of Our Lady;

- The presence of Volmar at and his witnessing of Hildegard's first "Visio," which indicates that the spontaneous or "out of the blue" occurrence of hallucinations is absolutely out of the question, or proves that Volmar, an "expert" on the application of the fly agaric to his tonsure, initiated and guided the experience, which was induced through the oral use of the Holy Mushroom. Besides, the "beaming" down of the fiery flames or the Holy Spirit from the ceiling of Hildegard's cell, touching and becoming attached to her head and brain, also proves the indoor use of entheogens that were responsible for the elicitation of Hildegard's "visions";

- The presence of both Volmar and Richardis [Plate 6] at the first "Schau" ("Vom Ursprung des Lebens") of the last ten "prophetic" visions, indicating that there, once again, was no spontaneity in the occurrence of this "Visio," but that it was yet another example of hallucinations "on call" and provoked through the use of entheogens, while Richardis "turns a blind eye" to the obvious hoax, or also experiences an "inner vision" or the sharing of a secret. Strikingly, this time the Holy Ghost descended from a window with wide-opened shutters in a cloud hovering above Hildegard's cell;

- There are several miniatures depicting the "rivers or flows of living water," or the recycling of urine containing muscimol, and one depicting this phenomenon associated with the ouroboros [Plate 48], the symbol of the circle of life;

- The depiction of numerous symbols and symbolic colors in the miniatures suggest they are full of hidden clues regarding the use of the fly agaric—including "living" water [Plates 7, 33, and 34], and the applications of psychoactive plants, of which the most striking evidence of the use of the Holy Mushroom—other than by Hildegard and Volmar—is found in the miniature "Von der Gliederung des Leibes" with a fuddled and "intoxicated" half-naked man resting his head on a red pillow and laying down underneath a tree in an orchard [Plate 8], after consuming the red "fruits." What strikes the eye in this miniature is that Hildegard (also) "turns a blind eye" to the "intoxicated" man, in this case nonverbally communicating the sharing of the secret of the consumption of the fly agaric as an entheogen [Plate 9];

- The application of an ointment containing small heaps of tiny white pellets with red flames between the labia majora and labia minora orgastic "yoni" ("Das Weltall") [Plates 2 and 49], along with the appearance of a diabolic monster in and from the loins and private parts of Hildegard posing as the golden crowned Holy Virgin ("Das Ende der Zeiten"), indicates the application of witches' flying ointment on or inside the female genitals [Plate 10]. Adding to this, from the reports of Hildegard's partially self-experienced effects of psychoactive plants in her *Physica* one can conclude that she was well informed of and familiar with the use of mind-altering substances. For the recipes and methods of application of seeds or flowers and leaves of psychoactive plants, either in dried form or soaked or dissolved in a (vinegar) potion, smoked (leaves, seeds), or used as constituents of ointments or ethereal oils, including witches' flying ointment [Plate 12], refer to the comments below.

From the numerous meetings and correspondence with kings and queens and emperors, including Barbarossa (Hildegard was granted a secret consultation in the private chambers of his palace), nobility, popes, or other high-ranking clergymen, one could conclude Hildegard was acting as a "pigmentarius" for the elite (Ruck 2007).

Hildegard's Works and Writings

4.0 Hildegard's Literary Work

Liber Scivias is derived from *Scito vias Domini*, or "Know the Ways of the Lord." The oldest illustrated version of the *Liber Scivias* is the so-called Rupertsberg Codex, which originated from the scriptorium at

Rupertsberg during Hildegard's life. The miniatures included in the *Scivias* were painted from 1141 until 1151, ergo shortly after Hildegard's first and seven years before her second "revelation." Its thirty-five miniatures, carefully executed in opaque gold and silver paint, thematically correspond to the visions. Almost the entire extensive literary works of Hildegard originate from the Rupertsberg period.

From 1151 until 1163, Hildegard writes her visionary works, *Book of Life's Merits,* or *Liber Vitae Meritorium,* and from 1163 until 1173–1174 the *Book of Divine Works,* or *Liber Divinorum Operum.*

From 1151 until 1158, coinciding with or shortly after the death of her amanuensis Richardis, Hildegard writes her *Works of Medicine and Natural Science,* or *Healing Herbs,* the *Liber Simplicis Medicinae,* and the *Liber Compositae Medicinae,* which later were named *Physica* and the *Causae et Curae.* Together they are better known as *Liber Subtilitatum,* or *Book of Subtletie,* in which she elaborates on medicinal plants, mineralogy and physics, cosmology, and astro(theo)logy.

Hildegard's views on mankind and the world were derived from ancient Greek cosmology and the theory of humors based upon the four elements, earth, water, air, and fire, with their respective qualities cold and dry, cold and moist, warm and moist, and warm and dry. With these elements, the four temperaments or humors of the body corresponded to melancholic (black bile), phlegmatic (slime), choleric (yellow bile), and sanguine (blood containing all elements). Strikingly in this respect, in her miniature "Das Weltall" depicting the "yoni," Hildegard positions the elements earth, water, air, and fire at the bottom of the vagina and at the entrance of the cervix, thus communicating that in her view the passage of the sperm through the vagina into the uterus and the following conception takes place where the four elements meet [Plate 13].

According to the Greeks, the human personality was determined by the dominance of one of these elements. Disease sets in when the delicate balance between the temperaments is disturbed. The balance could only be restored by eating the right plant or animal, which possessed the qualities the body needed. Hildegard especially was interested in finding out the qualities of a plant, animal, or mineral by describing the object, from which she derived the assumed healing properties and appliances of the "medicine."

From 1174 until 1178, Hildegard corresponds with various religious leaders and noblemen. The composition of her musical and theatrical works also originates from this period.

The *Book of Life's Merits* deals with the conflict between virtues and vices. It focuses on the struggle of man (and Hildegard) with good and evil.

The Book of Divine Works is considered to be her most mature and most creative achievement. In this work, consisting of three parts and ten visions, Hildegard unfolds a cosmologically supported history of salvation, from Genesis on to the Apocalypse. The central motive of this work on creation and the Creator and on the world of mankind is the *word* of God, which resulted in the creation and in the incarnation of Christ.

The "lingua ignota" and "litterae ignotae" are written in a secret language, which, in spite of modern cryptology and cryptography methods, has not been "cracked" or deciphered. These works were composed during the beginning of Hildegard's stay in Rupertsberg, preceding or around the time some of the nuns left the convent after a conflict with Hildegard and her inner circle of intimates. The music with religious lyrics was composed in the same period.

The mystery play, which had other-than-usual, self-fabricated texts not from the Bible, was performed onstage in the chapel of the Rupertsberg convent by Hildegard and her "sisters" and Volmar (Von Trotta, 2009). It was written and composed between 1151 and 1158. In the period 1151–1158, Hildegard also wrote about the rules of life of the Benedictine order.

4.1 The Significance of the Unknown Language

Preceding or around the time some of the nuns left the convent after a not-clarified conflict with Hildegard and her inner circle of intimates, Hildegard invented a new, unknown language, *"lingua ignota,"* and her own secret writing, *"literae ignotae."* For all of the letters of the alphabet, she uses her own new sign, with which she constructs new words or neologisms. Some words can be recognized as derivations of Latin or old high German, but words like *"korzinthio,"* for prophetess, are impossible to trace, although I wonder whether *korzinthio* could refer to the area east of the Corinthian Gulf in Greece, the dwelling place of the oracle of Delphi and the high priestesses or prophetesses in beautiful gowns, as documented on ancient Greek vases. As skilled fortune-tellers, the high priestesses would interpret the "answers" of the "intoxicated" oracle according to the expectations and desires of their customers, transcribing them on a handheld palm leaf, just like Hildegard depicts herself in some of her miniatures. Because of the absence of syntax and grammar for the secret language, the "lingua ignota" could not serve as a spoken language. Some sources suppose that the alphabet of the "literae ignotae" was used for communicating with other convents on "delicate" matters.

The written version of the secret language was completed before Hildegard started writing *Book of Life's Merits* in 1151. Once again, in spite of modern code-breaking methods it has only been possible to partly interpret the use and benefit of these forms of verbal and written communication.

Wilhelmy (1998) supposes it was meant to strengthen the bond among the nuns in the Rupertsberg convent. As one third, or approximately 900 words, of the handed-down vocabulary seem to refer to botany and medicine, I assume it was conceived to share her "secrets," such as the ingredients and recipes of the potions and ointments and the entheogens used by Hildegard and her intimates, with members of her circle of trust like Richardis, Volmar, and perhaps a few other nuns, including Richardis's niece Adelheid. As all intimated in her secrets had died before Hildegard passed away, by only trusting her secrets to parchment in a secret language, Hildegard, as long as the encoded texts have not been "cracked," took them to her grave. Obviously, Hildegard did not want to reveal to others than the members of her circle of trust, that psychoactive mushrooms such as the fly agaric, and other plants, were the source of her hallucinations, visionary and prophetic powers, and visions or epiphanies.

Hildegard more or less symbolically depicts, but for obvious reasons does not explicitly mention the fly agaric and the Liberty Cap. Because of Hildegard's exceptional knowledge of the medicinal qualities of fungi growing on trees, it is plausible to assume she also had knowledge of and experience with the mind-altering properties and effects of some of the psychoactive fungi growing on soil, such as psilocybin species, or their symbiotic association with tree roots, such as the *Amanita muscaria.* The unknown secret language ends with a listing of the names of trees, plants, herbs, and animals (Atherton 2001).

4.2 The Mystical Play

Hildegard's "Play of Virtues" is a mystical play, an opera for women's voices and one man's voice, which was put to music around the time of the move from Disibodenberg to Rupertsberg. With the musical instruments of that era, the play was performed onstage in the chapel of the Rupertsberg convent (Von Trotta 2009). Contrary to similar twelfth-century plays, Hildegard's mystical play does not make use of a text derived from a biblical source.

By means of the figure of *"anima"* (soul), the *"Ordo virtutum"* depicts an exemplary way of human life, probably her own life, symbolized in her playing the part of Mary, dressed in full regalia as if she were the Holy Mother herself. Initially happy, the soul is confronted with numerous unfavorable influences. It succumbs to them and is caught up in a web of estrangement. Eventually it feels pain and distress and longs for healing. Then curative powers advance, giving it the strength to return to its origin. They help with its fear, lending it the necessary support to turn away from the falsehood of life. They teach the soul to devote itself to the essence of life and to be wary in its dealings with itself and others. In the play, all vocal parts are performed by the nuns of the convent, with the exception of Hildegard's secretary and provost to the nuns, Volmar, who is staged as Diabolus, the devil. His part is a speaking role, which requires him to speak vociferously, creating a great pandemonium.

4.3 Music and Lyrics

Since ancient times, it was predominantly priestesses who used music and rhythm (snare drum, rattles) to obtain trance states (Redmond, 2012). Reviewing the history of classical and church music, Hildegard is the first composer known by name, and we can assume that she wrote poetry and composed music while under the influence of entheogens. About eighty of her compositions have been preserved, a repertoire that is the most elaborated among medieval composers.

Hildegard's compositions differ to such an extent from traditional medieval music that they can be regarded as a separate section in the Gregorian tradition. Inspired by her "visions," she altogether wrote seventy-six songs, of which there were forty-three antiphons, eighteen responsories, six sequences, seven hymns or hymn-like songs, one kyrie, and one alleluia, in her time all important musical and poetical parts of the liturgy.

The texts, which were especially meant for and understood by Hildegard herself, are of a poetical nature and characterized by lyrical outpourings. They mainly concern the glorification of the virginity and chastity of the Holy Virgin, with whom Hildegard strongly identified, or are dedicated to saints such as St. Ursula and St. Rupert. In the lyrics to the church music Hildegard composed, there sometimes is more or less direct or indirect reference to the symbols of the fly agaric elsewhere used in her texts and in her miniatures.

On Disibod, the founder of the first monastery on the Disibodenberg, she writes: "Sweet life, and blessed perseverance, which in this blessed Disibod built a constantly glorious light in heavenly Jerusalem. Now may praise be to God in the worthy form of a fine *tonsure*. And let the heavenly citizens rejoice for these *men who imitate them in this way*." Other lyrics say: "*Flame of the paraclete spirit, life of the life of every creature* … Around you clouds stream, the air flies, stones are moist, water draw out streams, and the earth irrigates *greenness*. You also constantly produce the learned, manmade happy by the inspiration of knowledge. Wherefore praise be to you

... giving the rewards of light." On Mary she writes: "*Flower,* you did not sprout forth from the dew nor from the droops of rain, and the air did not fly round above you, but *divine clarity produced you* on the noblest stem. Stem, *God foresaw your flourishing on the first day of his creation.* And from his word he made *golden material....* For this woman (Eve) ... plucked of his limbs...." (Summerly 2001).

In another poem she versifies: "O fighters of the *flower from the thornless branch,* you are the voice of the orbed world, encircling places of unbalanced senses.... O you disciples of the *most excellent being, in the most valued and most renowned symbol....* O sweet elected one who *burnt in the glow of the fiery one, a root,* and in the father's splendor elucidated mysteries ... and *your word* itself *took on flesh in a form that led directly to Adam....* O most splendid gem and serene elegance of the sun which into you was poured, a font springing from the heart of the father, which is his unique word, from which he made the *world's primal matrix which Eve threw into disorder.* For you the father effected this word as man, and so you are that *luminous substance* through which this word breathed all virtue, just as within the primal matrix he led forth all forms of life" (Summerly 2008).

The Physica or Book of Healing Herbs

In the years 1151 through 1158, Hildegard writes her encyclopedic works on medicine and natural healing, in which she describes and sometimes depicts numerous plants or herbs, trees, and fungi and their effects, including psychoactivity. In *Causae et Curae,* she describes the causes of diseases and ailments and their treatments and cures.

Only after Hildegard's death are the works are given the titles *Physica* and *Causae et Curae.* None of the surviving manuscripts of both works originate from Hildegard's lifetime. While the church attempted to gain mind control over "common" people through Church laws and rules forbidding the use of mind-altering and enlightening plants and fungi, in *Physica* and *Causae et Curae* Hildegard follows a strategy of pragmatic dualism, only describing and prescribing the parts of the entheogen plants that can be applied for medicinal purposes. In short, she avoids mentioning the psychoactive fungi and elaboration on the psychoactive qualities of the entheogen plants, or labels them as worthless, or only meant for herself and the "happy few" surrounding her and/or for "a selection of the rich, nobles and clergy, who also had access to or possessed the extremely rare and valuable manuscripts on witches' brews and ointments" (Rush 2011), which Hildegard likewise used as a source.

The *Physica* is divided into nine chapters in which Hildegard describes the preventive and curative use of plants, trees, fungi, animals, metals, precious stones, and the elements. Her so-called medical works were revealed by direct transmission from the Divine, in the same way as her more theologically based visions (Throop 1998). Her knowledge is based on her own observations of the local flora and fauna, but also on writings from antiquity and the early Middle Ages. Apart from Hildegard's personal experiments, hardly any empirical scientific research takes place. And the knowledge of entheogens may well have come from Jutta of Sponheim and/or Volmar of Disibodenberg, both guardians and trustees of Hildegard's secrets, and later shared with Richardis of Stade, who being an amanuensis probably also had some knowledge and experience of her own.

In the Middle Ages, all healing plants were regarded as symbols of (spiritual) well-being and eternal welfare. Most plants mentioned in Hildegard's work originate from the Mediterranean region, some came from Asian countries, and she also refers to indigenous plants, which was unusual in her time and age. Hildegard includes herbs, vegetables, flowers, and mushrooms, as well as honey, eggs, milk, butter and cheese, vinegar, sulphur, salt, and sugar. Trees are dealt with in a separate chapter. The recipes and prescriptions contain information on the preparation, doses, application, and the form of administration as a lotion, oil, ointment, pill, cake, bandage, or irrigation. Generally, the remedy is a juice, but it is also administered in pulverized form or as a powder dissolved in wine or vinegar (tonsure). Hildegard's medicophysical treatises were rooted in a "holistic" view of the world, and her writings were closely linked to her visionary cosmology. According to Throop, moderation—herself excluded in at least one respect—is Hildegard's key to good health. In a letter to Elisabeth of Schönau, another Benedictine visionary, she advices the use of discretion: "Do not lay on more strain than the body can endure. Immoderate straining and abstinence bring nothing useful to the soul" (Throop 1998). Hildegard endorsed the drinking of beer to her nuns, which was common practice in those days, because she believed the drinking water from their own well was not safe and beer gave their faces a rosy complexion.

In her search for remedies that might act as a cure for various dispositions or ailments and as stimulants enhancing well-being, she was very "intuitive" or experimentally orientated (ethereal oils, ointments, potions, living water, "medicinal" cannabis), possibly driven or motivated by constantly being in poor health herself and, probably not helping matters, by using mixtures of such psychoactives as *Amanita muscaria,* mandrake, henbane, and Datura, which she needed for her visions and physical experiences to (re)occur.

5.1 Animals

The chapters on existing and mythical animals, birds, reptiles, and fish are mainly based on her own observations, but also on superstition and magic. "Animals that eat others ... and give birth to many young, such as the wolf, the dog and the pig, are unsuitable for human consumption and repugnant for man ... because man's nature is not the same ... The cunning snake ... mislead us by its powers of persuasion" (Atherton 2001).

5.2 Psychoactive Plants Involved

5.2.1 Mandrake

Mandrake (*Mandragora officinalis*) is a perennial plant that belongs to the family of the nightshades. It has whitish-green flowers with five petals, dark green ovate-oblong to ovate, wrinkled, sinuate-dentate to entire, five-to-forty-centimeters-long leaves, somewhat resembling tobacco leaves, and growing in a rosette, and orange to red berries, which ripen in late spring. Its dark-brown parsnip-shaped roots are often bifurcated, looking like a two-legged "mannequin" or puppet, because of which they have long been used in magic rituals and in (neo-) pagan religions [Plate 11].

All parts of the plant are poisonous. Mandrake contains hallucinogenic alkaloids such as atropine, scopolamine, and hyoscyamine. Ingesting mandrake root, usually as a tea, can have some adverse effects on the user, including parasympathetic and hypnotic symptoms, anxiety attacks, sleeplessness, and hallucinations or delirium. In high doses it can even cause coma. The plant originally was used as a painkiller and for eliciting hallucinations and visions. Mandrake can also be used for the preparation of a dark green paste, one of the main ingredients of witches' flying ointments [Plate 12] (Van Elteren 2007).

Hildegard claims the following beneficial properties of mandrake: "And if someone is always sad and undergoes deprivations, thus constantly experiences pain and weakness in his heart, he should take (the root of) mandrake." She also recommends mandrake root as an aphrodisiac.

Mandrake finds its origin in today's Palestine and was already known as a talisman in ancient Egypt. The physicians from Alexandria left the root to soak in wine for a while and prescribed the brew as an anesthetic. The Greeks used the root in fertility rites and drank an extract of the root as a love potion. An early Christian story describes the mandrake root as a preliminary study for the creation of man (Godefridi 2011).

The use of mandrake is also mentioned in the Bible. "The rather peculiar story of Ruben's 'love apples' presumably can be traced back to Rachel becoming pregnant of her first child, Josef, as a result of her using mandrake … The root of mandrake often has a humanoid shape ['mannequin'], which literally rooted in the convictions of many cultures, that it had lust and fertility enhancing powers. The

Hebrew term for mandrake is associated with the verb 'loving'" (Porter 2003). Besides Rachel, other sources claim that Lea, another of the four wives of Jacob, succeeded in seducing her husband with the "love plant," mandrake. The Arab name for mandrake means "egg of the spirit."

Hildegard was the first author on medicinal herbs to mention mandrake (*Mandragora officinarum*) and even devotes a complete chapter to it: "Mandrake is hot and a little bit watery. It grew from the same earth that formed Adam, and [the root] resembles the human being a bit. Because of its similarity to the human, the influence of the devil appears in it and stays with it, more than with other plants. Thus, a person's good or bad desires are accomplished by means of it, just as happened formerly with the idols he made. When mandrake is dug from the earth, it should be placed in a spring ['queckborn'] immediately, for a day and a night, so that every evil and contrary humor is expelled from it, and it has no more power for magic and phantasms. But, if it is pulled from the earth, and set aside with earth sticking on it, and not cleansed in the spring water, it is harmful for many injurious acts of magic and for delusions, just as many evils were at one time done with idols" (Throop 1998). In a "docudrama" on Hildegard's life broadcast by the Zweite Deutsche Fernsehen (2010), it was suggested that Hildegard consumed mandrake roots to elicit hallucinations. In the transition from this subject to the "viridians" or "Grünkraft" of the plants Hildegard used, a few frames of a picture of the fly agaric were shown. Upon inquiry, the producer of the documentary stated that the photo was shown without ulterior motives or intent to link the psychoactive Holy Mushroom to Hildegard using entheogen fungi.

Hildegard suggests the possibility of substituting beech rootlets for mandrake if the latter is scarce. And because of its explicit shape, she classifies mandrake as magical and suppressant of sexual desires, although mostly mandrake is seen as an aphrodisiac and supposed to be erotically stimulating.

5.2.2 Datura

Datura (*Datura stramonium*) is an annual plant with five-to-ten-centimeters-long trumpet- or funnel-shaped white to whitish purplish flowers, dark green egg-shaped or elliptical leaves, and an egg-shaped capsule with or without spines containing the dark-brown seeds [Plate 13].

Hildegard refers to Datura (*Datura stramonium*) as the lily, depicts the plant with white, red, or greenish flowers [Plates 14 and 15], and, with a few additions in some miniatures, she symbolically depicts the total flowering plant as a golden fleur-de-lis staff [Plate 16]. "The real symbolic meaning of the white lily is not its purity, but the contact with the gods, the appearance of a god in the human world. In other words: an epiphany or a mystical experience" (González Celdrán 2001).

In eliciting a state of delirium, Datura is a dangerous drug, because it can lead to a fatal atropine poisoning causing cardiac failure. Datura also contains alkaloids like scopolamine. The dried and crumbled leaves are smoked fresh, or dried leaves and flowers are drunk as a tea. The seeds can be taken orally or smoked, which has a somewhat milder effect. The pulverized leaves and seeds also can be used for preparing ointments, which are applied to temples and armpits, on the penis or vulva, or inside the vagina, or on the soles of the feet. In this respect one has to bear in mind that atropine even can be absorbed through the intact skin.

The dried leaves and/or flowers of Datura are sometimes mixed with cannabis for smoking blends or ayahuasca brews. Depending on the dose, a trip can last from eight to eighteen hours and sometimes even a few days. During a trip, one experiences euphoria, surreal sensory delusions, and one can be absorbed in archetypal dreams with universal meaning or with a foreseeing or interpretive character, which can be significant for oneself or "mankind." The sensory delusions can temporarily cause amnesia and no awareness of being high, with dangerous extreme and bizarre behavior as a result. As side effects, headaches, dizziness, nausea, fear, anxiety or panic, confusion, sedation or stupor, difficulty breathing, dry mouth and eyes, uncoordinated movement or impaired mobility and speech, bad trips with depersonalization and being "half blind" for some days, because of inability to focus, have been reported.

On Datura Hildegard writes: "One should take the stem and leaves of lilies and pound them, expressing the juice from them. He should knead this juice together with some flower, and keep anointing the part of the body which suffers from rash ... The odor of the first bud of lilies, and indeed the odor or fragrance (Atherton 1991) of the flowers, makes a person's heart joyful and furnishes him with virtuous ideas" (Throop 1998).

5.2.3 Henbane

Henbane (*Hyoscyamus niger*) is an annual plant with yellow-greenish flowers with five petals and a purplish red center [Plate 18], green leaves, and dark-brown seeds. In ancient Greece, the priestesses of Apollo used henbane to yield the oracle. In the Middle Ages the plant spread over Western Europe up to England.

Scopolamine, hyoscyamine, and other alkaloids have been found in the foliage and seeds of the plant. Its psychoactive results include visual hallucinations and a sensation of flight. Common side effects of henbane ingestion include dilated pupils, restlessness, or flushed skin, and less common symptoms such as tachycardia, convulsions, vomiting, and hypertension. Historically it was used in combination with mandrake, nightshade, and/or Datura as an anesthetic potion, as well as for its psychoactive properties in "magic" brews.

Black henbane or Devil's Eyes (*Hyoscyamus niger*) is one of the ingredients of witches' flying ointment in use during the Middle Ages; the leaves and seeds can likewise be smoked. Hildegard writes: "If anyone eats it, or the oil made from its seed, it would become a deadly poison in him.... Oil made from its seed is not of much use; but when there is too much heat in one area of a person's limb, that place should be anointed with the oil. It will cool without other medicine" (Throop 1998). Originally seeds were mixed with beer to intensify the effect of the low-alcohol beverage until the seventeenth-century, when hops were introduced.

5.2.4 Nightshades

Black nightshade (*Solanum nigrum*) is an annual plant with small white flowers and yellow stamen, green egg-shaped leaves, and green berries turning black when ripe. It does not contain any of the alkaloids from plants like belladonna, henbane, or mandrake, but instead possesses the poisonous solanine, which is also a constituent of potato plants.

"Belladonna was used by the Inquisition to worm the secrets out of alleged witches. In the Middle Ages there were many herbalists who refused to cultivate the plant and monks … did not mention the plant in none of their works for a long time" (Wormhoudt 2008).

Hildegard prescribes Black nightshade (*Solanum nigrum*) as a remedy for pain in the heart, toothache, and swollen feet by means of placing cooked and squeezed nightshade on the chest or jaw or wrapping a cloth with nightshade inside around the feet. She neither warns of the deadly poisonous effects of belladonna or deadly nightshade (*Atropa belladonna*), nor does she mention the strong psychoactive effects of the tropane alkaloids it contains, if parts of the plant are used in ointments like the witches' flying ointment, in combination with mandrake and/or Datura.

5.2.5 Cannabis

Hemp, cannabis, or marijuana (*Cannabis sativa*) is a plant with long lancet-shaped green leaves, at the base joined together and arranged like a hand or a fan, with tiny greenish and brownish male and female flowers. Smoking or consuming the THC-rich buds of the plant both has psychological and physical effects. Cannabis can also be prepared as a tea, a cake, an oil, or an ointment. Medicinal cannabis is prescribed for nausea, pain, and alleviation of symptoms of chronic illnesses like multiple sclerosis. Acute effects while under the influence can include euphoria and anxiety. For an extensive documentation of the use of cannabis through the ages, I refer to the works of the cannabis historian Bennett (2010).

Hildegard depicts and describes hemp (*Cannabis sativa*): "its seeds are easy to digest, diminish bad humors, and fortify good humors," but warns, it should be avoided by "weak in the head" people: "Nevertheless, if one who is weak in the head, and has a vacant brain, eats hemp, it easily afflicts his head. It does not harm one who has a healthy head and full brain" (Throop 1998). She does not mention the possibility of smoking hemp or using it for oils or ointments or to bake a "space cake."

As Hildegard only mentions the medicinal qualities of cannabis and needed much stronger entheogens to (re-) produce her hallucinations, there seems to be no clear evidence of Hildegard smoking cannabis for recreational purposes as Rush suggested in stating: "Some of her vision passages can be read as a knowledgeable person rambling on cannabis.… " (Rush 2011).

Hemp is also presented in the "Codex" or "Vienna Dioscurides" written by the aforementioned Roman imperial princess Anicia Juliana, who lived in Constantinople from 462 until 527–528 CE.

Recently at an archaeological site on the Veluwe in the Netherlands, pollen of *Cannabis sativa* were found in a 4,200-year-old grave from the Stone Age.

5.2.6 Papaver

Poppy (*Papaver rhoeas*) is an annual plant with bright red flowers, green leaves, and capsules with tiny black seeds, which are used as a mild sedative. Although Hildegard neither discusses the effects of opium or *Papaver somniferum*, nor warns of its addictiveness, she does warn for the dangerous effects of the sap of poppies. And because she does not mention *Papaver somniferum*, it is unlikely that she was familiar with opiates.

At archaeological sites in the southern parts of the Netherlands, capsules and seeds of the indigenous poppy were found in settlements of primitive agricultural farmers, who lived in these areas around 5300 BCE and exchanged their products with local hunter-gatherers.

Hildegard also mentions the Common or Corn Poppy (*Papaver rhoeas*), a mild sedative. She writes: "It seeds when eaten, bring sleep and prevent prurigo.... They can be eaten after being steeped in water, but are better and more useful when eaten raw rather than cooked. The oil which is expressed from them does not nourish or refresh a person, nor does it bring him health or sickness" (Throop 1998).

5.2.7 Nutmeg

Nutmeg (*Myristica fragrans*) is the fruit or seed of an evergreen tropical tree with small white flowers and pointed egg-shaped leaves. Apart from the powdered form of the seeds used as a spice, essential oils and oleoresins are extracted from nutmeg. Nutmeg contains myristicin, a strong deliriant, of which large doses can create the so-called Finch-effect, that is to say, convulsions, palpitations, nausea, headaches, or generalized body pain, symptoms that can last longer than 72 hours. It can take about four hours before noticing any effects of a high, combined with the idea of free-floating, or before a sensation of the loss of limbs or a disturbance of the sense of time and space occurs. Hildegard mentions waking hallucinations and death by overdose as possible effects.

On the influence of nutmeg on mood and consciousness Hildegard writes: "If a person eats nutmeg [combined with cinnamon in baked cakes], it will open up his heart, make his judgment free from obstruction, and give him a good disposition.... [I]t will calm all bitterness of the heart and mind, open your heart and impaired senses, and make your mind cheerful. It purifies your senses and diminishes all harmful humors in you" (Throop 1998).

5.2.8 Wormwood

Wormwood (*Artemisia absinthium*) is prescribed as a principal remedy for all ailments. It is a remedy for head- and toothaches, and the juice of freshly pounded and pressed wormwood mixed with gently cooked wine and honey "will check your melancholy and sickness in the loins, and make your eyes clear." It was not until the end of the eighteenth-century that the plant became an ingredient of absinthe.

5.2.9 Ferns

And according to Hildegard, the fern [Plates 12 and 57] is of particular interest, because "It holds within itself great power, namely such a power that the devil flees from it.... In the place where it grows, the devils rarely practices his deceptions.... Magic and incantations of demons—as well as diabolic words and other phantasms—avoid a person who carries a fern with him.... In paradise, when the devil drew the human being to himself, a certain sign was made on the devil to remain on him, as a reminder, until the last day. When a person invokes the devil by some words, through which his deceptions are accomplished, the sign is touched. He is often invoked to injure a person, or to fulfill the will of the person over whom the words are spoken.... Fern sap has been placed for knowledge, and in its honest nature, goodness and holiness are signified. All evil and magic things flee and avoid it. In whatever house it is, poison and phantoms are not able to complete their work. Whence, when a woman gives birth to a child, fern is placed around her, even around the infant in his cradle. The devil besieges the infant less since, when he first looks at the infant's face, he hates him intensely.... Indeed, if a person who is forgetful and ignorant holds fern seed in his hand, his memory will return, and he will receive understanding; thus he who was incomprehensible will become intelligible" (Throop 1998).

5.2.10 Combination of Plants

The combination of nightshade and mandrake is found in green pastes or ointments made from the two extremely psychoactive plants: "witches' flying ointment," applied to skin tissue rich of capillaries; women preferred to rub it on and into the mucous membrane of the genitals or to insert sticks on which the ointment is smeared into their vagina and they "rode" on it (like a broomstick), in order to, after absorbing the psychoactive constituents, "fly to the Sabbath or engage in orgiastic ceremonies" [Plates 19 and 20] (Irvin and Rutajit 2008).

> Belladonna (*Atropa belladonna*) especially is known as one of the witches' herbs. Together with henbane and Datura it is an ingredient of witches' ointments. These three herbs contain hallucinogenic substances that reinforce each other … and cause a change of consciousness creating the illusion that one flies and perceives strong erotic images. In popular magic belladonna especially was used to evoke trances (Wormhoudt 2008).

5.3 Trees

5.3.1 Birch

Hildegard calls the birch—a pioneer with very light and tiny seeds, which are easily dispersed by wind over long distances and germinate and sprout in various types of soil, as found in the walled garden surrounding the inclusorium—the tree of "happiness and bliss." Considering that birches are one of the most important symbiotic partners of the fly agaric (and *Amanita pantherina*), it is valid to assume that the tree of "happiness and bliss" symbolically represents the fly agaric, as Hildegard does not refer to other qualities of birches' bark, sap, leaves, buds, and young shoots that incite happiness or bliss. Furthermore, birches are also the supplier of witches' brooms—a morbid growth of twigs caused by the mycelium of *Taphrina betulina*, and of broomsticks, which could be anointed with witches' flying ointment. Adding to this, since the early days of shamanism, the mythical holy birch tree of northern, eastern, and central Europe, and the Siberian people, has been associated with the Sacred Mushroom. Because of the association (of the roots) of birches with the fly agaric, the tree was chosen to be the symbol of the nine-step Staircase to Heaven. Of Bonifatius it is known that he called the birch tree "the Devil," in this way hoping to ban the pagan traditions around the tree and its symbiotic partner.

Birches infected by the mycelium of *Taphrina betulina*, as mentioned, produce branches with broomsticks that can be "harvested" and used at witches' Sabbaths, orgiastic ceremonies, or more private Wiccan rituals by women who sought the experience of "flying." Irvin (2008) states that on or at the tip of these branches witches' flying ointment was smeared, after which the witch literally made a ride on the broomstick while rubbing her private parts against it or by inserting the tip into the vagina to produce an orgasm [Plates 19 and 20]. The powerful orgasmic spasms reached through this procedure would have been mistaken for attempts to fly or obtaining a liftoff by witnesses, who out of fear of the Wiccan ceremonies, were hiding at a safe distance in the woods.

5.3.2 Beech

Concerning the beech tree, Hildegard writes: "And if someone is always sad and in hardship, so that he has pain and weakness constantly in his heart, he should take mandrake. If you do not have mandrake, take the first root mass that sprouts from the beech tree. Happily it has the same quality for this undertaking. You should pull it out entirely, without breaking the shoots, and carry the whole thing from the tree. Place it next to you in your bed, so that the roots get hot from you and receive the perspiration from your body.... [Y] ou will receive happiness and in your hart sense recovery. Likewise, you can do the same thing with cedar or aspen, and it will make you happy" (Throop 1998). The sprouting roots of all three trees mentioned are surrounded by ectomycorrhizal structures [Plate 62] of symbiotic macrofungi, which protect and defend the roots and from which they derive their energy source (sugars), help guard against bacteria and parasitic fungi or nematodes with self-produced antibiotics and fungicides. In fact the beech tree has the most tree-species-specific symbiotic mushroom partners of all three (Keizer 2012a), and it could well be that the described effect arrived from the powerful antibiotics secreted by the ectomycorrhizae were absorbed by and passed on through the skin.

Evidence of Hildegard having any knowledge of the antibiotics produced by microfungi such as *Penicillium digitatum,* however, was not found. It should be noted there is documentation that farmers living in the province of Drenthe in the Netherlands during the Middle Ages smeared the green mold of another *Penicillium* species fruiting on old rye bread on infected wounds. The antibiotics secreted by the mold killed the bacteria and the wounds dried out and healed within a few days (Keizer 1997).

5.3.3 Coniferous Trees

According to Hildegard, fir trees[11]—including the spruce, the symbol of Anna—with which *Amanita muscaria* and *Amanita pantherina* are associated, signify fortitude. "Spirits of the air hate, and avoid more than in other places, any place where there is fir tree wood. Magic thrives less and is less prevalent there than in other places." Hildegard describes how to make an ointment of fresh bark and needles, and how it can be used by someone who "ails in his head, so that he is 'vergichtiget,' raving, or mad, and if his heart is failing in strength, first anoint his heart well with this ointment. Then, having shaved his hair [tonsure], anoint his head with the same ointment. Repeat this on the second and third day, and his head will recover its health, and he will return to his senses" (Throop 1998).

The above, in its interconnection and natural contexts, leads to the conclusion that medieval herbalists had knowledge of the relationship between the fly agaric and birches and spruce, just as the shamans and druids did centuries before.

5.3.4 Other Tree Species

Apart from several fruit trees Hildegard includes, she discusses the cedar, cypress, juniper, oak, ash, plane, linden, hornbeam, willow, elm, alder, and the palm. Of these trees, only the oak, which Hildegard regards as neither the wood, nor the fruit being "good for medicine or a human being to eat," and the cedar could be symbiotic partners of *Amanita muscaria* and/or *Amanita pantherina.* The palm tree is the symbol of the Garden of Eden and its leaves were used by the high priestesses of the oracle of Delphi on which to write their messages. Regardless of the fact that palms are not indigenous to the German region, Hildegard depicts palm leaves [Plate 16] in the miniatures "Der neue Himmel und die neue Erde" and "Fünf Tugenden."

Van der Meer mentions that in the Qumran there are "numerous references … [in the miniature "Ecclesia" to] … Sophia and to secret knowledge.… The Qumran community describes itself as trees, as branches, as a garden with lots of water, as a plantation of Trees of Life next to a well, as eternal trees" (Van der Meer 2008).

5.4 Mushrooms and Other Fungi

Hildegard distinguishes between fungi of the soil and fungi growing on trees, the chapter on fungi being classified as excellent mycological work, which in its quantity and quality was unique for the Middle Ages. She regards mushrooms of soil and litter or dung as worthless, and urges to neglect and not to eat them, nor use them for medicinal purposes, which is quite astonishing for a German herbalist living in a country of fanatic mushroom collectors and consumers: "Mushrooms of any kind, which spring up on top of the ground, are like the foam and sweat of the earth, and are a bit harmful to the person who eats them. They create mucus and scum in him. Nevertheless, mushrooms growing in dry air and on dry land are more cold than hot, and are better than those that grow in damp air and on damp earth. Not much medicine is found in them. If a person eats mushrooms growing in damp air and on damp earth, they stir up a bad humor in him" (Throop 1998).

Although she never explicitly mentions the "Fliegenpilz" or "Kahlköpfe," the German names for *Amanita muscaria* and *Psilocybe* species, there is overwhelming evidence of her using psychoactive mushrooms such as the fly agaric and maybe to a small degree psilocybins, in the symbols and vivid colors of the human or nonhuman figures, clothing, and objects depicted in her miniatures and in the literary work in which she describes her "visions" or hallucinations.

Because of the controversy over pagan ceremonies rooted in shaman rituals that were integrated into the Catholic Mass, Heldegard decided to only share her secrets with a few members of her sectarian community. She did this by recording them in her secret language, thus withholding them from laymen and preventing them from experimenting with entheogens, like the ectomycorrhizal *Amanitas* and saprotrophic *Psylocybes*. The latter grows in poor grassland or on the excrement of cattle and horses and is much less depicted in Hildegard's miniatures than the fly agaric.

In contrast with the mushrooms of soil and litter, she regards parasitic or saprotrophic fungi growing on trees to be benignant: "However, the mushrooms which spring from certain trees, whether standing or lying on the ground, are of some value as human food.... They are less harmful to eat, and sometimes are valuable as medicine" (Throop 1998). And that is why the dark- and light-brown mushroom in the miniature "Die Seele und ihr Zelt," Müller-Ebeling (2010) calls "Fäulnispilz" [Plate 1], meaning a fungus causing wood decay, presenting as a sign of medieval mycophobia, an example of misinterpreting or misunderstanding the context of the depiction of the mushroom in the miniature.

About the mushroom growing on beech trees, with which she obviously means the Tinder or Hoof Fungus (*Fomes fomentarius*) or maybe includes the Artist's fungus (*Ganoderma lipsiense*), she writes that "it can be eaten in food by both healthy and sick people. Someone who has a cold, or a mucus rich stomach, should take a mushroom from the beech tree when it is fresh. He should cook it in water with good herbs and a bit of lard. He should frequently eat a bit of it after a meal. It will warm his stomach and remove mucus. But, if a pregnant woman is fatigued because her body is slow, heavy, and oppressed from the weight of the child, she should take a mushroom from the beech tree." After boiling it in water until it is completely broken down and straining it through a cloth, she should prepare a broth from its juice and "have some once or twice a day, after having eaten, and she will be gently released from the pain of her offspring" (Throop 1998). Note that the Tinder Fungus, along with the birch polypore (*Piptoporus betulinus*), was hanging from the belt of Ötzi, the Iceman, who lived 5,000 years ago and was found in the glacier ice on the Italian side of the mountains of Tirol. During the Middle Ages battered thin slices of the sterile interior of the fungus were used to cover open wounds to prevent bacterial infections (Keizer 2001, 2010).

It should also be mentioned that several tumor-inhibiting tripertenes have been isolated from annual brackets of the Chinese Reishi or Ling Zhi (*Ganoderma lucidum*) mushroom (Willard 1990), which also have been documented from the perennial brackets of the cosmopolitan *Ganoderma lipsiense.* Centuries ago, the Taoists used powered Reishi mushrooms, mixed with ginseng, as a longevity tonic.

Although rare, one can still find the so-called Pharmacists' bracket fungus, *Fomitopsis* (*Laricifomes*) *officinalis,* in the mountainous regions of Germany, Austria, and Switzerland (Keizer 2010b). Documents indicate that in centuries preceding the Middle Ages the powder of the ground annual brackets was a popular medicine used for the staunching of bleeding from a wound or against excessive sweating (Keizer 2001/2010). Strikingly, however, the Pharmacists' bracket fungus is not mentioned in *Physica.*

The mushroom growing on the willow tree, which probably is the Oyster Mushroom (*Pleurotus ostreatus*), is said to be "good to eat."

Besides, it is a medicine for people with glaucoma of their eyes and whose chest is oppressed because of pain in their lungs, or for pain in the stomach, heart, and spleen.

As for the mushroom growing on the pear tree, which is probably Sulphur Polypore or Chicken of the Woods (*Laetiporus sulphureus*), Hildegard states, "neither harms, nor profits the person who eats it. But, the person whose head is scabby, should take a fresh mushroom from the pear tree, squeeze its juice into olive oil, and then throw away the mushroom. He should often anoint his head with this oil, and he will be cured" (Throop 1998). Bear in mind that the bald spot of the tonsure can become scabby after repeated application of the red fleece of the fly agaric, which was sometimes soaked in vinegar to heighten the effect on the brain after putting the fleece on top of the head.

She also discusses the mushrooms growing on almond, elder, and aspen trees, which, in her opinion, are not valuable or good for eating, nor of much medicinal value. And she describes the beneficial effects from drinking a potion of water, milk, wine, or beer and "ligure" (ligurius), which is either a truffle (*Elaphomyces* spp.) or the "pietra fungaia," a pseudosclerotium of the Tuberous Polypore (*Polyporus tuberaster*), which in her day were believed to originate from the urine of the lynx, as stated by Hildegard too, or from the spilled sperm of rutting deer (Keizer 2001/2010).With this exceptional knowledge of the medicinal qualities of tree fungi, it is valid to assume that she, through her own experience, had an even greater knowledge of the effects of using "magic mushrooms" growing in the vicinity of trees or on soil or dung, even though she, for obvious reasons stated before, never mentioned one of them, including the species of *Gymnopilus* fruiting on trees, known to contain psychoactive constituents of which she obviously was not familiar.

5.4.0 Characteristics of the Psychoactive Fungi and Plants Involved

In the "disk of five" ("Die Chöre der Engel") [Plate 21] and "Der Tag der Grossen Offenbarung" [Plate 22], Hildegard depicts all the psychoactive fungi and plants involved in a more or less symbolic or explicit way.

5.4.1 The Fly Agaric

For a complete description of the characteristics of the fly agaric (*Amanita muscaria*) I refer to my *Encyclopedia of Fungi* (Keizer 1997), and *Interactive Guide to Mushrooms and other Fungi* (Keizer 2001/2010).

The fly agaric is a cosmopolitan ectomycorrhizal species with deciduous trees such birch, oak, beech, poplar, hornbeam, lime, and eucalyptus, or coniferous trees such as pine, spruce, fir, larch, and cedar as a symbiotic partner (Keizer 2001/2010). The toadstool or "paddenstoel" in Dutch develops and surfaces as a primordium, which is completely covered with a white to yellowish-golden velum universale, [Plates 23 and 24], in which, with the exception of the reproductive organs and the spores, all cells necessary for the development of the total mushroom are present.

The primordium often is depicted as a symbolic Cosmic Egg or Egg of the Universe and seen as the body of Christ symbolized by the host [Plate 17], bread, cheese ("Die Seele und ihr Zelt") [Plate 25], manna (red flakes, nuggets) [Plates 8 and 26], and the Living Stone, Stone of the Magi, or Philosopher's Stone. Hildegard twice depicts cut-in-half Cosmic Eggs in the ornamental frames surrounding the representations of the miniatures [Plate 27]. Once spread out, the edge of the red-to-golden cap curves upward and looks like a chalice, also known as the Chalice of Life or Holy Grail (Butler 2011a) [Plates 28 and 29]. Observed from beneath, the white gills or lamellae become visible, and look like the radiating rays of the sun representing the solar disk [Plate 30] or symbolized by the aureole worn by Jesus, Mary, and the saints, that sometimes has radial rays representing the gills or a red cross stretching out to four sides of the aureole [Plate 31]. After it dries out and shrinks, the color can change from red over orange to golden yellow; the remnants are known as the Golden Fleece [Plate 63] (Butler 2011b).

The fly agaric can be mistaken for the panther (*Amanita pantherina*), which has an ochraceous-to-dark-brown cap and is associated with some of the same trees the fly agaric has as a partner. It can also be mistaken for the King's fly agaric (*Amanita regalis*), which only seems symbiotically associated with spruce, compares with the Fly Argaric in its psychoactivity, and is mainly found in the mountainous areas of Scandinavia and the Levant.

Recent molecular research on the ancestors of the fly agaric has shown that *Amanita muscaria* was present in the Tertiair period—that is sixty-five to 2.4 million years ago—in the eastern Asian Siberian-Beringian region, and has spread over Asia, Europe, and North-America from there. In the distribution process, Alaska was the center of diversification of the three distinguished clades within the species.

The fly agaric probably derives its name from the former popular practice of soaking its red veil in sugared water or milk to kill flies. In naming the fly agaric *Amanita muscaria* (*musca* = fly), Linnaeus refers to using the red fleece for the destruction of the "disgusting beasts" while travelling in the Swedish Skåne region himself. The fly agaric contains muscimol, muscarine, and ibotenic acid, which changes into muscimol when dried. The effects reported after consuming fresh mushrooms are hallucinations accompanied by "sweats and shakes," which is a typical effect of muscimol, effects of "rivers of floating water (from one's belly)" [Plates 32, 33, and 34], or urine containing residues of muscimol (living water) to avoid the unintended side effects (nausea). "Amanitas are said to take one out of body … producing a quickening of the spirit" (Irvin and Rutajit 2009). The effects of consuming the panther (*Amanita pantherina*), which has a higher toxicity than the fly agaric, are comparable with the symptoms after eating fly agarics.

Apart from being eaten, dried fly agarics in a dissolved form often were used as an ingredient for elixirs, potions, and brews or for pastes, ointments, and essential oils, which were applied to the soft and mucous-membrane-rich parts of the body, such as the forehead, temples, armpits, and genitals. The first Christians residing in Rome, we are told, drank "blood," ergo an extract of the red fleece of the cap of the fly agaric, after which their ceremonies ended in orgies. The consumption of fly agarics often was a privilege claimed by shamans, druids, high priests or priestesses, prophets, and oracles, to strengthen their paranormal talents and make contacts with the gods. Although this is a well-documented historical fact, modern literature on pagan practice only sparsely discusses the role the Sacred Mushroom played and even nowadays plays in Wiccan ceremonies and rituals (Wormhoudt 2011).

Several centuries ago it was believed that the fly agaric, combined with the bufotenin-containing mucus of toads, was an ingredient of witches' brews, which made flying on their broomsticks possible. Even Santa Claus and Father Christmas are connected to Fly Argic and their reindeer, which, by the way, like their portion of fly agarics and "living" water. Originally this was taught to the reindeer by the Sami, which is a connection to the stories of fly agaric found in mythology and fungilore.

Under the influence of fly agarics oracles talked gibberish, which was interpreted by high priestesses according to their own judgment, and it was used by witches, shamans, and druids in performing pagan rituals and ceremonies. The purpose of tonsuring monks' heads is thought to have been to place the red veil on the shaven patch so that the psychoactive substance would be absorbed through the skin tissue rich in capillaries (Allegro 1970), without the nausea associated with oral consumption. As preparation for battle, the footmen used to drink the urine of the mounted Siberian warriors, from which they received the "living" water containing residues of digested fly agarics. The British mycologist Cooke was one of the first reporting the drinking of "living" water. The English expression "getting pissed" might be linked to becoming woozy or drunk after drinking "living" water instead of beer. When someone acts crazy, the Hungarians ask whether he has eaten from the "bolond gomba," ergo the fly agaric (Keizer 1997). The fact that in some languages the word for being drunk is being "mushroomy" also indicates the association of the use of the living water of the Sacred Mushroom and becoming intoxicated.

During the Swedish-Norwegian war at the beginning of the nineteenth-century, Swedish soldiers were fed dried fly agarics to heighten their courage (Keizer 2001/2010). In this respect they followed the Kamtsjatka tradition of drinking a liqueur brewed from fly agarics and an *Epilobium* species that, if used with modesty, lifted the strength and courage to withstand dangers and the enemy.

The Sacred Mushroom is commonly known from the Rigveda, anancient sacred collection of Vedic Sanskrit hymns from India, and is also mentioned in the medieval epic poems of the Old Edda from Iceland. Where foam from the mouth of Wodan's snorting horse fell on the ground, fly agarics emerged. Wherever Peter and Jesus spilled crumbs or spit pieces of bread on the ground, the Sacred Mushroom surfaced.

Experiencing trance after consuming fly agarics is documented for the Sami of Lapland and the Korjaks from northeast Siberia by a prisoner of war, the Swede Strahlberg, in his report of 1736. In Victorian times, returning travelers also told stories of the use of *Amanita muscaria* by Sami and Siberian tribes.

Although the use of fly agarics declined with the introduction of drinks with a high alcohol level, such as vodka (Keizer 1997), the women of the Turkic Sakha people or Yakuts of the Verkhoyansk area in Siberia nowadays still prepare and use a brew and ointments of the caps of fly agarics for rituals and ceremonies performed and coached by shamans. Among the Yakuts a masterly example of peaceful coexistence is found between the original shamanism and the Russian Orthodox Church. If someone wants to celebrate an important life event, first the shaman is asked to perform the traditional rituals, after which the Russian Orthodox priest is invited to perform the ceremonies of his church. From this can be concluded that the Russian Orthodox church shows far more tolerance toward its pagan roots and shamanism than in the Mediterranean region, the birthplace of the Church of Rome and then the Greek Orthodox Church. Their "flock" did not live so remotely, nor under such extreme conditions, and thus they could exercise much more control over their people.

After crossing the Bering Strait, the Siberian tribes were thought to have passed on their cult and use of the Sacred Mushroom to the local Native Canadian and American people.

Although forbidden and prosecuted by the authorities, there is a religious community in Switzerland called the "Kirche der Heiligen Pilze der Schweiz," of which the founder, pastor David Schlesinger, has made the consumption of *Amanita muscaria* the central element of the worship.

In today's homeopathic medicine the fly agaric is used for the treatment of psoriasis and chilblained hands.

5.4.2 The Liberty Cap

For a complete description of the characteristics of the Liberty Cap (*Psilocybe semilanceata*), I refer to my *Encyclopaedia of Fungi* (Keizer 1997), and *Interactive Guide to Mushrooms and other Fungi* (Keizer 2001/2010). The Liberty Cap grows on soil and grass debris in fairly poor to sparsely manured grasslands (Keizer 2001/2010). The Liberty Cap can be confused with other species of *Psilocybe,* mostly growing on excrement of cattle and horses, and with *Conocybe* species, which grow on dung or in fairly poor to sparsely manured grasslands.

The Latin "psilocybe" means "bold head," which is the same as "Kaalkopjes" in Dutch and "Kahlköpfe" in German. The Liberty Cap derives its name from its resemblance to the pileus [Plate 35], a cap originally worn by the Dioscuri Castor and Pollux and by the redeemed Roman slaves to cover their shaven heads with, later "transformed" into the Phrygian Cap worn by the French revolutionaries and the Magi [Plates 36 and 37]. The Dutch name "Libertijnenmutsje" refers to the Libertines, French agnostics, who, after being persecuted by the Inquisition, fled to Belgium and the Netherlands. Adding to this, the pileus is depicted as the blue bells of the carillon played by King David in a thirteenth-century psalm book from Norwich (Porter 2003).

Either a beehive, from which greenish-blue-colored mead spiked with Liberty Caps (ambrosia) may have been obtained, or the cap of a *Psilocybe* species served as a model for the navel stone of Delphi [Plate 38]. Psilocybin and psilocin, with the neurotransmitter serotonin-related psychoactive constituents of a few *Psilocybe* and *Panaeolus* species, used in Aztec rituals, were discovered at the beginning of the twentieth-century. After eating "magic mushrooms," one becomes euphoric, experiences visual hallucinations with a rich variety of shapes and colors and changes in perception, and has a distorted sense of time. Sometimes a trip is followed by flashbacks or ends in a bad trip. "The Liberty Cap is said to open the third-eye chakra" (Irvin and Rutajit 2009).

From the writings and miniatures of Hildegard alone, although more or less symbolically depicted in her miniatures, it is difficult to determine whether or not she used Liberty Caps herself or just depicted them, nor whether she was familiar with the effects of this entheogen from others' sources or from the experiences of contemporaries.

Recent physiological research has shown that by intravenously administering psilocybin, the blood stream to those parts of the brain that "tell" us who and what we are diminishes, after which rigid process thinking is put on hold or stopped, and hallucinations accompanied by intense experiences of color, moving images, and feelings of floating can arise. In the "cooling down" period after the trip, verbal incontinence and an urge to talk about the experiences sets in. Because of these effects it is therapeutic to administer psilocybin to depressive people to make them think more positively and let their gloomy thoughts and depressive feelings diminish (Carhart-Harris 2012).

By government order, a comparative research project was undertaken to study the addictive and detrimental effect of drugs and alcohol. The results of the study showed that, of all "stimulants," *Psilocybe mexicana* and *Psilocybe cubensis* were the least harmful for the physical and mental health of Dutch consumers (Van Amsterdam 2011).

Only a few month later, the Dutch government banned the cultivation and retailing of these "ecodrugs" in "smartshops," after which the smartshops changed to selling psychoactive "truffles" (sclerotia) instead.

5.4.3 The Combination of Fly Agarics and Liberty Caps

Combined, the two mushrooms strengthen the psychotropic effect because both fungi are keys to enlightenment on their own. "A combination of these two types of mushrooms is suggested to take you out of body with an open chakra system, and this was the goal of many alchemists and shamans. Could taking both types of mushrooms (*Psilocybe* and *Amanita*) at the same time be a deep cosmopolitan secret that directly relates to the 'Seal of God,' delivered by an angel … to humankind? When we consider that the angels are the messengers, Mercury is also the messenger and he carries the caduceus. The snakes forming the caduceus [Plate 39] represent both poisons (*Amanita* and *Psilocybe*). The consumption of these entheogens raise the kundalini in the body (forming the caduceus within), and the Seal of God suddenly becomes a tool for personal transformation, symbolized by the caduceus.… Uniting the opposites is considered the method of producing the philosophers' stone. It is also the method of achieving enlightenment in tantric philosophy and the soma ceremony" (Irvin and Rutajit 2009).

5.4.4 Ergots

For a complete description of the characteristics of *Claviceps* species and their reproductive transitional stages refer to *Encyclopaedia of Fungi* (Keizer 1997) and *Interactive Guide to Mushrooms and Other Fungi* (Keizer 2001/2010, 2010a).

Ergots of *Claviceps purpurea* are the dark-brown-to-black sclerotia of an ascomycete fungus, which lives as a parasite on grasses and corn. As ergots substitute for the seeds of the plants, they can easily be harvested, spiking the crop, and cause poisoning after eating bread or hardtack baked from flower of faulty gleaned grain. Ergots contain alkaloids causing ergotism, the "burning disease" of the poor, which is associated with fits of madness and epilepsy, spastic movements, blindness, a thirst impossible to quench, and necrosis and blackening of fingertips, toes, and earlobes (gangrene), and lysergic acid, a LSD-related compound, eliciting hallucinations. Before the introduction of fungicides in agriculture, poisonings with ergots often occurred.

The bizarre behavior of women suffering from ergot poisoning sometimes led to witch-trials, which ended in "witches" being burnt at the stake, as was probably the case in Salem in the United States in 1692. From history, there are several cases of more or less epidemic ergot poisoning documented, for instance in nineteenth-century Germany, which led to mass mortality within weeks of ingestion of the ergot-infected bread.

The last-known incidents were the thousands of deaths in Russia during the 1920s, the bread poisoning in 1951 in Pont-Saint-Esprit, France, and the numerous deaths during the famine of 1977 in Ethiopia after eating infected grass seeds (Keizer 2001/2010).

According to Wasson, et al (1978), the consumption of "kykeon," a special drink that contained psychoactive alkaloids coming from ergots, was a central aspect of the initiation ceremonies of the ancient Greek cult of worship of Demeter and Persephone. Whether Hildegard had knowledge of this potion seems improbable, because the use of the LSD-related component of ergots led to experiences that differ greatly from the character of the experiences Hildegard reports in the writings on her "visions."

Its Dutch and German name "mother's corn" comes from the use of ergots to stimulate labor contractions in women having difficulties giving birth. Despite the serious consequences of prolonged use, even as late as the 1940s ground ergots were used for the treatment of migraines (Keizer 2001/2010).

Hildegard warned against mistaking ergots for cumin seeds (*Cuminum cyminum*) and giving pregnant women ergots instead of cumin seeds, because of the ergot's strong abortive effects. Thus, she most likely would not have used ergots for psychoactive purposes.

Whether she used ergots to stimulate labor contractions or for an abortion, as may have been opportune after a monk impregnated one of her nuns, is not known. And adding to that, it is also questionable whether the use of ergots against migraine was already known and implemented in the Middle Ages. If Hildegard, for whatever reason or purpose, had regularly digested the powder of grinded ergots, after a while symptoms of gangrene and ergotism would have shown themselves; there is no evidence whatsoever of such symptoms.

5.4.5 A Note on Psychoactive Fungi in General

The effect of hallucinogenic mushrooms on the user's experience and behavior depends in part on his or her personality and genetic predisposition, which can vary to a great extent from person to person. As symptoms of psychiatric disorders can sometimes be elicited after one-off use, people with a genetic tendency to depression or psychosis should be discouraged from using psychoactive mushrooms.

6.1 Alchemy

Hildegard is said to be in search of the philosopher's stone (Rush 2011), which is not an actual stone but the primordium of the fly agaric, the Cosmic Egg or Egg of the Universe. Hildegard is also privy to certain aspects of alchemy, which can be derived from her descriptions of the supposed effect of gemstones, minerals, and metals. Traditionally, alchemists and magicians or magi [Plate 36] could choose from a wide range of secret knowledge encoded into cryptic symbolism and mystical language, leading to pure understanding of the word or Logos (Irvin 2009), or instruments used for performing "scientific" research.

6.2 Hildegard's Cosmology

The cosmology compiled by Hildegard is one of the most significant and complete conceptions of the world of the Middle Ages. Macrocosm, microcosm, the elements, the bodily fluids or humors, the temperaments, the seasons, and the stages of life all are inseparably linked: "God likewise created the elements of the world. All the elements of the world are found in man, and through them man does his work."

Hildegard claims that her astrological and cosmological "visions" were "beamed down" from above. Whether she used witches' flying ointment in order to elicit her "revelations" remains an unanswered question. Irvin (2009) reports that astro(theo)logical visions can be triggered by applying the paste or ointment to the temples and forehead.

As was said before, in antiquity the emphasis was on the four elements of the cosmos: earth, water, air, and fire. These were thought to correspond to man in the form of humors or temperaments, that is, melancholic (black bile), phlegmatic (mucus), sanguine (blood), and choleric (yellow bile). In the Middle Ages, the universe (macrocosm) and man (microcosm) are considered to be part of an analogous order: The course of the planets corresponds to the human blood circulation and both are evidence of God's creative hand.

In the miniatures "Das Weltall" [Plate 2] and "Von der Gliederung des Leibes," Hildegard depicts the constellation of the stars and moon at Christmas or the day of the supposed "birth" of Christ. The four corners of the earth or cardinal points [Plate 5], the wind directions or points of the compass [Plate 2], and the four seasons [Plate 8] are successively depicted in the miniatures "Die Seele und ihr Zelt," "Vom Bau der Welt," "Von der Natur des Menschen," and Von der Gliederung des Leibes." The signs of the zodiac [Plate 40] are represented in the miniatures "Vom Bau der Welt," "Von der Natur des Menschen," and "Von der Gliederung des Leibes."

Views, Conflicts, and Diminishing Influence

7.1 Conflicts and Diminishing Influence

In letters dated 1148–1150, which have received little attention, Tengswich, mistress of the Canones convent of St. Mary in Andernach, dares to criticize certain structures and habits within the Rupertsberg community. Her concerns centered on the inappropriate clothing, gems, and hairstyle worn during the performance of the Mass, the nuns or "brides of Christ," and in particular Richardis and Adelheid, who acted as seconds to the high priestess, Hildegard. She also criticized the lack of an ascetic lifestyle within the sectarian content. She comments: "We have also heard of certain unusual practices that you countenance. They say that on feast days your nuns stand in the chorus with unbound hair … and that as part of their dress they wear white silk veils.… Moreover it is said that they wear crowns of gold filigree, into which are inserted crosses … and that they adorn their fingers with golden rings. And all this despite the exact prohibition of the great shepherd of the church, who wrote: let women not comport themselves with plaited hair, or gold, or pearls, or costly attire. Moreover, what seems no less strange to us is the fact that you admit into your community only those women from noble, well-established families.…" This correspondence took place in the years 1148–1150, that is to say, before the move to the Rupertsberg convent, implicating that Hildegard and her sisters had already manifested themselves as a sectarian religious community during the last years of their stay in the Disibodenberg monastery.

Hildegard's reply is scanty and brusque, with an implicit appeal to her special and protected status recognized and legitimized by the Pope and the emperor. She defends the privilege of higher descent and explains that even God has drawn distinctions for people on earth. "Who would gather all this livestock indiscriminately into one barn—the cattle, the ass, the sheep, the kids? Thus it is clear that differentiation must be maintained in these matters, lest people of varying status, herded all together, be dispersed through the pride of their elevation, on the one hand, or the disgrace of their decline, on the other...." Self-confident Hildegard argues in favor of a splendid liturgical production and display. She justifies Rupertsberg nuns' practice of adorning themselves on feast days with silk and gold by pointing to the special position of the Blessed Virgin, impersonated by Hildegard, or as symbolized by the "virtues" Hildegard, Richardis, and Adelheid, and the other attendants, at Hildegard's ceremonies and stage plays, with Volmar playing the role of the devil.

The year before Hildegard's passing, she was in conflict with the clergy of the Mainz Cathedral over the burial of a nobleman in the cemetery at Rupertsberg, who was excommunicated but reconciled to the church before he died. After having been ordered to disinter the nobleman, she refuses to exhume his body, and bans the right to celebrate the holy office and the Holy Communion (host, body of Christ), ring the church bells, and to sing during Mass. Although she is convinced the nobleman was rightfully buried, she submits to the interdict, but as a precaution hides the grave. However, she fights for rectification by writing a long letter to the prelates in Mainz, describing the circumstances and urging them not to be moved "by indignation and unjust perturbation of spirit, or desire for revenge." Her personally delivered letter only succeeds in lifting the interdict for a short time.

When the ban is imposed again, Hildegard turns to the Archbishop of Mainz, Christian of Buch, who is staying in Rome, in the following rather threatening words: "Gentle father, our prelates in Mainz have instructed me to remove ... the body of a young man.... Otherwise we will have to stop the celebration of the sacraments. As always, this led me to turn to the True Light. In that light God ordered me: the corpse must never be removed with my willing permission, for God has taken this man.... To do anything contrary to this would bring upon us the shadow of great danger.... If the fear of almighty God had not hindered me, I would have immediately obeyed my superiors in all humility."

In response to her letter, the Archbishop of Mainz orders an exhaustive investigation of the circumstances, including a hearing of witnesses. Although on Hildegard's side, he reprimands her, showing that Hildegard's recognition as a visionary and prophetess and her claims of having a "hotline" with the Lord above diminishes, her influence declines, and she becomes less effective in maintaining her formerly church-instated privileges through blackmail and threatening with God's thorn, and is no longer getting away with whatever she pleases. In 1179, the year of Hildegard's death, the interdict is finally lifted.

Whether Hildegard wanted to have her special position reconfirmed and thus overplayed her hand by challenging the Church, or whether the Church was looking for a rightful pretense to make Hildegard and her nuns literally sing another tune, will never be clarified.

Possibly the conflict was an omen of the forthcoming turning of the tide in the church mores under the influence of the Cathars—in which Abbot Bernard of Clervaux (1090–1153), the founding father of the Cistercian order, played an important role—and of the first signs of the onset of the persecution of "heretics" and the Inquisition in Europe. The first call for persecution, imprisonment, and execution of heretics such as the Cathars is documented from the Council of Reims in 1157. On November 4, 1184, just five years after Hildegard died, the call was followed by the Decree of Reims, a pact or alliance was established between Pope Lucius III and Emperor Frederik II, however not leading to persecutions yet. With the Rules of Pamiers, drawn up in 1211, the Inquisition was installed at the level of a diocese, which defined the "cooperation" between church and state.

The Church persecuted the pagans brought in by the inquisitors, and the civil courts prosecuted and convicted the heathens and executed the verdicts. During the Fourth Lateran Council in 1215, Pope Innocent III called upon the Blood Council to intensify the persecutions of the heretics.

7.2 Hildegard's Views on Religious Controversies and the Position of Women

The Catholic Church persecuted the Cathars (derived from *catharsis*) as heretics, because they did not respect the authority and leadership of the Catholic Church. They regarded men and women as equals and lived according to an ascetic (vegetarian) lifestyle rejecting luxury, contradictory to Hildegard's clothing as high priestess and her nuns wearing silk veils, gemstones, and golden jewelry. "Cathars were the offshoot of Manicheans, who were heavily involved in the use of mind-altering substances" (Rushb 2011).

Between 1161 and 1163, Hildegard, in the second part of a letter to the Dome deacon and Clergy of Cologne, and in her sermons in Cologne (Atherton 2001), contrary to the Cathars, emphasized the unity of mind and body, and warned the behavior of the Cathars and their opinions on asceticism were threatening the Church: "[T]hey have lapsed to alcoholism.... The devil is among these people." Her critical position may well have been "inspired" by the competition she experienced as an expert on the use of entheogens and provider of psychoactives to the "happy few" surrounding her and her clients among the rich, noble, and clergy.

Hildegard, while today being regarded as a feminist and an advocate of women's emancipation and equal rights, in essence, considering her attacks on the Cathars, and her claiming a special and privileged position as a woman of nobility, she was not. "On the one hand [she] accepted many of the assumptions of the time about the inferiority of women ... called herself a 'paupercula feminae forma' or poor weak woman, and implied that the current 'feminine age' was thereby a less desirable age.... That God depended on women to bring his message was a sign of the chaotic times, not a sign of the advance of women. On the other hand, in practice, she exercised considerably more authority than most women of her time, and she celebrated feminine community and beauty in her spiritual writings. She used the metaphor of marriage to God (to present herself and her sisters as brides of Christ), though this was not her invention nor a new metaphor—but it was not universal" (Lewis 2011).

Hildegard called upon Bernard of Clervaux to interfere in the conflict with the Cathars by evangelizing and converting the "heretics" while traveling in France. Because his efforts went without success, Bernard returned home and died in 1153. Keep in mind that Bernard was one of the first patrons of King Philip IV, and he and Pope Clemens V persecuted Knights Templar (Butler 2011b).

7.3 Hildegard as an Example or Inspirational Source for Others

At the synod in Trier in the winter of 1147–1148, Pope Eugene III read from her work. From circa 1158 until 1171, Hildegard traveled and delivered sermons all over the German empire and France. She engaged in an extensive correspondence with male and female clergy and nobility from Germany, Austria, Switzerland, Italy, Belgium, and the Netherlands, and with the German king and Emperor Conrad III, King Henry II and Queen Eleanor of Aquitaine of England, and the empress of Greece.

In 1168, Hildegard wrote Emperor Barbarossa a letter, in which she lectured him on his conflict with the Pope and challenged him by taking sides with the Pope; Barbarossa did not acknowledge. Around 1154, Barbarossa ordered Hildegard to come to his palace in Ingolstadt for a consultation in the privacy of his quarters. As far as can be assessed from the left-behind correspondence, her written advice was stated in general terms (Atherton 2001).

In 2009, the movie *Vision* by Margarethe von Trotta was released, with Barbara Sukowa playing Hildegard, in which three years before the official canonization, Von Trotta crowns Hildegard as a Saint [Plates 14, 17, and 28].

The visionary nun Elisabeth of Schönau (1129–1165) partially imitated the scenes depicted in the miniatures of the *Scivias* in her *Liber viarum Dei.* And even nowadays artists like Sybil Archibald, who made a sculpture of Hildegard "pregnant" with a "Cosmic Egg," find inspiration in her.

In the nineteenth and twentieth-century, Hildegard was honored as a holy "prophetessa teutonica." She also was known as "Sybil of the Rine" and the "Gemstone of Bingen." Her contemporaries granted her the status of the most holy and pure virgin, a title she—not exactly a model of humility—out of false modesty rejected. In 2010, Ratzinger, that is, the German pope Benedict XVI, probably in anticipation of his recent canonization of Hildegard, delivered a speech entitled "Das Genie der Frau für das Werk der Kirche" ("The Genius of the Woman in the Workings of the Church"), in which he praised Hildegard and presented her as an example for modern Catholic women, who were summoned to take on the task of contributing to the church life of this day and age. With this, the personal denouncing of Hildegard in the past is carefully covered up with the papal red and white "cloak of charity." Haanappel (2012) states that Hildegard "today ... is considered to be the greatest mystic ever" and that she "was a 'donna universale' in her time."

Besides her "powers" as a visionary and a prophet, Hildegard was, and in certain respects still is, important as a mystic, poet, playwright, musician, and composer of church music and lyrics for the celebration of the Mass, and hourly prayers in her own two convents and, on request, for other monasteries, and because of her book on herbal medicine and gardening.

Colors

"The colors of the liturgical paraments (robes or garments and the tablecloth covering the altar) first appear in the ninth-century. White and red are the first colors that come into fashion. In the twelfth-century, the era of Hildegard, two other colors are added to the palette: green and black (for mourning). Purple (penance) and (pale) red or pink were added at a later date. Blue and yellow, both additions from an even later period, were banned by the Congregation of Rites. Gold cloth, golden brocade or golden-yellow silk can substitute for any other color except black" (Timmers 1978).

The colors of the liturgical garments serve to explicitly express and display the exclusive individual character of the secrets of the religious rituals performed. They also indicate and represent the clerical hierarchy. The symbols and symbolic colors depicted in miniatures, frescoes, and stained-glass windows together form a concise summary of the Christian faith, which is only meant to be completely understood by insiders and the artists assigned to produce them. Hildegard sticks to the medieval dressing code as far as Jesus, Mary, high-ranking clergymen, and saints are concerned.

8.1 Gold

Gold represents the color of the precious metal and is the color of:

- The sun, the solar disk [Plates 11 and 30], the rays of the sun, the moon, and the stars [Plate 5];

- The aureole with or without a red cross or gills [Plates 28, 31, and 32];

- The Cosmic Egg and golden nuggets [Plates 17 and 33];

- The Chalice of Life or Holy Grail [Plates 32, 34, and 42];

- The Golden Fleece, handheld by women while climbing the Cosmic Tree of Knowledge in "Die Mitarbeit am Erlösungswerk" [Plate 63];

- The host (body of Christ) [Plates 34 and 42];

- The golden nimbus (not depicted);

- "Living" water: recycling of divine knowledge [Plates 7, 32, 33, and 42];

- The fleur-de-lis staff [Plates 17 and 41];

- The palm leaf (of the priestess of Delphi) [Plates 17 and 41];

- The crown or tiara of Jesus and Mary [Plates 11, 14, 17];

- The trophy trumpet ("Vom Sinn der Geschichte");

- The symbolic color of enlightenment (flames or rays) [Plate 4].

8.2 Red

The color red symbolizes love and:

- The blood of Christ (wine) [Plate 31] or of the Lamb of God or Sacrificial Lamb;

- The fleece of the cap and of the "nuggets" on the ground [Plate 8] or the "flaces" falling from the sky (manna) [Plate 26] of *Amanita muscaria,* or the golden-red Golden Fleece [Plate 63];

- Head, hands, and feet [Plates 3, 40, and 53], and of the shoes worn by the pope and the Roman emperors, associated with the use and worship of the Sacred Mushroom;

- The flame, for "fiery red," "a flame red turning to white," or "a fireball" (Atherton 2001), for the Pentecostal flames or for the burning bush (not depicted);

- A rose or carnation substituting for the red cap of the fly agaric;

- The blushing of Adam (in "Der Erlöser") [Plate 15].

Vermillion red is the color of life and of fire. For liturgical paraments (vermillion) red (ruber) is often combined with white, the calotte or pileolus of a cardinal is red, and the pope sometimes wears a red hat or satumo. From the Middle Ages on, red is the color of the Pope, or supreme Shaman, of the Church of Rome.

8.3 White

White is the symbolic color of:

- Purity and innocence;

- The Lamb of God or Sacrificial Lamb (bleeding red);

- The velum universale of the fly agaric, which disintegrates into white dots on the cap [Plate 24];

- The Datura flower or virgin white lily [Plate 15 and 16];

- A white rose or carnation substituting for the primordium of the fly agaric;

- Virgin Mary, the forever pure lily;

- "The "flame glow white," "flame red turning to white," "white-shining energy," "white lilies, red roses" (Atherton 2001);

- The white-fur-lined red winter bonnet (camauro) and the white fascia of the pope;

- The white (albus) calotte or zucchetto worn by the pope, the symbol of his "top dog" or "alpha male" position in the hierarchy of the church, implying that the first-exposed white velum of the fly agaric is superior to or ruling over the later-exposed red of the fleece, thus representing the hierarchy among the pope and the cardinals. And the white garments worn underneath the red robe symbolize the stem, with its annulus, or the legs of Jesus hanging from the cross with a loincloth covering up his genitals.

8.4 Green

Green is the symbolic color of:

- Hope and the spruce (Anna) and other (evergreen) coniferous trees;

- "Veriditas," "greenness" in the "life cycle of men and trees," "green vigor" (Mary's womb), "fecundity" (Atherton 2001), or productivity and fertility;

- The leaves of Datura and other entheogen plants; dark green is the color of the paste of witches' flying ointment [Plate 12];

- The "fruit-bearing" evergreen spruce, which bears fruit at the trunk's base and brings forth the fly agaric, as is symbolically depicted in the "Tree of Jesse" (Lübeck) [Plate 43] and the painting of the "Baptism of Christ" of Andrea del Verrocchio.

In liturgical garments, green (viridis) becomes the dominant color if other colors are not obliged, which means that because gold can substitute for any other color, the colors red, white, green, and gold are dominant and worn most of the time.

8.5 Red-White-Green

The combination of red, white, and green, among others, is found in the interior decorating of the Marienkirche in Lübeck [Plate 44] and in the clothing of Pope Innocent III.

Red-white-green stands for:

- The evergreen spruce (Anna), which only in a restricted period of the year "bears fruit" from its roots as part of the life cycle of primordial or Cosmic Eggs of *Amanita muscaria;*

- The "three powers" red, white, and "moist green vigor" (Atherton 2001).

Liturgical paraments with a combination of these three colors are only worn on special occasions mainly associated with Jesus, Mary, and the saints.

8.6 Blue

Blue or pale blue is the symbolic color of heaven and the sky, of infinity, the chasing away of spirits, the supreme god and resurrection, and the pileus of the Liberty Cap and other psilocybins, and is represented by the pileus worn on a bold head [Plates 35, 36, and 37] and blue stains on white robes or bluing with golden tan of other objects. Mostly the pileus is depicted in blue, which is symbolic of the bluish-green discoloration occurring in psilocybin containing *Psilocybe* species. Blue also is "indicative for morning glories (and Lotus)" (Irvin and Rutajit 2009).

8.7 Indigo and Cyan

Indigo represents pure spiritual knowledge and dignity. According to the Church of Rome, cyan is the color of sin.

8.8 Purple or Pink

Purple stands for wisdom, spirituality, and magic, and, according to Atherton (2001), in the Catholic Church for "purple vigor" and lilies with "purple blooms." Henbane flowers are purplish-to-pink [Plate 18]. Royal purple is extracted from a rock snail and used to be more valuable than gold. Purple (violaceus) liturgical garments are worn during Advent and Lent.

8.9 Brown

Dark brown is the symbolic color of the seeds or pellets of Datura and mandrake [Plates 14 and 41], the roots (mannequin) of mandrake [Plate 11], and of the devilish figures with donkey's ears [Plate 4].

8.10 Greenish-Brown

Greenish-brown stands for a paste [Plate 12] with ingredients from psychoactive plants, or for witches' flying ointment.

Symbols

"The Hand of God reaches down from the sky, bringing mushrooms."

Andrea del Verrocchio, *The Baptism of Christ*

For the significance and symbolic meaning of the symbols used by Hildegard, I refer to the works of Rush (2008, 2011), Irvin (2008), Irvin and Rutajit (2009), Ruck et al (2007, 2010), González Celdrán (2001), Heinrich (2002), and Akers, et al (2011).

9.1 Fungi

9.1.1 The Fly Agaric (*Amanita muscaria*)

In the miniatures "Der Sündenfall" and "Der Erlöser," the fly agaric is depicted with a red cap and pronounced whitish dots on top of a mushroom tree [Plates 45, 46 and 47]. The most direct evidence of the use by others than Hildegard or Volmar of the Sacred Mushroom can be found in the miniature "Von der Gliedrung des Leibes." After consuming red "manna" or "fruits," descended from the sky a fuzzled or intoxicated half-naked man resting his head on a red pillow [Plate 8], Hildegard turning a blind eye to the scene [Plate 9]. In "Der Erlöser," together with a blue fold, a red bell-shaped fold in a man's clothing is shown, which according to Rush (2011) respectively stands for the Liberty Cap and the fly agaric [Plate 47].

The Sacred Mushroom is also symbolically represented in the combination of the colors red, white, and gold. The lower side of the cap is depicted as a solar disk [Plates 11 and 30] or an aureole with radiating rays or a red cross [Plate 31], or with gills in the form of flower petals or waves curling up [Plates 28 and 29], as is shown in "Der Allherscher und die erloschenen Sterne," and, "Der mystische Leib."

Omitting or not explicitly mentioning or showing the fly agaric in all its possible appearances forces Hildegard to substitute symbolically for the "invisible" but implicitly present mushroom or "fiery plant of God" (Heinrich 2002; Rush 2011) with:

- The bleeding Sacrificial Lamb or "Agnus dei" (blood and wool);

- Cosmic Eggs or red or golden "nuggets" [Plate 26] or "flakes" [Plate 8] laying on the ground or falling from the sky, being handheld or ornamentally attached to clothing and also shown as cut-in-half Cosmic Eggs in the ornamental frame [Plate 27] surrounding the miniature "Der dreieinige Gott" or "Christus in der Trinität";

- The chalice of life [Plates 34 and 61;

- "Living" water [Plates 33, 34, and Plate 42];

- The blood of Christ [Plate 31];

- Milk and cheese ("Die Seele und ihr Zelt)" [Plate 25] and the host (body of Christ) [Plate 42], either or not supplemented with the symbolical use of color. The chalice is also the symbol of St. Benedict.

9.1.2 The Liberty Cap (*Psilocybe Semilanceata*)

In Hildegard's miniatures the following more or less symbolic representations of the Liberty Cap are found:

- In "Die Chöre der Engel" Hildegard presents her entheogen "disk of five," in which a circular row of bluish men wearing an earth-colored pileus is depicted [Plate 35]. The color of the pileus probably refers to the substrate Psilocybin grow on;

- In "Der Wiedersacher," "Die Synagoge," and "Die Säule des Wortes Gottes," several alchemists or magicians with either a blue pileus or a blue (Phrygian) cap are acting "on stage" [Plate 36] or climbing the tree or staircase to heaven [Plate 37];

- On the stem and/or branches of some of the mushroom trees in the miniatures "Der Fall des Menschen," "Erschaffung der Welt, Sündenfall und Erlösung," "Der Sündenfall," and "Der Tag der grossen Offenbarung und der neue Himmel und die neue Erde," grow small long-stalked blue "leaves" or mushrooms shaped like the cap of Psilocybe species [Plates 45, 46, and 47];

- In "Der Erlöser," together with a red fold, a blue bell-shaped fold in a man's clothing is shown, which according to Rush (2011) respectively stands for the fly agaric and the Liberty Cap [Plate 47].

The above at least indicates Hildegard was well informed on the "magical" powers of these mushrooms, but, as said before, provides no evidence of being familiar with the use and effects of the Liberty Cap herself.

9.2 Sun, Moon, and Stars

Hildegard, either with or without rays, depicts the sun as the solar disk, twice with a blue circle in the center of a red and golden disk [Plates 11 and 30], possibly indicating both mushrooms joined together as in the caduceus.

A crescent moon as part of the sun or "pearl and oyster shell" [Plate 49], which, according to Irvin (2009), represents the virgin reproduction, is presented in the yoni of "Das Weltall." The Christmas constellation of the stars is depicted in "Das Weltall" [Plate 2], "Vom Bau der Welt," "Von der Natur des Menschen," and "Von der Gliederung des Leibes." In the three last mentioned miniatures, Hildegard also presents the astrological signs of the zodiac, the four wind directions, and the four corners of the world [Plate 5].

In medieval times, it was believed that a supermoon could cause insanity and mental disorders. The word "*luna*tic" comes from that notion.

9.3 Vesica Pisces

Apart from the irrefutably explicit vulva shown in "Das Weltall" [Plate 2], characterized by the labia majora and minora, clitoris, vagina, with the four elements, earth, water, air, and fire at the entrance of the womb and the "pearl and oyster shell-like" sun and crescent moon [Plate 49], Hildegard depicts the vesica pisces or yoni several times in a less realistic way [Plates 17 and 28]. Or as Irvin and Rutajit (2001) state, the multicolored vesica pisces "represents the sacred vulva, symbol of the Earth. The Goddess pulls apart the labia of her vulva to display exactly the same configuration as the entrance to Paradise."

9.4 Head and Eyes

In "Vom Ursprung des Lebens" and "Vom Bau der Welt," Hildegard shows a "head in head" or crown chakra [Plates 40 and 53], symbolizing an astral projection or out-of-body experience (under the influence of entheogens).

On the clothing in "Der Leuchtende," "Die Mitarbeit am Erlösungswerk," and "Vorbereitung auf Christus," on the wings in "Die Chöre der Engel," and in the tilted square or "kite" of "Die Seele und ihr Zelt," Hildegard depicts wide-open eyes [Plates 1 and 33] as a sign of inner vision or enlightenment by the living light of the Holy Ghost of the men and women involved.

Hildegard uses her and Volmar's and Richardis's eyes as a means of nonverbal communication with the observant spectator of her miniatures: Eyes are the mirror of the soul. Depicting looking one another straight in the eyes, as Hildegard and Volmar do when she is in her cell, suggests intimacy and bonding between the two of them [Plate 4]. Wide-open eyes stand for being a companion in or with an interest in following of external events. One eye shut (Hildegard, Richardis) represents inner vision or "entoptics": "one eye looking out, one eye looking into the soul" (Irvin 2009), the sharing of a secret, or turning a blind eye to the "hoax" in the scene [Plates 6 and 9]. Both eyes closed (Hildegard) symbolizes contemplation or delight or ecstasy, or experiencing or re-experiencing an (erotic) fantasy [Plate 50].

9.5 Mythical Animals

The ouroboros only once is presented as the first capital letter of the chapter accompanying the miniature "Der neue Himmel und die neue Erde" [Plate 48]. Of all other mythical animals and beasts, Hildegard depicts the snake, the phoenix, the dragon defeated by St. George, and the unicorn.

Adding to this, in "Der Wiedersacher," "Die Seele und ihr Zelt," "Die Seele verlasst ihr Zelt," "Der Wiederstand gegen die Versuchungen," "Das Ende der Zeiten," and "Der Tag der grossen Offenbarung," she depicts monsters with white fangs or shooting arrows at people [Plate 5], and devils with donkey or ass's ears [Plate 5] of king Midas "sticking out like horns from the sheaf of grain like ass's ears" (Celdrán 2001).

9.6 European and African Animals

Apart from mythical animals, Hildegard introduces the wild boar, bull (Taurus), red lion, red deer, wolf, dog, dove (with golden aureole or palm leave), a bird of prey (eagle), and a tortoise, bat, toad, scorpion, spider, and fish to some of the scenes in her miniatures.

9.7 Plants

9.7.1 Fleur-De-Lis

Hildegard often depicts the fleur-de-lis or Datura flower she calls the lily. In most instances they are golden, handheld fleur-de-lis staffs [Plate 17], or the flowers are depicted in more natural colors, such as white ("Der Erlöser") or red ("Fünf Tugenden," "Der Turm des Ratschlüsses") [Plates 15 and 16]. The seeds of Datura can be found in the miniature "Ecclesia" [Plate 14].

9.7.2 Henbane

The henbane flower twice is symbolically depicted in frames of miniatures [Plate 18].

9.7.3 Ferns

The description of the beneficial characteristics and depiction of ferns as the symbol of protection against the Devil's evil works, magic and demons, as is shown in "Die Säule der wahre'n Dreifalltigkeit" [Plate 12], is quite exceptional.

9.7.4 Palm Leaf

The palm leaf is the symbol of wisdom, held by the high priestess of Delphi, on which she wrote down her answers. The palm tree also is the symbol of the Garden of Eden and an attribute of Victoria, the goddess of invincibility, symbolizing the victory over death.

While posing as a high priestess or one of the virtues, Hildegard sometimes depicts herself holding a palm leaf as, for instance, is shown in "Die Chöre der Seligen" [Plate 16].

9.8 Mushroom Trees

Unlike in many paintings and frescoes of other artists, Hildegard's mushroom trees [Plates 45, 46, and 47] (Wilson 1983) are intact and do not lack the lower two to three caps, which otherwise would have been "harvested" for obvious reasons.

9.9 Cosmic Tree of Knowledge or World Axis

In "Die Säule der Menschennatur des Erlösers" and "Die Säule des Wortes Gottes," Hildegard shows the cosmic tree (of knowledge) or world axis [Plates 37 and 63].

9.10 Spinal Column

Adding to the depictions of the cosmic tree, the symbol of "the spinal column being the ladder to the brain on which steps the angels went up and down" (Irvin 2008) represented in Jacob's ladder or the staircase to heaven, is depicted several times in Hildegard's miniatures [Plates 54 and 55].

9.11 Fetal or Unborn Child

A rather peculiar phenomenon presented by Hildegard shows an almost full-grown child in the "belly" of the woman in "Die Seele und ihr Zelt" receiving its soul through an umbilical cord coming down from a golden tilted "kite" filled with cosmic eggs [Plate 60]. One might speculate on whether Hildegard in this miniature shows how according to Catholic law, the fetus is an embryo until forty-nine days after conception and not until the forty-ninth day the child becomes his soul, that is if these laws had been operational in medieval times. Or this, for once, could be evidence of the prophetic powers of Hildegard.

The Tree of Jesse of the Marienkirche in Lübeck

In the Marienkirche in Lübeck (Germany), in 2011, the author of this chapter discovered an Antwerp triptych from 1518, with a panel depicting the Tree of Jesse [Plates 43 and 58]. The Mary altar with the triptych is one of the few remaining examples of church art that "survived" the iconoclastic fury of 1566 initiated by Luther, because a friend and follower of his, who was in charge of the demolition of the interiors of Catholic churches in the Lübeck region, secretly disobeyed Luther and saved the beautiful interior of the church from the Lutheran vandals. Because of his acting as a patron of this church, an extremely rare specimen of church art remained intact for later generations to study and enjoy.

In a side panel of the triptych, the Tree of Life, the symbol of the development of consciousness, or Tree of Jesse regarded to be the family tree of Jesus, is depicted. Jesus is the immaculately conceived fruit of the loin of the Holy Virgin Mary, who herself is the immaculately conceived daughter of Anna. To save Mary from Eve's original sin, which, according to Allegro (1990/2009), was associated with the consumption of the Sacred Mushroom, the Catholic church introduced the myth of the immaculate conception of both women, by which Mary became the new "Eve," free of original sin, a principle that was not officially accepted until it was recorded in the dogma of 1854. This did not resolve the "chicken and egg" problem. Mary's mother, however, is not mentioned in the Bible.

To complete the family tree of Jesus, from the second-century on, Anna was introduced as the mother of Mary and grandmother of Jesus. It was not until many centuries later that Anna, Mary, and Jesus were depicted together in miniatures, paintings, frescoes, triptychs, and sculptures as a trinity called "Anna in three."

To avoid Mary's return to original sin, Anna also had to be immaculately conceived of a child. The "father" was supposed to be Joachim, which stands for "Jahweh prepares," "established by God," or "erected by the Lord." The panel shows Anna and her husband, Joachim, the mythical "parents" of the Virgin Mary and "grandparents" of Jesus.

Actually the Tree of Jesse represents the life cycle of the fly agaric. In the Bible, Jesus is presented as a sprout or shoots from the roots or base of, or the stump of, the Tree of Jesse, the father of David.

Anna is symbolized by the evergreen spruce and her symbolic color is green, the color of hope. Spruces, cedars, and cypresses are deep-rooting coniferous trees that are anchored firmly in the soil and reach to the sky, directing at the realm of the heavenly gods with their pointed, tapered tops. The Celts regarded the spruce as a symbol of the gift of knowledge and worshiped the conifer as the holy tree of life and death. The Romans planted cedars and cypresses at and surrounding their graveyards.

The spruce (as well as the birch) is one of the symbiotic partners of the ectomycorrhizal fly agaric, of which the mycelium associates with the roots of the tree and "fruits" from them in late summer and autumn. First, the mushroom completely develops inside a whitish to pale golden yellow primordium or Cosmic Egg or Egg of the Universe from which, in the second stage of development, the white dotted red cap emerges and spreads out.

It was not until the invention of the microscope in the beginning of the sixteenth-century that people could see and understand the functioning of the reproductive systems of humans (sperm) and fungi (spores). From Hildegard's observations of the fine rootlets of the beech can be concluded, however, that she at least had linked the appearance of certain species of fungi, such as *Amanita muscaria*, the Sacred Mushroom, with the roots of certain tree species.

In this way, a naturally occurring phenomenon—the symbiotic association of the entheogen fly agaric with the spruce (and birch)—is transformed into a religious symbol, and when the phenomenon repeats itself without human intervention and is "equipped" with a soul (animism), it's the first step toward humanizing or even deifying the fungus, as is the case with the Holy Mushroom. In the panel of the triptych of the Mary altar, as mentioned above, with the Tree of Jesse, the life cycle of the fly agaric is symbolically represented in the persons of Anna, Mary, and Jesus. From the chests or hearts of both of Mary's "parents," a root originates that is held with one hand by both parents. From the sides of the roots spruce cones emerge referring to Anna, the spruce, in this case, being the Tree of Life. Both roots join above the heads of Anna and Joachim, vertically "growing" as one root until it ends in a golden ball, a primordium or Cosmic Egg. The top of the "egg" opens up and unfolds as a "flower," ergo the cap of the fly agaric, complete with wide-apart "petals" or radial rays, symbolizing the lamellae or gills of the mushroom, in total looking like a shallow golden saucer or chalice, the Holy Grail. On top of the gilled cap, golden Mary sits with Jesus on her lap and with a horizontal lunar crescent supporting her lower back [Plate 59].

Contrary to the reproductive organs and pollen of the spruce, the spores and hyphae of fungi cannot be seen with the human eye. To come to a comprehensive "theory" on how mushrooms such as the fly agaric reproduce and to "solve" the "chicken and egg" problem associated with invisible phenomenon, the immaculate conception of Anna and Mary was fabricated. In the "womb" of Mary, with the roots of her "mother" Anna and connected to Mary (a "mature" fly agaric), there develops the Cosmic Egg, from which miraculously, through immaculate conception, Jesus, a "newborn" fly agaric, arises. A completely spread-out fly agaric takes on the form of a person hanging from a cross with a red upper body and spread-out arms, wearing a white loincloth—the annulus: remnants of the partial veil surrounding and hanging from the stem, ending in clenched-together white legs, the stem, coming down from underneath the cloth. The rim of the cap curls up, creating the chalice or Holy Grail with rainwater inside, saturated with dissolved muscimol from the red fleece, which is ritually drunk as the blood of Christ, later miraculously "turned into" wine (transubstantiation). "What washes, cleans my soul? No other well (fountain) I know other than the blood of Christ." It then slowly perishes and dries out, forming the Golden Fleece, until next year, often at or close to the same spot a new Sacred Mushroom is "born" or has resurrected or regenerated, a phenomenon that may have been the inspirational source of the born-again Christians. With this, the resurrection of Christ, the high priest of the New Covenant, is realized and according to the Bible "the order by virtue of an indestructible or infinitive live" is restored.

The fly agaric gives birth to himself, is "mother" Mary, God the Father, and Son, and according to Sabellius (third-century) holds the substance—"one substance of father and son" (consubstantiality)—that gives entrance to enlightenment by and internalization of the fire of the Holy Ghost, or the Trinity.

In the Tree of Jesse of the Mary altar, the Holy Virgin is depicted as an intermediary in the life cycle of the fly agaric. Seated on a horizontal crescent moon and in a "chair" of tree roots, Mary arises from a Cosmic Egg or Chalice of Life, and holds baby Jesus, the fruit of her loin, in her arms without her needing to have sexual intercourse to bear the child. Behind her back and head the tips of the roots of the spruce join like golden rays or flames while forming the back of a chair.

Apart from this, the panel presented mythological figures of the Holy Virgin, baby Jesus, and Anna; there are many examples of the use of color combinations of red, white, and green on pillars and arches [Plate 44] that are also referring to the fly agaric and the spruce. According to a woman working as a guide in the church, these colors were exclusively used because they were the cheapest, while the interior of the church is a paragon of the enormous wealth of the merchants, who, as counterparts to the Dome Church with only one bell tower, had the Marienkirche built with two towers.

In the Marienkirche of Lübeck, one also finds the remnants of how the territorial layout of the Catholic churches' interiors originally were designed and built. The high altar, at first, was the exclusive territory of the clergy and was separated from the ignorant and illiterate congregation by a rood screen, which made it impossible for the "flock of believers" to witness or participate in the secret and sacred "body and blood of Christ" rituals behind the scenes. In some churches, such as the Marienkirche, dividing walls ("doksaal" or "oksaal") were built between the high altar and the nave, with arches that could be closed with curtains. As time went on, however, in most churches the decorated "doksaal" was partially dismantled, after which the "sacraments," by then symbolically represented by the host and wine, were shared with the congregation.

Summary and Conclusion

Hildegard lived in a turbulent era characterized by ecclesiastical schisms and a continuously regenerating battle between secular and religious powers. In spite of or even thanks to these chaotic times, Hildegard succeeded in acquiring a special and unique position, which was not equaled by women within the Catholic Church until the present day.

In her work, and foremost in her correspondence as a reaction to Richardis's departure, it more than once becomes clear how her personality, because of traumatic experiences during childhood, but also at a later age, resulted in the development of a narcissistic personality disorder, with distinct symptoms of megalomania. As an example of this, in the miniatures "Vollendung der Kosmos" and "Das Ende der Zeiten," Hildegard even dares to depict herself in the full regalia of the high priestess [Plates 3 and 51] of her sectarian convent. Adding to this, she presents herself as Mary and plays the part of the Holy Virgin with the golden crown [Plates 17 and 29] in the mystery play she wrote and composed.

The fact that Volmar witnessed Hildegard's first "epiphany" proves that it is absolutely out of the question that the hallucinations were spontaneous, but that they were either self-induced or planned "revelations" initiated and guided by the "expert" Volmar by orally taking fly agarics. Besides, the descending of the fiery "flames" or the fire of the Holy Ghost from the ceiling of her cell, instead of straight from heaven, strongly speaks for the indoor use of entheogens, which were responsible for the luxation of Hildegard's "epiphany" at age forty-two [Plate 4].

The presence of both Volmar and Richardis several years after her first "Schau," her last ten "visions" indicates was not a matter of sudden and spontaneous visions, but of hallucinations, which were "delivered on call" after using entheogens such as the Sacred Mushroom, a presumption that is supported by Richardis's winking eye communicating the sharing of a secret or turning a blind eye to the hoax [Plate 6].

In the following nine miniatures of the last ten visions, Hildegard sits alone in her cell in the lower right or left corner and outside the frame, without any witnesses of her visionary images, while she is recording her "brainwaves" on a wax plate. The absence of witnesses of most of her "visions" justifies the conclusion that it mostly was not a matter of whether or not entheogens incited the hallucinations, but that they were an imaginative fantasy, pseudologica fantastica, and wishful thinking based on self-fulfilling prophesies, meant to confirm her "predictions." By only having two "revelations" on call in the presence of one or two of her intimates, who could "confirm" her foreseeing gift, Hildegard could again and again implicitly call upon the reliability and credibility of her prophecies and "visions."

If one takes the facial expressions of Hildegard, Richardis, and Volmar, and especially the depiction of wide open and one or both eyes shut into account, one realizes that Hildegard uses mimics and the eyes to communicate about how the miniature should be interpreted or "read" [Plates 4, 6, and 50]. In the miniature "Von der Gliederung des Leibes" Hildegard herself "turns a blind eye" to the "intoxicated" man, in this case nonverbally communicating the sharing of the secret of the consumption of the fly agaric as an entheogen [Plate 9].

From four miniatures one can conclude that Hildegard at least was informed of the recycling of "living" water or divine knowledge, that is, the drinking of urine saturated with muscimol produced by oneself or others consuming fly agarics. In the miniatures "Die Urmesse und die Messe" and "Der Leuchtende," whether or not fitted with golden Cosmic Eggs, "golden showers" respectively come from underneath the clothing of earlier users and Jesus [Plate 7]. In this case Christ does not wear the usual aureole, but a disk representing a flat disk of a cut-in-half Cosmic Egg [Plate 33]. The "living" water is poured upon the heads and over the bodies of human figures with or without a head or face and whether or not depicted with wide-open eyes on their clothing [Plates 7 and 33], which in more than one way symbolizes enlightenment after drinking "living" water. In addition to this, in "Das Opfer Christi und die Kirche," Hildegard shows how a golden stream flows from a cloud connected to the base of the cross into a golden chalice standing on a table, next to which a host or dissected Cosmic Egg—the "flesh" of Christ—is placed [Plate 32].

The miniatures "Das Ende der Zeiten" and "Das Weltall" demonstrate the effects of the application of witches' flying ointment on the vulva or inside the vagina [Plate 2] [Plate 10].

"Vom Wirken der Liebe" presents in a hardly concealing way the more than platonic love between Hildegard and Jutta and Hildegard and Richardis. On top of this, the miniature shows Jutta masturbating [Plate 52].

In retrospect, Hildegard seems to have been the last shaman tolerated (and even exploited) by the Church of Rome. She had an exceptional status for a woman of her day, a status for obvious reasons sanctioned by the emperor, clergy, and nobility.

In spite of the manifest presence of psychopathology, the unveiling of Hildegard's secrets did not lead to a lesser appreciation of her literature, art, and music by the author of this chapter; it just placed her work in a different "light" and gave cause to another understanding of its context.

Description and Analysis of the Miniatures

> "The art of painting is a mute, in her imagery however inexhaustibly communicative dialogue between the artist and his world—and all those, who go deeply into his works of art"
>
> (Temming 1968).

The oldest illustrated version of the *Liber Scivias* is the so-called Rupertsberg Codex, which originated from the scriptorium at Rupertsberg during Hildegard's life. Its thirty-five miniatures, carefully executed in opaque paint using gold and silver, correspond thematically to the visions. In the course of secularization, the Rupertsberg Codex comes to Wiesbaden in 1814, where it finds its place in today's Nassauische Landesbibliothek. During World War II the valuable manuscript is deposited in Dresden. Since 1945 it has been considered missing. The nuns of the Saint Hildegard Abbey have executed a true copy of the manuscript during the years 1927–1933.

12.1 In General

In the manuscripts with the miniatures, the first paragraph of the text mostly opens with a capital letter, depicting flower and leaf motives in the colors green, blue, purple, brownish, reddish-brown, golden-brown, and greenish with a golden background, and once depicting an ouroborus.

12.2 Differences and Similarities with Church Art and Writings of Others

In view of certain similarities in the miniatures of Hildegard, with depictions in the miniatures of the "Codex Aureus" or "Golden Evangeliarium" of Echternach (1020–1030), and the "Precious Evangeliar" of the holy Bernward (Brandt 1993) of the dome treasury of Hildesheim (960-1022), Hildegard, while traveling in Germany (1160—Echternach, Trier) may have found some "inspiration" in these evangeliars and other exemplary books for her later created works such as the *"Book of Life's Merits"* (1158–1163). Adding to this, there is a striking resemblance of one of her "angels" with wide-open eyes on her six wings, to a cherub in a fresco of the San Giovanni a Porta Latina in Rome from the same period (Timmers 1978).

Also in the twelfth-century Italian painting, there is a depiction of Our Lady of Guadalupe, the Holy Virgin, standing on a crescent moon inside a "vesica pisces" with all the characteristics of the female genitalia, including the clitoris and the labia (Irving 2009). Even though Hildegard restricts herself to a very detailed reproduction of the "yoni," her miniature "Das Weltall" shows striking resemblances to the vulva in the painting of Our Lady of Guadeloupe.

Although we do not know how far manuscripts and miniatures circulated or were exchanged or shared between the German empire and the French and English kingdom, or if they were even discussed in correspondence, there are certain similarities between Hildegard's work and the works of English and French colleagues that strike the eye. In any case, in the era of Hildegard's life, copies of richly illustrated evangeliars, representatives and reflections of the spirit of the times, existed and were circulated or were for perusal on the spot during Hildegard's travels.

Within the Russian Orthodox Church, which withdrew from the influence and jurisdiction of the Church of Rome, until the nineteenth-century model books with examples of symbols and prescribed use of colors circulated, which were regarded obligatory for the icon painters and can be found in icons up till 1813 (Rush 2011). According to Rush, the long-lasting use of these symbols can be traced back to the belief that the icons would lose their effects or power if they no longer contained the original symbols or if the icons were changed. The rather bizarre depictions of a red or golden-colored horizontally positioned baby Jesus "floating" inside a blood filled golden chalice especially catches the eye [Plate 61] . Besides, they are often illustrated with depictions of "mushroom trees," of which some of the lower caps have been "harvested," just like the Liberty Caps in the "Fall of Adam and Eve" from the bronze doors of the cathedral of Hildesheim (1015 CE) and lots of "mushroom trees" in other paintings and frescoes.

Within the Armenian Syrian Orthodox Church, the traditional combination of the symbolic colors red, white, and gold has best been preserved in the beautiful and bright-colored paraments of their bishops. Depending on the nature of the ceremonial celebration, such as the initiation of a bishop, the bishops carry and hold up a magnificent golden caduceus staff with double snakeheads and a cross in between and above them [Plate 39].

Recently the author found an altar piece with depictions of Anna, Mary, and Jesus, or Anna "in three," in a church in Austria, in which Anna holds a chalice filled with distinctly dotted caps of the fly agaric, which she presents to her "grandson." The interior of a brick Evangelical church from the end of the twentieth-century in Gerolstein (German Eifel) is decorated with marble floors and pillars and glass mosaic walls and ceilings, of which the design was "stolen with the eyes" during a visit to Florence. On the ceiling above the altar there are several Liberty Caps depicted at regular intervals.

In "Das Weltall mit seinen vier Elementen und den vier Windkräften," undated, Codex 2582, f. 237r, Östereichische Nationalbibliothek, Wenen (Schipperges 2007), instead of a vesica pisces, a simplified presentation of the "Weltall," shaped like a round ball, is shown that can be regarded as evidence of the deliberate depiction of a Cosmic Egg shaped like a vulva by Hildegard.

12.3 Other Possible Sources for Hildegard's Work (According to Atherton 2001)

- Herrad of Landsberg (died in 1196): female writer and from about 1178 head of a community of Augustinian canons at Hohenbourg near Strassbourg, author and compiler of the illustrated theological textbook *The Garden of Delights* (1160–1170);

- Hendrik of Velde: author of the Middle High German poem "Enit," based on classical sources, an early example of the vernacular literature that was beginning to flourish at the end of Hildegard's career;

- Hermas or Hermes Trismegistus: the Christian visionary author of the "Shepherd" from the second century; the "Shepherd" appears to have influenced Hildegard with its emphasis on visions, its teaching on the virtues, and its use of architectural imagery as in the later parts of the *Scivias;*

- Honorius of "Autun": the early-twelfth-century, living in Germany and England, author of *Elucidarium,* a survey of Christian doctrine with parallels to Hildegard's *Scivias* in the covering of themes; in his later work, "*Gemma animae,*" he used allegory and symbolism to discuss the liturgy, while in his *Imago mundi,* he treats cosmology and geography;

- Ældred of Rievaulx (1109–1167): an English Cistercian abbot, who, at the instigation of Bernard of Clairvaux, wrote *The Mirror of Love* (1142–1143), and was the author of *On Spiritual Friendship* (1150–1151), a classic expression of monastic friendship;

- Ambrosius Autpertus (died 784): a writer and theologian who, among other things, was the author of the *Conflict of the Vices and Virtues,* which appears to have influenced Hildegard's *Book of Life's Merits.*

12.4 Other Women and Men with Visions

- Rupert of Deutz (c. 1075–1129), a monk from the Belgian city of Luik, who in 1120 became abbot of the monastery of Deutz near Cologne. In his work *On the Glory and Honour of the Son of Men,* he reports having visions that show close similarity to those of Hildegard, visions he experiences for a long time without unveiling to others;

- Elisabeth of Schönau (1129–1165), the visionary nun who experienced her visions in an ecstatic state and not in the "awake" state Hildegard was in, a reason to assume she was not of the Sacred Mushroom persuasion (Atherton 2001);

- Saint Catherine of Genoa (1447–1510), the "apostle of the purgatory," who had comparable visions probably based on the use of "bitter tasting agarics" like the fly agaric, inducing ecstatic ruptures and hallucinatory images of Our Lady;

- A married woman from the fifteenth-century, who with consent of her husband dressed as a nun and started living a life as "deo devota," because she could not go without the holy "sacrament" (*Amanita muscaria*) administered at home by a priest, and the ecstatic state it incited in her (Schiewer 2009).

12.5 A Closer Look at Some of the Miniatures

As it is impossible within the context of this chapter to include the complete descriptions and analyses of all forty miniatures and the "Vorrede" (1150), only the most important and appealing aspects of the miniatures are highlighted and explained in some detail. The complete descriptions and the more or less tentative analyses will be available in an appendix to this chapter.

Explicit indications for the intentional eliciting of visions, epiphanies, or revelations in the presence of witnesses through the use of the fly agaric are to be found in the miniatures, "Die Seherin" ("Vorrede") [Plate 4] and "Vom Ursprung des Lebens" [Plate 8].

Solo experienced "Schau" or "Visio," or provoked conscious dreams, are especially found in the five miniatures, in which a quadrant with the Rupertsberger convent is the central theme [Plate 56].

Most of the miniatures are in the form of a "comic strip" without text "balloons," as, for instance, can also be found in frescoes on the walls and ceilings of early medieval churches in the northern parts of Germany, Denmark, and Romania (Voronet monastery); that is to say, if they have survived the iconoclastic fury, with this difference, that the depictions of Hildegard—for obvious reasons—are far more complicated and multi-interpretable and leave much more to the fantasy and imagination of the viewer.

Two miniatures are especially significant, because there (as always) is a separate frame attached to the left and the right lower corner showing Hildegard in her cell, while respectively Volmar [Plate 4] and Volmar and Richardis [Plate 6] are present as witnesses of Hildegard having her first ever epiphany ("Die Seherin"); and the first of the last ten visions ("Vom Ursprung des Lebens") coming down from "above," while she records her experiences on a wax plate.

In some miniatures, in a more or less symbolic way, the daily and ceremonial routine within the sectarian community is communicated. In accordance with this, often the beautiful and luxurious garments and gems worn by the high priestess [Plates 51 and 3] and her intimate seconds are on display, with Hildegard substituting for the Holy Virgin with a golden crown.

Adding to this, along with God and God's hand, Virgin Mary, Jesus, and Joseph, one finds angels [Plate 53], saints, among them St. George, the apostles including Peter guarding the key to heaven's door, the virtues, and (mythic) animals and devils with ass's ears [Plate 5] dominating the scenery. Hildegard, Richardis, and Jutta appear as figures representing Love, Humility, and Peace. In "Der mystische Leib," nobility and high-ranking clergy are brought onstage, which can be interpreted as an expression of appreciation or a symbolic reward for their (financial) support in building of the Rupertsberg convent [Plate 29].

As others did not witness the "conception" of "Vom Bau der Welt" and other visions associated with Hildegard's astrological concepts and ideas on the micro- and macrocosmos, it is more than obvious that these were copied from books, and not, as Hildegard claims, "beamed down" from above, because the necessary "flames" touching her head fail. Ergo, these visions probably do not have their origin in the use of entheogens, but are a product of fantasy and wishful thinking, combined with a recall of what Hildegard had seen before in library books. Because of this, Hildegard's astro(theo)logical concepts are a fine example of plagiarism without mentioning the source, and of attributing ideas to herself, which did not originate from her brain but from the brains of others.

Notes

1. Mycophobia is the fear of touching or consuming (poisonous) mushrooms or toadstools.
2. No clear evidence was found of Hildegard using cannabis or *Psilocybe*.
3. See 1.4, "The First 'Vision' or Epiphany."
4. See sections under "Personality Development."
5. It is known from developmental psychological research with young children who only have a limited vocabulary at their disposal that their memories of childhood as adults are not very reliable and often distorted, partially made up, or influenced by the need to make things seem better or worse than they really are or were.
6. "Inner vision" or "entoptics."
7. Note what Bolton Holloway (1992) before stated on Hildegard's reaction to Adelheid leaving the convent.
8. For instance, see: *Der mystische Leib*: "In the middle of this flower calyx a small woman dressed in red appears—Maria (is Hildegard), also known as "Sister of Wisdom" (Schipperges 2007).
9. See the text on the miniature "Vom Wirken der Liebe."
10. See: 5.3.2 "Beech."
11. For a summary of the effects after consumption of fly agaric, see 1.4, "The First 'Vision' or Epiphany."
12. Note the completion of the red-white-green combination, which stands for the fly agaric and the evergreen spruce (Anna).
13. Note pileolus referring to pileus, the cap of a (*Psilocybe*) mushroom.
14. Rush (2011) states that St. Ann or Anna is symbolized by a pine tree; it is, however, the spruce.
15. See "Die Seherin."
16. See: "Vom Ursprung des Lebens."

17. See respectively: "Die Seherin," "Vom Ursprung des Lebens," "Vom Sinn der Geschichte," "Vollendung des Kosmos" and "Vom Wirken der Liebe."

18. Nota bene: Jesus speaks of himself as "the water of life and the light of the world" and Hildegard calls him "that luminous substance."

Bibliography

Akers, B., Ruiz, J., Piper, A., and Ruck, C. 2011. "A Prehistoric Mural in Spain depicting Neurotrophic Psilocybe Mushrooms." *Economic Botany,* (XX)X, pp. 1–8.

Allegro, J. 1970. *De Heilige Paddestoel en het Kruis. Een studie van de aard en de oorsprong van het Christendom binnen de vruchtbaarheidskultussen van het Nabije Oosten.* Amsterdam: Bussum, De Haan.

Allegro, J. 2009. *The Sacred Mushroom and the Cross.* Gnostic Media.

Archibald S. 2010. *Statue of Hildegard of Bingen representing Virgin Mary pregnant of a Cosmic Egg.* http://www.youtube.com/watch?v=pmCSugTMKgw&feature= player_embedded.

Atherton, M. 200. *Hildegard of Bingen: Selected Writings.* New York: Penguin Classics.

Baird, J. 2006. *Personal Correspondence of Hildegard of Bingen.* New York: Oxford University Press.

Bär, N. 1987. *De vroegere wereld. Europese beeldende kunst tot de 19e eeuw.* Veenendaal: Gaade.

Barral i Altet, X., Avril, F., and Gaborit-Chopin, D. 1984. *Romanische Kunst. Zweiter Band. Nord-und Westeuropa,* (1060–1220). Munich: Verlag Beck.

Beane, W. and Doty, W. (eds.). 1976. *Myths, Rites, Symbols: A Mircea Eliade Reader,* Vol. II. New York: Henceforth.

Benedictus XVI. 2010a. *Speech of the pope on Hildegard of Bingen.* http://www.romereports.com/palio/pope-feminist-speech-on-the-woman-hildegard-of bingen-english-2650.html.

Benedictus XVI. 2010b. *Text of the speech of the pope on Hildegard of Bingen.* http://www.vatican.va/holy_father/benedict_xvi/audiences/2010/documents/hf_ben-xvi_aud_20100908_en.html.

Bennett, C. 2010. *Cannabis and the Soma Solution.* Trine Day, LLC: Waterville.

Borman, R. 2011. *Witte wieven en elfen.* A3 boeken, Geesteren.

Brandt, M., Kahsnitz, R., and H.J. Schuffels. 1993. *Das Kostbare Evangeliar des Heiligen Bernward.* Munich: Prestel Verlag.

Butler, A. 2011. *De Heilige Graal. Geschiedenis en geheimen.* Librero.

Butler, A. 2011b. *De Tempeliers. Geschiedenis en geheimen.* Librero.

Carhart-Harris, R., Erritzoe, D., Williams, T., Stone, J., Reed, J., Colasanti, A., Tyacke, R., Leech, R., Malizia, A., Murphy, K., Hobden, P., Evans, J., Feilding, A., Wise, R., and Nutt, D. 2012. "Neural correlates of the psychedelic state as determined by fMRI studies with psilocybin." *Proceedings of the National Academy of Sciences of the United States of America.*

Carotta, F. 2002. *Was Jezus Caesar? Over de Romeinse oorsprong van het christendom.* Soesterberg: Een onderzoek. Uitgeverij Aspekt.

Clausberg, K. 1980. *Kosmische Visionen. Mystische Weltbilder von Hildegard von Bingen bis heute.* Cologne: DuMont Buchverlag.

Devereux, P. 1997. *The Long Trip. A Prehistory of Psychedelia.* Brisbane: Daily Grail Publishing.

Dom- und Diözesanmuseum Mainz. (1998). 2010–2011. *Hildegard von Bingen.* Information and texts supporting the slides and illustrations of the exposition in the Historical Museum Am Strom in Bingen.

DSM-IV-TR. 2000. *Diagnostic and Statistical Manual of Mental Disorders,* 4th edition. Washington, DC: American Psychiatric Association.

Eliade, M. 2004. *Shamanism: Archaic Techniques of Ecstasy.* Princeton: Princeton University Press.

Every, G. 1970. *Christian Mythology.* London: Hamlin Publishing Group.

Fox, M. 2002. *Illuminations of Hildegard of Bingen.* Rochester, VT: Bear & Company.

Gnostic Media Exclusive Video. 2011. *Interview Allegro:* http://www.youtube.com/watch?v=mOu9tV6uy2E.

Godefridi, M. 2011. *Kruidwis. Leven* Celdrán *met kruiden.* Planten v Celdrán an A tot Z. (internet.)

Gombrich, E. 1969/1977. *Eeuwige Schoonheid. Inleiding tot de kunstgeschiedenis.* Haarlem: De Haan. Celdrán

González Celdrán, J. 2001. *Daturas for the Virgin.* POSTSCRIPTUM. I. *The MitraicTomb of Don Fernando of Avila.* Entheomedia.com.

González Celdrán, J. 2011. Personal communication with the author.

Gronau, E. 1999. *Hildegard von Bingen.* Stein-am-Rhein: Christiana-Verlag.

Haanappel, K. 2010. *Het Parijs van Isis.* Geesteren: A3 boeken.

Haanappel, K. 2012. *Herstory of Art.* Geesteren: A3 boeken.

Harner, M. 1973. *Hallucinogens and Shamanism. The Role of Hallucinogenic Plants in European Witchcraft.* Part III: *The Traditional Western World.* New York: Oxford University Press.

Haustein-Bartsch, E. 1991. *Russische Ikonen. Neue Forschungen.* Recklinghausen: Verlag Aurel Bongers.

Heieck, M. 2010. *Hildegard von Bingen. Wisse die Wege – Liber Scivias. Eine Schau von Gott und Mensch in Schöpfung und Zeit.* Werke Band I. Abtei St. Hildegard, Beuroner Kunstverlag: Rüdesheim/Eibingen.

Heinrich, C. 2002. *Magic Mushrooms in Religion and Alchemy.* Vermont: Park Street Press, Rochester.

Holloway, J. 1996. "Julian of Norwich, her 'Showing of Love' and its contexts." In *The Ordo Virtutum of Hildegard: Critical Studies,* edited by A. Ekdahl Davidson, 63–77. *Early Drama, Art and Music Monograph Series,* 18, Kalamozoo: Medieval Institute.

Hozeski, B. 2001. *Hildegard's Healing Plants: From Her Medieval Classic Physica.* Boston: Beacon Press.

Irvin, J. and Rutajit, 2007. A. *Astrotheology & Shamanism.* DVD, The Pharmacratic Inquisition. A version with subtitles is available on: http://www.gnosticmedia.com/the-pharmacratic-inquisition/the-pharmacratic-inquisition-with-subtitles-translated.

Irvin, J. 2008. *The Holy Mushroom. Evidence of Mushrooms in Judeo-Christianity.* Gnostic Media.

Irvin, J. and Rutajit, A. 2009. *Astrotheology and Shamanism: Christianity's Pagan Roots.* Gnostic Media.

Jaffé, H. 1985. *Schilderkunst door de eeuwen heen.* Weert: TrendBoek BV.

Johnson Lewis, J. 2011. *Hildegard of Binge: Visionary, Composer, Writer. The Legacy of Hildegard of Bingen.* About.com guide, Women's History.

Kahl, J. 1970. *Het onheil van het Christendom of pleidooi voor een humaniteit zonder God.* Utrecht: Bruna.

Keizer, G. 1988. *"Proxemics" en "pragmatics."* Tijdschrift Onderzoek over Omgeving en Gedrag (OOG), Technical University Eindhoven, pp. 19–32.

Keizer, G. 1991. *Systeemtherapie, persoonlijke ruimte en territorialiteit.* Systeemtherapie, derde jaargang, augustus. Houten: Bohn Stafleu Van Loghum, pp. 127–141.

Keizer, G. 1994. "Gezinstherapie." In *Hersenletsel: Gevolgen voor de getroffene en de omgeving* edited by L. de Vos and H. Eilander, 69–86. Psychologie & Praktijk. Swets & Zeitlinger, Lisse/Nederlands Instituut van Psychologen.

Keizer, G. 1996. Systeemtheorie and Deomgevingspsychologie. In Het Palet van de Psychologie. Coutinho: Bussum.

Keizer, G. 1997. *Illustrated Encyclopaedia of Fungi.* Lisse/London: Rebo.

Keizer, G. 2001/2010. *The Interactive Guide to Mushrooms and other Fungi.* CD-ROM. ETI BioInformatics (UNESCO), Amsterdam/Leiden: University of Amsterdam.

Keizer, G. 2010a. *Paddenstoelen.* ETI BioInformatics. Website: www.soortenbank.nl.

Keizer, G. 2010b. *Wie der Lärchenschwamm in die Eifel kam.* Der Tintling 16/5: pp. 68–69.

Keizer, G. 2011a. *A review of the second edition of Astrotheology & Shamanism.* Website: http://www.gnosticmedia.com/astrotheology-shamanism-a-review-by-gerrit-keizer.

Keizer, G. 2011b. *De wondere wereld van paddenstoelen en zwammen.* Website: http://fungikeizer.weebly.com.

Keizer, G. 2011c. *John Allegro. De Heilige Paddenstoel en het Kruis.* Website: http://www.allesoverpaddenstoelen.nl/downloads/Allegro.pdf.

Keizer, G. (2011d). *Von Pilzen und Menschen.* Der Tintling 71/5: pp. 84–87. Website: http://www.tintling.ch/fachbeitraege/buchkritik_keizer.html.

Keizer, G. 2012a. *De verborgen boom.* Geesteren: A3 boeken.

Keizer, G. 2012b. *De geheimen van Hildegard von Bingen.* Geesteren: A3 boeken.

Kidson, P. 1967. *De Wereld der Middeleeuwen.* Gaade's wegwijzers door het rijk der kunst. Bouw-, schilder- en beeldhouwkunst, manuscripten, metaal- en glaswerk. Den Haag: Uitgeverij Gaade.

Kohl Y. (no datre). *Migraine, mijn venster tot leven.* Website: http://people.zeelandnet.nl/vdwindt/migraine/yiri.htm.

Kohl Y. (no date). *Life & Works of Yiri T. Kohl.* Website: http://yiri.nl/paint/default.asp.

Lash C. 1980. *De cultuur van het narcisme. Leven in een tijd van afnemende verwachtingen.* Amsterdam: De Arbeiderspers, Synopsis.

Lehane B. 1978. *De Macht van de Planten. Hun macht over ons voedsel, over leven en dood, over de geest en over de ziel.* Amsterdam/Brussel: Elsevier.

Lemaire T. 1995. *Godenspijs of duivelsbrood. Op het spoor van de vliegenzwam.* Baarn: AMBO.

Levack B. 2006. *The Witchhunt in Early Modern Europe.* London/New York: Harlow/Pearson Longman.

Lewis-Williams, D. and Pearce, D. 2005. *Inside the Neolithic Mind: Consciousness, Cosmos, and the Realm of the Gods.* New York: Thames & Hudson.

Montelle, Y-P. 2009. *Palaeoperformance. The emergence of theatricality as social practice*. Londen: Seagull Books.

Monter, W. 2002. *Witch trials in continental Europe*. In *Witchcraft and magic in Europe*. University of Philadelphia: Pennsylvania Press.

Moreau. C. 1980. *Larousse Paddestoelen Encyclopedie*. Hasselt, Belgium: Heideland- Orbis/Kosmos.

Müller-Ebeling, C. 2010. *Der Fäulnispilz in Hildegard von Bingens Vision*. In C. Rätsch: *Pilze und Menschen. Gebrauch, Wirkung und Bedeutung der Pilze in der Kultur*. AT Verlag, pp. 156–157.

Pernoud, R. 1998. *'Hildegard von Bingen'*. Amsterdam: Uitgeverij Ooievaar.

Porter, J. 2003. *De Bronnen van het Geloof. Oude testament. Nieuwe testament. Het leven van Jezus. Vroege christendom. Jezus in de kunst.* Geïllustreerde gids voor de bijbel. Kok, Kampen/Lannoo, Tielt.

Redmond L. 2012. *En de drummers waren vrouwen*. Geesteren: A3 boeken.

Ruck, C., Staples, C., González Celdrán. J., and Hofmann, M. 2007. *The Hidden World: Survival of Pagan Shamanic Themes in European Fairy Tales*. Durham NC, Carolina Academic Press.

Ruck, C., Hoffman, M., and González Celdrán, J. 2010. *Mushroom, Myth and Mithras. The Drug Cult that Civilized Europe*. San Francisco, CA: City Lights.

Rush, J. 2008. *Failed God. Fractured Myth in a Fragile World*. Berkeley, CA: Frog Books.

Rush, J. 2011a. *The Mushroom in Christian Art. The Identity of Jesus in the Development of Christianity*. Berkeley, CA: North Atlantic Books.

Rush, J. 2011b.Personal correspondence.

Sacks, O. 1970/1992. *Migraine*. New York: Vintage Books.

Sauerma-Jeltsch, L. 1998. *Die Miniaturen im >>LIBER SCIVIAS<< der Hildegard von Bingen*. Ie Wucht der Vision und die Ordnung der Bilder. Wiesbaden: Reichert Verlag.

Schiewer, H-J. 2009. *Preaching and Pastoral Care of a Devout Woman (deo devota) in Fifteenth-Century Basel.* In *Medieval Christianity in Practice,* ed., M. Rubin, Princeton, NJ: Princeton University Press.

Schipperges, H. 2007. *Die Welt der Hildegard von Bingen. Leben, Werken, Botschaft.* Erftstadt: Verlag Hohe.

Schultes, R. and Hofmann, A. 1983. *Over de Planten der Goden.* Utrecht/ Antwerpen: Spectrum.

Simplistisch Verbond. 2010. *Interview of John Allegro by Kees van Kooten and Wim de Bie.* Part of a television program on the Fly Agaric, VPRO, Christmas Eve, December 23,1976; see Gnostic Media Exclusive Video.

Slavenburg, J. 1995. *Valsheid in geschrifte. De gespleten pen van bijbelschrijvers.* Zutphen: Walburg Pers.

Starr, M. *Hildegard of Bingen: Devotions, Prayers and Living Wisdom.* Veritas, 2010.

Sterkenburg, P. 1990. *Van Dale Handwoordenboek van hedendaags Nederlands.* Utrecht/Antwerpen: Van Dale Lexicografie.

Storch, W. 1997. *Hildegard von Bingen. Im Feuer der Taube: die Briefe.* Augsburg, Germany.

Summerly, W. and Camerata, O. 2001. *Hildegard von Bingen. Heavenly Revelations.* CD with texts. NAXOS.

Sommerly, W. and Camerata, O. 2008. *Abbess Hildegard von Bingen. Celestial*

Harmonies. Responsories and Antiphons. CD with texts, NAXOS.

Teleac/NOT. 2000. *Nederland in de Prehistorie. Een archeologische zoektocht.* Deel 4. *Eten en drinken.*

Temming, R. 1968. *Die Goldene Palette. Tausend Jahre Malerei in Deutschland, Östereich und der Schweiz.* Deutscher Bücherbund: Stuttgart/Hamburg.

Throop, P. 1998. *Hildegard von Bingen's PHYSICA: The Complete English Translation of Her Classic Work on Health and Healing.* Rochester, VT: Healing Arts Press.

Timmers, J. 1978. *Christelijke symboliek en iconografie.* Haarlem: De Haan.

Todorow, M., Lackner, S., Grohn H., and Schwarz, D. 1975. *Die Grossen Mahler: Altdeutsche Meister. Dürer, Grünewald, Holbein, Cranach.* Munich: Wissen Verlag.

van Amsterdam, J., Opperhuizen, A., and van den Brink, W. 2011. "Harm potential of magic mushroom use: a review." In *Regulatory Toxicoloy and Pharmacology,* Amsterdam: Elzevier.

van der Meer, F. 1972. *Oud-Christelijke kunst.* Bussum: De Haan.

van der Meer, A. 2008. *Van Sophia tot Maria.* Geesteren: A3 boeken.

van Elteren, G. 2007. *Hildegard, Femina Universalis.* Herba Sanitas.

von Trotta, M. 2009. *Vision.* Movie on the life of Hildegard of Bingen.

Trouw. *Al rond 1200 moest theater de kerk uit.* Religie & filosofie, 23 juli, 2010.

Wasson, R.G. 1968. *Soma: Divine Mushroom of Immortality.* NY: Harcourt Brace Javanovich.

Wasson, R.G., Hofmann, A., and Ruck, C. 1978. *The Road to Eleusis: Unveiling the Secret of the Mysteries.,* New York/London: Wolff Books.

Watzlawick, P., Beavin, J., and Jackson, D. 1967. *Pragmatics of Human Communication.* New York: W. W. Norton.

Wentinck, C. 1974. *Kunstschatten van Europa.* Amsterdam: Uitgeverij Amsterdam Boek.

Wilhelmy, W., Fels, G., Kotzur, H-J., and Koring, I. 1998. *Hildegard von Bingen.* 1098–1179. Ausstellungskatalog. Ausstellung Historisches Museum am Strom, Bingen (2010–2011). Mainz: Verlag Philipp von Zabern.

Willard, T. 1990. *Reishi Mushroom. Herb of Spiritual Potency and Medical Wonder.* Washington: Sylvain Press.

Willis, R. 2012. *Mythologie.* Wereldgeschiedenis: Librero.

Wilson, E. 1983. *Early Medieval Designs.* London: British Museum Press.

Wormhoudt, L. 2008. *Goden en sjamanen in Noordwest-Europa.* Geesteren: A3 boeken.

Wortmann, J. 1980. *Ikonen uit de collectie van Ikonengalerie Wortmann*, Zeist.

Zweites Deutsches Fernsehen 2010. Docudrama *Hildegard von Bingen und die Macht der Frauen.* Mainz.

Chapter 5

The Milk of the Goat Heiðrun

An Investigation into the Sacramental Use of Psychoactive Milk and Meat

Alan Piper

Alan Piper was born in 1953 in London, England. He participated in the psychedelic sixties and later became engaged with aspects of the new religious movements. Disillusioned by the cultic character of many of those movements, he entered university as a mature student in the mid-1980s to study the history of philosophy, religion, politics, and science, graduating in the History of Ideas. His studies included the practice of historical method, and since graduating he has applied the disciplines learned as an undergraduate toward investigating the role of mind-altering plant drugs in the history of human culture. Published works include "Bread of Heaven or Wines of Light: Entheogenic Legacies and Esoteric Cosmologies" (with Frederick Dannaway and Peter Webster) in *Journal of Psychoactive Drugs*, "The Lote Tree of the Furthest Boundary: Psychoactive Sacraments in Islamic Gnosis" in *Entheos: The Journal of Psychedelic Spirituality*, and "The Mysterious Origins of the Word 'Marihuana'" in *Sino-Platonic Papers.*

Introduction

Then the High One said: "A goat called Heiðrun stands up on its hind legs in Valhalla biting the buds off the branches of that very famous tree which is called Laerad. From her teats runs the mead with which every day she fills a cauldron, which is so big that all the Einjar can drink their fill from it."

Gangleri said: "What an exceedingly convenient goat for them. It must be a mighty good tree she feeds on!" (From *The Prose Edda of Snorri Sturluson*[1])

"Goats seem to enjoy absolute supremacy in the animal world as far as their passion for disparate drugs is concerned." (*Animals and Psychedelics*, Giorgio Samorini[2])

Of Milk and Other Sacred Inebriants

In traditional accounts, before the *mi'raj*, Mohammed's ecstatic ascent to Heaven to receive instructions for the faithful, the Prophet was offered three cups, one containing wine, one honey, and the third milk. Mohammed chose milk, for which choice he was commended.[3] However, one is tempted to ponder, why should drinking milk be associated with an ecstatic ascent to Heaven? In this investigation we shall discover that not only wine but also honey[4] and even milk can both be psychoactive in their own right and are associated with the major Indo-European traditions of psychoactive sacraments, from the Vedic soma and Zoroastrian haoma, to the cult of Dionysus and the Mysteries of Eleusis and later with the Christian Eucharist.

The sacred soma of the Vedas is mixed with milk and with honey:

> Fleet as swift steeds, thy drops, divine, thought-swift, have been, O Pavamana, poured with milk into the vat. The Rsis have poured in continuous soma drops, ordainers who adorn thee, Friend whom Rsis love.[5] The milk is blended with the honey of the bee: quickly come hither, haste, and drink.[6]

Zoroastrian scriptures record the preparation of haoma with milk:

> O haoma, endow the man who drinks thee mixed with milk; yea, more prosperous thou makest him, and more endowed with mind.[7]

According to Strabo, the Persian Magi pour a libation of "oil mixed with milk and honey" upon the earth when performing their sacrifices.[8] The very presence of Dionysus, who is associated with the Eleusinian Mysteries, promotes an effulgence of wine, milk, and honey, as recorded by Euripides:

> The land flows with milk, the land flows with wine, the land flows with honey from the bees. He holds the torch high, our leader, the Bacchic One, blazing flame of pine, sweet smoke like Syrian incense, trailing from his thyrsus.[9]

In the Homeric Hymn to Demeter, the goddess, like Mohammed, refuses an offer of wine and she asks instead for a drink of barley meal and water mixed with tender pennyroyal. Metaneira, wife of King Keleos of Eleusis, "filled a cup with sweet wine and offered it to her; but she refused it, for she said it was not lawful for her to drink red wine, but bade them mix meal and water with soft mint and give her to drink. And Metaneira mixed the draught and gave it to the goddess as she bade. So the great queen Deo received it to observe the sacrament."[10] The translator notes, "An act of communion, the drinking of the potion (*kykeon*) here described, was one of the most important pieces of ritual in the Eleusinian mysteries, as commemorating the sorrows of the goddess."[11] In the Christian tradition a ninth-century account of the Eucharist records that, "for the newly baptized the chalice is filled, not with wine, but with milk and honey, that they may understand that they have entered already upon the Promised Land."[12] While the refusal of wine is understandable in the context of Muslim injunctions against alcohol, given that Mohammed's drink of milk immediately precedes his ascent to heaven, the refusal of wine and choice of milk may reflect pre-Islamic traditions assimilated into accounts of the Prophet's life.[13]

Of Fumigants and Libations

A close connection between sacred libations and fumigants has been observed: "Since the same weed may appear in a maceration, infusion, tincture, or fumigation, it appears that incense, libation and ordeal are not fundamentally separable,"[14] Agni (fire) and soma (water) sacrifices of the Vedas are so intimately linked as to be aspects of each other and references are sometimes interchangeable.[15]

> Kalash people from the mountains of the Hindu Kush[16] in Pakistan make use of the juniper tree as a shamanic intoxicant.[17] Smoke of the burning foliage of juniper is inhaled as a psychoactive fumigant to enter altered states and the foliage is also soaked and chewed for the same purpose.[18] The Kalash are considered to be the descendants of the Central Asian peoples that called themselves the Aryani. These peoples are widely believed to have migrated from Central Asia around 2,000 BCE to the Iranian plateau, the Iranians (Ir-Aryans) and to the Indus valley, the Indo-Aryans. It was through the high passes of the Hindu Kush, in that era, that the migration from Central Asia brought the Indo-European language, a forerunner of languages still spoken throughout the region today. Those who settled in the Iranian plateau and the Indus valley recorded their use of a sacred plant drug, respectively the haoma of the Zoroastrian scriptures and the soma of the Vedic, latterly Hindu, scriptures. The Kalash and other speakers of Indo European languages are regarded as pockets of settlers from that migration, some of which have been largely untouched by Buddhism, Christian, and Islam, retaining features of the original Indo-European religion.[19] Like soma the juniper is sacred to Indra.[20] There is an extraordinary congruity between Kalash traditions concerning juniper and deceased shamans, and Christian traditions concerning the Tree of Life. The French anthropologists Jean-Yves Loude and Viviane Lièvre recorded this story concerning juniper and the grave of a Kalash shaman.
>
> A little bit before his death, Naga the *dehar* (shaman) gave three juniper berries to his son and said: "These three juniper berries,

> put them in my coffin and place a branch of juniper between my legs." Dehar Naga died and was interred according to his instructions. Three days later his son went by his grave. A juniper was growing at his feet and the other one at his head.[21]

In her book *The Quest of Seth for the Oil of Life,* [22] Esther Casier Quinn explores Christian traditions concerning the Tree of Life and the wood that formed the cross on which Christ was crucified, as well as how traditions concerning the former became conflated with those of the latter. Quinn considers that elements of these stories are pre-Christian and from the East. In certain variants of these traditions Adam, on his deathbed, asks his son Seth to return to the Garden of Eden and bring him the Oil of Mercy from the Tree of Life. Seth variously succeeds in recovering not the oil, but a sprig of the tree or its kernels. According to a summary by Quinn, Seth receives three kernels of the tree of life and places them in the mouth of his dead father.[23] From the kernels three trees grow—a cedar, a cypress, and a pine—and remain growing in the vale of Hebron until the time of Moses.

These three trees are uprooted by Moses and become the wands with which he sweetens the waters of Marah and brings forth water from a rock. David inherits the wands, which are now united to form a single staff. With it he changes the color and shape of some Ethiopians. The staff is replanted and grows into a tree. Moses discovers these rods when they appear, as in the case of the Kalash shaman at his head and feet, in a place where he has lain. Eventually, after various other incidents, the tree is used for the wood of the cross. Adam's skull has been buried at Golgotha and Christ's blood splashes onto the skull.

This image, where the white dome of Adam's skull, buried at the foot of a pine/cedar/cypress tree, is spattered with blood, can hardly but put one in mind of the psychoactive fly-agaric mushroom, *Amanita muscaria,* for which the pine tree is an essential host.[24] There is nothing else, however, suggestive of mushrooms in the traditions that Esther Quinn details, but they are filled with references to a Tree of Life that is cedar, cypress, pine, or juniper. All of these are trees from which oils are distilled, and resins collected, which contain potentially psychoactive compounds called terpenes. Quinn is clear that the motif of the Tree of Life is connected with the plant that enables heroic figures to enter the other world.

The twig or plant, then, is frequently represented in the ancient traditions of the Babylonians, the Jews, and the Greeks. Originally connected with fertility rights, the bough was also used in rainmaking ceremonies, in healing rituals, and in ceremonies surrounding the enthronement of the divine king. As a magic talisman, it enabled the hero to enter the other world; as a symbol of immortality, it was the object of the quest of Gilgamesh.[25]

Quinn connects this plant with that in Mesopotamian art where a figure, probably intended to represent the divine king, raises to his nose a plant with three leaves[26]and cites a reference, from the seventh-century BCE Assyrian royal inscriptions called the Sargonid Letters, stating that "the King gave us life by means of placing the Plant of Life under our nose." King Sargon II's conquests in Palestine caused a diaspora of the Israelites, which may explain their hatred of those that "lift the branch to the nose."[27] Quinn also refers to a repeated theme concerning the Tree of Life, namely something holy and mysterious that is in this tree. Sometimes it is a man, sometimes a marvelous child or a god, sometimes the phoenix bird. I will return to this mystery later.

The use of juniper and other plants and trees containing phytochemicals called terpenes[28] as sacred psychoactives is widespread throughout central Asia and the Middle East[29] and has been since biblical times.[30] It is described in Frazer's classic work of religious and cultural anthropology, *The Golden Bough.*[31] Some notion of what the experience of juniper intoxication is like can be gauged from the account of an anthropologist who tried it.[32]

One psychoactive terpene, thujone, derives its name from the Thuya tree, whose wood is so deeply imbued with essential oils that the interior of boxes made from its wood have a strong turpentine-type odor. The Thuya tree is commonly referred to as the arborvitae, the "tree of life," this name being derived from the medicinal qualities of its resin.[33] The Thuya is of the same family as the cypress and juniper, the *Cupressaceae*. Vessels made of juniper wood, whose oils have a similar character that of the Thuya, are so aromatic that they preserve their contents of milk or yogurt. The cedar, whose employment Frazer's account above refers, though a conifer has a genus to itself Cedrus, but is of the pine family, Pinaceae.[34] In India the Cedar is referred to as the "deodar," Hindi *deodAr,* from Sanskrit *devadAru,* literally, "timber of the gods," from *deva* god + *dAru* wood.

Of Fig Cakes, Sour Milk, and Turpentine Wood

Thujone, as absinthol, is also present in wormwood plants of the Artemisia family. The term wormwood refers to any bitter or aromatic herb or shrub of the genus Artemisia, which is distributed throughout many parts of the world. The leaves of the common wormwood, *Artemisia absinthium,* have been used since ancient times in medicines and such beverages as absinthe, in which it is the chief flavoring ingredient; other aromatic ingredients include hyssop, fennel, angelica root, aniseed, and star aniseed. Absinthe came to be considered dangerous to health because it appeared to cause convulsions, hallucinations, mental deterioration, and psychoses. These symptoms are attributed to its thujone content. Absinthe manufacture was prohibited in Switzerland in 1908, in France in 1915, and eventually in many other countries.[35] Absinthe has been deemed responsible for the artist van Gogh's madness and the eerie colors and swirling forms of some of his paintings. Another wormwood, cultivated commercially in the Middle East, is known as Levant Wormseed, *Artemisia cina* (alt. *Artemisia maritima*).[36] It contains the essential substance santonin, with recognized psychoactive potency. Its mental effects include delirium, excitability, and an inclination to dance and laugh. Pronounced visual effects include flickering before the eyes and the appearance of various figures and animals, objects seeming to totter and dance. Yellow may look red, gray may look yellow, blue may look green, or all objects may seem as if beheld through green glass. Red and blue may be seen in their complementary colors green and orange. All objects may become green and wavering, tinted green or yellow, as though one was looking through colored spectacles. The effects also include hallucinations of smell.[37] Santonin derives its name from the ancient Gallic tribe the Santones who, it appears, were partial to the effects of this herb.[38]

In Plutarch's *Lives,* describing parallel biographies of various noble Greek and Roman figures,there is an account of the initiation of the Achaemenid King of Persia Artaxerxes II (404–359 BCE). According to Plutarch, during initiation by the Persian Magian priesthood, the newly crowned king "must eat a cake of figs, chew some turpentine-wood, and drink a cup of sour milk. Whatever else is done beside this is unknown to outsiders."[39] The chewing of turpentine-wood, possibly only a symbolic dose in the king's case, is highly significant in mind of the chewing of juniper by the Indo-European Kalash tribal peoples. The turpentine-wood of Plutarch is the *tereminthoy* or terebinth tree, which the king must by implication swallow, katatragein meaning "chew down."[40] Especially significant in this context is the central role of chewing juniper in the initiation of daiyal (shamans) in the Hindu Kush.

In the Gilgit, to become daiyal, it is necessary to start chewing the leaves of the juniper very early. The future daiyal chews several leaves of juniper per day before their consecration. Purifier and intoxicant, the juniper holds a preeminent place in the shamanic ritual of the Hindu Kush/Karakoram.[41]

The terebinth was the original source of turpentine, used today for thinning paints and varnishes but traditionally having medical uses. Both the words turpentine and terpene, the sometimes psychoactive hydrocarbon compounds typically found in aromatic tree resins are derived from variations of *tereminth* and *terebinth.* Furthermore, terebinth resins have been used as additives to wine for thousands of years. Found at a Neolithic village site in Iran, a jar containing the remains of 7,000-year-old wine included residue on a potsherd dating to the time of the first permanent settlements in the Middle East. The sherd, c. 7,000 years old, came from one of six two-and-one-half-gallon jars excavated two decades ago from the kitchen area of a mud-brick building in Hajji Firuz Tepe, a Neolithic village in Iran's northern Zagros Mountains. Resin from the terebinth tree was also present, presumably used as a preservative, indicating that the wine was deliberately made and did not result from the unintentional fermentation of grape juice.[42]

Was this resin included for its intoxicating properties as well as preservation? I will return to the possible significance of the kingly initiate drinking sour milk, *oxygalaktos,* later in this paper. Meanwhile it should be noted in this connection that *oxys* can mean "pungent" or "sharp" and that *oxygalaktos* might not have meant soured milk, but milk pungently flavored in some other way.

Of Holy Smoke and Holy Goats

Inhaling fumes directly from burning foliage, either in a confined space such as a cave or a tent, or scooping up and breathing in the vapors from psychoactive plant materials scattered on a bowl full of hot coals, must be an extremely ancient practice. Herodotus's account from the fifth-century BCE, describing the use of small tents by the Scythians (a northwestern Iranian tribe) for inhaling the smoke of cannabis, [43] is probably the most famous account that confirms the antiquity of the use of cannabis as a ritual intoxicant. Less frequently quoted is his account of the islanders of the Araxes.[44]

The Islanders have also discovered another tree whose fruit has a very odd property: for when they have parties and sit around a fire, they throw some of it into the flames, and as it burns just like incense, and the smell of it makes them drunk just as wine does the Greeks, they get more and more intoxicated as more fruit is thrown on until they jump up and start dancing and singing.[45]

The Ossetes of the Caucuses, an Indo-European people, direct descendants of the hemp-inhaling Scythians of Herodotus,[46] were still practicing this means of self-intoxication in the nineteenth-century, as we shall soon see.[47]

The use of the familiar tobacco-type pipe as a drug delivery system in Eurasia is generally agreed to follow from the introduction of tobacco.[48] However, it may be safely assumed that the practice of simply inhaling the smoke of a narcotic plant in a suitably confined space is not only a practice of extreme antiquity, but probably one of the means by which the narcotic properties of certain plants were discovered. This likelihood has not escaped the observation of historians.[49] Likewise, informed scholarship has speculated that the use of incense in churches today is a relic of the ancient use of psychoactive fumigants. Many scriptural and other ancient references to the ritual use of incense may well be to psychoactive fumigants.[50]

Though the idea may be strange to most modern worshippers, drugs have played an important role in the history of religions. The ceremonial use of wine and incense in contemporary ritual is probably a relic of a time when the psychological effects of these substances were designed to bring the worshipper into closer touch with supernatural forces.[51]

The nineteenth-century traveler Jules Klaproth recorded practices, similar to those recorded by Herodotus on the islands of the Araxes, being employed by the Ossetians in the Caucasus Mountains, close to the modern river Aras (the ancient Araxes).

In the caves and the other places dedicated to Ilia (Elijah), they offer him goats, whose flesh they eat and whose skins they stretch out on a big tree. The day of the feast of Ilia, these skins are honored with particular reverence, so that the prophet will keep away hail and grant a rich crop. The Ossetians often go to those places and intoxicate themselves with the smoke of the rhododendron caucasicum[52;] they fall asleep on the ground and regard their dreams as an omen, according to which they regulate their actions. In addition, they have augurs that inhabit the sacred rocks, and who, in return for a gift, reveal to them the future.[53]

In the biblical account of the prophet Elijah, after trekking into the wilderness in despair, he falls asleep beneath a juniper tree and is woken by an angel. "And as he lay and slept under a juniper tree, behold, then an angel touched him, and said unto him, Arise and eat. And he looked, and, behold, there was a cake baken on the coals, and a cruse of water at his head. And he did eat and drink, and laid him down again."[54]

In the Islamic tradition Ilyas (Elijah) is identified with al-khidr, "the Green One," a legendary figure endowed with immortal life, who became a popular saint, especially among sailors and Sufis. The cycle of myths and stories surrounding al-khidr originate in a vague narrative, concerning an unnamed figure, in the Koran.[55] Arab commentators elaborated and embellished the Koranic story and named the "man of God," Khidr, claiming that he turned green as he dived into the spring of life, though variant interpretations identify Khidr with the vegetable world. Khidr's immortality and ability to assume a variety of local characteristics probably account for his widespread popularity among Arabs, Turks, Iranians, and other Muslims, despite orthodox Islamic opposition.[56] According to Franz Rosenthal the green color of hashish enabled it to claim the famous al-khidr, "the green one," as its patron saint, and amongst the many nicknames for hashish recorded by Muslim commentators, used among Sufi sheikhs, was a "visit from the green khidr."[57] According to Muslim tradition al-khidr was the companion-sage of Alexander the Great.[58] Alexander came from Macedonia, where Euripides wrote his *Bacchae* and *Euripides,* andmay have derived his accounts of the Dionysian rites from observations made while in Macedonia. Walter Otto, in his classic mythographic study of Dionysus,[59] remarks that the goat is the creature of Dionysus par excellence. One epithet of Dionysus is "Bacchus Tragephorus," the wearer of the goatskin.[60] The goat, as sacrificial victim, is celebrated in *Euripides* and *Bacchae,* notably in association with milk, animal skins, and sacred fumigants.

> Oh! happy that votary, when from the hurrying revel-rout he sinks to earth, in his holy robe of fawnskin, chasing the goat to drink its blood, a banquet sweet of flesh uncooked, as he hastens to Phrygia's or to Libya's hills; while in the van the Bromian god (Dionysus) exults with cries of Evoe! With milk and wine and streams of luscious honey flows the earth, and Syrian incense smokes.

The Kalash, like the Dionysian revelers, illuminate their nocturnal festivities with blazing pine branches, and in Morocco the Aissawa Sufi brotherhoods preserve ancient rites that may draw on the Dionysian ritual, as diffused through Hellenistic North Africa.[61] In their trance states the Aissawa tear apart sheep and eat their raw flesh.[62] This is, as far as I know, the only case of ritual omphagia, the ritual consumption of raw flesh, other than the similar practices of the Kalash, recorded in modern times. Omphagia is a term most closely associated with savage behavior of the Bacchantes, the followers of Dionysus in ancient Greek mythology. While they were under the god's inspiration, the Bacchantes were believed to possess occult powers, the ability to charm snakes and suckle animals, as well as preternatural strength that enabled them to tear living victims to pieces before indulging in their ritual feast of raw animal flesh.[63] The Aissawa are said to derive their ability to disembowel animals, with a gesture of their bare hands and at a distance, from a plant that also has alchemical powers.[64]

This plant must be picked in summer once the earth has "died," while digging around its root to the rising of the "Zohal" (Saturn). The hole must be large, not to wound the plant at the moment one withdraws it from earth. While digging, it is necessary to recite the following incantation: "I abjure you, oh terrifying plant, and harvest you under the auspices of the beneficent minds and God's holy names, the Expeditious, the Very Near, the One that always answers our invocations."[65]

The precautions described in its harvesting are reminiscent of those associated with the mandrake. However, with the kind help of Dr. Jamal Bellakhdar, I have identified this plant from its Arabic name as an aconite, Aconitum lycoctonum, whose common name is wolfsbane.[66] While the aconites appear as ingredients of witch's flying ointments, their presence is something of a mystery as they are very poisonous and without obvious psychoactivity. Their presence almost certainly means that their action was somehow complementary to the effects of henbane and other psychoactive ingredients.[67]

Of Goats, Goat-Men, and Goat-Songs

Walter Otto, in his investigation into the mythography of Dionysus, includes an ancient anecdote, in which the properties of the vine were discovered on the return of a giddy goat that had been browsing on vine leaves. It is supposedly a goat's regular departure from the herd and its later returns in the best of spirits that made Staphylus, the herdsman of Oineus, aware of the power of the vine.[68] Since vine leaves are not intoxicating in themselves, might this tale have been assimilated from a tradition concerning goats intoxicated by some other plant? Might there also be a clue here, in intoxicated animals, to the omophagia of the followers of Dionysus, the tearing apart of living animals and the consumption of raw animal flesh? Is this omphagia merely some ritual atavism, valued for its regressive authenticity and related to the ancestral hunt? If so, what is the meaning of the implicit spiritual dimension in the ritual omphagia of the Dionysians and the Aissawa? These questions led me to speculate on whether the flesh, blood, or even milk of ruminants foraging on entheogenic plants might itself be psychoactive and whether it might have functioned not only as a as a conduit for narcotics, but led to the discovery of the psychoactive properties of some plants. Might this be an explanation, in addition to their vital role in providing food and clothing in hunting and herding communities, for the ritual significance of goats, goat meat, and goatskins?

Those engaged in entheogenic studies have speculated that the discovery of the psychoactive properties of certain plants was accomplished through human observation of animal behavior.[69] Giorgio Samorini, in his recent study of the use by animals of psychoactives,[70] has confirmed such speculations through his personal ethnographic researches in West Africa and the observations of naturalists. When discussing the psychoactive potency of urine containing *Amanita muscaria* alkaloids and its use by man, Samorini comments: "It would seem that the Siberian peoples discovered its inebriating properties by observing the behavior of the reindeer. Anytime these creatures scent fungus-rich urine in the vicinity they make a mad dash for it."[71] According to Samorini we learned to observe these animal uses of healing plants for our own drug discovery and this may be how we developed most of our medical repertoire.[72] Samorini also recounts how local people in West Africa claim to have discovered the psychoactive properties of *Alchornea floribunda* and *Tabernanthe iboga*[73] by observing their use by gorillas and wild boars.[74]

Of all the creatures whose use of plant drugs Samorini describes, he singles out goats as enjoying "absolute supremacy in the animal world as far as their passion for disparate drugs is concerned."[75] A parallel tradition to that of Oineus, the goat, and the discovery of the properties of the vine referred to above, exists in Ethiopian and Arab legends concerning the discovery of the properties of the coffee berry by a goat herd, who is alerted by the frisky behavior of his herd to its stimulating properties.[76]

The anthropologists Jean-Yves Loude and Viviane Lièvre recorded not only the shamanic use of juniper as a psychoactive intoxicant amongst the Kalash of the Hindu Kush, but the antics of their goat-man. In Birir, the southernmost Kalash valley, it is said that in former times the return of the (goat) herdsmen gave rise to curious and disturbing events. During the last night of the harvest festival a herdsman, who had concealed his identity, took part in the dances disguised as a goat. His face was covered with flowers, and only his eyes were visible. He wore a pair of horns, and, as he passed among the women, he did his best to frighten them by charging them and touching them with his horns—those symbolic attributes—in an effort to impregnate them. The dance circle resounded to deep-throated "ho, ho, ho," mixed with the frightened cries of the girls.[77]

The Kalash goat-man's cry of "ho ho ho" might seem incongruous with its immediate echoes of our European figure of Santa Claus. However, Santa's cry of "ho ho ho" harks back to his earlier more sinister and ambiguous incarnations, when as "the devil's bluster" it heralded the appearance of figures dressed in animal skins or foliage participating in or leading the wild hunt, the revel rout.[78] The anthropologist Debra Denker recognized the echoes of

European seasonal figures in Kalash festivals: "Rolled woollen caps are decked with sprigs of holly oak and juniper, with feathers and beads. Baraman, a venerable old man with a strong-featured face is in the lead, his green and gold coat glittering in the sun. His dignity and bearing remind me unaccountably of the ghost of Christmas present."[79]

Kalash shamans show various traits in common with the wildman and other figures associated with the European revel-rout; namely, the wearing of bells, sexual displays, the wielding of a branch or sprig of a tree or bush, frightening women and children with pretended menace, and the distribution of nuts or other similar gifts.

At every spring festival, every morning of the fortnight of the holiday (the shaman) went through the village, brandishing bells without ringing them, banging them against each other, fanning them with a sprig of juniper. Thus he pursued the children with a feinted ferocity, throwing them nuts (a symbol of fertility), and come night, he deposited the bells and juniper on the threshold of the house elected by the supernatural entities to sacrifice for the pleasure of the gods.[80]

The figures, often masked, who feature in this kind of saturnalian pageant, which are associated with the protection of the fertility of animals, humankind, and crops, go back to prehistory. Figures similarly dressed in cave paintings are now interpreted as shamanic figures dressed in animal skins, associated with hunting magic.

Phyllis Seifker has contributed an important study of the figure of wildman, her term for the figures dressed in animal skins or foliage that take part in the revel-rout or wild hunt. Seifker shows that core elements of these traditions, while changing and evolving through the centuries, remain in place to this day throughout Europe, as well as being carried to the communities of the New World by European emigrants. Saint Nicolas and a helper figure called Black Peter are muted versions of the earlier wilder masquerading figures of the revel-rout associated with the solstice or equinoctial festivals.[81] One related European tradition, that of the "benandanti" of the Italian in Middle Ages, has been explored by Carlo Ginzburg.[82] In this case groups of young men, who took part in supernatural battles to protect their crops, carried the thyrsus, the herbalist's fennel stalk of the Bacchantes, the followers of Dionysus. Later Ginzburg further developed his initial researches and explored the evidence for a hidden shamanistic culture that flourished throughout Eurasia for thousands of years, and its persistence into the Middle Ages, including the likely role played within it by psychoactive plant drugs.[83] Ginzburg explores a number of motifs that link European folk traditions, classical mythology, and shamanism, including sacred animal skins. These themes show continuity between ancient Indo-European shamanism and the traditions of the classical world.

That the Greek word for their theatrical tragedies, *tragoidia,* derives from *tragos* goat and *oidos* singer is undisputed. However, whether the connection between goats and song is present in *tragoidia* because the original chorus was dressed in goatskins or because the songs originally accompanied the sacrifice of a goat to Dionysus remains a matter of debate.[84] Regardless, the association establishes the likelihood that Greek tragedy and its themes derive from religious ritual drama, whose origins recede into prehistoric shamanism. Walter Burkert hypothesizes that the *tragoidoi,* the goat singers, "were originally a troop of masked men who have to perform the sacrifice of the *tragos* that falls due in Spring; they perform with lamentation, song, and mumming, and in the end they may feast on the goat. Seriousness and fun may have interpenetrated in a curious way."[85] This description matches perfectly later incarnations of the revel rout, with its characteristic mixture of humor and menace. Jack Lindsay, in his study of the origins of tragedy, links modern Greek Christmas traditions and masqueraders in goat-man guise with the origins of tragedy in Dionysian rites.[86] He refers to an element of continuity over the millennia of "immemorial peasant guisings and mimings" in which "the persistence of goat costumes is striking." Burkert picks up on the ambiguity we have noted elsewhere in association with these rites, between the role of the sacrificer and victim.[87] He concludes that the tradition of the goat sacrifice "leads back to the depths of prehistoric human development, as well as to the center of tragedy."

Of the Besom, the Balsam, and the *Barsom*

Walter Burkert points out the likely extreme antiquity of use the branches of vegetation in ritual, extending probably to protohuman usage.[88] Uses would include the construction, clearing, and decoration of the sacred space, as a processional emblem, also for controlling those crowding round the sacred space, as well as for fumigation, and ritual beatings. The wildman and his companions in the revel-rout traditionally carry a primitive club with leaves still attached, obviously once a crude branch, or alternatively a bundle of sticks or leaves called a "besom." The word besom derives from the Old English *besema* or *besma,* meaning a bundle of twigs used as a broom or a flail.[89] The simplest form of broom or flail for threshing is simply a suitable shrub uprooted or a branch torn from a tree, thus "brush" and "scrub" as terms for stubby undergrowth suited for use as brush or scrubber. It is likely the wildman's club or besom originated, in part, in the ritual use of branches of sacred vegetation. Traditional European Christmas figures, Saint Nicholas and his helper Black Peter are still depicted holding the besom. According to tradition, it was the witchs' besom that enabled her to fly at her nocturnal meetings.[90] The Oxford Dictionary of Etymology regards the ultimate origin of the word *besom* as unknown.

Although various possible Indo-European (hereafter IE) roots for besom have been suggested,[91] a Semitic loan word carried into Indo-European seems possible, where ancient Hebrew *basam* and *boseme* carry the sense "sweet smelling" and denote balsamic plants or trees[92] and the etymology of balsam yields Syriac *besma,*[93] identical with Old English *besma* referred to above; balsam being an aromatic, usually oily or resinous substance flowing from various plants, or a preparation thereof, especially as used in medicine or as incense. According to Ethel Drower, who made a detailed study of Middle Eastern sacramental rites, the fragrant bundle of twigs that features in Zoroastrian ritual, variously rendered from the Avestan as *baresman, baresma* (Middle Persian *barsom*), is philologically related to "balsam."[94] The Greek *balsamon,* from which we derive the modern English balsam, is regarded as borrowing from one or another Semitic forms such as *basam* referred to above,[95] which, as well as having the general meaning of spices or perfume, probably denotes the balsam tree or plant itself.[96]

Mary Boyce dates the use of the *barsom* as a "recurrent device" from the Achaemenid period (550 to 330 BCE). According to Zoroastrian scriptures, there appear originally to have been two roles for the *barsom*. First, one where it is strewn, which may accord with Vedic rituals in which a bed of vegetation is constructed as a seat for the deity.[97] Secondly, that which is still in evidence in Zoroastrian liturgical practices today, where as a bundle of twigs it is held by the priest performing the haoma ritual. Various authorities have identified *barsom* with Vedic *barhis,* grasses heaped up as a seat for the gods attendant at a sacrificial ritual.[98] However, though *barsom* is frequently referred to in Zoroastrian scriptures as being "strewn," nowhere is it referred to as forming a "seat" for deity; and the connection between the roles of strewn *barsom* and that in which it is held in the hand of the officiating priest remain unclear.[99] The IE root invoked in connection with *barhis* is *bhars-/bhares-,* from which are derived words associated with being sharp or pointed, reflected in the modern English words "barb" or "beard."[100]

Also derived from the IE root *bhar-* is barley, which is intimately associated with the production of the Vedic soma, which is regularly described, in the Vedic scriptures, as an admixture.[101] Quite probably, given early European forms of "barley" such as *bere* (Old English) and *barr* (Old Norse), modern English "*beer*" shares a common etymology, given that barley malt is the usual source of beer.[102]

An etymological clue to the function of *barsom,* which appears to have eluded authorities to date, lies in the Albanian word *bar,* which means "grass" and "herb," as well as "medicine," "remedy," or "drug."[103] This calls to mind the fact that Arabic hashish means simply "grass," a fact duplicated in modern epithets for cannabis such as "herb," "weed," and "grass." In fact *bar-* is a prefix in a great many Albanian plant names, including many medicinal herbs[104] and in some Gaelic plant names.[105]

The identification of *bar* as referring to grass, herb, or medicine is important for two reasons. First, because Albanian is an IE language that is relatively close to its ancient roots, and can be traced directly to the ancient Illyrian or the Albanian peoples.[106] Second, because it may identify *barsom* as an entheogenic plant such as the *haoma* with which it is so closely associated. Tailleu suggests that barsom may simply be IE *bar-* (= grass, etc.) with the suffix -man/-men common to ritual objects, thus "sacred grass."[107] The importance of *barsom* and its intimate association with *haoma* is clear in Zoroastrian texts. For instance:

> We worship Mithra of wide cattle pastures with haoma-containing milk and baresman twigs, with skill of tongue and magic word, with speech and action and libations, and with correctly uttered words.[108]

Carved reliefs from the Sassanian period (224–633 CE) show the *barsom* being brandished like the Roman *fasces*, the insignia of official authority and penal power in ancient Rome. The *fasces* was carried by the lectors, or attendants, and was characterized by an axe head projecting from a bundle of elm or birch rods,[109] tied together with a red strap, representing punishment by flogging.[110] While I am not aware of any reason to directly connect the *fasces* and the *barsom* it remains a curiosity that both the *fasces* and the *besom* are regularly and independently described as "a bundle of rods" and are held as a symbol of authority. According to Eric Partridge, *fascis* is "probably akin to L *fascinus,* var. *fascinum,* a "magical spell," this being the root of "fascinate," in the sense of exerting a hypnotic or supernatural influence over someone,[111] which may return us to magical herbage. Clement Huart's study of ancient Iranian culture states that the *baresman* was used in ordeal. "The ordeal was frequently employed in cases of doubt to prove the guilt or innocence of an accused man. It was effected either by means of the sacred bundle of twigs used in religion (*baresma*) or by the fire."[112] Unfortunately, in this otherwise impeccably referenced work Huart does not give a source for this account. However, he is almost certainly referring to the Rashnu

Yasht (Yasht 12). "Then I shall come to you, I who am Ahura Mazda, to this instituted ordeal, to the fire and the *baresman,* to the full, overflowing (bowl of water), to the boiling ordeal—ghee and the vegetable oil."[113]

Both Dionysian rites and the antics of the participants of the revel-route of the wildman contain intimations of the ritual beating or flogging of sacrificial victims, initiates and those who have offended the community or even unwary spectators. One epithet for Dionysus is Bacchus *Narthecophorus,* "the one who carries the birch (narthex)."[114] Walter F. Otto, in a definitive study of Dionysus, describes the treatment of the *pharmakos,* the sacrificial victim, the scapegoat, whose death ensured fertility or cleansed the community.

> The chosen one was beaten with branches, as if he were being blessed, and he was led round to the music of the flute. As we are explicitly told once, he was clad in holy garments and wreathed with sacred plants. Previously he had been fed at public expense on especially pure foods.[115]

Rudolf Otto refers to evidence of ritual beatings associated with Dionysian festivals, as recorded by Pausinius.[116] Thus it appears that ritual beating with foliage might be a kind of blessing, a punishment by the members of the revel-rout, or precede being driven from the community, or being a sacrificial victim. Seifker's study of shamanistic traditions associated with the figure of the wildman refers to the continuation of "beating as blessing" or "prophylactic stimulation" into modern European culture.[117] The traditional Finnish sauna is not complete without a mutual and invigorating beating with birch stems that release fragrant oils. Such practices, in association with the steam bath, may relate to more ancient Eurasian bonding or initiation practices along the lines of the Native American "sweat lodge."

Some of the ambiguities in the characteristic representations of the wildman previously discussed are present in the North African figure of Bujlud. In North Africa there is a masquerade called *Bilmawn,* which takes place after the Great Sacrifice that follows

Ramadan, a month of fasting in the Muslim calendar. Local people dress up as a variety of characters with much in common with similar masquerades in Europe. One character in this masquerade is a goat-man called *Bujlud.* The word *Bujlud* is Arabic and means "man dressed in skins."

Bujlud indeed wears sheep or goatskins taken from victims that were sacrificed on the first day of the *Aid,* which are placed on his naked body.[118] The skin covering his arms is arranged so that the hooves dangle below his hands. His face, blackened with soot or powder, is hidden beneath an old goatskin container once used to churn butter, which he wears as a mask. His head is adorned with the horns of a cow or with a sheep's head. Sometimes his head or shoulders are covered with greenery. Powerful male attributes complete the outfit of the hideous character Bujlud.[119]

Bujlud exhibits a variety of the characteristics of the wildman; dressed in skins and greenery, he has exaggerated sexual characteristics, and chases and frightens the women and children. Armed with a stick, he threatens to beat those he catches but his touch is believed to be healing.

The more threatening aspects of earlier Saint Nicholas, wildman traditions involved the threat of a beating for children who had failed in their religious observations/learning their scriptures, as well as reward of gifts of nuts for those who had been good. The besom carried by the wildman, as well as being a broom or flail, could also mean a scourge for administering punishment.[120]

The wild hunt was the Bacchanalian revel-rout, whose participants are dressed in animal skins or foliage, and the ancient association of ritual intoxication with goats, sacrificial goat flesh, and people dressed in goat or other animal skins. The eating of raw sacrificial flesh and the close association of milk and soma/haoma and the intimate association of goats with the discovery of psychoactive plant drugs and the use of psychoactive fumigants, together with the carrying of sacred branches and the giving or receiving beatings with sacred vegetation. Vulgar sexual displays, exchanging (sexual) insults, and the mocking mummery of established religious ceremony and the temporary inversion of normal social values, the carrying of pine torches and the burning of sacred fumigants—all these are repeated thematic motifs recurring throughout Eurasian shamanic traditions.[121] Pondering these observations, a number of questions arise:

- Do plant phytochemicals turn up in the milk or flesh of ruminants?

- If phytochemicals turn up in ruminant's milk or flesh, do they retain their psychoactivity, and are there any records of milk or flesh of ruminants being known to cause intoxication in man?

- Are psychoactive plants used as forage by ruminants, either accidentally or deliberately as selected by man or animal?

- Is there any ethnographic, mythographic, or scriptural evidence in support of humans exploiting the properties of psychoactive milk or flesh?

I set out below the results of my investigations into these questions.

Do Plant Phytochemicals Turn Up in Milk or Flesh of Ruminants?

Emily of Wazan records in her autobiography that, in Algeria, the flesh of sheep that have fed upon wormwood is regarded as particularly well flavored and that large quantities of the fat so flavored can be eaten without injury.[122] Significant in this connection is the fact that Zoroastrian scriptures record that haoma was made with the fat of the sacrificial bull and that the haoma ceremony is intimately associated with the ritual sacrifice of bulls.[123]

Concerning artemisia, the wormwoods, Allen H. Godbey attests that, as they are almost the only fuel on the plains of North Syria, "wilderness wanderers from time immemorial have thus had clinical experience of their qualities."[124] Juniper holds a similar position amongst the Kalash as the only reliable fuel or forage available in the mountains of Hindu Kush.[125] Godbey draws on the accounts of a variety of nineteenth-century travelers and adventurers, who observed the effects of artemesia on men and animals. According to Godbey, the Bedouins used the gums of milder wormwoods for their stimulating or cordial properties, putting them in milk, curds, and *mereesy* (beer). The stimulating dose may be made very strong. Camels and goats eat the artemisia plants, and the milk is often made bitter because of this.[126] From this one may reasonably assume the degree of bitterness promises an equivalent degree of psychoactive potential.

In the Scriptural account of Zoroaster's conception, in which it plays an intimate part, haoma is clearly associated with the balsamic exudate of a tree.

> The haoma was constantly provided with a mouth, where it was suitable, and sap constantly oozed from the haoma where it was moist. And that haoma was connected with that tree; and on the summit of that tree, there where the nest of the birds was, it grew constantly fresh and golden-colored.[127]

Ambiguities in the description of haoma as plant, as tree, as something oozing from a tree or maybe growing in tree, may reflect not only the use of various substitutes over a period of time, but the use of a variety of different plants for the production of haoma.[128] This particular reference to haoma is profoundly suggestive of mistletoe. The verse, at least in translation, appears to refer to haoma as something growing in a tree, which sounds like mistletoe, based on several points[129]:

> 1. "The haoma was constantly provided with a mouth, where it was suitable, and sap constantly oozed from the haoma where it was moist." When the boughs of trees such as juniper or pine are affected by mistletoe and the dense spindly outgrowths called "witches brooms" that its presence provokes, they become especially resinous. A possible connection between these "witches' brooms" and the witchs' *besom* and the *baresman* must

be considered. In parts of Switzerland mistletoe, or perhaps the spindly outgrowths associated with it, are referred to as "thunder besom," because of their association with thunderstruck trees.[130]

2. "… haoma was connected with that tree." According to the description, the haoma was not part of the tree itself. Mistletoe grows as a parasitic outgrowth of a large variety of trees including, in connection with the themes explored in this paper, pine, cedar, and juniper in the Middle East. See also point 3.

3. "There where the nest of the birds was, it grew." Many birds feed on mistletoe and use the mistletoe or "witches' brooms" as cover or nests. The scripture further reveals "that Hom was also seen by (Zoroaster's father), when it had grown on that tree, on the inside of the nest."[131]

4. "It grew constantly fresh and golden-colored." Many mistletoes are golden in color and they grow throughout the year, causing them to become prominent when deciduous trees lose their leaves in winter or when evergreen trees lose their foliage due to the presence of the mistletoe.

5. Zoroaster's father declares "as there is no reaching by me up to that Hom, that tree must be cut down," indicating that the Hom grows high up in the tree, as mistletoe characteristically does.

Given mistletoe's possible psychoactivity, its prominent place in Indo-European folklore, and its connection with winter solstice celebrations, this tentative identification can't be ruled out. According to a line in Webster's seventeenth-century play *The White Devil*, "We seldom find the mistletoe, sacred to physic … without a mandrake by it."[132] Other investigators have suggested an association between mistletoe and the fly agaric mushroom.[133] Mistletoe is itself identified with the wood of the cross and is known as *Lignum Sanctae Crucis*, Wood of the Sacred Cross.[134] Quinn, in her exploration of the cycle of tales concerning Seth and the Tree of Life/Tree of the Cross, discusses the significance of the motif of a child/god/bird that appears in the Tree of Life, and she connects this with the figure of a dwarf beneath the Tree.[135] I wondered prior to speculating regarding a possible relation between haoma and mistletoe whether this might relate to a psychoactive fungus growing in a tree.[136] Note that the bird in the Tree of Life is identified in Middle Eastern folklore with the *phoenix, simurgh,* or *homa* bird, which is the symbol of IranAir.[137] A connection between the *homa* bird and haoma might seem tenuous were there no previous informed speculation on a possible connection.[138] In Zoroastrian cosmology haoma grows in the world tree in which dwells the Simurgh. Could mistletoe be the "nest of the simurgh"?[139]

> Where phytochemicals turn up in ruminant's milk or flesh, do they retain their psychoactivity? If so, are there any records of milk or flesh of ruminants being known to cause intoxication in man?

An eighteenth-century traveler in the Middle East records that "goats eat some shrub in such quantities that anyone who drinks the milk is made giddy by it."[140] The fact that phytochemicals from forage can turn up in the milk of ruminants is actually well recognized in veterinary science. For example, according to guidance issued by University of Kentucky College of Agriculture concerning White Snakeroot (*Eupatorium rugosum*), a poisonous alcohol is present in its leaves and stems. This toxic principle, tremolo, may be transmitted through the milk of poisoned cows to humans, causing the disease known as "milk sickness" or "trembles."[141] The same report confirms that although hemp is not ordinarily eaten by animals, it may be consumed in sufficient quantity to cause narcotic poisoning.[142] Cattle that become habituated to the intoxicating properties, or certain psychoactive forage plants termed "locoweeds," can pass the taste for these plants on to their offspring through their milk.[143]

The Nightshade family, Solanaceae, contains many plants used for food, including the potato and eggplant. Some solanaceous plants are moderately toxic if ingested in high concentrations. The most toxic of this family is the deadly nightshade, *Atropa belladonna.* Some grazing animals, such as rabbits, may eat the plant and berries without experiencing any effects, having developed a tolerance to their toxicity, while humans who eat the meat of these animals can suffer fatal results.[144]

Peter Lamborn Wilson, in his intriguing study *Ploughing the Clouds: The Search for the Irish Soma,*[145] describes the way in which such motifs of the soma ritual as a cow sacrifice have survived in Irish folklore and attached themselves to the figure of a late-medieval poet named Cearbhall O'Dálaigh. A folktale describes the magical initiation of this fourteenth-century bard:

One day he saw a cloud descend into a clump of rushes and a brindle[146] cow went and ate the rushes. When he told this in the evening, he was instructed to bring the first milk of that cow to his master. Cearbhall did diligently as he was told, but a drop of the milk spilled onto his finger, and thus he got the first taste of it. Immediately a great change came over him. His face became lustrous, and every word he spoke was in verse. Realizing that the boy had got the drink he intended for himself, the farmer ordered him to leave that place, and henceforth Cearbhall was a roving poet. Because of his first tasting the milk, he had not only genius at poetry, but also many kinds of magical powers.[147]

Where Wilson relates this imagery to the Vedic metaphor of soma as cow, we must ask ourselves at this point—could soma once have been the milk of a cow browsing on psychoactive vegetation? As Peter Lamborn Wilson points out, the *su* root of soma, meaning "pressed," whose currently accepted derivation is "that which is pressed," turns up in the Irish *súg* meaning "juice."[148] That which is "pressed" could have the connotation "that which is "squeezed out of an udder." Latin *sumen,* contracted from *sugmen,* means breast or udder. Thus also Latin *sudor* sweat and *sucus* juice, from which we have English "suck," "ex(s)ude" and so on. The Indo-European root *seu* carryies the senses of sap, juice, something dripping.[149] Least this seems a bridge too far, consider two observations made by the Vedic scholar Rajesh Kochhar. First, that soma, as with Cearbhall's drink of milk, is credited with granting poetic inspiration—it "enables the poetic drinker to compose a hymn, therefore soma is very frequently called a Kavi "poet"'; second, that "the process of juice extraction is called 'milking' in the Rgveda." The difficulty of explaining this allusion is emphasized by Kochhar's suggestion that this is "no doubt owing to the resemblance between the stalks and the cows teats."[150] The medieval Armenian epic "David of Sasun" is full of Mithraic imagery and contains references to soma-drinking and mushrooms. It refers to Mher's (Mithra's) "Milk Fountain of Immortality," and one hero has to "pass a test involving drinking huge amounts of 'milk,'" in a tale replete with many other indicators for the use of psychoactive substances.[151]

For Peter Lamborn Wilson the fact that the Celts are Indo-European peoples is sufficient explanation for allied traditions. According to Kochar, however, "soma/haoma was not known to the Indo-Europeans."[152] This is not the opinion, though, of Calvert Watkins, the renowned Indo-European scholar who discusses the various mixtures of honey, grains, and spices that appear in Greek literature and notes the parallels between the accounts of the Greek beverages and the soma ritual. His conclusion is that there was "a single Indo-European liturgical cultic practice" that gave rise to the Vedic and the Indo-Iranian soma ritual, to the act of communion of the Eleusinian mysteries, all involving a mixed potion.[153] The magical poetic initiation of Cearbhall O'Dálaigh , in fact , bears some extraordinary similarities to the scriptural account of Zoroaster's conception.

The Zoroastrian scripture the Denkard records that by the agency of two Zoroastrian Archangels, the nature of Zoroaster, transported via cloud-water, enters into vegetation that is eaten then by two cows and is mingled with the cows' milk. Zoroaster's father prepares haoma supplied from the tree that oozed resin, referred to previously. He mixes it with the milk from the cows and he and his wife drink it. It appears that the mixture is responsible for their desire to make love and thus Zoroaster is conceived. Though it appears that Zoroaster's bodily nature is conveyed via the cow's milk and it is haoma that supplies his guardian spirit, the entire process is immensely suggestive in the context of my speculative inquiry. Something of supernatural origin is transmitted into vegetation and from that vegetation into the cow's milk. That milk is mixed with haoma and the mixture is drunk. The mixture inspires erotic union whereby Zoroaster is conceived. His parents hear the voices of demons and afterward feel ashamed, but their union nonetheless is the source of the righteous Zoroaster, haoma incarnate.[154]

Are Psychoactive Plants Used as Forage Accidentally or Deliberately, as Selected by Man or Animal?

Cannabis is certainly fed as forage to cattle in Nepal,[155] where according to Mia Touw the sheer abundance of cannabis in the Tibeto-Himalayan region would encourage extensive use.[156] When F. Kingdon Ward[157] traveled through Tibet in the early part of this century, he frequently mentioned the large plantings of hemp close to villages.[158]According to Samorini, cannabis growers must "contend with animals greedy for their harvest. In the Hawaiian Islands, cows and horses must be guarded against, as they are particularly partial to the flowers of the plant. After browsing on them, these animals walk with a rolling gait, swaying gait. In Eastern Europe, lambs break into hemp fields, browse on the plants, and become 'merry and mad.'[159] In Poland the leaves of hemp together with leaves of calamus were given to cows if they were off their feed."[160] Another culturally important, though less well known, psychoactive plant, *khat* or *qat*, is also popular with goats.[161] The cultivation of *qat* is widespread in Ethiopia and the Yemen. Kevin Rushby, in his fascinating account of a journey from Ethiopia to the Yemen, in the footsteps of Sir Richard Burton, mixes accounts of contemporary *qat* culture with historical anecdotes and quotes widely on associations between *qat* and Sufism both in its uses, distribution, and origins.[162] According to Rushby the Yemeni saint Ahmed ibn Alwan is credited in legend with using *qat* in his meditations and prayers, the drug lifting him and his followers on their path to religious ecstasy. One sixteenth-century Yemeni mystic, Abdullah ibn Shariaf al-Din, declared, "I have made *qat* my way up." According to Al Biruni[163], the eleventh-century Persian scholar and scientist and one of the most learned men of his age, in one of the earliest references to *qat*, states it comes from Turkestan. Despite the fact that *qat* usage seems to have spread from Ethiopia in North Africa to Yemen in the Arabian Peninsula, in relatively recent historical terms,[164] suggesting an African origin, we must consider Al Biruni's suggestion a genuine possibility.[165]

Rushby quotes the Lebanese Christian writer Ameen Rihani on the role of *qat* in Sufi mysticism: [166]

> Even the Sufi poet descends from his starry heights to crown its "emerald leaves" with mystic rhymes. Here are two, which I am able to render into a tolerably English accent:

The winged horse of my heart, my spirit feeds and on it rides up to celestial meads.

> The winged horse, he calls Buraq, the steed of the prophet Mohammed: his heart is a ladder; and his ecstatic spirit is the angel Gabriel. Now, imagine the said angel riding upon Buraq—Ghat (*qat*)—and galloping up to the highest heaven, and you will get an idea of the poet's fancy.[167]

Given the intimate association between psychoactive fumigants and libations, it is not without significance when Rushby reports that, in one *qat* session in which he took part, a woman insists he waft a few drafts from a censer into his lungs. This suggests that parallel use of psychoactive plants as both fumigant and by mouth, as attested in the case of the Kalash with juniper, may well be an ancient tradition and practice.[168]

Is There Any Ethnographic, Mythographic, or Scriptural Evidence in Support of Humans Deliberately Exploiting the Properties of Psychoactive Milk or Flesh?

In his book *Soma: Divine Mushroom of Immortality,* R. Gordon Wasson, the father of ethnomycological studies, appends a selection of records by explorers, travelers, and anthropologists of the use of the fly agaric (*Amanita muscaria*) in Siberia. One of these comes from Adolph Erman, a nineteenth-century explorer. His native companions tell him about the fly agaric mushroom.

> Mukmor (the fly agaric), they said, was much rarer in Kamchatka and the Koryaks had only learned about its properties because the meat of reindeer which had eaten it had an effect that was as intoxicating as the mushroom itself.[169]

Professor Franco Fabbro, in a paper concerning possible use of *Amanita muscaria* by the early Christians, considers evidence from a mosaic in a third-century church depicting snails together with mushrooms. Fabbro speculates that the snails may have been fed on psychoactive mushrooms, before themselves being consumed in a ritual context. According to Fabbro, "the Romans were particularly familiar with snail-breeding techniques, knowing that the way they fed these animals determined their taste and postprandial effects."[170]

Since the consumption of *Amanita muscaria* may cause gastroenteric symptoms (e.g. nausea, vomiting, abdominal pain), most probably these complications were avoided with simple precautions: Instead of directly eating the mushrooms, it was good practice to first feed snails with these mushrooms for several days and then eat the snails. By doing so, the active hallucinogenic substances contained in *Amanita muscaria* could be ingested without having nasty gastroenteric side effects.[171]

This same principal may well have applied in the case of mountain goats or deer having browsed on juniper or mistletoe growing on juniper, or other terpene containing trees. Deer, goats, and other ruminants are fond of grazing on mistletoe, which provides fodder in the seasonal absence of other foliage. The chemical content of mistletoe varies according to that of the host that it parasitizes.[172]

The use of juniper as a psychoactive fumigant is intimately associated in the Hindu Kush with the goat sacrifice. In a description of the initiation process of the Danyal (shaman) in the Hindu Kush, the candidate first places his face over the hot coals above their on plate and starts inhaling the white smoke of dried juniper leaves for about five to ten minutes, then after a few rounds of dance he starts singing songs in which he tells about the departure of the spirits from the upper world to the human world. In his songs, he tells details of a spirit-journey from the upper world to the ceremony. The master Danyal listens to the candidate's songs carefully. Then the dramatic part of the ceremony is reached, when the candidate sings the song that his Makhakher Aji (spirit mother) has given him, with milk and blood in two horns of an ibex (a wild mountain goat).

After hearing this song, the master Danyal gives signal to the people for slaughtering the green goat[173] given by the mother's brother of the candidate for this ceremony. When the candidate smells the perfume of blood he runs from the circle to behind the gathering and tries to drink the blood of the slaughtered animal.[174]

Eventually the candidate falls unconscious whereupon he goes in a deep sleep for the whole day and night, when he wakes up he acquires a new status of a complete Danyal. A thread dipped in the goat's blood and scat is placed on his wrist, which suggests that what the goat has eaten is of significance. Goats and deer[175] certainly do browse on juniper, particularly where mountain scrub offers a limited choice of forage. The non-palatability of juniper foliage due to the presence of essential oils is overcome by hunger.[176] Goats eat more juniper and can better tolerate the toxicity of the essential oils it contains than other ruminants.[177] As it is likely the flesh of goats browsing on juniper is significantly infused with the psychoactive components of the plant,[178] this may explain their sacrifice and consumption in association with juniper as a psychoactive fumigant. If the Dionysian tradition of *omphagia* is connected with psychoactive animal flesh, the eating of meat raw may be explained by the necessity of eating the meat quickly to get the maximum effect. Wasson records that Erman's native informants explained to him:

> Wild reindeer that have eaten (fly agaric) are often found so stupefied that they can be tied with ropes and taken away alive; their meat then intoxicates everyone who eats it, but only if the reindeer is killed soon after being caught; and it appears that the communicability of the narcotic substance last about as long as it would have affected the animal's own nerves. [179]

The psychoactive properties of the flesh of stupefied animals may have been discovered through the ease of their capture.

Of Goats and the Tree of Life

Dr. Victor Sarianidi has investigated temple complexes in Turkmenistan dating from around 2000 BCE, at or around the time of the migration of the Indo-Aryans from Central Asia to the Iranian plateau and the Indus valley. In these temple complexes he found rooms apparently dedicated to the preparation of psychoactive brews for consumption in a ritual context.[180] Analysis of vessels from these rooms yielded evidence of the use of the opium poppy, cannabis, ephedra, and wormwood. In a note on Goats and the Tree of Life, Sarianidi states that on "the seals and amulets [found at sites in Turkmenistan] there are commonly depicted such antithetic [sic] compositions as a pair of goats flanking a centrally located tree, this being a common design on the pottery of Margiana." In images from Elam (in southwestern Iran) sometimes a poppy replaces the tree. "There are parallel compositions of a mountain with a tree, the only difference is that in Elam the tree is flanked by goats while in Margiana the goats are replaced by snakes standing on their tails." Snakes are a motif frequently associated with psychoactive plants, through the association of poisonous plants and venomous creatures, which were thought to derive their venom from eating poisonous herbage.[181] That the Tree of Life is substituted in some cases by the frankly psychoactive poppy, implies a psychoactive role for the Tree of Life, in this context.

Sugary tree resins may actually ferment on the bough and thereby intoxicate creatures that feed upon them. Dumont, in an important study of the role of the Ash as the world tree,[182] explores the link between sweet tree resins, used in brewing, and a tree of life that exudes mead. He does not, however, explore the psychoactivity of the bitter resins of cedar, pine, juniper, or their foliage. Dumont's study does, though, return us to the question of the role of goats, when he refers to the infant Zeus being suckled by one.[183] Present are the now-familiar motifs of caves, honey, milk, and the food of the gods. The *ambrosia* that Zeus takes from the goat, the food of the gods of Greek myth, is cognate with and etymologically related to the Hindu *amrita,* effectively the haoma/soma of the Indo-Europeans.[184] Dumont sees a parallel between the goat Amalthea and the goat Heiðrun of the Norse Eddas:

> The goat Amalthea recalls the goat Heiðrun of Norse mythology, which bites stalks off the branches of the world ash tree and then yields mead from its udders into large jars for the enjoyment of those feasting in Valhalla.[185]

The original reference to the goat Heiðrun in the Prose Edda is intriguing and draws this investigation towards its conclusion.

Gangleri (Odin) asked: "What do the Einherjar[186] have to drink in as much abundance as their food? Is water drunk here?" Then the High One said: "That is a queer question to ask now—whether All-father who invites kings and earls and other men of rank gives them water to drink! It is my belief that many a one coming to Valhalla would think a drink of water deadly paid for, if no better entertainment were to be found—and the enduring wounds and smarting to death. I can tell you a very different story about that place. A goat called Heiðrun stands up on its hind legs in Valhalla biting the buds off the branches of that very famous tree which is called Laerad. From her teats runs the mead with which every day she fills a cauldron, which is so big that all the Einjar can drink their fill from it." Gangleri said: "What an exceedingly convenient goat for them. It must be a mighty good tree she feeds on!"[187]

According to Helmut Baumann, the prophet Melampes,[188] reputed to understand the speech of all creatures, as a priest of Apollo decided to halt the spread of the cult of Dionysus among women. For this purpose he procured goat's milk from a goat that had eaten hellebore (*Helleborus cyclophylus),* and this instantly sobered them.[189] In Pliny's original account:

> Melampus is well known for his skill in the arts of divination. From him one kind of hellebore is called melampodion. Some

> hold that the discovery is due to a shepherd called Melampus, who noticed that his she-goats were purged after browsing upon the plant, and by administering the milk of these goats cured the daughters of Proteus of their madness.[190]

According to Herodotus it was Melampus who introduced the Dionysian arts to Greece.[191] Perhaps he knew both how to induce madness, divine or otherwise, as well as how to cure it.

Concerning the Bull of the Priestess of Enodia and the Bull Dream of the Druids

Walter Burkert, in his Transformations of the Scapegoat, [192] includes an account from the second-century collection of anecdotes on the ruses of war, the Stratagems of Polyaenus, a Macedonian Greek writer.

When the Ionians came to colonize Asia, Cnopus, from the family of Codrus, made war against those who held Erythrae.[193] The gods gave him an oracle that he should get the priestess of Enodia[194] from Thessaly as, his general. And he sent an embassy to Thessaly and informed them about the oracle; they sent him Chrysame, the priestess of the goddess; she was an expert in drugs. She took the biggest and finest bull from the herd, had his horns gilded and his body adorned with fillets and purple cloths stitched with gold; and she mixed into his food a drug that provokes madness, and made him eat it. The drug drove the bull mad, and would drive mad also whoever ate from him. Now the enemy was encamped on the opposite side. The priestess set up an altar and implements of sacrifice in full view of the enemy, and gave order to lead the bull along. But the bull, driven mad by the drug and filled with frenzy, made a sally and fled toward the enemy, bellowing loudly. The enemy, when they saw the bull with gilded horns, adorned with fillets, hurrying from the sacrifice of the adversaries toward their own camp, took this to be a good sign and an omen of good fate; they seized him, sacrificed him to the gods, and eagerly ate his meat, each of them, as if partaking of a demonic or divine sacrament. At once the whole army rose in a state of madness and insanity; they jumped up, ran hither and thither, began to dance, left their posts. When Chrysame saw this, she told Cnopus to call his army to arms at once and to lead them against their enemies, who were unable to defend themselves. And thus Cnopous killed them and became master of Erythrae, a big and prosperous city.

However apocryphal this tale, concerning the Ionian capture of Erythrae circa 1000 BCE, might appear on face value, it contains motifs that extend and develop the emerging picture of the use of psychoactive flesh. While it is impossible for the flesh of one bull to intoxicate an entire army, this account confirms ancient knowledge of the psychoactivity of the flesh of animals that have eaten entheogenic plant materials. Moreover, the feeding of the animal with psychoactive vegetable material takes place in a ritual sacrificial setting. The victims of the subsequent intoxication eat the meat "as if partaking of a demonic or divine sacrament." The results of eating this meat are not fatal in themselves, rather causing them to jump up, run hither and thither and dance. This behavior reminds one of the Bacchantes, the intoxicated followers of Dionysus. While the account in Polyaenus is one of the uses of this potency of psychoactive flesh as a stratagem of war, the account strongly suggests that this route of intoxication and its effects were a feature of sacrificial ritual. The only difference being that, in this case, the consumers of the psychoactive material are unaware of the potency of what they eat and that they are taken advantage of in their state of intoxication.[195]

A further account of the use of psychoactive bull's flesh has been recorded amongst the Celts, who are ultimately of Indo-European origin, and whose religious leaders, the Druids, have been repeatedly linked to the Brahmins, the priestly cast of the Vedas.[196]

One of the most interesting examples of trance is in an account of the choosing of a new king at Tara, when a bull was killed and a Druid gorged on its flesh. The Druid fell into a trance while incantations were recited over him, and on recovery he was able to prognosticate the distinguishing circumstances of the rightful claimant's approach to Tara. This rite was known as *tarbfeis,* "bull dream."[197]

According to Powells, "Frenzy, trance, and shape-shifting, all point to some generic connection between the Celtic magician, of whatever name, and the shaman of the North Eurasiatic zone. It is not at all unlikely that this aspect remounts to the early period of contacts over the Pontic steppes." The Pontic steppes border Northern Iran and this account of the *tarbfeis* has significant structural elements in common with the Zoroastrian tale of Arda Wiraz.[198] These are: (1) An individual is selected for the purposes of divining the answer to a question of great importance to the community. (2) He is put into a drugged sleep watched over by priests who chant over him. (3) On his return he is able to provide the answer to the community's question. Despite these common factors the link might be tenuous, were it not for R. C. Zaehner's account of the intimate association of haoma with the bull sacrifice. Zaehner informs us that, as in the Vedic preparation of soma: "The Zoroastrians too mix the haoma with milk, but we cannot be certain that this was the original, for the word for 'milk' (gaoman) may originally have meant 'ox-flesh,' which is how the Pahlavi translators understood it."[199] In Zaehner's reconstruction of the haoma rite, "in its original form there must have been a ritual immolation of a sacred bull or cow as well as the ritual pounding of the haoma plant. Both the sacrificial flesh and the haoma juice must have been consumed by the sacrificial priests. The flesh and haoma appear to have been mixed." According to Pliny the Druids sacrificed oxen in association with gathering mistletoe. They (the Druids) call the mistletoe by a name meaning "the all healing." Having made preparation for sacrifice and a banquet beneath the trees, they bring thither two white bulls, whose horns are bound then for the first time. Clad in a white robe, the priest ascends the tree and cuts the mistletoe with a golden sickle, and it is received by others in a white cloak. They then kill the victims, praying that God will render this gift of his propitious to those to whom he has granted it. They believe that the mistletoe, taken in drink, imparts fertility to barren animals, and that it is an antidote for all poisons.

Given that the Celts are an Indo-European people,[200] it is not surprising that the Druids have been persistently linked with the

Brahmins and the Magi, by both by the ancients and by modern Indo-European scholars.[201] Both Pliny and Hippolytus class the Druids and the Magi together. According to Pliny: "Even today Britain is spellbound by magic, and performs its rites with so much ritual that she might almost seem to be the source of Persian customs."[202] I am suggesting, of course, that the flow may have been in the other direction.

Conclusion

From the ethnographic, scriptural, and mythographic records and the observations of naturalists it appears likely that:

- The psychoactive properties of various plants were discovered anciently by human observation of the effects of plant drugs on animal behavior.

- The psychoactive properties of plants were sometimes also discovered through the consumption of milk or flesh of animals that had foraged on psychoactive plants.

- The first two points may be a partial explanation for the motif of the Tree of Life flanked by goats or deer and explain the prominence of goats in the rituals of various religious groups employing psychoactive plants.

- Ritual *omphagia* may have been established through the eating of the raw flesh of animals that had grazed on or had been fed psychoactive plants. This ritual may have been established because the plant was otherwise unpalatable, because this route mitigated its toxicity, or because the plant's psychoactivity was originally discovered in this way. In addition, it might be necessary to consume the flesh raw to preserve or maximize its psychoactive potency.

- Priests (covertly?) dosed animals with psychoactive plants prior to using their milk or flesh in sacrificial rituals, as well as mixing psychoactive substances with meat or milk, before dispensing them to the congregation. Chrysame, the priestess of Enodia, and the prophet Melampus both certainly knew this trick.

References

1. Young, Jean I., trans. "The Prose Edda of Snorri Sturluson." 1954. *Tales from Norse Mythology.* Cambridge, United Kingdom: Bowes & Bowes.

2. Samorini, G. 2002. *Animals and Psychedelics. The Natural World and the Instinct to Alter Consciousness.* Rochester, VT: Park Street Press.

3. There are various debates in the authoritative Islamic traditions, the hadith, concerning the significance of his choice.

4. On psychoactive honeys see Ott, J. 1997. *Pharmacotheon.* Kennewick, WA: Natural Products Company. The intoxicating effect of honeys, produced from certain flowers, is well attested in both the classical and modern periods. For example the account in Xenophon's Anabasis: "When they began running in that way, the enemy stood their ground no longer, but betook themselves to flight, one in one direction, one in another, and the Hellenes scaled the hill and found quarters in numerous villages which contained supplies in abundance.

   "Here, generally speaking, there was nothing to excite their wonderment, but the numbers of beehives were indeed astonishing, and so were certain properties of the honey. The effect upon the soldiers who tasted the combs was that they all went for the nonce quite off their heads, and suffered from vomiting and diarrhoea, with a total inability to stand steady on their legs. A small dose produced a condition not unlike violent drunkenness, a large one an attack very like a fit of madness, and some dropped down, apparently at death's door. So they lay, hundreds of them, as if there had been a great defeat, a prey to the cruellest despondency. But the next day, none had died; and almost at the same hour of the day at which they had eaten they recovered their senses, and on the third or fourth day got on their legs again like convalescents after a severe course of medical treatment."

From H.G. Dakyns' series, *The Works of Xenophon*, Anabasis 4:8. Which includes the note: "Modern travellers attest the existence, in these regions, of honey intoxicating and poisonous.... They point out the Azalea Pontica as the flower from which the bees imbibe this peculiar quality." Grote, *History of Greece*, Vol. ix. p.155. The events reported by Xenophon took place in the Pontic region South of the Caspian Sea. Time and again the references in this paper return us to the Pontus and adjoining regions beneath and between and adjoining the Black and Caspian Seas, Turkey, the Caucasus, Iran and Turkmenistan.

According to David Bedrosian: "Greek mythology provides some information on eastern Asia Minor and the Caucasus in the eighth-century BCE. The myths concerning (this region) are early reflections of the enduring image of the area as a place of magic/medicine/drugs. This reputation was based on the rich flora and fauna of the area. The naturalist V. Hehn, *Cultivated Plants and Domesticated Animals in their Migration from Asia to Europe* (1885), suggested that both the vine and cannabis, among a number of other plants, may have originated in or close to the area of our interest. Hehn calls Pontus 'the fatherland of poisons and antidotes.'" David Bedrosian, notes to Soma among the Armenians: www.rbedrosian.com/soma.htm. The origins of the goat and its earliest domestication are also traced to this area.

5. *Rig Veda*, Book IX, Hymn 86, v45.

6. Sama Veda, Book7, ch.3, Verse 17.

7. Yasna 10: 13.

8. Strabo, Bk. XV, ch. III, 14.

9. *Euripides, Bacchae,* lines 184–195.

10. *Hymn to Demeter*. Translated by Hugh G. Evelyn-White, Loeb Classical Library.

11. *Hymn to Demeter*. Translated by Hugh G. Evelyn-White, Loeb Classical Library.

12. Hatch, E. 1957. *The Influence of Greek Ideas on Christianity.* New York: Harper and Brothers.

13. This opposition may reflect adherence of certain cultural groups to psychoactive sacraments other than alcohol.

14. Godbey, A. 1930. "Incense and Poison Ordeals in the Ancient Orient," *The American Journal of Semitic languages and literatures,* Vol. XLVI, No. 4, July.

15. See, for example, Gonda, J., *Soma's Metamorphoses.* New York: North Holland Publishing Company, 1983, p. 15. "The names of Agni and Soma are so to say interchangeable." Note 48, "In the oldest parts of the Veda Agni and Soma have much in common." For extensive discussions of ambiguities concerning *haoma* as libation and a fire sacrifice, see Flattery, D. and M. Schwartz, 1989, *Haoma and Harmaline: The Botanical Identity of the Sacred Hallucinogen "Soma."* Berkeley, CA: University of California Press.

16. The Hindu Kush is one of the great watersheds of Central Asia, forming part of the vast Alpine zone that stretches across Eurasia from east to west. It runs from the Indus River where the borders of China, Kashmir, and Afghanistan meet, then Southwest through Pakistan and into Afghanistan.

17. The common name juniper refers to any of about 60 to 70 species of aromatic evergreen trees or shrubs constituting the genus *Juniperus* of the cypress family (*Cupressaceae*), distributed throughout the Northern Hemisphere. The juniper used by the Kalash is *Juniperus macropoda* (alt. excelsa).

18. 'If the smoke of juniper turns out to be valued for its stimulating qualities, another practice concerning this plant definitely confirms the recognition of its intoxicating properties by the peoples of Hindu Kush/Karakoram. Amongst the Kalash, as in the Gilgit, in quite recent past, the shamans ate leaves of juniper, sometimes first soaked in water (or blood): The dehar (shaman) Naga ate Juniper. "In trance, the dehar ate Juniper branches as thick as an arm!" attests Kasi Khoshnawas. (Various other shamans) ate

foliage of juniper, (some) solely during the feast of the Winter Solstice. No one else tried for fear of going mad. Concerning dehar Tanuk, the information proves to be ambiguous. Some say that he actually ate juniper soaked in water as well as the fragrant forage plants, named *namer,* (rhododendron?), Others affirm that he didn't fall in trance unless he ate juniper. . . Dehar Sindi, in ancient times, ate some branches (five) of *namer* at each of his trances after having ingested juniper (fifteen berries). The gods had commanded it of him. It helped him to make a 'good job' of it.' Lièvre, V. and J. Loude. 1990. *Le Chamanisme des Kalash du Pakistan.* Des montagnards polythéistes face à l'islam, CNRS Editions.

19. Lièvre, V. and J. Loude. 1988. *Kalash Solstice: The Winter Feasts of the Kalash of North Pakistan.* Islamabad, Pakistan: Lok Virsa.

20. "In Kafir mythology, Indra the ancient god himself planted the juniper in his garden in Wama, a plant that he brought back from meadows of the high mountain called Surmeiis." (Author's note: The Kalash and other hill tribes unconverted to Islam are commonly referred to as Kafirs, that is, "unbelievers"). "The Veda assures that to drink Soma procured a sort of intoxication which the gods—and especially Indra—were sensitive, as are men. In the same way, the Kafirs assign the revelation of the juniper to Indra, the plant whose smoke procures the drunkenness of the men and whose perfume 'pleases the gods.'" Lièvre, V. and J. Loude.1990. *Le Chamanisme des Kalash du Pakistan.* Des montagnards polythéistes face à l'islam, CNRS Editions.

21. Further: "Sindi, his son, returned to him, brought back a kid, performed an act of purification at the coffin of his father and went home. Katsata, a man 'who had mixed with the fairies' was buried with a twig of juniper in his turban. For seven days his coffin moved and the seventh day, a juniper pushed out of it and grew in the cemetery. Today, the tree, which was never cut, grows among the abandoned coffins at Birir." Lièvre, V. and Loude, J. 1990. *Le Chamanisme des Kalash du Pakistan.* Des montagnards polythéistes face à l'islam, CNRS Editions.

22. Quinn, E. 1962. *The Quest of Seth for the Oil of Life.* Chicago, IL: University of Chicago Press.

23. It seems highly likely to the author that this tradition is the source of the "Green Man" images present in Churches throughout Europe, which feature foliage growing out of the mouth, and sometimes nose and eyes of a human face. Despite the immense amount that has been written about the Green Man in recent years, I have found no other satisfactory explanation for this strange image.

24. In this connection note the Christian tradition that Christ was "hanged on a tree." Acts 5: 30 and Acts 10: 39, King James Bible.

25. Quinn, E. 1962. *The Quest of Seth for the Oil of Life.* Chicago, IL: University of Chicago Press, p.91.

26. Quinn, E. 1962. *The Quest of Seth for the Oil of Life.* Chicago, IL: University of Chicago Press, p. 156, note 15.

27. See note 94 below.

28. A class of hydrocarbons occurring widely in flora and fauna (largely through consuming plant material) and abundant in the essential oils of plants. The Cannabinols and Salvinorin are allied to the terpenes, as are the oils in Catnip, *Nepeta cataria,* that so stimulate and intoxicate cats.

29. Melikof, I. 2001. *La Montagne et L'Arbre Sacré de Hadji Bejtasch in Au banquet de Quarante: Exploration au Coeur du Bektachisme-Alevisme.* Istanbul: Les Editions Isis.

30. Godbey, A. 1930. "Incense and Poison Ordeals in the Ancient Orient," *The American Journal of Semitic languages and literatures,* Vol. XLVI, No. 4, July.

31. "The other mode of producing temporary inspiration, to which I shall here refer, consists in the use of a sacred tree or plant. Thus in the Hindoo Koosh a fire is kindled with twigs of the sacred cedar; and the Dainyal or sibyl, with a cloth over her head, inhales the thick pungent smoke till she is seized with convulsions and falls senseless to the ground. Soon she rises and raises a shrill chant, which is caught up and loudly repeated by her audience. So Apollo's prophetess ate the sacred laurel and was fumigated

with it before she prophesied. The Bacchanals ate ivy, and their inspired fury was by some believed to be due to the exciting and intoxicating properties of the plant" (Frazer, G. 1922. *The Golden Bough,* chap. VII., "Incarnate Human Gods").

32. "I tried chewing the leaves (of juniper). But the very bitter and resinous taste is barely tolerable for the uninitiated, even with a very small quantity. To confirm if the smoke of juniper has a narcotic effect, I tried to inhale the smoke of the nilo-chili (juniper). Inhaling was painful and only successful after several attempts. My view of the contents of the room was disturbed. When I closed my eyes, I had the feeling of being projected forward or upwards. I nodded my head as I had seen done by the *daiyal* in trance, and the feeling of being projected upwards intensified. A certain fear seized me, because every sound was intensified. As my fear increased and became uncontrollable, I interrupted the experience." (Adam Nayyar in his 1986 study on the Astor valley to the Southeast of Gilgit. In Lièvre and Loude 1990.)

33. Funk, W. 1978. *Word Origins: An Exploration and History of Words and Language,* New York: Wings Books.

34. Many other coniferous trees are known as "cedars" that resemble true cedars in being evergreen and in having aromatic, often red or red-tinged wood that in many cases is decay-resistant and insect-repellent; oils distilled from the wood are used in perfumery. See entries under Arbovitae and Cedar, *Encyclopædia Britannica.*

35. "Absinthe." *Encyclopædia Britannica.* Encyclopædia Britannica Online, 2012, Web. 29 Sep. www.britannica.com/EBchecked/topic/1731/absinthe.

36. *Artemisia maritima* also typically grows at similar heights as *Juniper macropoda* in the mountainous regions of Pakistan. Velle, K. 1998. *High Altitude Integrated Natural Resource Management.* Report no. 4: Natural forest inventory, Aga Khan Rural Support Programme Baltistan and Agricultural University of Norway.

37. Allen, T. 1964. *The Encyclopedia of Pure Materia Medica : A Record of the Positive Effects of Drugs upon the Healthy Human Organism.* Ridgewood, NJ: Gregg Press.

38. Godbey, A. 1930. "Incense and Poison Ordeals in the Ancient Orient," *The American Journal of Semitic languages and literatures*, Vol. XLVI, No. 4, July. Dioscorides mentions various wormwoods as being effective as a vermifuge, one of which was reported as growing in the country of the Santones in Gaul the name Santonin being derived from this classical association. See Grieve, M. 1971. *A Modern Herbal.* New York: Dover Publications.

39. Plutarch. 1926. *Lives,* Volume XI, Loeb Classical Library, Cambridge, MA: Harvard University Press.

40. David Flattery comments on this episode noting that: 'Among the situations where *sauma* seems most likely to have been used was at the inauguration of pre-Islamic rule. A reflection of the initiation of kings with *sauma* may be preserved in Plutarch's *Life of Artaxerxes.* Flattery and Schwartz, op. cit. p.98, note 4. David Flattery does not elaborate, but from the overall context, within his study, one must assume that his primary point of reference would be the sour milk as a preparation of *haoma.* Flattery also notes, (p.65, note 31), that the burning of juniper is associated with daeva-worshippers in the Avesta and that it is burned apotropaically in the Hindu Kush and that its burning with *hom* (=ephedra?) was recorded in Khorasan in the nineteenth-century. One might also note, in the context of this paper, that the word *tragein* used here, from the Greek verb *trogo* to chew, gnaw or nibble, is related to the Greek for "he-goat," *tragos,* meaning effectively the "nibbler."

41. Lièvre and Loude 1990.

42. *Archaeology,* Vol. 49 No.5 Sept./Oct., 1996.

43. Herodotus. 1996. *The Histories.* Book Four, pp. 73–75. New York: Penguin. Confirmed by modern discovery of such devices in frozen tombs from that area.

44. According to Plutarch, Mithra was born by the banks of the Araxes. *De fluviis,* 23: 4. The modern river Aras (Araxes), originates in Turkey and flows through Armenia before continuing along the shared border of Iran and Azerbaijan. The entire basin occupies the greater part of the South Caucasus.

45. Herodotus. 1996. *The Histories.* Book One, p. 202. New York: Penguin. One may only speculate as to the identity of this tree. Hedwig Schleiffer, places this text under the daturas. See Schleiffer, H. 1979. *Narcotic Plants of the Old World.* Montecello, NY: Lubrecht & Cramer LT.

46. The Caucasus lie to the north of eastern Turkey and western Iran between the Caspian and Black Seas.

47. Klaproth, J. 1823. *Voyage au Mont Caucase et en Géorgie.* Paris: Librairie de C. Gosselin.

48. There is little or no artifactual evidence for the familiar tobacco type of pipe in Eurasia prior to the introduction of tobacco. Opium was first smoked as an admixture to tobacco through soaking the tobacco in an opium wash, the development of the opium pipe for smoking pure opium came later. See Laufer, B. 1924. "Tobacco and its Use in Asia," *Anthropology Leaflet 18,* Chicago Field Museum of Natural History. This is not to say that straws or hollow bones might have been used to draw up psychoactive smoke or other ad hoc mechanisms used, such as earth pipes, (drawing off smoke from a fire in a small hollow in the ground), that would leave little or no artifactual evidence. On earth pipes see Laufer, B. Hambly, W., and Linton, R. 1930. "Tobacco and its use in Africa," *Anthropology Leaflet 29,* Chicago Field Museum of Natural History. On evidence for other possible ancient smoking implements see Merlin, M. 1984. *On the Trail of the Ancient Opium Poppy.* Cranbury, NJ: Associated University Press.

49. "As to the antiquity and genesis of such practices it is to be recognised, that they began when the primeval savage discovered that the smoke of his cavern sometimes produced queer physiological effects. First reverencing these moods of his fire, he was not long in discovering that they were only manifested when certain weeds or sticks were included in his stock of fuel. After finding out which ones were responsible, he took to praying to these kind gods for more beautiful visions of the unseen world, or for more fervid inspiration." (Godbey, A. 1930. "Incense and Poison Ordeals in the Ancient Orient," *The American Journal of Semitic languages and literatures,* Vol. XLVI, No.4, July.)

50. For cannabis in the Bible, see Benet, S. 1975. "Early Diffusion and Folk Uses of Hemp." In *Cannabis and Culture,* edited by V. Rubin. The Hague: Mouton Publishers. See also Rhode, E. 1966. *Psyche: The Cult of Souls and Belief in Immortality among the Greeks.* New York: Harper and Row. "The ancients were quite familiar with the practice of inhaling aromatic smoke to produce religious hallucinations," p.273, followed by references to classical authorities.

51. Clark, W. 2012. "Drug Cult." *Encyclopædia Britannica.* Encyclopædia Britannica Online, www.britannica.com/EBchecked/topic/172013/drug-cult.

52. The common name of *Rhododendron caucasicum* is the Snow Rose and it is marketed in the health food trade as Alpine Tea for its antioxidant properties. However, few species of Rhododendron are considered safe for human or animal consumption. Some rhododendrons contain grayanotoxins, which are amongst the common agents responsible for "mad honey," toxic honey due to bees collecting nectar from the flowers of certain plant species. Mad honey is recorded in literature of the ancient world, including its use as an early example of chemical warfare, where it was laid as a trap to disable an unwary approaching enemy. Maud Grieve's exhaustive and definitive Modern Herbal lists *Rhododendron chrysanthum,* giving the common name of this plant as the Snow Rose, habitat the mountains of Siberia, much used in Siberia as a remedy for rheumatism. She adds that the leaves contain a stimulant narcotic principle, which they yield to water or alcohol. In the Hindu Kush where the smoke of juniper is inhaled for shamanic purposes, as well as its leaves being eaten, the possible use of rhododendron species in conjunction with juniper has been recorded. See Lièvre, V. and J. Loude. 1990. *Le Chamanisme des Kalash du Pakistan.* Editions du CNS, pg. 495. Further information on the possible psychoactivity of Rhododendron species may be found in the journal, *Eleusis: Journal of Psychoactive Plants and Compounds,* No. 6, Dec., 1996.

53. Klaproth, J. 1823. *Voyage au Mont Caucase et en Georgie,* Paris , Vol. 1, pgs. 253–255. Author's translation.

54. 1 Kings 19, King James Bible.

55. Koran (18: 60–82).

56. "Al-Khidr." 2012. *Encyclopædia Britannica Online.* www.britannica.com/EBchecked/topic/316616/al-Khidr.

57. Rosenthal, F. 1971. *The Herb: Hashish versus Medieval Muslim Society.* Leiden: Brill.

58. Knappert, J. 1993. *The Encyclopaedia of Middle Eastern Mythology and Religion.* Rockport, MA: Element.

59. Otto, W. 1995. *Dionysus Myth and Cult.* Bloomington, IN: Indiana University Press.

60. "A goat-skin is often seen covering the god, particularly during orgiastic festivities." Cabello, F. 1997. *Notes on the Mythology of Wine.* London: Avon Books.

61. The *ghaytaoboe* becomes the Aissawa trademark as the ritual dancing leads into trance. "Even though a common feature of military orchestras in past centuries, its particular status within the fraternity hints at much older origins, preceding Islam, in the Dionysiacs of Antiquity." From notes by Christian Poche accompanying the CD, The Aissawa Confraternity, OCORA 1275.

62. Brunel, R. 1926. *Essai sur la confrérie religieuse des Aissaouas au Maroc.* Librarie Orientaliste, Paris: Paul Geuthner.

63. "Dionysus." 2012. *Encyclopædia Britannica Online.* www.britannica.com/EBchecked/topic/164280/Dionysus

64. The Aissawa, described as a Sufi brotherhood, also entertain audiences with feats such as eating glass and holding hot coals in their mouth. Throughout the world such feats are, of course, considered demonstrations of supernatural powers and religious devotion.

65. Brunel, R. 1926. *Essai sur la confrérie religieuse des Aissaouas au Maroc.* Librarie Orientaliste, Paris: Paul Geuthner.

66. Personal correspondence. See also Bellakhdar, J. 1997. *La pharmacopée marocaine traditionnelle: médecine arabe ancienne et savoirs populaires.* Paris: Ibis Press.

67. Although they might function as a crude deliriant, they are highly poisonous. They may have been included to sedate or induce

muscular paralysis while under the influence of other plants. Aconites are actually widely used throughout Eurasia as medicines, by those with knowledge of how to prepare and dose them, as well as being a favoured poison throughout the ancient world. See Bellakhdar, J. 1997. *La pharmacopée marocaine traditionnelle: médecine arabe ancienne et savoirs populaires.* Paris: Ibis Press.

68. Probus on Verg. Georg 1.9. See Otto, W. 1995. *Dionysus Myth and Cult.* Bloomington, IN: Indiana University Press.

69. "The pastoral herders of animals in the lonely mountains would, of course, be precisely the people who would note the marvellous appearance and properties of the god's entheogens, and its effects on the flocks that might graze upon it." See Jason, the Drug Man in: Heinrich, C., Ruck, C., and Staples, B. 2000. *The Apples of Apollo: Pagan and Christian Mysteries of the Eucharist.* Durham, NC: Carolina Academic Press.

70. Samorini, G. 2002. *Animals and Psychedelics. The Natural World and the Instinct to Alter Consciousness.* Rochester, VT: Park Street Press.

71. Samorini, G. 2002. *Animals and Psychedelics. The Natural World and the Instinct to Alter Consciousness.* Rochester, VT: Park Street Press. A case of *do* eat the yellow snow?

72. 'There are countless cases in which the psychoactive properties of certain plants have been discovered by human beings through observation of animal behaviour. For instance, in one origin tale from the New Hebrides, a man watches again and again as a rat gnaws on the root of the kava, dies, and later returns to life. Finally the man decides to test the effects of the root on himself and in so doing instigates the people's use of kava.' Samorini, G. 2002. *Animals and Psychedelics. The Natural World and the Instinct to Alter Consciousness.* Rochester, VT: Park Street Press.

73. Ibogaine, the hallucinogenic drug and the Samorini principal iboga alkaloid, is found in the stems, leaves, and especially in the roots of the African shrub *Tabernanthe iboga.* Ibogaine was isolated from the plant in 1901 and was synthesized in 1966. In small doses it acts as a stimulant. The peoples of West Africa and the Congo region have used iboga extracts or chewed the root of the plant in order to remain calm but alert while stalking game.

Chemically, ibogaine is an indole hallucinogen. In larger doses it is used as a potent initiatic ritual hallucinogen. "Ibogaine." 2012. *Encyclopædia Britannica* Online. www.britannica.com/EBchecked/topic/280882/ibogaine

74. "In the forests of Gabon and the Congo, natives relate that they long ago noticed wild boars digging up and eating the hallucinogenic roots of the iboga bush. In consequence, the boars became frenzied, leaping in every direction, displaying inexplicable fear reactions and suffering hallucinations. Porcupines and gorillas also intentionally feed on iboga for its effects. It was by observing and imitating these animals that natives deduced, and then experienced, the visionary properties of the plant.' www.britannica.com/EBchecked/topic/280882/ibogaine 75 Samorini, G. op.cit.

76. See, for example, "The Puzzled Boy and His Mad Goats," in Mark Prendergast, M. 2000. *Uncommon Grounds: The History of Coffee*. New York: Basic Books.

77. Loude J. and V. Lièvre. 1988. *Kalash Solstice: The Winter Feasts of the Kalash of North Pakistan*. Islamabad, Pakistan: Lok Virsa.

78. These are seasonal festivities, widespread throughout Europe until the early twentieth-century, in which groups of men decked out in animal skins, foliage or latterly patchwork and tatters, adorned with bells, often sporting artificial phalli—the original motley crew—paraded or ran through the community, inspiring sometimes laughter, sometimes terror with their bawdy and occasionally violent antics. Mean-spirited members of the community were liable to find their properties trashed. Winter solstice festivals often feature the inversion of normal social values, social superiors may be obliged to cook and serve their inferiors, as is the custom in the British army at Christmas. It may also be an opportunity to insult or assault others who have offended you at some other time, with relative impunity. Kalash men and women exchange good-humoured sexual insults at such times. See Seifker, P. 1997. *Santa Claus, Last of the Wild Men: the Origins and Evolution of Saint Nicholas, Spanning 50, 000 Years*. Jefferson, NC: McFarland.

79. Denker, D. 1981. "Pakistan's Kalash. People of Fire and Fervour," National Geographic, Oct.

80. Loude J. and V. Lièvre. 1988. *Kalash Solstice: The Winter Feasts of the Kalash of North Pakistan.* Islamabad, Pakistan: Lok Virsa.

81. See Seifker, P. 1997. *Santa Claus, Last of the Wild Men: The Origins and Evolution of Saint Nicholas, Spanning 50,000 Years.* Jefferson, NC: McFarland, and the equally fascinating book by Tony Van Renterghem. 1995. *When Santa Was a Shaman: The Ancient Origins of Santa Claus and the Christmas Tree.* St. Paul, MN: Llewellyn Publications.

82. Ginzburg, C. 1992. *The Night Battles: Witchcraft and Agrarian Cults in the Sixteenth and Seventeenth Centuries.* Baltimore, MD: John Hopkins University Press.

83. Ginzburg, C. 1991. *Ecstasies: Deciphering the Witches' Sabbath.* New York : Random House.

84. Funk, W. 1978. *Word Origins: An Exploration and History of Words and Language,* New York: Wings Books.

85. Burkert, W. 2001. "Greek Tragedy and Sacrificial Ritual." In Burkert, W. 2001. *Savage Energies,* Ch. 1, "Greek Tragedy and Sacrificial Ritual", Chicago, University of Chicago Press.

86. Lindsay, J. 1965. *The Clashing Rocks: A Study of Early Greek Religion and Culture.* London: Chapman & Hall.

87. Ibid. "Sacrificer and victim are so correlated as to be nearly identified."

88. Burkert, W. 1982. *Structure and History in Greek Mythology and Ritual.* Berkeley, CA:University of California Press.

89 Old High German *besmo, besamo* from Proto-Germanic **besmon.* Modern German *besen = broom.* Barnhart, R., ed., 1988. Bronx, NY: H. W. Wilson Co.

90. The precise significance of this is elusive. One suggestion, unlikely in my opinion, is that the broom-handle was used to apply flying ointment to the vaginal lips, whence it was absorbed. This appears to be an attempt to combine the notion that the witch actually

rode her broom in flight or pranced about with it hobby horse style, between her legs, with the witches known use of flying ointments, containing atropine or scopolamine of plant origin. I suspect there is also some kind of prurient assumption that the activities of a secretive magical sisterhood must involve deviant sexual activity. Regardless, the association of the besom with magical flight reinforces its possible entheogenic significance.

91. Partridge, E. 1959. *Origins. A Short Etymological Dictionary of Modern English.* London: Routledge & Kegan Paul, gives IE *bhes-*. Klein, E. 1971. *A Comprehensive Etymology of the English Language.* Amsterdam: Elsevier Scientific Publishing, gives IE *bheidh* "to bind, twist." But these speculations only account for the initial syllable of "besom."

92. Cheyne, T. and J. Black. 1899–1903. *Encyclopaedia Biblica: a Critical Dictionary of the Literary Political and Religious History the Archaeology, Geography and Natural History of the Bible.* New York and London: Macmillan/Adam and Charles Black.

93. Klein, E. 1971. *A Comprehensive Etymology of the English Language.* Amsterdam: Elsevier Scientific Publishing. In this connection Sula Benet derives cannabis from the Semitic *kanebosm,* composed of the words *kane* or *kene,* meaning 'cane,' and the Semitic root *bosm* or *busma,* meaning 'sweet smelling.' Benet, S. 1975. "Early diffusion and folk uses of Hemp." In *Cannabis and Culture,* V. Rubin (ed.), The Hague: Mouton.

94. Drower, E. 1956. *Water into Wine. A Study of Ritual Idiom in the Middle East.* London: John Murray. See her chapter, "Branch to the Nose." The author of Ezekiel 8: 17 rails against such abominations as the worship of Tammuz or the sun and those who "put the branch to their nose." This is interpreted by most OT authorities as a reference to Zoroastrian practices, where in the Haoma rite the priest holds the barsom in front of his face. The relevant Hebrew word *zemorah,* can actually mean branch, twig, or shoot. Ms Drower's study includes first-hand accounts, recorded in minute detail, of Zoroastrian, Mandean, Jewish, and Eastern Christian sacramental rites.

95. Neither Semitic nor Greek borrowings or influence in Avestan *baresman* are out of the question, because Aramiac was the lingua franca of the Persian Empire in the time of the Achaemenid Kings such as Artaxerxes II (404–359 BCE), whose initiation involved chewing on turpentine wood. Aramaic was gradually supplanted as the lingua franca of the Middle East by the Greek *koine* of the Hellenistic period inaugurated by the conquests of Alexander the Great in the early third-century BCE. *Koine* was the form of Greek spoken and written from the forth-century BCE until the mid-sixth-century CE in Greece, Macedonia, and the parts of Africa and the Middle East that had come under the influence or control of Greeks or Hellenized rulers. *Koine* is the language of the Greek translation of the Old Testament and of the New Testament. The Avestan alphabet used to record the Zoroastrian scriptures was created, for that purpose, in the third-century CE. Many of the letters are derived from Aramaic alphabet, via Pahlavi, Middle Persian. Greek influence is also present in the form of the full representation of vowel sounds. The Avestan alphabet was only replaced by the Arabic alphabet after Persia converted to Islam in the seventh-century CE and Greek loan words are attested in Sanskrit. See for example, "Indo-Aryan Languages." 2003. Encyclopaedia Britannica, 2003. www.britannica.com/EBchecked/topic/286348/Indo-Aryan-languages

96. Cheyne, T. and J. Black. 1899–1903. *Encyclopaedia Biblica: a Critical Dictionary of the Literary Political and Religious History the Archaeology, Geography and Natural History of the Bible.* New York and London: Macmillan /Adam and Charles Black.

97. "The baresman was apparently by origin a handful of herbage on which the sacrifice was laid, and its use goes back (as Brahmanic parallels show) to proto-Indo-Iranian times." Boyce, M. 1992. *Zoroastrianism. Its Antiquity and Constant Vigour.* Costa Mesa, CA: Mazda Publishers, p. 128. Flattery and Schwartz op. cit., reject the Vedic association and the conventional derivation from Vedic *bharis,* grasses strewn to produce a sacrificial bed and argue that barsom was originally the stems of Harmal (*Peganum harmala*), their botanical candidate for Soma/Haoma. They suggest that seed-heads or roots of which have been pounded in a mortar in the production of Haoma and are then casually strewn as a

consequence, thus coinciding with descriptions of barsom being strewn in worship. Their proposed etymology for barsom is a speculative combination of IE root words.

98. See Tailleu, D. 1997. "Baresman." *Acta Orientalia Belgica* X , (1995–96), pp. 165–171.

99. For a summary of the debate on the etymology of barsom and some proposed solutions to the strewn versus held barsom, see Tailleu op. cit. Dr. Tailleu struggles hard to untangle all the textual and etymological ambiguities in his study of Baresman and his observations must be taken into account. Nothing in his study precludes any of my observations and he accepts the possible identification with balsam by Ethel Drower (see note 94).

100. Note Lithuanian *barzd* = beard.

101. Modern English "barley' derives from the *bar-* root form plus *lic* meaning 'like,' thus Middle English barlic = barley. Modern Scottish retains *bar* as barley, see Renton, R. 1994. *Scottish Gaelic-English/English-Scottish Gaelic Dictionary.* New York: Hippocrene Books. In Celtic languages *bar-* words are linked to the harvest, carrying the sense of tip or top, thus Gaelic *bar maith* = good crop. Gaelic also yields *barrach* meaning both a hank of coarse hemp or flax to be used for spinning or weaving, or the top branches of tree, brush wood, or loppings of birch, which may return us to the besom. See, MacLennan, M. 1999. *Gaelic Dictionary.* Breton: Acair & Mercat Press, yields *barr* meaning "branch." Buck, C. 1949. *A Dictionary of Selected Synonyms in the Principal Indo-European Languages.* Chicago: University of Chicago Press. Also related is Latin *far* meaning "spelt," a kind of wheat, whence modern English "farina" for a cereal porridge and "farrago" meaning mixed fodder and so also a hodgepodge.

102. Partridge op. cit., is positive on this point. Commonly proposed is a derivation from Latin *bibere,* "to drink," though this etymology is uncertain.

103. Stefanllari, I. 1996. *Albanian-English: English-Albanian Dictionary.* New York: Hippocrene Books. There may be a connection with the Arabic term *bars* for a psychoactive confection of honey and spices mixed with various psychoactive ingredients such as cannabis,

opium, and Datura used for therapeutic purposes in Iraq from at least the twelfth-century and latterly throughout the Islamic world as a recreational drug. On *bars,* see: Lozano, I. 1998. Solaz del espíritu en el hachís y el vino: y otros textos árabes sobre drogas, Granada, Universidad de Granada 104 *Bar guimi* "slumber grass" = opium poppy, *bar-ethesh* fever grass = centaury, *bar-krend* = mistletoe. (*krënd* = dry thin branches or twigs as tinder also fodder of cut up twigs and leaves). Newmark, L. (ed.). 1999. *Oxford Albanian English Dictionary.* New York: Oxford University Press.

105. *Baraisd* = the herb borage, *bar-brhigeein* = silver weed, *barr-roc* = broad bladed tangle. From MacLennan, M. 1999. *Gaelic Dictionary.* Breton: Acair & Mercat Press, and, MacEachen, E. 1971. *MacEachen's Gaelic-English Dictionary.* Inverness: Highland Printers. The latter also yields *barrach* = branches of birch.

106. Albanian is also a 'satem' rather than 'centum' language, which groups it with Vedic and Avestan rather than the European IE languages The defining feature of these groups is that the word meaning 'one hundred', in Sanskrit (satam) and Avestan (satem), the initial consonant appears as an s-or sh-sound (a sibilant), whereas 'centum' in Latin, and the Greek, Old Irish, Welsh, and English words have a hard k-sound, (which is in some cases converted to h-).

107. Tailleu op. cit., who refers to the notion of power associated with (Proto) Indo-European *-men* formations such as Latin *carmen, numen* and Sanskrit *Brahman.*

108. From the *Khorda Avesta,* "Khwarshed Niyayesh" (Litany to the Sun).

109. Possible etymological connections with the birch and IE *bhars-* cannot be ruled out,where we have Latvian *berzs,* Russian *bereza* and Lithuanian *berzas* for 'birch.' Buck, C. 1949. *A Dictionary of Selected Synonyms in the Principal Indo-European Languages.* Chicago: University of Chicago Press.

110. *Fasces* is simply the plural of *fascis,* L. "a bundle (of sticks)." The word's origin is uncertain, but it is probably related to the modern English "fagot," also meaning a bundle of sticks. Macedonian Greek has *baskioi* "bundle of wood," from the Indo-European root *bhasko-*, from which English "bast" meaning plant-derived

fibres, including those of hemp used, in this case, to tie a bundle, maybe derived. Thus, also possibly, "basket," originally a bundle of goods. See, Klein, E. 1971. *A Comprehensive Etymology of the English Language*. Amsterdam: Elsevier Scientific, and Barnhardt, R. (ed.). 1988. *The Barnhardt Dictionary of Etymology*. New York: W. Wilson.

111. A *fascinum* being a small apotropaic phallic amulet. Partridge, E. 1959. *Origins. A Short Etymological Dictionary of Modern English*. London: Routledge & Kegan Paul. Note that the wearing of magical herbs for their apotropaic powers is a common practice. The original *fascinum* may have been a phallic man-root such as the Mandrake, either natural or carved. Klein op. cit., however, positively refutes a connection between *fasces* and *fascinum*. Shipley, J. 1984. *The Origins of English Words. A Discursive Dictionary of Indo European Roots*. Baltimore, MD: John Hopkins University Press, lists both under the IE root *bhasko-*.

112. Huart, C. 1972. &*Ancient Persia and Iranian Civilisation*. London: Routledge & Kegan Paul.

113. From Malanadra op. cit. Though clearly associated with more familiar means of ordeal, fire and boiling oil, the role of *baresman* in ordeal is unclear. However, it should be noted that psychoactive plants may be employed as entheogens or ordeal poisons according to dosage, and that the division between the two may not be clear cut.

114. "Bacchus is frequently pictured with stalks of this (birch) in his hand." Cabello, F. 1997. *Notes on the Mythology of Wine*. London: Avon Books.

115. Otto, W. 1965. *Dionysus: Myth and Cult*. Bloomington, IN: Indiana University Press, p. 39.

116. "After Stymphalus comes Alea, which too belongs to the Argive federation, and its citizens point to Aleus, the son of Apheidas, as their founder. The sanctuaries of the gods here are those of Ephesian Artemis and Athena Alea, and there is a temple of Dionysus with an image. In honour of Dionysus they celebrate every other year a festival called Sciereia, and at this festival, in obedience to a response from Delphi, women are flogged, just as the Spartan

lads are flogged at the image of the Orthian goddess." Pausinius 8.23.1. Otto, W. 1965. *Dionysus: Myth and Cult.* Bloomington, IN: Indiana University Press, p. 104.

117. The act of striking people, especially children, with sticks was once a common practice during holiday celebrations. In Poland on Dingus Day, the day after Easter, adults beat their children with twigs to aid growth and health. Beating people for luck was common in Germany and the Netherlands. In Swedish homes, the first person to rise from bed on a holiday gave other family members twigs, whereupon they set to beating each other. See Seifker, P. 1997. *Santa Claus, Last of the Wild Men: the Origins and Evolution of Saint Nicholas, Spanning 50, 000 Years.* Jefferson, NC: McFarland.

118. A Muslim festival, pronounced "eed."

119. Hammoudi, A. 1993. *The Victim and Its Masks: An Essay on Sacrifice and Masquerade in the Maghreb.* Chicago, IL: University of Chicago Press, pp.21–23.

120. For *besmen* as "a bundle of rods or twigs for flogging," see Kurath, H. (ed.). *Middle English Dictionary.* Ann Arbor, MI: University of Michigan Press, who quotes from St. Juliana, c. 1200, "ibeaton wið bittere besmen."

121. For a detailed account of a variety of recurrent motifs of Eurasian shamanism see Ginzburg, C. 1991. *Ecstasies: Deciphering the Witches' Sabbath.* New York: Pantheon Books.

122. "Emily, Shareefa Of Wazan, My Life Story, London Edward Arnold, 1911." In Godbey, A. 1930. "Incense and Poison Ordeals in the Ancient Orient," *The American Journal of SemiticLanguages and Literatures,* Vol. XLVI, No. 4, July. She was an Englishwoman who married the ecclesiastical head of Morocco in 1871, and bore him two children while living the lifestyle of a Moorish woman.

123. 'The Saoshyans and his helpers will perform the sacrifice of the raising of the dead, and in that sacrifice the bull Hadayans will be slain, and from the fat of the bull the white Haoma will be prepared, (the drink) of immortality, and it will be given to all men. And all men will become immortal for ever and ever." From the *Greater Bundahishn.* Translation in Zaehner, R. 1956. *The*

Teachings of the Magi. New York: Allen & Unwin. Also see Zaehner, R. 1961. *Dawn and Twilight of Zoroastrianism.* New York: Putnam.

124. Godbey, A. 1930. "Incense and Poison Ordeals in the Ancient Orient," *The American Journal of Semitic languages and literatures*, Vol. XLVI, No. 4, July.

125. "The juniper (*Juniperus excelsa, Juniperus macropoda*), (is) the final resource beyond the coniferous zone at 3500m altitude. The juniper, without which fire would be impossible at these heights and consequently the manufacture of cheese impracticable, keeps its greenery in winter, and thus allows the survival of the Markors and Ibex, (two kinds of wild goat)." Lièvre, V. and J. Loude. 1988. *Kalash Solstice: The Winter Feasts of the Kalash of North Pakistan.* Islamabad, Pakistan: Lok Virsa, p. 50.

126. Godbey, A. 1930. "Incense and Poison Ordeals in the Ancient Orient," *The American Journal of Semitic Languages and Literatures*, Vol. XLVI, No. 4, July.

127. *Denkard,* Book 7, ch. 2, Translated by E. West. (trans.) 1897. In *Sacred Books of the East,* vol. 5, New York: Oxford University Press, p. 128. One account of the ingredients of the libation prepared in the *haoma* ceremony includes "three ingredients, namely milk and the sap or leaves of two plants." Boyce, M. 1979. *The Zoroastrians: Their Religious Beliefs and Practices.* London: Routledge & Kegan Paul, p. 4. Mary Boyce is one of the foremost western scholars of Zoroastrianism and one of the few sources of modern translations of key texts. See, Boyce, M. 1984. *Textual Sources for the Study of Zoroastrianism,* University of Chicago Press. Other sources are, Zaehner, R. 1956. *The Teachings of the Magi: A Compendium of Zoroastrian Beliefs.* London: Allen & Unwin. See also the invaluable translations in Flattery and Schwartz op. cit., and Malandra, W. 1963. *An introduction to Ancient Iranian religion: Readings from the Avesta and Achaemenid Inscriptions.* Minneapolis, MN: University of Minnesota Press.

129. This information was gathered from Hawksworth, F. and Wiens, D. 1996. *Dwarf Mistletoes: Biology, Pathology, and Systematics Agriculture,* United States Department of Agriculture Forest Service, Handbook 709, (technical ed., D. Geils). Hawksworth and Weins include a section on ethnobotanical and medicinal uses

of mistletoe. The presence throughout the Near East, the Balkans, Greece and Western Europe of Dwarf Mistletoes, Arceuthobium, that affect juniper, cypress, pine, and thuya was confirmed by, Cielsa, W. 1997. *Dwarf Mistletoe in Balochistan: A Literature Review,* Forest Health Management," and supported by, Ciesla, W., Geils, B., and Adams, R. 2002. *Hosts and Geographic Distribution of Arceuthobium oxycedri,* United States Department of Agriculture Forest Service, Research Note. Many thanks to Brian Geils for answering my questions and referring me to further research material.

130. See Frazer, J. *The Golden Bough.* New York: Macmillan.

131. West, E. (trans.). 1897. *Denkard,* Book 7, ch.2, Translated by ibid., vol. 5. New York: Oxford University Press.

132. "I met the other day the following passage in the old dramatist Webster's play 'The White Devil': 'We seldom find the mistletoe sacred to physic, or the builder oak, without a mandrake by it.' Is this a piece of forgotten folklore, and is the fact alluded to by any other writer of the period? The mistletoe, very rarely seen on the oak, was supposed to have extraordinary virtues when found on that tree." Anonymous. 1880, *The Mistletoe and Mandrake,* Notes and Queries, 6th. Series. Many thanks to Dr. Brian Geils of the Mistletoe Centre (www.rms.nau.edu/mistletoe) for referring me to their annotated bibliography.

133. For references in Greek mythology to mistletoe as an entheogen and possible association with Fly-Agaric see: Heinrich, Ruck, and Staples op. cit., ch. 2: "Mistletoe, Centaurs, and Datura."I note that mistletoe is chiefly found in association with pine trees in Greece. See, Sfikas, G. 1990. *Medicinal Plants of Greece.* Athens: Efstathiadis Group.

134. According to folk traditions mistletoe was the tree originally used for the wood of the cross and shrank to its current size out of shame.

135. Quinn op. cit. For dwarves or gnomes as signifiers for psychoactive mushrooms see, Fericgla, L. 2001. *El hongo y la génesis de las culturas.* Marzo: La Libre de Marzo.

136. One possibility would have been Aloes, which is produced by the tree *Aquillaria agalloch.* In Southeast Asia, Aloes wood is also known as Eagle wood, Jinko. Aloes is a resin released by the tree to defend against fungus that attacks the tree in an effort to decompose the bark and other woody parts of tree. It is source of a sacred psychoactive incense. Garuda the magical bird of the Indian folklore is the discoverer and guardian of Aloes as well as being the thief of Soma. See Ratsch, C. Muller-Ebeling, C., Shahi, S., Rai, M., and Gurung, I. 2003. *Shamanism and Tantra in the Himalayas.* London: Thames and Hudson .

137. See: http://www.iranair.com/about/HomaBird.htm. Beneath Mount Elburz, which in Middle Eastern folklore is the home of the simurgh and world tree, one may find today the Homa Hotel. Elburz remains a modern site of mistletoe-infected forests.

138. "The concept of the immortal and ever flying bird, Homa, the symbol of good fortune and happy omen prognosticating a crown on every head it overshadows might be borrowed from the immortal drink, Homa." Quoted in, Dalal, G. 1995. *Ethics in Persian Poetry.* (With special reference to the Timurid Period), New Delhi, India: Abhinav Publications.

139. In folktales, burning a feather of the simurgh summons his presence and he rescues the hero carrying him away in magical flight. This could refer to the power of a fumigant to induce the experience of flight. On shamans as birds and bird-riders see, Lindsay, J. 1965. *The Clashing of Rocks: A Study of Early Greek Religion and Culture and the Origins of Drama,* London: Chapman and Hall, ch. 15, "Initiations and Shamans. Shaman as Bird."

140. Merrill, S. 1881. *East of the Jordan. A Record of Travel and Observation in the Countries of Moab Gilead and Bashan during 1875–1877.* New York: Scribner. The author was a distinguished American archaeologist who did early excavations in Jordan. He was US Consul to Jerusalem 1882–1907. Quoted in Godbey op. cit.

141. Herron, W. and D. La Bore. 1972. *Some plants of Kentucky poisonous to livestock.* Lexington, KY: University of Kentucky College of Agriculture.

142. Herron, W. and La Bore, D. 1972. *Some plants of Kentucky poisonous to livestock.* Lexington, KY: University of Kentucky College of Agriculture.

143. Siegel, R. 1989. *Intoxication. Life in Pursuit of Artificial Paradise.* New York: E. P. Dutton.

144. Deadly nightshade is known to have been a major active ingredient in witches' hallucinogenic "flying ointments" which also included aconite. See note 67 above.

145. Wilson, P. 1999. *Ploughing the Clouds: The Search for the Irish Soma.* San Francisco, CA: City Lights, in which the author uncovers traces of the Indo-European Soma tradition in Irish and other Celtic folklore.

146. Having obscure dark streaks or flecks on a grey or tawny ground.

147. O'Hogain, D. 1991. *DaithiÓhÓgáin, Myth, Legend and Romance. An encyclopaedia of the Irish folk tradition,* Prentice Hall. Wilson op. cit.

148. Wilson, P. 1999. *Ploughing the Clouds: The Search for the Irish Soma.* San Francisco, CA: City Lights, p. 57, note 31.

149. Shipley, J. 1984. *The Origins of English Words. A Discursive Dictionary of Indo European Roots.* Baltimore, MD: John Hopkins University Press.

150. Kochhar, R. 2000. *The Vedic People: Their History and Geography.* Hyderabad: Orient Longman.

151. See Bedrosian, D. 2000. *Soma among the Armenians:* www.rbedrosian.com/soma.htm.

152. Kochhar, R. 2000. *The Vedic People: Their History and Geography.* Hyderabad: Orient Longman, p. 97.

153. Watkins, C. 1977. "Let Us Now Praise Famous Grains." In *Indo-European Studies III,* Cambridge, MA, American Philosophical Society, pgs.468–498. For Indo-European sources of Nordic culture see also, Metzner, R. 2001. *The Well of Remembrance: Rediscovering the Earth Wisdom Myths of Northern Europe.* Shambhala Publications.

154. See, West, E. (trans.). 1897. *Denkard,* Book 7, ch. 2, *Sacred Books of the East,* Vol. 5, New York: Oxford University Press. The *Denkard* is a ninth-century encyclopaedia of the Zoroastrian religion, but with extensive quotes from materials thousands of years older, including (otherwise) lost Avestan texts. It is the single most valuable source of information on this religion aside from the Avesta.

155. Fisher, J. 1975. "Cannabis in Nepal: An overview." In V. Rubin. (ed.). 1975. *Cannabis and Culture.* The Hague: Mouton.

156. Touw, M. 1981. "The Religious and Medicinal Uses of Cannabis in China, India and Tibet." *Journal of Psychoactive Drugs,* Vol. 13 (1) Jan–Mar.

157. Ward, F. 1913. *The Land of the Blue Poppy.* New York: Cambridge University Press.

158. Touw, M. 1981. "The Religious and Medicinal Uses of Cannabis in China, India and Tibet." *Journal of Psychoactive Drugs,* Vol. 13(1) Jan–Mar.

159. Samorini, G. 2002. *Animals and Psychedelics. The Natural World and the Instinct to Alter Consciousness.* Rochester, VT: Park Street Press.

160. Knab, S. 1999. *Polish Herbs, Flowers and Folk Medicine.* New York: Hippocrene Books.

161. "Modern cultivators of khat are well aware that if a goat is given the chance to approach and browse upon the flower of paradise, it will cease feeding on other plants altogether and will charge, butt, and kick anyone who seeks to separate it from its 'heaven.'" Samorini, G. 2002. *Animals and Psychedelics. The Natural World and the Instinct to Alter Consciousness.* Rochester, VT: Park Street Press.

162. "Quite when this tree started on its long journey from innocuous and unnoticed tree to cultural mainstay is a mystery, but it seems likely that religious men first discovered its properties, using it to ward off sleep during long night-time meditations, and carried this useful spiritual helpmate with them on missionary journeys." Rushby, K. 1999. *Eating the Flowers of Paradise: A Journey through the Drug Fields of Ethiopia and Yemen.* New York: St. Martin's Press.

163. Born September 973 CE, in Khorasan, now in Turkmenistan. Died December 13, 1048 CE, Afghanistan. He possessed a profound and original mind of encyclopaedic scope; al-Biruni was conversant with Turkish, Persian, Sanskrit, Hebrew, and Syriac in addition to the Arabic in which he wrote. He applied his talents in many fields of knowledge, excelling particularly in astronomy, mathematics, chronology, physics, medicine, and history. He corresponded with the great philosopher Ibn Sina (Avicenna). Some time after 1017 CE he went to India and made a comprehensive study of its culture. Later he settled at Ghazna in Afghanistan. In religion he was a Shi'ite Muslim, but with agnostic tendencies. "Al–Biruni." *Encyclopædia Britannica Online,* www.britannica.com/EBchecked/topic/66790/al-Biruni.

164. Rushby op. cit., p.145.

165. Turkestan, also spelled Turkistan, is, in Asian history, the regions of Central Asia lying between Siberia on the north, Tibet, India, Afghanistan, and Iran on the south, the Gobi (desert) on the east, and the Caspian Sea on the west. Qat still grows wild in Turkestan (see *Khat, United Nations Office for Drug Control and Crime Prevention,* Bulletin on Narcotics, 1956, No. 4.), and wild populations of a species are one possible index of origin. Further, its origins and distribution are popularly associated with Sufism and Turkestan is an ancient centre of Sufi activities and hub of Sufi missionary activities. (See, for example, Smart, N. 2000. *Atlas of World Religions.* New York: Oxford University Press.

166. He visited Yemen in the 1930s and refers to *qat* in an account of the difficulties of rendering the obscurities of Sufi verse into English.

167. Rushby, K. 1999. *Eating the Flowers of Paradise: A Journey through the Drug Fields of Ethiopia and Yemen.* New York: St. Martin's Press.

168. Though usually chewed, *qat* leaves can be smoked. Note also the way that people commonly take pleasure in combining the drinking and smoking of a drug—coffee with a cigarette, a beer with a joint, brandy with a cigar.

169. Wasson, R. 1973. *Soma: Divine Mushroom of Immortality.* New York: Harcourt Brace Jovanovich.

170. Fabbro, F. 1999. "Mushrooms and snails in religious rituals of early Christians at Aquileia." *Eleusis, Journal of Psychoactive Plants and Compounds,* Vol.3.

171. Fabbro, F. 1999. "Mushrooms and snails in religious rituals of early Christians at Aquileia." *Eleusis, Journal of Psychoactive Plants and Compounds,* Vol.3.

172. See Heinrich, Ruck, and Staples op. cit., Ch. 2: "Mistletoe, Centaurs, and Datura."

173. The author of this text was unfortunately unable to explain the term 'green goat' use for the goat of sacrifice, though it is suggestive in the current context.

174. From a summarised version of an unpublished thesis submitted by Altaf Hussain to the department of Anthropology, Quaid-i-Azam University Pakistan, in partial fulfilment of the degree of Master of Science in Anthropology in 1990.

175. Juniper is only fair as deer forage in terms of nutritional quality, but deer may eat substantial amounts of juniper berries and foliage when desirable browse is unavailable. In late winter, up to 50 per cent of a deer's diet maybe juniper. Lyons, K. 1998. *Juniper Biology and Management in Texas.* College Station, TX: Agricultural Communications.

176. "Each juniper species has a unique combination of volatile oils, but the actual amount of each oil is affected by the environment. The types of oil and their relative proportions appear to influence which juniper species, which age of plants, and which individual plants are eaten by livestock. Oil content is lower in young juniper than in older juniper growth; consequently, goats prefer juniper seedlings and regrowth to mature growth. Goats regularly return to the same trees to harvest young regrowth. Leaf material appears to become less palatable as foliage ages." Lyons, Owens, and Machen op. cit.

177. Launchbaugh, K., Taylor, C., Straka, E., and Pritz, R. 1997. "Juniper as forage: An unlikely candidate?" *Juniper Symposium Proceedings,* Texas A & M University.

178. The bodies of Koala bears are so imbued with eucalyptus oil that they smell strongly of it, which may protect them from predators, through its unpleasant taste. Siegel, R. 1989. *Intoxication. Life in Pursuit of Artificial Paradise.* New York: E. P. Dutton. 179 Erman in Wasson op. cit.

180. Sarianidi, V. 1998. *Margiana and Protozoroastrianism.* Athens: Kapan Editions.

181. One should note in this connection that, in the Hindu Kush, goats are believed to be in the habit of trampling and devouring poisonous snakes. From this belief derives the *bezoar,* a miraculous stone that could neutralize and draw a snake's venom from a bite. Actually a shiny black fur-ball taken from a slaughtered goat's stomach, these are highly prized and often faked, truly a "stone that is not a stone," with marvellous powers.

182. Dumont, D. 1992. "The Ash Tree In Indo-European Culture," *Mankind Quarterly,* Vol. XXXII, No. 4, Summer.

183. "Rhea contrived to hide the infant Zeus from Kronos in this cave, and various stories are told about arrangements within the cave. Callimachus says that the Diktean Meliai and Adrastea took him into their arms, laid him in a cradle of gold, and gave him honeycomb to eat and the udder of the she-goat Amalthea to suck. It was at this time that bees first began to appear in the surrounding mountains ('Hymnus,' in Jovem 47). In Diodorus Siculus' version the nymphs mixed honey and milk and also gave him Amalthea's udder." Dumont op. cit.

184. In Zoroastrianism, Haoma is traditionally the first food that should pass a newborn's lips. It also administered as Last Unction, where in its priestly incarnation it functions as psychopomp, the guide for the soul of the deceased.

185. Dumont, D. 1992. "The Ash Tree In Indo-European Culture," *Mankind Quarterly,* Vol. XXXII, No. 4, Summer.

186. Heroes who have died bravely in battle and thus secured a place in Paradise, Valhalla.

187. Young, J. (trans.). 1954. *The Prose Edda of Snorri Sturluson: Tales from Norse Mythology.* Cambridge, England: Bowes & Bowes.

188. Melampes (L. Melampus), in Greek legend, a celebrated seer and physician, son of Amythaon and Eidomene, brother of Bias, mythical eponymous hero of the family of the Melampodidae. Two young serpents, whose life he had saved, licked his ears while he slept, and from that time he understood the language of birds and beasts. In the art of divination he received instruction from Apollo himself.

189. Baumann, H. 1996. *Greek Wild Flowers and Plant Lore in Ancient Greece.* London: The Herbert Press.

190. Pliny. 1989. *Natural History,* Book XXV, 47, Loeb Classical Library, Boston: Harvard University Press.

191. "I say, then, that Melampus acquired the prophetic art, being a discerning man, and that, besides many other things which he learned from Egypt, he also taught the Greeks things concerning Dionysus, altering few of them; for I will not say that what is done in Egypt in connection with the god and what is done among the Greeks originated independently: for they would then be of an Hellenic character and not recently introduced. Nor again will I say that the Egyptians took either this or any other custom from the Greeks. But I believe that Melampus learned the worship of Dionysus chiefly from Cadmus of Tyre and those who came with Cadmus from Phoenicia to the land now called Boeotia." Herodotus, *The Histories,* 2. 49.

192. Burkert, W. 1979. *Structure and History in Greek Mythology and Ritual.* Berkeley, CA: University of California Press.

193. An ancient city on the Kara Burun peninsula in western Turkey, held by the Cretans or Carians prior to the Ionian occupation.

194. Enodia as an incarnation of Hecate, mistress of plant drugs and mother of Circe, is associated with both Dionysian rites and the Mysteries of Eleusis.

195. A similar account of ancient chemical warfare using psychoactive tree resins exists in Strabo's *Geography* 12.1.18. Strabo describes how the Heptacomitae, inhabitants of the mountainous region close to the Causacus. "(They) cut down three maniples (600) of Pompey's army when they were passing through the mountainous

country; for they mixed bowls of the crazing honey which is yielded by tree twigs, and placed them in the roads, and then when the soldiers drank the mixture and lost their senses, they attacked them and easily disposed of them." This description again suggests the use of a substance, known and probably otherwise exploited for its psychoactive properties, for darker purposes of which there are other examples. Datura, widely used as a shamanic intoxicant in Asia, is also used as a knockout drop to render senseless the clients of prostitutes or unwary travellers in order to rob them.

196. Ellis, P. 1994. *A Brief History of the Druids.* London: Constable.

197. Powells, T. 1987. *The Celts.* London: Thames and Hudson. My thanks go to Allie Westfall, whose Internet paper on Druidism brought this passage to my attention and who kindly supplied a list of her sources. There are variant versions of such tales in different compendia of folktales. Here is one: "After that, the king, Eterscélae died. The men of Ériu (Ireland) then assembled at the bull feast: a bull was killed, and one man ate his fill and drank its broth and slept, and an incantation of truth was chanted over him; if the man lied about what he saw in his sleep he would die." From, *The Destruction of Da Derga's Hostel in Anon,* J. Gantz, J., trans., 1981. *Early Irish Myths and Sagas.* New York, Penguin. See also, Green, M. 1992. "Tarbhfhessin." In *Dictionary of Celtic Myth and legend.* London, Thames & Hudson,

198. According to the Arda Wiraf narrative, after a period of social upheaval in Iran following its conquest by Alexander the Great, the Zoroastrian priesthood needed to determine if their forms of worship were still pleasing to the gods. They selected blameless man, Arda Wiraf, to go on a drug-inspired journey to the other world, in order to determine the answer to their questions: "And Viraf washed his head and body, and put on new clothes; he fumigated himself with sweet scent and spread a carpet, new and clean, on a prepared couch. He sat down on the clean carpet of the couch, and consecrated the Dron (sacramental bread), and remembered the departed souls, and ate food. And then those Dasturs (priests) of the religion filled three golden cups with wine and narcotic of Vishtasp; and . . . he swallowed the wine and narcotic, and said grace whilst conscious, and slept upon the carpet. Those Dasturs

of the religion and the seven sisters were occupied, seven days and nights, with the ever-burning fire and fumigations; and they recited the Avesta and Zand of the religious ritual, and recapitulated the Nasks, and chanted the Gathas, and kept watch in the dark." On the seventh day Wiraf finally awakes from his "pleasant sleep" and supplies the answers to their questions. From, Haug, M. (trans.). 1917. *The Book of Arda Wiraf, The Sacred Books and Early Literature of the East,* Vol. VII: Ancient Persia.

199. Zaehner, R. 1961. *The Dawn and Twilight of Zoroastrianism.* London: Weidenfeld & Nicholson. Professors Zaehner and Mary Boyce, referred to above, are the two great twentieth-century European scholars of Zoroastrianism. Their opinions often differed. Zaehner was Professor of Eastern Religions and Ethics at the University of Oxford. He studied under the great Indo-European philologist Sir Harold Bailey. Prof. Boyce has long been associated with the School of African and Oriental Studies at the University of London.

200 The term "Indo-European designates peoples sharing a common linguistic and cultural heritage, traced to an original community based somewhere in Central Asia. Their initial dispersal east and west is believed to have occurred at a date in the second or third millennium BCE. Any notion of "Indo-European" or "Aryan" designating an ethnic category has long been abandoned by respectable scholarship.

201. See, for example, Dillon, M. 1975. *Celts and Aryans.* Simla: Indian Institute of Advanced Studies, and Hubert, H. 1994. *The History of the Celtic People.* London: Bracken Books. Also see Ellis, P. 1994. *A Brief History of the Druids.* London: Constable.

202. Quoted in Ellis, P. 1994. *A Brief History of the Druids.* London: Constable.

Chapter 6

The Significance of Pharmacological and Biological Indicators in Identifying Historical Uses of *Amanita muscaria*

Kevin Feeney

Kevin Feeney, JD, received his law degree from the University of Oregon in 2005, and is currently a student of Anthropology at Washington State University, where he is studying the religious use of psychoactive plants. His research interests include the study of folkloric and archaeological evidence for traditional uses of psychoactive mushrooms, and examining legal and regulatory issues surrounding the modern religious and cultural use of psychoactive substances, with an emphasis on ayahuasca and peyote. He is coauthor, with Richard Glen Boire, of *Medical Marijuana Law* (2007).

Introduction

Since the publication of R. Gordon Wasson's *Soma: Divine Mushroom of Immortality,* theories have abounded regarding potential historical mushroom cults involving the use of *Amanita muscaria* (Allegro 1971, Arthur 2003, Heinrich 2002, Irvin 2009, Irvin and Rutajit 2009). Subsequent researchers have relied largely upon studies of art, linguistics, and mythology, and have offered varying levels of support for their theories, drawing parallels between color schemes, mushroom shapes, and mushroom biology; however, Wasson's 1968 opus remains unparalleled in terms of breadth and sophistication. One of the fundamental contributions of Wasson's work was the proposition that soma was an entheogen, a point driven home through detailed comparisons of the known effects of entheogenic substances and descriptions of soma inebriation in the *Rig Veda.* In addition to Wasson's discussion of the ecstasies that can be produced by hallucinogenic mushrooms, he also argued that the soma cult involved ritual ingestion of *Amanita muscaria*–infused urine. Both of these factors provided a groundbreaking pharmacological depth to Wasson's theory.

Despite Wasson's pioneering efforts, however, he never adequately addressed how preparation, as described in the *Rig Veda,* affects the pharmacology of *Amanita muscaria,* and he also overlooked possible indicators of historical knowledge regarding the muscarinic properties of this mushroom. Another examination of the evidence for historical uses of this mushroom, which seeks to identify cultural knowledge of *Amanita muscaria*'s peculiar pharmacology, may further bolster theories identifying its use. In order to demonstrate the significance of such an investigation, evidence for use of this mushroom in India, Mesoamerica, and among Germanic and Celtic groups will be examined, with an eye to uncovering both pharmacological and biological evidence supporting a finding of historical *Amanita muscaria* use.

Understanding Amanita muscaria

Amanita muscaria is a cosmopolitan mushroom that can be found throughout the globe. While it occurs in both tropic and temperate climates, its potential habitats are limited due to the symbiotic nature of the mushroom. *Amanita muscaria* is a mycorrhizal mushroom, meaning that it only grows in association with certain trees, including birch, fir, pine, spruce, aspen and oak, and therefore can only be found in environments that support these arboreal species. This is an important property of *Amanita muscaria* because it helps us determine whether historical groups with suspected entheogen use may have had access to this mushroom.

While *Amanita muscaria* elicits some effects similar to *Psilocybe* mushrooms, including hallucinations, the properties and effects of *Amanita muscaria* are easily distinguishable from those caused by the *Psilocybes*. *Amanita muscaria* inebriation is typically characterized by confusion, delirium, hallucinations (often taking the form of size-distortion), muscle spasms, and alternating periods of excitation and lethargy or sleep. Although the pharmacology of *Amanita muscaria* is not entirely understood, there are three chemical constituents of which we are primarily concerned; these are ibotenic acid, muscimol, and muscarine.

The principal inebriating agents of *Amanita muscaria* are the isoxazole derivatives ibotenic acid and its decarboxylation product, muscimol. Ibotenic acid, a glutamate agonist, is the most abundant of the two principal compounds, although it readily decarboxylates into the more potent muscimol. Dehydration of the mushroom is the easiest way to promote decarboxylation of ibotenic acid to muscimol, which is five to ten times more potent than its precursor. It has been suggested that heating or cooking may also promote degradation of ibotenic acid to muscimol (Catalfomo and Eugster 1970), a suggestion that appears to be verified by more recent research (Tsunoda et al 1993a). Muscimol, a potent GABA agonist, is believed to be an artifact of ibotenic acid, rather than a biogenic feature of *Amanita muscaria* (Tsujikawa et al 2006). Both compounds are water-soluble, and muscimol is thermostable, meaning it will not degrade with cooking or boiling. The effects of these compounds, when used in isolation, have been shown to include: unsteadiness, dizziness, narrowed field of vision, mild visual spasms, altered auditory and visual perception, visual disturbances, loss of equilibrium, muscular twitches, and sleep (Chilton 1975, Waser 1979). Interestingly, the highest concentrations of ibotenic acid and muscimol in *Amanita muscaria* appear to occur in the skin of the cap and the yellow tissue immediately beneath it, while the lowest concentrations occur in the stipe, or stem (Michelot and Melendez-Howell 2003, Tsujikawa et al 2006, Tsunoda et al 1993b). The difference in potency between cap and stipe is an additional feature of *Amanita muscaria* that may be used to distinguish historical uses of this mushroom from use of *Psilocybes*.

Another notable constituent of *Amanita muscaria* is muscarine, a cholinergic agonist, which primarily affects the peripheral parasympathetic nervous system, instead of acting on the central nervous system as hallucinogens do. The effects of muscarine poisoning are generally marked by excessive perspiration and salivation, blurring of vision, abdominal pain, nausea, vomiting, and diarrhea. While the muscarine content of *Amanita muscaria* is generally considered insufficient to produce muscarinic effects (Catalfomo and Eugster 1970), recent research suggests that muscarine may in fact play an important role in the pharmacological effects of this mushroom (Feeney and Stijve 2011, Stijve 1982, Stijve 1981), a role that has apparently not gone unnoticed by cultures familiar with this mushroom's properties. In the following pages I will outline how these idiosyncratic features of *Amanita muscaria*'s pharmacology and biology can be used to help identify potential historical uses of this mushroom.

Saliva and the Gift of Intoxication

The folklore surrounding the use of *Amanita muscaria* in Europe and Asia seems to suggest that cultures familiar with this mushroom recognized its muscarinic effects and considered them important components of *Amanita muscaria* inebriation. In several folk stories the muscarinic effects of *Amanita muscaria* appear to play an important role in the mushroom's origins. In Siberia, Koryak legend tells us that *Amanita muscaria* was created by the spittle of Vahiyinin, the God of Existence (Schultes and Hofmann 1992). Similarly, a Croatian variation on the myth of Wotan's (Odin) wild hunt describes how *Amanita muscaria* was formed by the bloody spittle that fell from the mouth of Wotan's horse (Morgan 1995). The connection between salivation and the creation of *Amanita muscaria* strongly suggests a cultural familiarity with the muscarinic effects produced by the mushroom, and provides a basis for further investigating stories that connect muscarinic effects, like salivation, with sacred inebriants and magical objects.

While there is no direct evidence of *Amanita muscaria* use amongst the Germanic tribes, the above account of Wotan's wild hunt combined with stories describing the origins of the famed Mead of Inspiration are highly suggestive that early Germanic peoples were familiar with, and revered the properties of this mushroom. According to myth, as recorded in Snorri Sturluson's *Skaldskaparmal*, the rival gods of the Aesir and Vanir sealed a truce by spitting into a cauldron. From the spittle a being known as Kvasir was created. Kvasir came to be celebrated for his wisdom and teachings, but was subsequently killed by two dwarfs who mixed his blood with honey to create the Mead of Inspiration. It was said that anyone who drank of this Mead would become a wise poet. The Mead, which later came into the possession of Suttung the Giant, was eventually recovered by Wotan, who convinced Suttung's daughter to let him have a taste. Wotan slyly consumed the entirety of the Mead and escaped to Asgard in the form of an eagle. On Wotan's journey some of the Mead was "dropped," making the Mead available to mortals. Upon arrival at Asgard the Mead was spit into containers and provided to the Gods.

The importance of this story lies in the repeated connections between saliva and the creation of the Mead of Inspiration. First, saliva is used in the formation of Kvasir, who can be seen as an embodiment of the sacrament, as suggested by Eliade (1982). In order to gain the wisdom of the sacrament, Kvasir must be sacrificed so that he may be consumed in the form of the Mead of Inspiration. After Wotan steals the Mead we are told that some of the Mead is lost on his journey, and what remains is spit up again when he returns to Asgard. In this account saliva is connected twice with the creation of the Mead, first through the creation of Kvasir, and second through regurgitation of the Mead in Asgard. The way the Mead is lost, however, is equally important. The account of Wotan "dropping" some of the Mead on his journey is ambiguous at best, but since Wotan consumed the Mead there are a limited number of ways that it could have been lost. Presumably the Mead was lost through salivation, urination, or defecation. While diarrhea is a potential effect of muscarine, the psychoactive properties of *Amanita muscaria* are known to be preserved in the urine, which is collected amongst some Siberian tribes for repeated use (Wasson 1968). Knowledge of either of these qualities could be indicated here, in addition to the obvious connections between saliva and the creation of the inebriant, which are clearly paralleled in the Koryak and Croatian myths mentioned earlier.

A similar creation story is recounted in the *Popol Vuh* of the Quiche Maya (Goetz and Morley 1950, Tedlock 1996), recorded shortly after the Spanish Conquest, although the connection to ritual inebriant use is less clear. In this story two youth, Hun-Hunahpú and Vucub-Hunahpú, find themselves in the Underworld, Xibalba, where they are challenged to a life or death ball game by the Lords of Xibalba. The two youth are overcome by the Lords of Xibalba, and are sacrificed in their defeat. Hun-Hunahpú's decapitated head is hung in a tree where he is visited by Xpuic, a daughter of the Xibalbans. Hun-Hunahpú spits in the maiden's hand, impregnating her. Xpuic eventually gives birth to the Hero Twins, who will later defeat the Lords of Xibalba.

Although the above story does not appear directly connected to inebriant use, the story remains striking for several reasons. First and foremost is the act of creation through expectoration, a clear parallel with the Koryak and Croatian myths recounting the origins of *Amanita muscaria.* Second, *Psilocybe* mushrooms are still used among certain Mexican indigenous groups, although no modern use has been confirmed among any Mayan groups. Psychoactive mushroom use was documented at the time of the conquest, around the same time that the *Popol Vuh* was recorded, and earlier archaeological artifacts depicting mushrooms have been found throughout Mesoamerica. Some of these artifacts clearly appear to be representations of *Amanita muscaria* (Figure 1, *see also* Schultes & Hofmann 1992: 82; Figure 2), although modern uses of *Amanita muscaria* in Mesoamerica remain unconfirmed (Schultes and Hofmann 1992).

Third, and finally, is a parallel story among the Aztecs, which identifies the Hero Twins as the god Quetzalcóatl and his twin aspect Xólotl. Quetzalcóatl, which may be translated as either "plumed serpent" or "precious twin," is a god with a variety of attributes, who is known by different names depending on what particular attribute is emphasized. His appearance as Ehecatl, the wind god, and Xólotl, the twin, are the most significant to our discussion.

Quetzalcóatl, in his form of the Wind God, is often depicted with fangs and dangling eyeballs (Borhegyi 1980). The appearance of dangling eyeballs has been interpreted as representing a type of remorseful weeping, or perhaps some pervasive type of eye disease (Vankirk and Bassett-Vankirk 1997). However, Carl de Borhegyi (2010), son of the renowned archaeologist Stephan de Borhegyi, recently suggested that the dangling eyeball represents a mushroom. This is most clearly illustrated by a stone bust of Ehecatl, found on the south coast of Guatemala, which features both the fanged teeth and dangling eyeballs (Figure 3). Upon closer inspection, a clear picture of an *Amanita* mushroom emerges. The eyelids of the bust appear to represent mushroom caps, while the eyeballs can be seen as representations of the typical bulbous base of an *Amanita.* The only prominent features missing are the distinctive warts that typically decorate the cap of the mushroom and the characteristic ring left by remnants of the universal veil. Further supporting

Borhegyi's observation is the fact that one of the effects of muscarine is lacrimation, or tear production. As a result, Ehecatl's dangling eyes may double as both representations of the mushroom and of tears, perhaps an acknowledgment of this peculiar property of the mushroom.

Xólotl, the God of Twins, and twin of Quetzalcóatl, is also occasionally depicted with a dangling eyeball. In the *Codex Borgia,* a pre-Columbian religious manuscript believed to originate in either the state of Puebla or Oaxaca, Mexico, Xólotl is depicted with this strange feature (Figure 4; *Codex Borgia* Plate 10). The dangling eyeball also appears in connection with a solar deity (Xólotl, perhaps) depicted in a birthing pose (*Codex Borgia* Plate 43), as well as in representations of women who died during childbirth (*Codex Borgia* Plates 47, 48). The *Codex Borgia,* however, also features images of individuals having their eyes ritually gouged (Plates 15 and 16), as well as a figure who can be seen gouging his own eye out (Plate 10). Ultimately, the purpose of this feature remains unclear. It has been suggested that it may represent penitent weeping, a form of eye affliction, or perhaps may represent the results of some type of ritual sacrifice. Nevertheless, the similarity between the stylized "dangling eyeball" and a mushroom is remarkable, particularly when one recognizes the pharmacological connection between muscarine and tear production.

Other Muscarinic Indicators

Aside from creation stories, there may be other indicators that a particular culture is familiar with the muscarinic properties of *Amanita muscaria.* A passage from the *Rig Veda,* known as the Frog Hymn, may suggest such knowledge among the Indo-Aryans. In this passage frogs are compared to perspiring Brahmins gathered around the soma bowl:

> Like Brahmins at the overnight soma-sacrifice speaking around as it were a full lake, ye celebrate that day of the year which, O Frogs, has begun the rain.
>
> Soma-pressing Brahmins, they have raised their voice offering their yearly prayer, Adharvu priests, heated, sweating, they appear; none of them are hidden (MacDonell 2006: 145).

While it has been asserted that the Brahmins in this passage are sweating because they are gathered around a heated cauldron of milk (Doniger 2005), a new possibility arises if soma is the *Amanita muscaria* mushroom, as suggested by Wasson.

Another suggestive account of soma intoxication comes from Phillipe de Félice. Referencing a story from the *Satapatha Brahmana* in 1936, de Félice provided the following description of soma inebriation: "It happens sometimes that the inebriation is accompanied by organic disturbances, which are in reality symptoms of an acute intoxication. Men know and fear the baleful effects of the drug, and, though he was a god, Indra himself did not escape them, since one day the soma came forth from every opening in his body" (Wasson 1968:135, *citing* Félice 1936). The experience of the god Indra, as described above, suggests typical muscarinic symptoms, which include: salivation, perspiration, vomiting, and diarrhea. There are few orifices that are left unaffected by the properties of muscarine.

Importance of Preparation

Historical accounts of how long-lost inebriants were prepared, as well as archaeological artifacts that evidence particular preparation techniques, can provide important clues in identifying these enigmatic substances. Wasson, in his attempt to identify the three filters used in the preparation of soma, clearly recognized the importance of preparation in unearthing the hidden identity of this sacred inebriant. Wasson (1968) identified these three filters as (1) a celestial filter, or filter of sunlight; (2) a filter of woolen cloth; and (3) the human body, and relied on a combination of relevant passages from the *Rig Veda,* and on explanations of *Amanita muscaria*'s pharmacology, in making his case. Wasson focused heavily on the first and third filters in his theory but placed little emphasis on the second, a weakness pounced upon by several critics. Vedic scholar John Brough (1971: 338) argued that, "if the soma-plant had been a mushroom, it would be strange that the elaborate Vedic process of pounding out and filtering the juice should have been necessary. Why should the plant not have been simply eaten?"

Others have similarly argued that the elaborate process of preparation for soma, as outlined in the *Rig Veda,* would be unnecessary and inexplicable if the same effects could be obtained by simply chewing and swallowing the mushroom (Flattery and Schwartz 1989, Greene 1992).

While some have argued that these objections are nonsensical (i.e., who would make this argument about Japanese use of tea: Ott 1998: 25-26), evidence of complex preparations are often examples of a sophisticated understanding of plant properties and toxicities (Johns and Kubo 1988). However, the idea that the Aryans may have had an advanced understanding of plant properties and preparations was also rejected by Brough (1971: 336), who definitively stated that "there are no grounds for believing that the Indo-Iranians were sufficiently skilled herbalists to have made such discoveries."

Methods of detoxifying and processing plants for human use are known throughout the world, and include a variety of techniques, including dehydration, application of heat, leaching, and fermentation, among others (Johns and Kubo 1988). While it is difficult to trace the origins of these methods, or to answer the question of how certain groups learned to detoxify and process useful plants in their environment, to make a blanket claim that certain cultures were incapable of discovering plant properties, and the methods necessary for rendering them safe and useful, seems naive at best. Regarding the processing of fungus specifically, the Chinese have long made use of various polypore mushrooms for medicinal purposes, most of which require a hot water extraction in order to render the medicinal properties available for human use. Similarly, methods of parboiling are used among the Karelians in Northern Europe to render certain mushrooms edible, including *Gyromitra esculenta* and certain species of *Lactarius* (Härkönen 1998). In Nagano, Japan, as another example, villagers are known to pickle *Amanita muscaria,* a process that removes both hallucinogenic and toxic components of the mushroom, thereby making them edible (Phipps 2000). Nevertheless, while preparations of foods and inebriants may employ arbitrary methods that merely reflect cultural preference, rather than serving a practical function, it would be a mistake to simply make such an assumption. As a result, a closer look at Wasson's three filters is warranted.

Wasson's first filter, a celestial filter of sunlight, represents the process of dehydration. As mentioned earlier, dehydration of *Amanita muscaria* causes ibotenic acid to degrade into the more potent compound muscimol. Additionally, recent investigations have indicated that the process of dehydration significantly reduces the incidence of vomiting following *Amanita muscaria* ingestion (Feeney 2010). These pharmacological features of *Amanita muscaria* are recognized by Siberian tribes familiar with the mushroom, many of whom have taboos against consumption of the fresh mushroom, which is considered toxic and potentially deadly (Jochelson 1905, 1908, Maydell 1893). Wasson, relying on ethnographic accounts of the disparate attitudes towards fresh and dried mushrooms among these Siberian tribes, makes a strong argument that dehydration, or a "filter of sunlight," was the first of three filters applied in the preparation of soma as described in the *Rig Veda*.

Wasson's second filter, a filter of woolen cloth, is based on numerous verses from the *Rig Veda* describing the mixture of soma with water, being pressed with stones, and finally filtered through a woolen cloth. The term soma can be translated as meaning "the pressed one," with the prefix "su-" signifying "to press," indicating the import of this procedural step (Nichols 2000: 113, Wasson 1968: 62). While clear pharmacological information is lacking, my own research has demonstrated that extractions of *Amanita muscaria* in water significantly reduce the frequency of toxic effects (nausea and vomiting) caused by fresh or dried specimens of the mushroom (Feeney 2010). These findings are significant in that they counter one of the major criticisms of Wasson's theory, that the elaborate process of preparation for soma, as outlined in the *Rig Veda*, would be unnecessary and inexplicable if the same effects could be obtained by simply chewing and swallowing the mushroom (Brough 1971, Flattery and Schwartz 1989, Greene 1992).

While water extractions are not necessarily conducted for functional purposes, the fact that such an extraction method significantly alters the effects of *Amanita muscaria* makes such preparatory techniques, when combined with corroborating evidence, potential indicators that the Indo-Aryans were familiar with the pharmacological properties of this mushroom. Notably, the creation of the Mead of Inspiration in Germanic mythology shares some significant parallels with soma and its preparation. According to the *Skaldskaparmal*, the Mead of Inspiration was created by two dwarfs, who captured and killed Kvasir the Wise. The Mead was produced by mixing Kvasir's blood with honey, and any who drank of the potion would become "poetically" inspired. Interestingly, Kvasir's name begins with the prefix "kvas," which can be translated as "wort of" (Nichols 2000: 113). Here we have several peculiar parallels: first, both the god soma and the supernaturally born Kvasir can be seen as divine embodiments of a sacred inebriant; and second, each name suggests a particular type of preparation associated with the embodied inebriant, specifically that the inebriant should be extracted as an infusion or decoction.

One rebuttal offered by Wasson to Brough, and others, was that indigenous groups in Mexico are known to make aqueous extractions of *Psilocybes* for use in curing ceremonies, a point meant to undermine the argument that preparation of mushrooms is unnecessary (Ott 1998). While the point is well taken, and as Jonathan Ott (1998) pointed out, no one would question the Japanese preference for infusions of tea over consuming whole tea leaves, it does not obviate the potential that preparation serves a particular pharmacological function. While evidence supporting the historical use of *Amanita muscaria* in Mesoamerica is tentative (Schultes and Hofmann 1992), an argument can be made that the extraction methods used with *Psilocybes* may be a remnant of earlier practices involving the use of *Amanita muscaria.*

In Mexico, the Mixtec are known to prepare aqueous extractions of *Psilocybes,* generally grinding the mushrooms on a metate and mixing them with water (Borhegyi 1961). Interestingly, sets of metates and manos (grinding stones) have been found in association with mushroom stones in Guatemala, artifacts that are thought to date back to the Early or Late Preclassic Mesoamerican periods (1000 BCE–200 CE) (Borhegyi 1961). While the mushroom stones remain an enigmatic feature of Mesoamerican archaeology, the association of metates with mushroom stones tends to support the prevailing theory that the mushroom stones are connected with the ritual use of hallucinogenic mushrooms (Borhegyi 1961, Wasson & Wasson 1957). The grinding of mushrooms on a metate also recalls the Vedic descriptions of "pressing stones" used in the preparation of soma.

While my own investigations suggest that aqueous extractions of *Amanita muscaria* produce effects that are significantly less toxic than when the mushroom is consumed fresh or dried (Feeney 2010), there does not appear to be any clear preference for aqueous extractions among Siberian groups with traditional uses of this mushroom. While there are general taboos against consumption of fresh mushrooms, which are considered toxic and potentially lethal (Jochelson 1905, 1908), the mushrooms are consumed in a variety of manners, including dried, cooked in soups, and both aqueous and alcohol extractions (Saar 1991). Although there is no ethnographic evidence suggesting a preference for aqueous solutions among Siberians with traditional uses of *Amanita muscaria,* evidence suggesting this extra step of processing by the Mixtec remains significant, particularly given the adeptness of traditional cultures at identifying and eliminating toxins from food sources (Johns and Kubo 1988).

Wasson proposed that the third filter was represented by the human body, which would filter and emit the purest variety of soma in the form of urine. This conjecture was based upon several key passages in the *Rig Veda,* combined with evidence of urine-recycling practices in Siberia, where the urine of intoxicated individuals would be consumed to produce additional bouts of intoxication. In support of his theory Wasson pointed to several passages in the *Rig Veda,* suggestive of an association between soma and urine, including the following:

> 9.74.4: The swollen men piss the flowing [soma] (Wasson 1968: 29).
>
> 8.80.3: In the belly of Indra the inebriating soma clarifies itself (Wasson 1968: 56).

Wasson's assertion that the third filter mentioned in the *Rig Veda* is the human body, and that mushroom-infused urine is the purest form of soma, has perhaps been the most contentious component of his theory. Daniel Ingalls, a Harvard professor of Sanskrit, raised several significant challenges to Wasson's position that merit mention. First, Ingalls took issue with Wasson's assertion that "priests appointed to impersonate Indra and Vayu" urinate the divine inebriant (Wasson 1968: 30), pointing out that there is no evidence in the *Rig Veda* "that priests ever impersonate the gods in any capacity" (Ingalls 1971: 189). Ingalls' second point of contention is based on both the scarcity and ambiguity of passages connecting soma and urine, of which he notes "the verb to urinate is used in connection with the word soma only twice in the *Rig Veda*" (Ingalls 1971: 189).

Most important to our present considerations, however, is a point raised by Jonathan Ott (1998) that *Amanita muscaria* is not the only substance where substantial amounts of inebriating compounds are discharged in the urine. Consumption of both *Psilocybe* mushrooms and mescaline-containing cacti are both followed by significant amounts of the inebriating compounds psilocin and mescaline being eliminated in the urine (Grieshaber et al 2001, Kalberer et al 1962, Ott 1998). As a result, consumers of either of these drugs could theoretically consume their own urine in order to prolong the effects of inebriation. In part, it was the distinctiveness of this feature of *Amanita muscaria* that made the mushroom so compelling to Wasson as a candidate for soma, though the strength of his theory does not rise or fall depending on the validity of this part of his argument, as some critics have argued (Letcher 2008). While Ott's observation clearly calls into question the significance of this component of Wasson's theory, his assessment is not entirely satisfactory. First, there is no ethnographic record of cultures that ingest urine in order to prolong the effects of *Psilocybe* mushrooms or mescaline-containing cacti, while the historical record clearly shows this practice among the Siberians with regards to the use of *Amanita muscaria*. Secondly, Wasson's argument goes beyond mere recognition of this odd property of *Amanita muscaria* by additionally arguing that the process of filtering soma through the human body is a process with pharmacological significance. This assertion is clearly outlined by Wasson in the following speculation:

> In modern experience the fly-agaric causes nausea. If the agent that provokes vomiting is not the same as the one that leads to ecstasy, the former might be eliminated in the digestive track and urine be thus freed from this inconvenience (Wasson 1968: 31).

Wasson goes even further, claiming that "the soma juice that is drunk by 'Indra' and 'Vayu' in the course of the liturgy is filtered in their organisms and issues forth as sparkling yellow urine, retaining its inebriating virtue but having been purged of its nauseating properties" (Wasson 1968: 55).

From a pharmacological perspective Wasson may indeed be correct. While ibotenic acid, one of the mushroom's active constituents, passes in the urine unmetabolized, it is likely that other components of *Amanita muscaria* that contribute to nausea and vomiting, such as muscarine, have been metabolized (filtered) into inactive byproducts. This biological process would leave a fairly pure extraction of ibotenic acid in the consumer's urine. This filtering effect also appears to be supported by ethnographic accounts from Siberia, including the following observation from Carl von Dittmar:

> People generally claim that the effect of the mushroom poison becomes more intense and more beautiful when it has already passed through another organism. Thus an intoxicated man will often be followed by someone else who wants to collect his urine, which is supposed to possess this effect to a particularly high degree (Wasson 1968: 257, *reprinting* Dittmar 1900).

While it is important to realize that *Amanita muscaria* is not unique in the sense that its properties can be recycled through urine consumption, the more important question is, why does this practice come about? And why is this practice not observed among indigenous groups in Mexico with traditional uses of *Psilocybe* mushrooms? There are two possible answers to these questions, the first being scarcity. If a resource is scarce, which has been suggested by accounts that a single mushroom might be exchanged for a reindeer in Siberia (Erman 1833–1848), then we are likely to see cultures maximizing the use of particular resources. Wasson's theory suggests that soma was only available in the mountains, and would have been scarce in the Indus Valley, where the Indo-Aryans came to reside. Recycling urine, as Wasson asserts is described in the *Vedas,* makes sense in an environment where the principal inebriant is scarce and highly valued.

The second possible answer is that the urine of *Amanita muscaria* consumers has been relieved of toxic qualities that are evident in fresh or dried specimens of the mushroom, thus making the urine a more pure and desirable drug. More information is needed about the pharmacology of *Amanita muscaria* before such an answer can be given with confidence, but an answer in the affirmative would provide a clear reason why *Amanita muscaria*–infused urine is valued and used, whereas *Psilocybe*-infused urine is not so valued. I have not, as of yet, uncovered other examples of urine being associated with a divine inebriant, but the two above-stated reasons provide a potential basis for drawing a connection between ritual urine consumption and use of *Amanita muscaria,* and not with *Psilocybes* or other inebriants.

The Potent Head

The concentration of ibotenic acid and muscimol in the cap of *Amanita muscaria* is another unique pharmacological feature of this mushroom. While the pharmacology of *Amanita muscaria* is not completely understood, if the distribution of muscarine, and other toxic compounds that may be present, are uniformly distributed throughout the mushroom, then removal of the stem could be seen as a method of preparation that decreases the mushroom's overall toxicity. Among the Khanty of Western Siberia, only the cap of the *Amanita muscaria* is consumed, though the reasons for this practice are unknown (Saar 1991). Another example of this type of preparation can be found among the Mixe of Oaxaca, Mexico, who prepare *Psilocybe* mushrooms in this way (Wasson and Wasson 1957). The Mixe consume the caps of the mushroom only, the stems are saved and later left in front of a cross as an offering. While the stem retains a ceremonial purpose, there is no clear pharmacological reason for the stem of a *Psilocybe* mushroom to be discarded. This practice could signify an earlier use of *Amanita muscaria,* where the practice of discarding the stem would have potentially decreased the negative effects of the mushroom. While this is largely speculative, it seems certain that the scarlet cap of *Amanita muscaria* would have caught the eye of indigenous peoples before the generally drab appearance of the *Psilocybes,* and that its properties would similarly have been discovered much earlier. Although *Amanita muscaria* is equally as effective an inebriant as *Psilocybe* mushrooms, the potency and resulting effects of the mushroom are more highly variable, both factors that may have contributed to a subsequent preference for *Psilocybe* varieties and an eventual discontinuance of *Amanita muscaria* use.

Aside from clues we might garner from preparation techniques that favor mushroom caps, there are recurring themes regarding decapitation and the spiritual potency of the head in the Vedic, Germanic, Celtic, and Mesoamerican cultures. In the *Brahmanas*, an ancient Indian text that follows the *Vedas*, one of the cups of soma is referred to as the head of Gayatri, Gayatri being the eagle who bore Indra down from the heavens after beheading the dragon Vrtra and obtaining the holy soma. Here, not only is soma represented by the image of a head, but it is procured only after beheading Vrtra. Similarly, the giant Mimir, who guards the Well of Wisdom in Germanic mythology, is beheaded by the Vanir gods who wish to gain access to the sacred Well. The Well of Wisdom is generally considered a permutation of the Mead of Inspiration, from which Odin drinks. The close association of Mimir with the Well, and the subsequent preservation and use of his head as an oracle by Odin, suggests that Mimir's head may itself be a representation of an inebriant.

The Celts believed that the head was the container of the soul, as well as a source of truth, wisdom, and healing (Cowan 1993). In this view, the head is essentially a source of spiritual potency, much like the cap of the *Amanita muscaria* is the source of the mushroom's mind-altering properties. In Celtic myth, there is a faery tree bearing scarlet berries that "cheer like wine" and is guarded by a giant (Wilson 2001). The giant was slain by Diarmuid, a Fenian warrior, who took refuge in the tree in order to hide from Finn McCool, leader of the Fianna, whom he had betrayed. Finn sent nine men into the tree after Diarmuid, and each was beheaded, their heads falling from the tree like "ripe berries." The berries appear to be frequently equated with the head (Wilson 2001), a connection that again combines the symbolism of the head with a divine inebriant. Interestingly, both Celtic and Germanic myth have examples of giants guarding divine inebriants, with Odin beheading nine thralls of the giant Suttung in his pursuit of the Mead of Inspiration.

Ritual decapitation, as a form of sacrifice, was practiced by the Aztecs in Mesoamerica (Baquedano and Graulich 1993). As described earlier, Hun-Hunahpú, the father of the Hero Twins in the *Popol Vuh,* was decapitated after losing a ball game with the Underworld Xibalbans. His head was hung in a tree and became like fruit, also a potential embodiment of the sacred inebriant.

The persistent connection between spiritually potent decapitated heads and inebriating fruits and beverages is striking, however it is important to note that symbols are often multivocalic, representing a multiplicity of meanings, including ideas that may appear contrary from an outside perspective (Turner 1965). It is not asserted here that the practice of decapitation is directly related to, or even results from, the use of psychotropic mushrooms, but rather that the particular pharmacology of *Amanita muscaria* is highly compatible with the symbolism implicit in "cults of the head." When addressing historical uses of psychoactive mushrooms this peculiar feature of *Amanita muscaria,* and related symbolism, could be an important factor in distinguishing ritual use of *Amanita muscaria* from ritual uses of *Psilocybes.*

Feats of Strength

As mentioned earlier, the Koryak believe that *Amanita muscaria* was created by the god of existence, Vahiyinin, but some further elaboration is required. The origin story begins with Big Raven, who encounters a beached whale. Big Raven sought to help the whale return to the sea, but was unable to lift the large creature. Big Raven pleaded with Vahiyinin for assistance, and Vahiyinin responded by spitting upon the ground, causing *Amanita muscaria* to grow. The deity told Big Raven to "go to a level place near the sea: there thou wilt find white soft stalks with spotted hats. These are the spirits wa'paq. Eat some of them and they will help thee" (Wasson 1968: 268, *reprinting* Jochelson 1905, 1908). Big Raven ate the mushrooms and was imbued with great strength, whereupon he returned the whale to the sea and proclaimed, "Let the Agaric *[Amanita muscaria]* remain on earth, and let my children see what it will show them" (Wasson 1968: 268, *reprinting* Jochelson 1905, 1908). *Amanita muscaria* mushrooms have been used for both strength and endurance among Siberians, and reportedly keep hunters nimble when pursuing prey. According to Georg Heinrich von Langsdorf (1809), who spent time among the Kamchadal in the early nineteenth-century, a man was reported to have carried a 120-pound sack of flour for ten miles after consuming *Amanita muscaria,* a feat he would normally have been incapable of. Similarly, a woman from Kamchatka proclaimed that "under the influence of the fungus it is a trifle to walk 50km" (Saar 1991: 164). A more recent account describes how Koryak women will chew small pieces of *Amanita muscaria* while tanning fur, or attending other tasks, in order to relieve muscle soreness and provide endurance (Irimoto 2004).

The connection between *Amanita muscaria* and feats of strength led to the proposal by Samuel Ödman in 1784 that *Amanita muscaria* was the intoxicant of the Viking Berserkers (Fabing 1956). The Berserkers were warriors, associated with the cult of Odin, known for their ecstatic battle frenzy and seeming imperviousness to pain (Buchholz 1984). The Berserkers have been described as warriors who rode into "battle without coats of mail and acted like mad dogs or wolves. They bit their shields and were as strong as bears or bulls. They killed people, and neither fire nor iron affected them" (Hollander 2002: 10). This theory was later supported by F.C. Schuber, a Norwegian physician and botanist, who noted that the symptoms of Berseker rage are consistent throughout different accounts (Fabing 1956), and also by Rolf Nordhagen, who in 1930 uncovered an 1814 report from the Varmland regiment (Swedish Army) where an officer had taken note of troops that were raving and foaming at the mouth (Morgan 1995: 116). Upon inquiry the officer was informed that the soldiers had taken *Amanita muscaria* in order to prepare for battle (Morgan 1995: 116). Other accounts suggest that the Berserker rage begins with particular symptoms, including shivering, chattering of teeth, chills in the body, and flushing in the face (Fabing 1956). Such symptoms suggest that some sort of substance was ingested that would regularly cause such effects, effects that are often associated with the beginning stages of *Amanita muscaria* inebriation. Laws were passed outlawing Berserkers and robbers in 1015 CE in Norway, and later in 1123 CE in Iceland (Fabing 1956). The practice ceased in Iceland shortly after its prohibition (Fabing 1956), a fact that may have more to do with ecological changes in Iceland rather than a respect for law.

Interestingly, Wasson dismissed the Berserker theory out of hand, claiming that symptoms caused by *Amanita muscaria* were opposite of those associated with the Berserker rage (Wasson 1968: 176–178). Perhaps Wasson had concerns about linking *Amanita muscaria* with such a violent tradition, however the known symptoms of the Berserker rage appear to be compatible with ethnographic accounts of the mushroom's use in Siberia, including a report that the mushrooms are eaten among the Koryak when one is "resolved toward murder" (Morgan 1995: 103). It is also worth noting that soma is most commonly associated with Indra, a god of war, who consumes soma prior to his great battle with Vrtra.

A parallel to the Berserker tradition can also be found among Celtic myths detailing the deeds of the hero Cú Chulaind (Riedlinger 1999). Cú Chulaind was known for his ferociousness in battle, and parallels have been drawn between descriptions of his battle-fury and symptoms caused by *Amanita muscaria* (Riedlinger 1999). As Cú Chulaind's fury builds, his behavior becomes manic, his hair bristles, and his heart booms, symptoms that Thomas Riedlinger has connected with the agitation and tachycardia caused by *Amanita muscaria.* More curiously, however, are descriptions of Cú Chulaind's fury, in which one eye is described as protruding while the other recedes into the back of his head, a description that Riedlinger argues is indicative of the visual distortions caused by *Amanita muscaria* inebriation.

The accounts of the Berserkers and of Cú Chulaind are certainly suggestive of the effects of *Amanita muscaria,* which makes it surprising that Wasson so readily denied any connections between the Berserkers and this mushroom. The Berserker rage also has a counterpart, as the rage is generally described as being followed by a period of lassitude (Fabing 1956: 234), which brings us to the next topic: mushroom-induced sleep.

The *Muscaria* Slumber

One of the noted properties of *Amanita muscaria* is the inducement to sleep. Waldemar Bogoras, a Russian anthropologist exiled to Siberia in the late nineteenth-century, observed the use of *Amanita muscaria* among the Chuckchee, and noted that many users of the mushroom would succumb to a period of sleep (Bogoras 1904–1909). Bogoras noted that some individuals would fall asleep immediately after consuming the mushroom, only to wake up a few hours later while fully inebriated. Others would pass through three stages of inebriation, including stimulation, hallucination, and stupor, before succumbing to a heavy slumber (Bogoras 1904–1909). This experience was also noted by other early explorers including Joseph Kopec, who was given mushrooms by a medicine man to treat his illness and to provide sleep. Kopec reported that a long restful sleep followed, one filled with vivid dreams which he described thus:

> Flowers of different colors and shapes and odors appeared before my eyes; a group of most beautiful women dressed in white going to and fro seemed to be occupied with the hospitality of this earthly paradise. As if pleased with my coming, they offered me different fruits, berries, and flowers. This delight lasted during my whole sleep, which was a couple of hours longer than my usual rest (Wasson 1968: 244).

Gordon Wasson himself reported a tendency toward sleep in his own experiments with *Amanita muscaria*, and periods of sleep have been reported elsewhere as a consistent symptom of *Amanita muscaria* ingestion (Cosack 1998, Irimoto 2004, Saar 1991).

According to Snorri Sturlson, Odin could change shape and send his spirit out on errands "while his body lay as if asleep or dead" (MacCulloch 1930: 47). This sort of spirit travel is a common feature of shamanism, yet the description of Odin appearing as if asleep or dead, while having a supposedly "ecstatic" experience, is particularly suggestive given his close association with the inebriating Mead of Inspiration. Interestingly, shamanic practices among the Saami share similarities with this description of Odin's spiritual travel. The practices of the Saami are of particular interest since they are reported to have used *Amanita muscaria* as a shamanic inebriant (Itkonen 1946), and because they are linguistically related, as members of the Uralic language family, to Siberian tribes that continue to use *Amanita muscaria* today. During shamanizing it is reported that the Saami shaman "falls down dead" (Backman and Hultkrants 1978: 45). As the shaman lays "as if asleep or dead" he completes his shamanic tasks and afterward wakes up in a sweat, as if he had been involved in some strenuous activity (Backman and Hultkrantz 1978: 102), perhaps suggesting the muscarinic effects of *Amanita muscaria.* It is plausible that shamanic practices, and perhaps use of *Amanita muscaria,* were introduced to the Germanic peoples by the Saami.

Another example of mystical slumber is provided by a Pahlavi translation of the *Avesta,* which describes an event where Zoroaster falls into a seven-day slumber after consuming a substance described as "liquid omniscient wisdom" (Flattery and Schwartz 1989: 21). Flattery and Schwartz (1989: 23) proposed that this liquid represents soma, and maintained that "the Pahlavi accounts show that sauma [soma] brought about a condition outwardly resembling sleep in which visions of what was believed to be a spirit existence were seen." While the original identity of soma was almost certainly lost by the time the Pahlavi texts were written, it is possible that Zoroaster's sleep following consumption of soma is a remnant of earlier accounts of soma's properties.

The infamous Berserker rage, detailed above, is also described as being followed by a period of feebleness and lassitude, a state that was said to persist for a day or more (Fabing 1956: 234). A similar description of the Celtic warrior Cú Chulaind is provided by Thomas Riedlinger (1999), who recounts an episode where Cú Chulaind's battle-fury is followed by a yearlong torpor filled with visionary and prophetic dreams. The combination of agitation and feats of strength with periods of lassitude and sleep in accounts of the Berserkers and tales of Cú Chulaind are clearly suggestive of *Amanita muscaria* use.

While little is known about the pharmacological mechanisms that induce these periods of sleep, the ethnographic record and accumulated anecdotal reports appear to suggest that a period of slumber is a common symptom produced by *Amanita muscaria* inebriation. This "sleep effect" provides us another tool that can be used to further bolster theories regarding use of *Amanita muscaria* in the historical record.

The Sacred Tree and the Mushroom

The *Amanita muscaria,* as a mycorrhizal mushroom, only grows in association with particular trees, a feature that may have become apparent to cultures with traditional uses of the mushroom. In Siberia, the *Amanita muscaria* grows in association with birch, which figures as the world-tree within the cosmology of several Siberian tribes (Eliade 1992, Wasson 1968). Dried *Amanita muscaria* are often kept wrapped in birch cloth or birch containers (Dittmar 1900). In certain Siberian myths, an eagle is described as perched in the tree, while a serpent dwells at its base (Wasson 1968: 214), an image paralleled in Germanic myths of the world tree (Leto 2000: 61). Interestingly, the name for the Germanic World Tree, Yggdrasill, translates as Ygg=Wotan (Odin), drasill=horse, or Wotan's horse (Eliade 1992: 380). This dual identity of Yggdrasill, as both the World Tree and as Wotan's horse, suggests that the horse's saliva, which gives birth to *Amanita muscaria,* fell to the base of the World Tree, perhaps demonstrating recognition of the symbiotic relationship between *Amanita muscaria* and the sacred tree.

While mushrooms are never clearly discussed in relation to the World Tree, Mimir's Well of Wisdom is described as residing under one of its roots. It is from this Well that Odin receives the gift of poetic inspiration. Another interesting story is provided in the *Havamal,* where Odin is described as sacrificing himself on a tree (presumably the World Tree). Odin hangs on the tree for nine days without food or water, before discovering the sacred Runes at the base of the tree. The story contains clear shamanic implications, suggesting a period of fasting before receiving a vision, and is also suggestive of the first stage of preparing the mushroom, dehydration. The lack of food and water can potentially be seen as having the dual meaning of shamanic fasting, as well as desiccation of the sacrament, as personified by Odin. Each of these stories suggests that something important may be found at the base of the World Tree, and when taken together the implication that a sacred inebriant will be found growing at the base of the tree is powerful. That *Amanita muscaria* is clearly specified in one of these stories is a further indicator that the properties of this mushroom were understood, and held in high esteem, perhaps representing both the contents of Mimir's Well as well as the Runes themselves.

Celtic mythology also associates intoxicating "berries" with trees. In "The Voyage of Maeldvin," a tree with magical berries is encountered on a mystical island (Laurie and White 1997). The berries, which produce intoxication and sleep, are described as large as an apple with a tough rind, a description which fails to bring to mind any known fruit trees in Ireland, or the British Isles more generally (Laurie and White 1997). The fact that these berries are found on an island has potentially important implications. With most of Ireland's forests depleted over a thousand years ago, the last remnants of Irish forests would be found on islands (Laurie and White 1997). Because *Amanita muscaria* requires a symbiotic relationship with trees to grow, the mushroom would have been rare on the Irish mainland.

The issue of deforestation is also significant in the case of Iceland and the disappearance of the Berserkers. Iceland had dense forests when it was first settled in 870 CE (Nichols 2000), but most of these forests had disappeared by 1123 CE, when the Berserker rage was outlawed (Leto 2000). Accounts that the Berserkers disappeared around this time perhaps have less to do with the outlawing of "going berserk," and more to do with the lack of forests. Without forests, *Amanita muscaria* would have become unavailable, and cases of *Amanita muscaria* intoxication would have disappeared.

In Mexico there also appears to be a connection between trees and some mushrooms. In the *Annals of the Cakchiquels* there is reference to use of "mushrooms [which grow at the foot] of the trees" as a sacrifice to one of the gods (Recinos and Goetz 1953: 83). In the *Vocabulario Castellano-Zapoteco*, a Zapotec lexicon compiled by Fray Juan de Cordoba, there is a reference to an intoxicating mushroom, *Nocuana peneeche*, which apparently grew in trees (Wasson and Wasson 1957: 228). There is also, of course, the story of Hun-Hunahpú, whose head is hung in a tree, and whose expectoration later results in the birth of the Hero Twins. In this case, Hun-Hunahpú's head could potentially be seen as an embodiment of the mushroom.

More convincing, however, is a myth that comes from the Tzutuhil, telling the creation story of the god Maximon. In this story the Nahuales, gods of the Tzutuhil, were looking for a tree that could rule over the men of earth, and learned of a tree surrounded by mushrooms that grew at the base of a volcano (Lowy 1981). Upon approaching the tree a great wind arose, and the tree was struck by a bolt of lightning, splitting the tree. Inside the tree an ambiguous countenance was encountered, which was then carved into the figure of Maximon. When Maximon was fully formed he was imbued with special powers by the Nahuales. A deaf mute was brought from the village to test Maximon's healing powers. Maximon gave the man a piece of a mushroom found growing at the base of the tree, thereby curing the man of his condition (Lowy 1981). Again, we find a connection between a sacred tree, which gives birth to a god, and healing mushrooms that appear to grow in association with the tree. Interestingly, *Amanita muscaria* is known among the nearby Quiché Maya as Kakuljá, or lightning bolt (Lowy 1974, Lowy 1981), which provides another potential connection between *Amanita muscaria* and the legend of Maximon.

Mushrooms and Mystical Birth

The growth patterns of mushrooms are difficult to view since they come and go so quickly, appearing and disappearing overnight as if by magic. Their apparent lack of seed is another feature that was likely observed by early peoples who encountered them, perhaps providing further mystery as to the origin of these strange organisms. Wasson asserted that the lack of any mention of roots, leaves, blossoms, or seeds in association with descriptions of soma was highly suggestive of a non-plant fungal candidate. Regarding seed specifically, Wasson pointed out that "there is positive evidence that soma was thought to lack seed: soma was procreated from on high, the Somic germ having been placed by the gods" (Wasson 1968: 18). Wasson later went on to discuss Aja Ekapād, a deity connected with soma, whose name roughly translates as "un-born single-foot" (Wasson 1971). The name suggests both a type of miraculous birth or origin, and can also be seen as an anthropomorphism of a mushroom, which has only "one foot."

Among the Mazatec in Oaxaca, Mexico, mushrooms are referred to as *si to,* or "that which springs forth" (Wasson and Wasson 1957: 251). A similar idea, of "springing-forth," also occurs in Germanic mythology in descriptions of how the world was born. According to myth, Odin and his brothers slayed the giant Ymir, and from his body the world was created. Dwarfs, who would later create the Mead of Inspiration, spontaneously appeared "like maggots from the flesh of Ymir" (Leto 2000: 61). This story is noteworthy not only because of the connection between dwarfs and the Mead of Inspiration, but because the miraculous appearance of the dwarfs parallels the miraculous appearance of mushrooms. It is not insignificant that the dwarfs are compared to maggots, organisms that occur abundantly in mature specimens of *Amanita muscaria,* and other mushrooms. Interestingly, the names of the first two dwarfs who emerge are Muódsognir, which roughly translates as "one who guzzles courage," and Durinn, which can be broken down to the term durr, "to sleep" (Leto 2000:61). The first name, Muódsognir, suggests a connection to the Mead of Inspiration, or Dwarfs Mead as it is sometimes called, while the second name suggests a connection between the inebriant and slumber. The apparent embodiment of the mushroom in the dwarfs is also significant because of the characteristic hallucinations of size distortion caused by both *Amanita muscaria* and *Psilocybe* mushrooms.

Size Distortion

The effect of mushrooms on perceptions of size was most famously illustrated by Lewis Carroll in his classic book *Alice in Wonderland.* It is generally believed that Carroll's description of a mushroom that could make one either large or small was inspired by accounts of *Amanita muscaria* use in Siberia. One such account may have come from Stepan Krasheninnikov (1755), who described how a man under the influence of *Amanita muscaria* "might deem a small crack to be as wide as a door, and a tub of water as deep as the sea." While perceptions of space are clearly affected, another interesting feature is the prevalence of diminutive beings in *Amanita muscaria* visions.

In Siberia both the Chukchee and Yurak report visions of "Fly Agaric Men," dwarflike creatures that look like mushrooms, with no neck or legs, which sometimes guide bemushroomed individuals on journeys, and other times are the source of mischief (Bogoras 1904–1909, Lehtisalo 1924). It is believed that the number of these mushroom spirits one encounters depends on the number of mushrooms consumed. As a result, it has become practice among Yurak shamans to eat only two and a half mushrooms, and in this way they can keep up with the half-man while on their journey (Lehtisalo 1924). Similar mushroom spirits are recognized by the Khanty, and other Siberian tribes (Saar 1991).

In Japan, the *Amanita muscaria* is known as *beni-tengu-take,* or long-nosed goblin mushroom (Wasson 1973). The Tengus, or goblins, are considered trickster spirits in Japan. While pickled *Amanita muscaria*s are consumed in Japan without effect, no traditional uses of the mushroom for its psychoactive properties are known. Nonetheless, the name of the mushroom suggests a level of familiarity with its peculiar properties.

As mentioned previously, dwarfs are responsible for the creation of the Mead of Inspiration, which was made by mixing honey with the blood of Kvasir. Dwarfs are strongly associated with the Underworld and appear as anthropomorphized mushrooms in the myth describing the creation of the world. Interestingly, giants are also closely associated with the Mead of Inspiration. The giant Suttung extorts the Mead of Inspiration from the dwarfs, and keeps it hidden within his mountain home, where it is eventually retrieved by Odin. More recent Germanic folklore connects mushrooms with elves, specifically with the elf king, who is commonly depicted as resting under a toadstool. According to folklore, it is said that "whoever carries a toadstool about him grows small and light as an elf" (Nichols 2000: 114; *citing* Grimm 1966: 1412).

Mushrooms and Language

With soma, the Mead of Inspiration, and among other implied sacraments, there is a strong connection between inebriation and the production of language. Indeed, the ninth book of the *Rig Veda* is full of hymns dedicated principally to the god and sacrament soma. Soma, in the *Rig Veda,* is connected with exalted speech and with the origins of poetry. The Mead of Inspiration, sometimes referred to as the Mead of Poetry, is said to provide "poetic inspiration" to those who consume it (MacCulloch 1930). A connection between language and the Germanic sacrament is also apparent in the myth of Odin's self-sacrifice on the World Tree, where he hangs for nine days and nights without food and water before discovering the runes, an early Germanic form of written language.

Among the Celts there is also clear mythology that connects the ideas of poetic inspiration with sacred inebriation. In Celtic mythology there is a story of a tree that drops "hazelnuts" of knowledge into a nearby spring, producing what the Celts referred to as either *bolg fis,* or *bol imbais,* which respectively translate as "bubbles of wisdom" and "bubbles of poetic inspiration" (Laurie and White 1997: 57). According to Laurie and White (1997), the term *bolg* is often found in Irish and Scots Gaelic names of mushrooms, suggesting a possible link between mushrooms and bubbles of wisdom. In a related story,

"The Boyhood Exploits of Finn," Finn MacCool travels to learn poetry from Finn Éices. The boy is asked to catch and cook the salmon of Féc's pool, but told not to eat any part of it. Unbeknownst to the boy, the salmon has fed on the "bubbles of wisdom," and will transfer knowledge to anyone who consumes it. While cooking the fish Finn accidentally burns his thumb; in response the boy places his thumb in his mouth and inadvertently absorbs the power and knowledge of the fish. In this way, Finn becomes a poet, and master of language.

Notably, a direct connection between mushrooms and language can be found among Siberian groups with traditional uses of *Amanita muscaria* and also among Mexican groups who use *Psilocybes* in divinatory and healing rituals. Among the Khanty of Siberia, *Amanita muscaria* plays an important role in the recitation of heroic epics and in the production of ritual song. Storytellers will consume several mushrooms in order to inspire their performances and to "sing heroic epics in a ferocious voice all the night long" (Saar 1991: 164). The *chirta-ko*, a specific type of Khanty shaman, will sing and drum as part of traditional divination rites. Each *chirta-ko* has his own mushroom song, which is understood to be spontaneously bestowed by the mushroom. It is believed that "each fly agaric (*Amanita muscaria*) song is different because it is that particular fly agaric that gives the words to the shaman's song" (Wiget and Balalaeva 2001: 87).

In Mexico, the Mazatec believe that "he who eats these mushrooms [*Psilocybes*], if he is a man of language, becomes endowed with an inspired capacity to speak" (Munn 1973: 88). In interviews with Álvaro Estrada (1981), María Sabina recounted how she received a book of wisdom from the mushrooms, and how she cured "using the language of the children," as the mushrooms are called by the Mazatec (Estrada 1981: 49).

Unlike many of the other traits discussed in this chapter, which are distinctive of *Amanita muscaria*, the connection between mushrooms and language production does not appear to be entirely unique. The use of song and percussive instruments are prevalent in psychedelic forms of shamanism, and also prevalent in religious uses of related inebriants. Song plays an important role in ceremonies of the Native American Church, which uses peyote as a sacrament, and both song and chanting play an important role in the Brazilian ayahuasca religions. Additionally, the apparent miraculous birth of mushrooms also extends to *Psilocybes*, as well as the visual impacts on perceptions of size. While some of the discussed traits can be extended to other psychedelic candidates, I propose that the above traits, when considered as a complex, can ultimately provide an increasingly compelling basis for theories identifying historical uses of *Amanita muscaria*.

Conclusion

Due to their soft bodies and ephemeral nature, it is unlikely that biological evidence of mushrooms will ever be discovered in the archaeological record. This fact poses certain difficulties in determining the antiquity of modern cultural uses of psychoactive mushrooms, like those in Mexico and Siberia, and makes it even more difficult to determine whether psychoactive mushrooms were recognized and used by historical culture groups that are now extinct. These limitations, however, should not discourage the pursuit of these investigations.

Even though Wasson was not an anthropologist, or a historian, his approach to research was generally measured and thoughtful, combining data from historical texts and both the ethnographic and archaeological record, in addition to his own on-the-ground data collection. While Wasson's investigations into the identity of the *Vedic* soma were groundbreaking, his line of argumentation was limited by an incomplete understanding of the pharmacological properties of *Amanita muscaria.* In the preceding pages I have endeavored to detail the variety of unique pharmacological and biological properties of *Amanita muscaria* and, through examples based on historical cultures in India, Mesoamerica, and Europe, to illustrate how the idiosyncratic properties of *Amanita muscaria* can be used as tools to help flesh out theories attempting to identify historical and ritual uses of this mushroom. While many of the examples provided are speculative, they all suggest that a more comprehensive examination of these historical cultures may bear *fruit*. New investigations with an eye to *Amanita muscaria*'s unique properties, including evidence of appropriate detoxification methods, muscarinic symptoms, and variations between feats of strength and slumber, may help to bolster existing theories regarding historical uses of *Amanita muscaria*, as well as to develop promising new lines of inquiry.

References

NOTE: references marked with an * have been cited after the book by Wasson (1968).

Allegro, J. M. 1971. *The Sacred Mushroom and the Cross*. New York: Bantam Books.

Arthur, J. 2003. *Mushrooms and Mankind: The Impact of Mushrooms on Human Consciousness and Religion*. Escondido, CA: The Book Tree.

Bäckman, L. and Å. Hultkrantz. 1978. *Studies in Lapp Shamanism*. Stockholm: Almqvist & Wiksell International.

Baquedano, E. and Graulich, M. 1993. "Decapitation among the Aztecs: Mythology, Agriculture, Politics, and Hunting." *Estudios de Cultura N´ahuatl* 23:163–177.

Bogoras, W. 1904–1909. The Chukchee, Memoir of the American Museum of Natural History. Jesup North Pacific Expedition, Parts 1, 2, and 3. New York.*

Borhegyi, C. de. 2010. *Soma: "Divine Mushroom of Immortality" in the New World*. Hidden in Plain Sight. Available at: http://www.mushroomstone.com.

Borhegyi, S. F. de. 1980. "The Pre-Columbian Ballgames: A Pan-Mesoamerican Tradition." *Contributions in Anthropology and History*, Vol. 1. Milwaukee Public Museum.

Borhegyi, S. F. de. 1961. "Miniature Mushroom Stones from Guatemala." *American Antiquity* 26: 498–504.

Brough, J. 1971. "Soma and *Amanita muscaria.*" *Bulletin of the School of Oriental and African Studies* (BSOAS) 34: 331–62.

Buchholz, P. 1984. "Odin: Celtic and Siberian Affinities of a Germanic Deity." *The Mankind Quarterly* 24: 427–437.

Catalfomo, P. and Eugster, C. H. 1970. "*Amanita muscaria:* Present Understanding of its Chemistry." *Bulletin on Narcotics* 22 (4): 33–41.

Chilton, W. S. 1975. "The Course of an Intentional Poisoning." *McIlvainea* 2: 17–18.

Cosack, R. 1998. "*Amanita muscaria* and the Curing Sleep." *Yearbook for Ethnomedicine and the Study of Consciousness* 6–7(1997/1998): 273–282.

Cowan, T. 1993. *Fire in the Head: Shamanism and the Celtic Spirit.* San Francisco: HarperSanFrancisco.

Dittmar, C. 1900. "Reisen und Aufenthalt in Kamtschatka in den Jahren 1851–1855." In *Beiträge zur Kenntniss des Russischen Reiches und der angrenzenden Länder Asiens,* Series 3, Vol. 8 (pp. 98–100). St. Petersburg.*

Doniger, W. 2005. *The Rig Veda.* London: Penguin Classics.

Eliade, M. 1992. *Shamanism: Archaic Techniques of Ecstasy.* Princeton: Princeton University Press.

Eliade, M. 1982. *A History of Religious Ideas, Vol. 2.* Chicago: The University of Chicago Press.

Erman, A. 1833–1848. *Reise um die Erde durch Nord-Asien und die beiden Oceane in den Jahren 1828, 1829 und 1830 ausgeführt.* Berlin.*

Estrada, Á. 1981. *María Sabina: Her Life and Chants.* Santa Barbara: Ross-Erikson.

Fabing, H. D. 1956. "On Going Berserk: A Neurochemical Inquiry." *The Scientific* Monthly 83(5): 232–237.

Feeney, K. 2010. "Revisiting Wasson's Soma: Exploring the Effects of Preparation on the Chemistry of *Amanita muscaria.*" Journal of Psychoactive Drugs 42(4): 499–506.

Feeney, K. and Stijve, T. 2011. "Re-examining the Role of Muscarine in the Chemistry of *Amanita muscaria.*" *Mushroom: The Journal of Wild Mushrooming* 106: 32–36.

Félice, P. de. 1936. *Poisons Sacrés, Ivresses Divines: Essai sur quelques forms inférieures de la mystique.* Paris.*

Flattery, D. S. and Schwartz, M. 1989. "Haoma and Harmaline: The Botanical Identity of the Indo-Iranian Sacred Hallucinogen 'Soma' and Its Legacy in Religion, Language, and Middle Eastern Folklore." *Near Eastern Studies* 21: 1–211.

Goetz, D. & Morley, S. G. 1950. *Popol Vuh: The Sacred Book of the Ancient Quiché Maya.* Norman: University of Oklahoma Press.

Greene, M. T. 1992. *Natural Knowledge in Preclassical Antiquity.* Baltimore: The Johns Hopkins University Press.

Grieshaber, A. F., Moore, K. A., and Levine, B. 2001. "The Detection of Psilocin in Human Urine." *Journal of Forensic Sciences* 46: 627–630.

Grimm, J. 1966. *Teutonic Mythology.* New York: Dover.

Härkönen, M. 1998. "Uses of Mushrooms by Finns and Karelians." International Journal of Circumpolar Health 57(1): 40–55.

Heinrich, C. 2002. *Magic Mushrooms in Religion and Alchemy.* Rochester, VT: Park Street Press.

Hollander, L. M. 2002. *Heimskringla: History of the Kings of Norway.* Austin, Texas: University of Texas Press.

Ingalls, D. H. H. 1971. "Remarks on Mr. Wasson's Soma." *Journal of the American* Oriental Society 91 (2): 188–91.

Irimoto, T. 2004. *The Eternal Cycle: Ecology, Worldview and Ritual of Reindeer Herders of Northern Kamchatka.* National Museum of Ethnology. Osaka, Japan.

Irvin, J. 2009. *The Holy Mushroom: Evidence of Mushrooms in Judeo-Christianity.* Gnostic Media Research & Publishing.

Irvin, J. and Rutajit, A. 2009. *Astrotheology & Shamanism: Christianity's Pagan Roots.* BookSurge Publishing.

Itkonen, T. I. 1946. "Heidnische Religion und späterer Aberglaube bei den finnischen Lappen." *Mémoires de la Société Finno-ougrienne* 87. Helsinki.

Jochelson, W. 1905/1908. *The Koryak: Memoir of the American Museum of Natural History, New York.* A Publication of the Jesup North Pacific Expedition. Vol. VI, Part I. Religion and Myth, New York, 1905. Part II. Material Culture and Social Organization of the Koryak, 1908.*

Johns, T. and Kubo I. 1988. "A Survey of Traditional Methods Employed for the Detoxification of Plant Foods." *Journal of Ethnobiology* 8(1): 81–129.

Kalberer, F., Kreis, W., and J. Rutschman. 1962. "The Fate of Psilocin in the Rat." *Biochemical Pharmacology* 11(4): 261–269.

Krasheninnikov, S. 1755. *Description of Kamchatka Land.* St. Petersburg.*

Langsdorf, G. H. von. 1809. "Einige Bemerkungen, die Eigenschaften des Kamtschadalischen Fliegenschwammes betreffend." Wetterauischen Gesellschaft fur die gesammte Naturkunde, Annalen Vol. I, No. 2 (pp. 249–259). Frankfurt.*

Laurie, E. R. and T. White. 1997. "Speckled Snake, Brother of Birch: *Amanita muscaria* Motifs in Celtic Legends." *Shaman's Drum* 44 (Mar/May): 52–65.

Lehtisalo, T. 1924. "Entwurf einer Mythologie der Jurak-Samojeden." *Mémoires de la Société Finno-Ougrienne,* Vol. LIII. Helsinki.*

Letcher, A. 2008. *Shroom: A Cultural History of the Magic Mushroom.* New York: Harper Perennial.

Leto, S. 2000. "Magical Potions: Entheogenic Themes in Scandinavian Mythology." *Shaman's Drum* 54 (Winter): 55–65.

Lowy, B. 1974. "*Amanita muscaria* and the Thunderbolt Legend in Guatemala and Mexico." *Mycologia* 66: 188–191.

Lowy, B. 1981. "Ethnomycological Inferences from Mushroom Stones, Maya Codices, and Tzutuhil Legend." *Revista/Review Interamericana* 10(1): 94–103.

MacCulloch, J. A. 1930. *The Mythology of All Races: Eddic Mythology, Vol. II.* Boston: Marshall Jones Company.

MacDonell, A. A. 2006. *A Vedic Reader for Students.* Delhi: Motilal Banarsidass Publishers.

Maydell, B. G. von. 1893. "Reisen und Forschungen im Jakutskischen Gebiet Ostsibiriens in den Jahren 1861–1871." In *Beiträge zur Kenntniss des Russischen Reiches und der angrenzenden Länder Asiens,* Series 4, Vol. 1–2 (pp. 298–300). St. Petersburg.*

Michelot, D. & Melendez-Howell, L. M. 2003. "*Amanita muscaria:* Chemistry, Biology, Toxicology, and Ethnomycology." *Mycological Research* 107(2): 131–146.

Morgan, A. 1995. *Toads & Toadstools: The Natural History, Folklore, and Cultural Oddities of a Strange Association.* Berkeley, CA: Celestial Arts.

Munn, H. 1973. "The Mushrooms of Language." In *Hallucinogens and Shamanism,* edited by M. Harner, pp. 86–122. New York: Oxford University Press.

Nichols, B. 2000. "The Fly-Agaric and Early Scandinavian Religion." *Eleusis: Journal of Psychoactive Plants & Compounds* 4: 87–119.

Ott, J. 1998. "The Post-Wasson History of the Soma Plant." *Eleusis: Journal of Psychoactive Plants and Compounds* 1: 9–37.

Phipps, A. G. 2000. "Japanese Use of Beni-Tengu-Dake *(Amanita muscaria)* and the Efficacy of Traditional Detoxification Methods." Masters Thesis. Florida International University.

Recinos, A. & Goetz, D. 1953. The *Annals of the Cakchiquels.* Norman: University of Oklahoma Press.

Riedlinger, T. J. 1999. "Fly-Agaric Motifs in the Cú Chulaind Myth Cycle." Paper presented 29 October 1999 at the Mycomedia Millennium Conference, Breitenbush Hot Springs Retreat and Conference Center, Detroit, Oregon. Available at: http://www.erowid.org/plants/amanitas/amanitas_writings5.shtml

Saar, M. 1991. “Ethnomycological Data from Siberia and North-East Asia on the Effect of *Amanita muscaria.*” *Journal of Ethnopharmacology* 31: 157–173.

Schultes, R. E. and A. Hofmann 1992. *Plants of the Gods.* Rochester, VT: Healing Arts Press.

Stijve, T. 1981. “High Performance Thin-Layer Chromatographic Determination of the Toxic Principles of Some Poisonous Mushrooms.” *Mitt. Gebiete Lebensm. Hyg.* 72: 44–54.

Stijve, T. 1982. “Het Voorkomen van Muscarine en Muscimol in Verschillende Paddestoelen.” *COOLIA* 25(4): 94 – 100.

Tedlock, D. 1996. *Popol Vuh: The Definitive Edition of the Mayan Book of the Dawn of Life and the Glories of Gods and Kings.* New York: Simon & Schuster.

Tsujikawa, K., H. Mohri, K. Kuwayama, H. Miyaguchi, Y. Iwata, A. Gohda, S. Fukushima, H. Inoue, and T. Kishi. 2006. “Analysis of Hallucinogenic Constituents in *Amanita* Mushrooms Circulated in Japan.” *Forensic Science International* 164: 172–178.

Tsunoda, K., N. Inoue, Y. Aoyagi, and T. Sugahara. 1993a. “Change in Ibotenic Acid and Muscimol Contents in *Amanita muscaria* during Drying, Storing or Cooking.” *Journal of the Food Hygienic Society of Japan* 34(2): 153–160.

Tsunoda, K., Inoue, N., Aoyagi, Y., and T. Sugahara. 1993b. “Changes in Concentration of Ibotenic Acid and Muscimol in the Fruit Body of *Amanita muscaria* during the Reproduction Stage.” *Journal of the Food Hygienic Society of Japan* 34(1): 18–24.

Turner, V. 1965. “Ritual Symbolism, Morality, and Social Structure among the Ndembu.” In *African Systems of Thoughts,* edited by M. Fortes and G. Dieterlen, pp. 75–95. London: Oxford University Press for the International African Institute.

Vankirk, J. and Bassett-Vankirk, P. 1997. *Remarkable Remains of the Ancient Peoples of Guatemala.* Norman: University of Oklahoma Press.

Waser, P. G. 1979. "The Pharmacology of *Amanita muscaria.*" In *Ethnopharmacologic Search for Psychoactive Drugs,* edited by D. Efron, B. Holmstedt, and N. S. Kline. New York: Raven Press.

Wasson, R. G. 1968. *Soma: Divine Mushroom of Immortality.* Italy: Harcourt Brace Jovanovich, Inc.

Wasson, R. G. 1971. "The Soma of the Rig Veda: What Was It?" *Journal of the American Oriental Society* 91(2): 169–187.

Wasson, R. G. 1973. "Mushrooms and Japanese Culture." *Transactions of the Asiatic Society of Japan,* Vol. 11: 5–25.

Wasson, R.G. and Wasson, V.P. 1957. *Mushrooms, Russia and History.* New York: Pantheon.

Wiget, A. and Balalaeva, O. 2001. "Khanty Communal Reindeer Sacrifice: Belief, Subsistence and Cultural Persistence in Contemporary Siberia." *Arctic Anthropology* 38(1): 82–99.

Wilson, P. L. 2001. *Ploughing the Clouds: The Search for Irish Soma.* San Francisco: City Lights Publishers.

Figures

Figure 1. The above statuette comes from Nayarit, Mexico, and is believed to date back to 100 CE. Here a man, perhaps a *curandero,* is seated beneath a giant *Amanita muscaria.* (Illustration by Laura Boergadine Sapp ©).

Figure 2. This panel taken from the *Madrid Codex* features God M (right) presenting what appears to be an *Amanita muscaria* to a seated figure. Alternatively, it has been speculated that the object represents an incense burner. (Illustration by Laura Boergadine Sapp ©).

Figure 3. This stone sculpture represents the Wind God, Ehecatl, and prominently features his dangling eyeballs, generally considered to be tears. Upon closer inspection, however, the tears can easily be seen as the stalk and bulbous base of an *Amanita,* with the eyelids providing the cap of the mushroom. Only the characteristic warts are missing. (Photo by Jacques VanKirk ©).

Figure 4. This panel taken from the *Codex Borgia* features the God of Twins, Xólotl. Here, and elsewhere in the *Codex,* he is featured with a dangling eyeball, or what appears to be a mushroom. The similarities between this stylized "eye" in the *Codex* and those in the sculpture of Ehecatl are noteworthy and require further investigation. (Illustration © by Laura Boergadine Sapp).

Chapter 7

Enter the Jaguar

Mike Jay

Mike Jay has written widely on the history of science and medicine, and is a specialist in the study of drugs across history and cultures. His books on the subject include *Emperors of Dreams: Drugs in the Nineteenth Century* (2000, revised edition 2011), *The Atmosphere of Heaven* (2009), and, *High Society: Mind-Altering Drugs in History and Culture* (2010). His website is http://mikejay.net.

Introduction

The monumental ruins of Chavín de Huantar, 10,000 feet up in the Cordillera Blanca of the Peruvian Andes, are officially a mystery. The vast, ruined granite and sandstone structures—cyclopean walls, huge sunken plazas and step pyramids—date from around 1000 BCE, but although they were refashioned and augmented for close to a thousand years, the evidence for the material culture associated with them is fragmentary at best. Chavín seems to have been neither a city nor a military structure, but a temple complex constructed for unknown ritual purposes by a culture that had vanished long before written sources appeared. Its most striking feature is that its pyramids are hollow, a labyrinth of tunnels connecting hundreds of cramped stone chambers. These might be tombs, but there are no bodies; habitations, but they are arranged in a disorienting layout in pitch-blackness; grain stores, but their arrangement is equally impractical. Instead, there are irrigation ducts honeycombed through the carved rock, elaborately channeling a nearby spring through the subterranean maze, and in the center a megalith set in a vaulted chamber and carved with a swirling, baroque representation of a huge-eyed and jaguar-fanged entity.

The archaeological consensus is that Chavín was some kind of ceremonial focus; some have tentatively located it within a lost tradition of oracles and dream incubation. But the mystery remains profound, and is considerably heightened by the bigger picture that it represents. By most reckonings, and depending on how the term is defined, "civilization" emerged spontaneously in only a handful of locations around the globe: Mesopotamia, the Indus Valley, China, Mexico, perhaps the Nile. To this short list, especially if civilization is defined in terms of monumental architecture, must now be added Peru. It was only proposed in the 1930s that Chavín is 3,000 years old, and it has only recently been recognized that huge ceremonial structures of plazas and pyramids were being constructed in Peru at least a thousand years earlier. The coastal site of Caral, only now being excavated, turns out to contain the oldest stone pyramid thus far discovered, predating those of Old Kingdom Egypt. So the mystery of Chavín is not an isolated one: It was the flowering of a pristine and unique culture, and one that still awaits interpretation.

But there's a salient and largely unexamined feature of the Chavín culture, which offers a lead into the heart of the mystery: the presence of a complex of powerful plant hallucinogens in its ritual world. The San Pedro cactus (Trichocereus/Echinopsis spp.) is explicitly featured in its iconography; like the Mexican peyote cactus, San Pedro contains mescaline, and is still widely used as a visionary intoxicant in Peru today. Objects excavated from the site also include snuff trays and bone tubes similar to those still used in the Peruvian Amazon for inhaling seeds and bark containing the powerful hallucinogen dimethyltryptamine (DMT). The leading Western scholar of the culture, Yale University's Richard Burger, whose *Chavín and the Origins of Andean Civilization* (Thames & Hudson 1992) is the most authoritative survey of the territory, states plainly enough that "the central role of psychotropic substances at Chavín is amply documented."

It's not special pleading for a drug-centric view of ancient cultures (at least, not necessarily) to observe that the presence of mind-altering plants offers a bridge between remains and ritual, by indicating the state of consciousness in which the latter would have taken place. It also opens up collateral evidence from the deep-rooted traditions of mind-altering plant use, which still exist in the region, and from modern understanding of the drugs in question. The combination of mescaline- and DMT-containing plants has been surprisingly little-explored even in the dedicated fringes of contemporary drug culture, but the preparations in question remain legally obtainable, relatively simple to prepare in high-potency doses, and powerfully effective. Such observations may have limited explanatory power, since a state of consciousness is not a belief system and offers little evidence for the content of the ceremonies in which drugs are used. Nevertheless, the effects of these particular drugs set logistical parameters for their use, to which the design of the Chavín complex may have been a practical response.

First, I will give a brief survey of the culture from which Chavín emerged, and then follow this with some thoughts on the role that plant hallucinogens might have played in the temple's mysteries.

For many thousands of years the Pacific coast of Peru has been as it is today, that is a barren, moonscape desert. Rain never falls except in El Niño years; fresh water is only to be found in the few river valleys, which punctuate it; for the best part of a thousand miles, rocky shores meet a cold ocean in a misty haze. But the harsh terrain has its riches, for the Humboldt current, sweeping up from the freezing depths of the southern ocean, is loaded with krill and alive with fish; its biomass is 100 times greater than the balmy Atlantic at the same latitude off Brazil. For 10,000 years a substantial human population has been sustained by this current: rancid industrial fishmeal factories today, but in the Stone Age groups of itinerant hunter-gatherers whose presence is attested to by massive shell middens. Some of these hills of organic detritus—oyster shells, cotton twine, dried chilies, crushed bones—are a hundred feet high, and remained in continuous use for 5,000 years or more.

It was out of this seasonally nomadic coastal culture, shuttling between the arid coasts and the fertile mountain valleys, that the first monumental sites emerged. Dates are still being revised, but are now firmly set some time before 2000 BCE. The sites may have been used much earlier as huacas, natural sacred spots, around which ceremonial stone and adobe structures gradually accreted and expanded. Caral, a massive site a hundred miles north of Lima where substantial excavation is finally under way, is perhaps an example of this process. Its sprawling complex of dusty mounds centers on a megalith, perhaps originally upended into the valley by an earthquake; from the vantage point of this stone the oldest pyramid precisely mirrors the peak of the mountain that towers over it, suggesting that the megalith may have been the original focus for this alignment. The pyramids, at Caral as elsewhere, seem to have begun as raised platforms for fire-pits, which were subsequently extended upward in layers as the site grew to accommodate increasing human traffic. Below Caral's pyramids is another feature that would endure for millennia and spread from the coast to the high mountains: a sunken circular plaza, large enough for a gathering of several hundred participants, with steps leading up to the platform of the pyramid above.

This plaza-and-pyramid layout, reproduced in dozens of sites spanning hundreds of miles and thousands of years, seems to have evolved for a ceremonial purpose, but there's still little consensus about what this might have entailed. Beyond the general problem of reconstructing systems of meaning and belief from stone, these early sites are sparse in cultural materials. Graves are few, and simple; the early monumental building predates the firing of pottery (hence the archaeological term for the era, "Preceramic"). There's little general evidence of human habitation, although there are some chambers in the Caral pyramids that may have housed those who attended the site. Some scholars have sought to cast these as a "priestly elite" ruling caste of a stratified society, but they may equally have been no more than a class of specialist functionaries without particularly exalted status in the community. Certainly a site like Caral would have been no prize residence: It's not a palace at the center of a subjugated settlement so much as a monastic perch on its desolate fringes. Its barren, windswept desert setting overlooks a fertile valley, taking up none of the precious irrigated terrain.

The size of the complex suggests that the fertile valley attracted visitors, and that Caral was a site of pilgrimage for more than its local community. The earliest agriculture on the coast emerged in such valleys, especially cotton and gourds, which were used for making fishing nets and floats; it may be, therefore, that the ceremonial site grew in size as the use of these cultivated commodities spread ever more widely through the loose network of fishing communities up and down the coast. This would suggest a very different picture from the one presented by better-known pristine civilizations such as Mesopotamia or the Indus Valley, where archaeologists have tended to associate the origins of monumental architecture with the control of complex power relations—a centralized state, coercive labor, irrigation systems, a powerful priest craft or military might. Peru seems to tell a rather different story: one of structures emerging largely unplanned, piecemeal and over generations, within a shifting, stateless network of hunter-gatherers.

A further clue to the culture of these Preceramic coastal sites is provided by Sechin, a complex a few centuries later than Caral (around 1700 BCE), several river valleys to the north. Here, for the first time, the temple is adorned with figurative carvings. But if these are a clue, they're an oblique one: graphic but inscrutable representations carved in relief on stone blocks. Most are of human forms, some of them dismembered, but their most distinctive motif is wavy trail lines, often ending in finger-like tips, emanating from various parts of the bodies. Some of these seem to be intestines, and some emerge from the mouths of the carvings, but others coil from heads, hands, and ears, suggesting they aren't literal representations of blood, guts, or bodily fluids. Their significance remains disputed. Early interpretations tended to claim that they were savage warrior figures commemorating tribal battles, victories, and annihilated populations, but many of the figures are hard to fit into such a scheme. Recent interpretations, by contrast, have tended to focus on visionary, perhaps shamanic states, just as the Paleolithic cave art of Europe is now increasingly interpreted not as realistic representations of "hunting scenes" but of an imagined dreamtime previously visited in a heightened state of consciousness—see, for example, David Lewis-Williams, *The Mind in the Cave* (Thames and Hudson 2002). Within this reading, the numinous swirls and halos would commemorate not military victories but the mysteries the ceremony at Sechin engendered.

There is circumstantial evidence for interpolating the use of plant drugs into this ceremonial world. Part of this comes from Chavín, where the same structures would emerge later with images of these plants explicitly represented. Part of it comes from nearby archaeological finds of chewed coca leaf quids and rolls of plant material, which may be cored, skinned, and dried San Pedro cactus. The coca, along with other plant remains, implies a trade network that connected the coast and the mountains—a symbiosis that would later characterize the Chavín culture. Coca doesn't grow on the coast, but at an altitude of 1,000-2,000 meters up the mountain valleys; San Pedro begins to colonize the steep mountain cliffs at the upper end of this belt, continuing up to 3,000 meters. Given that more bulky mountain plant foodstuffs were being supplied to the barren desert coast two or three days' journey away, and dried and salted fish traded in return, fresh or dried San Pedro could have been brought down in quantity, as it still is today.

Chavín culture, when it emerged, would testify to the existence of such cross-cultural contact, and more besides. Yet Chavín wasn't the first ceremonial center in the mountains. The Preceramic site of Kotosh, a hundred miles away from it across the inland ranges, dates from a similar period as Sechin, and its remains show similar structures: altar-like platforms around stone-enclosed fire pits, stacked on top of one another through several layers of occupation. One gnomic Preceramic symbol also survives: a molded mud-brick relief of a pair of crossed hands, now housed in the national museum in Lima. Centuries before Chavín, perhaps as early as 2000 BCE, Kotosh demonstrates that trade links between the mountains and the coast had also generated some commonality of worship.

***

The emergence of Chavín as a ceremonial center, probably around 900 BCE, adds much to this earlier picture: It's more complex in construction than its predecessors, and far richer in symbolic art. It's set not on a peak or commanding ridge, but in the narrow valley of the Mosna River, at the junction of a tributary, with mountains rising up steeply to enclose it on all sides. Similarly, the temple structure itself isn't designed to be spectacular or visible from a distance, but is concealed from all sides behind high walls. The approach to the site would have been through a narrow ramped entrance in these walls, whose distinctive feature was that they were studded with gargoyle-like, lifesize heads, some human, some distinctly feline with exaggerated jaws and sprouting canine teeth, and some, often covered in swirling patterns, in the process of transforming from one state to the other. This process of transformation is clearly a physical ordeal, as the shape-shifting heads grimace, with teeth exposed in rictus grins. In a specific and recurrent detail, mucus emanates in streams from their noses.

Inside these walls—now mostly crumbled, and with the majority of the heads housed in the onsite museum—there are still substantial remains of a ceremonial complex, which was reworked and expanded for nearly a thousand years, its last and largest elements dating to around 200 BCE. The basic arrangement is the by-now-traditional one of plaza and step pyramid, but these are adorned with far more complexity than their predecessors. Many lintels, columns, and stelae are covered with relief carvings, swirling motifs featuring feline jaws, eyes and wings. The initial impression is amorphous and chaotic, but on closer inspection these motifs unfurl into composite images, their interleaved elements in different scales and dimensions, the whole often representing some chimerical entity composed of smaller-scale entities roiling inside it. As the architecture develops through the centuries it becomes larger in scale, reflecting the increased scale of the site; at the same time, the reliefs gradually become less figurative and more abstract, discrete entities melting into a mosaic of stylized patterns and flourishes.

It was only in 1972 that the most striking of these reliefs were uncovered, on faced slabs that line the oldest of the sunken plazas, running like a frieze around its circle at knee height. These figures are presumably from the site's formative period; the most remarkable is a human figure in a state of feline transformation, bristling with jaws, claws, and snakes, and clutching an unmistakable San Pedro cactus like a staff or spear. Beneath this figure—the "Chaman," as he's become informally known, runs a procession of jaguars carved in swirling lines, with other creatures, birds of prey, and snakes, sometimes incorporated into the whorls of their tails.

These reliefs are all carved in profile, and all face toward the steps that lead up from the circular plaza to the old pyramid, at the top of which is the familiar altar-like platform. But at the back of this platform is something entirely unfamiliar: a pair of stone doorways disappearing into the darkness inside the pyramid itself. These lead via steps down into tunnels around six-foot high and constructed, rather like Bronze Age long barrows, from huge granite slabs and lintels. The tunnels take sharp, maze-like, usually right-angled turns, apparently designed to disorient and cut out the daylight, zigzagging into pitch-blackness. Opening out from these subterranean corridors are dozens of rock-hewn side chambers, some large enough for half a dozen people, others seemingly for solitary confinement. There are niches hacked in some of the chamber walls that might have housed oil lamps, and lintels which extrude like hammock pegs.

Running through the bewildering network of tunnels and chambers are smaller shafts, some of them air vents, others water ducts, which allowed the nearby spring to gush and echo through this elaborately constructed Underworld.

Right in the heart of the labyrinth is a stela carved in the early Chavín style, a clawed, fanged, and rolling-eyed humanoid form, boxed inside a cramped cruciform chamber that rises to the top of the pyramid. The loose arrangement of stones in the roof above, which form a plug at the crown of the pyramid, have led to speculation that they might have been removable, allowing the Lanzon, as the carved stela is known, to point up like a needle to a gap of exposed sky. Other fragments of evidence from the site, such as a large boulder with seven sunken pits in the configuration of the Pleiades, suggest that an element of the Chavín ritual—perhaps, given the narrow confines around the Lanzon, a priestly rather than a public one—might have involved aligning the stela with astronomical events.

This plaza and pyramid was Chavín's original structure, but over the centuries more and grander variants were added. There are several shafts, some still unexcavated, that lead down into larger underground complexes, their stonework more regular than the old pyramid and their side chambers typically more spacious. There is a far larger sunken plaza, too, square rather than circular and leading up to a new pyramid and surrounding walls on a more massive scale. Whatever happened at Chavín, the architecture suggests that it carried on for centuries, and for an increasing volume of participants.

The term most commonly applied to what went on at Chavín is "cult," although elements of meaning might perhaps be imported from other terms like pilgrimage destination, sacred site, oracle, or, in its classical sense, temple of mysteries. This is a conclusion partly drawn from lack of evidence that it represented an empire, or a state power: There are no military structures associated with it, nor centralized labor for major public works like irrigation or housing. During the several centuries of its existence, tribal networks would have risen and fallen around it, changes in the balance of power apparently leaving its source of authority untouched. Its cultic—or cultural—influence, though, spread far and wide. Throughout the first millennium BCE, "Chavínoid" sites spread across large swaths of northern Peru, and preexisting natural huacas began to develop Chavín-style flourishes: rock surfaces carved with snaky fangs and jaws, standing stones decorated with bug-eyed, fierce-toothed humanoid forms. People were clearly coming to Chavín from considerable distances, and carrying its influence back to far-flung valleys, mountains, and coasts.

Was Chavín, then, a religion? There has been some speculation that the carvings on the site represent a "Chavín cosmology," with eagle, snake, and jaguar corresponding to earth and sky and so forth, and the humanoid shape-shifter, as represented on the Lanzon, a "supreme deity." But Chavín was not a power base that could coerce its subjects to replace their religion with its own: The spread of its influence indicates that it drew its devotees from a wide range of tribal belief systems with which it existed in parallel. It is perhaps better understood as a site that offered an experience rather than a cosmology or creed, with its architecture conceived and designed as the locus for a particular ritual journey. In this sense, the Chavín figures would not have been deities competing with those of the participants, but graphic representations of the process that took place inside its walls.

The central motif of this process is signaled clearly enough by the shape-shifting feline heads that studded its portals: transformation from the human state into something else. It is here that Chavin displays the influence of a new cultural element not conspicuous in the sites preceding it. The prominence of the jaguar and shape-shifting motifs suggest the intertwining of traditions not just from the coast and the mountains, but also from the jungle on the far side of the Andes. While the monumental style of Chavín's architecture builds on earlier coastal models, its symbolism points to the feline transformations that still characterize many Amazon shamanisms. The trading networks on the Pacific Coast had long ago joined with those in the mountains; at Chavín, where the river Mosna runs east into the Rio Marañon and thence into the Amazon, it seems that these networks had also reached down the humid eastern Andean slopes into the jungle, and had transmitted the influence of another hunter-gatherer culture: one characterized by powerful shamanic technologies of transformation, in many cases with the use of plant entheogens.

These twin influences—the coastal mountains and the jungle—are mirrored by the presence at Chavín not of one entheogenic plant but two. The San Pedro cactus, as depicted on the wall of Chavín's old plaza, may have been an element of the earlier coastal tradition, but is in any case native to Chavín's high valley: A magnificent specimen, which must be at least 200 years old, towers over the site today. Local villages still plant hedges with it, and traders to the curandero markets down in the coastal cities still source it from the area. But the mucus pouring from the noses of the carved heads, combined with material finds of bone sniffing tubes and snuff trays, all point with equal clarity to the use at Chavín of plants containing a second drug, DMT, and a tradition with a different source: the Amazon jungle.

Today, the best-known ethnographic use of DMT-containing snuffs is among the Yanomami people of the Amazon, who traditionally blow powdered Virola tree bark resin up one another's noses with six-foot blowpipes, a practice which produces a short and intense hallucinatory burst accompanied by spectacular streams of mucus. But there are various other DMT-containing snuffs used in the region, including the powdered seeds of the tree *Anadenanthera colubrina,* whose distribution—and its artistic depiction in later Andean cultures—makes it the most likely ingredient in the Chavín brew. Anadenanthera-snuffing has been largely replaced in many areas of the Amazon by ayahuasca-drinking, a more manageable technique of DMT ingestion, but this displacement is a recent one, and Anadenanthera is still used by some tribal groups in the remote forest around the borders of Peru, Colombia, and Brazil. Even today, the tree grows up the Amazonian slopes of the eastern Andes and as far west as the highlands around Kotosh. The transformation offered at Chavín was, it seems, mediated by the combination of these two extremely potent psychedelics.

The presence of these two plants at Chavín, without necessarily illuminating the purpose or content of the rituals, has certain implications. The effects and duration of San Pedro and Anadenanthera are very distinct from each other, and characterized by quite different ritual uses. San Pedro, boiled, stewed, and drunk, can take an hour or more before the effects are felt; once they appear, they last for at least ten hours. The physical sensation is euphoric, languid, expansive, and often with some accompanying nausea; in many Indian traditions, such effects are dealt with by setting the participants to slow, shuffling three-step dances and chants. The effect on consciousness is similarly fluid and oceanic, including visual trails and a heightened sense of presence: The swirling lines that surround the figures at Sechin could perhaps be read as visual representations of this sense of energy projecting itself from the body—particularly from the swirling, psychedelicized intestines—into an immanent spirit world.

Anadenanthera, by contrast, is a short, sharp shock, and one that's powerfully potentiated by a prior dose of San Pedro. At least a gram of powdered seed needs to be snuffed, enough to pack both nostrils. This process rapidly elicits a burning sensation, extreme nausea, and often convulsive vomiting, the production of gouts of nasal mucus, and perhaps half an hour of exquisite visions, often accompanied by physical contortions, growls, and grimaces that are typically understood in Amazon cultures as feline transformations. Unlike San Pedro, which can be taken communally, the physical ordeal of Anadenanthera tends to make it a solitary one; the subject hunched in a ball, eyes closed, absorbed in an interior world. This interior world is perhaps recognizable in the new decorative elements that emerged at Chavín. Images like the spectacular glyph that covers the Raimundi stela—a human figure that seems to be flowering into other dimensions and sprouting an elaborate headdress of multiple eyes and fangs—are reminiscent not just of ayahuasca art in the Amazon today but also of the fractal, computer-generated visual work associated with DMT in modern Western subcultures.

The distinct effects of these two drugs suggest a functional division between two elements or phases of the ritual, mirrored in Chavín's contrasting architectural elements. Like the kiva in Southwestern Native American architecture, which it so closely resembles, the circular plaza is readily interpreted as a communal space, used for gathering and mingling, and thus perhaps for dancing and chanting through a long ritual accompanied by group intoxication with San Pedro: It may be that the cactus was already a traditional element of the coastal ceremonies where the form of the plaza originated. The innovative addition of chambers inside the pyramid, by contrast, seems designed for the absorption in an interior world engendered by Anadenanthera, an incubation where the subject is transformed and reborn in the womb of darkness.

Chavín's architecture, in this sense, can be understood as a visionary technology, designed to externalize and intensify these intoxications and to focus them into a particular inner journey. This in turn offers an explanation for why so many might have made such long and arduous pilgrimages to its ceremonies. It wasn't necessary to visit Chavín simply to obtain San Pedro or Anadenanthera. Both grow wild in abundance in the Andes; there could hardly have been, as in some cultures ancient and modern, a priestly monopoly on their use. Those who came to Chavín weren't coerced into doing so; it drew participants from a wide area, over which it exercised no political or military control. The Chavín ceremony, rather, would have offered a ritual on a spectacular scale, where the effects of the plants could be experienced en masse within an architecture designed to enhance and direct them.

Within this environment, participants could congregate to enter a shared otherworld, and also submit themselves to a highly charged individual vision quest. The sunken plaza might, as the reliefs suggest, have harnessed the heightened consciousness of San Pedro to a mass ritual of dancing and chanting; the participants might subsequently have ascended the temple steps individually to receive a further sacrament of powdered Anadenanthera seeds administered to them by the priests via bone snuffing tubes. As this was taking hold, they would be led into the chambers within the pyramid, where they could experience their DMT-enhanced visions in solitary darkness. Here, the amplified rushing of water and the growls and roars of the unseen participants around them would enclose them in a supernatural world, one where ordinary consciousness could be abandoned, the body itself metamorphosed and the world seen from an enhanced, superhuman perspective—analogous, perhaps, to the uncanny night vision of the feline predator. The development of the subterranean chambers over centuries would reflect the logistical demands of ever-greater numbers of participants willing to enter the jaguar portal and submit themselves to a life-changing ordeal that offered a glimpse of the eternal world beyond the human.

So Chavín remains a mystery, but perhaps in a more specific sense. If we want an analogy for its function drawn from Western culture it might be the Eleusinian Mysteries, originating as they did in subterranean chambers near Athens a little later than Chavín, around 700 BCE. Like Chavín, Eleusis persisted for nearly a thousand years, under different empires, in its case Greek and Roman; like Chavín—and like the Hajj to Mecca today—it was a pilgrimage site drawing its participants from a diverse network of cultures spanning virtually the known world. Classical written sources attest to some of the exterior details of the Eleusinian mysteries: its seasonal calendar, its processions, the ritual fasting, and the breaking of the fast with a sacred plant potion, the kykeon. But over the thousand years that these mysteries endured, the deepest secrets of Eleusis—the visions that were revealed by the priestesses in the chambers in the bowels of the earth—were never revealed, protected under penalty of death. At Chavín the only surviving records are the stones of the site itself, but the mystery is perhaps of the same order.

Chapter 8

Ravens' Bread and Other Manifestations of Fly Agaric in Classical and Biblical Literature

Edzard Klapp

Edzard Klapp was born in 1937 in Elbing (formerly East Prussia, now Poland) and now lives south of Stuttgart, where he has worked as a public prosecutor, now retired. He corresponded with John M. Allegro and published a variety of essays mainly about the history and ritual use of *Amanita muscaria* in diverse German periodicals. Because of these publications he is well known for his research specialty. His essay "Raven's Bread" (*Rabenbrot*) was printed for the first time in the German periodical *Curare* (1982).

Introduction

By order of the Lord the prophet Elias withdrew to the creek Krith and lived there on the bread God's raven brought him. Many Christian artists took up this theme. In parts of the Middle East, the name "ravens' bread" has been used for the hallucinatory fly agaric *(Amanita muscaria)* to the present day.[1] It may be supposed that that popular botanic name represents the keynote of the Elias legend.

In his painting "Elias and the Angel in the Desert"[2], Dieric Bouts hinted at the toadstool nature of the food of Elias. He set a supposedly harmless roll of bread in the shape of a toadstool on a pitcher. Has there been—at least up to recent times—a continuous folk tradition that ravens' bread is a name for fly agaric? St. Jerome wrote the story of St. Anthony's visit to St. Paul of Thebes. While on his way, Anthony meets a centaur.[3] Later, when he meets Paul and the saints are exchanging compliments, the heavenly raven rushes down with a double ration of bread. Gruenewald portrayed this moment on one of the tables of the Isenheim altar. Anthony's temptation is the companion painting—the symmetry discloses the inner relationship[4]. Those demonic phantasms, do they originate in the use of ravens' bread?

In the Biblical Psalms, hobgoblins of the kind oppressing St. Anthony are named enemies, opponents, calumniators, or atheists again and again. Indeed, they seem to have a dominating or constitutive role within the rite. Research on the psalm has so far failed to identify those enemies within their historic context. However, from the angle of psychopharmacology one might come to a new interpretation of the genesis and mission of the Psalms of Lament. It would have been their purpose to support and guide the sacral user of psychedelic toadstools in a beneficial way.

Therefore we are confronted with a religiously relevant phenomenon of a psychosis arising from external factors. As an argument in favor of this circumstance we can consider that the "enemies" of the psalmist usually fade away like smoke or chaff in the wind as soon as they have fulfilled their role. On the other hand, modern clinical psychiatry supplies us with appropriate stereotypical statements from intoxicated patients. A pot smoker: "in the station and in the train, they all grinned at me so stupidly...."

A significant characteristic of many psychoses is that the patient generally relates everything he experiences to himself and so judges it in a distorted manner: "For it was not an enemy that reproached me; then I could have borne it; neither was it he who hated me that did magnify himself against me; then I would have hid myself from him: But it was thou, a man mine equal, my guide, and mine acquaintance. . . ." (Psalm 55: 12-13). Since inexpensive editions of the psaltery may easily be bought in any local bookshop, we need no lengthy citations here. One can find many paraphrases for the rescuing "Realm of God," ardently sought and the counterpart to the world of those nightmares. To garner this glory the supplicant undergoes a previous depression ("hangover"): "The LORD is nigh unto them that are of a broken heart; and sayeth such as be of an contrite spirit. Many are the afflictions of the righteous; but the LORD delivereth him out of them all. He keepeth all his bones: not one of them is broken" (Psalm 34, 18–20).

> Probasti cor meum deus // Visitasti nocte // Igne me examinasti

> "Thou God hast proved mine heart; thou hast visited me in the night; thou hast tried me with fire . . ." (Psalm 17: 3)

In the martyr painting within the Isenheim altar, as a consequence, He hovers in a heavenly aureole above the tormented believer.

Samson, conqueror of the lion and sweet tooth, married a Philistine woman. On their wedding, he posed a riddle to his guests: "Out of the eater came forth meat, and out of the strong one came forth sweetness" (Judges 14, 14). Rembrandt depicts this scene—Samson posing riddles at table[5]. The central figure is the bride, looking puzzled, as if she wanted to say to the gallery visitor: "Hey, don't you notice anything?" Before her, there stands a curious centerpiece: a plate, decorated with diverse herbs and a slender chalice at its center. Seen separately it looks like a mushroom upside down. Well, the Philistines, for their part, answer back with another question: "What is sweeter than honey? And what is stronger than a lion?" (Judges 14: 18) We believe that the clues to this enigma lie somewhere in the following reasoning:

"Honey" might mean the "honey of the rock" (Psalm 81: 16; Deuteronomy 32: 13), or the substance of the miracle of the rock (Exodus 17: 6). Could it have been the juice of squeezed fly agarics?

If that were true the association of lion and honey, hidden in the mystery riddle, would be solved: He who had been able to overthrow his "enemies" [the lion] may enjoy the "honey"[6.] [*Strictly speaking*]: Meat came out of the eater and sweetness came out of the strong one. For both parts of that riddle the answer may be deduced as follows: The word of the Lord, that is God's incarnated word. The latter, the word "made flesh" or the "Son of God"[7] is the drug of fly agaric. Using it results in a horror trip preceding the blessed flash of enlightenment.

I will leave it to the maturity and wisdom of the user to recognize the nightmares looming from the depth of his unconscious as reflections of his own soul[8.] Is here the right place to ask for the original and genuine sense of the commandment to love one's enemies (St. Matthew 5: 44)? If so, the surmounting of the psalmist's own attitude would lie in that commandment: "Break their teeth, O God, in their mouths; break out the great teeth of the young lions, O LORD" (Psalm 58: 6). Henceforth the solution would be not to deny one's shady sides but to acknowledge them; in fact, to "love" them. In this sense "the love of enemies" would be prerequisite to brotherly love[9.] It deserves notice that the commandment to love one's enemies [included in the Sermon on the Mount] is closely associated with the so-called Beatitudes. As to the Beatitudes, corresponding verses of the psalms can be cited:

> But the meek shall inherit the earth; and shall delight themselves in the abundance of peace (Psalm 37: 11).

> The sacrifices of God are a broken spirit; a broken and contrite heart, O God, thou wilt not despise (Psalm 51: 17).

The phalanx of theologists who are instructed to subordinate exegesis to dogmatism *ex officio* are afraid up to present times to take note of those things or even to discuss them. Afraid of what? And afraid of what about? If you explained to a well-read Buddhist that Boddhisattva Avalokitesvara never had a human existence, he would answer: "So what?" A Gallus, a priest of Kybele [if one still existed] consulted about where and when Attis had lived on earth, would only shrug his shoulders. In vain you would ask for the "historical" context of the heroic activities of Mithras. Every insider knows these questions have no answer. They did not stop their cults from growing. Besides, there is every reason to believe that fly agarics were ritually used in those cults as well. The same could be stated for the mysteries of Dionysus. As to the latter example, remember those classic pictures of maenads known from Greek vases: These maenads clothed in panther skins carry roe kids and other "animals" in their bare hands. There can be no doubt that these examples are explicit allusions in an intentional language of symbolism.

The Lobdengau-Museum at Ladenburg, not far from Heidelberg, possesses a Mithraistic religious symbol, which is its most significant treasure. It shows Sol and Mithras at their banquet. They sit on the skin of the Celestial Bull that had been killed elsewhere. In heroic nudity Sol raises his drinking horn before the disk of the so-called "Sun Tree," thus demonstrating the origin of his power. The "Sun Tree" can easily be identified as the bottom side of the pileus of a toadstool; you would not be wrong to declare it a fly agaric.

Some typical features of the Mithraistic iconograms are well known as toadstool-born, such as Mithras's birth from a rock, his Phrygian cap, his peeping out of a tree, his miracle of the rock [shooting on a cloudy rock with an arrow], and many others.

If you browse among the large stock of the Corpus Cybelae Attidisque[10] you will discover many other icons of Attis formed like mushrooms. The legend of Attis also suggests connections to mushrooms. The figures of Attis tristis and Attis hilaris describe the typical states of consumers of fly agaric. As to the correlation of tears and joy, see Psalm 126: 5, "They that sow in tears shall reap in joy."

But no supporter of the official churches would openly dare to combine the mysteries of Good Friday and Easter with the effects of eating fly agaric. He would have to expect to be banned from the pulpit and removed from office. If such fears continue it will take at least 500 years to experience a change of views. This change need not take that long. Only lame habits of thinking slow down such a change.

When discussing Hieronymus Bosch, Charles de Tolnay[11] interprets hell and heaven. According to him Bosch replaces the paradise and hell of the Middle Age, which were objective pictures of the celestial and infernal hierarchies, with subjective visions, which correspond to the conceptions of the great mystics and exist in their souls only. In this phrase the terms "objective" and "subjective" clang a bit treacherously. Which came first? Was it the spontaneous view of future life in which the bodiless soul—freed from the bonds of time and space—comes to know perpetual salvation? Or was it the incidental discovery of hallucinatory plants, which arouse a feeling of euphoria, disturb consciousness, and widen time and space to new dimensions? Such an experience would have a virtually explosive effect upon the sleeping mind of men. It would bring them to believe in things they never thought before. That is, if we may say so, direct Revelation.[12]

Appendix

We have a hint to magical power and sacred mushrooms thanks to Sergius Golowin,[13] who interprets the embodiments of Vishnu—here in the case of Avatar as a dwarf (Vamana). In addition I would like to emphasize a trait of Avatar as a lion (Narasimha). In usual pictures, Avatar the Lion is somebody who intensively gnaws in the adept's ("enemy's") stomach, but carefully dresses the wound with pink bandages. The [esoteric] drama of initiation, which is indicated in such a picture, is blocked [for exoteric use] by a popular cover story. To decipher that kind of pictures, one should remember that the pink color (of the bandages) is reserved for the Brahmanic caste. I do know verre-églomisé paintings of Northern India of the nineteenth-century, made for ritual use, on which exactly this color can be seen clearly. And the ritually "killed" man shows a relaxed and awake facial expression.

Note: Images may be found at www.clinicalanthropology.com.

Basic Literature

Wasson, R. 1969. "Soma: Divine Mushroom of Immortality." *Ethno-Mycological Studies* 1. New York: Harcourt Brace Jovanovich.

Allegro, J. 1970. *The Sacred Mushroom and the Cross*. London: Hodder and Stoughton.

Notes

1. Said, G. and Geerken, H. 1979. "Die Halluzinogene Muscarin und Ibotensaeure im Mittleren Hindukusch—Ein Beitrag zur volksheil—praktischen Mykologie in Afghanistan." *Afghanistan Journal* 62.
2. Church of St. Peter, Leuven [1464]; plate III 8, in M.W. Alpatow [1964], *Geschichte der Kunst*, vol. II, Dresden: VEB Verlag der Kunst.
3. Fly agaric is said to have been the favourite food of the centaurs, indeed! See the foreword, which gave Robert Graves the introduction to his profound book, *The Greek Myths*, (New York: Penguin Books, 1992). Since revising *The Greek Myths* in 1958, I have had second thoughts about the drunken god Dionysus, about the centaurs with their contradictory reputation for wisdom and misdemeanour, and about the nature of divine ambrosia and nectar. These subjects are closely related, because the centaurs worshipped Dionysus, whose wild autumnal feast was called "the Ambrosia." I no longer believe that when his Maenads ran raging around the countryside, tearing animals or children in pieces and boasted afterwards of travelling to India and back, they had intoxicated themselves solely on wine or ivy-ale. The evidence, summarized in my *What Food the Centaurs Ate* (Steps: Cassell and Co, 1958, pp. 319–343), suggests that satyrs (goat-totem tribesmen), centaurs (horse-totem tribesmen), and their Maenad womenfolk, used brews to wash down mouthfuls of a stronger

drug: namely a raw mushroom, *Amanita muscaria*, which induces hallucinations, senseless rioting, prophetic sight, erotic energy, and remarkable muscular strength. Some hours of this ecstasy are followed by complete inertia; a phenomenon that would account for the story of how Lycurgus, armed only with an ox-goad, routed Dionysus's drunken army of Maenads and Satyrs after its victorious return from India.

On an Etruscan mirror the *Amanita muscaria* is engraved at Ixion's feet; he was a Thessalian hero who feasted on ambrosia among the gods. Several myths are consistent with my theory that his descendants, the centaurs, ate this mushroom; and, according to some historians, it was later employed by the Norse "berserks" to give them reckless power in battle. I now believe that "ambrosia" and "nectar" were intoxicant mushrooms: certainly the *Amanita muscaria*; but perhaps others, too, especially a small, slender dung-mushroom named *Panaeolus papilionacaeus*, which induces harmless and most enjoyable hallucinations. A mushroom not unlike it appears on an Attic vase between the hooves of Nessus the Centaur. The "gods" for whom, in the myths, ambrosia, and nectar were reserved, will have been sacred queens and kings of the preclassical era. King Tantalus's crime was that he broke the taboo by inviting commoners to share his ambrosia.

Sacred queenships and kingships lapsed in Greece; ambrosia then became, it seems, the secret element of the Eleusian, Orphic, and other mysteries associated with Dionysus. All the events, the participants swore to keep silence about what they ate or drank, saw unforgettable visions, and were promised immortality. The "ambrosia" awarded to winners of Olympic footrace when victory no longer conferred the sacred kingship on them was clearly a substitute: a mixture of foods the initial letters of which, as I show in *What Food the Centaurs Ate*, spelled out the Greek word "mushroom." Recipes quoted by classical authors for nectar, and for *cecyon*, the mint-flavoured drink taken by Demeter at Eleusis, likewise spell out "mushroom."

I have myself eaten the hallucinogenic Mushroom, *psilocybe*, a divine ambrosia in immemorial use among the Masatec Indians of Oaxaca Province, Mexico; heard the priestess invoke Tlaloc, the Mushroom God, and seen transcendental visions. Thus I wholeheartedly agree with R. Gordon Wasson, the American discoverer of this ancient rite, that European ideas of heaven and hell may well have derived from similar mysteries. Tlaloc was engendered by lightning; so was Dionysus; and in Greek folklore, as in Masatec, so are all mushrooms—proverbially called "food of the gods" in both languages. Tlaloc wore a serpent-crown; so did Dionysus. Tlaloc had an underwater retreat; so had Dionysus. The Maenads' savage custom of tearing victims' heads may refer allegorically to tearing off the sacred mushroom's head—since in Mexico its stalk is never eaten. We read that Perseus, a sacred King of Argos, converted to Dionysus worship, named Mycenae after a toadstool which he found growing on the site, and which gave forth a stream of water. Tlaoc's emblem was a toad; so was that of Argos; and from mouth of Tlaoc's toad in the Tepentitla fresco issues a stream of water. Yet at what epoch were the European and Central American cultures in contact?

These theories call for further research, and I have therefore not incorporated my findings in the text of the present edition. Any expert help in solving the problem would be greatly appreciated. Deyá, Majorca, Spain, 1960, Robert Graves.

4. Cf. pp. 167 and 183 in Max Seidel (1973/1980), Mathis Gothart Nithard Gruenewald, "Der Isenheimer Altar," Stuttgart: Chr. Belser Verlag.

5. Nowadays Dresden, pictures 168 and 169 in M. W. Alpatow [1966], *Die Dresdner Galerie*, Dresden: VEB Verlag der Kunst.

6. Cf. Revelation of St. John the Divine, 10: 9 and 10.

7. "Mushrooms and tubers are called creatures of the gods because they don't develop from seeds as other living things."—Porphyrius, cited after L. Lionni [1978], Parallele Botanik, p. 8, Cologne: Middelhauve.

8. "Behold, the figures—may they be as they will—you can see in the state of Bardo, are unreal dream-visions, called and given off by yourself, being unable to recognize them as your own work, and

frightening you." Bardo Thodol, cited after, A. David-Neel [1962], *Unsterblichkeit und Wiedergeburt: Lehren und Gebraeuche in China, Tibet und Indien*, p. 54, Wiesbaden: Brockhaus.

9. "Every love is built on self-love," says Meister Eckhart.

10. Published by Brill, Leiden, edited by M. Vermaseeren.

11. German edition (1963), Baden-Baden: Holle, p. 110 ; mentioning "Heaven and Hell" [Palace of Doges].

12. M. Barnard [1968], "The God in the Flowerpot," *The American Scholar*, Autumn 1963; cited after R. E. Masters / J. Houston, *Psychedelic Art*, German edition [1969], Munich: Droemer-Knaur, pp. 109 and 110.

13. Sergius Golowin in, Bildlexikon der Symbole (1980), by Wolfgang Bauer et al, Abi Melzers Productions, Dreieich, p. 82, right column. Cf. beyond that: W. Vollmer, *Vollstaendiges Woerterbuch der Mythologie aller Nationen* (1836), Stuttgart, pp. 1542–1543. We took further the picture, printed here, of the Lion-Avatar [Vollmer, plate CXIX]. Vollmer borrowed those pictures of Vishnu's Avatars from Philippus Baldaeus' (1632–1672) book, *Description of the East Indian Countries of Malabar, Coromandel, Ceylon, etc.*, (in Dutch, 1671).

Chapter 9

Democracy and the Dionysian Agenda

Carl A. P. Ruck

Carl A. P. Ruck is Professor of Classics at Boston University, and authority on the ecstatic rituals of the god Dionysus. With the ethnomycologist R. Gordon Wasson and Albert Hofmann, he identified the secret psychoactive ingredient in the visionary potion that was drunk by the initiates at the Eleusinian Mystery. In *Persephone's Quest: Entheogens and the Origins of Religion,* he proclaimed the centrality of psychoactive sacraments at the very beginnings of religion, employing the neologism "entheogen" to free the topic from the pejorative connotations for words like "drug" or "hallucinogen."

Introduction

Thespis

In the year 264 BCE, a calendar of important events was carved on a marble stele and set up on the Greek island of Páros. Two pieces were found in the early seventeenth-century and offered for sale.[1] A third fragment comprising the base of the monument and the end of the text was later found in 1897.[2] Known as the *Parian Chronicle* or the *Marmor Parium,* it lists important events, dating them backward from the date of the establishment of the monument. The earliest event is the supposed kingship of Cecrops in the city of Athens in 1582/1 BCE. Cecrops was a man with the body of a serpent, and many of the events, such as the Flood of Deucalion and the sailing of Jason and the Argonauts in quest of the Golden Fleece, belong to the realm of myth. For the year 534 BCE, it records that the poet Thespis produced a drama[3] in the city of Athens[4] and was the first to speak in the role of an actor,[5] for which the prize was a goat.

This was an event of extreme significance for the development of Athens as a cultural center, since what would become the Theater of Dionysus was largely responsible for the enduring image of Athens long after the failure of its attempt to achieve political dominance as a supposed democracy among the Greeks in the fifth century in the classical age of Pericles. "Thespian" is now a term for an actor.

What exactly Thespis did, if he even existed apart from myth, became elaborated in the later tradition, and he was credited with inventing tragedy.[6] The fourth-century Aristotle does not mention him in his treatise on drama, although he claims that the genre developed from choral dances, when one of the dancers stood apart to assume the role of a dramatic persona.[7] The choral dances, called "dithyrambs," however, were circular, whereas the chorus in tragedy employed a rectilinear choreography; and dithyrambs, moreover, were eventually performed as a separate contest in the theater. In any case, the dramatic impersonation of personae was probably already established by the rhapsodists, who recited the Homeric oral poems, which by their nature alternate narrative portions with sections purporting to represent the words of the characters in the tale.

As Thespis became more mythologized, or perhaps from sources no longer extant, it developed that he came from the village of Ikaria on the slopes of Mount Penteli, now the upscale residential suburb of Dionysos. Horace, in the late first-century BCE, claimed that Thespis went about in a cart with performers, their faces oiled with wine dregs.[8] This was the common view as seen in the third-century BCE Egyptian Hellenistic Greek epigrammatist Dioscorides, who described the dancers as stained with wine and added a basket of figs to the prize.[9] Thespis entered the canon as the inventor of tragedy, attested by the first-to-second-century Christian theologian Clement of Alexandria[10] and the second-to-third-century Egyptian Greek rhetorician Athenaeus.[11] By the tenth century, however, the Byzantine encyclopedia called the *Suda,* "The Fortress" (or by the mistaken idea of its author as *Suidas*), noted that Thespis was similar to other performers and may have been preceded by Epigenes of Sicyon (near Corinth) as either the second or sixteenth in line. Several sources even list titles of tragedies ascribed to Thespis and quote verses, although all are now deemed forgeries.[12]

Crab Dance

The earliest mention of Thespis is by the fifth-century comic playwright Aristophanes in his *Wasps* (produced in 422 BCE, roughly a century after the introduction of Thespis into the city).[13] It is a parody of the sort of dancing performance for which Thespis was known.[14] Although its intention is comic, it must have been recognizable as an exaggeration of Thespis and thus it is our most authentic evidence about the supposed founder of tragedy.

The episode concludes the *Wasps,* and apart from involving the previous characters of the comedy, the old man with a passion for serving on the jury (*Philokleon,* "Love-Cleon"), his son (*Bdelykleon,* "Loathe-Cleon"), and the slave (*Xanthias,* "Reddy"), it seems to bear no relationship to the plot of the comedy. It appears to be a self-contained set piece, as the playwright himself claims, a novel and unprecedented way to end a comedy, namely with a dance, as he says in the final words of the play[15]:

> Come, if you love us, go out dancing, since there's no one who's done this ever before, dismissed his chorus dancing.[16]

Aristophanes describes it as a *trugedy,* the last word of the play, which is a pun on tragedy, substituting *trux* for *tragos* or "goat." The *trux* is the "must," which is the unfermented wine, containing the newly pressed juice, grape skins, stems, and seeds; after fermentation, this deposits at the bottom of the cask as the "lees" or "dregs." As the conclusion of this Thespian vignette, it recalls the tradition of Thespis and his dancing troupe with their faces smeared with the wine dregs. Aristophanes thus concludes by claiming that he has reinterpreted the supposed tragedian Thespis as a comedian, or presented a comic parody of his tragic dancing.

The slave, as the beginning of the vignette, announces that his old master has become possessed by some demon that has entered the house like a whirlwind. The old guy has been drinking for a long time and has been erotically aroused by the music of the flute, which would have been played for him by his sex-for-hire female companion or *hetaera.* So pleased is he with the whole business that all night he hasn't stopped dancing, the sort of old stuff with which Thespis used to compete in the contests, and he intends now to come out to show that the tragic poets of today know nothing about dancing compared to Thespis.

The old guy bursts out of the house, probably with his hetaera and her flute, and the choreography of a mad dance begins, contorting his body, with creaking spine-joints and bellowing nostril, gapping ass and legs kicked sky-high. It is clear that it is a drunken madness for which the remedy would be a drink of hellebore.[17] As a remedy, the psychoactive hellebore functions as "a hair of the dog that bit you."[18] The contorted body, bellowing nostril (*mukter mukatai*), and creaking spine probably indicate the gigantism of his aroused phallus. Such sexual exertion in a decrepit old man would appear inherently comic. The remarkable phrase *mutker mukatai* encodes multiple punning that the visible presentation would have made explicit, the penis as a *mukes* or mushroom and the metaphoric association of its rapidly erecting fruit with the bellowing of a bull (*mukema*) and of its slimy cap with the mucous discharge (*muxa*) of the nostril (*mukter*) as the ejaculating semen. The mushroom itself is named in Greek for this same mucous metaphor, there being no name for the plant itself except through metaphors, which indicates a religious taboo.

The comedy had begun with an obscene routine employing similar metaphoric motifs as the two slaves who had been sent to keep guard over the old man to keep him from jury duty attempt to relieve the tedium of their boredom by escaping into the drug-induced visionary world of the Thracian version of the god Dionysus.[19] The god is Sabazios, tended as a bull, and it marches like a Persian over their eyelids, causing visionary dreams. A similar routine opens the *Knights*, where the slaves "bolt," punning on masturbate as "come of themselves" and "run-off and desert." It develops into mutual fellatio, as they drink each other's ejaculation as a draught of "bull's blood," potent wine drunk straight from the source, the phallus in its metaphoric metamorphosis as a psychoactive mushroom.[20]

The old man in the Thespian vignette now summons his competitors, and the only takers are the sons of Karkínos. Karkínos seems to have served as a naval general in the year 431 BCE,[21] and to have been a member of the priestly class.[22] This is apparently the reason that Aristophanes refers to him as the "Sea-ruling Lord" at verse 1531, as a stand-in for the sea god Poseidon. The parody links him with Phrynichos at verse 1523, who was a tragedian of the previous generation.[23] Aristophanes is so pleased with his parody of Karkínos in the *Wasps* vignette that he repeated it the next year in the *Peace*. The only drama ascribed to Karkínos, however, is entitled the *Mice* (*Múes*),[24] which would be the title of a comedy, instead of a tragedy. The only words that survive from a play by him are, "Alas! O me, O me!" This is hardly distinctive, but Karkínos seems to have put crybaby gods on the stage, again something more expected in a comedy than a tragedy.[25] The *Mice* play is apparently the point of the joke about him in the *Peace*. There it is claimed that he "strangled the cat" in his drama, or that the "cat strangled his drama."[26]

Karkínos may have actually been a comedian or *trugedian*, instead of a tragedian.[27] His was a family of playwrights, however, and his son Xenokles, his grandson Karkínos II, and perhaps his great-grandson Xenokles II, were all tragedians. It was customary not to name a child after a living relative. Thus Karkínos II was born after the death of his grandfather, as was Xenokles II, and hence they were never all alive at the same time and certainly not all simultaneously poets. Nonetheless, what interests us here is the joke about the crab dance by the little sons of Karkínos in the Thespian vignette. All of these children would have been too young to be poets in 422. Xenokles II wasn't active as a playwright until the 370s, which is fifty years later.

So what is the joke, and what relevance does it have to do with the nature of the supposed Thespian invention of tragedy and its role in the development of Athenian democracy?

Karkínos means "crab," and one would expect his sons, therefore, to look like crabs. This, indeed, they do. They are described in the *Peace* as dancers (*orchestras*), but their necks, like that of the crab, are no neck at all, but resemble a knapsack or soldier's packsack (*guliauchenas*).[28] As costumed for their dance, they would wear the phallus, and thus they are presented with the metaphor of the penis as a bird. They are "quails, homebred" (*ortugas oikogeneis*). In the *Birds*, produced in 415 BCE, Aristophanes lists the quail, along with the goose and the cock, as an irresistible gift to make even the most reluctant virginal boy at last open his thighs for his lover.[29] The quail has a crest that resembles the claw of the crab. These crab-quails are specifically described as homebred, which implies that they were raised for the popular sport of bird fights, and thus we may infer that Aristophanes is describing the dance in the *Wasps* as a cockfight between the puny sons of Crab and the gigantic erection of old Philokleon. The old man, in fact, announces that his performance will put to shame the great tragedian Phrynichos, who cowers like a cock.[30] The cock is the Persian bird and the reference is to the great tragedian's *Capture of Miletos* (produced 493), which so saddened the Athenian audience that they wept and then pelted the cowering poet with stones for reminding them of the event.[31] Thus the slave Xanthias replies that Philokleon, too, will be "stoned."[32] A verse of Phrynichos's tragedy reads: "[the Persian] cowered like a cock folding his slavish wing."[33]

The crab dancers may actually have been played by children, whose penis would be no match for an adult's. Perhaps, in fact, they don't wear the phallus at all, but merely dance essentially nude, displaying their baby version of the penis. There are three of them in the *Wasps,* the "middle-one," his brother, and finally the "smallest" or youngest, all of them small enough to eat as the produce of the sea, brothers of the shrimps, no bigger than spiders.[34] Gulping and drinking them down in victory, in this context, would have obscene connotations. "What a plethora of sons!" Philokleon exclaims of the good fortune of their father. The three sons of Karkínos who would have been alive in 422 would be Xenotimos, Xenarchus, and Xenokles I. Only the last was a playwright, the smallest of the lot (verse 1511). As the youngest son of a man in his prime, he would at most have just begun his career and hardly been worth the parody, except for the convenient name of his daddy as Crab. Only the words of the comedy survive. In performance, each of Philokleon's introductory remarks about the crab sons would have been interspersed with enough time for the child dancer to perform his separate routine.

Their smallness is not merely a matter of their puny erections or baby penises. The *Peace* further describes them as dwarfish (*nanophueis*), tricky (*mechanodiphas*), and dung pellets (*sphuriadon apoknismata*), what we might term "rabbit turds" or "bird droppings." It is hardly likely that Karkínos fathered a whole family of dwarfs.

These crab sons are the crab lice (*Phthirus pubis*) that infest the genitals.[35] They are about three millimeters in size and are recognizable as resembling crabs with the unaided eye, hence its name. They are "tricky" because it is hard to catch them all. Thus in the *Wasps,* they have fallen as a plethora from wrens (*orchilon*), with a pun on *orchis* or "testicles" (as in the medical term "orchidectomy," or "orchid," so named for the resemblance of the flower to a testicle). Similarly, Karkínos himself enters at the end of the dance, well pleased with the performance of his falcon-sons (*triorchois*), punning on a triad (*tri-*) of such testes and also upon the *orche*stration of their dancing, like the wheeling flight of the falcon. The smallest son, who writes tragedies, is specified as the parasitic pinna-guard crab (*Pinnotheres pisum*), commonly called the pea crab from its appearance as a little ball, like a dung pellet. It infests the pinna mollusk (*Pinna noblis*), which anchors itself vertically, with the tiny crab lurking in the proffered slimy opening, like a sexual aperture of the body.

Their dance in the *Wasps* describes them as spinning like tops, slipping sidewise round and round, and slapping their belly-penises with knees sky-high. The action of the play pauses to give them time to perform their little routine ensemble (1516–1517).

> OK, now. Let's all give them a little room so that they can spin themselves about up front without us in the way.

Three very young boys, as required for their minuscule size, too young for professional training, would have played these parasitic crabs twirling their little penis "foot" (*poda kuklosobeite*)[36] around the gigantic bellowing *mukter* nostril of the maddened enthusiast for the old style of Thespian *trugedy,* and giving the spectators a charming pederastic spectacle as the children kicked their "leg up high" so that spectators shout "bravo" (*ozosin hoi theatai*), a tasty morsel to gulp down.

> Twist, twirl, tap your bellies, toss you leg sky high. [OK. That's enough.] Now be gone.[37]

It must have been a memorable performance. The next year in the *Peace,* as the hero Trugaeus, named as the *trux*-man, who flew to heaven on the back of a dung beetle to rescue the goddess Peace, prepares to celebrate his nuptials with her handmaiden "Harvest," imagining himself making love and fondling her breasts, he will be more blessed than those parasitic twirler sons of Crab,[38] who understandably are excluded as uninvited guests.[39]

In addition to this crab routine, Aristophanes used the head louse (*Pediculosis capitis*) and the mosquito for his parody of Socrates's "mystery" teachings in the *Clouds* (423 BCE, thereafter revised and apparently performed on tour at other venues), and the bed bug (*Cimex lectularius*), later in the comedy.[40] The chorus of the *Wasps*, moreover, was costumed as insects, with the phallus serving as their stinger.

Democracy

The Athenians rewrote their early history to make the mythical hero Theseus, of the generation before the Trojan War (c. 410 BCE), the founder of their democracy.[41] The Athenians considered themselves autochthonous, which is to say, the indigenous population of Attica. They were originally Pelasgian, one of the pre-Greek peoples, largely bypassed by the Indo-European migrations, and later assimilated into the developing Greek-speaking Hellenic culture.[42] Like their neighbors, the earliest government was a kingship,[43] probably replacing an earlier matriarchal and matrilineal culture, as mythologized in Euripides's drama *Ion* (c. 410s BCE), about the supposed founder of the Ionian tribal group (in the generation after the Flood of Deucalion, c. 1500 BCE), as distinct from the Dorians, Aeolians, and Achaeans. The same cultural transition is mythologized in the goddess Athena's suppression of the Gorgon Medusa and in her supplanting of the "goat" goddess Pallas as the patroness of the city of the Athena sisterhood, Athens.[44] A similar transition from matriarchy to patriarchy is discernible in the myth of Theseus's birth from his "goat" father Aegeus and the expulsion of his father's mistress Medea (Medusa, "queen") and her matrilineal son Medos.

The king was not necessarily always the most able in battle, and he came to share his power with a warlord or *polymarch*, and eventually other chieftains as magistrates for specific tasks, advised by a council of nobles. By the eleventh-century, the role of king had been reduced to a hereditary magistracy, which continued into the Classical Age as one of the ten archons or "rulers," the *basileus* or nominal "king" in charge only of the religious functions of kingship. The king was eventually replaced by an oligarchy of aristocratic families, who rotated the magistracies among themselves and whose power was derived from their preeminence as warlords, with adequate wealth to raise horses and serve as knights or chivalric mounted warriors.

In the eighth-century, the invention of the shield and battle armament led to new techniques of warfare and the emergence of an ancillary military force of infantry soldiers derived from families with sufficient means to supply the requisite body armor.[45] These were people of a new class that had acquired wealth through the produce of their lands or from commerce, often surpassing the inherited wealth of the aristocracy; and their participation in the city's defense justified their demand for a voice in its government. Eventually, in the early fifth-century, the development of the Athenian navy built at public expense from the income of the newly discovered silver mines at Laurion (c. 483 BCE) allowed poor, landless people to participate as oarsmen in the city's defense and similarly demand a voice in the democracy.[46] The sailors were the lowest class and tended to be the most democratic, owing allegiance to their aristocratic captains.

These new classes were a potential source of support for any aristocrat to rise above the fellow members of the oligarchy. Such aristocrats might attempt a coup d'état and assume the role of tyrant as solitary leader. This happened in several Greek cities in the sixth century, and the tyrant was seen as beneficial to his support group, and as a threat to his peers. The pejorative connotations of tyranny spread to the lower classes only when the tyrant became unpopular, usually for failing to deliver on his promises, and sought to maintain his supremacy by a mercenary force and political suppression.

The first to attempt tyranny in Athens was Cylon (Kulon), who was a member of perhaps the noblest family going back to the great-grandson of Nestor of the Trojan War. He used his recent celebrity as a victorious Olympian athlete to secure a dynastic marriage to the daughter of the tyrant of neighboring Megara, but he failed to gain sufficient popular support within the city, probably because of the suspicion of foreign interference. He sought asylum in the old Temple of Athena, but Megacles, the official chief archon at the time (632 BCE), put him and his supporters to death. This was an act of sacrilege that put a curse upon him and his noble family of the Alcmaeonids. Despite periods of temporary exile, however, the family would return to supply Kleisthenes, the founder of the navy and the democracy, Pericles (Perikles), and his nephew Alcibiades (Alkibiades).

Peisistratos

The second attempt at tyranny two generations later was more successful. Peisistratos (Latinized as Pisistratus) as archon *polymarch* rose to prominence in 565 BCE by reclaiming the disputed territories of Eleusis and Salamis from Megara and ending its unofficial trade embargo, which had been causing food shortages in Athens for several decades. The family of Peisistratos (the Neleids) also traced its lineage back to Nestor, via Nestor's father Neleus.[47] It should be noted that both the Alcmaeonids and the Neleids derive from the southern Peloponnesus and that hence they were Indo-Europeans as very early immigrants among the original Pelasgian peoples of Attica.

Three political factions at that time were competing to control the government of Athens: the landholder agrarian people of the plains, who were the most numerous; the wealthy non-noble merchant traders of the coastal region; and the herdsmen mountain or hill people. Although these last were the poorest and the fewest, they were also the most revolutionary since they had the most to gain, and Peisistratos espoused their cause and leveraged his popularity from the Megarian conflict and its beneficial effect upon trade to collude with Megacles, the grandson of the Alcmaeonid who had led the first attempt, for the support of the coastal dwellers, thus producing a coalition that was still outnumbered by the aristocratic plainsmen.

Peisistratos staged an assassination attempt on his own life and convinced the assembly to provide him with a group of bodyguards like a private army, with which he seized control of the Acropolis.[48] The plainsmen and the coastal dwellers, however, reunited to drive him into exile. He returned several years later, when the united opposition fell apart, and Megacles supported his reinstatement, on the condition that he take his daughter as wife. Again using a theatrical ruse, he rode into the city on a golden chariot accompanied by a tall woman dressed as the goddess Athena, convincing many that his tyranny had divine sanction.[49] He was again driven into exile when he angered Megacles by avoiding having a child from his wife, since she was accursed as an Alcmaeonid. He returned a third time with a foreign mercenary force and retained the tyranny until his death in 527 BCE. He ruled as the dominant citizen, without changing the constitution and the traditional magistracies.

He was a model tyrant, reduced taxes, distributed largess to the poor, and tried to spread the opportunities for wealth, to relieve strife between the classes. His son Hippias inherited the position and continued his father's liberal policies. The tyranny only became repressive and despotic when his brother Hipparchos was murdered in 514 BCE, not for political reasons, but because of a homoerotic involvement. The Alcmaeonid family with Spartan aid deposed him in 510 BCE.

Primus inter Pares

In his role of leading citizen, Peisistratos commissioned public building projects that provided employment for the lower classes, attracted foreign craftsmen and artists, and enhanced the image of Athens as a cultural center,[50] thereby replacing regional clan-based loyalties with a civic allegiance. He may have sponsored a definitive edition of the Homeric poems for recitation at the Panathenaean Festival,[51] adding, as it is suspected, a few references to Athens,[52] which probably as a still-Pelasgian city had not played a very significant role in the tradition of the Trojan War. In any case, the model kingship of old Nestor in the *Odyssey* (book 4) and the companionship of his son Peisistratos and Telemachus could not but enhance the legitimacy of the Neleid family. Even if there were no interpolations, the rhapsodic recitations, which Peisistratos made an event of the Panathenaean Festival, associated Athens with the rich epic cultural identity of the Greeks.

He cleared a large area on the north slope of the Acropolis for the public marketplace or Agora as the civic center of the city and built his own large palace at its southwest edge,[53] adjacent to the Royal Stoa, which was the administrative center of government, and beneath the temple of Athena Polias that he constructed above on the Acropolis. A temple was the house of the god, and he similarly surrounded himself with cult altars, shrines, and other temples, equating himself with the religious and political cultural identity of the city. By establishing religious festivals, which were celebrations that brought the entire populace together for a common feasting and drinking, he further unified the diverse peoples into a cohesive family. It was a style of governance that set the pattern for the Alcmaeonid Pericles a century later. Although in name a democracy, according to Thucydides, its first citizen governed Athens.[54] It was only after his death that the government passed into the control of demagogues ("leaders of the demos or people"), who competed to satisfy the populace. Aristophanes in the *Knights* parodied the Demos as anally receptive to the demagogue Kleon, a maker of leather dildos, by inventing someone to oppose him with the more satisfying real object.

Among the building projects of Peisistratos was the construction of the largest temple ever envisaged as the house of Olympian Zeus in the open area north of the city walls. Although it wasn't completed until the time of the Roman Emperor Hadrian almost seven centuries later, it was an extravagant expression of the tyrant's devotion to the father of his patroness goddess, and inevitably made Athens the most Greek of all the cities. Similarly, he brought the great shrine of the goddess Demeter at Eleusis under the control of Athens and built the first major initiation hall for the Mysteries, attracting numerous pilgrims from abroad. The gateway to the Mysteries became the city of Athens, essentially identifying the city with the cult of Eleusis.

The religion, with its psychoactive Eucharist, offered a visionary experience that assured even the poorest initiate of a beneficent relationship with the deities of the afterlife as reciprocal guests in one another's homes.[55]

The Alcmaeonids, who eventually deposed his son Hippias, followed a similar building program under Pericles, and prepared for their return to Athens by building a new temple for Apollo at Delphi to confirm their legitimacy with their aristocratic Spartan Dorian allies. When the "democratic" Alcibiades fell from power, he sought asylum first with these Spartan allies, and then with the Persian aristocracy.

Country Manners

It was in this spirit of unifying the diverse classes of the populace by the use of religion that Thespis was welcomed into the city in the year 534 BCE from his homeland in the hill territories near where Peisistratos and his family had their ancestral estates at Brauron. The Thespian performance would have been something local and familiar to the Neleids. Although a much older man than the tyrant, the great lawgiver Solon was his relative. Solon's mother was a cousin of the mother of Peisistratos, and as was often the custom, it was reputed that Solon was both the mentor and lover of his handsome younger relative.[56] Solon is reported to have relaxed his sober severity in his old age and in a "spirit of wine and song," as his biographer Plutarch described it six centuries later, indulged himself with attending one of the performances of Thespis when it was still a rural event.[57] He didn't like it much and reprimanded the actor for lying in public, claiming that soon the same deceit would infect the legal system. Solon's relative Plato[58] in the next century would argue the same danger of theatrical impersonation in his *Republic*. Solon subsequently thought he saw the proof of his suspicion when Peisistratos enacted the ruse of the supposed assassination attempt. Odysseus had done something similar in disguising himself as a maltreated beggar to sneak into Troy, but Peisistratos was deceiving his friends instead of his enemies.[59]

The comparison indicates how readily myth provided a framework for interpreting reality. The second ruse with the girl who impersonated Athena as his sponsor is the common motif of the goddess aiding her chosen hero[60] and was accepted as true since it was expectable in myth. Solon's rejection of Thespis was not the disgruntled opinion of a man who had lived beyond his time, but he saw the true danger of dramatic impersonation in that it confused the boundaries of reality.

This was probably the origin of drama as a shamanic ritual to channel a spirit from the dead into the person who would impersonate its myth.[61] What sort of performance Solon saw, however, has become mythologized history, influenced by the claim that Thespis invented a mask of some sort, either coloring his face with white lead (*psimúthion*), as would be appropriate for the white face of a revenant's spirit,[62] or similarly draping it with white linen.[63]

The same Byzantine lexicon preserved a tradition that he supposedly "shaded his face with purslane." Although there are traditions of fig leaves and various floral wreaths,[64] only the purslane is specifically associated with Thespis. Purslane (*Portulaca oleracea*) is an edible wild succulent. If used as a pigment, it would at most impart a greenish tint, perhaps also appropriate for a revenant, but in medieval lore no doubt representing much more ancient traditions, it was supposed to ward off evil spirits.

The plant, however, is called *andrachne* and *komaros* in Greek, and its identification as purslane was arbitrary on the part of Linnaeus. In Theophrastus,[65] it is a kind of arbutus, the strawberry tree, *Arbutus unedo,* which describes it as a "little tree." Its strawberry-like fruits ferment while still on the bush and are mildly intoxicating.[66] Today it is used to fortify wine,[67] although it certainly has less alcoholic concentration than that produced by the fully fermented grapes and its use is probably symbolic as a surrogate for something else. It is also commonly crushed into a preserved condiment with additional sugar. Thespis, however, according to the lexicographer, shaded his face with it, probably a quotation from a lost poem, which implies that he wore it as a wreath. Its sanctity is suggested by its occurrence in the ancient escutcheon of the city of Madrid with a bear, perhaps derived from it both as a host for the *Amanita muscaria* mushroom and as a little tree metaphoric surrogate, with intoxicating scabby red fruits.[68] In Greek mythology, the baby Hermes was nourished beneath a strawberry tree, which was still preserved in his sanctuary in Boeotian Tanagra, where he was honored for having averted a plague.[69] The nursing beneath the tree suggests that it was something like divine milk or nectar and ambrosia. Since he is the deity who escorts souls to and from the otherworld, it is emblematic of a psychoactive agent that would open the pathways between the realms, which would make it a suitable plant to be associated with Thespian dramatic shamanism.

The botanical name for purslane as *portulaca* is supposedly derived from Latin as a diminutive of *porta* as the "little door" (*portula*), although its milky sap may be responsible for its name as the "milk-carrier" (*portare lac*). The "little tree" and the "little door" would both be metaphoric for a shamanic agent. It may also be connected to the word for little "sow," *porcula, porcella,* which was a colloquialism for the "vulva," also appropriate as the mystical gateway.[70] It was used medicinally for uterine complaints. Its name in English as purslane derives from the Italian *procellina* for the cowrie shell, which resembles the slit in the vulva. Its nacreous shell resembles the porcelain glaze Marco Polo saw in China, hence the milky sap of the purslane.

The Rural Dionysia

The wine dregs supposedly smeared on the dancers' faces identified them as acting in the service of the god in the rural Dionysian rites, what would eventually be canonized as the Rural Dionysia in the month of December, as part of the total Dionysian agenda. This agenda is characterized by the dichotomy of the wild rural as contrasted with the cultivated urban ceremonies. To the wild belonged the Rural Dionysia and the winter maenads, while the urban ceremonies were the symposia or "drinking parties" of the men and the tragedies of the theater. Mediating the dichotomy were the Lenaean ceremonies of the *lenai* and the great three-day festival of the Anthesteria.

Aristophanes depicts the Rural Dionysia in the *Acharnians* (425 BCE). It takes place in the hill town of Acharnes, in the same region as the village of Thespis. The farmer Dikaiopolis prepares to enjoy the benefits of his private peace treaty, while the general Lamachos gets dressed for war. Prominent in the festival is drinking and the procession of the phallus, escorted by obscenities. To judge from the Thespian vignette in the *Wasps,* this may have been the essence of the rural celebration, which is parodied as the twirling crabs dancing around the drunken old man's burgeoning *mukter* "nostril," bellowing like a *mykes* mushroom-bull. In any case, the rural Thespian performance, not only in the *Wasps* parody, was a popular intensely drunken revel, obscene and boorish country manners, still enacted in the villages of French viticulture as the drinking of the *vin bourru,* the intoxicating still-fermenting effervescent wine.

The invitation to perform it in the city could not have coincided with the inauguration of the theater competitions since, as mythologized, it was only Thespis and his troupe, with no competitors, who came in from the hillside. Its serious tragic nature, moreover, is read back as historical revisionism from what the theater became, whereas the Aristophanic vignette as a *trugedy* may be closer to the truth. The records of the victories in the contests go back only to the year 501 BCE, almost a decade after the Alcmaeonids had deposed the Neleid tyranny, and three decades after the Thespian performance in the city. Kleisthenes reformed the constitution of Athens as a democracy in 508 BCE, and what the tyrant Peisistratos had inaugurated by inviting these country manners of drunken revelry into the city became inseparable from the democratic identity of the Athens of the fifth-century.[71]

Dionysus in the City

As the drama festivals became regularized in the course of the ensuing century, the willingness to receive Dionysus into the city was demonstrated annually at the end of March for the celebration of the Great Dionysia (called the Dionysia in the City, to distinguish it from the Rural Dionysia), by escorting the ancient wooden cult statue of the god into the theater, along with a parade of wooden or bronze phalloi and an even larger phallus carried in a cart. The etiology of the event was the incorporation of the mountain village of Eleutherai on the frontier with Boeotia into Athens. The name of the town as the "Liberated Sisterhood" would suggest *eleutheria* or "freedom," and the god had the cult name of Eleuthereus or "Liberator,"[72] a liberation both political as a democracy and psychological as the basic religious nature of the theatrical experience. Supposedly the town was named for its eponymous hero Eleutheros, who was the first to erect a cult image of the god clad in a black goatskin.[73] His daughters derided it and went mad and were cured when their father established the cult of the Dionysus of the Black Goatskin.[74] The village of Eleutherai is in the neighborhood of Mount Kithairon, noted as the locale of the maenadic or bacchant ceremonies described in Euripides's *Bacchae;* the "liberated sisterhood" of Eleutherai is the same group of maddened female devotees of the god under a related metaphor. The escort of the cult image and the gigantic phallus into the theater supposedly was intended to commemorate the tradition that the Athenians had at first rejected the cult from Eleutherai and were visited by a plague upon the genitals of the men, which was cured also only when they accepted the rural god into the city.

A similar myth about the god's initial rejection involved Ikarios, the eponymous hero of Ikaria, the mountain village of Thespis.[75] Ikarios received Dionysus and gave the god's newly invented wine to his fellow herdsmen. They thought that they had been poisoned and killed Ikarios in a drunken revel. When they regained their senses the following morning, they threw his corpse into a well. When the dog of his daughter Erigone (the "Early Born") led her to his grave, she hanged herself from a tree above it and the dog leapt into the well. For retribution, the god made all the maidens of Athens commit suicide in the same way, and then visited the land with a drought, which was relieved only when the Athenians accepted his cult. Erigone became a maenadic bride of the god and was placed among the stars as the constellation Virgo. A similar stellar transformation occurred with the god's bride Ariadne into the Corona Borealis, the Northern Crown. Erigone's father became the Plowman Boötes and the dog Maira became Procyon, the alpha star or brightest in the constellation Canis Minoris.

The myth was the etiology of the ritual of swinging at the Anthesteria, the February festival of Dionysus, when the wine casks were first opened. Young girls hung ribbons and dolls and little wine cups from the boughs of trees and had themselves pushed on a swing above the newly broached casks. Similar swinging rituals were also enacted in the rural festivals.[76]

The classic version of this myth of the god's rejection is the plot of Euripides's *Bacchae,* which contrasts the suffering of the Theban king Pentheus, whose name means "pain," with the beatific mystery of the joyous rites celebrated by the maddened bacchants on Mount Kithairon.[77] The message is clear: Reject the blessings of drunken madness only at your peril.

Urban Rowdiness

At some point, a dramatic festival was added for the performance of comedies, which took place in January. It became part of the Lenaia festival, which takes it name from the sisterhood of the *lenai* maidens, who are maenads or bacchants named by another metaphor for the *lenós* or "wine-vat."[78] They are not the same as the mountain revels of the maenads as depicted in Euripides's *Bacchae,* and unlike the maenads, they are depicted on vases ladling out the wine and entering states of ecstasy. The mountain maenads, in contrast, are never seen drinking, but the nature of their revel is symbolized by the *thyrsus* that is their emblem. It symbolizes the activity of herb-gatherers and they are honoring the pre-viticultural manifestation of the god, symbolized by the wild toxic ivy as the antecedent of the cultivated vine of the god and the fermented toxin of the grape.[79] Another name for the *thyrsus* is *narthex,* which is etymologically derived as the "narcotic receptacle." The *lenai,* moreover, enacted their ritual in the city, whereas the maenads are outside the city on the mountainside.

The gathering of magical plants traditionally involves rituals of sexual mimesis under a plethora of metaphors.[80] For the maenads, these included sexual assault by satyrs or goat-men, dismemberment of a living bull with the bare hands, suckling of wild beasts, fire handling,[81] rabbit hunting without nets, and the dismemberment and ingestion of their own children. These are all obviously metaphors, since the women did not bring their children to the mountain revel and it is inconceivable how women could dismember or pull a bull to pieces bare-handedly. The "rabbit" hunt is metaphoric of their offering their "bunny" sexually to the god. Needless to say, moreover, satyrs don't exist except as something materialized from another reality. The infant god is sometimes cradled in the basket of a winnowing fan (*mystica vannus Iacchi,* "the mystical fan of Iacchus"[82]), associating him with the ergot fungus of the Eleusinian potion.

Originally, the Lenaean comedic performances may have been produced in some area of the marketplace improvised as a theater or from moveable carts or floats. Eventually they were moved to the Theater of Dionysus, and comedies were added to the schedule of competitions at the Great Dionysia and tragedies were also performed at the Lenaia.[83] The first recorded comic victor at the Dionysia is Chionides, who the *Suda* lexicon says won eight years before the Persian Wars, which would be around 487 BCE, but so early a date is doubtful. The dramas, both tragic and comedic, were so popular that troupes from the city performances toured the countryside for presentations at the Rural Dionysia, which was not everywhere celebrated on exactly the same date, allowing theatrical groupies to view a great variety of plays.[84] By its nature, comedy enacts democratic free speech and the insulting of eminent citizens, commemorating the overthrow of the old aristocracy.[85] Thematically, as comedy evolved into a fixed genre, it enacted the victory of the lower class or of the disenfranchised females.

Unlike the Lenaia in January, however, the March Great Dionysia coincided with the opening of the seas for navigation after the season of dangerous winter storms, and many foreigners flocked to the city for the spectacle and also to attend to legal issues that had to be adjudicated in the Athenian court. The festival also had an influence on the city's political agenda since it was followed soon after by the election of the annual magistrates, the meeting of the public assembly, and the beginning of the year's military campaigns. The Dionysia became a showcase for the city's military supremacy. Gifts and tributes from the allied cities and weapons were paraded into the theater on the first day of the festival, along with bulls to be sacrificed for the common state-sponsored feasting. The procession included the dancers, performers, playwrights, and their patrons, and floats displaying the extravagant paraphernalia and costumes for the dramas. The entire holiday, with its variety of dancing and dramatic genres, together with the feasting and the execution of civic business, could occupy a week. The feasting at both the rural and at all the city rites dissolved class distinctions, and even the slaves took part.

The first day ended with a second procession in the evening, a *komos,* which was a drunken revel through the streets of the city. Comedy takes its name from the *komos.* It was not uncommon, as might be expected, that such urban revelry resulted in violence and lawless behavior.[86] The *Wasps,* in fact, enacts such a rowdy brawl as the outcome of old Philokleon's drinking party, calling him the "nouveau riche dregs" of society (*veoploutos trux*), using the term that will culminate in the *trugedy* of the Thespian vignette.[87] The hero in the comic genre was a member of the lowest class, and the old man is a lover of the aristocratic democratic demagogue Kleon.

> Then when he was thoroughly drunk, he started back home, hitting whoever was in his path. Here he comes tottering along. I'm getting out of the way before he gets me (1299-1449).

Since it was customary to drink throughout the daylong performances,[88] it is likely that the street revelry was the normal conclusion each night as the spectators wended their way home.

Strong Wine

The wine drunk in the theater contained a special herbal additive.[89] Greek wine in general was extremely intoxicating, even when drunk, as was the custom, diluted with three or four parts water, since its toxicity was enhanced by a variety of toxins and preservatives that intensified its potency far beyond its alcoholic content, which could not exceed the concentration achieved through natural fermentation, which at most would be about fourteen percent, before dilution.[90] The additives altered the wine to produce various types of intoxication suitable for its particular use or ceremony, but there can be little doubt that small amounts were capable of inducing ecstatic states and even visionary experience.

Like the Eleusinian ergot potion, wine was a magical and symbolic mingling of elements that reconciled the dichotomy of wild natural toxins, for which the ivy and similar plants were emblematic, and the civilized product of cultivation, the controlled fungal growth of the yeasts of fermentation upon the body of the god slain in the harvest of the grapes grown from the vine. Both the Eleusinian potion and wine represent the taming of the seedless wild mushroom by inducing a similar fungal growth upon a cultivated host, the grape of Dionysus or the grain of Demeter. Wine itself is emblematic of the political agenda enacted by the integration of the rural Thespian routines into the very heart of the city on the southern slope of the Acropolis.

The philosopher Plato, who himself had written tragedies and who's our most authentic witness to the dramas of the fifth-century, described the theater experience as a communal rapture or public spiritual possession, proceeding from the other world through the entranced actors on to the spectators seated in the natural amphitheater of the hillside, producing a harmonious togetherness like the pattern revealed by a magnet's alignment of iron rings drawn ineluctably into a continuous chain of bondage.[91] As such, in his opinion, it produced a dangerous homogeneity of indoctrination.

The Thracian Sabazios

What survive of these performances in the theater are only the script, the words without music, and no designation of stage action or choreography for the most part, except what can be inferred from the text. Thus the *Wasps* comedy begins with the two slaves trying to relieve the tedium of their guard duty through the use of a mind-altering drug. This must have involved some activity that would have been readily identifiable to the audience. They both feel a pleasant sleepiness coming upon them. This will result in dream visions, which they will later expound, interpreting the political references in the puzzling riddle of what they have seen.

The first effect is that they might be becoming crazy and out of their minds (*paraphroneis*, verse 7), or perhaps ecstatic like corybants (*korubantiais*). The reference to the corybants (*korybantes*) indicates a particular type of very ecstatic dancing associated with Phrygia (central Anatolia), practiced by young males as a Mystery initiation or a sexual puberty ritual into a brotherhood in the service of the goddess Cybele. Only the initiates would know their exact identity, but Plato hints that the ceremony involved the sodomizing of the young initiate,[92] as also happened in Mithraism, where the initiate, either nude or dressed as a woman, became the male bride of the supreme initiator, the Father.[93]

The *korybantes* are analogous to similar fraternities devoted to the chthonic great goddess with a variety of names localized at different Mystery sanctuaries, in particular the Kabeiroi (*Cabiri*) of Thrace, the islands of Lemnos and Samothrace, and Boeotian Thebes; and the

Kuretes and the Daktyls of Crete. What characterized the *korybantes*, as their name indicates, is their ecstatic "dancing" (*bantes*), dressed in military armor with a crested "helmet" (*korys*). The old man's son in the *Wasps* had tried to cure his father's juridical mania by initiating him as a *korybant*, but he ran off with tympanum right back to the court (119–120).

But that isn't what they are doing, as one of the slaves in the *Wasps* says. Instead the sleep that is taking hold of him comes from Sabazios, to which the other agrees. They are both tending the same Sabazios bull, and it feels like some nodding Persian sleep has just marched across their eyelids. There must be a pause in the action while they have their trance before they go on to narrate what marvelous dreams they had.

Obviously they are taking a drug, clearly identifiable from a distance by the spectators. It is Persian, visionary, metaphorically a bull, associated with a Mystery initiation, and identified as the god Sabazios. If we supply the missing stage direction, they are probably eating mushrooms, in which case the *mukter mukatai* routine of the Thespian vignette at the comedy's conclusion was introduced at the beginning and is the source of the old Philokleon's intense "spinal" erection from his nightlong binge. There is nothing else but the phallus as mushroom that would be visually identifiable to the audience and have these connotations. Performance in the open-air theater, moreover, would require an economy of stage props. The metaphoric transmutations of the performers' phallus usually are all that is required. The mushroom was a common metaphor for the penis.[94]

Sabazios was a Mystery god of the Phrygians and Thracians. Mythically, he may be identical with a version of Dionysus as Phanes, born as the son of Rhea and protected from the jealous Hera as a nursling of Cybele.[95] This mystery identity is recalled in Euripides's *Bacchae* as the homeland of his troupe of bacchants[96]; the tragedy was composed for production in Macedonia-Thrace.[97] The second element of his name (*zios*) is the Indo-European word that produces Zeus, Ju(piter), day (Latin *dies*), and god (Greek *theos* and

Latin *deus*). The native country of the "redhead" slave Xanthias is apparently Thrace, where the name Rufus (Latin "red") often occurs on tombstones. Thracians were noted as blue-eyed and redheaded.[98] The cult of Sabazios came with the Indo-European migration in the first millennium BCE, and he was assimilated as a version of both Dionysus and Zeus. He is depicted as a bearded horseman, a father god associated with the sky, wearing a Phrygian cap, wielding his staff of power, and trampling the serpent or the lunar bull of the Anatolian goddess beneath his horse's hooves. Several bronze hands from the Roman period survive, intended as the finial for the god's staff raised in benediction, with enigmatic decorations, such as a pinecone, serpent's head, scorpion, amphorae, and banquet table laden with loaves of psychoactive bread for the cultic meal. His cult was espoused by the Macedonian warrior elite and is responsible for such dynastic names as Philip, as a "lover of horses."

In Athens at the time of Aristophanes, the cult involved ecstatic initiation by women,[99] supposedly allowing a serpent to slither between their breasts. "God between the breasts" was the secret password,[100] and Alexander the Great's mother and father first met while they were being initiated in the sanctuary on Samothrace.[101] Alexander's mother may have indoctrinated Alexander with the notion that a deity in the initiation was his actual father. The cult was apparently monotheistic and involved Chaldean astrology, and in Rome of the second-century BCE, the Jews were expelled from Rome along with the astrologers,[102] since Sabazios was equated with Yahweh Sabaoth.[103] Artifacts from Mithraea of the Roman period indicate that Sabazios had also been equated with the Persian Mithras, the fraternity that bound the emperors, soldiers, and bureaucrats who administered the Roman Empire.[104] Mithraism was the way that Zoroastrian monotheism spread the mushroom *haoma* sacrament of the Persians into Europe as an element in the sevenfold stages of its secret drug-induced initiation.

For Aristophanes of the *Wasps* routine, this would have been known as the sacrament of the Persian aristocracy, whose kings Darius and his son Xerxes had invaded Greece at the beginning of the century with their elite military forces of the *haomavarga,*[105] the "haoma wolves," whose battle fury, like that of the Nordic berserkers, was induced by the ingestion of *Amanita muscaria.*[106] The Dacians, who were a northern branch of the Thracians, at the time of the Emperor Trajan were still arousing the werewolf fury of their warriors by the ingestion of mushrooms.[107] Stone mushroom monuments at sacred sites and rock carvings from this region indicate that the ecstatic cult of Dionysus-Zeus-Sabazios-Zalmoxis was practiced perhaps as early as the eighth-century, although mythologized as of much greater antiquity.[108]

The Thracian version of the rejection myth about the arrival of the god Dionysus involves the ancient king of the Edoni, whose city Amphipolis the Athenians had conquered just before the beginning of the Peloponnesian War. He was Lycurgus. His father and his son were named Dryas, for the oak tree, implying that they were Druids, whose sacred plants were the mistletoe and the *Amanita muscaria,* which both are parasitic on the oak and intertwined in folkloric motifs.[109] Lycurgus is named as the person "who acts the wolf," like the werewolf warriors that Trajan fought among the Dacians. Like the Theban Pentheus, Lycurgus banned the new religion and imprisoned the maenads, but Dionysus drove him mad, and either in his altered vision or in blindness to ordinary reality, he killed his wife and mistook his own son for the ivy, which he pruned away, cutting off his limbs, nose and ears, fingers and toes.[110] Another version of the myth records that he cut off his own foot, thinking it was the ivy,[111] rendering him effectively a one-foot like a mushroom. In attacking the ivy, he is associated with the primitive antecedents of viticulture, the wild mushroom and the ivy, as opposed to the fungus cultivated in the fermentation of the grape.[112]

Ironically, Kleon, whom Philokleon so much admires in the *Wasps,* would not outlive the year of this comedic parody. He died that summer on campaign in Thrace, where he confronted the Spartan general Brasidas, who also died there in the battle for Amphipolis. Kleon had risen to prominence as a demagogue after the death of Pericles and was a staunch opponent of his fellow aristocrats, employing numerous paid informants to gather evidence against them to present in court. He was a particular favorite of the jurists, who are the wasps of the chorus, because he raised their pay to three obols, approximately a day's wages for unskilled labor. In so doing, he had tapped another demographic group to tip the balance of support in his favor, enlisting the unemployed jurors, many of them in their dotage. They constitute the equivalence of his private army, working within the democratic judicial system and paid for at public expense. The *Wasps* makes clear that without the jury dole, the families of the old jurists will have nothing to eat (303 *et seq.*) The deaths of Brasidas and Kleon removed the main obstacles to peace and a treaty was signed the next year, although the peace did not last.

Snuff and Snot

The wasps who are the jurors obviously have a phallus to serve as stringer.

> They have a stinger from their groin, real sharp, with which they prod, and shouting, they leap and toss it about with a tip burning like sparks (225–227).

The obvious target is the asshole of their enemies. They can also launch a frontal attack on the genitals, aimed at the "pair of eyeballs" (testes) and the "fingers" (penises).[113] As the chorus of old jurists enters, a boy accompanies each. It is still dark before dawn and the burning tip of the phallus serves as lantern. The routine is obscene. The boy is the keeper of the lamp, directing the elder to watch out for the rocks of turd and fecal mire that lie in the path. The elder directs the boy to pick up a twig to trim the oil lamp's wick, but the boy instead uses his "finger."

> Where did you learn to push the wick with your finger, stupid? Now you've made me ejaculate, spill the oil. It doesn't bother you how costly it is.

> If you hit us again, we'll put out the lamp and go home, and without this here [asshole] you can just stir up the muck in the dark waddling about like ducks.

> I can take care of "bigger" ones than you! But look at this muck I'm in. The lamps have mushrooms now—see them! That's a sign that I'm going to have to pee. Rain, with a cold autumn wind, brings on a good crop of them (248–265).

The homoerotic badinage continues when the boy asks the father for a gift. The father suggests knucklebones, which were used as dice. The best throw was called Aphrodite, when all four came up different. The boy says he prefers figs since they are sweeter. Obviously the opposition involves a metaphor since knucklebones aren't eaten. The father says you wouldn't think so if you were hung. "Hung" is a colloquialism connoting a large penis or being the recipient of the same. The cleft fig immediately suggests the image of the receptive vulva, commonly noted as the obscene fig gesture, a clenched fist with the thumb as the clitoris protruding between the forefinger and middle finger, to which the reply is the finger gesture (*digitus obscenus, digitus infamis,* or *digitus impudicus*) as the erect penis.

The knucklebones lend themselves to the fantasy that the erect penis has bones, like the creaking vertebrae of old Philokleon's bellowing snozzle. Thus Philokleon proclaimed that he would triumph over the first of the crab-sons to enter by a knucklebone *pas de deux.*[114] A Corinthian bronze mirror cover (c. 350 BCE) is etched with a scene depicting the nude Aphrodite playing knucklebones with the goat-man Pan.[115] He is her frequent attendant and is usually seen with an aggressive exaggerated erection. Behind Aphrodite is Eros. Beneath the bench where they are playing is a "goose" whose long and in this context obscene neck drives home the metaphor. Aphrodite was particularly fond of geese. By one etiological version of the myth, Zeus invented "knucklebones" so that his boy-lover Ganymedes would have a toy with which to play.

The father's strange reply about being hung implies the threat of anal penetration, which was the obscene mimesis of their entry with the sparking mushroom lantern. Thus the boy replies that he won't "escort" or "send forth" (masturbate) the old man anymore.[116] The fig gesture also resembles the penis with the scrotum below it. A sycophant is an abusive term for a paid informant. It means someone who "shows the fig," implying the baseness of the creature who displays the vulva or anus as an invitation for penetration. It is these sycophants that the demagogue Kleon employs for evidence against his democratic rivals.

The lantern routine encodes another fungal metamorphosis for the phallus. The burnt end of the lamp wick is called a mushroom (*mukes*), as it still is in French today as the *champignon*. The sparking of the wick with the formation of the mushroom is supposedly a presage of winter rain.[117]

This mushroom on the wick is called "snuff" in English, but "snot" in former times, from the metaphor of the wick dangling from the lamp like snot from the nostril,[118] and the human action of snuffling back the snot of a mucous nasal discharge. In Greek "snot" is *muxa*, but also the nose or nozzle of the oil lamp. The mushroom was linked with nasal mucus because the *membrum virile* discharges a mucous liquor of magical potency. The lamp-nozzle with its dripping wick carries the same idea with fire involved. Ancient medical writers and Pliny attributed a sexual character to the *Amanita muscaria.* There is a startling association in the complex of words and figures of speech for fire, the nose and its mucus, and mushrooms, and various erotic connotations. The same fossilized figures survive in French, Spanish, and English. "Punk" in English (Irish *sponnc*) is the name applied to a powdered fungus used as tinder; it also means a harlot who sparks her client. In French, the word for "punk" is *amadou.* "Spunk" in colloquial English means seminal fluid. It is a doublet for punk, and both are cognate with Greek *spongia* "sponge"(and Latin *fungus*), which is cognate with German *Schwarmm,* meaning both "mushroom" and "sponge." *Champignon* is the penis in colloquial French; a synonym is *chandelle,* which means both a tallow taper and a running nose. In Shakespeare, "tallow" is the semen and equated with piss:

> Send me a cool rut-time, Jove, or who can blame me to piss my tallow? (*Merry Wives of Windsor,* act 5, scene 5)

A "long nose," as in the triumphant declaration of the *mukter mukatai* vignette, is an erect penis. From the Greek word for mucus (*muxa*) is derived the English word "match." Nothing could be more obvious, however, once the erotic act is linked with a mucous emission and with the punk that leaps into flame when sparked. In Spanish, the word for snuff or the burnt end of a wick is *seta,* meaning mushroom, and also *moco,* meaning mucus.

On the comic stage, a mere lewd gesture is all that would be required to elucidate the multiple obscene transformations of the god's phallus.

A God for All Seasons

Only Dionysus, and perhaps Demeter of the Eleusinian Mystery, could be considered a patron of democracy. Apollo was much closer to the aristocratic ideals of the Dorian Spartans, whose response to popular dissent was to enslave those outside the wealthy noble oligarchy.[119] They also discouraged the rise of a competing plutocracy by adopting an unwieldy archaic monetary system with little value as an international currency.

With the importation of the Thespian mountain mushroom rites into the official calendar of the city's religious celebrations, Athens became a democracy, or more exactly an aristocratic oligarchy of demagogues vying against one another for popular support. Aristophanes, in all likelihood, like the other playwrights, was a member of an upper class.[120] No one else would have had the leisure and wealth to acquire the requisite education. The joke about Euripides's mother as a vegetable-peddler does not derive from his family's poverty. They had extensive estates on the island of Salamis. Instead, it implies that she is a whoring herbal pharmacist.[121]

Only Dionysus and Demeter's daughter Persephone experienced the mystery of death and the return. Although both were children of

Zeus, they were only visitors among their relatives in the Olympian family, whose life was eternal and ageless. The grain must die and enter the earth to be *reborn.* So too must the grape be harvested, drained of its juice like blood, and interred in vats beneath the ground to gestate through the controlled putrefaction of fermentation and emerge as the old god rejuvenated in the persona of himself as the newborn infant. Through the winter months when the god of viticulture lay in the netherworld, his primitive antecedents were celebrated in the phallic misbehavior of the Rural Dionysia and the mountain orgies of the bacchants, who acted out the rituals of gathering the ivy and the wild naturally toxic inebriants. Emblematic of these were the uncultivable mushroom and the thyrsus-narthex that they carried as the container for the gathered entheogens. For both men and women, these were the months for the wildest sexual fantasies.

In January, as the cultivation of the fungus in the fermenting casks neared completion, the women of the Lenaean rite ladled out the still-incomplete product, drinking it from *skyphos* mugs, in the presence of a masked pillar hung with the god's maenadic robes or beside his tombstone. The choice of cup traditional for each ritual was significant; the *skyphos* was a mug, easily handled, while the *kylix,* with its broad cup and slender stem, was a challenge to handle with sobriety. They struck the tympanum, to imitate the sound that the quaking earth makes when it parts to open up a passage from the lower depths, and they experienced ecstatic rapture, which unlike the mountain revel was induced by the still-fermenting brew.

January was the month for marriage, when, as the Greeks saw it, the sexual exuberance of males, which had wilted in the heat of the summer's sun, was at its peak, while the lusting of the females decreased with the colder season. The god mediated this sexual dichotomy, dressing as a female for his mountain bacchants, who were his nymphs or "brides," and assaulting them in fantasy only through the irrepressible priapism of his ithyphallic satyrs. The female dress of the dead god now hangs on the phallic pillar at the ladling ceremony. The fermenting god is still in the other world.

In February, the fermentation was completed, and the resurrection of the god was celebrated as the three-day festival of the Anthesteria. When the casks were broached, it opened up a pathway not only for the reborn infant god, but also for the entire entourage of the dear departed. Spirits of the dead wandered abroad and were invited to partake of the feasting, with special procedures to share the wine and meat at separate tables and from separate pitchers (*choes*), in order to avoid contamination from the dead. It was a time to celebrate family values, men, their wives and nubile daughters, and the children, who were initiated into their first experience of drunkenness at the age of three or four and are seen on the child-sized version of the drinking pitchers cavorting with spirits or playing beside the tombs and imitating some of the most sacred rituals of the god. There can be little doubt that the three days of drinking induced a visionary reality.

> This is my second curse for that guy who did me in so that I didn't get a chance to put on my comedy at the Lenaea. I hope that as he makes his way home from the drinking, with his brain on fire, some raving drunken ghost of Orestes breaks open his head, and as he tries to fight back, he picks up in the darkness, instead of a rock, a freshly passed turd.[122]

The visit of the maddened Orestes to Athens was the etiology of the ritual of drinking from the *choes,* to keep his pollution at a distance.

It was at this time also that the Lesser Mystery was celebrated at the sanctuary of the huntress Artemis, just outside the city on the banks of Ilissos River. As an element of that preparatory purification for the Greater Eleusinian Mystery, the wife of the "king" archon united sexually with the god Dionysus through the medium of his bull sacrament, which was probably the wild mushroom,[123] which in the potion ingested by the thousands of initiates later in September at Eleusis had similarly yielded to cultivation as the ergot fungus on the grain grown throughout the rainy winter months.

Two months later, as the cultivated vines begin to sprout,[124] the other civilized aspect of the god takes precedence at the city

Dionysia, where originally the performances in the Theater were tragedies. The dual personae of the god are expressed in his two names, the Bacchus of the wild vegetation, as opposed to the cultivated Dionysus. Although the seas were now navigable, the timing of the city Dionysia was influenced by religion, rather than convenience, since the climate in late March, even on the south-facing and protected slope of the Acropolis, is still cold and not ideal for outside daylong performances.

Perhaps in the rural Thespian celebration, these tragedies (or *trugedies*) were sung for the goat as the prize or pay of the dancers. As the genre developed, however, tragedy enacts the necessary sacrifice of the goat, as the primitive persona of the god and, in fact, a real threat to the cultivation of the vine of viticulture. The tragic hero generically represents the necessary downfall of someone worthy enough to bear the burden of primitivism and pollution in order to allow the emergence of its counterpoise in someone who is more essential for the foundations of culture and society. Comedy is exactly the opposite. Satyr plays, which along with the old dithyrambic dances, formed part of the entire theatrical bill, mediated between the two genres as a kind of comedic tragedy. The comedies and satyr plays would be the send-off for the audience to wend their way back home through the streets of the democratic city that the tyrant first put on the path of demagoguery by inviting Thespis in from the countryside.

Aristophanes parodied this as a dance of the genital crab-son *trugedians* around the old Thespian lover of demagoguery, with his gigantic mushroom of a phallus.

Notes

1. It is now in the Ashmolean Museum of Oxford University. It was deciphered and published among the Arundel Marbles (*Marmora Arundelliana,* London, 1628–1629), nos. 1–21, 59–119), Felix Jacoby, *Fragmenta graecorum historicorum* (1923–1959), 239A, epoch 39.

2. Now in the museum on Páros.

3. The number is partially illegible and read as a restoration, but the date falls between 541/0, when Cyrus the Persian king took control of the City of Sardis, and 520/1, when Darius became king of the Persians. It is further ascertained by the restoration of the name of the archonship in Athens for that year.

4. The technical term for producing a drama is used, *edidaxe dram[a]*, "he taught (his troupe) a doing (i.e., a drama)."

5. As restored, *[en a]stei*, "in city."

6. The technical term used to indicate that Thespis took an actor's role is restored as *[hypokrita]to*, "he answered as a hypocrite."

7. The extant testimony is assembled in Pickard-Cambridge, Sir A.W., *Dithyramb, Tragedy, and Comedy,* second edition revised by T. B. L. Webster (London: Oxford Clarendon Press, 1962), 69–89.

8. Aristotle, *Poetics,* 1449a10–15. Pickard-Cambridge, *Dithyramb, Tragedy, and Comedy,* 89–97.

9. Horace, *Ars Poetica,* 275–277: *Ignotum tragicae genus invenisse Camenae dicitur et plaustris vexisse poemata Thespis quae canerent agerentque perunti faecibus ora* ("Thespis is said to have invented the [previously] unknown genre of the tragic muse and to have carried his poems about in carts, which [his troupe] sang and acted, their faces smeared with wine-lees").

10. *Greek Anthology,* 5.410. Dioscorides composed a series of epigrams on prominent writers, both past and contemporary, with a particular interest in the history of literary genres, and also erotic and funerary pieces that depict daily life in Egypt.

11. Clement of Alexandria, *Stromata,* 1.79.1.

12. Athenaeus, *Deipnosophistae,* 2.11.40a.

13. August Nauck, *Tragicorum graecorum fragmenta* (Leipzig: Teubner, 1822–1892), 832.

14. Aristophanes, *Wasps,* 1479.

15. The ensuing episode is so unlike the mythologized image of Thespis as the inventor of tragedy that an ancient scholiast

found an otherwise unknown cithara-singer as the object of the parody. Aristophanes, however, calls this "the old pieces with which Thespis fought the competitions." The unknown cithara-player wouldn't seem to be famous enough to warrant the parody. Moreover, the *Wasps* routine compares Philokleon's opponent in the contest to the famous old tragedian Phrynichos, which would be meaningless if the Thespian is the cithara-player, who, in any case, would not be noted for his dancing.

16. Aristophanes, *Wasps*, 1535–1537.

17. If unprecedented, it became used in other plays. William Walter Merry, *Aristophanes, The Wasps: Introduction and Text* (Oxford: Clarendon Press, 1893), 102.

18. Horace, *Satires*, 2.3.82.

19. As a colloquial phrase in English, this refers to the belief that placing a few hairs of the dog in the wound could treat a rabid dog bite. It is a common medical notion going back to Classical Greek medicine that *similia similibus curantur,* "cures are effected by using the same thing that caused the malady for a cure."

20. Carl A.P. Ruck, Mark A. Hoffman, and José Alfredo González Celdrán, *Mushrooms, Myth, and Mithras: The Drug Cult that Civilized Europe* (San Francisco, CA: City Lights Books, 2011), 153 *et seq.*

21. *Ibid.*, Chapter 4, "Death by Bull's Blood," 77–86.

22. Thucydides, *History of the Peloponnesian War,* 2.23.2; Diodorus Siculus, 12.42.7.

23. *Inscriptiones graecae*, I' 365.30–40 [= 22 296]; 22 1498.69.

24. There was a contemporary dancer named Phrynichos (Andocides, *On the Mysteries*, 47), but the joke about being stoned (verse 1491) requires the tragedian.

25. Scholiast on Aristophanes, *Peace*, 793 and 795–796.

26. Scholiast on Aristophanes, *Clouds*, 1259. *Ió moí moi*, which sounds like the lament of one of Karkínos' gods, according to Strepsiades, Aristophanes, *Clouds*, verse 1261.

27. Aristophanes, *Peace*, 793.

28. Kenneth S. Rothwell, Jr., "Was Carcinus I a Tragic Playwright?": 241–245, in *Classics Faculty Publication Series,* University of Massachusetts Boston, vol. 1, no. 1 (1994).

29. Aristophanes, *Peace,* 788–789. Aristophanes uses the word *gulios* with the meaning as a "soldier's pack-bag" in verse 527. It apparently could be metaphorically extended to describe a "hedgehog" on the basis that it, as the scholiast notes, has no neck, which is the point here, not that the crab son is compared to a hedgehog, contrary to the opinion of E.K. Borthwick, "The Dances of Philocleon and the Sons of Carcinus in Aristophanes' *Wasps*": 4–51, in *The Classical Quarterly,* new series, vol. 18, no. 1 (May, 1968). The lack of a neck (*atrachilos*) is the defining characteristic of the crab in *Palatine Anthology* (*Anthologia Graeca*), 6, 196.2. The *gulios* is clearly the soldier's "knapsack" in Aristophanes, *Acharnians,* 1097, as the general Lamachos arms for war. Hence, it is weird that the L-S-J lexicon glosses the adjective *guli-auchenen* as "long-necked, scraggy-necked," since the point is just the opposite, no neck at all.

30. Aristophanes, *Birds,* 707.

31. Aristophanes, *Wasps,* 1490.

32. Herodotus, *Histories,* 6.21.

33. Reading the verb as a future passive (*ballesei*) with Dindorf's emendation.

34. August Nauck, *Tragicorum graecorum fragmenta* (Leipzig: Teubner, 1856), frag. 17.

35. Borthwick, "Dances of Philocleon," emends "spider" (*phalagx*) to "blind-rat or mole" (*sphalax*) at verse 1509, since he sees no point in a spider, especially since he emends "vinegar cruet" (*oxis*) to "owl" (*otos*); the two animals go better as describing an imagined type of dancing. However, a crab son should look like a crab, which a spider does, as also does the vinegar cruet, which would have been a ceramic in the shape of a cup, perhaps with side-handles resembling the claws of the crab. Both the spider and the vinegar cup would have no neck. The Latin for the vinegar cup is *acetabulum,* which is used now in anatomy to designate the

shallow "socket" of the hipbone because of its resemblance to the "vinegar cup."

36. On the antiquity of louse infestation, see J. Bondeson, MD, PhD, "Phthiriasis: The Riddle of the Lousy Disease": 328–334, in *Journal of the Royal Society of Medicine*, vol. 91 (1998).

37. Aristophanes, *Wasps*, 1523.

38. *Ibid.*, 1529–1530.

39. Aristophanes, *Peace*, 863 *et seq.*

39. *Ibid.*, 775 *et seq.*

40. Aristophanes, *Clouds*, 146–168; 627 *et seq.*

41. Euripides (fifth-century), *Herakles; Suppliant Women; Children of Herakles.* Isocrates (fourth-century), *Helen; Panathenaicus.* Barry S. Strauss, *Fathers and Sons in Athens: Ideology and Society in the Era of the Peloponnesian War* (London: Routledge, 1993), 112–118.

42. Herodotus, *Histories*, 1.56–58.

43. Aristotle, *Politics*, 1297B.

44. Athens with the final "s" is an anglicized version of the Greek plural *Athenai* as the plurality of the Athena-s. This is commonly explained as the result of the gathering together of the villages of Athena into a single civic identity (*sunoikismos*) under the rule of Theseus. Comparison with other feminine pluralities as the designation of cities (Mycenae, Thebes), however, suggests that these were settlements originally presided over by a goddess and her similarly named sisterhood. Of particular significance in this regard is the name of Delphi (a Latinized version of a masculine plural *Delphoi*) as "male womb-mates or brothers," replacing the probably female sisterhood that presided there before it passed into the patronage of Apollo and the male-dominant Olympians.

45. Tyrtaeus, frag. 12.15–20.

46. Xenophon, *Constitution of the Athenians*, 1.1–2.

47. Herodotus, *Histories*, 5.65.

48. Aristotle, *Constitution of the Athenians,* 13; Herodotus, *Histories,* 1.59; Plutarch, *Life of Solon,* 185.

49. Aristotle, *Constitution of the Athenians,* 14; Herodotus, *Histories,* 1.60.

50. Sarah B. Pomeroy, *Ancient Greece: A Political, Social, and Cultural History* (Oxford: Oxford University Press, 1999), 172; Terry Buckley, *Aspects of Greek History, 750–323 BC: A Source-based Approach* (London: Routledge, 1996), 87–89.

51. Our extant texts derive from the work of the second-century BCE Hellenistic scholar Aristarchus of Samothrace, librarian of Egyptian Alexandria, working from earlier compilations. The subject of the Pisistratean recension, although based on ancient tradition (Cicero, *De oratore,* 3.13.137), remains questionable. J.A. Davison, "Peisistratus and Homer": 1–21, in *Transactions and Proceedings of the American Philological Association,* vol. 86 (1955).

52. M.J. Apthorp, *The Manuscript Evidence for Interpolation in Homer* (Heidelberg: Carl Winter, 1980). The text was constantly evolving through oral performances: G. Nagy, *Poetry as Performance: Homer and Beyond* (Cambridge, UK: Cambridge University Press, 1996).

53. Building F, dated *ca.* 550–525.

54. Thucydides, *History of the Peloponnesian War,* 2.65.

55. R. Gordon Wasson, Albert Hofmann, and Carl A.P. Ruck, *The Road to Eleusis: Unveiling the Secret of the Mysteries* (New York, NY: Harcourt Brace Jovanovich, 1978; reprinted and enlarged, twentieth anniversary edition, Los Angeles: Hermes Press, 1998; thirtieth anniversary edition, Berkeley, CA: North Atlantic Books, 2008); Carl A.P. Ruck. *Sacred Mushrooms of the Goddess; Secrets of Eleusis* (Berkeley, CA: Ronin Publishing, 2006).

56. Plutarch, *Solon,* 1.2–4.

57. *Ibid.*, 29.4–5.

58. Diogenes Laërtius (third century CE), *Lives of the Philosophers,* 3.1.

59. Ibid., 30.1–2. Solon, frag. 11. 1–4 (Bergk).

60. Carl A.P. Ruck and Danny (Blaise) Staples, *The World of Classical Myth: Gods and Goddesses, Heroines and Heroes.* Durham, NC: Carolina Academic Press, 1994), 150.

61. E. Rozik, *The Roots of Theatre: Rethinking Ritual and Other Theories of Origin* (Iowa City: IW: University of Iowa Press, 2002), chap. 4.

62. Aristophanes, *Ecclesiazusae,* 1072–1073.

63. Suidas, *s.v.* Thespis. The phrase is "linen alone": the meaning is uncertain since it may mean "of linen only, not of cork or wood," or of "linen without paint or coloring," or of "linen without any stiffening."

64. Suidas, *s.v. thríambos;* cf. Athenaeus, *Deipnosophistae,* 14.622.

65. Theophrastus, *History of Plants,* 3.16.6: cf. Pliny, *Natural History,* 13.130.

66. *Unedo* is supposed to mean, "I eat only one" (*unum solum edo*).

67. Kerényi, K., *Dionysos: Archetypal Image of Indestructible Life.* Princeton, NJ: Princeton University Press, 1976), 327.

68. Carl A.P. Ruck, Blaise Daniel Staples, José Alfredo González Celdrán, and Mark Alwin Hoffman, *The Hidden World: Survival of Pagan Shamanic Themes in European Fairytales* (Durham, NC: Carolina Academic Press, 2006), 77–79.

69. Pausanias (second century CE), *Description of Greece,* 9.22.1–2.

70. Compare the Celtic goddess Sheila-na-gig, stretching wide her vulva. Ruck, *Sacred Mushrooms of the Goddess,* 12–13.

71. P. Easterling, *The Cambridge Companion to Greek Tragedy* (Cambridge, UK: Cambridge University Press, 1997), 23.

72. R. Rehm, *Greek Tragic Theater* (London: Routledge, 1992), 14.

73. Hyginus (first-century CE), *Fabulae,* 225.

74. Pausanias, *Description of Greece,* 9.20.1.

75. Apollodorus (second-century BCE), *Bibliotheca,* 3.14.7.

76. B. Dietrich, "A Rite of Swinging during the Anthesteria": 36–50, in *Hermes,* vol. 89, no. 1, (1961), 36–50.

77. Ruck, "The Wild and the Cultivated: Wine in Euripides' *Bacchae.*" 179–223, in R. Gordon Wasson, Stella Kramrisch, Jonathan Ott, and Carl A.P. Ruck, *Persephone's Quest: Entheogens and the Origins of Religion* (New Haven, CT: Yale University Press, 1986).

78. Matthew Dillon, *Girls and Women in Classical Greek Religion* (London: Routledge, 2002), 149–152.

79. Wasson *et al., Road to Eleusis,* 88.

80. Ruck *et al., Hidden World,* 133–137, on gathering mandrake in Rumania. Wasson *et al., Road to Eleusis,* 103–108.

81. This survives in a Christianized version in the fire walk performed at the Anastenaria in Greece. L. Danforth, *Firewalking and Religious Healing: The Anastenaria of Greece and the American Firewalking Movement* (Princeton, NJ: Princeton University Press, 1989).

82. Virgil, *Georgics,* 1.166.

83. Edward Capps, 1903. *The Introduction of Comedy into the City Dionysia: A Chronological Study in Greek Literary History* (Chicago, IL: University of Chicago Press, 1903).

84. Plato, *Republic,* 475d.

85. Martin Litchfield West, *Studies in Greek Elegy and Iambus* (Berlin: Walter de Gruyter, 1974), 27–28. Scholiast on Dionysius Thrax (second-century BCE Greek grammarian), *Ars grammatica* (*Techne*), 18.15 Hilgard.

86. Michael Rinella, *Pharmakon: Plato, Drug Culture, and Identity in Athens.*

(Lanham, MD: Lexington Books, 2010).

87. Aristophanes, *Wasps,* 1290–1387.

88. Felix Jacoby, *Fragmente der griechischen Historiker* (Leiden: Brill, 1923–1959), fragment 171.

89. Hesychius (fifth-century CE, lexicographer), *s.v., trimma.*

90. Ruck, *Sacred Mushrooms of the Goddess,* 85–100.

91. Plato, Ion, 533d et seq. Wasson et al., Persephone's Quest, 219–223.

92. Plato, Euthydemus, 277d.

93. Ruck, et al., Mushrooms, Myth, and Mithras, 122–126.

94. Archilochus, frag. 34, Diehl; cf. Hesychius, Herodian.

95. Nonnus (fourth or fifth-century CE Greek Egyptian Christian), Dionysiaca, 9.136 *et seq.*

96. Euripides, Bacchae, 64 *et seq.*: "Happy he who, blest man, initiated in the mystic rites, is pure in his life, ((lacuna)) who, preserving the righteous Orgies of the great mother Kybele, and brandishing the thyrsos on high, and wreathed with ivy, doth worship Dionysos. Come, ye Bakkhai, come, ye Bakkhai, bringing down Bromios, god the child of god, out of the Phrygian mountains into the broad highways of Greece.... But ye who left Mt. Tmolos, fortress of Lydia, revel-band of mine, women whom I brought from the land of barbarians as my assistants and traveling companions, uplift the tambourines native to Phrygian cities, inventions of mine and mother Rhea."

97. The play was written for King Archelaos of Macedon, but was found in the papers of the poet after his death and produced in Athens by his son. E.R. Dodds, *Euripides Bacchae* (Oxford: Clarendon Press, 1044, 2edition 1960), xxxix *et seq.*

98. Xenophanes, frag. B16 (Diels, Die Fragmente der Vorsokratiker, 1903).

99. Demosthenes, *De corona*, 260.

100. Clement of Alexandria (first century CE), Protrepticus, 1.2.16.

101. Plutarch, Alexander, 2.2.

102. Valerius Maximus, *Epitome of Nine Books of Memorable Deeds and Sayings*, 1.3.2.

103. Plutarch, Symposiacs, 4.6. Helmut Koester, *History, Culture, and Religion in the Hellenistic Age* (Berlin: Walter de Gruyter & Co., 1995), 187.

104. Ruck et al., *Mushrooms, Myth, and Mithras*, 153–157.

105. Ludmila Koryzkova and Andrej Vladimirovich, *The Urals and Western Siberia in the Bronze and Iron Ages* (Cambridge, UK:

Cambridge University Press, 2007), 225. Herodotus, *Histories,* 1.201–202. Herodotus calls them "nomads" or Saka Scythians, and records a garbled account of their ritual, confusing it with an aromatic burnt fruit that is probably cannabis.

106. Ruck et al., *Mushrooms, Myth, and Mithras,* 54.

107. Dio Cassius, History, epitome, 68.8. Mircea Eliade, *De Zalmoxis à Gengis-Khan. Études comparatives sur les religions et le folklore de la Dacie et de l'Europe orientale,* (Paris: Payot, 1970).

108. Stavros Kiotsekoglou, "Upaithria Iera tes Archaias Thrakes (Open-air Sanctuaries of Ancient Thrace)": 4–21, in *Aeropos* (July–August, 2009).

109. Ruck and Staples, "Mistletoe, Centaurs, and Datura": 15–40, in Carl A.P. Ruck, Blaise Daniel Staples, and Clark Heinrich, *The Apples of Apollo: Pagan and Christian Mysteries of the Eucharist* (Durham, NC: Carolina Academic Press, 2001).

110. Homer, *Iliad,* 6.130–140.

111. Servius, commentary on Virgil, *Aeneid* 3.14; Hyginus, *Fabulae,* 123.

112. Andrew Dalby, *The Story of Bacchus* (London: British Museum Press, 2005).

113. Aristophanes, *Wasps,* 430–431. The joke would be insipid without recognizing the eyeballs and the finger as the corresponding other side of the opponent's anatomy. Surprisingly, the placement of the phallus on the wasps costume has been a subject of debate, with some preferring it to dangle uselessly from behind. Ulrich von Wilamowitz-Moellendorff, "Über des Wespen des Aristophanes" (1911, reprinted in *Kleine Schriften* vol. 1, Berlin: Weidmann, 1971), 302.

114. Aristophanes, *Wasps,* 1503. The *emmeleia* is a technical term for the stately dance of tragedy.

115. British Museum, London.

116. Aristophanes, *Wasps,* 291–30). Carl A.P. Ruck, "Euripides' Mother: Vegetables and the Phallos in Aristophanes": 13–57, in *Arion,* new series vol. 2, no. 1 (1975).

117. Virgil, *Georgics,* 1.390.

118. These observations are quoted from a letter to Professor Pease from R. Gordon Wasson and his wife Valentina Pavlovna, dated June 28, 1953, Wasson Archives, Harvard Botanical Museum.

119. C. Scott Littleton, *Gods, Goddesses and Mythology* (Tarrytown, NY: Marshall Cavendish, 2005), 598.

120. Antony Andrewes, *Greek Society* (New York: Penguin, 1981, originally published 1967 as *The Greeks*), 247–248.

121. Ruck, "Euripides' Mother."

122. Aristophanes, *Acharnians,* 1164–1170.

123. Ruck, *Sacred Mushrooms of the Goddess,* 73–84.

124. Virgil, *Georgics,* 2.319–320, places the planting of the sprouting vine with the return of the migratory crane to Europe, which announces the beginning of spring in March.

Chapter 10

Virgil's Edible Tables

Carl A. P. Ruck and Robert Larner

Carl A. P. Ruck is Professor of Classics at Boston University, an authority on the ecstatic rituals of the god Dionysus. With the ethnomycologist R. Gordon Wasson and Albert Hofmann, he identified the secret psychoactive ingredient in the visionary potion that was drunk by the initiates at the Eleusinian Mystery. In *Persephone's Quest: Entheogens and the Origins of Religion,* he proclaimed the centrality of psychoactive sacraments at the very beginnings of religion, employing the neologism "entheogen" to free the topic from the pejorative connotations for words like "drug" or "hallucinogen." Robert Larner earned a BA at the University of Washington in English in 2003, and an MA in English Literature from Western Washington University in 2005.

Introduction: Food Too Awful to Eat

When Aeneas and his men finally land on the Italian shore, the fortuitous fulfillment of a dire prophecy that had seemed almost a curse signals that they have arrived at the promised new homeland. The Harpy Celaeno (the "dark one") delivers what Phoebus Apollo, on the authority of the omnipotent father Jupiter, had predicted to her:

> *ibitis Italiam portusque intrare licebit.*
> *sed non ante datam cingetis moenibus urbem*
> *quam dira fames nostraeque iniuria caedis*
> *ambesas subigat malis absumere mensas.*[1]

> "You will go to Italy and be allowed to enter the harbors, but you will not build the city granted you before terrible hunger and the injury you have inflicted upon us by our slaughter forces you to consume tables gnawed with your jaws."

Strangely, when the prophecy is fulfilled at the beginning of Book VII, Aeneas recalls not Celaeno, but his father, Anchises. It is something he had almost forgotten until his son Iulus remarked, "Hey, we've even eaten the tables" (*heus, etiam mensas consumimus*, 7.116):

> *hic domus, haec patria est. genitor mihi talia namque*
> *(nunc repeto) Anchises fatorum arcana reliquit:*
> *"cum te, nate, fames ignota ad litora vectum*
> *accisis coget dapibus consumere mensas,*
> *tum sperare domos defessus, ibique memento*
> *prima locare manu molirique aggere tecta."*
> *haec erat illa fames, haec nos suprema manebat*
> *exitiis positura modum.*[2]

> "This is our home, this, our country. Now I remember it, for my father Anchises left me just such hidden knowledge of the fates. "When, my son, borne to unknown shores with nothing to eat, hunger forces you to consume your tables, then, exhausted,

> hope for home, there be thee mindful to place your first roofs and build a rampart." This was that hunger, this was the last thing remaining to put an end to our wanderings."

At the time of the Harpy's curse, however, Anchises certainly had no clue as to its meaning. Instead, he had prayed to the gods to keep it from ever happening:

> *"di, prohibete minas; di, talem avertite casum*
> *et placidi servate pios."*[3]

> "Gods, fend off those threats! Gods, avert such an event and peaceful save the pious!"

Since Anchises died abruptly at the end of Book III, in order conveniently to be in the underworld when Aeneas visits there, he had no time to convey the meaning of this prophecy to his son.

> *hic pelagi tot tempestibus actus,*
> *heu, genitorem, omnis curae casusque levamen,*
> *amitto Anchisen. hic me, pater optime, fessum*
> *deseris, heu, tantis nequiquam erepte periclis!*[4]

> "Here, after I've been driven by so many tempests of the sea, I loose, alas, my father Anchises, the comfort of my every care and mischance. Here, O best of fathers, you desert me, alas, snatched in vain from so many dangers."

Aeneas even reproaches Celaeno for not having foretold him of the loss. When Aeneas sees Anchises in the underworld in Book VI, the father reveals the whole destiny of the Roman nation, but makes no mention of the edible tables.

Ironically, the Harpy's prophecy that the event would signal that Aeneas has finally reached his homeland had come in retaliation for his having driven the "innocent Harpies" (*harpyias insontis,* 3. 249) from their own new homeland and kingdom (*patrio … regno*), since they have been chased away from their indigenous Thrace. They, too, are starving, "faces always sallow from hunger" (*pallida semper ora fame,* 3.217–218), but everything they approach is inevitably "defiled by their own foul stench and filthy touch" (*contactuque omnia foedant immundo… taetrum … inter odorem,* 3. 227–228), laden with excrement, the "foulest discharge of their stomachs" (*foedissima ventris proluvies,* 3.217–218). Aeneas's men have slaughtered ownerless (*nullo custode,* 3.221) free-roaming cattle and goats. This is the customary food for the Harpies,[5] but they render the meat disgusting to the men. Like the loathsome tables (*mensas,* 3.231) laden with the meat of the slaughtered herd, defiled by the touch and stench of the Harpies, the tables that would signal the site for the founding of Aeneas's first Italian settlement are something that one would eat only as a last resort, driven by an obscene hunger (*obscenamque famem,* 3.367), a hungering for "filth."

The loathsome cattle are Virgil's calque of Odysseus's Cattle of the Sun episode.[6] Odysseus's men ate the meat, despite the fact that the gods sent an ominous warning: The hides of the slaughtered beasts began to creep along the ground and the meat, both the raw and that roasting on the spits, began to bellow with the lowing of cattle.[7] So great was the hunger of Odysseus's starving men that they continued to consume the writhing flesh. It was Virgil's invention to link the Harpy tables with the disgusting still-living meat of the slaughtered mooing beasts. These two repulsive foods are both metaphoric for the same tabooed and awful sacrament. Despite several attempts, Aeneas does not manage to eat the defiled banquet. For Odysseus's crew, it was the reason that they all would perish.

Obs Fatalis Crusti, a Disk of Deadly Crust

When the prophecy is fulfilled in Book VII, the eating of the tables, in fact, is described as a "violation by touch" with "audacious jaws" of "disks of deadly crusts."

> *violare manu malisque audacibus orbem*
> *fatalis crusti*[8]
> *"to violate by touch and audacious jaws the disk of fatal crust."*

The adjective *fatalis* means "fateful," but it also has the implication of fatal doom.

What they are eating obviously must resemble a round table (*orbis,* "circle, ring, hoop"), rather than the rectangular tables customarily used in dining rooms, bordered on three sides by the "reclining couches" or *triclinia* on which the diners reclined, leaving the fourth side free for the access of the servers. Round tables could be supported on three legs, usually ornamented as fantastic beasts, giving the table a zoomorphic identity. Such a table was called a *cilliba.* The three-legged table is ideally suited for steadiness on an uneven floor. In Greek dining at a symposium, the *triclinium* ("triple recliner") would accommodate three symposiasts each, and the tables, called *trapezai* ("three-feet"), were round and used to serve the morsels to accompany the drinking.

Virgil, however, specifically calls the table an *orbis* or "disk." This is the word used for the *monopodium* ("one leg"), a pedestal table,[9] a table of Asiatic design introduced into Rome in the second-century BCE by the consul Gnaeus Manlius Vulso.[10] In the nineteenth-century neoclassic revival, the term *monopodium* was used to designate the legs carved to resemble fantastic beasts. Although in the encounter with the Harpies Aeneas has reclining mattresses (*toros,* 3.224) as well as proper tables (*mensae*) for the banquet, he lost most of his ships in the storm at the beginning of Book I, but presumably his surviving ships were reequipped when they set sail from Dido and Carthage, or in any case there is no reason they would have lost their former dining paraphernalia. The banquet that signals the end of their wandering, however, makes no use of ordinary dining furniture and is a kind of picnic, with the men seated on the ground. Such dining arrangements are depicted in Egyptian frescoes, with the diners seated cross-legged around a low pedestal table.

Requirements of History

Virgil died before completing the *Aeneid.* According to his biographer, he expected that the poem would require three more years of work and he left instructions for it to be destroyed.[11] In composing the epic, Virgil worked from a prose narrative version, which he then versified, a few lines per day, not in sequential order. As published, although complete, the poem has several unfinished half-lines, indicating areas still under revision. His literary executors were allowed no editorial additions, although Book II was switched with Book I, and the first four verses identifying the author and his previous works were deleted.[12] Both the Harpy episode and the fulfillment of the prophecy are incomplete (half-lines at 3.218 and 7.129). Although some scholars have argued that the half-lines are an intentional innovation in Virgil's metrical scheme,[13] there are only about sixty of them in the entire poem of 17,896 verses, or 0.003 percent. It is highly unlikely that in the projected three additional years of revision the completion of these unfinished half-lines was not on the author's agenda. The edible tables were an essential item in the historical traditions he was obliged to include in his epic and he appears to have been struggling with the motif.[14] Thus he left unresolved whether Celaeno or Anchises was the source of the "edible tables" prophecy.

The Trojan prophetess Cassandra's prediction about the renewal of the defeated Trojans in the founding of Rome was recorded in the enigmatic poem *Alexandra,* attributed to Lycophron, a third-century BCE Alexandrine Greek tragedian.[15]

> Someday, my descendants, lifting up the foremost crown by force of battle, will exalt again the fame of the race of my ancestors to the highest, grasping the scepter and monarchy of land and sea. Nor in the darkness of oblivion, my unhappy fatherland, shall you hide your withered glory.[16]

Despite the difficulty of its arcane traditions and obscure language, the poem was popular in antiquity. It identifies Aeneas, without naming him, by a series of the most abstruse references, and narrates that he "would chance upon a [single] table full of edibles, which was later eaten by his companions, and he then would "remember ancient prophecies" (1250–1252) and there found thirty cities in the land of the aboriginal inhabitants.[17]

This brief mention of the mythical event was apparently something recorded in some now-lost work preserved in the Alexandrine library, probably elaborating some ethnographic anthropological motif, which was a particular interest of the scholar-writers who presided over the library and its vast collection of texts. The table, by this tradition, was something already there that Aeneas apparently came upon. He "chanced" upon it and then "remembered" something.

The story had become common knowledge by Virgil's time. Various attempts were made to rationalize it, especially in view of Rome's emerging political and cultural dominance. The Greek historian and geographer Strabo (64 BCE–c. 24 CE) claimed that for lack of a better table, a large loaf of bread was put down and eaten up along with the meats upon it.[18] The Athenian mythologist Konon (36 BCE–17 CE) made them tables at a sacrifice and called it a ritual.[19] Dionysius of Halicarnassus (c. 60 BCE–after 7 CE) claimed that the men strewed either parsley (celery, *apium*) or wheaten cakes under the food to keep it off the ground and then after the food was consumed, they inadvertently went on to eat the underlay, before realizing that they had fulfilled the prophecy by eating their tables.[20] Dionysius was resident in Rome and similarly patronized by Augustus, making it likely that Virgil discussed the matter with him.

Harpy Tables

It was Virgil's innovation, however, to link the prophesied "edible tables" with the customary food of the Harpies, the obscene tables laden with their excrement, and the repulsive bits of mooing flesh from the prohibited wild untended herd of Helios. He also linked the starving Harpies with the dire Odyssean hunger that would at last afflict Aeneas and his men, both groups foreigners in a new land.

As Virgil describes the fulfillment of the prophecy, the men dispose their bodies on the ground at the roots of a single tall tree, they set up the banquet and put down flat-cakes made of spelt flour throughout the grass for the feast, in accordance with Jupiter's monition (*sic Iuppiter ipse monebat,* 7.110), and then heaped wild fruits on top of the cereal base:

corpora sub ramis deponunt arboris altae,
instituuntque dapes et adorea liba per herbam
subiciunt epulis (sic Iuppiter ipse monebat)
et Cereale solum pomis agrestibus augent.[21]

"They disposed their bodies beneath the roots of a high tree,
and instituted the feast and tossed down spelt flatbreads upon
the grass for plates—That was exactly Jupiter's monition—and
they heaped the wheaten base with rural fruits."

A cross, moreover, is incised to mark these flatbreads or fatal crusts (*patulis ... quadris,* 7.115). This detail is obviously intended to be significant, given the paucity of descriptive items: "quartered platters." Such quadrant markings were meant to imitate the crossing of the solar elliptic and the celestial equator, symbolically linking the bread astrologically to the cosmos as something similarly "heaved up" as a "heaven."[22] The sacramental bread of the Mithraic initiation had such a marker with this significance. The Mystery initiation of Mithraism had been introduced into Rome just recently in 69 BCE when Pompey took the Cilician pirates captive to the city,[23] and by the time of Nero, a hundred years later, there were already well-established Mithraic lodges in Rome. Earlier versions of the initiation lodges were already established in Anatolia, traceable back to well before the sixth-century, when the worship of Mithras comprised the warrior cult of the Persian Achaemenid dynasty and the elite royal guard. These spelt cakes are leavened rounds of flatbread, which is another essential detail of their metaphoric identity as heavenly bread.

The comment that Jupiter had given precise directions, however, is the first time that the event has been anything more than an inadvertent fulfillment of the prophecy. Aeneas is following precise directions, monitions from Jupiter, without knowing what they mean. Otherwise, he would have unloaded the tables and the mattresses from the ship for a proper feasting.

Heroic Destiny

Aeneas, as a hero, has a serious character flaw with which Virgil certainly had to contend. He is a hero that no reader can love since he has a predetermined program to fulfill as an agent of destiny in founding the Roman nation and authenticating the divine legitimacy of his patron Caesar Augustus. Even his love affair with Dido ends simply because he is told he must move on to complete his duty: *Italiam non sponte sequor,* "I go on to Italy not by my own freewill" (4.361). Here the "monition of Jupiter" signals that the ever "pious" hero is enacting a precise formula for this prophetic picnic, which even he does not understand until his son Iulus (Julius) "jokingly" (*nec plura adludens,* 7.117) remarks that they have consumed their tables.

"Now I remember (*nunc repeto,* 7.123)," Aeneas says. It makes little sense to designate the feasting procedure as divinely dictated and then realize that the feast fits the parameters of the curse, unless the "monition" is separate from the curse that it fulfills. Aeneas clearly does not know what the point of the prescribed banquet procedure is until Iulus makes the joke.

Thus the precise recipe dictated by Jupiter deserves careful attention. It prescribes *adorea liba* ("spelt-cakes") strewn around the trunk of a tall tree as metaphoric tables. Since the ultimate source of the Harpy's prediction came to her from Apollo and he is conveying knowledge that Jupiter (Zeus) originally declared at his shrine of Dodona in northwestern Greece,[24] the tall tree is inevitably an oak, with its associations with Druidism.

Fodder Food in Days of Yore

Servius, the late fourth-century commentator on Virgil, attempted to offer help with certain details of the episode. Both the type of flat cake (*libum*) and its flour from spelt required notice. The *libum* cake should be composed of flour, honey, and oil, and is flat (*placenta*), often used as sacrificial offerings. "Spelt" is an ancient type of wheat

(*Triticum spelta*), so named because it fruits with spikelets containing only two "split" red grains. Ordinarily, it is called *far* in Latin. *Ador* is a rare enough archaic word to require definition as a "type of spelt" (*genus farris*). It is named simply as something edible, derived from *edere*, "to eat."[25] It is, however, etymologically more like "fodder" than "food."

The earliest extant occurrence of the word as a noun is contemporary with Virgil in Horace's *Satires* (2.6.89), where the country mouse, who offers dainty morsels of other foods to his city visitor, is content himself to dine on *ador* and ergot-infested darnel: *(cum) esset ador loliumque, dapis meliora reliquens* ("while he ate *ador* and darnel, leaving the better parts of the feast for his guest"). Pliny records that *ador* is what the ancients used to call *far*.[26] Cato the younger (second-century BCE), the earliest occurrence of the adjective, advised that one plant it in poor soils and damp fields,[27] where inevitably, like the darnel, it, too would be a host for the toxic ergots. *Far* itself is cognate with *bar*-ley.

Ador, like darnel (*lolium*), was seen as the primitive weedy antecedent of the hybridized cultivated grains:

> *pulcher fugatis*
> *ille dies Latio tenebris,*
> *qui primus alma risit adorea*[28]
>
> "that beautiful day, when the shadows fled, which first smiled on Latium with bountiful spelt."

Horace is speaking of the removal of the threat of war, and here the archaic spelt (*ador*) connotes a return to the utopian days of yore. Horace's country mouse may dine on old-time foods, but as any city dweller would know, the mouse is delusional. *Ardor*'s association with darnel (*Lolium temulentum,* "drunken *lolium*") involves it in the traditions of altered eyesight from the psychoactive ergot toxins, which manifest on darnel as red enlarged kernels of *Claviceps purpurea* on its host weed grass, similar to the two red kernels of a corn of spelt.

Darnel was "cheap flour" (*vile triticum*) and "feeding on it" (*lolio victitare*) made you see things that weren't there.[29] Ovid described it as "making the eyesight faulty, vitiating the eyes" (*lolium oculos vitians*).[30] Bread made from it caused vertigo.[31] Its biblical Greek name as *zizania* is derived from the Arabic *ZDN* for "nausea."[32] Greek bath-keepers tossed the ergots ("seeds," *semina*) on the fire as an intoxicating fumigation.[33] Cattle and other herded animals, like the Cattle of the Sun, that grazed upon it would become ecstatic. These effects are due entirely to the ergot toxins since darnel in itself is devoid of toxicity.[34] The ergots were thought to be seed kernels, exceptionally enlarged by the heat of the sun. They resemble the cock's spur (cockle), like the talons of the Harpies (*uncaeque manus*, "barbed hands," 3.217).

The ergot is actually a fungal growth, the mycelium completely permeating the host seed kernel, and it is clearly recognizable as a fungus when the mycelium under suitable conditions fruits into a cluster of tiny red mushrooms visible to the naked eye. The ergots, moreover, are a deadly poison, tabooed. Without the requisite pharmaceutical science for accessing their potential, the visions and the ecstasy were the prelude to death. Darnel was a wild weed that like a disease could attack the cereal grains, and, as it was thought, might reverse their hybridization back to the primordial spelt or the primitive grasses. The spread of the fungal infection from the darnel to the cultivated grains was a clear demonstration of its recidivist threat. Mushrooms are largely uncultivable and represent the wild antithesis to the cultivated foods. The Romans, like other ancient cultures, were well aware of the toxicity of the ergots and removed them from the grain spikes by hand. They also propitiated the chthonic deities by the annual festival of the Robigalia (named for the "redness" of the "rust," a common designation of the ergots) by an animal sacrifice of a red dog, an animal that it was taboo to eat, as an offering to the netherworld Hecate, goddess of witchcraft and herbalists.

It should be noted that the flat cakes (*liba*) of *ador* would be red circular disks (*orbes*), here in the picnic as prescribed by Jupiter, heaped with something defined as wild fruits (*poma agrestia*), specifically the "fruits" of trees, substituted for the noisome offal of the Harpies and the repulsive writhing still-living bits of flesh from the Cattle of the Sun. These flatbreads, as prescribed by Jupiter, symbolically represent the food of bygone times, the recidivist toxic fodder of primitivism. They resemble small pedestal tables.

Innocuous Mimesis

This is the folkloric motif of the aversion of a dire curse by the substitution of an innocuous surrogate. Aeneas unwittingly has followed the exact directions from Jupiter that will mitigate the curse by fulfilling it, which when recognized by Iulus has turned it into a joke. This fulfills the prayer of Anchises immediately after Celaeno had delivered the curse, that the gods avert or turn aside (*talem avertite casum*, 3.265) such a happening. Prophecies, if from an authentic source, which this certainly is, from Jupiter himself, must prove true. Otherwise, the non-fulfillment invalidates the divine dimension. The classic example is Sophocles's *Oedipus Rex*, where the hero accepts his role as the ally of the god by disclosing himself as the foreordained murderer of his father, and thereby restoring faith in the Delphic oracle. The only way to piously thwart a valid prophecy or authentic curse is to fulfill it in some other way. The curse of Celaeno was that they would be forced to eat the equivalent of the repulsive tables laden with writhing flesh defiled by the Harpies, that is to say, to eat "Harpy tables." Thus the type of flat cake specified by Jupiter's monition is a *libum*, which was the equivalent of a birthday cake,[35] here celebrating the inauguration of the first Trojan-Roman settlement, and one with theological associations primarily with Bacchus, the god of rural intoxication:

> *et te, Bacche, vocant per carmina laeta, tibique*
> *oscilla ex alta suspendunt mollia pinu.*
> *hince omnis largo pubescit vinea fetu,*
> *complentur vallesque cavae saltusque profundi*

et quocumque deus circum caput egit honestum.
ergo rite suum Baccho dicemus honorem
carminibus patriis lancesque et liba feremus,
et ductus cornu stabit sacer hircus ad aram,
pinguiaque in veribus torrebimus exta colurnis.[36]

"And thee, Bacchus, they summon through happy songs, for thee they hang pliant little masks from a tall pine. Hence every vineyard grows to maturity with large produce, and the hollow valleys and profound forests are filled to completion, and wherever also the god bore his honored head. Therefore, accordingly to custom we will sing proper respect to Bacchus with ancestral songs and bear platters and *liba*-cakes. And the goat, led by his horn, will stand sacred at the altar, and we will roast its rich entrails on skewers of hazel wood."

Although there isn't much for Aeneas's men to eat as set out for the picnic (*penuria edendi,* "penury of eating," 7.117), they are not starving (*dira fames,* 3.255; *haec erat illa fames,* 7.128). After all, they apparently have a full store of adorean flatbreads on the ships. Nor is there any reason they didn't unload the *mensae* and couches. The surrounding country, moreover, was the source for the wild fruits heaped on the flatbreads and there is no reason they couldn't have gathered more. They nibble away (*vertere morsus,* 7.112) at the scant bit of bread (*exiguam in Cererem,* 7.113) almost absentmindedly, before they realize what they have done. This may be a rite or ritual, but it is not a violated sacrifice. There is no altar. There were no prayers. Although the breads could have been a consecrated offering, it wasn't divine practice to load them with fruits, with only the fruits intended for consumption and the bread alone designated for the god. If the cakes were to be offered to the gods, they would have to be burned; otherwise, they were intended to be eaten by the worshipper or left for consumption by the poor or distributed to the priests' assistants or the slaves. Such was the custom.[37] Only tabooed foods like dogs would be left to rot entire as an offering to the netherworld. In general, the sacrificial meal was one shared with the gods, as in the *Georgic* feast quoted *in extenso* above, and the divine portion would have to be burned to become accessible to the deity. The portion of the gods was ordinarily the parts not considered suitable for human consumption, like the bones and hide. Only in the direst occasion of a holocaust offering meant to appease the divine wrath by a penitential act would the entire offering be committed to the flames. The ancients could not afford to throw food away. The "violation" (*violare manu,* 7.114) and "audacious chewing" (*malisque audacibus,* 7.114) fulfill the prophecy that the Trojan refugees would be forced to eat something repulsive. *Audax* has a positive meaning as well, "bold and daring," and "violation with the hand" implies that they dared touch it.

Aeneas encounters the half-bird Harpies on the Strophades, two small islands southeast of Zakynthos in the Ionian Sea. After the Strophades episode, he landed at Buthrotum (modern Butrint, Albania) northward on the opposite mainland shore of Epirus.[38] Aeneas would have traveled two days march inland from Buthrotum to Dodona,[39] where he received the "monition" of Jupiter for the picnic procedure, although he obviously does not connect it with the curse of the Harpy. Virgil, however, omits the visit to Dodona and leaves unresolved how Aeneas received the "monition." He probably would have included the visit to Dodona in further revision. Another tradition claimed that he had received the monition even earlier from the Erythraean sibyl, well before he ever departed from Anatolia.[40] The "monition" (*Aeneid,* 7.110) and the prophecy (*Aeneid,* 7.123) are not the same; otherwise Aeneas could not have forgotten it in the space of thirteen verses.

Isles of No Return

The Srophades are named as the "Turning Point," since it was here that either their sister Iris, the rainbow messenger of the gods, or Hermes turned back the pursuit of the two sons of Boreas, Zetes and Calais, who journeyed with the Argonauts and chased the Harpies away from their torment of Phineus in Thrace. Like the Harpies, they too are winged and thus capable of flying after them in the wild pursuit. The islands had formerly been called the "Floating Isles," *Plotai*,[41] which means that, like Delos, they had floated here from the otherworld[42]; or more descriptive of their barren landscape, they could be called the "Sea-Urchins," *Echinades*.[43] Today the desolate islands are, appropriately, a refuge for birds. They belong to the Orthodox Church and are uninhabited except for a single monk.

The pursuit had ranged over most of the mythological topography of the otherworld, including the Hyperboreans and the African Ethiopians[44]:

> [The Boreades chased the Harpies] to the lands of the [Persian] Massagetae and of the proud Half-Dog men, of the Underground-folk and of the feeble Pygmies, and to the tribes of the boundless Black-skins and the Libyans.[45]

The Strophades were the specific entrance of the Harpies to the underworld, and Aeneas encounters them again in the vestibule to the jaws of Orcus, along with a motley catalogue of monsters that includes the Gorgons.[46] There, they continue their torment of Phineus by the defilement of his food.[47] Like the Gorgons, the Harpies were once beautiful,[48] often interchangeable with other ornithological human hybrids, like the Sirens and the nightingale,[49] but the general misogynist bias of Classical myth and the dread of the deposed goddess rendered them increasingly demonized and monstrous.[50] They are a version of the Minoan bird-goddess. Thus another of their topographical lairs is the Dictaean Cave on Crete.[51]

They are named as "Snatchers" ("Raptors"). More specifically, they are spirit-abductors, personified as a whirlwind,[52] and like the fairies of Celtic tradition, they were accused of stealing people away to their netherworld realm in a blast of fairy wind (elfin eddy).[53] A person was apt suddenly to disappear from sight in this world, in a fit of rapture possessed in the clutches of these ravishing "flying virgins."[54] In Greek lore, all winds blow from chthonic caverns and return with the person they have possessed. The classic example is the rapture of Oreithyia by the north-wind Boreas while she was consorting with her herbalist sisterhood of the "Pharmacists" or "drug-girls."[55]

The way that the Harpies settled upon the table of Phineus, laden with the abundant buffet of morsels of food brought him by his compassionate neighbors,[56] suggests their obvious metaphoric materialization as a swarm of monstrous flies.[57] In addition to the defilement by their stench and excrement, they were toxic in their own right. Their feathers figure among various fabulous ingredients in a spell compounded by the witch Medea,[58] including the blood of Herakles, poisoned by the psychoactive botanical essence of the monsters he defeated.[59] Their ravenous appetite, moreover, is a necessary consequence of their defilement of the tables of dainty morsels, since they, no less than Phineus, have nothing but Harpy tables to eat. Like their victim, they, too, are involved in the traditions of clairvoyance since the prophetic horses of Achilles were the daughters of a Harpy,[60] and Virgil knew the tradition that mares could become pregnant by the wind.[61] This was how the equine Medusa conceived her horse child Pegasus by Poseidon.

Like the other monsters and the Gorgons, the Harpies are zoomorphic anthropomorphisms of a psychoactive agent or botanical shamanic sacrament. The Gorgons are specifically linked in the Perseus myth of the founding of Mycenae and in the Golden Apples of the Hesperides to their manifestation as mushrooms.[62] The particular nature of the torment of Phineus represents a perversion of the taboo upon the agency for his prophetic clairvoyance. His sin was that he was too good a clairvoyant, and thus he has been blinded to the sight of this reality and the entheogen that inspired his prophetic visions is now denied him as taboo, the edible turned inedible. It is appropriate for a sacred plant to be taboo and supposedly repulsive, shielding it from profane use. Since he continues to live, however, the only sustenance he is afforded is the now-abominable diet of Harpy tables in the netherworld.

Monitor of the Gateway

Phineus (Phineas) has no Greek etymology. It may be cognate with Hebrew Phinehas, which is Egyptian (*Pe-nehasi*) designating a bronze-skinned Ethiopian,[63] although a Hebrew speaker may have understood it as meaning an "oracular mouth of brass."[64] Phineus was originally from Phoenicia, a brother of Cadmus (Kadmos), both of them sons of Agenor, whose father was Belus (Baal) of Egypt, hence an African; another brother settled in Ethiopia, which in Greek means the land of the "burnt-faces."

There was a dwarfish version of Cadmus (Kadmilos), who was depicted as a black-skinned pygmy and was involved in the Mystery religion of the Kabeiroi, perhaps as the *pais* or "boy" associated with the god Dionysus in the religion's iconography. The name appears to be Phoenician, meaning "great gods." The most famous initiation sanctuaries were in Boeotian Thebes, which Cadmus founded, and on the islands of Samothrace and Lemnos, off the coast of Thrace.[65] The Pelasgian (pre-Indo-European) inhabitants of Lemnos were called *Tyrsenoi,* which was interpreted as "Etruscans."[66]

The Wee Folk

Three things are certain about the religion: drunken intoxication, dwarfish Ethiopians, and phallic symbolism. Aeschylus staged a satyr play entitled the *Kabeiroi,*[67] in which they were portrayed as addicted to drinking and they make Jason and his men drunk. The main archaeological remains from the Mystery sanctuaries are the characteristic two-handled drinking mugs, depicting the grotesque ithyphallic little pygmies, often as comic caricatures of Greek heroes. It was customary to smash these vessels in the course of the ceremonies, indicating the sacramental nature of their content. Wine was always a medium for psychoactive additives, and the two-handled design of the Kabeiroi mugs indicates that the drink was a powerful potion, not like the symposium's customary cylix, which was a challenge to manage decorously when deeply intoxicated.

There was a version of the Kabeiroi as the great creator god Ptah (Hephaestus) in a temple in Egyptian Memphis, where the mad Persian King Cambyses mocked them since they were portrayed as ithyphallic dwarfs, little Ptahs or *pataiki,* interchangeable with the dwarf Bes, as protectors of the household.[68] Volcanic Lemnos was the site of the forge of Hephaestus, and the Kabeiroi also were seen as his attendants, like the "one-eyed" Cyclops brotherhood.[69] The religion varied at different sanctuaries, sometimes being mainly a male initiation, and was assimilative, involving Demeter and Persephone, often with secret different names. The number of the Kabeiroi deities varied, but they could be confused with the twin Dioskouroi sons of Zeus, Castor and Pollux. The Dioskouroi were both born from a single red egg; the two half shells were still preserved a thousand years later, and each twin was characterized by the shell cap he wore as a hat, a depiction that suggests their fungal anthropomorphosis.[70] The involvement of Hephaestus (Vulcan) and the volcanic forge testifies to the great antiquity of metallurgy as metaphoric of alchemic spiritual transmutation. The origin of the cult was Trojan and definitely a version of the Anatolian mother goddess Cybele (and her analogues) and her little male attendants, interchangeable with the Cretan Rhea, and the birth of the divine child, as either Zeus or Dionysus, who in Thracian tradition was the Mystery god Sabazios, whose cult persisted late into the Roman period under a variety of names, which included the Jewish Yahweh.

Penates

The Romans identified the Cabiri (Kabeiroi) with the household *Penates*, which Aeneas took with him from Troy.[71] They were ostensibly named as the guardians of the household's food "storehouse" or pantry (*penus*). The food store is the center of the family's well-being, and hence the *Penates* preside over the "penetration" into the building's "interior" (*penetralia*),[72] which was the "hearth" or *lar,* hence their coupling with the other household deity, the *Lar,* sometimes made plural as the *Lares,* associated with the goddess of the hearth, Vesta. This penetration into the inner sanctum of Vesta obviously once had sexual innuendoes,[73] and a more mystical version of their etymology derived them from the "inner core" (*penitus*), the innermost secret of being.[74] The Romans obviously were not quite sure what the *Penates* were, except that they were very ancient and Trojan and probably Etruscan.

Although the function of the penis is penetration, it is not, however, derived from a related root, but is Greek (*péos*), metaphorically a "tail." Phallus is an erect penis and is derived from the Indo-European root **bhel-*, meaning to "inflate or swell up," hence cognate with "bull," "blow," and "balloon" in English, but also with *bólinthos,* Thracian for "wild bull." The bellowing of the bull, however, is involved in the folklore of the mushroom, which was thought to fruit amid the thunderous sound, as it suddenly emerged from the ground,[75] swelling into its phallic shape like a sponge (*spongos,* fungus), absorbing the moisture of the rainfall and materializing as a dwarfish one-footed android.[76] The sponge-fungus is analogous to leavened bread, a fungal growth. "Bread" is a metaphor for the mushroom, in particular the "raven's bread," which is a name for the *Amanita muscaria,* derived from the bird's fondness for eating the mushroom.[77] It bears mentioning that the sound emitted by the Gorgon sisterhood, apart from the hissing of their serpent hair, was the mooing of cows.[78]

The *Penates* were honored at each family dinner by burning a small portion of the food as an offering to them before the meal could commence. This was not the ordinary sacrifice as a sharing with the deities, but more in the way of removing a taboo. Total silence was observed until the slave announced *dei propitii,* "The gods are propitious,"[79] which is to say, "It is safe to eat, the curse on the food has been lifted." The divinities of Lavinium, which is the colony that Aeneas founds on the banks of the Tiber at the site of the edible tables, were these *Penates,*[80] and they were supposedly Samothracian,[81] which probably means Cabiric. In addition to each household's private *Penates,* the original Trojan (Samothracian) antique figurines were supposedly preserved in a temple in Rome, but although they were national relics, they probably were forgeries. When a magistrate left office, he would travel to Lavinium to sacrifice to the *Penates* and Vesta, as testimony of the tradition of their first arrival to the Italian shore with Aeneas.

Although by the Roman period the *Penates* were anthropomorphized as male youths, often a pair of them, holding a cornucopia of abundance and a libation *patera,* or as a soldier with lance, the most ancient version was probably a Cabiric dwarf in an exaggerated state of sexual arousal, basically an anthropomorphic phallus. Significantly, the *Penates* were always statuettes or figurines, little people. Among the enigmas posed by Cassandra's prophecy in Lycophron's *Alexandra* about the arrival of the Trojan Aeneas in Italy is the tradition that he met his former enemy Odysseus as a dwarf (*nấnos*) at the site of the edible tables.[82] The dwarf Odysseus is depicted on a Boeotian Kabeiroi drinking vessel as black-skinned and ithyphallic, impelled on a raft formed by two amphorae, blown by a blast of wind from the head of Boreas. The opposite side of the cup depicts the dwarf Odysseus recoiling from the cup of drugged potion offered him by an African dwarfish version of Circe.[83] This Odysseus *nấnos* could also be identified as the Pelasgian King Nánas, the founder of the Etruscans in Italy.[84] He would also be interchangeable with the female dwarf Nána, who was the botanical virgin mother of Attis, the castrated lover of the Anatolian goddess Cybele.[85] This mother goddess cult is the origin of all the anthropomorphized phallic dwarfs involved in the ecstatic Pelasgian/Etruscan Mysteries. These include the Cretan dactyls and the warrior corybantic ecstatic dancers.

The Kabeiroi may have joined the two sons of Boreas in their pursuit of the Harpies.[86] Inasmuch as they appear to have personified the spirit of Phineus's tabooed sacrament, it is appropriate that they were instrumental in freeing him from the curse.

Phineus was king of Salmydessos (modern Kirklareli, Turkey), a Thracian town on the north shore of the Black Sea. His realm controlled both sides of the narrow Bosporos passage, and Jason encountered him on the European side, since his expertise involves the dangerous journey through the Clashing Rocks (*Symplegades*), which has long been recognized as a shamanic metaphor for the trip to the other realm.[87]

Toadstools and Fairy Tables

Recently, a large number of natural rock formations in Thrace have been identified as sacred sites marked by "mushroom stones,"[88] probably linked to the mushroom cult of the Thracian manifestation of Dionysus as Sabazios.[89] Some of these natural formations show signs of human modification to make them more resemble mushrooms. Stone slabs are also found throughout Thrace carved with a mushroom image; these slabs are often concentrated in Christian cemeteries, where they were reused as grave markers. Additionally a large number of grave markers in the shape of mushrooms have been found throughout Greece, some of them as early as the archaic period. These mushroom tombstones are particularly common from Thrace. A remarkably explicit example is the tombstone of Lysandra, daughter of Alexander, from Daskylion on the southern shore of the Black Sea.[90] In the view of the authoritative scholars of Greek burial customs:[91]

> It would be easier to accept these as *phalloi* if any one of them bore the slightest resemblance to the organ with which Greek artists were well familiar. The asymmetry of the *glans,* and the duct and testicles are never shown, and the knob is often flat, hemispherical or spherical. The only group of objects which all these "*phalloi*" can be said to resemble is fungi.

The Lysandra tombstone has a niche carved into the mushroom's cap, where the deceased is shown enthroned, flanked on each side by a winged Psyche ("soul butterfly" fairy) and a coiled serpent. Psyche is named for the "soul breath" and is also the word for "butterfly," whose remarkable metamorphosis and emergence from the cocoon are emblematic of spiritual transcendence. She is traditionally depicted as the closest analogue to the Celtic fairy,[92] whose name is derived from the Latin *fata* or "fate." The fairy creatures on the mushroom tombstone are each offering her a hoop or fungal fairy ring. The stipe is also carved with a niche in which the god Hermes is seen as a herm pillar, with erect phallus, flanked by chthonic dogs.

The mushroom thus is itself the phallic marker of the axis to the other realm. The extraordinary splendor of the Lysandra tombstone probably indicates that Alexander's daughter was an initiate into a Mystery, perhaps a presiding priestess of the rite.

The Clashing Rocks were also known as the Cyanean Rocks (*Kyaneai*) for their color, *kuaneos*, commonly translated as something dark blue or purple, but more probably the dark hue of bronze.[93] This would match the color of the king-prophet Phineus, whose brazen oracular mouth presides over the dangerous shamanic rapture. The passageway has metaphoric connotations of the sacred food that negotiates the journey through the two opposing cliffs. Each day a dove flew through them, delivering ambrosia to Zeus on Olympus in the form of a golden apple from the tree in the Garden of the Hesperides.[94]

Virgil's edible tables, therefore, are round red pedestals, placed under a tall oak, heaped with morsels of food, associated with spiritual toxic raptors that materialize like a swarm of flies that render them ostensibly taboo, and involved in the tradition of ambrosia and the magical Golden Apples, the latter specifically identified as the head of the Gorgon Medusa and a zoomorphic metamorphosis of a mushroom. These tables could also be anthropomorphized as a penis dwarf. The Harpy tables seem to be an analogous classical version of the fairy tables of Celtic lore.[95]

> A little mushroom table spread,
> After short prayers, they set on bread
>
> (Robert Herrick, Oberon's feast in *Hesperides*, 1648)

> Upon a mushroom's head,
> Our table we do spread.
>
> (Anonymous, *Queen Mab's Invitation*, c. 1658)

The *Amanita muscaria* or fly agaric is the fairy mushroom. Its botanical nomenclature (*muscaria*) and its numerous common names reflect its attractiveness to flies. With the epithet of the toadstool, it demonstrates the taboo on its ingestion and the demonizing of its indwelling spiritual raptors. The scabby white remnants of its universal veil that shatters as the cap fully expands to the likeness of a tabletop immediately suggest the bits of forbidden food with which it is spread. In fairy lore, moreover, in addition to their mushroom tables spread with dainty morsels, they were said to leave round cakes or breads of barley or oatmeal about on the ground, but the food was cursed and should never be eaten except in times of the severest hunger.[96] Conversely, a piece of bread was the surest amulet to ward off a blast of the dangerous kidnapping fairy wind.

Etruscans and Caesar's Mushroom

There is no reason that Virgil would not know of the mushroom. He spent nearly a decade composing his *Georgics*, dedicated to his Etruscan patron Maecenas,on the subject of agriculture, and was himself devoted to his farm near Mantua.[97] The town today is the site for a mushroom festival in late September. In medieval lore, the poet was said to have delighted Augustus with a meal of truffles.[98] The Roman emperors were so fond of mushrooms that another of the Amanitas bears the name *caesarea* or "Caesar's mushroom." Claudius was assassinated by a meal that contained a poisonous variety of this same family of Amanitas.[99] The Roman cookbook of Apicius records six recipes for preparing or preserving mushrooms.

The most unambiguous depictions of the mushroom are extant in vases from southern Italy that have survived destruction since they were sequestered safely in Etruscan tombs. The placement in tombs indicates their sacral nature. One of these is the Perseus amphora already referenced above. The other is a large platter depicting the abduction or rapture of Persephone; raised knobs in the likeness of mushrooms ornament its rim.[100] In addition to burial in underground tombs, the Etruscans placed the cremated remains of the deceased in above-ground necropolises in stone urns with hemispherical covers resembling mushrooms. A large number of them are found in the Etruscan cemetery of Tarquinia, dating from the eighth-century.

Less elaborate versions consist of cylindrical pits containing a clay cinerary urn covered with an inverted one-handled bowl or helmet. The same design is expanded in the elaborate multi-chambered tombs, which are cylindrical and topped with a grassy mound. The Mausoleum of Augustus is essentially an Etruscan tomb.[101]

Robert Graves identified an object as a mushroom on an Etruscan mirror depicting the torment of Ixion, bound spread-eagled on a rotating carriage wheel.[102] Such mirrors, like the vases, survive since they also were frequently placed in tombs and depicted funereal themes symbolic of the interrelation of this world with the other. A whirling wheel denotes the rapturous transport of the shamanic journey. The configuration of the object and the myth of Ixion, however, better suit the identification of the "flower" as a psychoactive Datura.[103] A common motif on South-Italian Greek-Etruscan vases, moreover, is a head with a Phrygian cap emerging from lily blossoms that should probably be identified as the Datura.[104] The Phrygian cap is descriptive metaphorically of the *Amanita muscaria* mushroom and thus equates the two plants in the ritual pharmacopeia of shamanism.

The Etruscans originally occupied the central and southern coastal regions of the Italian peninsula, with close ties to the Corinthian Greek colonies on the island of Sicily. In Corinthian lore, Sisyphus created the first indigenous people of their tribe out of mushrooms.[105] The closeness of the Etruscan ties with Corinth is demonstrated by the story of Demaratus the Corinthian, a member of the royal family of the Bacchiadae, whose legendary ancestor had founded the city of Syracuse in 734 BCE. Accused of sedition, Demaratus fled from Sicily with his great wealth to the Etruscan city of Tarquinia (Corneto) in 655 BCE and is credited with introducing Greek cultural arts to the mainland. He married an Etruscan noblewoman and fathered Lucius Tarquinius Priscus, the fifth King of Rome. Supposedly, he introduced the art of writing to the Etruscans,[106] but this is a claim commonly made of founder heroes, like Cadmus at Thebes, and may mean only the use of the Phoenician-Greek writing symbols, which isn't documented in Greece before the eighth-century

BCE,[107] whereas Cadmus arrived well in the Minoan period several generations before the Trojan War. Herodotus dated Cadmus back to around 2000 BCE,[108] and the inscriptions he saw in ancient Cadmean writing with Greek letters in the Theban temple of Apollo[109] must have been a pious forgery since the Phoenician consonantal signs were not developed until around 1020 BCE.

In all probability, the arrival of Aeneas in Campania was an Etruscan foundation legend.[110] New DNA evidence links human and animal samples from Etruria and Anatolia.[111] The legendary Aeneas is obviously remembered as a Trojan, of the same generation as Hector and Paris. His father Anchises is a maternal cousin of King Priam. The mother of Aeneas, however, is Aphrodite, which in ritual terms involves him in the mythology of the great Anatolian mother goddess, making him an analogue of Sabazios and the Cretan-Minoan Zeus-Dionysus. The Aeneas legend, however, is probably mythologized history since it is unlikely that his mother was a goddess and the Etruscan domination of the region of the Italian peninsula corresponding roughly to modern Tuscany dates back to the ninth-century, 300 years after the supposed war fought at Troy. It is generally agreed that the Etruscans entered the Italian peninsula around 800 BCE. The assimilation of King Nanas with the dwarfish Odysseus is more an indication of the proselytizing of the Kabeiroi Mystery than of events contemporaneous with the postwar generation.

Trojans and Etruscans

The language of the Trojans was Luwian, a branch of the Indo-European language family, related to Hittite. The language of the Etruscans survives only in inscriptions and a single codex, the *Liber Linteus,* so-called because it was written on linen, apparently a ritual calendar, used as a mummy wrapping in Ptolemaic Egypt. The language was long considered an "isolate," unrelated to any known family group, going back to the time of Virgil himself,[112] but it now is recognized as belonging to the Tyrsenian family, related to a language spoken in the eastern Alps, the northeast Caucasus, and the northern Aegean, particularly the island of Lemnos, where Etruscan inscriptions have been discovered.[113] These languages became extinct because its speakers eventually adopted the prevailing languages of Greek, Latin, and, later in the Alps, Vulgar Latin. Etruscan, however, may actually be Indo-European, a language of Anatolia, a dialect of Luwian, with some borrowings from neighboring Phrygian peoples.

Latin belongs to the Italic-Celtic group of the Indo-European family. Various waves of migration from eastern and central Europe penetrated the Apennine peninsula from the north as early as the mid-second millennium BCE, although the region was inhabited by modern man already in the upper Paleolithic, around 34,000 years ago, and by Neanderthals in the late Pleistocene. They all left remains of their cultures, which include burial sites of the third-millennium Beaker People and rock drawings in the Alpine valley of Camonica in Lombardy, starting in the ninth millennium. These peoples predate the waves of Indo-European migration and some appear to have entered the peninsula through Apulia from the south. The rise to military and political dominance of the inhabitants of the plain of Latium supplanted Etruscan autonomy after the traditional founding of Rome in 733 BCE, although the site was inhabited as early as the Bronze Age. The early history of the city recounts a succession of seven kings as rulers; two of the last three were said to be at least partially Etruscan. The dominant Latin speakers, however, prevailed, and the last person known to be able to read Etruscan was the Emperor Claudius, whose first wife was Etruscan and who wrote a treatise on the Etruscan subject and compiled a lexicon of the language.

The legendary Aeneas is obviously a Trojan-Etruscan and a descendant of Dardanus, the ancestor of the Trojans who instituted the religion of the Kabeiroi on the island of Samothrace, but when the migrating Aeneas's first settlement on the island of Crete, the land of the Curetes (another version of the Kabeiroi brotherhood), is visited by plague, the Phrygian *Penates*[114] that he has carried from the burning Troy appeared before his eyes in a waking dream that was no dream:

nec sopor illud erat, sed coram agnoscere vultus
velatasque comas praesentiaque ora videbar.[115]

"That was no dream, but I seemed to recognize them face to face, their wreathed hair and living faces."

They tell him that the true origin of these *Penates* is in the west, in a land that the Greeks called Hesperia, now renamed Italy after their present king Italus, among a people called Oenotrians (Enotrians) for their cultivation of the wine (*w-oinos*, "wine"). When told of the vision, Anchises confirms the dual origin and twin parentage (*prolem ambiguam geminosque parentis*)[116] and admits that he had made a mistake, although it was something Cassandra had often told him. The Enotrians had disappeared through assimilation by the sixth-century BCE, but some writers speculated that they had arrived from Arcadia in Greece as early as the time of the Trojan War. By this accounting, Dardanus was an Etruscan already resident in Italy, and then brought the Kabeiroi Mystery in the other direction, eastward to Thracian Samothrace and the Phrygian mountain town of Dardania, near Troy.[117] Arcadia in the mountainous highlands of the central Peloponnesus has no access to the sea and did not develop colonizing cities; if such a migration occurred earlier even than the thirteenth century BCE Trojan War, it was probably cultic proselytizing, rather than a movement of people.

Although the traditional founding of Rome mythologizes the emergent dominance of the Latin-speaking populace, the city in its religion, design, and governance was largely Etruscan.[118] Caesar as a cognomen or inherited "nickname" was given various implausible folk etymologies (such as a caesarian "cut" birth or an ancestor who was a "hairy" infant) and despite wide speculation, it remains unknown. It may be something preserved from Etruscan, and is the origin of later names like Charles and Karl. As the third in the tri-nominal system of personal names, it should describe some physical feature of an ancestor. Although intermarriage of the Roman patricians and the noble Etruscans would have been expectable, Augustus's claim to the heritage of Aeneas depends solely on the name of the Julia family. He supposedly is related to the Iulus who was Aeneas's son. The family name Iulius (Julius) might be an adjectival form of the god Iovis(Jove), but in the mythologized claim to Trojan lineage it was interpreted as derived from Aeneas's son (Euryleon/Iulus), whose name was supposedly changed to Ascanius after he fled from Troy (Ilium).[119] Both the derivations from Jove and from the Ilus of Ilium are the "usual playful etymologies of no consequence."[120] It was natural for the name of Caius Julius Caesar to elicit attempts to explain his divine status as back-formations after the fact of his deification. Euryleon is not attested as the name of Ascanius before the Augustine period.[121] Ilus (*Ílos*), not Iulus, was known both as a son of Dardanus and as a son of Dardanian Tros, the latter being the origin of both Ilium and Troy. In any case, as an Indo-European Latin-speaker, Augustus could claim the Homeric connection only though his Julio-Claudian family's possible Etruscan relatives.

Etruscan Wizardry

The Etruscans had a reputation for expertise in medicine and the occult arts of divination, magic, and religion. Medicine, moreover, is a catchall category that does not distinguish healing arts from the proficiency in herbal agents for accessing ecstatic experience. Maecenas was from a noble Etruscan family, a "descendant of kings,"[122] which probably means he was particularly knowledgeable of this heritage. The Etruscans believed that a tiny male creature named Tages, who popped up out of the ground in the path of a ploughman, had founded their religion.

> *haut aliter stupuit, quam cum Tyrrhenus arator*
> *fatalem glaebam mediis adspexit in arvis*
> *sponte sua primum nulloque agitante moveri,*
> *sumere mox hominis terraeque amittere formam*
> *oraque venturis aperire recentia fatis:*
> *indigenae dixere Tagen, qui primus Etruscam*
> *edocuit gentem casus aperire futuros.*[123]

> "Not less astounded was [Hippolytus, the Amazon's son], than when the Tyrrhenian ploughman saw a fateful clod of earth first move of its own accord in the middle of his fields with no one disturbing it, and soon assume the shape of a human and lose the form of earth, and then its newly acquired mouth open with disclosures of things that were to come; the indigenous people called him Tages, who first taught the Etruscan people how to disclose the future."

People gathered around this miraculous apparition and in the presence of the entire populace of Etruria, what it said was written down by dictation as the foundation of the Etruscan science of divination.[124] The prophetic little creature was either the grandson of Jupiter, via his father Genius,[125] or he was born autochthonous from the earth itself. Genius was a creature, sometimes winged fairylike, that personified the individual manifestation of divine nature, not only human, but resident in all aspects of creation, including vineyards and even festivals and social and religious rites like matrimony and the circus.

Tages is the Latinized version of his name, which in Etruscan would have been *Tarchies,*[126] probably a variant of Tarchunus, an Etruscan version of the Latin name Tarchon, the legendary founder of the Etruscan city of Tarquinia. Tarchon is sometimes identifiable as the ploughman who received Tages from the ground, or portrayed with him.[127] In the *Aeneid,* King Tarchon leads the Etruscans in their alliance with Aeneas against Turnus and the other tribes of Latium.[128] Sometimes Tages is depicted as just a talking head emerging from the ground. In appearance he was young, but also wizened, a *puer senex.* He usually wears a conical Phrygian cap. An early-third-century BCE small bronze figure of a child, presented to Pope Clement XIV in 1771, is thought to represent Tages.[129] It depicts him as an infant nude, seated on the ground, one thigh horizontal, the other with knee raised exposing his penis, and with his head as an adult turned upward. He has a pouch or "bulla" suspended as a locket around his neck, of the sort that Roman children wore as a protective amulet, usually containing phallic symbols, until the age of sixteen and then stored as a memento and brought out for display at special adult honorary occasions.

Haruspicy and Alchemy

The special knowledge that Tages entrusted to Etruscans was divination through the inspection of the liver of a sacrificed animal, haruspicy (hepatoscopy). It is an art of great antiquity that can be traced back to Mesopotamia and even earlier, with references both in the Bible[130] and Homer.[131] An Etruscan mirror from Vulci depicts the Homeric seer Calchas inspecting a liver; he is winged, probably as an indication of his shamanic rapture.[132] He is bent over with one foot on a rock, and the entire scene is framed by a vine with leaves and bunches of grapes; the pitcher or ewer on the ground behind him probably contains wine, which is to say, an intoxicant. It is highly unlikely that the pitcher is an extraneous detail. A coin of the Emperor Sestertius Herennius Etruscus (227–251 CE), which celebrates his Etruscan heritage[133] and the "Piety of the descendants of Augustus" (*Pietas Augustorum*), depicts his cult implements as the ewer flanked on the left by the *lituus* (crosier) of a haruspex above a *simpulum* basin with an aspergillum for sprinkling its holy (baptismal) water in the ritual of aspergation, and on the right a serpent coil. The pose of the Etruscan haruspex with one foot raised and resting on a rock is apparently traditional, indicating the seer's mediation between earth and the celestial realm. It occurs on another mirror depicting Tages (*Parva Tachies*) inspecting the liver with Tarchon (*Avi Tarchunus*).[134] The entire scene is support by a winged male on the base handle, the traditional motif of the ecstatic flight.

Since the liver is essential for life, the largest and weightiest of the entrails and containing the greatest amount of the life force in the form of blood, it was considered the center of personal existence. The basic tenet of alchemy is that what is below is as above. Thus the liver is a microcosm of the vitality of the universe. The liver of a sheep was most commonly used since that animal is relatively inexpensive and most frequently butchered or sacrificed. A Babylonian sheep's liver molded from clay (c. 1900–1600 BCE) is marked as a map.[135] An Etruscan version from Piacenza in bronze from the Hellenistic Period (c. 100 BCE) is labeled with the names of the gods controlling each area.[136] As with alchemy, however, the inspection of the microcosm not only gave a clairvoyant reading of the cosmos, but it also offered the possibility of influencing the upper realm. In Virgil, the Etruscan Asilas has the power to change the world by the manipulation of the victim's liver:

> tertius ille hominum divumque interpres Asilas,
> cui pecudum fibrae, caeli cui sidera parent,
> et linguae volucrum et praesagi fulminis ignes ...[137]

> "Third [was] that interpreter of men and gods, whom the entrails of sacrificed sheep obey, whom even the stars obey, and the speech of birds and the fires of the prescient lightning."

Since both the chattering of birds and the interpretation of lightning flashes were also clairvoyant techniques of the seer, Asilas can not only predict the future, but also influence what happens.[138] Such power was seen as a threat to the established order and astrologer-seers were on occasion either banned or executed by a succession of Roman emperors.[139]

The liver was the organ that was the site of the daily torment of the chained Titan Prometheus as punishment for his creation of man. Prometheus is the mythical prototype of the clairvoyant seer, named as the "Fore-thought." The liver is the organ that functions in hemolysis, the cleansing of the blood from toxins, and thus it is a motif in botanical agencies for shamanic rapture. Although it is unlikely that the ancients knew of the filtering function of the liver, it was thought to be the organ through which the digested food from the stomach and intestines entered the bloodstream.[140] When that food is psychoactive, the whole animal's flesh becomes a source of the toxin,[141] and the liver would have the highest concentration, reabsorbing what the kidneys did not eliminate into the urine.[142] The myth of Prometheus, who stole "fire" in a narthex or "narcotic box-plant," associates the clairvoyant liver with psychoactive plants.[143] The bitter brownish or greenish-yellow secretion of the liver called bile or gall (Latin *bilis,* Greek *cholé,* both derived from the Indo-European root *ghel-* for "shine," yellow like gold) is another element in the motif. It is enlisted as two of the basic humors of the body (melancholic, choleric) and was associated in Roman thought with rancor and madness. "Gall" was further implicated in the motif of botanical psychoactive toxins by its association with the venom of serpents,[144] which contaminate plants by contagion. Eating your enemy's liver was equivalent to mastering his soul,[145] and in the initiation of an Eskimo shaman or *angakok,* the initiator eats the liver of the novice, which gives them both the power to travel in the spirit.[146]

The Paradigmatic Foundation Myth

The Etruscan foundation myth of the little talking head called Tages that popped up out of the ground and revealed the arcane secrets of the cosmos that empowered the shaman-seer Tarchon, the legendary founder of the Tarquinii, to change the world belongs to the motif of foundation stories. The most blatantly entheobotanical (i.e., involving the role of a psychoactive botanical pharmaceutical agent) is Perseus's role in founding the citadel of Mycenae by plucking a mushroom at the site, causing the spring to flow and providing a new etymology for the city from *mykes,* the "mushroom," metaphorically as the "mucous thing."[147] In cultures where the mushroom is sacred, it has no name, but is denoted only by metaphoric identities.[148] As mentioned above, the Perseus myth seems to have been a popular theme for the Etruscans. Perhaps the most famous of the foundation myths is the arrival of Cadmus (Kadmos) at Thebes. His name is derived from the Phoenician-Semitic root *QDM,* meaning the "east" or "Orient."[149]

Cadmus went in search of his sister Európe (Europa, which to a Greek would suggest "broad-face," probably descriptive of one of the manifestations of the Gorgon Medusa), who was abducted by Zeus in the form of a bull from Phoenicia. Európe is derived from the Phoenician-Semitic root *RB* meaning "west" and recognized as such at least as early as the Byzantine period.[150] She lent her name to the geographical Europe as early as the Homeric "Hymn to Apollo."[151] The myth is thus the major foundational etiology of the northern continent's relationship to the Middle East and the African continent to which it belongs. For her part, Európe's birthing of Minos on Crete and his wife's sexual passion for one of her husband's bulls are the foundational story of Phoenician traditions in the formation of Minoan pre-Greek culture centered at Knossos.

Cadmus passed through Samothrace in his search of his sister. He was initiated there into the cult of the Kabeiroi, and his brother or nephew Thasos is credited as the "founder" of the nearby island of Thasos. Another brother Cilix (Kilix) founded Cilicia, on the southern shore of Anatolia. The Phoenicians had mastered the art of navigation and were instrumental in the founding of numerous colonies.[152] Since they could sail out of sight of land, they may have discovered the Azores, and perhaps even beyond.[153]

At Delphi, Cadmus received instructions to follow a special cow with a half-moon on her flank and found a city where she lay down. Európe's abduction by a bull and Cadmus's instructions to follow a cow in search of her are obviously versions of the same motif, probably traceable back to the bull-cow sanctuaries uncovered at Çatal Hüyük in Anatolia, dating from the Neolithic period and considered the precedent for the later Minoan culture. The half-moon that marked the Európe-cow involves her in the metaphoric motif of the goddess and the lunar periodicity of her menstrual cycle, still commemorated by Hera's ancient epithet as "cow-faced" (*Boöpis*), a trait she shares with the Egyptian goddess Isis.[154]

The Serpent Lady of the Spring

A giant serpent already inhabited Thebes with his Lady when the cow revealed the site to Cadmus in the plain destined to be called Boeotia ("Cow-land"), and following Athena's instructions, he slew the serpent and planted its fangs. The serpent is metaphoric for the consort of the Lady and probably indicates the totemic animal assumed by a shaman and represents the sacred beast with which the ruling couple claimed kinship. The ritual slaughter of the serpent was a surrogate sacrifice of the human whose spirit could be ritually induced to inhabit the animal.[155] There were various symbolic ways that the Lady's consort could access the serpent's power or reside within its persona, but the simplest and most direct would be to eat the animal or its consubstantial sacred psychoactive plant or entheogen. The beast is usually called a dragon with teeth, but a dragon is a serpent and serpents have fangs, not teeth. The customary translation obscures the toxicity of the planted seeds, and the role of serpents in ecstatic religious rites. In some cases, they were probably "milked" to extract their venom.[156] The same procedure was used for toads, yielding the metaphor of the toadstool.[157] Both the "toe of frog" and "lizard's leg" figure in the witches' cauldron of Shakespeare's *Macbeth*, along with "adder's fork" and a variety of herbs with zoomorphic names.[158]

A red-figured *krater* (wine-mixing vase) from Paestum near Naples in the Italian Campania[160] depicts the encounter of Cadmus and the serpent with the traditional motif of the transmutation of the serpent's wild toxicity into a cultivar: As usual in the depiction of the heroic encounter, an olive grows between Cadmus and the serpent, the olive being emblematic of a wild useless plant that is pruned into the fruit-bearing tree.[161] The Lady with the serpent has an unidentifiable sprig of some plant in her hand, which she has obviously picked or gathered. The Dionysian motif of the ecstatic nature of the event is further indicated by the presence of Pan and a satyr with *thyrsos* (narthex) watching the event. The *thyrsos* is the emblem of herb-gatherers.[162] As a culinary term, moreover, the stipe (or "trunk," *stipes*) of a mushroom was called a *thyrsus* in Vulgar Latin.[163] This is particularly significant. First, it documents the extraordinary longevity of the metaphoric link between mushrooms and the maenadic ecstatic rites over a period of a millennium. Secondly, it equates the *thyrsos* of the receptacle for the gathered drug-plants (narthex) with the stipe of the *Amanita muscaria,* whose psychoactive cap or *pileus* is analogous to the entheogen stuffed into it. In the case of the *thyrsos* itself, the gathered herb is depicted as wild ivy, the primitive and toxic antecedent to the vine and the wine grown by human intervention through the controlled fungal fermentation. These two aspects of the god, contrasting the wild natural toxic plants (Bacchus) and the cultivated intoxicant grown from the grape (Dionysus), are an essential aspect of his symbolism and rituals, and it is commemorated by the herbal intoxicants mixed with the wine. Essentially, the vinous potion mediates or combines the wild and cultivated persona of the god. It should be noted also that *stipes* inevitably equate the mushroom to a tree and that *pileus* anthropomorphizes it as a little capped creature.

The Theban encounter of Cadmus and the serpent is analogous to Apollo's claiming of Delphi by slaying the Python and its Lady on the adjacent Mount Parnassus, since the Theban serpent lurked in a spring that is sometimes equated with the Delphic Castalian Spring,[164] a day's journey away and where Cadmus has just been. Alternatively, there is a sacred spring, Ismene, which is local to Thebes. This latter is associated with Dionysus and the death of the Theban Dirke, and she provides us another name for the Lady with the serpent. Dirke is named for the "double cleft," which is descriptive of the Delphic Castalian Spring that flows from the base of the twin Shining Cliffs that loom ominously over the sanctuary of Delphi. It suggests also that the cleft where the two cliffs converge is the vulva. Dirke was identified in botanical lore as the psychoactive Datura lily (*dirkaion,* jimsonweed). The extraordinary complexity of the Theban foundation myth, requiring several generations to be completed, is probably due to the city's location at the base of Mount Parnassus, making it part of the whole motif of the mountain's Corycian Cave as a cosmic axis, a pathway of shamanic rapture extending from the womb of earth to the celestial realm.[165] Hence, the Castalian Spring is not unrelated to the local Ismenian fountain. At the base of the pathway lay Ogygia, where Odysseus languished in the embrace of Calypso,[166] before his ascent back home.[166]

Alternatively, the indigenous goddess may have been named Thebe, equated with the Antiope who several generations later birthed the founding twins Amphion and Zethos. These latter warring brothers play the same role as Romulus and Remus in building the circuit wall surrounding the Cadmean acropolis citadel. A red-figured vase from Paestum depicts the Lady of the spring and her serpent, with Athena instructing Cadmus to toss the stone and with a heavenly apparition of Harmonia above Athena, suggesting that both Athena and Harmony are the transmutation of the Lady of the spring.[167] By one account, Harmonia was the daughter of the serpent,[168] appropriately since the serpent of Ares thus yields to the harmonious union of Cadmus and Harmonia.

The Crop of Indigenes

From the sown fangs a race of men arose and Cadmus instigated internecine strife by tossing a stone in their midst. These men are the autochthonous people, called the "Sown-men" or Spartoi. Among the races of fantastic creatures are the *Kaulomyketes,* mushroom warriors, named as "cover-mushrooms," who use their mushroom caps as a shield.[169] They are probably a version of the "shade-foots" (*Skiapodes*), a one-legged anthropomorphism of the mushrooms who use their parasol foot as a cover when they have exhausted their strength from the extraordinary effort of leaping from the ground.[170] It should be obvious, in any case, that what rises from the plowed field is both toxic and botanical. When only five remained, the battle ended. The number five is significant because the little "digital" (*dakyl*) ecstatic attendants of the goddess traditionally form a pentad, representing her dismembered phallic digits. They built the citadel of Thebes, and the success of the reconciliation between the immigrant founder and the Spartoi was commemorated as the marriage of Cadmus and "Harmony," the daughter of the warlike Ares, who formerly had presided over the spring of the serpent and the Lady.[171] One of their daughters, Agave, was married to Echion, the "serpent," one of the sown-men. Another way of telling the story has the marriage to Harmony signal the success of the foundation event on Samothrace. Harmonia is listed as Samothracian by birth.[172]

In either case, the event signals the successful evolution of the deities into their Olympian identities, transmuting their former Pelasgian theophanies in the religious traditions of the dominant Anatolian goddess. The same motif of the stabilizing event for the Olympian deities occurs with the only other marriage that the gods attended, the marriage of Peleus and Thetis, which ended the threat to the Olympian hierarchy by voiding the possibility of the birth of a son who would replace Zeus. That marriage, however, to which Strife understandably was not invited, led to the Trojan War, the final test of female suppression through the reluctant acquiescence of Helen in the bonds of male-dominant matrimony.

Thus Athena plays the same role as adjuvant with Cadmus as with Perseus and numerous other founding heroes. She is the most complete transmutation of that former goddess into the male-subservient motherless daughter of her father Zeus. Since the Theban story is a sacred etiology, analogous to the mystery tradition of the Kabeiroi on Samothrace and elsewhere, there are understandably numerous divergent accounts, which are only superficially different. The actual event is subject to the prohibition of silence guarding the secret of a mystery. Such mysteries universally involve a visionary experience accessed by a psychoactive sacrament or entheogen or by an innocuous symbolic surrogate. The founder hero is a shaman who first establishes the cosmic pathway that allows the new city to flourish with the blessings of the deities, above and below.

Et Tu Spectabere Serpens

The myth of the unfounding of Thebes, the reversal of its founding, makes the entheobotanical theme even clearer. In Euripides's *Bacchae,* Echion's son Pentheus rejects the mysteries of the Thracian Sabazios-Dionysus; and Cadmus, as Dionysus, the cult leader of his own religion foretells:

> You will become a serpent metamorphosed, and your wife as zoomorphism will take on the shape of a snake. You will drive a cart with your wife drawn by cows, as the prophecy of Zeus proclaims, a leader of foreigners, and you will destroy with your countless troops many cities. When you finally plunder the Delphic sanctuary, then only will you have your miserable homecoming. Then Ares will rescue you and Harmony and set you up to live in the land of the blessedly departed.[173]

Ovid makes the theme even clearer. When the victorious Cadmus examines the gigantic size of the serpent he has just defeated, a voice out of nowhere is heard:

> *quid, Agenore nate, peremptum*
> *serpentem spectas? et tu spectabere serpens.*
>
> "Why, son from Agenor, do you inspect the serpent. You, too, will be the object of inspection as a serpent."[174]

When Harmonia saw her husband's metamorphosis, she begged to share his fate and she, too, became a serpent.[175] Pentheus is identified in the *Bacchae* with a temperament caused by the ingestion of wild poisonous plants, the opponent of the Sabazios cult that brings a drug that alleviates suffering and inspires beneficial heroism and intelligence.[176]

Cadmus's troubled legacy as founder continued in his only son's great-grandson, Oedipus, still replete with entheobotanical controversy in the confrontation with the Sphinx, and the warring of his two sons, Eteocles and Polyneices. The latter used the magical necklace of Harmony to bribe an alliance of foreigners to fight his brother's Theban defenders to the death at the seven gates of Thebes. Even that act of mutual annihilation did not end the controversy, but the sons of the seven came back to retake the city finally ten years later.

The serpent's fangs had a further resurgence in the myth of Jason and Medea. Jason had to plow a field with a team of brazen fire-breathing bulls, the invention of Hephaestus, no doubt cast in his volcanic forge with his dwarfish workmen, and then plant the fangs, with the same result of internecine strife caused by the stone thrown in the midst of the men born from the ground.

Jason was protected in his task by the anointment or chrism that gave him his name as the "drug-man" (*Iason*).[177] Medea gathered the pharmaceutical agent for the chrism from the immortal blood of Prometheus, tormented on the nearby mountain. The plant has a "double stem," which is descriptive of the *Amanita muscaria* in its early egg-like stage, as the stipe begins to push the base and cap apart to form a dumbbell shape.[178] Since mushrooms have no roots, this dumbbell shape can be fantasized as a tree trunk or "stipe" growing both upward and downward, two stems separating the opposing spread of the little tree's foliage or cap. It is the only plant with a double stem.

Alternatively, the Greek *kaulos* for "stem" could be interpreted as a "covering" or shield, as in the anthropomorphized warriors called the *Kaulomyketes*. The *muscaria* also characteristically has a double covering, the universal veil, covering the entire primordial egg, and the annulus ring, covering the spore-bearing gills.

The Prometheus *pharmakon* is a mushroom. It is the color of the Corycian crocus, raised up on a stem growing in two opposite directions and with a double covering, about a cubit tall, the size of a dwarf wearing a cap, and the root of this anthropoid when cut is like newly cut flesh. It grows from the *ichor* of the Titan, the ethereal fluid that flows in the veins of the gods.[179]

The Corycian crocus is usually associated with the cave where Echidna dwells, the mother of all monsters; it is there that Zeus defeated her consort Typhon (Typhoneus). In the contest, Zeus lost what is euphemistically called his "sinew." Similar euphemisms abound in the Bible, and the Jewish dietary restriction avoiding eating the sinew that runs between the thighs is generally fulfilled by not eating the hindquarters of the animal for fear of contamination with the genitals.[180] The association of the magical plant with the Corycian Cave suggests that the operative metaphor for the crocus is phallic. "Mushroom" in Greek was slang for erect penis.[181] The "queen" Kreousa of Athens (*kreousa* is participle in Greek meaning "reigning female," the same as *medousa*) encountered Apollo in a cave beneath the Acropolis while gathering such a crocus to conceive Ion, the founder of the Ionian tribal group of the Greeks.[182] The actual location of the Corycian Cave was a matter of debate in antiquity. One version placed it in Syria among the primordial Arimoi people,[183] whose language from the ninth-century on would become Aramaic. It could also be found in Lydia, Cilicia, and Sicily.[184] There is a famous version of this so-named cave at Delphi, where Apollo performed the contest that refounded the sanctuary as an oracle of Zeus.

The basic pattern in the foundation myth is mediation with primitivism, which on one level is expressed botanically as wild plants yielding to cultivation, and on another the intermingling of indigenous autochthonous people with the immigrant founder, usually celebrated as a miscegenetic marriage. Thus Aeneas will marry Lavinia, whom he will have to defend from her indigenous lover Turnus. The gods have instructed Lavinia's father, Latinus, to marry his daughter to a foreigner.

Indigenous Foreigner

The foreign founder, however, is often no outsider at all. Cadmus, after the undoing of his founding of Thebes, would rule with the exiled Harmonia over the Illyrian tribe of the Encheleans, named as the "Eel-people." An eel is an aquatic "snake," which in the Slavic language of the Illyrians was cognate with the Greek and Latin words for eel.[185] They could be found closer to Thebes in the Boeotian Lake Copais, which was famous for the eels that it provided as a culinary treat in Athens.[186] Its waters were what were left of the Ogygian deluge. Ogyges was the primordial ruler of Thebes,[187] now found in the furthest watery depths beneath the city, below the subterranean aquifer. It was the realm of the underworld, home of the "avenging" Furies (*Erinyes*),[188] daughters of Night,[189] and they first sprang from the blood of the castrated genitals of Ouranos. This magical realm of Ogygia lay beneath many cities, Athens as well as Thebes.

The theme of the indigenous foreigner is repeated with Oedipus, the fourth generation descended from Cadmus's only male child. He returned to Thebes as an outsider to confront the Sphinx and earn the meaning of his name as the "Know-foot," solving her riddle about the feet, only to discover that he had been born there and named from birth for the maiming that left him with feet united as the "Swollen-foot."[190]

> —I untied your pierced ankles [foot-sockets-joints, *arthra*].
> —That was a terrible deformity I got from birth.
> —So that you are named from this mischance who you are.

When Oedipus learns the true meaning of his name as a "One-foot," he tears the brooches from the dead Jocasta's robe and blinds himself, striking his eye "sockets-joints" (*arthra,* 1270) as ratification of his newly acquired vision. That Oedipus is a "One-foot" "One-eye" is a botanical metaphor and eventually Oedipus will reside among the *Erinyes* as a foreign friend in the Ogygian realm beneath Athens.[191] The "foot" and the "eye" are both euphemisms for the erect penis. The "marked foot" or lameness is a characteristic of the founder hero and indicates his closeness to the earth.[192] Oedipus (*Oidipous*) was originally a "finger-creature" or little *dakyl,* born from the earth, with the name of *Oidyphallos* or "Swollen-phallus."[193] In this manifestation, he is equivalent to the *Kabeiroi* and an anthropomorphized mushroom. The identification of the swollen foot with the phallus is a commonplace of psychology.[194]

A south-Italian Campanian red-figure wine pitcher vase (*oinochoë*) (c. 350–325 BCE) depicts a burlesque version of Oedipus confronting the Sphinx.[195] He wears a Phrygian cap and appears as a scrawny, pot-bellied dwarf, a *daktyl* with spindly legs and a giant erection, leaning on his walking staff. By one account, the Sphinx was the half-sister of Oedipus.[196] Like the Gorgon Medusa and all such monsters, she is probably a botanical anthropomorphism. In other burlesque depictions, she may appear as a winged (i.e., ecstatic) hag with sagging breasts and pubic hair, but hermaphroditic like the Medusa, with a penis for a tail. She may even appear as a man with a giant phallus, ejaculating over Oedipus, and so excited that she seems to be defecating.[197] The two, Oedipus and the Sphinx, are comparing sexual apparatus, with the male Sphinx clearly superior. This particular vase is probably a parody influenced by Aristophanes's *Knights,* depicting the demagogue Cleon in his role of the dildo-maker who services the annually receptive populace with his leather wares.

The Sphinx is a sexual predator, attacking or menacing adolescent males, either heterosexually or homosexually, even in depictions that are not burlesque, as on the base of the statue of Zeus from the Temple of Olympia.[198] She is named as the (spell) "binder," etymologically linked to the English "sphincter." She lent her name to the Boeotian Mount Phikios, which was her haunt.[199] Although usually imagined as a woman with the haunches of a lion, the wings of a great bird, and a serpent tail, she could be caricatured also as a hound. One burlesque shows the tables turned, with the hound of Oedipus sexually mounting the Sphinx.[200] One version of her origin is from the Syrian Corycian Cave of the Arimoi, a child of the mother of all monsters, Echidna and her mate Typhon,[201] inevitably confusing her with the nearer Cave on Mount Parnassus. She is not related to the Egyptian Sphinx, which is male and was called a sphinx by the Greeks because of its similarity to their mythical monster.

The indigenous foreigner is also the motif of Cadmus's daughter Semele, who conceived Dionysus. His other three daughters fared no better. Autonoë joined her sister Agave in dismembering Pentheus, and she was the mother of Actaeon, who was similarly dismembered by his own hunting hounds in exactly the same spot as the ordeal of Pentheus. Inó was the foster nurse of Dionysus, and she was instrumental in the sacrifice of Phrixus, which led to Jason's voyage of the Argonauts. At Corinth, where Jason seeks asylum with his foreign Lady, the sorceress Medea, she actually is no foreigner at all, but is returning to her father Aeëtes's native land.[202]

The Gorgon's Venom

As we have seen, Aeneas is actually returning to his ancestral home.[203] The journey of the Etruscan Dardanus from Italian Corythus (Cortona[204]) to Samothrace and Phrygian Mount Ida is matched by the return of Aeneas to the land of his Arcadian Greek forefathers. There he will form an alliance with Evander, the Arcadian, who brought the alphabet to Italy sixty years before the Trojan War and founded Pallantium on the future site of Rome, commemorating the victory of Hercules over the giant cattle-thief Cacus on the Palantine Hill. Heracles was returning from the Hesperid Garden with the cattle of Geryon, an episode replete with the traditional fungal motifs. The episode of the cattle of Geryon is a doublet for the Homeric Cattle of the Sun.[205] The event was the etiology for the Great Altar of Hercules in the Forum Boarium, the cattle market of Rome.

Aeneas's opponent is Turnus, probably an Etruscan,[206] king of the Rutuli (*Rudhuli*, the "redheads," a trait associated with the Thracians). In Dionysius of Halicarnassus, his name is Tyrrhenus, of which Turnus is an apparent corruption. His lineage, as displayed on his shield,[207] is from the Argive river Inachus, the father of the cow-maiden Io; and his totemic monster, which he wears on his helmet crest, is the chimera, the doublet of the Gorgon Medusa, which Bellerophon, the doublet of Perseus, sought in Anatolia. Bellerophon's conquest of the chimera is a Corinthian version of the Mycenaean Perseus's conquest of the Gorgon. Turnus is as foreign as Aeneas, as Amata, Lavinia's mother explains to her husband Latinus:

> *si gener externa petitur de gente Latinis,*
> *idque sedet, Faunique premunt te iussa parentis,*
> *omnem equidem sceptris terram quae libera nostris*
> *dissidet externam reor et sic dicere divos.*
> *et Turno, si prima domus repetatur origo,*
> *Inachus Acrisiusque patres mediaeque Mycenae.*[208]

> "If a son-in-law is needed foreign from the Latins, and that is settled and the commands of your father Faunus weigh upon

> you, every land free from our rule I deem foreign, and the gods agree. Turnus, in fact, if the first origin of his house be sought, has Inachus and Acrisius as forefathers, and straight in the middle, Mycenae."

This is astounding: *mediae Mycenae*, "smack in the middle—Mycenae," with Acrisius, its king, the grandfather of Perseus, as ancestor. Mycenae is also the homeland of Agamemnon, who as leader of the Greeks at Troy is the archenemy of Aeneas. She speaks maddened with the poisons of the fury (*Erinys*) Allecto. "Straightway Allecto, infected with the Gorgon poisons..." (*exim Gorgoneis Allecto infecta venemis...*) sought out the lofty fortification of the city of Latinus and sat silent on the threshold of Amata's chamber. It is the Mycenaean heritage from Perseus's Gorgon that infects her mind and drives her into a Bacchic frenzy.

> *huic dea caeruleis unum de crinibus anguem*
> *conicit, inque sinum praecordia ad intima subdit,*
> *quo furibunda domum monstro permisceat omnem.*
> *ille inter vestis et levia pectora lapsus*
> *volvitur attactu nullo, fallitque furentem*
> *vipeream inspirans animam.*[209]

> "The goddess flung a single serpent from her Stygian [blue-purple] hair at her, and in her breast it applied itself to her very heart, by which monster driven to madness she would disrupt her entire house. It slipped beneath her robe between her breasts and coiled, unfelt, undetected, inspiring her frenzied viperous soul."

The serpent slithering between the breasts of Amata with its Gorgon venom could not but recall the reputed initiation into the *Kabeiroi* Mystery. Alexander's mother Olympias is the most notorious example.[210] Her husband Philip, according to tradition, refused to sleep with her after he found her in bed with the serpent, and she encouraged her son with the belief that Zeus Amon (i.e., Egyptian-African) was actually his father. The password for the initiate into these mysteries of the Thracian Sabazios was "the deity over the breast—the deity being this serpent crawling over the breasts of the initiated."[211] Such serpent worship can be documented from the Minoan period, where idols survive of female snake handlers, sometimes with the serpents crawling over the woman's entire body.[212]

It persisted into a wide range of Christian heretical sects, largely interchangeable under a variety of names such as Marcion, Valentinus, Basilides, Apelles, Peratae, Sethians, the simplest being the Ophites, named for the *ophis* or "serpent" and the Naassenes, which is the Hebrew for "serpent." The evidence for these cults, apart from the Nag Hammadi Library of apocryphal texts, is pejorative from Christian apologists, and some of the sects may not even be Christian. The one thing that is common about them all is that they had an ecstatic orgiastic visionary ritual, and the serpent, which became the serpent in the Garden of Eden, offered Gnosis. In these Christian cults, the serpent was held to the breast and caressed, or allowed to slither over the Eucharist bread to impart its essence to the communion sacrament, indicating that the bread is symbolic or a surrogate for a plant that might impart the ecstatic wisdom that the serpent embodied.

Augustine Sobriety

One of the earliest Old Latin documents is a brass tablet dated 186 BCE, the transcript of an official letter from the Roman consuls to the people of the *Ager Teuranus* in the land of the Bruttii (Pelasgian Oenotrians), opposite the Sicilian Straits.[213] It informs them of a decree passed by the senate (*senatus consultum de Bacchanalibus*). It had come to the attention of Rome that men there were engaging in Bacchic rites and henceforth it forbade all Bacchic lodges (*Bacanal*) without a prior license; attendance of men at meetings with female Bacchants (*Bacas*); male Bacchic priests; masters, both male and female, of communal moneys; communal contracts; secret ceremonies; unlicensed rites, either public or private, whether in or outside the city; and unlicensed gatherings of more than five, two men and three women. The lodges were to be dismantled, unless by chance they contained a holy altar, which could not be destroyed. Failure to comply with this decree was a capital offense.[214] The contagion of this foreign religion had spread to other cities and was even established in Rome. The secret nature of the rites was seen as a political threat and in the event, 4,000 people were put to death. What we can decipher from the decree and Livy's extended account is that the rites were an outrage to Roman sensibilities, involving secret nocturnal gatherings, with drum-beating and cymbals, extreme intoxication, soothsaying and prophecies, sexual abandon, in particular the sodomizing of young recruits, and illicit sacrifices, perhaps even with human victims. Roman officials feared that it was something that would tend to effeminate the men enlisted in the Roman army.

The Romans had a similar problem when they imported the rites of Cybele to Rome in 204 BCE. It was intended as an additional Trojan ally in the war against Hannibal, and the sacred image of the goddess was escorted into the city with ceremonial pomp and installed in a newly built temple, but the ecstatic nature of the religion, which involved extreme maddened states culminating in self-castration, was offensive to Roman sensibilities. The goddess's sanctuary was isolated behind a walled enclosure and the participation of Roman citizens in the rites was restricted, until the official policy was finally liberalized in the time of the Emperor Claudius.[215] In the *Aeneid,* Virgil used the tradition that Cybele had provided the timbers for the Trojan ships, making them indestructible, until Aeneas finally gets to Italy. When Turnus tries to burn them, the ships turned into sea nymphs.[216]

The opposition of the two rival foreigners and their Ladies and the foundational sacrament form the basic structure of the final six books of the *Aeneid.* This matches the balance of the first and second halves of the epic in the opposition of the two of them as lovers—Turnus, driven by the Gorgon frenzy of Amata, and pious Aeneas, who deserted his beloved Dido to follow his destiny in founding Rome. In this context, the depiction of the cow-maiden Io on Turnus's shield (*iam saetis obsita, iam bos,* "now sown with bristles, now a cow," 7.790) is indicative of Turnus's Mycenaean heritage, Io, driven against her will with the estrual stinging of the gadfly (*oistros*), which is the spirit of "Argus, the keeper of the virgin" (*custos virginis Argus,* 7.791). The estrus (heat, or the period of sexual excitement in mammals preceding ovation) is named for this stinging fly. "Sown with bristles" metaphorically associates Io's bovine metamorphosis with plants, and in particular the sown men. Dido similarly had the frenzy of love inflected upon her by Venus, turning her into an unfortunate demented deer, struck by a poisoned arrow.[217]

Virgil characterizes Turnus as a variety of wild and dangerous beasts (a lion, tiger, wolf, or eagle[218]), supported by Amata and her troop of maenadic women. Even her name as "Beloved" in this context of sobriety is ominous.[219] Significantly, as Aeneas approaches Italy, he skirts but does not land on the "dire shores" (*litora dira,* 7.22) of Circe's island, where men are turned into beasts by the sorceress's potion (*potentibus herbis,* "potent herbs," 7.19), enslaved as her love objects.[220] They hear the roaring of chained lions and the raging of pigs, bears, and wolves, which once were men.

In the confrontation of Turner with the other foreigner, Aeneas represents all the virtues that Augustus hopes to instill in the Roman people, after the terrors of the recent Civil War. The motif of the foreign Lady inevitably has reverberations with Cleopatra's enslavement of Marc Anthony and Julius Caesar. Her reported suicide with the caressed asp is the motif of the serpent between the breasts.

In this same vein, one can consider the benign transmutation of the founding Harpy tables that Aeneas and his men innocuously eat, as opposed to the wild Mystery rites of his antithesis in the figure of the Gorgon-infected Tyrrhenus and his mother. At the final moment, as Aeneas hesitates to deliver the coup de grace, it is the sight of the belt of Pallas, his beloved friend and ally, that Turnus wears as a trophy from his murder, that decides the contest, a moment of irrational passion from the otherwise so pious hero. The name of Pallas cannot be divorced from the goddess who so often acts as adjuvant in encouraging heroes to aid her in overcoming her former persona as the Queen of the Gorgon sisterhood. The baldric of Pallas depicts the Danaids's slaughter of their husbands on their marriage night, the "bridal chamber running with blood" (*thalamique cruenti,* 10.498). The death of Turnus is the final triumph over the ecstatic Lady's power.

Notes

1. Virgil, *Aeneid,* 3.254–257.
2. *Ibid.*, 7.122–127.
3. *Ibid.*, 3.265–266.
4. *Ibid.*, 3.708–711.
5. Michael C.J. Putnam, *Virgil's Aeneid: Interpretation and Influence*

(Chapel Hill, NC: University of North Carolina Press, 1995), 64.

6. Servius (fourth-century CE), *In Vergilii carmina commentarii, ad Aeneidem*, 3.220.
7. Homer, *Odyssey,* 12.260 *et seq.*
8. Virgil, *Aeneid,* 7.114–115.
9. Sir William Smith, *Dictionary of Greek and Roman Antiquities* (London: Walton and Marberly, 1853), *sc. mensa.*
10. Pliny, *Historia naturalis,* 34.8.
11. Aelius Donatus (fourth-century CE), *Vita Virgilii,* 35 *et seq.*
12. *Ibid.*, 42.
13. James J. O'Hara, "The Unfinished *Aeneid*?": 96–106, in Joseph Farrell and Michael C.J. Putnam (eds.), *A Companion to Vergil's Aeneid and its Tradition* (Chichester, UK: Blackwell Publishing Ltd., 2010).
14. Lowell Edmunds, "Epic and Myth": 31–44, in John Miles Foley (ed.), *A Companion to Ancient Epic* (Oxford, UK: Wiley-Blackwell, 2005).

15. The third-century BCE Lycophron was a tragedian; there is also a second-century BCE Lycophron, who may have been the author.

16. Lycophron, *Alexandra,* 1226–1232.

17. Called the *Boreigonoi,* explained by the Byzantine commentator Tzetzes on Lycophron as a corruption of *aborigines.* Compare Strabo, 13.1.53.

18. Strabo, 13.1.53.

19. Konon, 26 F 1, Felix Jacoby, *Die Fragmente der griechischen Historiker.*

20. Dionysius of Halicarnassus, *Roman Antiquities* (*Rhomaike archaiologia*), 1.55.3–4. So also the anonymous probably fourth-century CE *Origo gentis Romanae,* 12.1, citing some unknown Domitius.

21. Virgil, *Aeneid,* 7.108–111.

22. Carl A.P. Ruck, Mark A. Hoffman, and José Alfredo González Celdrán, *Mushrooms, Myth, and Mithras: The Drug Cult that Civilized Europe* (San Francisco, CA: City Lights Books, 2011), 151–176.

23. Plutarch, *Life of Pompey,* 4.

24. Servius, *ad Aeneidem,* 3.256, citing Varro (first century BCE), *Antiquitates rerum humanarum et divinarum.*

25. Calvert Watkins, "An Indo-European Agricultural Term: Latin *Ador,* Hittite *Hat-*": 187–194, *in Harvard Studies in Classical Philology* (Wendell Clausen *et al.*, eds.), (Cambridge, MA: Harvard University Press, 1973).

26. Pliny, *Historia naturalis,* 18.81: *far, quod veteres adoreum apellavere.*

27. Cato, *de Agricultura,* 34.2: *in creta ... et ager qui aquosus erit, semen adoreum potissimum serito. Creta* is 'Cretan earth,' chalky poor fields, suited for weedy growths.

28. Horace, *Odes,* 4.4.36–38.

29. Plautus, *Miles Gloriosus,* 321: *Mirumst lolio victitare te tam vili tritico.*

30. Ovid, *Fasti,* 1.691: *et careant loliis oculos vitiantibus agri,* 'may our fields be free of eyesight corrupting darnel.'

31. Pliny, *Historia naturalis,* 18.62 (translation 18.44): *cum est in pane, celerrime vertigenes facit,* 'when it is in bread, it very quickly causes dizziness.'

32. William Smith, *Dr. William Smith's Dictionary of the Bible: Comprising its Antiquities, Biography, Geography, and Natural History* (Boston, MA: Houghton, Mifflin and Co., 1890), *sc.* tares.

33. Pliny, *Historia naturalis,* 18.62. Although LSD is quickly destroyed by fire, there are numerous contemporary testimonies to its efficacy when smoked, and the procedure of the ancient bath-keepers produced an intoxicating steam, rather than burning it.

34. R. Gordon Wasson, Albert Hofmann, and Carl A.P. Ruck, *The Road to Eleusis: Unveiling the Secret of the Mysteries* (New York and London: Harcourt Brace Jovanovich, 1978), reprinted and enlarged, twentieth anniversary edition, Los Angeles: Hermes Press, 1998; thirtieth anniversary edition, Berkeley, CA: North Atlantic Books, 2008).

35. Juvenal, *Satires,* 16.38. Virgil, *Eclogues,* 7.33–34: *sinum lactis et haec te liba, Priape, quotannis expectare sat est,* 'A bowl of milk and these liba-cakes, Priapus, are all you can expect each year (from me, a poor farmer).' Priapus is a rural ithyphallic version of Bacchus, the son of the god and Venus.

36. Virgil, *Georgics,* 2.388–396.

37. Andrew Dalby, *Food in the Ancient World from A to Z,* (London: Routledge, 2003, reprinted 2003), *sc.* sacrifice.

38. Virgil, *Aeneid,* 3.29–2293. Dionysius of Halicarrnasus, *Roman Antiquites,* 1.51.

39. Varro, cited by Servius, *Ad Aeneidem,* 3.256.

40. Dionysus of Halicarnassus, *Roman Antiquites,* 1.55. Sarolta A. Takács, "Forging a Past: The Sibylline Books and the Making of Rome": 15–28, in Judith Ryan and Alfred Thomas (eds.), *Cultures of Forgery: Making Nations, Making Selves* (New York, NY: Routledge, 2003).

41. Apollonius Rhodius, *Argonautica,* 2.297.

42. Ruck, "The Offerings from the Hyperboreans": 225–256, in R. Gordon Wasson, Stella Kramrisch, Jonathan Ott, and Carl A.P. Ruck, *Persephone's Quest: Entheogens and the Origins of Religion* (New Haven, CT: Yale University Press, 1986).
43. Pseudo-Apollodorus, *Bibilioteca,* 1.121–123.
44. Hesiod, *Catalogue of Women,* fragment 150 (Merkelbach-West), from *Oxyrrhynci Papyri* 1358 fragment 2, column I (Grenfell-Hunt).
45. H.G. Evelyn-White, Loeb translation.
46. Virgil, *Aeneid,* 6.289.
47. Seneca, *Hercules Furens,* 747 *et seq.*
48. Hesiod, *Theogony,* 265 *et seq.*
49. Lycophron, *Alexandra,* 653: "the rock (islands) of the Harpy-limbed nightingales." See commentary of Tztetzes, *ad loc.*
50. Aeschylus, *Eumenides,* 50.
51. Apollonios Rhodius, *Argonautica,* 2.434.
52. Homer, *Odyssey,* 20.66, 77.
53. Patricia Monaghan, *The Encyclopedia of Celtic Mythology and Folklore* (New York, NY: Facts on File, Inc., 2004), *sc.* 'fairy blast' and 'fairy kidnapping.'
54. Ovid, *Metamorphoses,* 7.4: *volucres virgineae.*
55. Plato, *Phaedrus,* 229. Carl A.P. Ruck, *Sacred Mushrooms of the Goddess: Secrets of Eleusis* (Berkeley, CA: Ronin Publishing, 2006), 73 *et seq.*; Ruck, "The Wild and the Cultivated: Wine in Euripides' *Bacchae*": 179–223, in Wasson *et al., Persephone's Quest.*
56. Apollonius Rhodius, *Argonautica*, 2.185.
57. Apuleius, *Golden Ass,* 10.15: uti... *cellulam suam tam immanes vilolare muscas, ut olim Harpyiae fuere, quae diripiebant Phineias dapes.* (They could not believe) 'that such monstrous flies, as once were the Harpies, who snatched away Phineus's banquet, had violated their prison cell.'
58. Seneca, *Medea,* 777.

59. Euripides, *Herakles,* 822 *et seq.;* Sophocles, *Trachinae.* Carl A.P. Ruck, "On the Sacred Names of Iamos and Ion: Ethnobotanical Referents in the Hero's Parentage":235–252, in *Classical Journal,* vol. 71. no. 3 (1976); "Duality and the Madness of Herakles": 53–76, in *Arethusa,*vol. 9 (1976).

60. Homer, *Iliad,* 16.150.

61. Virgil, *Georgics,* 3.274.

62. Ruck, *Sacred Mushrooms of the Goddess;* Carl A.P. Ruck, Blaise Daniel Staples, and Clark Heinrich, *The Apples of Apollo: Pagan and Christian Mysteries of the Eucharist* (Durham, NC: Carolina Academic Press, 2001), 41–85; Ruck *et al.,Mushrooms, Myth, and Mithras,* 87–95.

63. R. Laird Harris, Gleason Archer, Gleason Leonard Archer, Jr., and Bruce Waltke, *Theological Wordbook of the Old Testament* (Chicago: Moody Publishers, 2003).

64. *The New English Bible* (Cambridge, UK: Cambridge University Press, 1961). There are three persons of this name in the Bible, the grandson of Aaron, the younger of Eli's evil sons, and the father of the priest Eleazar.

65. Walter Burkert, *Greek Religion* (Cambridge, MA: Harvard University Press, 1985, translation of *Griechische Religion der archaischen und klassischen Epoche,* Stuttgart: Verlag W. Kohlhammer, 1977), 281 *et seq.*

66. Herodotus, *Histories,* 1.94. G.A. Wainwright, "The Teresh, the Etruscans and Asia Minor": 197–213, in *Anatolian Studies,* vol. 9 (1959). Lycophron, *Alexandra,* 1240 *et seq.*

67. *Tragicorum Graecorum Fragmenta* (August Nauck), 94–97a.

68. Herodotus, *Histories,* 3.37.2–3: 'For the image of Hephaestus is very like the Pataicoi of the Phoenicians, wherewith they ornament the prows of their ships. For persons who have not seen these, I will explain in a different way—it is a figure resembling that of a pygmy.'

69. Sandra Blakely, *Myth, Ritual, and Metallurgy in Ancient Greece and Recent Africa* (Cambridge, UK: Cambridge University Press, 2006).

70. Ruck *et al.*, *The Apples of Apollo*, 120–126.

71. Virgil, *Aeneid*, 2.293–294.

72. Cicero, *De natura deorum*, 2.68. Yves Bonnefoy, *Roman and European Mythologies* (Chicago, IL: University of Chicago Press, 1992), *sc.* Penates.

73. Luigi Zoja, *The Father: Historical, Psychological, and Cultural Perspectives* (Sussex, UK/Philadelphia, PA: Routledge/Taylor and Francis, Inc., 2001, originally published as *Preistoria, storia, attualità e scomparsa del padre*, Torino: Bollato Boringhieri, 2000), 136 *et seq.*

74. Festus (second-century CE), epitome of Verrius Flaccus (Augustine Age), *De verborum significatu*, 2961; Macrobius (fifth-century CE), *Saturnalia*, 3.4.8–9, citing Varro (first-century BCE).

75. Ruck, in Wasson *et al.*, *Persephone's Quest*, 256.

76. Wasson *et al.*, *Persephone's Quest*, 13, 67, 152 *et seq.*

77. *Ibid.*, 136.

78. Ruck *et al.*, *The Apples of Apollo*, 79–81.

79. Servius, *AdAeneidem*, 1.730.

80. Ovid, *Fasti*, 3.615; Servius, *Ad Aeneidem*, 2.296; Varro, *De lingua Latina*, 5.144.

81. Lewis Spence, *An Encyclopaedia of Occultism* (New York, NY: Cosimo, Inc., 2006, originally published New Hyde Park, NY: University Books, 1920), *sc.* Cabiri.

82. Lycophron, *Alexandra*, 1244. Odysseus met Aeneas in Italy, Hellenicus of Mytilene (fifth century BCE), cited by Dionysius of Halicarnassus, *Roman Antiquities*, 72.

83. H.B. Walters, "Odysseus and Kirke on a Boeotian Vase": 77 *et seq.*, in *Journal of Hellenic Studies*, vol. 13, (1892–1893).

84. Timothy Peter Wiseman, *Remus: A Roman Myth* (Cambridge, UK: Cambridge University Press, 1995), 51.

85. Ruck *et al.*, *Mushrooms, Myth, and Mithras*, 101–118.

86. Hesiod, *Catalogue of Women*, fragment 150.17–18, restored. Blakely, *Myth, Ritual, and Metallurgy in Ancient Greece*, 52.

87. Jack Lindsay, *The Clashing Rocks: A Study of Early Greek Religion and Culture and the Origins of Drama* (London: Chapman and Hall, Ltd., 1965).

88. Stavros Kiotsekoglou, "Upaithria Iera tes Archaias Thrakes (Open-air Sanctuaries of Ancient Thrace)": 4–21, in *Aeropos* (July–August, 2009).

89. Carl A.P. Ruck, "Democracy and the Dionysian Agenda," see Chapter 10 above. Ruck, "The Great God Sabazius and the Crab Dance in Athens": 193–220, in *The Stone Mushrooms of Thrace*, Proceedings of the Conference (Alexandrouplois, Greece: EKATAIOS, 2009).

90. Wasson *et al.*,*The Road to Eleusis*, 132; Ruck, *Sacred Mushrooms of the Goddess*, 61.

91. Donna Kurtz and John Boardman, *Greek Burial Customs* (London: Thames and Hudson, 1971), 242–244.

92. E.g., Psyche and the sleeping Eros, Roman mosaic, third-century CE. Antakya Museum, Turkey, inv. no. 1021.93. William Edwart Gladstone, *Der Farbensinn: Mit besonderer Berüsichtigung der Farbenkenntnis des Homer* (Brelau: Kern Verlag, 1878, reprinted *in Juventus Mundi: The Gods and Men of the Heroic Age*, Whitefish, MT: Kessinger Publishing, 2005), cited in Sir Norman Lockyer (ed.), *Nature: International Journal of Science*, vol. 18, October 31, 1878, 701 *et seq.*

94. Homer, *Odyssey*, 12.63; Euripides, *Hippolytus*, 748.

95. Margaret Bennett, "Balquhidder Revisited: Fairylore in the Scottish Highlands, 1690–1990": 94–115, in Peter Narváez (ed.), *The Good People: New Fairylore Essays* (Lexington, KY: The University Press of Kentucky, 1991), 110: "And sometimes they just sit on these little toadstools and eat off the big ones. Sort of like a dinning room? Yes. Is it like furniture? Yup! You could say that…."

96. Monaghan, *Encyclopedia of Celtic Mythology*, *sc.* 'fairy food.'

97. H. Bennett, "The Restoration of the Virgilian Farm": 87–95, in *Phoenix*, vol. 5, no. 3/4 (winter, 1951).

98. *Gesta Romanorum,* a thirteenth-fourteenth-century popular collection of anecdotes, intended as a sourcebook for preachers.

99. Tacitus, *Annales,* 12.66; Cassius Dio, *Historia Romana,* 61.34; Suetonius, *De vita caesarum, vita Claudii,* 44.

100. Art Institute of Chicago.

101. Mark J. Johnson, "The Mausoleum of Augustus: Etruscan and Other Influences on its Design": 217–240, in John Franklin Hall (ed.), *Etruscan Italy: Etruscan Influences on the Civilization of Italy from Antiquity to the Modern Era* (Bloomington, IN: Indiana University Press, 1996).

102. Robert Graves, *Food for Centaurs* (Garden City, NY: Doubleday, 1960). Michael Ripinsky-Naxon, *The Nature of Shamanism: Substance and Function of a Religious Metaphor* (Albany, NY: State University of New York Press, 1993), 157.

103. Ruck and Staples, "Mistletoe, Centaurs, and Datura": 15-40, in Ruck *et al, The Apples of Apollo.*

104. Ruck *et al., Mushrooms, Myth, and Mithras.*

105. Ovid, *Metamorphoses,* 7.392–3; (Pseudo-Apollodorus, *Bibliotheca,* 1.9.3.

106. Tacitus, *Annales,* 3.14.

107. Walter Burkert, *The Orientalizing Revolution: Near Eastern Influence on Greek Culture in the Early Archaic Age* (Cambridge, MA; Harvard University Press, 1992, translated from the German edition of 1984), 26.

108. Herodotus, *Histories,* 2.145.4.

109. *Ibid.,* 5.59.1.

110. Peter Mountford, "Aeneas: An Etruscan Foundation Legend," in *Australian Society for Classical Studies,* Proceedings, vol. 32.

111. Marco Pellechia *et al.,* "The Mystery of Etruscan Origins: Novel Clues from *Bos taurus* Mirochondrial DNA": 1175–1179, in *Proceedings of the Royal Society, Biological Sciences,* vol. 274, no. 1614 (7 May 2007).

112. Dionysius of Halicarnassus, *Roman Antiquities,* 1.30.2.

113. The Lemnos Stele, a funerary monument of the sixth-century BCE. Additional examples have been found on pottery fragments and on an inscription from the village of Efestia.

114. Virgil, *Aeneid,* 3.148.

115. *Ibid.,* 3.173–174.

116. *Ibid.,* 3.180.

117. *Ibid.,* 7.205–211.

118. John F. Hall, "From Tarquins to Caesars: Etruscan Governance at Rome": 149–181, in John Franklin Hall (ed.), *Etruscan Italy* (Provo, UT: Brigham Young University of Art, 1996).

119. Dionysius of Halicarnassus, *Roman Antiquities,* 1.65.

120. Stefan Weinstock, *Divus Julius* (Oxford: Clarendon Press, 1971), 9.

121. Dionysius of Halicanassus, *Roman Antiquites.* Appian (second century CE), *De regibus Romanis,* 1.

122. Horace, *Odes*, 1.1: *atavis edite regibus;* 3.29.1: *Tyrrherna regum progenies,* 'Etruscan descendant of kings.'

123. Ovid, *Metamorphoses,* 15.553–559.

124. Cicero, *De diviniatione,* 2.50–51.

125. Festus, *De verborum significatu,* 359.14.

126. Giuliano Bonfante and Larissa Bonfante, *The Etruscan Language: An Introduction* (Manchester, UK: Manchester University Press, 1983), 205.

127. Nancy Thomson de Grummond, *Etruscan Myth, Sacred History, and Legend* (Philadelphia, PN: University of Pennsylvania Museum of Archaeology and Anthropology, 2006), 23–27.

128. Virgil, *Aeneid,* 8.506, 603; 10.153, 290; 11.727, 746.

129. Museo Gregoriano Etrusco, Rome, inv. no. 12108.

130. *Ezekiel,* 21.21; *Proverbs,* 7.23.

131. Homer, *Iliad,* 20.469 *et seq;* 24.212 *et seq.*

132. Museo Gregoriano Etrusco, Rome, inv. No. 12240.

133. His mother was apparently an Etruscan, Herennia Etruscilla.

134. Bronze mirror from Tuscania (*c.* 300 BCE), Museo Archeologico Nazionale, Florence.

135. Probably from modern southern Iraq, British Museum, London, Western Asia Collection, catalogue no. ME 92668.

136. Piacenza Museo Civico.

137. Virgil, *Aeneid,* 10.175–177.

138. Asilas is a master of the *Etrusca disciplina.* Christine G. Perkell. *Reading Vergil's Aeneid: An Interpretive Guide* (Norman, OK: University of Oklahoma Press, 1999), 191 *et seq.*

139. Tiberius, Claudius, Vespasian, Domitian. Matthew Bunson, *Encyclopedia of the Roman Empire* (New York, NY: Facts on File, Inc., 1994, 2002), *sc.* astrology.

140. Galen, *De usu partium,* 4.15. Plinio Prioreschi, *A History of Medicine: Roman Medicine* (Omaha, NE: Horatius Press, 1998), 521.

141. Alan Piper, "The Milk of the Goat Heidrun: An Investigation into the Sacramental Use of Psychoactive Milk and Meat" (2004).

142. Gregory Möller, University of Idaho, course curriculum: "Natural Toxins in Plants and Fungi: The Ecological Biochemisty of Food." Robert M. Julien, *A Primer of Drug Action: A Concise, Nontechnical Guide to the Actions, Uses, and Side Effects of Psychoactive Drugs* (New York, NY: Worth Publishers, 2001, revised reprint of Henry Holt and Co., 1975), 15 *et seq.*

143. Ruck *et al., The Apples of Apollo,* 131–135.

144. *Job, mererah,* 20.25. In Matthew's account of the crucifixion, *chole* (2.34) is a decoction of some product in wine, probably derived from a plant. The various plants defined as 'gall' in the Bible include hemlock, opium, henbane, and delphinium.

145. Hecuba wishes to eat Achilles' liver raw, Homer, *Iliad,* 24.212.

146. Harlan I. Smith, "Notes on Eskimo Tradition": 209–216, in *Journal of American Folklore* (American Folklore Society), vol. 8 (1894).

147. Ruck *et al.*, *The Apples of Apollo,* 42–45.

148. Carl A.P. Ruck, "Fungus Redivivus: New Light on the Mushroom Controversy": 353–381, addendum in republication of John Allegro, *Sacred Mushroom and the Cross: a study of the nature and origins of Christianity within the fertility cults of the ancient Near East,* with an introduction by Allegro's daughter Judy Brown (Los Angeles, CA: Gnostic Media Research and Publishing, 2010).

149. R.B. Edwards, *Kadmos the Phoenician: A Study in Greek Legends and the Mycenaean Age* (Amsterdam: Hakkert, 1979).

150. Hesychios. See Burkert, *The Orientalizing Revolution.*

151. Homer, *Hymn to Apollo* (perhaps 522 BCE), 251–252: 'people who inhabit the rich Peloponnesus and all those who inhabit Europe and throughout the wave-washed islands.'

152. Maria Eugenia Aubet, *The Phoenicians and the West: Politics, Colonies, and Trade* (Cambridge, UK: Cambridge University Press, 1993, translation of *Tiro y las Colonias Fenicias de Occidente,* Ediciones Bellaterra, 1987).

153. Mark McMenamin, *Carthaginian Cartography: A Stylized Exergue Map* (South Hadley, MA: Meanma Press, 1996).

154. Henry Brugsch-Bey, "On Hera Boöpis": appendix 8, 740–751, in Heinrich Schliemann, Ilios: *The City and the Country of the Trojans* (London: J. Murray, 1880).

155. Sir James Frazer, *The Golden Bough: A Study in Magic and Religion,* (Whitefish, MT: Kessinger Publishing, 2003, reprint of 1927), vol. 4, 82 *et seq.*

156. Cynthia Palmer and Michael Horowitz, "Introduction": 21–22, in Cynthia Palmer and Michael Horowitz (eds.), Shaman Woman, *Mainline Lady: Women's Writings on the Drug Experience* (New York, NY: William Morrow and Co., 1982).

157. Jonathan Ott, *Pharmacotheon: Entheogenic Drugs, their Plant Sources and History* (Kennewick, WA: Natural Products Co., 1996), 177–179.

158. Shakespeare, *Macbeth,* act 4, scene 1. For the association of serpent venom and psychoactive plants, see Ruck, in Wasson *et al., Persephone's Quest,* 199.

159. Musée du Louvre, Paris, catalogue no. N3157, attributed to Python, *c.* 360–340 BCE.

160. Carl A.P. Ruck and Daniel (Blaise) Staples, *The World of Classical Myth: Gods and Goddesses, Heroines and Heroes* (Durham, NC: Carolina Academic Press, 1994), 62–63.

161. Theophrastus, *Historia plantarum,* 9.16.2.

162. Apicius (fourth-fifth-century CE), *De re coquinaria,* 7.13.6: *boletos aliter: thyrsos eorum concisos in patellam novam perfundis, addito pipere* . . . ('Another way to cook mushrooms: you toss their thyrsus chopped up in a new pan, with some pepper added . . .').

163. Pseudo-Hyginus, *Fabulae,* 6. This detail is sometimes discredited as an error, but Hellenistic scholars merely copied what they found in another source.

164. Ruck, *et al., Apples of Apollo,* 27.

165. Homer, *Odyssey,* 1.88.

166. Ruck and Staples, *The World of Classical Myth,* 288.

167. A.D. Trendall, *Paestan Pottery: A Study of the Red-Figured Vases of Paestum* (London: Macmillan, 1936), 24.

168. Dercylos, quoted by a scholiast on Euripides, *Phoenissae,* 7. *Fragmenta historicorum Graecorum* (Müller), 4.387.

169. Lucian of Samosata, (Greek, second century CE), *Vera Historia,* 1.16. The *kaulos* is the 'stem' or 'stalk' of a plant. However, the *Kaulomyketes* are described as using mushrooms for a shield and asparagus stalks for spears.' A 'Stalk-mushroom' is meaningless. The *kaul-* is derived from Indo-European *kel-*, designating a 'covering,' as in hull, cell, and conceal. The English word caul for the birth membrane adhering as a covering derives from Old French *cale,* meaning a skullcap, of unknown origin. As a covering, it probably derives from the same root. Apocalypse is the 'un-covering.' See Ruck *et al., Apples of Apollo,* 101, footnote 38. A monk's hood or

even the entire covering habit is called a cowl, probably from the same root, derived from Latin *cucullus.* The reduplication of the *c-* indicates a loss of initial *s-*, relating the word to a shield, *scutum.* See Carl A.P. Ruck and Mark A. Hoffman, *The Effluents of Deity: Alchemy and Psychoactive Sacraments in Medieval and Renaissance Art* (Durham, NC: Carolina Academic Press, 2012), 278–283.

170. Wasson *et al., Persephone's Quest,* 63–72, 151–152.

171. Matia Rocchi, *Kadmos e Harmonia: un matrimonio problemmatico* (Rome: Bretschneider. 1989).

172. Diodorus Siculus, 5.48.2.

173. Euripides, *Bacchae,* 1330–1339.

174. Ovid, *Metamorphoses,* 3.97–98. So also Apollodorus, 3.5.4; Strabo. 7.7.8; Hyginus, *Fabulae,* 6; Nicander, *Theriaca,* 607 *et seq.*

175. Hyginus, *Fabulae,* 1.6.

176. Euripides, *Bacchae,* 326–327. Ruck, "The Wild and the Cultivated: Wine in Euripides' *Bacchae*": 179–223, in Wasson *et al., Persephone's Quest.*

177. Carl A.P. Ruck, "On the Sacred Names of Iamos and Ion: Ethnobotanical Referents in the Hero's Parentage": 235–252, in *Classical Journal,* vol. 71, no. 3 (1976).

178. Ruck, *et al., Apples of Apollo,* 67–142.

179. Apollonius Rhodius, *Argonautica,* 3.844–857.

180. Ruck and Hoffman, *The Effluents of Deity: Alchemy and Psychoactive Sacraments in Medieval and Renaissance Art,* 10 *et seq.*

181. Archilochus, fragment 34 (Diehl). Cf. Hesychios, Herodian. Wasson *et al., Road to Eleusis,* 131 *et seq.*

182. Euripides, *Ion,* 88. See Ruck *et al., Apples of Apollo,* 54–58.

183. Homer, *Iliad,* 2.780–785; Pindar, fragment 13, *Pythian Odes,* 1.17, 8.16.

184. Strabo, 13.4.6.

185. Marjeta Sasel Kos, "Cadmus and Harmonia in Illyria": 113–136, in *Arhcoloski Vestnik*, vol. 44 (1993).

186. Pausanias, *Description of Greece*, 9.24.1–2; Aristophanes, *Acharnians*, 880–895.

187. Pausanias, *Description of Greece*, 9.5.1.

188. Aeschylus, *Eumenides*, 1037.

189. *Ibid.*, 321.

190. Sophocles, *Oedipus Tyrannus*, 1034–1036. Compare 718: '[Laius] joined together the sockets of his feet.'

191. Sophocles, *Oedipus in Colonus.*

192. Lois Bragg, Oedipus Borealis: *The Aberrant Body in Old Icelandic Myth and Saga* (Cranbury, NJ: Associated University Presses, 2004), 46 *et seq.*

193. Karl (Károly) Kerényi, *Heroes of the Greeks* (London: Thames and Hudson, 1978, translation of *Die Heroen-Geschichten*, 1958), *sc.* Oedipus.

194. Sandro Ferenczi and Otto Rank, *The Development of Psychoanalysis* (Whitefish, MT: Kessinger Publishing, 2006, reprint of 1925).

195. Boston Museum of Fine Arts, inv. no. 01.8036, reputedly from Capri. Ruck and Staples, *World of Classical Myth*, 250. David Walsh, *Distorted Ideals in Greek Vase-Painting: The World of Mythological Burlesque* (Cambridge, UK: Cambridge University Press, 2009), plate 83.

196. Pausanias, *Description of Greece*, 9.26.2–4.

197. Corinthian *kylix*, Sam Wide Group, *c.* 375–350, Oxford, Ashmolean Museum. Walsh, *Distorted Ideals*, plate 108.

198. Pausanias, *Description of Greece*, 2.3.10.

199. Lycophron, *Alexandra*, 1465. Sphinx in the Boeotian dialect is Phinx.

200. Boeotian black-figure cup, *c.* 450–400 BCE, Oxford, Ashmolean Museum, inv. no. 1966.1006. Walsh, *Distorted Ideals*, 81.72a–b.

201. Hesiod, *Theogony,* 326; Apollodorus, 3.5.8; scholiast on Euripides, *Phoenissae*, 46.

202. Pausanias, *Description of Greece,* 2.3.10.

203. Virgil, *Aeneid,* 3.96: *antiquam exquirite matrem,* 'seek out your ancient mother.'

204. Servius, *Ad Aeneidem,* 3.167, 7.207, 10.719.

205. Carl A.P. Ruck, Blaise Daniel Staples, José Alfredo González Celdrán, and Mark Alwin Hoffman, *The Hidden World: Survival of Pagan Shamanic Themes in European Fairytales* (Durham, NC: Carolina Academic Press, 2006), 256–268.

206. Nicholas Hammond and Howard Scullard, *Dizionario di antichità classiche* (Milan: Edizioni San Pacio, 1995), 1836.

207. M.R. Gale, "The Shield of Turnus (*Aeneid* 7.783–92)": 176–196, in *Greece and Rome,* second series, vol. 44, no. 2 (Oct., 1997).

208. Virgil, *Aeneid,* 7. 367–372. Compare Dionysius of Halicarnassus, *Roman Antiquities,* 1.61.

209. Virgil, *Aeneid,* 7.346–351.

210. Plutarch, *Life of Alexander,* 2.6.

211. Clement of Alexandria, *Protrepticus* (or *Exhortation to the Heathen*), 2.8.

212. Large (height 34.2 cm.) faience 'snake Goddess' statuette from the underground treasure repository of the central shrine, Knossos, with snakes coiled around her arms, shoulders, and hips, forming a knot in front, characteristic of the belt worn by the Gorgon Medusa. Her right hand holds a snake's head; a second snake appears over her turban. Herakleion Museum, Crete.

213. Now in Vienna. Compare Livy, 39.8–19.

214. E.H. Warmington, *Remains of Old Latin* (Cambridge, MA: Harvard University Press, 1940, 1953, Loeb Library), vol. 4, Archaic Inscriptions, no. 26 (pages 254–259).

215. Ruck *et al.*, *Mushrooms, Myth, and Mithras,* 101–118.

216. Virgil, *Aeneid,* 9.99–147.

217. *Ibid.*, 4.69–73.

218. Virgil, *Aeneid*, 9.59–64, 9.563–564, 9.565–566, 9.730, 9.792–796, 10.454–456, 12.4–9. Viktor Pöschl, *The Art of Vergil: Image and Symbol in the Aeneid* (Ann Arbor, MI: University of Michigan Press, 1962, translated by G. Seligson), 98–99.

219. Dionysius of Halicarnassus calls her Amita ('paternal aunt'), which is taken as a misprint. Her intended son-in-law Turnus, however, is her nephew. She is sometimes called Palanto.

220. Virgil, *Aeneid*, 7.10–24.

Chapter 11

The Genesis of a Mushroom/ Venus Religion in Mesoamerica

Carl de Borhegyi
with Suzanne de Borhegyi-Forrest, PhD

Carl de Borghegyi is the author of the Internet research site *Breaking the Mushroom Code: Mushroom Religion Before Columbus* at www.mushroomstone.com. Carl is a self-taught art historian. He was first introduced to Mesoamerican art and archaeology as a child by his archaeologist parents, Stephan and Suzanne de Borhegyi. The effect of these early experiences were everlasting. Although Carl opted for a major in physical education at the University of Wisconsin, he read extensively in Mesoamerican archaeology, took classes at Hamline University, and, as a board member of the Maya Society of Minnesota, worked on programs and attended workshops by visiting scholars. His introduction to the online research site FAMSI (*Foundation for the Advancement of Mesoamerican Studies, Inc*) led him to the vast Justin Kerr database of photographs of Mesoamerican codices, ceramic figurines, wall and cave paintings, and Maya vase paintings. He began his studies of Maya ceremonial iconography in 1989.

Suzanne de Borhegyi-Forrest graduated from Ohio State University with a degree in Biological Sciences and began graduate studies in physical anthropology at the University of Arizona in 1948. There she met and later married Stephan de Borhegyi, a postdoctoral student of archaeology. Suzanne worked closely with Steve, assisting in all phases of his research as well as editing his publications. After her husband's death in 1969 she completed a Master's degree in History at the University of Wisconsin-Milwaukee, and in 1974 she assumed the directorship of the Albuquerque Museum of Art and History. In 1981 she began doctoral studies at the University of Wyoming, and she received her PhD in 1987. Her dissertation, published in 1989 by the University of New Mexico Press, is entitled *The Preservation of the Village: New Mexico's Hispanics and the New Deal.* She has worked as an independent scholar and authored books and articles on Maya archaeology, Southwestern U.S. history, and museums.

Introduction

More than a half century ago, the late Mesoamerican archaeologist Stephan F. de Borhegyi (better known by contemporaries as Borhegyi) published the first of several articles in which he proposed the existence of a Mesoamerican mushroom cult in the Guatemalan highlands as early as 1000 BCE This cult, which was associated from its beginnings with ritual human decapitation, a trophy head cult, warfare, and the Mesoamerican ballgame, appears to have had its origins along the Pacific coastal piedmont.

He developed this proposition after finding a significant number of small, mushroom-shaped sculptures in the collections of the Guatemala National Museum and in numerous private collections in and around Guatemala City. While the majority of these small stone sculptures were of indeterminate provenance, a sufficient number had been found during the course of archaeological investigations as to permit him to determine approximate dates and to catalog them stylistically. These small sculptures had long been labeled "mushroom stones" (Figure 1).

The late ethnomycologist, R. Gordon Wasson, published Borhegyi's first article on the subject in his monumental work *Mushrooms, Russia, and History* (Wasson and Wasson 1957). From the time of their initial meeting in Guatemala in 1952 until Borhegyi's untimely accidental death in 1969, the two scientists worked in close cooperation and shared a voluminous correspondence. As the result of their collaborative efforts, as well as Wasson's extensive research into mushroom symbolism in Siberia and Southeast Asia, Wasson postulated the existence of a belief system, shared by both continents, that was so ancient that its most basic elements may have been carried to the New World with the first human settlers. The origin of this Pan American belief system, he believed, was early man's discovery of the mind-altering effects of various hallucinatory substances found in nature, among them the *Amanita muscaria* mushroom. Wasson described the experience as *entheogenic*, or "god generating."

Borhegyi's proposal of an ancient mushroom cult met with limited, highly skeptical acceptance at best, among his archaeological colleagues. Few in the Mesoamerican archaeological community seriously considered the possibility that the mushroom sculptures had an esoteric religious significance. The renowned authority of the time, Maya archaeologist J. Eric S. Thompson, scoffed at the proposition, arguing that they were more likely used as stools, though he conceded that they would not have been very comfortable! (Thompson to Borhegyi, March 26, 1953, MPM Archives) In the years that followed Borhegyi's death, the existence of entheogenic mushroom ceremonialism in ancient Mesoamerica, and specifically among the Maya, was denied or essentially dismissed as inconsequential.

I believe there are several reasons for this lamentable gap in our understanding of indigenous New World magico-religious origins. One has to be the universal human trait of selectively "seeing" primarily what is of interest to us, and what we are already disposed to believe. Another is the well-known Western bias against any mind-altering substance other than alcohol, combined with a great distaste for the widespread experimentation with psychedelic substances in the 1960s and 1970s that followed Wasson's rediscovery of mushroom ceremonialism among the Mazatec Indians of southern

Mexico. Fortunately for future researchers, cultural anthropologist Peter Furst, and a few mycologists, Guzmán, Lowy, and Schultes and Hoffman, continued to research and publish books and articles on the significance of hallucinogenic mushrooms in the development of Mesoamerican art and culture.

It was not as if Borhegyi's study was not well grounded in substantial, verifiable evidence. Besides citing his own and others' archaeological studies, Borhegyi referred frequently to writings by the chroniclers who witnessed and recorded what they saw of native mushroom ceremonies during the early years of the Spanish Conquest. Their firsthand reports tell us that the Aztecs ate mushrooms or drank a mushroom beverage in order to induce hallucinatory trances and dreams. During these dreams, they reportedly saw colored visions of jaguars, birds, snakes, and little gnomelike creatures. In 1651, the physician to the King of Spain, Dr. Francisco Hernandez, wrote a guide for missionaries in the Spanish colonies, *Historia de las Plantas de Nueva España,* in which he stated that the Indians worshipped three kinds of narcotic mushrooms. After describing a lethal species of mushroom, he wrote that another species of mushroom when eaten caused madness and uncontrolled laughter. Other mushrooms, he continued, "without inducing laughter, bring before the eyes all kinds of things, such as wars and the likeness of demons" (Wasson 1962: 36; see also Furst 1990: 9).

Franciscan friar Bernardino de Sahagun was the first to record the use of mushrooms in his *Historia General de las Cosas de Nueva España.* This multivolume compilation of priceless Mexica ethnographic information, known as the Florentine Codex, was written between 1547 and 1582. In it Sahagun wrote that the Indians gathered mushrooms in grassy fields and pastures and used them in religious ceremonies because they believed them to be the flesh of their gods (Teonanacatl). Mushroom intoxication, he wrote, gave their sorcerers the power to seemingly change themselves into animals, as well as to have powerful visions during which they heard voices they believed to be from God. It was through sacred mushroom rituals that their priests summoned the deities of creation to manifest themselves in the Underworld, where, they believed, life regenerated from death. In another passage he wrote that:

> Toltecs were, above all thinkers for they originated the year count, the day count; they established the way in which the night, the day, would work; which sign was good, favorable; and which was evil, the day sign of wild beasts. All their discoveries formed the book for interpreting dreams.... Through sacred mushroom rituals priests summoned the deities of creation to manifest themselves in the underworld where life regenerates from death.

Sahagun also described the use of mushrooms at the coronation of the Aztec high priest Montezuma II:

> For four days there was feasting and celebration and then on the fourth day came the coronation of Montezuma II, followed by human sacrifices in numbers.... At the very first, mushrooms had been served. They ate them at the time when the shell trumpets were blown. They ate no more food; they only drank chocolate during the night, and they ate the mushrooms with honey (Sahagun 1950).

Another Spanish chronicler, Fray Toribio de Benevente, better known as Motolinía, recorded:

> They had another way of drunkenness, that made them more cruel and it was with some fungi or small mushrooms, which exist in this land as in Castilla; but those of this land are of such a kind that eaten raw and being bitter they ... eat with them with a little bees honey; and a while later they would see a thousand visions, especially serpents, and as they would be out of their senses, it would seem to them that their legs and bodies were full of worms eating them alive, and thus half rabid, they would sally forth from the house, wanting someone to kill them; and with this bestial drunkenness and travail that they were feeling, it happened sometimes that they hanged themselves, and also against others they were crueler. These mushrooms, they called

> in their language teonanacatl, which means “flesh of God” or the devil, whom they worshiped (Wasson 1962).

The Spanish clergy and Conquistadores were understandably horrified at what they interpreted as a devil-inspired misinterpretation of the Holy Eucharist. In the years that followed the Spanish Conquest, all aspects of native ceremonial life were banned, temples and idols were destroyed, and hundreds of the colorfully illustrated books, known as codices, were burned. Despite these official sanctions, however, some conscientious historians continued to describe what they had observed, albeit with a heavy dose of sixteenth-century cultural and religious bias. One of the more renowned Spanish chroniclers, Fray Diego Duran, wrote that his writings would likely go unpublished because many of his contemporaries feared that they would revive ancient customs and rites among the Indians. He added that: “They [the Indians] were quite good at secretly preserving their customs.” Duran was correct about the fate of his work. His *Histories of New Spain* (1537–1588) was hidden away in the Madrid Library, where it was rescued from obscurity only in the nineteenth century. Duran records that wild mushrooms were consumed during feasts and ceremonies involving sacrifice, the word for which, nextlaoaliztli in the Nahuatl language of the Aztecs, meant either “payment,” or the act of payment (for gifts received from the gods). Young children were taught that death by the obsidian knife was a most honorable way to die, as honorable as dying in battle or for a mother and child to die in childbirth. Those who were sacrificed by the obsidian knife were assured a place in Omeyocan, the paradise of the sun, the afterlife (Duran 1971).

While most accounts of mushroom use in the early Spanish chronicles concern the Aztecs, also known as the Mexica, there is evidence that Maya mushroom ceremonial use, associated with a mushroom stone cult, lasted well into the Colonial Era. In 1554, mushroom images were described as symbols of dynastic power in the Maya Quiche document “Title of Totonicapán” (Recinos 1953):

> The lords used these symbols of rule, which came from where the sun rises, to pierce and cut up their bodies for the blood sacrifice. There were nine mushroom stones for the Ajpop and the Ajpop Q'amja, and in each case four, three, two, and one staffs with the Quetzal's feathers and green feathers, together with garlands, the Chalchihuites precious stones, with the sagging lower jaw and the bundle of fire for the Temezcal steam bath.

Another Colonial period document, "The Annals of the Cakchiquels" (Recinos 1953: 82–83), records:

> At that time, too, they began to worship the devil. Each seven days, each 13 days, they offered him sacrifices, placing before him fresh resin, green branches, and fresh bark of the trees, and burning before him a small cat, image of the night. They took him also the mushrooms, which grow at the foot of the trees, and they drew blood from their ears.

In 1998, I began my own investigations into the subject. Curious to know just what had derailed the promising line of inquiry my father had opened, I began looking for mushroom imagery in Mesoamerican art. My task was greatly facilitated by new photographic technology, the computer, and the Internet, all of which are modern-day miracles unavailable to earlier researchers. The online research site FAMSI *(Foundation for the Advancement of Mesoamerican Studies, Inc)* provided a link to Justin Kerr's remarkable compilation and database of roll-out photographs of Maya vase paintings, murals, and codices, and Mesoamerican stone and ceramic sculptures. These photographs contained a treasure trove of visual information. It was this site, above all, that made possible a detailed study of Mesoamerican artistic imagery. This study, together with a raft of new insights into Mesoamerican iconography and Maya hieroglyphic writing by other scholars, has enabled me to expand this subject far beyond my father's pioneering efforts.

While I have presented here only a few of the many images I found relating to ancient Mesoamerican magico-religious mushroom worship, many more examples can be viewed and studied on Kerr's database, accessible through his website or through FAMSI. The encoded mushroom imagery contained therein occurs with such frequency and in such indisputably religious context, that I believe there can no longer be any doubt as to the importance of mushrooms and other hallucinogens in the development of Mesoamerican indigenous religious customs and belief.

Hidden in Plain Sight: Images of Mushroom Ceremonialism in Mesoamerican Art

> When we look at the mushroom stones we must always remember that in pre-Conquest times most art, if not all, was religious, as it once was in Europe. And we must remember that the hold on the inner life of the Mesoamerican peoples of entheogeny [meaning "god within"], notably the entheogenic mushrooms, was all-powerful, as it is to this day in remote corners of highland Mexico. Those who have not explored the role of the entheogens in the cultural past of Mesoamerica easily overlook that role or assume that it was of minor importance, solely because for us it is of no importance(Wasson, 1980:189).

The earliest examples of mushroom imagery in Mesoamerica appear in Olmec art and coincide with the beginnings of the first complex civilizations in the New World. The Olmecs have long been associated with a powerful unitary religion that we call "Olmec." This religion, which spread with great rapidity following Olmec trade routes throughout much of Mesoamerica, shared elements of its belief system with the Andean area of South America, from which it may have derived, or to which it later spread.

Coe suggested some time ago that hallucinatory substances may have figured into the earliest religious rituals based on the discovery of numerous toad bones in Olmec burials at the Formative site of San Lorenzo in Chiapas, Mexico (Coe 1994: 69, Furst 1990: 28). The presumption was that the Olmecs may have been using toad toxin, a well-known hallucinogen. However, the Olmecs also revered hallucinogenic mushrooms. Some of the earliest mushroom stones, which date to Olmec times, bear toad images carved on their base. These have been found throughout Chiapas, Mexico, the Guatemala highlands, and along the Pacific slope as far south as El Salvador (Borhegyi 1957, 1961, 1963, 1965a, 1965b). The late scholar and art historian Tatiana Proskouriakoff demonstrated that in Mayan glyphs the toad is the divine symbol of rebirth (Coe 1993: 196). Numerous images of mushrooms also appear in association with Olmec figurines; both in the Olmec heartland at the site of San Lorenzo in Veracruz, and at other Olmec-influenced sites such as Tlatilco and Tlapacoya in the Mexico highlands near modern-day Mexico City (Figures 2a, 2b, 18).

Some of the most obvious examples of mushroom veneration, and the association of mushrooms with shamanic rituals, come to us through the ancient, realistic, and very appealingly humanistic art of Western Mexico shown in Figures 3, 4, 5, 6. Figurines such as these, alone or in miniature village scenes, though well-known and sought after by collectors, were long dismissed as simply secular and "anecdotal" folk art. Only recently have scholars such as Furst (1998), Guzman (2003, 2009), and Schultes (1979) called attention to the sacred, symbolic, supernatural, and shamanic component to these ancient mortuary ceramics.

One of the reasons that mushrooms have for so long escaped identification by the anthropological community as sacred symbols is surely the fact that, for the most part, the images of mushrooms were simply not "seen" at all. Figure 7 is an example of the clever way in which the ancient artist obscured sacred mushrooms from the eyes of the uninitiated by "hiding them in plain sight." In this case this carved stone image of a bearded Quetzalcoatl has long been described as "weeping." The tears were explained by a Toltec legend in which a semi-historical Toltec king known as Quetzalcoatl Ce Acatl Topiltzin wept when he was expelled from his beloved city of Tollan (Tula). A second look at this image will reveal mushrooms encoded into the eyes. While the significance of the encoded mushrooms is not well understood, they clearly link this deity with mushroom worship.

The painted images in Mesoamerican art, and especially those on Maya cylindrical funerary vases, are especially complex and confusing to the uninitiated. In some cases the mushroom symbolism is quite obvious once you begin to "see" it. In other cases mushrooms are so cleverly encoded that they easily escape detection until pointed out. A good example is the mushroom encoded into the headdress of the scribe depicted in Figure 8.

Scholars agree that most of the images depict gods and rituals from Mesoamerican legends. We know this was a rich oral and written tradition from the tantalizingly tiny portion that has been preserved in the few pre-Hispanic codices that escaped the Spanish cultural holocaust. We have learned a bit more from the historical and religious texts recorded during the immediate post-Conquest period. However, the task of relating these legends to the rich profusion of carved and painted imagery has been very complicated. Not only did the imagery evolve over a span of four millennia, it was produced and interpreted by many different but related Mesoamerican subcultures.

These beliefs, recorded over time in different native languages, spawned a great variety of gods bearing different names in different culture areas, but with numerous identifiable similarities. Efforts by archaeologists and art historians to sort out and catalog the many overlapping names and identities have been frustrated by the fact that ordered and demarcated categories run counter to the fluidity that characterizes Native American belief systems. A multiplicity of identities is a basic feature of the Mesoamerican supernatural realm.

The great god Quetzalcoatl, among the most ancient of the Mesoamerican gods, is a good example of the synthesizing that occurred over the centuries. Best known by his Nahuatl name meaning "Quetzal-serpent," he combines the green plumage of the Quetzal bird and the scales of a serpent, while often displaying jaguar fangs as well. Early notions of Quetzalcoatl date as far back as the Preclassic Olmec culture (refer to Monument 19 at La Venta).

Depicted in his earliest form, he is a serpent ("coatl" in the Nahua language) covered with the brilliant green plumage of the Quetzal bird—to this day the national bird of Guatemala.

Images of a bearded god king associated with images of the Feathered Serpent go back to the beginnings of religious imagery in Mesoamerica. Two early Olmec paintings of a bearded, fanged deity with feline, serpentine, and bird-like features have been found in caves in the southern Mexico state of Guerrero. A revered Olmec shrine deep within Juxtlahuaca cave in Guerrero, Mexico, depicts a bearded figure in a yellow and red striped tunic. He extends his right hand to a dwarf or monkey. According to Coe (2002: 89) he holds a trident, but it could possibly be an Amanita mushroom. In Mesoamerican mythology monkeys represent the survivors (humans turned to monkeys) of the previous world age and are related to Quetzalcoatl, who was their ruler. If, on the other hand, the small black figure represents a dwarf, it is significant inasmuch as, in Mesoamerican mythology, dwarfs represent the mythical guide to the Underworld. Two other paintings in the cave depict a red Feathered Serpent with green plumes, and a red Underworld jaguar.

When depicted in human form Quetzalcoatl is a bearded man with a cone-shaped hat, who often wears a conch-shell breastplate, known as the "wind-jewel." In late pre-Conquest times he is identified with a semi-historical ruler of Tollan (Tula) known as Ce Acatl Topiltzin Quetzalcoatl. The Maya knew this god as Kukulcan.

We find Quetzalcoatl linked with the Mexican rain god Tlaloc, and his Maya counterpart, Chac, through rain, lightning, and water. He is linked with the Mexican wind god, Ehecatl, and with the Vision Serpent, and its Maya equivalent, the Manikin Scepter god, K´awil, through lightning, ceremonial blood offerings, and concepts of birth and rebirth. And he is linked with Venus, the dualistic Morning Star and Evening Star, through concepts of death and resurrection of the Sun God. Despite the complexity of these images, I believe the common denominator that unites them all is the centrality of the hallucinogenic mushroom experience, and the path that it offered for maintaining the daily resurrection of the Sun (and thus metaphorically of humankind) through mediation by the planet Venus. For the purposes of this paper, I have taken the liberty of identifying all of the various manifestations, or avatars, of this great culture-hero known best by his Toltec/Aztec name of Quetzalcoatl.

The Mushroom/Venus Connection

The mushroom-Venus religion, as I see it, was spawned by early man's reverence for the sun and rain as the source of all life, combined with the fear that the world and all mankind would perish should this cosmological order not be maintained through appropriate shamanic rituals. It is more than likely that the discovery of the mind-altering effects of various hallucinogens such as *Amanita muscaria* and psilocybin mushroom led to both the power of the shamans and to the rituals through which they assured the survival of the world. Judging from the visual imagery, mushrooms so closely associated with death and rebirth. They are also so closely associated with sacrifice and ritual decapitation that their ingestion may have been considered essential to the ritual itself, whether in real life or symbolically in the Underworld. In this sense, it is important to note that mushroom images often occur in association with period endings in the Maya calendar.

To the Maya, Venus ranked second in importance only to the Sun, with which it was closely associated. As the Evening Star, Venus appeared to follow the Sun into the Underworld when it disappeared at night. Then, as the Morning Star, it seemed to herald its rebirth. This dualistic aspect of Venus is why the planet was venerated as a God of both Life and Death, and therefore resurrection. As recorded in the colonial period document known as *The Title of the Lords of Totonicapán,* the Quiche gave thanks to the sun and moon and stars, but particularly to the Morning star, "the star that proclaims the day, the day-bringer" (Recinos 1953, 1974: 184).

Venus, instantly recognizable as the brightest star in the sky, was also noticeable for its periodic comings and goings as either a Morning Star or an Evening Star. The early shamans who charted its mysterious movements came to realize that, when viewed from the same spot on Earth from Morning Star to Morning Star, it completed a cycle every 584 days. Remarkably, five of these synodic Venus cycles equaled eight solar years precisely to the day. Special calendar priests plotted the stations of Venus over periods of 52- and 104-year cycles, and measured lunar phases, eclipses, solstices, equinoxes, and other celestial movements. They, like many other ancient peoples, regarded these movements as a divinely inspired avenue for understanding man's relation to time, space, and immortality, and used them to regulate their lives. Hundreds of years later this ancient astronomical wisdom was recorded in the remarkable Venus Almanac preserved in the Dresden Codex, one of only four remaining Maya codices.

A very early representation of the sacredness of the mushroom and its relationship to Venus worship is the petroglyph in Figure 9. This petroglyph was found carved into a rock surface at the early Classic period site (200–750 CE) of La Sabana near Acapulco, Guerrero, Mexico (Manzanilla and Talavera 2008). Itappears to bear a number of calendric symbols, including a solar disc in front of the monkey's abdomen and a possible Long Count date of 3.3.4.3.2 above the monkey's left shoulder (Manzanilla and Talavera: 58–66). In Mesoamerican iconography, the monkey is a sacred symbol associated with learning, wisdom, intelligence, and tradition. Therefore, the petroglyph is not only associated with mushroom and Venus worship, it is linked as well with the god Quetzalcoatl, the culture hero who brought these qualities as gifts to mankind. Moreover, in his guise as the Wind God, Ehecatonatiuh, Quetzalcoatl presided over the second sun until it was destroyed by great winds. The survivors of that era were turned into monkeys and Quetzalcoatl became their ruler (Miller and Taube 1993: 118). Archaeoastronomer Susan Milbrath reports (1999: 257) that an analysis of the Dresden Codex identifies the Monkey as possibly related to Venus as the Morning Star.

The monkey leaping from the mushroom may represent the first of the Nine Lords of the Night, known as G1 of theBolon Ti Ku.The monkey, as the first of these lords, is associated with the act of creation. Quetzalcoatl, as G9, the last god, presided over the ritual of time's completion. The Nine Lords of the Night were responsible for guiding the Sun, identified as the Underworld jaguar, into the Underworld to be sacrificed by decapitation and reborn as a baby jaguar. The word *K'uh* in Classic Mayan glyphs was assigned to the monkey god, and in glyphs his monkey-like profile was used to describe "holy" or "sacred," a word referring to "divinity" or "god" (Coe 2001: 109).

The Mushroom/Quetzalcoatl-Tlaloc Connection

According to their ancient mythologies, the Nahua, the Mixtec, and the Maya, all cultures which developed from the same Olmec roots, shared the belief that the mushroom ritual established direct communication between Earth and Heaven (sky) and united man with god. Numerous Nahua, Mixtec, and Maya legends establish the belief that the very essence in the world of the great god and Aztec/Toltec culture hero, Quetzalcoatl, was to establish this communication. Quetzalcoatl, who legends and codices reveal was believed to have brought mushrooms to mankind (refer Figure 23), also taught that mankind must make sacrifices and transcend this world in order to achieve immortality. To demonstrate the need for self-sacrifice, one version has him immolate himself in a divine fire. As told in the *Popol Vuh*, the sacred book of the ancient Quiche Maya, the sun-god of the Maya, Kinich Ajaw, and his Aztec equivalent, Huitzilopochtli, would suffer death in the Underworld if not nourished with the blood of human hearts.

There is also much evidence in Mesoamerican mythology that links the many avatars of Quetzalcoatl, Jaguar-Bird-Serpent, to the duality of the planet Venus. The Spanish chronicler Motolinía describes a star he calls Lucifer. He writes: "[T]he Indians adored this star more than any other save the sun, and performed more ritual sacrifices for it than for any other creature, celestial or terrestrial.... The final reason why their calendar was based on this star, which they greatly revered and honored with sacrifices, was because these misguided people believed that when one of their principal gods, called Topiltzin or Quetzalcoatl, died and left this world, he was metamorphosed into that radiant star" (La Faye 1987). That star was the planet Venus.

In Aztec mythology, Quetzalcoatl's twin brother, Xolotl, representing the Evening Star, guides the Sun on its nightly journey into and through the Underworld. Resurrected in the morning by the Morning Star, Quetzalcoatl's avatar, the harpy eagle, carries the newly reborn Sun back into the heavens. Among the Quiche Maya, Venus in its form as the Morning Star was called *iqok'ij,* meaningthe "sunbringer" or "carrier of the sun or day" (Tedlock 1993: 236).

Caves have always figured prominently in Mesoamerican mythology because of their significance as portals to the Underworld. Because mushrooms are often found growing in damp caves there is evidence of a close association of mushrooms and caves from earliest times. Archaeologists Brent Woodfil and Jon Spenard found ceramic mushroom-shaped pots in the Candelaria cave system in the San Francisco Hills near the lowland Maya site of Cancuén, Petén, Guatemala (Spenard 2006). According to Spenard, the cave was named Ocox, meaning "mushroom" in Q'eqchi Mayan, because of the large quantity of mushrooms growing from the floor of the rock shelter (personal communication 2011).

Mushrooms are also linked with Quetzalcoatl's alter ego, Tlaloc, through rain and lightning. The late ethnomycologist Bernard Lowy found convincing evidence of a linkage between the *Amanita muscaria* mushroom and lightning in the languages and folklore of the modern-day Maya of southern Mexico and Guatemala (1974: 188–191).

In Figure 10, the artist has encoded a mushroom into the forehead of K'awil at the base of his projecting trademark axe/smoking tube. According to Freidel, "the axe through the forehead signaled … a state of transformation embodied by the power of lightning" (1993: 194, 199). The Maya believed that mushrooms sprouted where lightning had touched the ground, so the one-leg may possibly refer to the mushroom's stem or stipe, as well as to a bolt of lightning. For this reason both K'awil and his one-legged Mexican counterpart

Tezcatlipoca likely represent the divine mushroom. Here, at last, may be the reason the ancient Maya carved stones to resemble mushrooms. They may have carved the mushroom stones in order to worship K'awil as a one-legged god of divine transformation. These effigies were then venerated with the blood of humans and animals.

Although images of the *Amanita muscaria* mushroom predominate in Preclassic period art, the psilocybin mushroom seems to have become widely used in the later Postclassic period. The Toltec / Maya vessel in Figure 11 depicts a diving god. The Harpy Eagle headdress links this deity to Quetzalcoatl as the Morning Star and the god of Underworld resurrection. I would argue strongly that the objects in the hands of the diving Quetzalcoatl (Kukulcan in Yucatec Mayan), are the severed caps of psilocybin mushrooms and not, as other scholars have suggested, balls of incense. The removal of the head of the mushroom or mushroom cap is a symbolic reference to ritual decapitation in the Underworld. The legend that Quetzalcoatl opposed human sacrifice may well be a post-Conquest interpretation propagated by Spanish missionaries. In actuality he was the god of self-sacrifice and, according to Aztec legends, immolated himself as a sacrificial example to mankind. Wasson writes that the stems of sacred mushrooms were removed and the mushroom caps consumed ritually in pairs prior to self-sacrifice. Interestingly, the stem of the psilocybin mushroom turns blue when the mushroom is picked or bruised, an observation that may explain the use of blue as the color of sacrifice. That characteristic blue color is, in fact, the best and safest way to identify a *psilocybin* mushroom (Guzman 2009: 261).

The Mushroom and the Were-Jaguar

Olmec cultural remains are easily recognized through the powerful art style featuring adult and baby "were-jaguars," a style so pervasive that archaeologist Matthew Stirling in 1955 named the Olmec the "people of the jaguar." He speculated that the Olmecs believed that at some time in their mythical past a jaguar had copulated with, and impregnated, a human female.

Much of the mushroom imagery I discovered was associated with an artistic concept I refer to as jaguar transformation. Aztec legends relate that the Sun, as a jaguar, descends each night into the Underworld to battle the forces of death in order to be resurrected and returned to the sky by the Morning Star in its form as the Harpy Eagle. Under the influence of the hallucinogen, the "be-mushroomed" emulates, metaphorically, the nightly death of the Sun God and his transformation into the Underworld Jaguar. Individuals shown as undergoing this transformation in the Underworld are depicted with such jaguar features as spots, fangs, claws, a tail, and/or the snarling mouth commonly found in Olmec art. This esoteric association of mushrooms and jaguar transformation was earlier noted by Furst (1976: 78, 80).

I believe the mask in Figure 12 symbolizes the soul's journey into the Underworld, where it will undergo ritual decapitation, jaguar transformation, and spiritual resurrection. Mexican art historian Miguel Covarrubias demonstrated that later images of Quetzalcoatl, feathered serpents, and rain gods like the Mexican god Tlaloc and the Maya god Chac were all derived from the Olmec were-jaguar associated with sacrifice and the Underworld (Miller and Taube 1993).

The Mushroom and the Ritual of Sacrifice

There are numerous historical reports as well as visual images that link mushroom consumption to the ritual of sacrifice. These include bloodletting, penis perforation, and even the improbable act of self-decapitation. Scenes of Underworld jaguar transformation not only contain mushroom imagery, but are often preceded by scenes of decapitation. With so much visual evidence suggesting that hallucinogenic mushrooms were consumed prior to ritual decapitation, it seems reasonable to propose that they were considered essential to the ritual itself, whether in real life or symbolically.

Wasson believed that the origin of ritual decapitation lay in the mushroom ritual itself. In a letter to Borhegyi he writes:

> The cap of the mushroom in Mije [or Mixe] is called kobahk, the same word for head. In Kiche and Kakchiquel it is doubtless the same, and kolom ocox is not "mushroom heads," but mushroom caps, or in scientific terminology, the pileus of the mushroom. The Mije in their mushroom cult always sever the stem or stipe [in Mije *tek* is "leg"] from the cap, and the cap alone is eaten. Great insistence is laid on this separation of cap from stem. This is in accordance with the offering of "mushroom head" in the Annals [of the Cakchiquels] and the Popol Vuh (June 7, 1954, MPM archives).

Figure 13, Maya vase K6608, depicts three Underworld jaguars. The Underworld jaguars all wear mushroom-shaped earplugs, and wear sacrificial scarves symbolic of Underworld decapitation. The scarves metaphorically bear the colors and spots of the *Amanita muscaria* mushroom.

Interestingly, the individuals about to, or in the process of, undergoing the sacrificial knife, are frequently shown as unbound, and either assume postures of submission or are depicted as active participants.

Like many other Late Classic–period carved and painted vessels, the Maya vase K1490 (Figure 14) depicts the ritual of self-decapitation. The third individual from the right has no head. He holds in his left hand the obsidian knife with which he has decapitated himself. In his right hand he holds the cloth in which he will wrap the head. The fourth individual from the right is shown holding the severed head by the hair with his right hand, and a knife in his left hand. In this scene, which is rife with mushroom imagery, the Lord of the Underworld is depicted as a white skeleton known as Skeletal God A. He holds the severed head in one hand and a serpent-bird staff in the other. His fleshless body represents death and decay, but also the transformation at death from which life is regenerated.

Not all decapitation sacrifice was done willingly, however. In a similar manner as above, Maya vase painting K638 (Figure 15) depicts a prisoner stripped of his clothing, his arms bound behind his back, being led by priests into the Underworld to undergo the ritual of Underworld decapitation. The prisoner is followed by a priest holding an axe. He is dressed in the guise of the Underworld jaguar. That the prisoner is an offering to a Venus God is indicated by Venus glyphs in the cartouche at the lower right. The artist encodes the four cardinal directions and its sacred center in the mushroom-inspired shields. The priest leading the way into the Underworld wears a robe decorated with symbolic mushrooms. The portion of his headdress painted red forms a scroll, which I have identified as a symbol of the religion.

The priest on the far right wears a red tunic with white spots symbolic of the *Amanita muscaria* mushroom. The priest directly behind the prisoner wears an Amanita-inspired hat with the same colors. The artist infers they all journey into the Underworld under the influence of *Amanita* mushrooms, including the prisoner, who will be ritually decapitated by a priest dressed as the Underworld Jaguar. Dictionaries of Maya highland languages compiled after the Spanish Conquest mention several intoxicating mushroom varieties whose names clearly indicate their ritual use. One type was called *xibalbaj okox,* "Underworld mushroom," in reference to the belief that the magic mushroom transported one to a supernatural realm known as the Underworld (Sharer 1994: 542).

Two pages from Codices that escaped the Spanish cultural holocaust depict mushrooms. The first, Figure 16a, from the Codex Tro-Cortesianus, clearly depicts mushroom glyphs. The second, Figure 16b, from the Madrid Codex, shows a scene related to mushrooms and ritual sacrifice. This codex, the longest of the Maya books, making up some fifty-six pages painted on both sides, dates from sometime in the fourteenth or fifteenth-century. It is now in the American Museum in Madrid.

The top panel of Figure 16b shows four individuals cutting themselves for ritual bloodletting and possibly self-decapitation. The panel below it depicts a ruler on a throne confronted by a black Death god, ruler of the Underworld. Lowy (1980) has definitively identified the object he holds in his right hand, though oversize, as an Amanita mushroom. The god holds a flint knife in the other hand. In the bottom panel three gods, one of them the long-nosed Maya god Chac, hold an axe in one hand and a severed head in the other. The scene, I believe, represents the Underworld Sun God prior to self-sacrifice. Since Quetzalcoatl sacrificed his own life at Teotihuacan in order to create humanity, I believe that the shamans (priests) taught that the ruler's divine resurrection after death came through their own acts of self-sacrifice in the Underworld.

Another common form of sacrifice was bloodletting. Mushroom-induced bloodletting rituals were likely performed in caves, which were revered as portals to the Underworld. In the latter ritual, blood was drawn from the penis and sprinkled upon the remains (cremated ashes or exhumed bones and most likely skulls) of deceased ancestors. The resurrection ritual was likely timed astronomically to the period of inferior conjunction, when the planet Venus appears to sink below the horizon and disappear into the "Underworld" for eight days. It then rises as the Morning Star, thereby appearing to resurrect the sun.

The Mushroom/Ballgame/Warfare Connection

The Mesoamerican ballgame was closely associated with ritual decapitation. The sacred book of the Quiche Maya, a colonial-period document known as the *Popol Vuh* (Tedlock 1985), records that the Lords of the Underworld *(Xibalba)* challenged the Hero Twins to a ball game. The Hero Twins, Hunahpu and Xbalanque, were ball-playing culture heroes who, after losing a ballgame with the Lords of the Underworld were decapitated and then resurrected into the sky as the sun and the moon (Thompson 1967: 27–28). In Mexican mythology the twins are Quetzalcoatl and his Underworld brother named Xolotl. Both represent the patron gods of the ballgame, and both deities represent the dualistic aspects of the planet Venus, as a Morning Star and Evening Star.

Sacred mushrooms such as the *Amanita muscaria* and psilocybin were likely consumed before the ritual ballgame. The effect would have been to greatly enhance the player's perception of strength and bravery and give him an illusion of invincibility. Numerous ballplayer figurines have been found at Xochipala and at such other Preclassic sites as Tlatilco and Tlapacoya in the Valley of Mexico. Not all of them were male, however, as illustrated by Figure 17.

In Mesoamerica even wars were linked to mushrooms and sacrifice. The planet Venus is perhaps best known in Mesoamerican studies through its connection with the special kind of warfare called Venus-Tlaloc warfare, or "Star Wars." Beginning in about 378 CE, these wars were timed to occur during aspects of the Venus astronomical cycle and were conducted primarily to capture prisoners from neighboring tribes for ceremonial sacrifice. Hostilities were timed to begin upon the ascent of Venus into the morning sky (Schele and Freidel 1990: 130–31, 194). Hallucinogenic mushrooms appear to be linked to "Tlaloc warfare" or "Venus star-wars" as illustrated by Figure 18. The gold Aztec figurine depicts a warrior wearing a mushroom-inspired nose plug. Note that the warrior holds a shield depicting the "quincunx," a Mesoamerican Venus symbol identifying the four cardinal directions of the universe and its cosmic center, the sacred portal into the spirit world.

It is likely that warriors consumed mushrooms before going into battle because, as for ballplayers, it induced a feeling of invincibility and gave them super strength. Spanish chronicler Fray Sahagun, who was the first to report mushroom rituals among the Aztecs, also suggested that the Chichimecs and Toltecs consumed the hallucinogen peyote before battle for the same reason (Furst 1972: 12).

We know from the Spanish chronicles quoted earlier in this article that mushrooms were eaten with honey. They were also likely crushed or powdered and consumed in a liquid mixed with honey, or by means of an enema device. A mushroom infusion administered by means of an enema would have a much quicker and more powerful effect on the body than one ingested orally.

The ritual use of intoxicating enemas for spiritual transformation has been described in the earliest Spanish accounts of native customs. This ritual use of enemas, although poorly understood, is commonly represented in Maya vase paintings.

Mushroom consumption by means of such a device would avoid problems with nausea and vomiting and quickly bring the individual receiving it to the altered state of consciousness required for self-sacrifice. In Figure 19, the priest holds a small vase containing the mushroom mixture, which he has poured from a larger jar marked with a twisted X-icon symbolizing the portal to the Underworld. This X-icon, like the sacred ball court in the Underworld, identifies the holy place of rebirth and deified resurrection. Through this portal, identified with the planet Venus, a divine bird, symbolized by eagles or vultures as avatars of the Morning Star, carries the deified dead to the heavens.

Figure 20, Scene 1, shows a priest or shaman preparing an enema for the sacred mushroom ceremony. Scene 2 depicts a large plate-size Amanita mushroom in the lap of the priest. Scene 3 depicts the priest holding the enema device. In Scene 4, on the far right, the enema device is filled with the mushroom infusion ready to be injected.

Mushrooms in the Mesoamerican Economy

The rich volcanic soils of the Guatemala Highlands and its Pacific slope are a natural habitat for a number of species of hallucinogenic mushrooms, including both the Psilocybin and *Amanita muscaria*. According to mycologist Guzmán, the psilocybin mushroom is easy to propagate. I propose that they may have been cultivated in the many large bottle-shaped pits that have been excavated in the environs of Kaminaljuyu. The fact that this species of mushroom is easily propagated suggests that it was probably grown in quantity for purposes of trade, an activity suggested by Figure 21. Judging from this Maya vase painting, merchants may have carried large bags of mushrooms on their backs (Guzmán 2010). If so, this highly prized commodity would have provided an important and very lucrative source of wealth for the rulers of the period.

A thousand years of history is recorded in the Mixtec Codices, and page 24 of the Codex Vindobonensis, shown in Figure 22, appears to sum up, according to Mixtec mythology, the entire history and significance of the Mushroom/Venus/Quetzalcoatl/Tlaloc religion. In it Quetzalcoatl, as the Wind God Ehecatl (9-Wind), who is cited as the great founder of all the royal dynasties, is the pervasive character. The Codex Vindobonensis, also known as the Codex Vienna, was produced in the Postclassic period for the priesthood and ruling elite. Page 24 of this codex relates how and why the god Quetzalcoatl, in his guise as the wind god Ehecatl, brought mushrooms to mankind.

Snouted and fanged anthropomorphic individuals with dangling eyeballs are a feature commonly associated with the god Quetzalcoatl in his form of Ehecatl the Wind God (Borhegyi 1980: 17). In the second row from the top, the last figure on the right wearing a bird mask has been identified as the Wind God, *Ehecatl*, an avatar ofQuetzalcoatl. As long ago as 1929, German archaeologist Walter Lehmann noted that many of the figures depicted in this Codex held objects resembling mushrooms in their hands. Mexican archaeologist Alfonso Caso later confirmed this identification (Wasson 1980: 214). Here Quetzalcoatl, as the Ehecatl, is shown in the act of bestowing divine mushrooms to mankind. The Figure receiving mushrooms from the Wind God Quetzalcoatl has been identified as *Pilsintecuhtli*, a manifestationof theAztec god Xochipilli, a child god who was the prince or lord of psychedelic flowers (Aguilar 1996: 80). Note that this individual not only has mushrooms in his hand, but also is shown with fangs, denoting Underworld jaguar transformation.

According to Aztec legend, *Ehecatl-Quetzalcoatl* created mankind from the bones he stole from the Underworld Death God, whose severed head Quetzalcoatl holds in his hand. Note the tears of gratitude on the individual sitting immediately opposite Quetzalcoatl. This individual, and those who sit behind Quetzalcoatl on the left, also hold sacred mushrooms and all appear to have fangs. Fangs suggest that, under the magical influence of the mushroom, they have been transformed in the Underworld into the Underworld jaguar.

In the middle of the page on the left side, Quetzalcoatl gestures to the god Tlaloc, directly in front of him, to open the portal to the Underworld. Furst, who describes this iconography, describes this scene as depicting the divine establishment of the ritual consumption of sacred mushrooms. He identifies the triangular or V-shaped cleft in the basin of water on the left, which may be a sacred ball court, as a cosmic passage. Through it, deities, people, animals, and plants pass from one cosmic plane to another (1981: 151). Here an individual plunges head-first through the opening.

On the bottom left, two figures stand beside another V-shape portal of Underworld resurrection. The figure on the left pointing to the sky also has fangs. He appears to be a human transformed at death into the Underworld Sun God, or mythical "were-jaguar." This gesture probably signifies resurrection from the Underworld. The Janus-faced deity in front of him holds what appear to be sacred psilocybin mushrooms similar in shape to the ones illustrated in Figure 11. This Janus-faced deity is, in all likelihood, the dualistic planet Venus, representing both the Morning Star and the Evening Star. Note that this deity is painted black (signifying the Underworld) and wears a double-beaked harpy eagle headdress (signifying the sun's resurrection). The five plumes in the harpy eagle's headdress refer to the five synodic cycles of Venus. The three mushrooms in his hand refer to the Mesoamerican trinity—the three hearthstones of creation, the sun, the morning star, and the evening star.

Soma in the Americas?

Reopening Old Roads of Archaeological Inquiry

No discussion of the beginnings of mushroom/Venus worship in the New World would be complete without at least a brief mention of possible Old World origins. The prevailing anthropological view of ancient New World history is that its first human inhabitants came from Asia, but having arrived and spread throughout the length and breadth of the two continents, they developed their own complex cultures totally independent of outside influence or inspiration. Beginning with Franz Boas, American anthropologists adopted an essentially isolationist point of view. The peoples of the New World, they argued, were fully capable of developing civilizations as sophisticated as any found in the Old World. Suggestions to the contrary were dismissed as, at best, lacking in hard archaeological evidence, and at worst, fanciful, racist, or demeaning. As a result, Americanists, in general, ruled out all considerations of possible trans-oceanic contact as lacking in legitimacy.

This view was strongly challenged by a number of anthropologists around the middle of the twentieth-century. Among them were Robert Heine-Geldern, an Austrian pioneer in the field of Southeast Asian studies, and Mesoamerican archaeologist Gordon Ekholm. While Heine-Geldern was fascinated by, and wrote about, the significant parallels he found in the symbolic arts of Southern Asia and Middle America, Ekholm made an investigation of possible Old World/ New World connections a major focus of his career. Ekholm proposed multiple transpacific contacts between the New World beginning as early as 3000 BCE, and both he and Heine-Geldern speculated that the Chinese, during the Chou and Han dynasties, undertook planned voyages to and from the western hemisphere as early as 700 BCE.

At the time, an abundance of convincing evidence appeared in print, supplied by Ekholm and other anthropologists as well as by scholars from different disciplines (Riley et al 1971). In addition to providing examples of probable animal, plant, and technological exchange between the continents, they argued that most American prehistorians, being landlubbers, underestimated the ability of ancient seamen to build craft capable of navigating the oceans. These well-reasoned and documented arguments notwithstanding, acceptance by American anthropologists of the possibility of significant trans-oceanic contacts between the Americas prior to 1492 CE was not forthcoming. Even with the recent awareness that early humans used boats to explore their world as early as 50,000 years ago, when they reached the shores of Australia, this denial has remained as intractably lodged in the minds of New World archaeologists as the possibility of a New World mushroom-based religion.

It is therefore particularly interesting that my study of mushroom symbolism in art has led me to a number of striking parallels between the visual imagery of Mesoamerica and that of Southeast Asia. Some of these parallels surely derive from common roots in a Paleolithic shamanic mushroom cult brought to the New World by the first comers from Asia, as suggested by Wasson, but others appear far too sophisticated and complex for such an explanation. While this is a subject that will be further explored in a later publication, I will close by presenting a few intriguing similarities that bear further investigation.

Figures 23 a and b—two female figurines with encoded mushroom imagery in their headdresses from Harappa in the Indus Valley of southwest Asia—are a case in point. Dated to the first and second millennium BCE, these figurines have been identified as Mother or Earth goddesses. The use of mushroom imagery in connection with the head in areas as far distant as Southeast Asia and Central Mexico (compare with Figure 2b) is both striking and intriguing. While one can argue that the simultaneous appearance of mushroom imagery in the early cultures of the Indus Valley and the Olmec culture of Mesoamerica could be the result of parallel outgrowths of the same Paleolithic shamanistic cult proposed by Wasson, there are other more complex similarities that suggest possible transpacific contacts between the two areas. One of these is the method of extraction of the hallucinogenic drink used in both areas. This evidence supports Wasson's identification of the revered plant, called soma in Indo-Aryan folklore, and known in Zoroastrian and later Persian mythology as haoma, as the *Amanita muscaria* mushroom. The earliest of the hallucinogenic mushrooms to be recorded visually in the art of Mesoamerica, the Amanita is also the first of various hallucinogens to have been deified in the history of human culture (Furst 1972: 201).

According to the sacred book of Hindu hymns known as the Rig Veda, a mysterious plant called soma was the source of an intoxicating drink known by the same name. While the actual identity of this sacred plant has been lost through time, both its description and the details of its preparation seem to point to the *Amanita muscaria* mushroom. The flesh of the plant was crushed, using "soma stones," and the juices were filtered through wool into large jars. In a like manner, mushroom stones, when they have been found *in situ* in the course of archaeological excavation, are often accompanied by stone-grinding tools known as *manos* and *metates* (see Figure 1). Accounts of mushroom ceremonies still in practice among the Zapotec Indians of Mexico confirm the use of these tools in the preparation of hallucinogenic mushrooms for human consumption. One must conclude that these *manos* and *metates* were used for the same purpose as the sacred stones described in the Rig Veda that were used to prepare soma.

The earliest records of the use of soma in Asia are in connection with a nomadic people living in northwestern Siberia. Possibly as early as the Paleolithic, their shamans developed an ecstatic cult based on the consumption of a hallucinogenic plant. Around 1600 BCE, when these people known today as Aryans moved down into what is known today as Afghanistan and the Indus Valley, they brought with them their religious cult and its hallucinogenic drink, along with the observance and celebration of certain celestial laws that they believed were essential to keeping the world in balance. This balance was maintained through acts of ritual sacrifice. By this time these people called themselves Aryans, and at some point in their history the simple shamanism of their Siberian homeland was expanded into a rich and complex religious tradition based on the worship and ecstatic experience achieved by consuming the plant known in Proto Indian-Iranian as "sauma." It is this religious tradition that is later recorded in the hymns in the Rig Veda.

The earliest evidence of a mushroom-based religious cult in the New World appears to date to approximately the same time period, around 1500 BCE, and the beginnings in Mesoamerica of Olmec culture. This sophisticated culture, with its distinctive art style and mythology, pyramids, and megalithic stone sculpture adorned with the images of gods and rulers, appeared quite suddenly in full blossom, first along the Pacific coast of Guatemala and Mexico, and shortly thereafter in what is now the state of Veracruz, Mexico. We know very little about the religious beliefs of the Olmecs and their contemporary neighbors, other than that they apparently revered the hallucinogenic *Amanita muscaria* mushroom, which they portrayed in small stone sculptures known as Mushroom Stones and also depicted in association with pottery figurines. It is likely that they also practiced ritual decapitation in connection with an esoteric cult of the human head associated with trophy heads, and with the Mesoamerican ballgame. As the first complex religion in Mesoamerica, the Olmec set the tone for future religious developments throughout much of the New World.

Both in the Old World and the New, human sacrifice and the ritual of decapitation was believed necessary to save mankind from calamity and the cosmos from collapse. Since the greatest gift one could offer the gods was one's own life, the purpose of human sacrifice was to preserve life rather than to destroy it. I believe strongly that this concept of life from death via decapitation was mushroom-inspired. Both Indian and Mesoamerican religious traditions believed in a three-tiered cosmos with celestial gods traveling back and forth from the Heavens to the Underworld, and both saw a triadic unity in their gods (Hindu triad, and Palenque triad) that was related to such cosmic forces as wind, rain, lightning, and fire. The early Vedics, Hindus, Buddhists, and Persian Zoroastrians, like the Mesoamericans, also believed in four great eras or world periods that ended in cataclysm prior to the present, fifth, and final world.

These are but a few of many parallels between the religious beliefs of the two areas. Rather than belabor the subject at this time, I will close with the hope that historians will be open-minded to the concept that the oceans, thousands of years ago, were highways, not barriers. It is equally important to acknowledge the capability of ancient peoples to explore their environment and disperse their intellectual baggage to its far corners.

Bibliography

Aguilar, M. 1996. *Nahualism and ethnomedicine in Mesoamerica*. In, U Mut Maya VI,

Advanced Seminar led by L. Schele, C. Jones, and T. Jones, eds., Austin, TX: University of Texas, pp. 125-132.

Borhegyi de, S. 1957b. *Mushroom Stones of Middle America. In, Mushrooms, Russia and History* by V. Wasson and R. Wasson, eds., New York: Pantheon.

Borhegyi de, S. 1961. *Miniature mushroom stones from Guatemala. American Antiquity*, Vol. 26: 498-504.

Borhegyi de, S. 1963. *Pre-Columbian pottery mushrooms from Mesoamerica. American Antiquity*, Vol. 28: 328-338.

Borhegyi de, S. 1965a. *Archaeological Synthesis of the Guatemalan Highlands*. In, G. Willey, ed., *Handbook of Middle American Indians*, Vol. 2, pp. 3-38, Austin, TX: University of Texas Press.

Borhegyi de, S. 1965b. *Some Unusual Mesoamerican Portable Stone Sculptures in the Museum für Volkerkunde*. Baessler Archiv 13 (1): 171-206, Berlin, Germany.

Borhegyi de, S. 1980. *The Pre-Columbian Ballgame: A Mesoamerican Tradition*, Milwaukee, WI: Milwaukee Public Museum Archives.

Borhegyi de, S. 1957 – 1969. Correspondence files, Milwaukee, WI: Milwaukee Public Museum Archives (hereon designated MPM Archives).

Carlson, J. 1981. *Olmec Concave Iron Ore Mirrors: the Esthetics of a Lithic* Technology and the Lord of the Mirror. In, E. Benson, ed., *The Olmec and Their Neighbors*, Cambridge, MA: Harvard University Press, pp. 117-147.

Coe, M. 2002. *Mexico*. New York: Thames & Hudson.

Coe, M. 1993. *The Maya*. New York: Thames & Hudson.

Colas, P. and Voss, A. 200. *A Game of Life and Death: the Maya Ball Game*. In, N. Grube (ed.), Maya, Divine Kings of the Rain Forest. Oxford: Konemann Verlagsgesellschaft.

Davis, R. 1981. (ed.). *Images, Miracles, and Authority in Asian Religious Traditions*, Boulder: Westview Press.

de Landa, D. 1560 (1959). *Relación de las Cosas de Yucatán*. Mexico: Porrúa.

Duran, Fray Diego de. 1971. *Book of the Gods and Rites and the Ancient Calendar*. F. Horcasitas and D. Heyden, trans, Norman, OK: University of Oklahoma Press.

Eguiluz Selvas, Pedro de, n.d., "*Origins of the Long Count*," internet article.

Ekholm, G. 1971. "*Diffusion and Archaeological Evidence*."In, C. Riley, J. Kelley, J. Pennington, and R. Rands, eds., Man Across the Sea: Problems of Pre Columbian Contacts. Austin, TX: University of Texas.

Freidel, D., Schele, L., and Parker, J. 1993. *Maya Cosmos: Three Thousand Years on the Shaman's Path*. New York: William Morrow.

Furst, P. 1972 1990. *Flesh of the Gods: The Ritual Use of Hallucinogens*, Long Grove, IL: Waveland Press.

Furst, P. 1976. *Hallucinogens and Culture*. Novato, CA: Chandler and Sharp.

Furst, P. 1981. *Jaguar Baby or Toad Mother: A New Look at an Old Problem in Olmec*

Iconography. In, E.P. Benson, ed., *The Olmec and their Neighbors*. Cambridge, MA: Harvard University Press.

Furst, P. 1998. *Shamanic Symbolism, Transformation, and Deities in West Mexican Funerary Art*. In, R. Townsend, ed., *Ancient West Mexico: Art and Archaeology of the Unknown Past*. Chicago, Il: Art Institute of Chicago, pp. 169-189.

Guzmán, G. 2003. *Fungi in the Maya Culture: Past, Present and Future. Three Millennia at the Human/Wildland Interface*, Binghamton, NY: Haworth Press, pp. 315-26.

Guzmán, G. 2009. *The Hallucinogenic Mushrooms, Diversity, Traditions, Use and Abuse with Special Reference to the Genus Psilocybe*. In, J.K. Misra and S.K. Deshmukh, eds., Fungi from Different Environments, Enfield, New Hampshire Science Publishers, pp. 256-275.

Guzmán, G. 2010. "*The Hallucinogenic Mushrooms in the World: Traditions, Taxonomy, and Distribution*," unpublished paper.

Kidder, A., Jennings, J., and Shook, E. 1946. *Excavations at Kaminaljuyu, Guatemala*, Carnegie Institution of Washington Pub. 561, Washington, DC.

LaFaye, J. 1987. *Quetzalcoatl and Guadalupe: The Formation of Mexican National Consciousness*. Chicago, Il: University of Chicago Press.

López, M. and Talavera, A. 2008. *Las Manifestaciones Gráfico Rupestres en los Sitios Arqueológicos de Acapulco*, Instituto Nacional de Antropología e Historia, México D.F.

Lowy, B. 1974. *Amanita muscaria and the thunderbolt legend in Guatemala and Mexico*. Mycologia 66: 188-190.

Lowy, B. 1980. *Ethnomycological inferences from mushroom stones, Maya codices and Tzutuhil legend*. Rev. Interamericana 10: 94-103, Puerto Rico: Interamerican University.

Milbrath, S. 2000. *Star Gods of the Maya*. Austin, TX: University of Texas Press.

Miller, M. and Taube, K. 1993. *The Gods and Symbols of Ancient Mexico and the Maya: An Illustrated Dictionary*. London: Thames & Hudson.

Proskouriakoff, T. 1950. *A Study of Classic Maya Sculpture*, Carnegie Institution of Washington, Publ.593, Cambridge, MA.

Recinos, A. and Delia Goetz, D. (trans.). 1953. *The Annals of the Cakchiquels/Title of the Lords of Totonicapán*, 3rd ed. Norman, OK: University of Oklahoma Press.

Riley, C., Kelley, J., Pennington, C., and Rands, R. (eds.). 1971. *Man Across the Sea: Problems of Pre-Columbian Contacts*. Austin, TX: University of Texas Press.

Sahagún, Bernardino de, *Florentine Codex* (1540-1585). 12 vols. Translated and edited by A. Anderson and C. Dibble, 1950, School of American Research and University of Utah, Santa Fe: NM.

Schele, L. and Freidel, D. 1990. *A Forest of Kings: The Untold Story of the Ancient Maya*. New York: William Morrow.

Schultes, R. and Hofmann, A. 1979. *Plants of the gods: origins of hallucinogenic use*. New York: McGraw-Hill.

Sharer, R. 1994. *The Ancient Maya*, 5th ed. Stanford, CA: Stanford University Press.

Spenard, J. 2006. "*The Gift in the Cave for the Gift of the World: An Economic Approach to Ancient Maya Cave Ritual in the San Francisco Hill-Caves, Cancuén Region, Guatemala.*" Masters Thesis, Florida State University, Tallahassee, FL.

Tedlock, D. (trans.). 1985. *Popol Vuh: The Mayan Book of the Dawn of Life*. New York: Touchstone Books.

Tedlock, D. 1993. *Breath on the Mirror: Mythic Voices and Visions of the Living Maya*. New York: Harper Collins.

Thompson, J. 1967. *The Rise and Fall of Maya Civilization*, 2nd ed., Norman, OK: University of Oklahoma.

Vankirk, J. and Bassett-VanKirk, P. 1996. *Remarkable Remains of the Ancient Peoples of Guatemala*. Norman, OK: University of Oklahoma.

Wasson, R. and Pavlovna, V. 1957. *Mushrooms, Russia and History*, two vols. New York: Pantheon Books.

Wasson, R. and. Pau, S. 1962. *The Hallucinogenic Mushrooms of Mexico and Psilocybin, A Bibliography*, Botanical Museum Leaflets, Harvard University, Vol. 20(2): 25-73.

Wasson, R. 1968, *Soma, Divine Mushroom of Immortality. Ethno-Myco-Sabina and her Mazatec Mushroom Velada*. New York: Harcourt-Brace Jovanovich.

Wasson, R. 1972. "*The Divine Mushroom of Immortality*," In, P. Furst, P., ed., Flesh of the Gods: The Ritual Use of Hallucinations. Long Grove: Ill: Waveland Press.

Wasson, R. 1980. *The Wondrous Mushroom: Mycolatry in Mesoamerica* New York: McGraw Hill.

Whittington, E. 2001. *The Sport of Life and Death*. London: Thames & Hudson.

Williams, R. 2009. "*Soma in Indian Religion:*" *Entheogens as Religious Sacrament*, www.rwilliams.us/archives/Etheogens.pdf.

Woodfill, B. and Spenard, J. 2001. *"Investigaciones espeleo-arqueologicas regionales en Cancuén."* *Informe Preliminar*, #3, pp.235-250, Dept. of Anthropology, Vanderbilt University of Nashville, Nashville, TN.

Chapter 12

Sacred Mushrooms and Man

Diversity and Traditions in the World, with Special Reference to *Psilocybe*

Gastón Guzmán

Gastón Guzmán was born in 1932 in Xalapa, Mexico, and is Emeritus National Research in Mexico and Emeritus Research in the Instituto de Ecologia at Xalapa, and Curator of the Fungus Collection in that Institute. This Fungus Collection was founded by him in 1980, and now it is the second most important in the country. Guzmán started to work as a botanist in 1953 in the jungles of Mexico and Central America in field explorations. Late in 1955, he was assistant to the Botany Laboratory at the Biological School of Polytechnic Institute, where he studied biology, and then Professor of Botany and Mycology during 1956–1982. He founded the Fungus Collection in that institution in 1955, now the biggest in the country. He is a biologist and earned his PhD at the same institution in 1967. He was a fellow in 1965 at the University of Michigan, under the direction of Dr. A.H. Smith, and in 1970 at the Guggenheim Foundation, as well as a visiting researcher in several mycological institutions in South America, USA, Europe and Japan, from 1970 through 1980. He has published more than 350 mycological papers, and fourteen books, all on mushrooms, among them the first book, in 1977, on the identification of mushrooms published in Mexico, and the first world monographs of the genera *Scleroderma* and *Psilocybe,* in 1970 and 1983, respectively. He collected more than 38,000 fungi in Mexico, South America, USA, Europe, Japan, and Nepal. Dr. Guzmán has described more than 250 new taxa (including two genera) of mushrooms. He is an honorary member of the Colombian Academy of Sciences at Colombia, Mycological Society of America (USA), Latin American Mycological Association, Baracaldo Mycological Society (Spain), Mexican Society of Mycology, and Mexican Association of Medical Mycology.

Introduction

Fungi and man have shared a close relationship since the beginning of civilization, especially with those species that when consumed affect the nervous system by creating impressions of brilliant colors, visions, voices, and noises. These mushrooms are the famous hallucinogens that, since rediscovered to science in the 1950s in Siberia and Mexico, acquired widespread attention in medical circles, but mainly in popular society. An article by Wasson (1957) and the books by Wasson and his wife (Wasson and Wasson 1957), and Heim and Wasson (1958), followed by papers by Heim and Wasson, and Singer and Smith (1958) laid the basis for our current knowledge of the use of sacred mushrooms in Europe, Africa, Papua New Guinea, and North, Central, and South America.

Presented here is a critical review of the importance of these mushrooms from prehistoric times to the present, along with a discussion of the decline in their traditional use in native cultures and their abuse in modern society. The *Psilocybe* species are the most important, but I will also consider other fungi such as *Amanita muscaria,* ergot, and some species of bolets, these latter from China and bolets and russulas from Papua New Guinea. Among the psilocybin I will consider *P. aztecorum, P. caerulescens, P. cubensis, P. hispanica, P. hoogshagenii, P. kumaenorum, P. mairei, P.*

mexicana, P. moseri, P. muliercula, P. semilanceata, P. subcubensis, P. yungensis, and *P. zapotecorum,* hallucinogenic species that are distributed throughout almost all the world, mainly in Mexico. I will also discuss the confusion with *Panaeolus sphinctrinus,*which was mistakenly recorded as the first narcotic mushroom in Mexico. Although *Cordyceps* and *Elaphomyces* are not included in the present contribution, *Cordyceps capitata* and *Elaphomyces muricatus* were discussed by Heim and Wasson (1958) as mushrooms involved with *Psilocybe muliercula* ceremonies in Mexico, information confirmed by Guzmán (1983). It is also considered in the knowledge of the fungi among the Maya in Guatemala. As an example of the complex diversity and confusion around the hallucinogenic fungi, Heim, Singer, and Guzmán in the 1950s and 1960s discussed as sacred mushrooms species of *Clavaria, Conocybe, Copelandia, Dictyophora, Gomphus, Lycoperdon, Psathyrella,* and *Vascellum,* mushrooms without any ethnomycological importance. I will also attempt to clarify the variation in species of *Psilocybe;* e.g. recently I found that *P. zapotecorum* has sixteen different names (Guzmán 2012). See below, in the almost end of the "teonanácatl" time, the confusion of *P. zapotecorum* with *P. hoogshagenii.* Figures 2–15 show the most important fungi treated here.

The Beginning

The use of neurotropic fungi in shamanistic practices began during the Paleolithic, as can be seen in some petroglyphs in Siberia, and in prehistoric murals in the Sahara Desert and in Spain. The Paleolithic figures in Siberia were studied by Dikov (1971) and reviewed by Samorini (2001). They were found in the Chukotka region of Northeastern Siberia. These are depicted as small humans with what appear to be mushrooms crowning (or growing on) their heads, as if these mushrooms meant some mental possession. About Dikov the mushrooms are probably *Amanita muscaria.* Other petroglyphs in that area depicted figures resembling fat mushrooms, similar to species of bolets (see below). Dikov's (1971) hypothesis that *A.*

muscaria was used in shamanic ceremonies by primitive tribes in northern and northeastern Siberia was developed from information reported by Wasson and Wasson (1957), among others.

Concerning the bolets, there is some interesting information published by Stijve (1997) and Arora (2008) about a trip that Arora made to China. Arora observed some bluing bolets being sold in the markets as food. The sellers told him that it was necessary to stir-fry the mushrooms for ten to twenty minutes before eating because, if the mushrooms were not well cooked, they produced visions and people saw "little men." Using this information, Arora interviewed other people, and a student reported that he had seen a whole regiment of little soldiers marching over the table after consuming insufficiently cooked bolets. Another case was reported by a young woman who told him that she remembered eating some bluing bolets when she was a child and seeing very clearly that walls and shapes were moving. When she stared at a dripping water faucet, each droplet falling into the sink turned into an insect and crawled away. The sensation endured for two days. These cases in China are related to the information reported by Heim (1962) and Heim and Wasson (1965), in which they describe the use of bolets by several tribes in Papua New Guinea, as I will discuss below.

Prehistoric murals discovered in the Sahara Desert in Africa, in the Tassili caves of southern Algeria (Samorini 1992, 2001), depict a line of running human figures each holding a mushroom in the right hand (figures 16–18), appearing to be depositing the mushrooms in the bottom of the cave. In another mural of that place, two shamans are depicted in a state of ecstasy. They are shown wearing masks and their entire bodies, including arms, hands, and legs, are covered with mushrooms. Guzmán (2012) has suggested that the mushrooms depicted are *Psilocybe mairei* (Figure 2), a hallucinogenic mushroom described by Maire (1928) from Algeria and later by Malençon and Bertault (1970) from Morocco. Presumably the Sahara Desert was not as arid as it is today, and there were forests of oaks and conifers at this time like those that grow today in other parts of Algeria and Morocco where *P. mairei* has been found.

A prehistoric mural related with mushrooms (Figures 19 and 20) has also been recently discovered in the Selva Pascuala Region in Cuenca Province, northeast of Spain close to the Pyrenees Mountains. Akers et al (2011), with the assistance of Guzmán, studied that mural and identified the mushrooms depicted as *Psilocybe hispanica* (Figure 3). Guzmán (2000) described this mushroom from the Pyrenees, where it is found growing on dung, and where young people consume it as a form of recreation (Fernández-Sasia 2006). The mural shows a hunting scene with several men, bulls, and deer, and a row of thirteen fruiting mushrooms. It is supposed that these mushrooms are related in a shamanic relationship with the dung of the animals. It is interesting to note that some of the mushrooms depicted are shown with their stems bifurcated at the base, which could have led to an anthropomorphic interpretation as legs. Similar anthropomorphic figures are also found in other Spanish murals, but without any depicted mushrooms.

Amanita muscaria in the Traditions

I present here the most important ethnomycological information on *Amanita muscaria* in order to discuss its important role in the ancient cultures of Eurasia and Mesoamerica. In so doing I hope to avoid duplicating or contradicting the contributions by K. Feeney and E. Klapp in this book. *Amanita muscaria* (Figure 14), which grows in pine and beech forests throughout the world, attracted human attention because of its brilliant color and form and, when ingested, it induced gigantic colored visions (macropsia) and a sensation of euphoria, even though it sometimes also produced gastrointestinal distress. We know that this mushroom was used and still is probably in use by some primitive Siberian tribes (Wasson and Wasson 1957, Schultes and Hofmann 1979). The Siberian tribesmen also drank the urine of those who had eaten the mushrooms in order to achieve the same effects. *Amanita muscaria* is a taxonomic complex of at least four varieties, the most common being the *kamtschatica, americana,* and *flavivolvata,* the latter two occurring only in America (Singer

1986). It is curious that, in addition to the neurotropic effect of this mushroom on men, it was also observed early on that it stupefied flies. It was for this reason that it acquired its common English names of "fly mushroom" and "fly agaric." Linnaeus observed this property and named this mushroom *Agaricus muscarius*.

Amanita muscaria was especially important in the Nordic countries of Europe, where it was used in the early religions (Nichols 2000). A chapel in Plaincourt, France, from the Middle Ages has a mural depicting Adam and Eve in the Garden of Eden. They are on opposite sides of a tall tree in the shape of an *A. muscaria.* A serpent coiled on the long stem of the mushroom offers them the traditional apple. Both Adam and Eve have their hands on their stomachs, as if they have abdominal pain. Here we can see the effect of the macropsia produced by this mushroom, inasmuch as Adam and Eve are of the same stature as the tree. This mural shows how this mushroom was linked with the Church (Ramsbotton 1953, Wasson and Wasson 1957, Gartz 1996, Samorini 1997, 2001). Wasson (1968) claimed that *A. muscaria* was the origin of the enigmatic soma of ancient Indo-Aryan religion. As for the chemistry of the fungus, there is still confusion concerning its chemical composition. The first substance studied was muscarine, a toxic glycoside that produces gastrointestinal distress. Then bufotenin was isolated, an indolic substance first known from the skin of the toad *Bufo*. Somewhat later it was realized that rather than bufotenin, *A. muscaria* contains ibotenic acid, another indolic substance, which produces color visions. Still later, muscimol and muscazone were isolated, both of them derivatives of ibotenic acid (Schultes and Hofmann 1973).

Amanitas and Diffusion

It is generally believed that *A. muscaria* came into use in America during the Ice Age, after people from Siberia crossed the Bering Strait into what is now Canada and the United States. The Ojibwa Indians in the Great Lakes region between Canada and the United States still consumed *A. muscaria* in the traditional way (Wasson

1979, Navet 1988). Emigrating southward, humans reached Mexico and Guatemala, where a number of carved and painted images in the ancient and Spanish Colonial art have recently been identified as representing this mushroom (de Borhegyi 2011). However, in contemporary Indian cultures as well as in their traditions, *A. muscaria* is not used as it once was. In Mexico, at the archaeological place of the Capacha Culture near Nevado de Colima, a clay figure of a little Indian was found, seated under a gigantic *A. muscaria* (Figure 21). Here we see the macropsia effect, as well as an appearance of ecstasy on the countenance of the man. He has his arms raised in front of him and a somniferous smile on his face. This piece is now in the Regional Museum in Guadalajara (Schultes and Hofmann 1979; Wasson, in Kramrisch et al, 1986; Guzmán 2012). Another Mexican example is a small stone in the shape of an *A. muscaria* button (Figures 22–23). This artifact was found at an archeological site near Pátzcuaro, Michoacán, attributed to the Purepecha Indian group. The Indians of the region, who do not eat *A. muscaria* at the present, say that it is poisonous, especially in its button stage (Figure 24). This fact may explain why this small stone carving bears a skull on one side, a possible warning of the danger of eating this fungus in its button stage.

As for the use of *A. muscaria* by the Náhuatl Culture (also named Aztec), two interesting archaeological pieces represent the relationship of this mushroom with the mind (Figures 25–26). A carved stone piece (Figure 25) shows an *A. muscaria* in each eye socket instead of an eye, and the face of the person is distorted. In Figure 26 the right side of the face of this terra-cotta head has a hat and nose in the shape of an *A. muscaria,* while the left side of the face is completely distorted. Both figures show how important this mushroom was in the Aztec culture, and its relationships with the mind.

Art and Amanitas

Lowy (1972) found interesting representations of *A. muscaria* in the Maya culture in Dresden, Galindo, and Madrid codices, and suggested that they might relate to the sacred mushroom cult among the Maya, an observation first proposed by de Borhegyi (1957). Lowy (1974) also discussed finding a Thunderbolt legend in Guatemala and Mexico (Chiapas) relating lightning and thunder with *A. muscaria.* These two natural phenomena inspired fear, respect, and reverence for the power displayed. The ancient Maya thought this phenomenon was related to a magical alliance with the mushroom. Today the Indians say that *A. muscaria* is born where thunderbolts fall, and that is the reason that mushrooms have such strong power, as discussed also by Guzmán (2003a). There is another legend on the thunderbolt and the *Psilocybe zapotecorum,* which I will discuss below. Nyberg (1992) compared the traditional use of *A. muscaria* in Siberia with the traditional use of the psilocybin among the Mesoamerican cultures. He reported that the Siberians take *Amanita muscaria* as a means of communicating with the spirits, as a treatment for disease, and to relieve dangerous situations, but not for religious reasons, while the Mesoamerican Indians take the psilocybin for religious purposes. However, the Mexican Indians use psilocybin to cure or protect from disease, or to communicate with relatives from the past, as noted by Wasson and Wasson (1957) and verified by the author in his numerous field trips.

The "Teonanácatl" Time

While the Mesoamerican Indians used *Amanita muscaria* as a sacred mushroom for many years (we do not know for how long), they eventually switched to other mushrooms and even to other plants, such as peyote (*Lophophora williamsii,* a narcotic cactus found in desert areas). In the course of this change, they discovered the hallucinogenic properties of several species of psilocybe. This change may have occurred because *Amanita muscaria* is not abundant, and it causes stomach distress. The psilocybin, on the other hand, are found in abundance, as reported by Sahagún in the sixteenth-century in his relation to the mushroom known by the Aztecs as "teonanácatl." Moreover, their ingestion does not result in gastrointestinal troubles.

There is much evidence of the pre-Hispanic use of psilocybin as sacred mushrooms, not only in Mexico, but in all Mesoamerica and even in South America. The earliest information comes from the Capacha Culture in the Nevado de Colima region of Mexico, with a piece (Figure 27) found in the same place as Figure 21 and related to *Amanita muscaria*. This piece of Figure 27 was first discussed by Furst (1974), and later commented upon by Schultes and Hofmann (1979), as well as, more recently by Guzmán (2009, 2012). Furst, Schultes, and Hofmann interpreted the figurine as a group of Indians in a mushroom ceremony, or as dancers, respectively. Regarding this mushroom, because of the thick stem, form of the cap, and robustness, Guzmán (2012) identified the species as *Psilocybe zapotecorum* (Figure 15), a common mushroom in the region. Schultes and Hofmann (1979), however, thought it could be *P. mexicana* (Figure 4). As for the Schultes and Hofmann (1979) interpretation of dancing Indians, this is erroneous because the people of the figure appear more likely to be under the neurotropic influence of the mushroom. They are portrayed with their eyeballs out of their sockets, and the mushroom is depicted as gigantic due to the macropsia effect. For this reason the persons cannot remain standing, much less dancing, and so they hold their arms around each other. The most important observation concerning this figure, according to Guzmán (2012), is that both hats and arms of the four Indians are snakes. This observation accords with the fact that snakes were of great importance in the Náhuatl and other Mexican Indian groups; they were considered sacred and represented the important god Quetzalcóatl. Moreover, both Schultes (1939) and Wasson (1980) observed representations of Quetzalcóatl in relation with some mushrooms in the Vindobonensis Codex.

The relationship of Quetzalcóatl in Figure 27 is confirmed by another Capacha piece (Figure 28), also from the Nevado de Colima region of Mexico. In this miniature assemblage, five Indians embrace in a circle surrounding another individual, and all of them also have snake hats and arms. Donitz et al (2001) reported this interesting piece, but without any comment. The two above figures (Figures 27 and 28) are very similar and differ only in that the second, instead of a mushroom, has another person in the center of the circle. This central figure probably represents Quetzalcóatl. We conclude, therefore, that the ingestion of sacred mushrooms such as psilocybe is related to the god Quetzalcóatl.

Náhuatl Culture

Sahagún (1530), in his important treatise on the Náhuatl Culture, described some devilish mushrooms that the Indians ate, which gave them terrible visions. These mushrooms were known as "teonanácatl" (teo=sacred, nanácatl=mushroom). For several centuries both the mushroom and even the word "teonanácatl" were unknown. Then, early in the twentieth-century, Saffor (1915) proposed that "teonanácatl" was the peyote that some Indians consumed as a narcotic (see above). He isolated an indolic substance from this plant, which he named mescaline, because he confused peyote with the fruits of the *Agave,* which is used to produce the Mexican alcoholic drink known as "mezcal." Meanwhile, Reko, who was studying the Indian traditions of Oaxaca, heard about some mushrooms that they ate in nocturnal ceremonies. When this news reached Schultes, who was at Harvard University, he established contact with Reko in order to learn more about these rare mushrooms. Reko and Schultes visited the village of Huautla de Jiménez, where the Indians were supposed to use these mushrooms, and obtained two packages of mushrooms from the Indians. The next day, Reko and Schultes searched for these mushrooms in the field, and placed specimens in a third package. Schultes deposited the three packages at Harvard University for study. However, only the mushroom in the package gathered by Reko and Schultes was identified, because the others were unknown (Guzmán 1983, 2012).

The mushroom identified at Harvard University was *Panaeolus campanulatus* var. *sphinctrinus.* With this information, Schultes (1939) published the first identification of Sahagun's "teonanácatl." Later, in the 1940s, Singer studied the other packages of mushrooms brought by Schultes to Harvard University. The first package he identified better as *Panaeolus sphinctrinus* (Figure 11), and one of the others as *Psilocybe cubensis* (Figures 7 and 29), an important mushroom considered sacred by the Indians. Singer presented this new and outstanding information in two small paragraphs in his great book of more than 800 pages on the taxonomy of Agaricales (Singer 1949). One paragraph concerned *Panaeolus sphinctrinus,* and the other *Psilocybe cubensis,* both species considered as narcotics among the Indians discussed by Schultes. Later Singer removed the information on *Panaeolus* in subsequent editions of his book (e.g. Singer 1986), after Guzmán informed him in a letter that no species of *Panaeolus* used in Mexico was considered sacred. Nevertheless Schultes continued to insist that Indians used *P. sphinctrinus* (Schultes and Hofmann 1979). This case is similar to the auditory *Lycoperdon* species reported by Heim et al (1966) and rejected by Guzmán (in Ott et al 1975), because those lycoperdaceous mushrooms are a mixture of *Lycoperdon, Vascellum,* and *Scleroderma,* all with auditory properties, the two former edible and the latter poisonous. However, Schultes and Hofmann (1979) presented that information as fact. Guzmán showed in several papers that *Panaeolus* and the lycoperdaceous were not used by the Indians at any time (e.g. Guzmán 1983, 2008, 2009, 2012). The problems with *Panaeolus* probably began when Reko and Schultes heard the Indians' descriptions of sacred mushrooms. One is a fungus growing on soil in grasslands (*Psilocybe mexicana,* Figure 4) while the other is a mushroom growing on dung (*P. cubensis,* Figure 29). When Reko and Schultes searched for these mushrooms in the field, they could not find any, but instead found the common *Panaeolus,* easy to find on dung and presenting smaller fructifications as *Psilocybe mexicana.* Concerning the third package of mushrooms at Harvard, Guzmán (1983) identified it as *P. caerulescens,* a common sacred mushroom among the Mazatec (Figure 5).

When Wasson and his wife were in Siberia studying why there are people who eat mushrooms and enjoy them, and others who are afraid to eat any kind of mushroom, a friend sent them a picture of a Maya mushroom stone and an article published by the Maya archaeologist de Borhegyi (Wasson and Wasson 1957, de Borhegyi 1957). They decided thereupon to look for the origin of that Maya piece, but in so doing came across the paper on "teonanácatl" by Schultes (1939). In 1953, the Wassons went to Guatemala to meet de Borhegyi and went with him to look for evidence of current use of hallucinogenic mushrooms in Guatemala. Finding none, they continued to Mexico and visited Huautla de Jiménez. During several trips to that village in 1954–1956 they came to know María Sabina, a shaman (*curandera*) who used sacred mushrooms in nocturnal ceremonies. Although the Wassons knew the hallucinogenic mushrooms, they required help from Heim for their identification. Later, after Heim and Wasson visited several other parts of Mexico in order to study these mushrooms, they found that the most important species were *Psilocybe* followed by *Stropharia cubensis* (known today as *Psilocybe cubensis*) (Figures 4–9, 13bis, 15, 29), and *Conocybe siligenoides*, and not *Panaeolus* (Wasson 1957, Heim and Wasson 1958). Singer, who had studied several different mushrooms in South America, explored Mexico in 1957 looking for hallucinogenic mushrooms. He and Smith, from the University of Michigan, published the first world taxonomic monograph on hallucinogenic mushrooms, all of them belonging to the genus *Psilocybe* (Singer and Smith 1958). They reported that there were thirteen species of hallucinogenic *Psilocybe* known at that time. However Guzman, who began his study of hallucinogenic mushrooms in 1957, first as assistant of Singer, published later a world monograph on the genus (Guzmán 1983) in which he considered around ninety species.

The Magliabechiano Codex

The Magliabechiano Codex, which Sahagún attributed to the Indians in his great work on Aztec culture, includes a color drawing of an Indian eating the "teonanácatl" (Figure 30). Among the mushrooms, which the Indian presumably gathered, are three fruiting bodies with green caps. Moreover, there is a gigantic and frightful personage standing behind the Indian, which is probably the god of sacred mushrooms, as Guzmán (2012) stated. The frightful personage clutches the Indian to take him to the mushroom world. Since the Catholic Church had forbidden the consumption of these mushrooms, because they were considered to be demonic, Sahagun probably asked the "tlacuiles" (the scribes who drew the codices) to represent the devil. The Indians, who did not know what the devil looked like, painted the mushroom god. From the form and color of fungi shown in this drawing, Guzmán (2012) believes that they belong to *Psilocybe zapotecorum,* which is common in the Tetela del Volcán, a region on the southern slope of the Popocatépetl volcano, close to the ancient Aztec capital Tenochtitlán (the site of modern-day Mexico City). Guzmán (2008) first identified the mushrooms in the Magliabechiano Codex as *P. caerulescens* (Figure 5), but later, after considering that this species is not common, and is unknown in the all surrounding area of Mexico City, identified it as *P. zapotecorum.*

It is confusing that the name "teonanácatl," which Sahagún (1530) assigned to the mushroom, is not used by any ethnic group in Mexico. Neither is it to be found in any Spanish Colonial source other than Motolinia (1541), who seems to have taken the word from Sahagún. Notwithstanding, this word has been extensively cited in the bibliography ever since hallucinogenic mushrooms were rediscovered in Mexico (e.g. Schultes 1939, Wasson and Wasson 1957, Heim and Wasson 1958, Singer and Smith 1958). Although Guzmán has looked in vain for the name "teonanácatl" among the different Mexican ethnic groups, he did find the name "teotlaquilnanácatl" in his explorations in 1959 in the State of Puebla (Guzmán 1960). This word is very similar to the one used by Sahagún, but differs from it only in the prefix "tlaquil," which means paint. Guzmán heard that name in a dialogue with some Indians after showing them some hallucinogenic mushrooms, for example, *Psilocybe caerulescens, P. cubensis,* and *P. zapotecorum.* The Indians were at first quite surprised because, at that time, it was highly unusual for a white man to have sacred mushrooms in his hands. The sacred mushrooms had been kept a secret from the white man because the Church forbade them. That is probably the reason why Sahagún was unable to report the name correctly. The Indians tried to keep the use and name of such mushrooms a secret. However, the correct word seems to be "teotlacuilnanácatl," because of its relation to "tlacuil," meaning paint or painting. As for the secrecy with which the Indians kept all knowledge of the sacred mushrooms, it is interesting to note that Sahagún did not hear the word "apipíltzin" used in the eastern area around the Popocatépetl volcano, where he was evangelizing the Indians. "Apipíltzin" is the name the Indians give to *P. aztecorum* (Figure 8), a small sacred mushroom that grows in the high pine grasslands on that mountain (Guzmán 1978, 1983).

Two other Indian codices depicting mushrooms are Codex No. 27 (Figure 31) and the Lienzo de Zacatepec No. 1 (Figure 1), in each of which is a glyph of a hill in the shape of a human head with mushrooms on or inside the head. In Codex 27, the glyph depicts a hill with two mushrooms. Caso (1963) identified it as "nanacatépetl." The glyph of the hill in the Lienzo de Zacatepec is shaped like the head of an Indian with four mushrooms above (inside of him?). Wasson (1980) believed that both codices related to the use of hallucinogenic mushrooms. Guzmán (2012) tentatively identified the mushrooms in both codices as either *P. zapotecorum* or *P. muliercula* (Figure 9), both of them common in the regions in which the codices were painted.

Another interesting legend of the sacred mushrooms was obtained by Wasson, who through an interpreter learned that the Indians related hallucinogenic mushrooms to lightning bolts. According to the Zapotec shaman (brujo) named Aristeo Matias, *P. zapotecorum*, which he called "piule," was considered sacred because lightning bolts bred mushrooms and put blood into them (Wasson, in Kramrisch et al 1986). In 1957 Guzmán, while looking for information on the "piule" (mushroom) or "corona de Cristo" (Christ crown), met with Don Aristeo, a wise man who lived alone in an isolated Indian house situated in a field some distance from the town of San Agustín Loxicha. Guzmán asked him, through an interpreter, where the mushroom "corona de Cristo" grew and how it was used in ceremonies. Guzmán learned many interesting things from Don Aristeo, among them the swampy habitat of *P. zapotecorum,* where Guzmán gathered that mushroom and sent it to Singer for study (Guzmán 1983). Singer identified this mushroom as *P. zapotecorum.* However, sometime later, Guzmán identified that collection from the muddy habitat as *P. hoogshagenii,* which the Indians also considered sacred and identified as "piule" or "corona de Cristo," but different from *P. zapotecorum* (Guzmán 1983, 2012).

Mushroom Secrets

Wasson's claim that the Indians kept the use of the hallucinogenic mushrooms as a secret is not true, as stated in Kramrisch et al (1986), and confirmed several times by Guzmán (1960, 2008, 2009, 2012). The eating of these mushrooms was, however, kept secret from the white man, who did not understand why the Indians ate the "terrible" and sacrilegious mushrooms. The Church followed the problem of the natural mycophobia of the Spanish population when it first opposed the use of these and other mushrooms and began a vigorous persecution of the Indians through the Inquisition. Just as happened in Europe in the Middle Ages (with *Psilocybe semilanceata,* Figure 10, and *Amanita muscaria,* Figure 14, see ahead), the native people in the Spanish Colony in Mexico were forced to conduct their mushroom ceremonies in secret. This is the reason why the Indians live today in the high mountains (e.g. Huautla de Jiménez), to which they escaped in the hope of being left alone by the Spaniards and the Church. Despite these intentions, the friars and missionaries established themselves in all of the Indian towns and gradually changed the Indians' reverence for their own gods and cults to today's worship of the God of the Christian religion. In this connection, it is interesting to note that in one little church in Chignahuapan, Puebla, a mushroom is still venerated. They named this church "El Señor del Honguito" (The Lord of the Mushroom). Guzmán et al (1975) studied this church and found that it was built in honor of the fungus *Ganoderma lobatum,* the cap of which has on the pore face a sketch of the crucified Christ. The hypothesis is that, because the Indians preferred to worship Christ by eating psilocybin at improvised Christian altars carved into the walls of ravines, where these mushrooms commonly grow, the religious of the church decided to find the mushroom that the Indians would eat, and that would instead persuade them to go to the church. Nevertheless, they could not gather those rare fungi, but found a woody *Ganoderma* and, after making a drawing of Christ on the pore layer of the mushroom cap, left it in the road. When the Indians found it, they declared it to be a miracle, and believed that they must go to the church to worship Christ. After that, the Indians built a special little church to the miraculous mushroom.

Other Central and South American Artifacts Related to the Cult of the Hallucinogenic Mushrooms

In the Maya Culture of Guatemala and El Salvador (both in Central America) many ancient stone artifacts have been found that are carved in the shape of mushrooms (Figures 32 and 33). These are the famous "mushroom stones" first reported by de Borhegyi (1957, 1961). Although de Borhegyi was convinced that they represented mushrooms because of their shape, there has been much debate about their meaning (Wasson and Wasson 1957). In this debate some anthropologists have related these figures with phallic symbols. In this connection some very large mushroom stones have recently been reported from Peru (Torres, C., personal communication). These stand approximately 1.5 meters in height and have a phallic form. Some of them even have an apical fissure. Recently, Trutmann (2012) published a review of the anthropological pieces from Peru, among them these "mushroom stones," in which he supposed they are mushrooms or phallic representations. However, Wasson (1980), based on some pieces found by Lowy and Heim (Figures 34 and 35), which represent individuals with heads held downward and eyes out of their sockets, stated that it is probable that these pieces depict individuals under the influence of neurotropic mushrooms, because it seems they are positioned head-first, as if they are returning to reality after sensing that they were flying. This sensation is frequent when these kinds of mushrooms are eaten. Also Guzmán (2012) relates these Maya mushroom stones with the cult and use of *Psilocybe zapotecorum,* known for its robustness and form, a species common in Guatemala as well as in Mexico.

Schultes and Bright (1979) illustrated some interesting small gold pectorals that were found originally in the Darién region of Panama and are now housed in the Gold Museum of Bogotá. These anthropomorphic figures (Figures 36, 37, and 38) are depicted with two mushrooms on the head and big round earrings or wings growing from the sides of the head or neck. Schultes and Bright (1979) and Schultes and Hofmann (1979) relate these figures to the use of sacred mushrooms and explained the depiction of wings or large round earrings as indicating that they feel as if they were flying, which is the psychotropic effect of ingesting this kind of mushroom. One of these figures is a woman (Figure 38) sitting with an expression of meditation. Guzmán (2012) suggests that, based on the form and size of the mushrooms and their tropical locality, these mushrooms could be *Psilocybe moseri,* a hallucinogenic species belonging to the group of *P. zapotecorum* that grows in tropical regions. In another case, a metal figure (Figure 39) recently found in Colombia (Torres, C., personal communication) appears to be related to the above-mentioned golden figures from Panama. It represents a woman sitting with a mushroom in each hand. The figure belongs to the Quimbaya culture, and the mushrooms also appear to be *P. moseri.* Another figure, this one found at Lake Titicaca, belongs to the Puccara Culture of Peru (Figure 40). It is an Indian with his eyes out of orbits, where a mushroom is engraved on his hat and he holds another in one of his hands. Guzmán (2012) believes this piece also relates to hallucinogenic mushrooms. Finally, Furst (1974), discussing early Jesuit missionaries, reported that the Yurimagua Indians in Peru ate a tree mushroom to get drunk. Presumably this mushroom is *Psilocybe yungensis* (Figure 13 bis), a species that grows on rotten wood in temperate forests from Bolivia to Mexico (Heim and Wasson 1958, Guzmán 1983).

Sacred Mushrooms in Europe from Greek Times to the Middle Ages

In addition to the examples cited earlier on the use of *Amanita muscaria* in Europe in the past, there is information of the use of other hallucinogenic fungi in the Middle Ages. However, the earliest use of fungi in relationship to religion began in ancient Greece, where in a city named Eleusis near Athens, a sacramental drink was used in mysterious rites (Kramrisch et al 1986), drunk from special porcelain vessels. On these vessels are depicted tassels of wheat, because of the relationship of the tassels with a hallucinogenic fungus. The nature of the drink remained a puzzle for centuries, until research conducted by Hofmann in the team of Wasson et al (1978) revealed it to be related to the indolic substance LSD (lysergic acid diethylamide), the first psychotropic substance known to science. Hofmann isolated LSD as early as 1937, although its hallucinogenic properties were not recognized until 1943. Hofmann studied the special ceremonies that took place in Eleusis, and based on his chemical and physiological research on the Eleusis drink, Wasson et al (1978) concluded that the Greeks in Eleusis used the sclerotia of the ergot, *Claviceps purpurea* (Figure 12), which is a parasite on the tassels of wheat, rye, or barley.

These sclerotia of the fungus have thirteen alkaloids, which produce contractions on the even musculature and in addition vertigo, trembling, cold perspiration, and visions. Hofmann observed that of these alkaloids, the ergonovine, which is the basis of LSD, is hallucinogenic and a water-soluble indolic substance. Hofmann experimentally drank the water solution and experienced symptoms like those from psilocybin. In this way, Wasson et al (1978) stated, therefore, that the Eleusian secret of why and how the Greeks got drunk in a psychotropic way was from ergot, which they drank dissolved in water. Moreover, Samorini and Camilla (1994) studied a Greek representation of a mushroom they found in the Louvre museum at Paris. Here Demeter and Persephone are apparently talking about a mushroom, an unknown agaric in the hand of Persephone. This mushroom is an indication of how little we know about the ethnomycology of the Greek culture. We also do know that *Claviceps purpurea,* through its sclerotia, produced great epidemics in Europe during the Middle Ages, when the flour used for baking bread became accidentally mixed with sclerotia. People intoxicated by eating the bread experienced psychedelic hallucinogenic perceptions. It is interesting to note, moreover, that in Europe and North America sclerotia were also used pharmaceutically, as a uterotonic agent in the control of postpartum hemorrhages, because of its action on the uterine musculature (more information on the uses of the ergot is in Ramsbottom 1953, Kramrisch et al 1986, García-Terrés 1994, and Samorini 2001).

As for the Roman culture, in which edible mushrooms were very important (e.g. *Amanita caesarea*), an interesting carved stone mushroom was found in an old market in Algeria (Figure 41, Harshberger 1929). The mushroom is identified as an edible variety, probably *Volvariella volvacea,* which is a common species in tropical regions. On the other hand, two Roman mosaics in Tunisia depicted mushrooms (Samorini, 1998), which appear to be large agarics identified as *Psilocybe mairei.* This hallucinogenic species, which is known only from Algeria and Morocco (see above), produces macropsia, as do all hallucinogenic species. It is probably for this reason that the mushrooms in the mosaics are so very large, and linked with their profane use.

There are several reports of the use of hallucinogenic mushrooms in Europe during the Middle Ages. All relate to the *Amanita muscaria* (Figures 14 and 24) or *Psilocybe semilanceata* (Figure 10) and are linked with either the mushroom-trees of early Christianity, or with colloquial expressions. Nevertheless, some churches contain frescoes of Genesis, depicting Adam and Eve with the tree in the Garden of Eden. The most famous mural is the one discussed here earlier from

Plaincourault in France. Samorini (1998, 2001) studied another mural in the abbey of Saint Savin, France, where a scene from the Old Testament depicts two mushroom-trees, one of them resembling a *Panaeolus,* according to Samorini, or *Psilocybe coprophila,* according to Guzmán. Whichever the case, both mushrooms are poisonous, and their representation in the mural may imply that these mushrooms are dangerous. Additionally, Samorini (2001) and Gartz (1996) discussed the bronze doors of the cathedral in Hildesheim, Germany, which depict Adam and Eve below a mushroom-tree in the form of two tall *Psilocybe semilanceata.* Close by is God shown asking Adam, "Who ate the forbidden fruit?" As if in answer, Adam points to Eve and both cover their genitals with one of their hands. In this scene the macropsia produced by *P. semilanceata* is clearly evident. In another way, Gartz (1996) and Samorini (1998) discussed certain colloquial Catalan expressions such as "estar tocado de bolet" (to be touched by the mushroom) and "bruja picuda" (witch with a point). Both seem to relate to the practice of witchcraft, with the former referring to the effect of the mushrooms, probably *Amanita muscaria,* which when eaten causes a kind of craziness, while the second is related to *Psilocybe semilanceata,* a mushroom with a cone-shaped papillate cap. Samorini (1998) also comments that in Milan, Italy, in the ninth-century, the *Amanita muscaria* was famous for its property of producing pleasure. It was said that this mushroom "makes you sing."

Hallucinogenic Mushrooms in Papua New Guinea

Traditions relating to hallucinogenic mushrooms in Papua New Guinea are poorly known, despite the fact that they were studied many years ago; for example, Ross (1936), Gitlow (1947), Wasson and Wasson (1957), Singer (1958, 1960), Reay (1960), Heim (1962, 1965, 1966), Heim and Wasson (1965), and Heim et al (1966). Nevertheless, Treu and Adamson (2006) recently presented a good review. We know that Heim (1962) and Heim et al (1966) described the hallucinogenic *Psilocybe kumaenorum* (Figure 13), but did not relate it to mushrooms in use by the local people. Other hallucinogenic species of psilocybe in Papua New Guinea, such as *P. brunneocystidiata* and *P. papuana,* have been described by Guzmán and Horak (1978), but also without ethnomycological information. As for the use of hallucinogenic mushrooms in Papua New Guinea, there are bibliographical reports of several tribes, namely the Kuma, Mogei, Papus, and Sina-Sina, which use these mushrooms in the Mount Hagen or Waghi Valley, both in the Western Highlands of that country. Among the names given to the mushrooms are "nonda," "ngam ngam," "wonda bingi," and "koobl tourroum." These mushrooms are apparently eaten in ceremonies, where everyone exhibits some madness, sorrow, or excitement. They run about crazily and occasionally individuals are even killed in a collective frenzy. They also attack members or neighboring clans with spears or other weapons.

The mushrooms reported by Heim (1962, 1965, 1966) and Singer (1958, 1960) are listed in Table 1. All belong to the genera *Boletus, Heimiella,* and *Russula,* but not to *Psilocybe.* Hofmann used chromatography to reveal indolic substances in some of the samples of bolets sent to him by Heim. Moreover, when Heim consumed *Boletus manicus* he saw brightly colored visions. Schultes and Hofmann (1979) present a review of the information published by Heim on Papua New Guinea. Similar cases of *Boletus* have been reported in China (see above). Apparently, the people of Papua New Guinea no longer use these narcotic mushrooms. The civilization has brought about deforestation of the woodlands. This in turn has caused a decline in the number of bolets and russulas, which are associated with trees through the mycorrhiza, and is changing the traditions (see the following chapter).

Table 1. Narcotic mushrooms other than the Psilocybe *that were used traditionally in Papua New Guinea and produced madness (see text).*

Boletus flammeus

B. kumaeus

B. manicus

B. nigerrimus

B. nigroviolaceous

B. reayi

Heimiella anguiformis

Russula agglutinata

R. kirinea

R. maenadum

R. nondorbingi

R. pseudomaenadum

R. wahgiensis

The Present: Loss of the Traditions

Just as the traditional use of intoxicating mushrooms has declined among the indigenous people of Papua New Guinea, so has the traditional use of hallucinogenic mushrooms declined in Mexico. In this latter case it is in large part due to the fame of these mushrooms, especially among young people, who use them for recreational purposes. Maria Sabina and other shamans (*curanderos* or *brujos*) in Mexico insisted that improper use by white people, who took the mushrooms without any ceremonial respect, caused the sacred mushrooms to lose their power. Young Indians seized the opportunity to sell sacred mushrooms to young white people, and a prosperous trade began in the 1970s. At the same time, when white youth discovered how easy it was to cultivate these hallucinogenic mushrooms at home, they established a good business, which, though primarily in the USA, Europe, and Japan, now extends to almost the whole world. In Indonesia, and in particular in Bali, restaurants commonly offer scrambled eggs mixed with such hallucinogenic mushrooms as *Psilocybe cubensis* or *Copelandia cyanescens* (Allan, personal communication, Schultes and Hofmann 1979, Gartz 1996).

It is truly unfortunate that the wide experience and knowledge of the indigenous people concerning both sacred mushrooms, and edible mushrooms in general, is being lost. Guzmán (2001), in the course of numerous field trips, became acquainted some time ago with this extensive and important knowledge. In 1953, when he first started to study mushrooms, the Musquitias Indians of Honduras showed him *Psilocybe subcubensis* as an important mushroom in their traditions. They called that mushroom "suntiama," but he did not obtain more information about the use. It is very probable that this tradition has now been lost. In 1957 Guzmán established a good friendship with Isauro Nava, an intelligent Mazatec man from the region of Huautla de Jiménez in Mexico, who spoke and wrote well in both Spanish and Mazatec. He explained many important things about mushrooms both to Singer and Guzmán. Figure 42 is an example. One might ask here, who is teaching, the Indian or the scientist? Nocturnal ceremonies in Mexico using sacred mushrooms, which were common when these mushrooms were first reported by Wasson (1957), are either now very rare, or have disappeared entirely in many of the towns. In Huautla de Jiménez, these ceremonies are now conducted for tourists and business has become more important than traditions.

Abuse of Use Without Context

Guzmán (2001, 2003b, 2009) discusses both the traditions related to sacred mushrooms, and their abuse as recreational hallucinogens. He suggests some solutions to combat their trade and recreational use, and warns the public of the dangers of eating these mushrooms without following the wise recommendations of the Indians. Their precautions are very simple. First, the mushrooms should be eaten only at night in order to avoid noises and distractions, in order to concentrate only on the visions, voices, and noises that are the effect of these mushrooms. An experienced person should be present when they are eaten to assure that they are taken properly; never eat these mushrooms alone. However, unnecessary people should be avoided or must remain silent. Alcoholic drinks should be avoided before, during, or after their ingestion, together with any food, medicine, coffee, or smoking. Finally, the person should rest and not attempt to work during the following five days, because the mind needs that amount of time to return to its normal state. With these simple rules, we can understand how shamans such as Maria Sabina and Aristeo Matias lived many years without any mental problems, in spite of their frequent use of the mushrooms.

Corollary

It is hoped that this contribution has revealed something of the complex world of sacred hallucinogenic mushrooms, among which *Amanita muscaria,* many species ofpsilocybe, and some bolets and russulas, among others, are the most important, even though their traditional use is being lost, along with the knowledge of these mushrooms and their proper use, as is the case of the ergot in Greece. It is interesting to observe that in spite of the worldwide distribution of hallucinogenic mushrooms (Guzmán et al 1998), only some tribes from Siberia and Indians in Canada, the USA, and Mexico continue to use these mushrooms in their religious traditions.

The loss of native traditions began with the spread of European civilization throughout the world. The colonization of new lands brought change to the native cultures by introducing new customs and forms of life. Much of the original vegetation was destroyed by the introduction of plantations for agriculture (e.g. banana, citrus, sugar cane) or for cattle. The introduction of new plants, such as *Araucaria, Casuarina, Eucalyptus,* and *Grevillea* trees, changed not only the lifestyle of the natives, but also changed the habitat of the mushrooms, as discussed by Buyck (2008) in Madagascar, and Treu and Adamson (2006) in Papua New Guinea, and observed by the author in Mexico and Central and South America. On the large tropical island of Madagascar change has been so drastic that, incredibly, despite the numerous mycological explorations made in the past and the studies by Hennings, Patouillard, and Heim, no species of *Psilocybe* or other hallucinogenic mushrooms, which surely grew or grow there, has ever been recorded.

Today, unlike during the 1950s, it is difficult to find a shaman or even a wise older Indian in Mexico who knows about sacred mushrooms. Hallucinogenic mushrooms are now considered a drug in Mexico, as well as in many other countries, despite the fact that these mushrooms are not drugs. Scientific studies on them have been delayed or legally prohibited, also forbidding their remittance to specialists or the exchange of specimens. Barron et al (1964) asked an interesting question: Could not their constructive potential outweigh their admitted hazards?

We have no clear information about the use of hallucinogenic species of psilocybe from the great continent of Africa, despite its thorough exploration in the past. We have only some confused data from Nairobi and Kenya by Cullinan et al (1945), who reported some rare poisoning. The mushroom described by them agrees more or less with *P. cubensis,* although Pegler and Rayner (1969) believe it to be *P. merdaria,* a non-hallucinogenic mushroom. Guzmán (1983) believes that the *Stropharia aquamarina* from Kenya described by Pegler (1977) may be *P. subcubensis,* or *P. aquamarina,* true hallucinogenic mushrooms. However, it is important to note that Guzmán, with assistance from Nixon and Cortés-Pérez, is studying a new hallucinogenic species of *Psilocybe* from the Republic of the Congo. Nixon, who collected the mushroom, heard from a native that they talk about some old rituals on Mount Thsiaberimu (which means "mountain of the spirits"). However, the mushroom he collected and sent to Guzmán was found in grassland, and it is not familiar to the local people.

In contrast with the few cases where hallucinogenic mushrooms are still used in the traditional way, we have numerous cases of their past use, as is shown in the map in Figure 43. At present the only two ethnic groups that still use *Amanita muscaria* are in Siberia and the Ojibwa Indians of Canada and the USA. Psilocybe is used by only a few ethnic groups in Mexico. The use of some bolets and russulas in Papua New Guinea seems to have been lost. Prehistoric depictions of mushrooms are known only from Siberia, the Sahara Desert, and Spain. The former relate to *Amanita muscaria* and some bolets, and the others with psilocybe. However, in pre-Hispanic Mexico and Central and South America we have evidence of the use of *Amanita muscaria* and several species of psilocybe (Furst 1974, de Borhegyi 2011), although *Amanita muscaria* may have been used only in Mexico and Guatemala. Referring to Europe, we also have references to the use of *Claviceps purpurea,* ergot, in ancient Greece, several references to the use of *Amanita muscaria* before and during the Middle Ages, and references to psilocybin linked to warlocks in the early Christian religion, these latter identified with *Psilocybe semilanceata.*

Given the panorama above, it is obvious that we need many more studies if we wish to understand the past and present use of sacred mushrooms throughout history. We also need to be aware of numerous confusions, for example, Williams (2012), who reported new archaeological gold figures from Panama without any apparent knowledge of other similar figures from Panama described by Schultes and Bright (1979), which were erroneously reported from Colombia. An example of the contradictory nature of the present panorama is in *Champignons Magazine* (No. 56: 2007), in which a review of studies by Wasson, Heim, Hofmann, and Guzmán is presented in shocking contrast with an article with color illustrations on the use of the hallucinogenic mushrooms for recreation among the young people of France.

In summary, it is interesting to note that neurotropic or hallucinogenic mushrooms, which when eaten affect the central nervous system, have been linked from the beginnings of human existence with warlocks or religious practices. In Mexico, the Nahuátls associated these mushrooms with their great god Quetzalcóatl. After the Spanish Conquest, the Catholic Church, through the Inquisition, prohibited the use of these "devilish" mushrooms. However, it is surprising to find that Indians today eat these mushrooms to honor Christ and to "talk" with Him. Despite the fact that the effects of the mushrooms are simple biochemical reactions in the brain to the mushrooms' indolic substances, humans, worldwide, continue to believe that their effects are linked with religious significance.

Acknowledgments

The author expresses thanks to his work team, Florencia Ramírez-Guillén, Alonso Cortés-Pérez, Manuel Hernández and Juan Lara. He also acknowledges B. Akers, E. Fanti, R. Fernández-Sasia, E. Gándara, L. Guzmán-Dávalos, R. Halling, D.L. Hawksworth, T. Herrera, D. Martínez-Carrera, E. Navet, S. Nixon, J. Ott, A. Piper, J.A. Ruiz, J. Rzedowski, G. Samorini, S. Somerlin, P. Stamets, T. Stijve, C.M. Torres, and M. Ulloa, all of whom contributed to his research with mushrooms, pictures, or bibliographic references. He also thanks the curators of the Algeria Herbarium and Denver Museum. His early research was supported by R.E. Schultes, R. Singer, R. Heim, and R.G. Wasson, through information, methodologies, fungi, or bibliography. He also expresses his appreciation to Carl de Borhegyi for permission to reproduce mushroom figures, and to Suzanne de Borhegyi-Forrest, who kindly and generously assisted to improve the English in this work.

Bibliography

Akers, B., Ruiz, J., Piper, A., and Ruck, C. 2011. "A prehistoric mural in Spain depicting neurotropic *Psilocybe* mushrooms?" *Economic Botany* 65: 121–128.

Arora, D. 2008. "Notes on economic mushrooms. Xiao ren ren: the 'little people' of Yunnan." *Economic Botany* 62: 540–544.

Barron, F., Jarvik, M., and Bunnell, S. 1964. "The hallucinogenic drugs." *Scientific American* 210 (4): 29–37.

Buyck, B. 2008. "The edible mushrooms of Madagascar: an evolving enigma." *Economic Botany* 62: 509–520.

Caso, A. 1963. "Representación de hongos en los códices." *Estudios de Cultura Náhuatl* 4: 27 38.

Cullinan, E., Henry, D., and Rayner, R. 1945. "Fungus poisoning in the Nairobi district." Eastern Afric. Medic. Jour. 22: 252–255.

de Borhegyi, C. 2011. "Breaking the Mushroom Code: Mushroom Imagery in the Art of Ancient Mesoamerica." http://www.mushroomstone.com.

de Borhegyi, S. 1957. "A Typological, Chronological, and Distributional Chart of Mushroom Stones in Middle America," Appendix 1. In R. Wasson and V. Wasson, eds., *Mushrooms, Russia and History.* New York: Pantheon Books.

de Borhegyi, S. 1961. Miniature mushroom stones from Guatemala. *American Antiquity* 26: 498–504.

Dikov, N. 1971. *Rock art puzzles of ancient Chukotka: Pegtymel petroglyphs.* Muscow: Nauka.

Donitz, R., de los A. Olay, M., and Reyes, J. 2001. Museo Universitario de Arqueología de Manzanillo y Museo Universitario Alejandro Rangel Hidalgo In: Los Tesoros de Colima. *Arqueología Mexicana,* Ed. Especial 9, Mexico City.

Fernández-Sasia, R. 2006. "*Psilocybe hispanica* Guzmán, un taxón novedoso en nuestro entorno. *Revista Errotari* 3: 73–76.

Furst, P. 1974. "Hallucinogens in Precolumbian Art." In *Art and Environment in Native America* edited by M. King and I.R. Taylor. Lubbock, TX: Texas Technological University.

García-Terrés, J. 1994. "Nuestro camino a Eleusis." *Biblioteca de México* 9: 15–21.

Gartz, J. 1996. *Magic Mushrooms Around the World.* Los Angeles, CA: Lis Publications.

Gitlow, A. 1947. "Economics of the Mont Hagan Tribes, New Guinea." *Monographs American Ethnological Society,* 12.

Guzmán, G. 1960. "Nueva localidad de importancia etnomicológica de los hongos neurotrópicos mexicanos" (Necaxa, Puebla, México). *Ciencia* (Méx.) 20: 85–88.

Guzmán, G. 1978. "Variation, distribution, ethnomycological data and relationships *of Psilocybe aztecorum,* a Mexican hallucinogenic mushroom." *Mycologia* 70: 385–396.

Guzmán, G. 1983. "The genus *Psilocybe.*" *Beih. Nova Hedwigia* 74: 1–439 + 40 plates.

Guzmán, G. 2000. "New species and new records of *Psilocybe* from Spain, the USA and Mexico, and a new case of poisoning by *P. barrerae.*" *Documents Mycologiques* 29(116): 41–52.

Guzmán, G. 2001. "Hallucinogenic, medicinal, and edible mushrooms in Mexico and Guatemala: traditions, myths, and knowledge." *International Journal of Medicinal Mushrooms* 3: 399–408.

Guzmán, G. 2003a. Fungi in Maya culture: past, present, and future. In *The Lowland Maya Area. Three Millennia at the Human-Wild Land Interface* edited by S. Fedick, M. Allen, J. Jim?nez-Osornio, and A. Gomez-Pompa, New York: Food Products Press.

Guzmán, G. 2003b. "Traditional uses and abuses of hallucinogenic fungi: problems and solutions." *International Journal of Medicinal Mushrooms* 5: 57–59.

Guzmán, G. 2008. "Hallucinogenic mushrooms in Mexico: an overview." *Economic Botany* 62: 404–412.

Guzmán, G. 2009. "The hallucinogenic mushrooms: diversity, traditions, use and abuse with special reference to the genus *Psilocybe.*" In *Fungi from Different Environments* edited by J. Misra and S. Deshmukh. Enfield, England: Science Publications.

Guzmán, G. 2012. "New taxonomical and ethnomycological observations on *Psilocybesps.* from Mexico, Africa and Spain." *Acta Botánica Mexicana* 100: 81–108.

Guzmán, G. and Horak, E. 1978. "New species of *Psilocybe* from Papua New Guinea, New Caledonia and New Zealand." *Sydowia* 31: 44–54.

Guzmán, G., Allen, J., and Gartz, J. 1998. "A worldwide geographical distribution of the neurotropic fungi, an analysis and discussion." *Ann. Mus. Civici di Rovereto* 14: 189–280.

Guzmán, G., Wasson, R., and Herrera, T. 1975. "Una iglesia dedicada al culto de un hongo, 'Nuestro Señor del Honguito,' en Chignahuapan, Puebla." Bol. Soc. Mex. Mic. 9: 137–147.

Harshberger, J. 1929. "An ancient Roman toadstool carved in stone." *Mycologia* 21: 143–144.

Heim, R. 1962. "Les champignons toxiques et hallucinogènes." *Société Nouvelle Editions Boubée,* Paris.

Heim, R. 1965. "Les champignons associés à la folie des Kuma. Étude descriptive et iconographie." *Cahiers du Pacific* 7: 7–64.

Heim, R. 1966. "Le *Boletus flammeus.*" *Cahiers du Pacific* 9: 67–68.

Heim, R., R. Cailleux, R. Wasson, and P. Thévenard. 1966. "Nouvelles investigations sur les champignons hallucinogènes." *Muséum Nat. d'Hist. Naturelle,* Paris.

Heim, R. and R. Wasson. 1958. "Les champignons hallucinogènes du Mexique." *Archives du Muséum National d'Histoire Natural,* sér. 7, VI, Paris.

Heim, R. and R. Wasson. 1965. "The 'mushroom madness' of the Kuma." *Botanical Museum Leaflets,* Harvard University 21: 1–36.

Kramrisch, S., J. Ott, C. Ruck, and R. Wasson. 1986. "Persephone's quest: Entheogens and the origin of religion." *Ethnomycological Studies* 10, Verona: Yale University Press.

Lowy, B. 1972. "Mushroom symbolism in Maya Codices." *Mycologia* 64: 816–821.

Lowy, B. 1974. *Amanita muscaria* and the thunderbolt legend in Guatemala and Mexico. *Mycologia* 66: 188–191.

Maire, R. 1928. "Diagnoses des champignons inédits de l'Áfrique du Nord." Bull. Soc. Mycol. Fr. 44: 37–56.

Malençon, G. and R. Bertault. 1970. *Flora des champignons supérieurs du Maroc.* Vol. I. Centre National Recherches Scientifique et Faculté de Sciences, Rabat.

Motolinia, F. de (pseudonym for T. de Benavides). 1541. *Libro de las cosas de la Nueva España.* Mexico City. Reprinted several times, e.g. 1971, Universidad Nacional Autónomade México, Mexico City.

Navet, E. 1988. "Les Ojibway et l'Amanita tue-mouche (*Amanita muscaria*): Pour une ethnomycologie des Indiens d'Amérique du Nord." Jour. *Société des Américanistes* 74: 163–180.

Nichols, B. 2000. "The fly-agaric and early Scandinavian religion." *Eleusis* 4: 87–119.

Nyberg, H. 1992. "Religious use of hallucinogenic fungi: a comparison between Siberian and Mesoamerican cultures." *Karstenia* 32: 71–80.

Ott, J., G. Guzmán, J. Romano, and J. Díaz. 1975. "Nuevos datos sobre los supuestos licoperdáceos psicotrópicos y dos casos de intoxicación provocados por hongos del género *Scleroderma.*" *Bol. Soc. Mex. Mic.* 9: 67–76.

Pegler, D. 1977. "Preliminary agaric flora of East Africa." *Kew Bulletin.* Add. ser. VI, London.

Pegler, D. and R. Rayner. 1969. "A contribution of the agaric flora of Kenya." *Kew Bulletin* 23: 347–412.

Ramsbottom, J. 1953. *Mushrooms and Toadstools.* London: Collins.

Reay, M. 1960. "Mushroom madness in New Guinea highlands." *Oceania* 31: 137–139.

Ross, W. 1936. "Ethnomycological notes on Mt. Hagen tribes (Mandated territory of New Guinea). With special reference to the tribe called Mogei." *Anthropos* 31: 341–363.

Saffor, W. 1915. "An Aztec narcotic." *Journ. Hered.* 6: 291–311.

Sahagún, B. 1530. *Historia general de las cosas de la Nueva España.* Several volumes, Mexico City (with many reprints in Spanish and English, besides two Indian Codices, Florentino and Magliabechiano, both in Náhuatl and Spanish. Cited also as 1569–1582. Book IX reported the name "nanácatl" and XI "teonanácatl." One of the Spanish reprints is in 1955 from Ed. Alfa, at Mexico City, in three vols, where, in Vol. II, there are the words "nanácatl" and "teonanácatl."

Samorini, G. 1992. "The oldest representation of hallucinogenic mushrooms in the world (Sahara Desert, 90000–70000 BP)." *Integration* 2/3: 69–78.

Samorini, G. 1997. "The mushroom-tree of Plaincourault." *Eleusis* 8: 29–37.

Samorini, G. 1998. "The 'Mushroom-Trees' in Christian Art." *Eleusis* 1: 87–108.

Samorini, G. 2001. "Funghi allucinogeni." *Studie etnomicologici,* Telesterion ed., Dozza.

Samorini, G. and Camilla, G. 1994. "Rappresentazioni fungine nell'arte Greca." *Ann. Mus. Civici di Rovereto* 10: 307–326.

Schultes, R. 1939. Plantae Mexicanae II. "The identification of teonanácatl, a narcotic Basidiomycete of the Aztecs." *Botany Museum Leaflets,* Harvard University 7: 37–56.

Schultes, R. and Bright, A. 1979. "Ancient gold pectorals from Colombia: mushroom effigies?" *Botany Museum Leaflets,* Harvard University 27: 113–141.

Schultes, R. and Hofmann, A. 1973. "The botany and chemistry of hallucinogens." Springfield, IL: Charles C. Thomas.

Schultes, R. and Hofmann, A. 1979. *Plants of the Gods: Origins of Hallucinogenic Use.* New York: McGraw-Hill.

Singer, R. 1949. "The Agaricales (mushrooms) in modern taxonomy." *Lilloa* 22: 5–832 + 29 pls.

Singer, R. 1958. "A *Russula* provoking hysteria in New Guinea." *Mycopathologia et Mycologia Appl.* 9: 275–279.

Singer, R. 1960. "Sobre algunas especies de hongos presumiblemente psicotrópicas." *Lilloa* 30: 117–127.

Singer, R. 1986. *The Agaricales in modern taxonomy,* fourth ed. Koenigstein: Koeltz Scientific Books.

Singer, R. and Smith, A. 1958. "Mycological investigations on teonanácatl, the Mexican hallucinogenic mushroom II. A taxonomic monograph of *Psilocybe,* section *Caerulescentes.*" *Mycologia* 50: 262–303.

Stijve, T. 1997. "Hallucinogenic bolets in China?" *Eleusis* 7:33.

Treu R. and Adamson, W. 2006. "Ethnomycological notes from Papua New Guinea." *McIlvainea* 16: 3–10.

Trutmann, P. 2012. "The forgotten mushrooms of Ancient Peru." *Global Mountain Action, Fungi and Mountains Publication,* Series 1, Oreslina.

Wasson, R. 1957. "Seeking the magic mushroom." *Life,* May 13. Reprinted in June 10. Translated to Spanish in June 10 (this latter also in http://www.imaginaria.org/wasson/wasson.htm). Also published in Spanish without the color plate, in *Espacios* 14(20), 1996, pp. 21–27.

Wasson, R. 1968. *Soma: Divine Mushroom of Immortality.* New York: Harcourt Brace Jovanovich.

Wasson, R. 1979. "Traditional use in North America of *Amanita muscaria* for divinatory purposes." *Journal of Psychedelic Drugs* 11: 25–28.

Wasson, R. 1980. *The Wondrous Mushroom: Mycolatry in Mesoamerica.* New York: McGraw-Hill.

Wasson, R. and V. Wasson. 1957. *Mushrooms, Russia and History.* New York: Pantheon Books.

Wasson, R., A. Hofmann, and C. Ruck. 1978. *The Road to Eleusis. Unveiling the Secret of the Mysteries.* New York: A Helen and Kurt Wolff Book.

Williams, A. 2012. "Los Señores Dorados de Panamá (El Dorado de Panamá). Las tumbas de los antiguos jefes de Centroamérica." *National Geographic*, January Spanish issue, Mexico City.

Chapter 13

The Soma Function in Jung's Analytical Psychology

Dan Merkur

Dan Merkur, PhD, is a psychoanalyst in private practice in Toronto, Canada. He teaches at both the Toronto Institute for Contemporary Psychoanalysis and the Living Institute, a transpersonal psychotherapy school in Toronto. He earned his doctorate in comparative religion, has taught religious studies at five universities in Canada and the United States, and is currently a Visiting Scholar at the Department and Centre for the Study of Religion at the University of Toronto. His publications include a book of short fiction, twelve books of scholarship, and many articles.

Introduction

The analytical psychologist Carl G. Jung is well known as the foremost expositor of Western esotericism of the twentieth-century. Time and again, he addressed topics that had previously belonged to Western esotericism; but in place of the magical and metaphysical valences that they had traditionally possessed, he provided them with original psychological assessments of his own (Hoeller 1982:

4–50; Wehr 1992, 2002). His procedure was consistent with his claim of being a scientist and his dislike of being called a mystic (Jaffé 1992: 1–2, 27). Jung is often credited with salvaging topics such as alchemy from disrepute and neglect, by asserting their value for depth psychology (Hanegraaff 2012: 293–94). At the same time, Jung's writings functioned as exposures or exposés that introduced the general public to many topics on which occultists had previously been partly or wholly reticent.

Jung's access to Western esotericism can be determined only in part. His background in spiritualism pertained to matters in the public domain (Charet 1993) and proceeded as a psychiatrist from the standpoint of German Romantic Mesmerism (Hanegraaff 2012). There is no evidence that he was ever initiated in any esoteric society. He acknowledged that he read books of theosophy and anthroposophy and knew "very many" people, including patients, who adhered to one or the other "gnostic" organization (Jung 1973a: 203; see also Ljunggren 1994). Jung's knowledge of esotericism was nonetheless noticeably flawed. Rudolf Steiner, the leader of the German Theosophical Society who broke away to found anthroposophy in 1913, responded in a 1917 lecture to Jung's first collection of essays:

> Psychoanalysts have made us aware that the reality of the soul is to be accepted as such. They have done that. But … they are neither able nor willing to approach spiritual reality (Steiner 2001).

Anthroposophists have understood Steiner to have credited Jung with "understanding soul but not spirit" (Ahern 1984: 169).

A comparison of Freud's discussion of Logos in *The Future of an Illusion* (1927), and Jung's writings on Logos throughout his collected works, will sustain Steiner's critique. For Freud, as for the Johanine gospel, Logos was the Stoic term for the *nous* of Aristotelian psychology (Merkur 1992); for Jung, Logos instead signified the rational faculty of Aristotle. Rather than conform to the tripartite, learned psychology of spirit, soul, and body that descended through the Aristotelian and Neoplatonic traditions to influence St. Augustine of Hippo, pseudo-Dionysius the Areopagite, Ramon Lull, Paracelsus, Jacob Boehme, Franz Hartmann, Steiner, and many others, Jung adhered simplistically to the dualistic folk psychology of body and soul that Protestantism had received from St. Gregory the Great and the monastic tradition (on learned and folk medieval psychologies, see Merkur 2007: 96–114). In his *Visions* seminar, Jung taught:

> For practical uses, it is really best—though terribly shocking, I admit—to assume that everything has a double existence: a known tangible surface and at the same time an invisible, unknown existence. And you can call the unconscious and unknown side of the thing its soul, as the unconscious invisible life in us is called soul or essence or whatever term you like to use (Jung 1997: 206).

One cannot be certain that he misunderstood and did not merely disagree with views that he misrepresented. He was capable, for example, of publishing such a howler as the following: "The Christian principle which unites the opposite is the *worship of God*, in Buddhism it is the *worship of the self* (self-development)" (Jung 1921: 221). In point of fact, the Buddhist teaching of *anatta*, "no-self," explicitly opposed and contradicted the Upanishadic Hindu doctrine of *atman*, "self," that Jung appropriated for analytical psychology (Jung 1921, Coward 1985). Jung (1938c: 191) repeated the same error elsewhere. "When the Buddhists say that progressive perfection through meditation awakens memories of former incarnations, they are no doubt referring to the same psychological reality, the only difference being that they ascribe the historical factor not to the soul but to the self (*atman*)." Attributing the Hindu *atman* doctrine to Buddhists allowed Jung to generalize about "the East," and he was a sufficient dilettante (and racist) to be indifferent to the facts.

On the whole, I think it possible that Jung had very little access to aspects of Western esotericism that were not in the public domain. In *Memories, Dreams, Reflections*, Jung briefly discussed his family's coat of arms.

> The Jung family originally had a phoenix for its arms, the bird obviously being connected with "young," "youth," "rejuvenation." My grandfather changed the elements of the arms, probably out of the spirit of resistance toward his father. He was an ardent Freemason and Grand Master of the Swiss lodge. This had a good deal to do with the changes he made in the armorial bearings. I mention this point, in itself of no consequence, because it belongs in the historical nexus of my thinking and my life.
>
> In keeping with this revision of my grandfather's, my coat of arms no longer contains the original phoenix. Instead there is a cross azure in chief dexter and in base sinister a blue bunch of grapes in a field d'or; separating these is an estoile d'or in a fess azure. The symbolism of these arms is Masonic, or Rosicrucian. Just as cross and rose represent the Rosicrucian problem of opposites ("*per crucem ad rosam*"), that is, the Christian and Dionysian elements, so cross and grapes are symbols of the heavenly and the chthonic spirit. The uniting symbol is the gold star, the *aurum philosophorum.* The Rosicrucians derived from Hermetic or alchemical philosophy (Jung 1973b: 232).

This passage is typical of Jung's handling of Masonic and Rosicrucian topics throughout his writings and seminars. He tells us little or nothing about Freemasonry yet waxes eloquent about the Rosicrucian tradition within alchemy. This pattern is very much in keeping with Masonic practice, where oaths of silence pertain to Masonic topics but do not inhibit discussions of alchemy. There is no evidence that Jung was ever a Freemason (Sonu Shamdasani, personal communication, 2011). However, his grandfather and namesake Carl Gustav Jung had been a prominent Swiss physician who was elected Grand Master of the United Swiss Freemason lodges in 1850 (Bair 2003:12). We may reasonably assume that the asymmetry of Jung's discussion, silent on Masonry and eloquent on Rosicrucianism, originated with his grandfather, though Jung did not know his grandfather, who predeceased him. Jung presumably depended on his father, and perhaps other family members, for his grandfather's teachings about the family's coat of arms. What secret lore Jung knew was no more, I suggest, than was symbolized by the coat of arms. Near the end of *Memories, Dreams, Reflections,* the editor Aniella Jaffé placed Jung's remark: "I am conservative to the bone. I fill my pipe from my grandfather's tobacco jar and still keep his alpenstock, topped with a chamois horn, which he brought back from Pontresina after having been one of the first guests at that newly opened *Kurort*" (Jung 1973b: 358). I have found no esoteric lore in Jung's corpus that would be inconsistent with an interpretation of the jar and the alpenstock as allusions to the grail and the lance, respectively, of medieval Arthurian romance (on the grail as a psychedelic motif, see Merkur 2000: 111–26).

At the same time, Jung was not always fully forthcoming. It is often said that Jung was an appallingly bad writer, who was at the best of times unable to communicate his ideas easily (Storr 1973: 31-32). But there were also ideas that he only hinted at or alluded to, sometimes because he could not formulate the ideas better, but often because he chose to leave the ideas unfinished and enigmatic. In many, many cases, Jung becomes comprehensible when his scattered remarks on single topics are gathered together. The Persian alchemist Jabir ibn Hayyan, writing in the eighth or ninth-century, introduced the esoteric literary technique known as *dispersion,* dividing a topic up into small portions that are dispersed through a larger body of writings (Crosland 1962); dispersion was famously discussed and utilized in the twelfth-century in the *Guide of the Perplexed* by Rabbi Moses Maimonides (Bakan, Merkur, and Weiss, 2009). Whether by accident or design, Jung was a master of dispersion. Jung also resorted to secrecy. He wrote an introductory essay about his mental imagery technique, "The Transcendent Function," in 1916, but he allowed it to remain unpublished for over forty years. Students at the C. G. Jung Institute mimeographed it in 1957; it was first published for the general public in his *Collected Works* in 1958. Jung neglected to publish anything else about his mental imagery technique until he discussed "active imagination," as he then called it, in his Tavistock lectures, which he gave in 1935 and published the year after. Lachman (2010) noted that, "Jung discussed the ideas in seminars and lectures, but usually only with his closest students, rather like an initiate sharing the most profound mysteries with only his most devoted pupils" (2010: 116). Jung's reticence was not limited to the topic of active imagination. A careful comparison of Jung's published remarks on topics of esoteric interest with his treatment of the same topics in the posthumously published seminars that he gave to the Zürich Psychological Club will disclose that Jung reserved a great many teachings for oral instruction. The gap between the public and private presentations of analytical psychology was shared by the club members. When the foundation of the C. G. Jung Institute of Zürich was first proposed, with the prospect of opening the doors to the general public, the club members opposed it "as they were quite content to keep the dissemination of analytical psychology to themselves and for themselves only" (Bair 530–531).

Jung owed at least part of his reticence, I suggest, to his engagement in exposure. Like Freud, he wanted to speak publicly and psychologically of matters that polite society shunned. Where Freud shocked people with candid discussions of sexuality, Jung instead shocked people with explicit discussions of spirituality. Bair (2003) relates that when, in the 1930s, Jung decided to research alchemy systematically, he asked his mistress Toni Wolff to contact antiquarian booksellers to arrange for the purchase of a number of books.

> She was so aghast she would not even listen to his theories, let alone work with him. With more overt opposition than she had ever shown, she argued that to make such ideas public, let alone declare alchemy the foundation of his psychology, would marginalize him within the medical-psychological community and lead to ridicule and scorn in the world at large (Bair 2003: 399).

The upshot of Wolff's opposition to his alchemical researches was her replacement by Marie-Louise von Franz as his primary conversation partner (Bair 2003: 370). The expansion of Jung's corpus to include not only dualism (1921), Eastern religions (1929 onward), and alchemy (1935 onward), but also, in his last decade, synchronicity (1951), the image of God (1952), UFOs (1958), active imagination (1958), and conscience (1958), may easily be seen as a process of increasing candor that included, but was not limited to, increasing exposure of esotericism. What held him back, I suggest, was less a devotion to secrecy than a concern to maintain his public reputation as a responsible, levelheaded, and scientific psychologist.

In this article, I propose to explain the secret place of psychedelic drugs within Jung's analytical psychology.

Extraversion and Introversion

No one, to my knowledge, has previously remarked that Jung's concepts of introversion and extraversion were central to Jung's psychologization of Western esotericism. The original presentation of the two ideas in 1912 antedated his introduction of the typology. The ideas may be found in passing in *Wandlungen und Symbole der Libido,* the text over which he famously broke with Freud. What a year later he would call extraversion he discussed in 1912 in Freud's terminology as libido directed toward objects.

> It is ... the *incapacity to love which robs mankind of his possibilities.* This world is empty to him alone who does not understand how to direct his libido towards objects, and to render them alive and beautiful for himself, for Beauty does not indeed lie in things, but in the feeling that we give to them. That which compels us to create a substitute for ourselves is not the external lack of objects, but our incapacity to lovingly include a thing outside of ourselves (Jung 1916: 193).

In agreement with Freud that object-love is healthy and desirable, Jung discussed the inability or incapacity to love as introversion and attributed it to the resistance.

> The resistance, which opposes its unwillingness to the will, alone has the power to produce that pathogenic introversion

> which is the starting point of every psychogenic disturbance. The resistance against loving produces the inability to love (Jung 1916: 294).

Jung introduced the terms *extraversion* and *introversion* in "A Contribution to the Study of Psychological Types" (1913). Where Freud accounted for the opposition of love and resistance by postulating two "drives," which is to say, two types of psychic energy, Jung proposed that a single type of psychic energy underwent two movements, turning outward (extraversion) and turning inward (introversion).

> I propose to use the terms *extraversion* and *introversion* to describe these two opposite movements of libido.... We speak of extraversion when he gives his whole interest to the outer world, to the object, and attributes an extraordinary importance and value to it. When, on the contrary, the objective world sinks into the shadow, as it were, or undergoes a devaluation, while the individual occupies the center of his own interest and becomes in his own eyes the only person worthy of consideration, it is a case of introversion (Jung 1913: 500).

In the same publication, Jung associated his psychological types with the philosophy of Friedrich Nietzsche.

> The Apollinian state ... as Nietzsche conceives it, is a withdrawal into oneself, or introversion. Conversely the Dionysian state is the unleashing of a torrent of libido into things (Jung 1913: 507; see also Jung 1988: 143, 145, Jung 1997: 189).

Freud's English translators favor the terms *instincts* and *instinctual drives* where Freud had written *Triebe,* "drive," a term that he had taken over from Nietzsche. The mistranslation makes Freud appear more biological and less psychological than he was. It simultaneously conceals his debt to Nietzsche. In reverting directly to Nietzsche, Jung was reverting to Freud's source in order to develop an alternative to Freud's formulation of the consensually agreed psychological phenomena.

In a second article on the two psychological types, first published in 1916, Jung suggested that "monism" was "a general psychological tendency" that proceeded "from the desire to set up one function or the other as the supreme psychological principle" (1966: 288). Jung was to elaborate his clinical opinion that "the defect of one-sidedness" was the major concern of psychotherapy for the remainder of his life. The 1916 article included the statement, however, that "The introverted type knows only the principle of *thinking*, the extroverted type only that of *feeling*" (Jung 1966: 288). In a lecture that he gave at Dornach, Switzerland, in 1917, Steiner reacted against Jung's presentation. He remarked that "Jung's theory is simply a paraphrase of the banal and trite division of people into feeling and rational types without adding anything to the facts" (2001: 42). Word of Steiner's critique possibly reached Jung in Zurich through his patient and friend Emilii Medtner, a Russian Symbolist who frequently visited his closest friend, the writer Andrei Belyi, who was an Anthroposophist in residence in Steiner's community at Dornach (Ljunggren 1944). Jung nevertheless took his time conceding the point. According to Jung's pupil C. A. Meier, who participated in the study group out of which *Psychological Types* (1921) emerged, it was Hans Schmid who persuaded Jung that extraversion was not necessarily related to feeling (Shamdasani 2003: 68); and it was only in 1919, in correspondence with Sabina Spielrein, that Jung announced his intention to "revoke the original identity of extraversion and feeling, as well as that of introversion and thinking" (Bair 2003: 284–85). *Psychological Types* (1921) contained his public repudiation of his previous thinking. "In my earlier publications I identified the introvert with the thinking and the extravert with the feeling type … it became clear to me only later that introversion and extraversion are to be distinguished as general basic attitudes from the function-types" (Jung 1921: 149).

Jung's 1921 book presented a more complicated system. In addition to the two basic *attitude*-types, introversion and extraversion, "distinguished by the direction of their interest, or of the movement of libido" (1921: 330), Jung identified four subsidiary *function*-types, thinking, feeling, sensation, and intuition. Jung also took the occasion to indicate differences between Nietzsche's formulations and his own.

The state of introversion, if habitual, always entails a differentiation of the relationship to the world of ideas, while habitual extraversion involves a similar differentiation of the relation to the object. We see nothing of this differentiation in Nietzsche's two concepts. Dionysian feeling has the thoroughly archaic character of affective sensation. It is therefore not pure feeling, abstracted and differentiated from instinct and becoming a mobile element, which, in the extraverted type, is obedient to the dictates of reason and lends itself to them as their willing instrument. Similarly, Nietzsche's conception of introversion is not that pure, differentiated relation to ideas that has freed itself from the perception of inner images whether sensuously determined or creatively produced, and has become a contemplation of pure and abstract forms. The Apollinian mode is an inner perception, an intuition of the world of ideas. The parallel with dreaming clearly shows that Nietzsche thinks of this state as on the one hand merely perceptive and on the other merely eidetic (Jung 1921: 144).

Although Nietzsche's drives had contrasted thinking and emotion, Jung's attitude types did not. In Jung's system, *feeling* named the type of value-laden cognition that is involved with value judgments, ethical and aesthetic judgments, judgmentalism, and subjective opinions. It was not a term for emotion. All six of Jung's categories were cognitive; none pertained to emotions or affects.

Without acknowledging his debts to Freud's (1914) concepts of object-libido and narcissistic-libido, Jung took pains to conform his attitude types to Freud's findings.

> The attitude-types … are distinguished by their attitude to the object. The introvert's attitude is an abstracting one; at bottom he is always intent on withdrawing libido from the object, as though he had to prevent the object from gaining power over him. The extravert, on the contrary, has a positive relation to the object. He affirms its importance to such an extent that his subjective attitude is constantly related to and oriented by the object (Jung 1921: 330).

Jung admitted that his typology was arbitrary. "As a principal of classification, one can choose any likeness or unlikeness if only it is general enough, be it anatomical, physiological, or psychological" (Jung 1964: 217). What was important was not his concern with attitude types but his attention to "the problem of opposites."

> Most readers have not noticed this because they are first of all led into the temptation of classifying everything typologically, which in itself is a pretty sterile undertaking. I have therefore stressed in the preface to the Spanish edition that my typology is essentially a critical apparatus for sifting the empirical material collected by analysis. So it is not the case at all that I begin by classifying my patients into types and then give them the corresponding advice, as a colleague of mine whom God has endowed with a peculiar wit once asserted. In general I use these technical terms in my practical work only when I have to explain to certain patients the one-sidedness of their behavior, their remarkable relations with other people, and such things (Jung 1973a: 186).

Jung's early publications introduced the attitudes and functions as a typology, that is, as a set of unchanging, static categories; but he later arrived at the appreciation that every person possesses both attitudes and all four functions, in differing measures and prominence.

> If we consider that no man is simply introverted or simply extraverted, but has both attitudes potentially in him—although he has developed only one of them as a function of adaptation—we shall immediately conjecture that with the introvert extraversion lies dormant and undeveloped somewhere in the background, and that introversion leads a similar shadowy existence in the extravert. And this is indeed the case (Jung 1943: 56).

Jung also came to appreciate that the spontaneous processes of the psyche continuously alter the relations among the types, bringing unconscious types to consciousness, attending to them selectively, and allowing the remainder to lapse again into unconsciousness.

These processes were active regardless of the particular opposites that became conscious and unconscious in any individual. "The circular movement … has the moral significance of activating the light and dark forces of human nature, and together with them all psychological opposites of whatever kind they may be" (Jung 1938a: 25). In his writings for publication, Jung referred only summarily and confusingly to his understanding of the process of transformation.

> The way to the goal seems chaotic and interminable at first, and only gradually did the signs increase that it is leading anywhere. The way is not straight but appears to go around in circles. More accurate knowledge has proved it to go in spirals: the dream-motifs always return after certain intervals to definite forms, whose characteristic it is to define a center (Jung 1952a: 28).

Jung's oral communications during his seminars at the Psychological Club provide a more complete understanding. "Individuation takes place when it is realized, when someone is there who notices it; otherwise it is like the eternal melody of the wind in the desert" (Jung 1997: 1314).

> It is a process of continuous transformation with no end if we don't interfere. It needs our conscious interference to bring it to a goal—by our interference we make a goal. Otherwise, it is like the eternal change of the seasons in nature, a building up and a pulling down, integration and disintegration without end (Jung 1988: 236–37).

A passing remark on the union of opposites indicates that the ebb and flow within the unconscious, arising from its continual compensations for the one-sidedness of consciousness, pertained specifically to the two attitude types, introversion and extraversion. "The union of opposites is necessary, and in particular the difficult task of reconciling extraversion and introversion by means of the transcendent function" (Jung 1954c: 501). Implicitly, there is at all times both a movement of the libido toward introversion and its return from introversion to extraversion.

The circular process gains significance when it is brought into conjunction with Jung's dispersed remarks about mystics, mystical experiences, and mysticism as instances of introversion. "The peculiar nature of introverted intuition, if it gains the ascendancy, produces a particular type of man: the mystical dreamer and seer on the one hand, the artist and the crank on the other" (Jung 1921: 401). "Negation … is itself an attitude to the world … that on the one hand is purely intellectual and rational, and on the other a profound feeling of mystical identity with the world. This attitude is introverted" (Jung 1921: 191).

> An introverted attitude, therefore, which withdraws its emphasis from the external world (the world of consciousness) and localizes it in the subjective factor (the background of consciousness) necessarily calls forth the characteristic manifestations of the unconscious, namely … the sense of indefiniteness, timelessness, oneness. The extraordinary feeling of oneness is a common experience in all forms of "mysticism" (Jung 1954c: 491).

The unceasing ebb and flow of introversion-extraversion is the same circular process that Neoplatonists in late antiquity discussed as the decline or declension of the one into the many, together with the *epistrophe,* or "reversion" of the decline through the ascension of the many to the one (see Lloyd 1990: 126). The continual fragmentation and reintegration of all-being is known in Hinduism as *lilla,* the "play" of the divine. Jung psychologized Neoplatonic and Hindu mysticism when he insisted on seeing psychological experiences where Neoplatonists and Hindus had been convinced they had access to metaphysical truths.

Jung's attitude types informed his views on meditation. Because Hindu yoga had the psychological effect of producing introversion, it was able to attain mystical experiences.

> The Indian conception teaches liberation from the opposites, by which are to be understood every sort of affective state and emotional tie to the object. Liberation follows the withdrawal

> of libido from all contents, resulting in a state of complete introversion.... As a result of the complete detachment of all affective ties to the object, there is necessarily formed in the inner self an equivalent of objective reality, or a complete identity of inside and outside, which is technically described as *tat tvam asi* (that art thou). The fusion of the self with its relations to the object produces the identity of the self (*atman*) with the essence of the world (i.e., with the relations of subject to object), so that the identity of the inner with the outer *atman* is cognized.... Yoga is a method by which the libido is systematically "introverted" and liberated from the bondage of opposites (Jung 1921, pp. 118-19).

Jung was aware that the term *yoga* might refer to a variety of techniques, but he considered all of them to be introvertive in their effects.

> Yoga was originally a natural process of introversion, with all manner of individual variations. Introversions of this sort lead to peculiar inner processes which change the personality. In the course of several thousand years these introversions became organized as methods, and along widely differing lines. Indian yoga itself recognizes numerous and extremely diverse forms (Jung, 1936, p. 536).

Jung contrasted the attitude types that were favored in the East and the West. "Introversion is, if one may so express it, the 'style' of the East, and habitual and collective attitude, just as extroversion is the 'style' of the West. Introversion is felt here as something abnormal, morbid, or otherwise objectionable" (Jung 1954c: 481). Yoga was appropriate for the East, but the style of the West warranted different procedures, such as active imagination.

> I do not apply yoga methods in principle, because, in the West, nothing ought to be forced on the unconscious. Usually, consciousness is characterized by an intensity and narrowness that have a cramping effect, and this ought not to be emphasized still further. On the contrary, everything must be done to help

> the unconscious to reach the conscious mind and to free it from its rigidity. For this purpose I employ a method of active imagination, which consists in a special training for switching off consciousness, at least to a relative extent, thus giving the unconscious contents a chance to develop (Jung 1936: 537).

Jung did not imply that active imagination was extravertive. Active imagination widened consciousness, whereas yoga was inhibitive. Jung would likely have classed active imagination together with Freud's psychoanalysis, which "aims at an artificial introversion for the purpose of making conscious the unconscious components of the subject" (Jung 1936: 536).

Jung's recognition of two subcategories of extreme introversion, the inhibitive variety exemplified by yoga, and the consciousness-expanding alternatives of active imagination and free association, may be brought into comparison with a discussion of floral symbolism by Rudolf Steiner. In a 1909 lecture, Steiner, who was then a theosophist, provided a "Rosicrucian" interpretation of *Flor et Blancheflor,* an Old French romance that Konrad Fleck had rendered into German verse in 1230.

> An old couple are spoken of, named "Flor" and "Blancheflor." In modern language this means approximately "the flower with red petals," the rose, and "the flower with white petals," the lily.... Flor and Blancheflor are souls, embodied in human beings, who have lived before.... One could see in the rose, in Flor or Flos, the symbol for the human soul who has taken into itself the personality-impulse, the ego-impulse, allowing the spiritual to work out of the individuality, who has brought into the red blood the ego-impulse. In the lily, however, was seen the symbol of the soul who can only remain spiritual because the ego remains without, comes only to the boundary of the soul's existence. Thus rose and lily are polar opposites. The rose has taken the consciousness of itself wholly into itself; in the lily it has remained outside. But there has once been a union between the soul who is within, and the soul who, outside, enlivens the world as World-Spirit. Flor and Blancheflor express the

> finding of the World-Soul, the World-Ego, by the human soul, the human ego.... In the lily is expressed the soul which finds its higher egohood. In this union of lily-soul and rose-soul was seen that stream of European initiation ... through which is united exoteric and esoteric Christianity (Steiner 1909: 439-40).

Steiner assumed that the names *Flor* and *Blancheflor,* which mean "Flower" and "White Flower," were to be identified with the rose and the lily. The assumption possibly depended on the biblical verse, "I am a rose of Sharon, A lily of the valleys" (Song of Songs 2:1). His exposition interpreted the poem's characters allegorically. "Rose and lily are polar opposites," he asserted. The rose symbolized the human soul that has absorbed a spiritual "ego-impulse," which manifests within the soul's individuality. In this respect, the rose represents the *principium individuationis* that Nietzsche had called Apollinian—and Jung introversion. In Steiner's system, however, the rose is simultaneously a spiritual ego-impulse, an individuality that strives for spirituality. It accomplishes this goal when it has "taken the consciousness of itself wholly into itself," obliterating its individuality in the process. The rose thus symbolizes the absorption of the many into the one or, to put the same matter in experiential terms, an absorptive type of impersonal mystic union (Merkur 1999) in which there is no distinction between the ego and the "higher egohood."

The lily symbolized a different type of religious experience. Here the ego, meaning now the higher egohood or world-spirit, remained outside the human soul, coming "only to the boundary of the soul's existence." Steiner's phrasing implied a communion between soul and world-soul, which engaged each other as an "I" and a "Thou" in a personal or non-absorptive type of mystic union (Merkur 1999). For Steiner, the experience of communion was not theistic. Elsewhere, in an extended account of what he termed "initiation," Steiner (1982: 29pp34) described an experience of communion that proceeded, successively, with the spirits of one's own youth and old age. Importantly, Jung referred frequently to experiences of active imagination that consisted of an inner voice, arising from the unconscious, that could be engaged in an inner dialogue that he termed *Auseinandersetzung,* "having it out with" or "coming to terms with" the unconscious (Jung 1934: 184pp5, 1938b: 38–41, 45, 1950a: 131–33, 1952a: 274–75, 277–79, 1952b: 665, 1954a: 40–41, 1954d: 226, 289, 1958b: 87–88, 90, 1970: 497, 973a: 195–96, 1984: 512–13, 516, 638–40, 642).

The pairing of yoga with active imagination was Jung's personal practice from 1913 until 1917 (Shamdasani 2005: 108–9). In *Memories, Dreams, Reflections,* where he discussed his own experiences of having it out with his unconscious, Jung reminisced:

> I was frequently so wrought up that I had to do certain yoga exercises in order to hold my emotions in check. But since it was my purpose to know what was going on within myself, I would do these exercises only until I had calmed myself enough to resume my work with the unconscious. As soon as I had the feeling that I was myself again, I abandoned this restraint upon the emotions and allowed the images and inner voices to speak afresh. The Indian, on the other hand, does yoga exercises in order to obliterate completely the multitude of psychic contents and images (Jung 1973b: 177).

Jung's alternation between active imagination and yoga was an alternation, in Steiner's typology, between the lily and the rose. Jung achieved two types of introversion, the one consciousness-expanding and the other inhibitory, which permitted introspective access to the ebb and flow of extraversion and introversion within the unconscious. For Steiner, these states were occult and metaphysical; for Jung they were psychological, numinous, and sometimes synchronistic.

Jung appreciated that conscious intervention within the circular process of introversion-extraversion induces an alteration that transforms the circularity into a spiral.

> It is a process which moves in a circle if you do nothing about it. You can see that with insane people where the conscious is absolutely unable to accept what the unconscious produces,

> and in that case the unconscious process simply makes a circle, as an animal has its usual way where it always circulates; deer or hares or any other wild animals move like that when they are pasturing. And that is so with us in as much as the conscious is divorced from the unconscious. But the moment the conscious peeps into the unconscious and the line of communication is established the unconscious no longer moves in mere circles, but in a spiral. It moves in a circle to the moment when it would join the former tracks again, and then find itself a bit above (Jung 1988: 955).

"It is a sort of spiral movement in which she sees the central problem from all sides, from below as well as from above, from all sides at all times" (Jung 1997: 267). "There is an eye that sees it; his consciousness looks into the process and so hinders it from being a mere circle. It is a spiral which is moving up to a certain goal. And that process is dramatic" (Jung 1988: 956). The reconception of the Neoplatonic circle as an ascending spiral had been a *leitmotif* of German Romanticism (Abrams 1971) that was much more widely spread than its best-known form in the thesis-antithesis-synthesis of Hegelian dialectic. Once again, Jung interpreted psychological processes, where his historical predecessors had naively assumed that they dealt with metaphysical ones.

Because Jung psychologized both the mystic circle and its Romantic elaboration into a spiral, he conceptualized not a metaphysical One, All-Being, or God that was itself the helpless subject of unending repetition, but a psychological self, *atman,* or image of God that was a product and subject of psychological process.

> The goal of psychic development is the self. There is no linear evolution; there is only a circumambulation of the self. Uniform development exists, at most, only at the beginning; later, everything points toward the center (Jung 1973b: 196–97).

Jung's further steps, of integrating the self within consciousness through the ego's cooperation with it, completed what he called "the individuation or rebirth process" (Jung 1997: 871; see also 1954b: 35,

1984: 301). Jung (1921: 118) had rejected as inadequate the South Asian procedure of effecting "liberation from the opposites" through "complete introversion." He similarly faulted the "Rosicrucian solution" in Goethe's poem *Geheimnisse,* which consisted of "the union of Dionysus and Christ, rose and cross" (Jung 1921: 186, n. 31), "a blend of Dionysian joyousness and Christian self-sacrifice" (Jung 1921: 188). Jung's solution was nearer that of Steiner who, having abandoned theosophy for anthroposophy, united souls rather than deities. The rose, "the soul who is within," obliterates the human soul in absorptive union; yet the rose is simultaneously no other than the lily, "the soul who, outside [the human soul, and yet in communion with it], enlivens the world as World-Spirit." In other words, a spiritual alchemist who has performed the alchemical wedding, realizing both the rose and the lily within his or her own soul, achieved self-understanding of both being and not being the world spirit. Going further than Steiner, Jung psychologized the alchemical wedding. His approach entailed the thesis that "[t]he self … is a God-image, or at least cannot be distinguished from one" (Jung 1969: 22, see also 1948: 194, 1958a: 339). What subjectively appear to be experiences of the divine are actually experiences of the self. The harmonization of two types of introvertive experience, the one inhibitory and the other consciousness-expanding, is a psychological event that integrates the psyche. It does not exceed the psyche and move mysteriously in metaphysical or supernatural realms.

Having embarked on a psychological reformulation of the alchemical wedding—possibly his grandfather's Rosicrucian version, rather than either Goethe's or Steiner's—Jung came to appreciate that the conscious attention to the circular process that converts it into a spiral also gives rise to the concept of a center, a midpoint where the opposites find their balance. This concept of a center, which Jung called the self, advanced importantly beyond the thinking of both the Neoplatonists and the Rosicrucians. For the mystics, there had been the human soul and its God. In Jung's conception, the two types of introvertive experience could be mapped at opposite points along the circumference of the circle or spiral. Jung's idea of a superordinate process, to which soul and image of God were alike subordinate, implied the self as a third quiddity, at the center of the circle or spiral, something that was neither soul nor image of God but was instead symbolic of the process that governed both.

The Soma Function

> Freud had followed Nietzsche in linking the Dionysian to the unconscious and the Apollinian to consciousness. Jung ignored the relation to consciousness and instead drew attention to Nietzsche's association of the Apollinian and Dionysian with alternate states of consciousness.

We find another parallel in Nietzsche's contrast between the *Apollinian* and the *Dionysian*. The example which Nietzsche uses to illustrate this contrast is instructive—namely, that between dream and intoxication. In a dream the individual is shut up in himself, it is the most intimate of all psychic experiences; in intoxication he is liberated from himself, and, utterly self-forgetful, plunges into the multiplicity of the objective world (Jung 1913: 506; see also 1921: 138, 144).

In "Dreams and Myths" (1908), the psychoanalyst Karl Abraham had linked the Dionysian principle of Nietzsche not only to sexual desire, but specifically also to soma, a psychoactive beverage that was consumed ritually in the ancient Hindu Rig Veda. Abraham wrote:

> In the oldest Indian sources the name for nectar is amrita; later it is called soma and in the Zendavesta haoma. The names nectar and ambrosia are familiar to us from Greek mythology. Various miraculous and mysterious effects are attributed to nectar: it vitalizes, inspires, and confers immortality. This latter quality is clearly expressed by the word "amrita" and its etymological equivalent "ambrosia." Nectar, too, has a similar meaning.

> All peoples of whom we have any knowledge have produced intoxicants whose consumption induces the familiar deceptive sensations. They make man feel vitalized, inspired and elated. At the same time they give him an increased feeling of warmth and arouse his sexual desire. The Dionysian revels are invariably erotic in character. Drink thus induces in man two kinds of fire: bodily warmth and the fire of passion. Man obtained intoxicating drink from the juices of certain plants. In myths these plants are called soma (Abraham 1909: 200–1).

We know from their private correspondence that Freud had advised Abraham in May 1908 to include a discussion of soma in his article. In Freud's view, soma was a psychoactive substance whose natural occurrence in the human body he termed libido, but whose chemical composition remained unidentified. "The legend of the soma potion contains the highly important presentiment that all our intoxicating liquors and stimulating alkaloids are merely a substitute for the unique, still unattained toxin of the libido that rouses the ecstasy of love" (Freud and Abraham, 1965, p. 40). Freud publicly discussed the idea of a "toxic" basis to libido at a meeting of the Vienna Psychoanalytic Society on November 4, 1908, when he suggested that such an intoxicant underlied the legends of a love potion (Kerr 1988: 147; citing Nunberg and Federn 1967: 36–37).

Jung's discussions of soma in *Wandlungen und Symbole der Libido* were contributions to the same early psychoanalytic conversation. Jung referred to soma in two passages. In the first, he discussed the distinction between intellect and soul in the late antique philosophy of Plotinus, the founder of Neoplatonism. Intellect conceptualizes the Platonic ideas in their unchanging, eternal, being; soul is the principle of life, dynamism or becoming that puts the ideas into motion in the world we know. Jung wrote:

> According to Plotinus, the world-soul has a tendency towards separation and divisibility, the *sine qua non* of all change, creation, and *reproduction*. It is an "unending All of life" and wholly energy; a living organism of ideas which only become

> effective and real in it. The intellect is its progenitor and father, and what the intellect conceives the world-soul brings to birth in reality. "What lies enclosed in the intellect comes to birth in the world-soul as Logos, fills it with meaning and makes it drunken as if with nectar." Nectar, like soma, is the drink of fertility and immortality (Jung 1967: 138, compare Jung 1916: 148).

Where the quotation from Plotinus had analogized Logos to nectar, Jung's commentary removed the analogy. Jung asserted that nectar, like soma, was—and was not merely analogous to—an intoxicant that makes the soul drunk with Logos.

Jung's second reference to soma in *Wandlungen und Symbole der Libido* retained Freud's association of soma with libido.

> Agni is the soma, the holy drink of inspiration, the mead of immortality. Soma and fire are identical in Vedic literature. The ancient Hindus saw fire both as a symbol of Agni and as an emanation of the inner libido-fire, and for them the same psychic dynamism was at work in the intoxicating drink ("fire-water," Soma-Agni as rain and fire). The Vedic definition of soma as "seminal fluid" confirms this view. The "somatic" significance of Agni has its parallel in the Christian interpretation of the Eucharistic Blood as the body of Christ.
>
> Soma is also the "nourishing drink." Its mythological characteristics coincide with those of fire, and so both are united in Agni. The drink of immortality, Amrita, was stirred by the Hindu gods like the fire (Jung 1967: 167-68; compare Jung 1916: 185).

What was missing from these two passages in 1912, as compared with Abraham's discussion in 1908, was the linkage to Nietzsche that Jung introduced in 1913. Jung repaired the omission not in print, but as an oral teaching that he gave in his seminar on *Dream Analysis*. On November 20, 1929, Jung initially addressed soma as a mythological symbol, but immediately continued by mentioning its psychoactive properties.

> Soma is a mythological drink in the Vedic religion, magical like the wine in the Christian sacraments, or in the Dionysian mysteries. It is a revivifying drink which is also intoxicating (Jung 1984: 396).

After a further brief reference to soma as an "intoxicating drink" (1984: 397), Jung wrote at length in a manner that clarified what he meant by calling soma "revivifying."

> The soma drink is an apotropaic drink.... When one drinks this, one cannot die; that medicine comes from the land of the dead, moonland, the moon-tree, it is the medicine of immortality. Gilgamesh travels toward the Westland, to the land of the setting sun. Then there is the myth of the Babylonian Utnapishtim, which antedates the Noah legend by a thousand years. They both cross over a great flood and are removed to the Westland, to live an eternal life. They are seeking immortality in the land of the dead....
>
> Then there is the other side of the moon, the lunatic side, which Dr. Harding has mentioned, the moon madness which has to do with the moon as mind. Intoxication is artificial madness. A small dose is exceedingly important in order to bring up one's irrational side; a little madness is good—to be a bit upset—but more is dangerous. In the soma ceremonies, if one gets very drunk one falls from grace. St. Paul in writing to the Corinthians complained that they ate and drank too much; it was a terrible misuse of something sacred. The temptation is to drink deep gulps. In the asylums, the insane are permitted to take communion but they ask for a whole bottle full, and one has to rescue the chalice.
>
> That middle line suggested by the mystery cults is exceedingly critical and delicate. Drink more and one comes down into the flesh with a bump; drink too little and one is not irrational enough. The purpose is to do away with our ordinary cramped consciousness. Even the primitive is just as intense as we are on our daily habits, our routine. The real purpose of the religious ceremonial is to revivify. It was created to lift man out of the ordinary, to disturb his habitual ways, that he may become aware

> of things outside. Many a man, from his accursed circle, has drunk to escape, and discovered the extraordinary beauty of the world and embraced the world, when ordinarily they are terrible beasts. They have discovered the beauty of drunkenness and embrace wine for the divine quality of it, opening their hearts, opening up avenues to mankind. One real moment like that may be a moment of revelation (Jung 1984: 398–99).

Earlier in the seminar on *Dream Analysis*, Jung had associated spiritual experiences with the sense of immortality. "You may have had a spiritual experience which convinced you, quite unmistakably, that you were in the presence of God, filling you with the conviction of immortality" (1984: 353–54). In a later seminar on the *Spiritual Exercises* of St. Ignatius Loyola, Jung employed the same trope in reference to the Eleusinian Mysteries: "The main idea seems to have been the idea of transformation: human consciousness had to be changed until it was capable of experiencing the feeling of immortality while still in this life" (Jung 1977: 185). Jung claimed that the philosopher's stone of the alchemists signified an intoxicant similar to soma: "The stone has the significance of a panacea, of a drink of immortality" (Jung 1980: 800). "The medicine man … gives *pharmakon athanasias,* the medicine of immortality which makes the new man. When you take the *tinctura magna* of the alchemist you are cured forever" (Jung 1984: 128). It was similarly with reference to its provision not of physiological longevity, but of an experience of immortality, that Jung asserted, "According to its oldest definition, soma is a life-giving or intoxicating drink" (1988: 1439).

Jung interpreted the experience of immortality not metaphysically but psychologically. It is an experience of the timelessness of the unconscious.

> The intuition of immortality which makes itself felt during the transformation is connected with the peculiar nature of the unconscious. It is, in a sense, non-spatial and non-temporal. The empirical proof of this is the occurrence of so-called telepathic phenomena, which is still denied by hyperskeptical critics, although in reality they are much more common than is

> generally supposed. The feeling of immortality, it seems to me, has its origin in a peculiar feeling of extension in space and time (Jung 1950a: 142, see also Jung 1938c: 191).

We may note, in passing, that Jung's references to psychoactive drugs in his professional publications were limited to the discussion of soma, together with passing remarks on drinks of immortality. Jung did not publish the explanation that drinks confer immortality by inducing a sense of the presence of God. He reserved to oral presentation in his seminars the explanation that mythical drinks of immortality were psychoactive beverages that induced spiritual experiences. He knew that his students were taking notes of the seminars, out of which they prepared transcripts for mimeograph circulation among themselves; but the publication of his seminars was not envisioned in his lifetime. In other words, Jung taught in public that myths and rites contained motifs that concerned medicines of immortality; but he reserved as a private teaching to his seminar students the further information that he was speaking not of a fabulous fictional drug that produced physiological longevity, but of an entirely real, psychoactive substance that produced spiritual experiences. His discussion of dosage in the Dream Analysis seminar may possibly have been based on equally private experience. "Drink more and one comes down into the flesh with a bump; drink too little and one is not irrational enough."

In contrast with the majority practice of proposing a botanical candidate for the identification of soma, Greene suggested that we concern ourselves with soma's function:

> What if we should take the texts at their word and say that the external form and color of soma vary, that the substitutes for soma are even more varied, and that we may not even be talking about a specific plant at all, but about a pharmacological principle common to a number of plants? If this were the case, then instead of searching for soma through the study of plant morphology we would take the search for soma to be essentially a *biochemical* rather than a *botanical* problem (1992: 113).

Any of several psychoactive plants might conceivably fulfill the function of soma or another drink of immortality, and different plants and preparations may have been employed over time and across cultures. Once the shift is made methodologically from seeking a specific botanical source to seeking a cultural-historical drug effect, we may treat as unduly speculative Swales's (1983) claim that Freud's experiences with cocaine inspired his "toxic" theory of libido (cited by Kerr 1988: 147–48). One could as easily and as inconclusively argue that an experiential acquaintance with Nietzschean "drives," dating to the early 1870s, may have inspired Freud's cocaine experiments in the mid-1880s.

What remains significant is the legend, promoted by Freud and Jung alike, that they broke over the question of libido. After amply refuting the legend, Stepansky (1976: 186) concluded that "the real issue to be examined is not why Jung 'broke' with Freud, but why Freud felt impelled after seven years to elevate relatively long-term differences with Jung to the status of major obstacles that would preclude any collaboration at all." Stepansky suggested that substantive issue arose from Freud's ambitions to institutionalize psychoanalysis (1976: 192), a history that has now been chronicled minutely by Borch-Jacobsen and Shamdasani (2012). When, however, Freud and Jung's differing attitudes toward libido are understood in terms of the soma function on which they agreed, the legend gains new meaning.

Edward Glover (1950: 56–57), a classical psychoanalyst polemicizing against Jung, remarked: "It is not at all clear, nor in the present writer's opinion is it likely ever to become clear from Jung's writings, why, having originally committed himself, whether he knew it or not, to Freud's dualistic theories of instinctual conflict, Jung embraced with such enthusiastic haste a monistic theory of mental energy." Glover's subscription to the standard legend took it at face value, as a discussion of two energies or one, when, I suggest, it was a way of alluding publicly to the underlying question about naturally occurring neurochemical intoxicants and their plant equivalents. Jung, no less than Freud, had proposed a theory of two toxins that occur naturally in the human psyche, only one of which has the soma function. What was at stake in their debate was the identity of the second toxin.

In Freud's view, the second toxin was responsible for resistance, repression, and other inhibitory functions that were consistent with the neuroses. "Of all the clinical pictures which we meet with in clinical medicine, it is the phenomena of intoxication and abstinence in connection with the use of certain chronic poisons that must closely resemble the genuine psychoneuroses" (Freud 1905: 113). "The similarity of the neuroses to the phenomena of intoxication and abstinence after the use of certain alkaloids, as well as to Graves' disease and Addison's disease, is forced upon our notice clinically" (Freud 1906: 279, see also Freud 1916–17: 388, Freud 1925: 214–15). Freud (1920) eventually went so far as to identify the inhibitory trend in the psyche as a death drive; but at the very end of his life Freud (1939: 76) dropped his metaphysical speculations and acknowledged that he had evidence only of negative reactions to traumas that proceed through avoidances and may intensify into inhibitions and phobias.

Where Freud was a neurologist concerned with psychoneuroses, Jung was a psychiatrist seeking to expand Freud's psychoanalysis to account additionally for the evidence of psychoses; and he could not agree to Freud's formulation of the second toxin. To postulate an inhibitory toxin might explain the inhibitions and fixations that characterize the neuroses, but something more was needed to explain schizophrenia. At the Salzburg Congress in the spring of 1908, Jung proposed that a nonspecific and as yet unidentified toxin was responsible for schizophrenia. The paper has been lost; its abstract reads as follows:

> The depotentiation of the association process or *abaissement du niveau mental,* which consequently has a downright dreamlike quality, seems to indicate that a pathogenic agent [*Noxe*] contributes to dementia praecox which is absent in, say, hysteria. The characteristics of the *abaissement* were assigned to the pathogenic agent, which was construed as organically

> conditioned and likened to a symptom of poisoning (e.g., paranoid states in chronic poisoning) (Jung 1908: 335).

In Freud's model, where fantasy is produced by libido and resistance by the second toxin, neurosis appears as an overactivity of the second toxin; but the circumstance of psychosis required a different formulation. One could plausibly argue, with Freud, that neurosis involved an inhibition of unconscious libido; but how was one then to account for the loss of reality-testing in psychosis? Jung proposed that an inhibitory toxin, such as Freud had postulated responsible for the inhibition of unconscious libido, acted in psychosis to inhibit conscious reality testing. Owing presumably to its failure to find endorsement, Jung dropped his proposal; but his concern with the puzzle of psychosis abided. In *Wandlungen*, Jung remarked that the contents of psychoses were not invariably sexual, for which reason he proposed that libido not be restricted to psychosexuality, but instead must be redefined as psychic energy, whether or not psychosexual. With this amendment, neuroses could be attributed to introvertive movements of libido, without need to postulate an inhibitory toxin of the sort imagined by Freud. Implicitly, the concept of a second and inhibitory toxin could be reserved to account for the inhibition psychosis.

What goes unexplained in Jung's model, as also in Freud's, is why their thinking began with a pair of toxins. They shared the unearned, axiomatic assumption, *a priori*, that precisely two toxins were to be contemplated, neither more nor less. As I have hoped to make clear, the theories of two toxins dovetailed with Jung's distinction between free association (and presumably active imagination) as a consciousness-expanding sort of introversion, and yoga as an inhibitory one. These were psychologizations of metaphysical, Rosicrucian categories that Steiner had symbolized by the lily and the rose.

Correspondence on Psychedelics

In addition to Jung's remarks on soma and equivalent drinks of immortality, his demonstrable involvement with psychedelics consist of several letters he wrote in the last decade of his life, in response to inquiries regarding the psychiatric research that was being done with mescaline and LSD in the mid-1950s. Jung was first made aware of the research by John Smythies, who was Humphry Osmond's co-worker at the Saskatchewan Hospital in Weyburn, Saskatchewan, before Abram Hoffer joined the team (Hoffer, Osmond, and Smythies, 1954; Osmond and Smythies 1952; Smythies, 1952). It was presumably through Smythies that the distinctively Jungian concept of "heightening" or "widening" consciousness entered the lexicon as consciousness-expansion and inspired Osmond to coin the term *psychedelic,* "mind expanding." Jung had earlier corresponded with Smythies regarding their shared interest in parapsychology research (Jung 1976: 127).

Jung's opinions about psychedelics were first sought by his friend Father Victor White, an English Dominican and a scholar of Thomist theology whose expertise in Jungian psychotherapy had led to White's consultation by Dr. Ronald A. Sandisonof the Powick Hospital in Worcester. Powick had done a study tour of Swiss hospitals in September 1952 that included a visit to the Sandoz Laboratories in Basel, where Albert Hoffman, the inventor of LSD, advocated the therapeutic value of the drug (Roberts 2008: 21). Sandison becamethe first psychedelic psychotherapist in England (Crocket, Sandison, and Walk 1963; Sandison 1954, 1955, 1957, 1959a, 1959b, 1960, 1963, 1964a, 1964b, 1968, 1975; Sandison and Hopkin 1964; Sandison, Spencer, and Whitelaw 1954; Sandison and Whitelaw 1957). Jung's letter to White, dated 10 April 1954, referred to Aldous Huxley's (1954) writings on mescaline and immediately remarked "I don't know either what its psychotherapeutic value with neurotic or psychotic patients is" (Jung 1976: 172). Jung next asserted that he was content with the techniques of analytical psychology. "I only know there is no point in wishing to *know* more of the collective unconscious than one gets through dreams and intuition. The more you know of it, the greater and heavier becomes your moral burden, because the unconscious contents transform themselves into your individual tasks and duties as soon as they begin to become conscious" (1976: 172). Jung felt that were he to take mescaline without "a legitimate need," it could only be "out of idle curiosity," which would be improper.

> I should hate the thought that I had touched on the sphere where the paint is made that colors the world, where the light is created that makes shine the splendor of the Dawn, the lines and shapes of all form, the sound that feels the orbit, the thought that illuminates the darkness of the void. There are some poor impoverished creatures, perhaps, for whom mescaline would be a heaven sent gift without a counter poison, but I am profoundly mistrustful of the "pure gifts of the Gods." You pay very dearly for them (Jung 1976: 172–73).

The "counter poison," the second toxin whose identification he and Freud had disputed, was evidently still on his mind forty years later.

Jung expressed concern that mescaline provides more access to the unconscious than the drug-taker is able to assimilate and integrate.

> If you are too unconscious it is a great relief to know a bit of the collective unconscious. But it soon becomes dangerous to know more, because one does not learn at the same time how to balance it through a conscious equivalent (Jung 1976: 173).

In summarizing and recapitulating his argument, Jung suggested that physicians administering mescaline to patients should first take the drugs themselves.

> It is quite awful that the alienists have caught hold of a new poison to play with, without the faintest knowledge or feeling of responsibility. It is just as if a surgeon had never learned further than to cut open his patient's belly and to leave things there. When one gets to know unconscious contents one should know how to deal with them. I can only hope that the doctors

> will feed themselves thoroughly with mescaline, the *alkaloid of divine grace*, so that they learn for themselves its marvelous effect (Jung 1976: 173, Jung's italics).

Jung's italicization of the phrase "alkaloid of divine grace" presumably took for granted the Thomist conception of grace in which White was expert. It also explicitly placed mescaline in the category of soma, the philosopher's stone, and other drinks of immortality.

Rather a different tone informs Jung's letter of February 15, 1955 to Alfred M. Hubbard. During Prohibition, Hubbard had been either a rumrunner, or a Treasury Agent undercover as a smuggler, or both. He was recruited by the Office of Strategic Services (OSS) in 1939 to smuggle weapons and war material from the United States into Canada and became a high-level OSS officer. He was allegedly introduced to LSD by Dr. Ronald Sandison of the Powick Hospital in England, in advance of learning through wartime associates of the CIA's clandestine research. After an ecstatic religious experience, he became a proselytizer of LSD use, becoming known as the "Johnny Appleseed of LSD." Hubbard contacted Dr. Humphry Osmond, who was working with LSD and mescaline at Weyburn Hospital in Saskatchewan, and urged him to abandon the aversive use of the drugs, that is, the attempt to induce nightmarish, psychotomimetic experiences in the hope of scaring alcoholics into sobriety, and to replace the aversive technique with one that was calculated to precipitate religious experiences. Hubbard used the phrase "set and setting," referring to the mental mindset of the drug-taker and the physical setting of the event, which he manipulated proficiently in the drug experiences that he administered (Lee and Shlain 1992: 44–45, 49, 52; Stevens 1987: 54, 59). After working with Osmond, Hubbard worked as an LSD therapist of alcoholism at Hollywood Hospital in Vancouver, where he lived (MacLean, MacDonald, Byrne, and Hubbard 1961).

Jung's letter declined Hubbard's invitation to participate in his "mescaline scheme." Jung expressed the same clinical reservations that he had explained to White.

> The analytical method of psychotherapy (e.g., "active imagination") yields very similar results, viz. full realization of complexes and numinous dreams and visions. These phenomena occur at their proper time and place in the course of the treatment. Mescaline, however, uncovers such psychic facts at any time and place when and where it is by no means certain that the individual is mature enough to integrate them (Jung 1976: 222).

To Hubbard, Jung advanced the theory that mescaline acts by "paralyzing the normal function of apperception and thus giving free reign to the psychic factors underlying sense perception." The removal of the rational coherence that organizes sense impressions into meaningful perceptions allows "a rich display of contingent colors, forms, associations, etc., from which under normal conditions the process of apperception selects the correct quality." It also provides an opportunity for the unconscious to add other, non-sensory imagery (Jung 1976: 222-223; see also pp. 300, 318–319).

Jung next repeated his assertion that the techniques of analytical psychology were preferable means to achieve the same ends as mescaline.

> In psychotherapy and psychopathology we have discovered the same variants (usually, however, in a less gorgeous array) through amplification of certain conscious images.... But if he reaches and experiences [them in this way], he has not only acquired them by legitimate endeavor but he has also arrived at the same time in a mental position where he can integrate the meaning of his experience. Mescaline is a shortcut and therefore yields as a result only a perhaps awe-inspiring aesthetic impression, which remains an isolated, unintegrated experience contributing very little to the development of human personality (Jung 1976: 223).

Jung neglected to remark that analytical psychology provides the opportunity to indoctrinate patients with Jungian teachings before allowing their unconscious to express itself. Mescaline makes a greater demand on integration precisely because it allows a greater voice to the patient's own unconscious and a considerably lesser opportunity to the therapist's pedagogy.

Jung's dishonesty is evident in his flat rejection of the religious significance that Hubbard had attributed to mescaline experiences:

> The idea that mescaline could produce a *transcendental* experience is shocking. The drug merely uncovers the normally unconscious functional layer of perceptional and emotional variants, which are only psychologically transcendent but by no means "transcendental," i.e., *metaphysical*. Such an experiment may be in practice good for people having a desire to convince themselves of the real existence of an unconscious psyche. It could give them a fair idea of its reality. But I never could accept mescaline as a means to convince people of the possibility of spiritual experience over against their materialism. It is on the contrary an excellent demonstration of Marxist materialism: mescaline is the drug by which you can manipulate the brain so that it produces even so-called "spiritual" experiences (Jung 1976: 223–224).

To White, a Catholic priest who had no intention of advocating the religious use of mescaline, Jung had asserted that mescaline was an "alkaloid of divine grace," but to Hubbard, who wished to proselytize the religious use of psychedelics, Jung dissembled. Jung had always rejected claims of the transcendental and metaphysical by psychologizing them. He avoided materialism only by recourse to phenomenologism. He reduced everything spiritual to the psyche, but did not go the step further to materialism by reducing everything psychical to the brain. This said, Jung did not inform Hubbard of the casuistic distinctions that he was making and instead allowed Hubbard to misunderstand him.

Jung's letter to Hubbard also expressed concern that mescaline might prove to be pathogenic for some drug-takers.

> There is finally a question which I am unable to answer … the possibility that a drug opening the door to the unconscious could

> also *release a latent, potential psychosis.* As far as my experience goes, such latent dispositions are considerably more frequent than actual psychoses, and thus there exists a fair chance of hitting upon such a case during mescaline experiments. It would be a highly interesting though equally disagreeable experience, such cases being the bogey of psychotherapy (Jung 1976: 274).

Like Jung's concept of consciousness-expansion, which pertained not generally to waking cognition but only to recursive or reflective thinking, his concept of latent, potential psychosis was specific to his model of the mind and is not necessarily meaningful in other psychotherapeutic discourses. In Jung's view, psychosis was always the result of a relative weakness of the ego.

> The possibility of a future psychosis has nothing to do with the peculiar contents of the unconscious. But it has everything to do with whether the individual can stand a certain panic, or the chronic strain of a psyche at war with itself. Very often it is simply a matter of a little bit too much, of the drop that falls into a vessel already full, or of the spark that accidentally lands on a heap of gunpowder (Jung 1939: 240; see also 1928: 153; 1950b: 351; 1953: 520; 1954a: 40; 1958: 269).

In some cases, the failure of the ego-complex to control the unconscious is caused by an unusually strong unconscious; in others, by an unusually weak ego (Jung 1939: 244).

A third letter that discussed psychedelics was written to Betty Grover Eisner on August 12, 1957. Eisner was an LSD researcher at the University of California at Los Angeles (Cohen, Fichman, and Eisner 1958, Eisner and Cohen 1958, Cohen and Eisner 1959, Eisner 1959, 1963, 1964). A coworker of Sidney Cohen (Stevens 1987, p. 63), she was responsible in 1959 for the first appreciation that the contents of psychedelic experiences exhibit a sequence or progression over time. The phenomenologies advanced by Robert E. L. Masters and Jean Houston (1966), Stanislav Grof (1975), and myself (Merkur 1998) built on Eisner's insight. Whether consciously or unconsciously, Eisner was presumably inspired by Jung's claim that the individuation process—the point where the unconscious circling finds linear direction and transforms into a spiral—involves a sequential manifestation of archetypes: the shadow first, followed by the anima in men or animus in women, and so forth. Far from welcoming Eisner's interest in his work, Jung recycled objections to mescaline experience that he had earlier written to White and Hubbard. This time he deprecated religious experience by comparison with a religious way of life.

> Experiments along the line of mescaline and related drugs are certainly most interesting, since such drugs lay bare a level of the unconscious that is otherwise accessible only under peculiar psychic conditions. It is a fact that you get certain perceptions and experiences of things appearing either in mystical states or in the analysis of unconscious phenomena, just like the primitives in their orgiastic or intoxicated conditions. I don't feel happy about these things, since you merely fall into such experiences without being able to integrate them. The result is a sort of theosophy, but it is not a moral and mental acquisition.... To have so-called religious visions of this kind has more to do with physiology but nothing with religion.... Religion is a way of life and a devotion and submission to certain superior facts—a state of mind which cannot be injected by a syringe or swallowed in the form of a pill (Jung, 1976, pp. 382–83).

Concluding Reflections

Jung's attitude types and his concept of individuation were originally designed as psychologizations of Rosicrucian esoterica that involved their partial exposure to public knowledge. Not in his publications, but in their oral elucidation in his seminars at the Zurich Psychology Club, Jung made rare but explicit references to soma, the philosopher's stone, drinks of immortality, and other mythological references to psychedelics. With the passage of time and the movement of psychedelics from rare, learned lore to popular culture, Jung's maintenance of his habitual style of part-exposure and part-reticence had the ironic effect of motivating him to dissemble in order to protect the secrets of the alchemical marriage.

What was the big secret of Rosicrucianism? That drugs were used to induce spiritual experiences. That there were two classes of drugs, symbolized as lily and rose, Luna and Sol, the Queen and the King, and so forth, that produced markedly different effects, and led to markedly different theologies or metaphysics. Both the use of drugs and the resultant theologies were inimical to traditional Christianity and punishable, for many centuries, by execution. In our more enlightened times, of course, these same crimes are punishable merely by prolonged imprisonment, blacklisting, defamation of character, and so forth.

I am not in any way suggesting that Freud and Jung were occultists. Rather, the two pioneers of depth psychology happened to know these secrets that late-eighteenth-century Rosicrucianism had bequeathed to German Romanticism. In fashioning their theories of the mind, Freud and Jung took into account both the scientific evidence in the public domain, and the further, largely secret evidence of drug-based spirituality. Neither depth psychologist was interested in engaging in the sort of controversy that would have been necessary to expose the occult sufficiently to establish the two classes of psychoactives as historical knowledge. And neither had any interest whatever in occult metaphysics. It was simpler, and sufficient for their purposes, to postulate two toxins in the human brain, without troubling to explain how they had come by their speculations.

Jung's analytical psychology is an excellent example of the process by which the soma function can be installed within a religious or psychological system while use of the drug is itself abandoned. In Jung's view, dreams, intuitions, and active imagination disclosed the same depths of the unconscious psyche as psychedelic drugs did; but he favored the phenomena that were gentler, slower, less risky, and easier to control through indoctrination.

References

Abraham, Karl. (1909). "Dreams and Myths: A Study in Folk-Psychology." In *Clinical papers and essays on psycho-analysis*. London: Hogarth Press, 1955; reprinted New York: Brunner/Mazel, Publishers, 1979, 151–209.

Abrams, M. (1971). *Natural Supernaturalism: Tradition and Revolution in Romantic Literature*. New York: W. W. Norton.

Ahern, G. (1984). *Sun at Midnight: The Rudolf Steiner Movement and the Western Esoteric Tradition*. Wellingborough, UK: Aquarian Press.

Bair, D. (2003). *Jung: A Biography*. New York & Boston: Little, Brown and Company.

Bakan, D., D. Merkur, and D. Weiss. (2009). *Maimonides' Cure of Souls: Medieval Precursor of Psychoanalysis*. Albany, NY: State University of New York Press.

Borch-Jacobsen, M. and S. Shamdasani. (2012). *The Freud Files: An Inquiry into the History of Psychoanalysis*. Cambridge: Cambridge University Press.

Charet, F. (1993). *Spiritualism and the Foundations of C. G. Jung's Psychology*. Albany: State University of New York Press.

Cohen, S. and Eisner, B. (1959). "Use of Lysergic Acid Diethylamide in a Psychotherapeutic Setting." *Archives of Neurology and Psychiatry81*: 615–619.

Cohen, S., Fichman, L., and Eisner, B. (1958). "Subjective Reports of Lysergic Acid Experiences in a Context of Psychological Test Performance." *American Journal of Psychiatry115*: 30–35.

Coward, H. (1985). *Jung and Eastern Thought*. Albany: State University of New York Press.

Crocket, R., R. Sandison, and A. Walk (eds). (1963). *Hallucinogenic Drugs and Their Psychotherapeutic Use*. Springfield, IL: Charles C. Thomas.

Crosland, M. (1962). *Historical Studies in the Language of Chemistry*. Reprinted New York: Dover Publications, 1978.

Eisner, B. (1959). "Observations on Possible Order within the Unconscious." In *Neuro-psychopharmacology: Proceedings of the First International Congress of Neuro-pharmacology (Rome, September 1958)* edited by P. Bradley, P. Deniker, and C. Radouco-Thomas. Amsterdam, London,and New York: Elsevier Publishing Company, pp. 438–441.

Eisner, B. (1963). "The Influence of LSD on Unconscious Activity." In *Hallucinogenic Drugs and Their Psychotherapeutic Use* edited by R. Crocket, R. Sandison, and A. Walk. Springfield, IL: Charles C. Thomas, pp. 141–145.

Eisner, B. (1964). "Notes on the Use of Drugs to Facilitate Group Psychotherapy." *Psychiatric Quarterly 38:* 310–328.

Eisner, B. and Cohen, S. (1958). "Psychotherapy with Lysergic Acid Diethylamide." *Journal of Nervous and Mental Diseases* 127: 529–39.

Freud, S. (1905). "Fragment of an Analysis of a Case of Hysteria." *Standard Edition of the Complete Psychological Works of Sigmund Freud* 7: 7–122. London: Hogarth Press, 1953.

Freud, S. (1906). "My Views on the Part Played by Sexuality in the Aetiology of the Neuroses." *Standard edition* 7: 271–79. London: Hogarth Press, 1953.

Freud, S. (1916–17). "Introductory Lectures on Psycho-Analysis." *Standard Edition* 15–16: 9–463. London: Hogarth Press, 1961–63.

Freud, S. (1920). "Beyond the Pleasure Principle." *Standard Edition* 18: 7–64. London: Hogarth Press, 1955.

Freud, S. (1925). The Resistances to Psycho-Analysis. *Standard edition* 19: 213–222. London: Hogarth Press, 1961.

Freud, S. (1927). The Future of an Illusion. *Standard Edition21:* 5–56. London: Hogarth Press, 1961.

Freud, S. (1939). Moses and Monotheism: Three Essays. *Standard Edition23:* 6–137. London: Hogarth Press, 1964.

Freud, S. and Abraham, K. (1965). *A Psycho-Analytic Dialogue: The Letters of Sigmund Freud and Karl Abraham 1907–1926*. H. Abraham and E. Freud, ed., trans., B. Marsh and H. Abraham. NewYork: Basic Books.

Glover, Edward. (1950). *Freud or Jung?* New York: W. W. Norton.

Greene, M. (1992). *Natural Knowledge in Preclassical Antiquity.* Baltimore and London: Johns Hopkins University Press.

Grof, S. (1975). *Realms of the Human Unconscious: Observations from LSD Research.* New York: The Viking Press.

Hanegraaff, W. (2012). *Esotericism and the Academy: Rejected Knowledge in Western Culture.* Cambridge: Cambridge University Press.

Hoeller, Stephan A. (1982). *The Gnostic Jung and the Seven Sermons to the Dead.* Wheaton, IL: Theosophical Publishing House.

Huxley, A. (1954). *The Doors of Perception.* (1956). *Heaven and Hell.* London: Granada Publishing, 1977.

Jaffé, A. (1989). *Was C. G. Jung a Mystic? And Other Essays.* Einsiedeln, Switzerland: Daimon Verlag.

Jung, C. (1908). "On Dementia Praecox." In *The Symbolic Life: Miscellaneous Writings*, 2nd ed., translated by R. Hull. *Collected Works of C. G. Jung* Vol. 18, p. 335. Princeton: Princeton University Press, 1980.

Jung, C. (1913). A Contribution to the Study of Psychological Types. In *Psychological Types* translated by R. Hull and H. Baynes. *Collected Works of C. G. Jung* Vol. 6, pp. 499–509, Princeton: Princeton University Press, 1971.

Jung, C. (1916). *Psychology of the Unconscious: A Study of the Transformations and Symbolisms of the Libido. A Contribution to the History of the Evolution of Thought* translated by Beatrice M. Hinkle. New York: Dodd, Mead and Company; reprint, 1947.

Jung, C. (1928). "The Significance of the Unconscious in Individual Education." In *The Development of Personality* translated by R. Hull. *Collected Works of C. G. Jung* Vol. 17, pp. 149–164, Princeton:Princeton University Press, 1970.

Jung, C. (1934). The Development of Personality. In *The Development of Personality* translated by R. Hull. *Collected Works of C. G. Jung* Vol. 17, pp. 167–186, Princeton: Princeton University Press, 1970.

Jung, C. (1936). "Yoga and the West." In *Psychology and Religion: West and East,* 2nd ed., translated by R. Hull. *Collected Works of C. G. Jung* Vol. 11, pp. 529–537, Princeton: Princeton University Press, 1969.

Jung, C. (1938a). "Commentary on 'The Secret of the Golden Flower.'" In *Alchemical studies,* translated by R. Hull. *Collected Works of C. G. Jung* Vol. 13, pp. 1–56. Princeton: Princeton University Press, 1967.

Jung, C. (1938b). "Psychology and Religion." In *Psychology and Religion: West and East,* 2nd ed., translated by R. Hull. *Collected Works of C. G. Jung* Vol. 11, pp. 3–105, Princeton: Princeton University Press, 1969.

Jung, C. (1938c). "The Relations Between the Ego and the Unconscious," 3rd ed. In *Two Essays on Analytical Psychology,* 2nd ed., translated by R. F. C. Hull. *Collected Works of C. G. Jung* Vol. 7, pp. 121–241. Princeton: Princeton University Press, 1966.

Jung, C. (1939). "On the Psychogenesis of Schizophrenia." In *The Psychogenesis of Mental Disease,* translated by R. F. C. Hull. *Collected Works of C. G. Jung,* Vol. 3, pp. 233–24, Princeton: Princeton University Press, 1976.

Jung, C. (1943). "On the Psychology of the Unconscious," 5th ed. In *Two Essays on Analytical Psychology,* 2nd ed., translated by R. F. C. Hull. *Collected Works of C. G. Jung* Vol. 7, pp. 1–119.Princeton: Princeton University Press, 1966.

Jung, C. (1948). "A Psychological Approach to the Dogma of the Trinity." In *Psychology and Religion: West and East,* 2nd ed., translated by R. Hull. *Collected Works of C. G. Jung,* Vol. 11, pp. 107–200. Princeton: Princeton University Press, 1969.

Jung, C. (1950a). "Concerning Rebirth. In *The Archetypes and the Collective Unconscious,* 2nd ed., translated by R. C. Hull. *Collected Works of C. G. Jung,* Vol. 9, Part I, pp. 111–147. Princeton: Princeton University Press, 1969.

Jung, C. (1950b). "A Study in the Process of Individuation." In *The Archetypes and the Collective Unconscious*, 2nd ed., translated by R. Hull. *Collected Works of C. G. Jung*, Vol. 9, Part I, pp. 290–354. Princeton: Princeton University Press, 1969.

Jung, C. 1952a). *Psychology and Alchemy*, 2nd ed., trans. R. Hull. *Collected Works of C. G. Jung*, Vol. 12. Princeton, NJ: Princeton University Press, 1968.

Jung, C. (1952b). "Religion and Psychology: A Reply to Martin Buber." In *The Symbolic Life: Miscellaneous Writings*, 2nd ed., translated by R. Hull. *Collected Works of C. G. Jung* Vol. 18, pp. 663–670. Princeton: Princeton University Press, 1980.

Jung, C. (1953). "Psychological Commentary on 'The Tibetan Book of the Dead.'" In *Psychology and Religion: West and East*, 2nd ed., translated by R. Hull. *Collected Works of C. G. Jung* Vol. 11, pp. 509–526, Princeton: Princeton University Press, 1969.

Jung, C. (1954a). "Archetypes of the Collective Unconscious." In *The Archetypes and the Collective Unconscious*, 2nd ed., translated by R. Hull. *Collected Works of C. G. Jung* Vol. 9, Part I, pp. 3–41. Princeton: Princeton University Press, 1969.

Jung, C. (1954b). "Psychological Aspects of the Mother Archetype." In *The Archetypes and the Collective Unconscious*, 2nd ed., translated by R. Hull. *Collected Works of C. G. Jung* Vol. 9, Part I, pp. 73–110. Princeton: Princeton University Press, 1969.

Jung, C. (1954c). "Psychological Commentary on 'The Tibetan Book of the Great Liberation.'" In *Psychology and Religion: West and East*, 2nd ed., translated by R. Hull. *Collected Works of C. G. Jung* Vol.11, pp. 475–508, Princeton: Princeton University Press, 1969.

Jung, C. (1954d). "Transformation Symbolism in the Mass." In *Psychology and Religion: West and East*, 2nd ed., translated by R. Hull. *Collected Works of C. G. Jung* Vol. 11, pp. 201–296, Princeton:Princeton University Press, 1969.

Jung, C. (1958a). "Flying Saucers: A Modern Myth of Things Seen in the Skies." In *Civilization in Transition*, translated by R. Hull. *Collected Works of C. G. Jung* Vol. 10, pp. 307–433 Princeton:Princeton University Press.

Jung, C. (1958b). The Transcendent Function. In *The Structure and Dynamics of the Psyche,* 2nd ed., translated by R. Hull. *Collected Works of C. G. Jung* Vol. 8, pp. 67–91, Princeton: Princeton University Press, 1969.

Jung, C. (1964). Symbols and the Interpretation of Dreams. In *The Symbolic Life: Miscellaneous Writings,* 2nd ed., translated by R. Hull. *Collected Works of C. G. Jung* Vol. 18, pp. 183–264, Princeton: Princeton University Press, 1980.

Jung, C. (1966). The Structure of the Unconscious. In *Two Essays on Analytical Psychology,* 2nd ed., R. F. C. Hull trans., *Collected Works of C. G. Jung* Vol. 7, pp. 269–304, Princeton: Princeton University Press, 1966.

Jung, C. (1967). *Symbols of Transformation: An Analysis of the Prelude to a Case of Schizophrenia,* 2nd ed., translated by R. Hull. *Collected Works of C. G. Jung* Vol. 5. Princeton: Princeton University Press.

Jung, C. (1969). *Aion: Researches into the Phenomenology of the Self,* 2nd ed., translated by R. Hull. *Collected Works of C. G. Jung* Vol. 9, Pt. 2. Princeton: Princeton University Press.

Jung, C. (1970). *Mysterium Coniunctionis: An Inquiry into the Separation and Synthesis of Psychic Opposites in Alchemy,* 2nd ed. *Collected Works of C. G. Jung* Vol. 14. Princeton: PrincetonUniversity Press.

Jung, C. (1973a). *Letters, Volume 1: 1906–1950.* G. Adler and A. Jaffé, eds., R. Hull trans., Princeton, NJ: Princeton University Press.

Jung, C. (1973b). *Memories, Dreams, Reflections,* 2nd edition. A. Jaffe, ed., R. Winston and C. Winston, trans., New York: Pantheon Books/Random House.

Jung, C. (1976). *Letters, Volume 2: 1951–1961.* G. Adler and A. Jaffé, eds., R. Hull trans., Princeton, NJ: Princeton University Press.

Jung, C. (1977–78). "*Exercitia Spiritualia* of St. Ignatius of Loyola: Notes on Lectures" (1939), Part I. *Spring 1977,* 183–200.

Jung, C. (1980). "On the 'Rosarium Philosophorum.'" In *The Symbolic Life: Miscellaneous Writings,* 2nd ed., translated by R. Hull. *Collected Works of C. G. Jung* Vol. 18, pp. 797–800, Princeton: Princeton University Press, 1980.

Jung, C. (1984). *Dream Analysis: Notes of the Seminar given in 1928–1930.* William McGuire, ed., Princeton: Princeton University Press.

Jung, C. (1988). *Nietzsche's* Zarathustra*: Notes of the Seminar given in 1934–1939.* James L. Jarrett, ed., 2 vols. Princeton, NJ: Princeton University Press; rpt. London: Routledge, 1994.

Jung, C. (1997). *Visions: Notes of the Seminar given in 1930–1934, Vol. 1.* Claire Douglas, ed., Princeton, NJ: Princeton University Press.

Kerr, J. (1988). "The Devil's Elixirs,Jung's 'Theology' and the Dissolution of Freud's "Poisoning Complex." *Psychoanalytic Review, 75:* 1–34; reprinted in Paul Bishop, ed., *Jung in Contexts: A Reader* London and New York: Routledge, 1999: 125–153.

Lachman, G. (2010). *Jung the Mystic: The Esoteric Dimensions of Carl Jung's Life and Teachings: A New Biography.* New York: Jeremy P. Tarcher/Penguin.

Lee, M. and Shlain, B. (1992). *Acid Dreams: The Complete Social History of LSD: The CIA, the Sixties, and Beyond,* 2nd ed. New York: Grove Press.

Ljunggren, M. (1994). *The Russian Mephisto: A Study of the Life and Work of Emilii Medtner.* Acta Universitatis Stockholmiensis, Stockholm Studies in Russian Literature. Stockholm: Almqvist & Wiksell International.

Lloyd, A. (1990). *The Anatomy of Neoplatonism.* Oxford: Clarendon Press.

MacLean, J, MacDonald, D., Byrne, U., and Hubbard, A. (1961). "The Use of LSD-25 in the Treatment of Alcoholism and Other Psychiatric Problems." *Quarterly Journal of Studies on Alcohol, 22:* 34–45.

Masters, R. and Houston, J. (1966). *The Varieties of Psychedelic Experience.* London: Turnstone Books, 1973.

Merkur, D. (1992). "Spirit and the Problem of Social Instincts: Exceptions to Freud's Critique of Religion." *The Psychoanalytic Study of Society, 17:* 249–87. L. Boyer and R. Boyer, eds. Hillsdale, NJ: Analytic Press.

Merkur, D. (1998). *The Ecstatic Imagination: Psychedelic Experiences and the Psychoanalysis of Self-Actualization*. Albany, NY: State University of New York Press.

Merkur, D. (1999). *Mystical Moments and Unitive Thinking*. Albany: State University of New York Press.

Merkur, D. (2000). *The Mystery of Manna: The Psychedelic Sacrament of the Bible*. Rochester, VT: Park Street Press.

Merkur, D. (2007). *Crucified with Christ: Meditation on the Passion, Mystical Death, and the Medieval Invention of Psychotherapy*. Albany, NY: State University of New York Press.

Nunberg, H. and Federn, E. (eds.). (1967). *Minutes of the Vienna Psychoanalytic Society, Volume II: 1908–1910*. New York: International Universities Press.

Roberts, A. (2008). *Albion Dreaming: A Popular History of LSD in Britain*. London: Marshall Cavendish Limited.

Sandison, R. (1954). "Psychological Aspects of the LSD Treatment of the Neuroses." *Journal of Mental Science*, 100:508–15.

Sandison, R. (1955). "L.S.D. Treatment for Psychoneurosis: Lysergic Acid Diethylamide for Release of Repression." *Nursing Mirror*, 100:1529–1530.

Sandison, R. (1957). "The Contribution of L.S.D. Therapy to Analytical Theory and Practice." *Bulletin of the British Psychological Society* 33:24.

Sandison, R. (1959a). "The Role of Psychotropic Drugs in Group Therapy." *Bulletin of the World Health Organization*, 21:505–15.

Sandison, R. (1959b). "The Role of Psychotropic Drugs in Individual Therapy." *Bulletin of the World Health Organization*, 21:495–503.

Sandison, R. (1960). "The Nature of the Psychological Response to LSD." In H. Abramson, ed., *The Use of LSD in Psychotherapy: Transactions of a Conference on d-Lysergic Acid Diethylamide (LSD-25) April 22, 23, and 24, 1959, Princeton, N.J*, New York: Josiah Macy, Jr., Foundation, pp.81–150.

Sandison, R. (1963). "Certainty and Uncertainty in the LSD Treatment of Psychoneurosis." In *Hallucinogenic Drugs and Their Psychotherapeutic Use,* edited by R. Crocket, R. Sandison, and A. Walk. Springfield, IL: Charles C. Thomas.

Sandison, R. (1964a). "Hallucinogens." *The Practitioner* 192: 30–36.

Sandison, R. (1964b). "The Role of the Psycholytic Agents in the Therapeutic Process" [abstract]. *Bulletin of the British Psychological Society* 46: 67.

Sandison, R. (1968). "The Hallucinogenic Drugs." *The Practitioner* 200: 244–250.

Sandison, R. (1975). "Group Therapy and Drug Therapy." In *Group Psychotherapy and Group Function,* edited by M. Rosenbaum and M. Berger. New York: Basic Books, pp. 608–621.

Sandison, R. A. & Hopkin, I. (1964). "Psychotherapy Using LSD." *Nursing Times* 60: 529–32, 556–57.

Sandison, R., Spencer, A., and Whitelaw, J. (1954). "The Therapeutic Value of Lysergic Acid Diethylamide in Mental Illness." *Journal of Mental Science 100:* 491–507.

Sandison, R. and Whitelaw, J. (1957). "Further Studies in the Therapeutic Value of Lysergic Acid Diethylamide in Mental Illness." *Journal of Mental Science 103:* 332–343.

Shamdasani, S. (2003). *Jung and the Making of Modern Psychology: The Dream of a Science.* Cambridge: Cambridge University Press.

Steiner, R. (1909). "On the History of Christian Rosenkreutz." In *A Christian*

Rosenkreutz Anthology, edited by P. Allen. Blauvelt, NY: Rudolf Steiner Publications, 1968: 439–441.

Steiner, R. (1982). *Rosicrucianism and Modern Initiation: Mystery Centres of the Middle Ages (Six Lectures Given in Dornach, 4th–13th January, 1924),* 3rd ed., M. Adams, trans., London: RudolfSteiner Press.

Steiner, R. (2001). *Freud, Jung, and Spiritual Psychology: Five Lectures held in Dornach and Munich between February 25, 1912, and July 2, 1921.* M. Laird-Brown, trans., rev., S. Seiler andR. Smoley. Hudson, NY: Anthroposophic Press.

Stepansky, P. (1976). "The Empiricist as Rebel: Jung, Freud, and the Burdens of Discipleship." *Journal of the History of the Behavioral Sciences12*: 216–39. Rpt. in R. Papadopoulos, ed., *Carl Gustav Jung: Critical assessments, Volume 1: Jung and his method in context.* London and New York: Routledge, 1992: 169–199.

Stevens, J. (1987). *Storming Heaven: LSD and the American Dream.* New York: Harper & Row.

Storr, A. (1973). *Jung.* New York: Routledge.

Swales, P. (1983). *Freud, Cocaine, Sexual Chemistry: The Role of Cocaine in Freud's Conception of the Libido.* New York: Privately published by author.

Wehr, G. (1992). "C. G. Jung in the Context of Christian Esotericism and Cultural History." In *Modern Esoteric Spirituality,* edited by A. Faivre and J. Needleman. New York: Crossroad Publishing Company, 381–399.

Wehr, G. (2002). *Jung and Steiner: The Birth of a New Psychology.* In Lauer, H. *The Riddles of the Soul: Depth Psychology and Anthroposophy.* Hudson, NY: Anthroposophic Press.

Chapter 14

R. Gordon Wasson: The Man, the Legend, the Myth

Beginning a New History of Magic Mushrooms, Ethnomycology, and the Psychedelic Revolution

Jan Irvin

Jan Irvin is an independent researcher, author, and lecturer, speaking at both academic and public venues. He hosts the popular Gnostic Media podcast at www.gnosticmedia.com. He's the author of *The Holy Mushroom: Evidence of Mushrooms in Judeo-Christianity; A Critical Re-Evaluation of the Schism Between John M. Allegro and R. Gordon Wasson Over the Theory on the Entheogenic Origins of Christianity Presented in The Sacred Mushroom and the Cross.* He coauthored *Astrotheology & Shamanism: Christianity's Pagan Roots,* 2006/2009, and co-produced the DVD *The Pharmacratic Inquisition,* 2007. See www.gnosticmedia.com. He's the curator of the official website for John Marco Allegro, the much-criticized Dead Sea Scrolls scholar, and has contributed much to the reexamination of many of Allegro's theories. With the Allegro family, he republished Allegro's famous 1970 classic, *The Sacred Mushroom and the Cross,* in a fortieth-anniversary edition published in 2009. See www.johnallegro.org. He's the editor of the upcoming *Entheogens: A Comprehensive Overview of the Psychedelic*

Sciences, a two-volume set of interviews done with more than fifty of the world's leading independent and academic researchers in psychedelic studies.

Introduction

> Legends are often history processed to point some moral. They are misleading as history, but they help us to understand the people who invent and believe in them. Usually the world recognizes as legends only the outgrown cables of earlier generations. But this is merely because, believing as we do our own legends, we do not recognize them for what they are
>
> (Wasson 1948: v ff.).

The fields of ethnobotany and ethnomycology often pertain to studying the myths and legends (and fables) of the many cultures around the world, including our own, and attempting to understand how these myths and legends have been influenced by entheogens, or psychedelic plants and drugs. A curious idea that has come about as a result of focused research is that the entire genesis of the field of ethnomycology, the stories about its origins and history, about the discovery of magic mushrooms, and the start of the psychedelic movement, may themselves be based upon myths and legends.

The word myth is derived from the Greek *mythoi*, or *mythos* (μῦθος). *Webster's Third New International Dictionary* 1986[1] defines the word, in part, as:

> **1**: a story that is usually of unknown origin and at least partially traditional, that ostensibly relates historical events usually of such character as to serve to explain some practice, belief, institution, or natural phenomenon, and that is especially associated with religious rites and beliefs—compare EUHEMERISM, FABLE, FOLKTALE. **2 a**:*a story invented as a veiled explanation of a truth*... [emphasis mine]

The word *legend* is derived from the Latin *legenda,* meaning "what is read." Webster's, in part, defines the word *legend* as:

> **1 a:** the story of the life of a saint **b:** a collection of such stories **c:** ACCOUNT, HISTORY [...] **2 a:** LECTIONARY 1 **b:** PASSIONAL *3 a: a story coming down from the past; especially: one handed down from early times by tradition 1997: 10....* **b:** the total body of such stories and traditions; especially: the collective stories and traditions of a particular group... [emphasis mine]

The myths and legends that surround psychedelic culture, our culture, are rarely questioned. Specifically, I mean the stories that grew up about the pioneers and founders of the field itself. For instance, it was believed for decades that John M. Allegro stole his ideas from Gordon Wasson for his book, *The Sacred Mushroom and the Cross* (1970/2009). But by going line by line through Allegro's research, as I showed in my 2008 book, *The Holy Mushroom,* I proved there was no evidence to substantiate these *myths* against Allegro—myths that had been started by *Gordon Wasson himself* and propagated by Jonathan Ott for over a decade. On the contrary, Allegro had not taken his ideas from Wasson and had been very careful in checking his citations, though he had left a few very minor errors, such as transposed numbers and letters.

Due to working on *The Holy Mushroom* book, I came to study the legends and myths surrounding R. Gordon Wasson—the popularizer of magic mushrooms, one of those considered responsible for launching the psychedelic movement, and also considered to be the founder of the field of ethnomycology. We're told that his work is solid, and that he would turn over every stone in his tireless quest for truth. We're told that this pioneer's work is unassailable, and that as the father of ethnomycology his research is almost unquestionable.

> His apparent contradictions were the outward indications of an enigmatic, complex personality. He [Wasson] was both a respectable banker and, like it or not, a "founder" of the psychedelic movement; an elitist about sacred mushrooms but also, through his article in *Life,* their popularizer; a level-

> headed scientist whose scholarly writings, while grounded in fact, yet inspire many readers to regard the sacred mushrooms with religious awe and reverence; the Father of Ethnomycology but also, to many a kind of New Age patriarch (Riedlinger 1990/1997:10).

And while R. Gordon Wasson really existed as a man, and he really was a mushroom researcher—which gives us a nucleus of historical fact—it seems we are dealing with a partly fictitious narrative, and apparently actions and events, embodying some popular ideas concerning a historical phenomenon.

This is a difficult and sensitive topic for many in the various fields of psychedelic studies. Many people have based their work in the field on apparently unquestionable foundations. Over the years, when I have raised the issues covered within this essay with various professionals, I've been told time and again that, "I knew Wasson personally, and he couldn't have acted this or that way"—often in the face of primary documentation proving otherwise, *in Wasson's own words*, right before them. Some will feel that because they met or had conversations with Wasson, that he could not have possibly acted outside their perceived relationship with him, as if he had no life prior to or outside his interactions with them.

How do we approach a topic that many will feel personally threatened about? Should we bother to tiptoe around common sensitivities and beliefs? Or should we let the evidence speak for itself, and accept as truth only what we can verify through actual research? It is my opinion that we should let the evidence speak for itself. We should follow the proper process of discovery, emotionally detached from the findings, asking *who, what, where,* and *when* along the way. We will amass the evidence and check each citation, letting it stand on its own. Once we've gathered the evidence, rather than allowing our emotions or our longstanding bias in favor of Wasson to intervene, and so that we can understand *why*, we'll sort out any contradictions in that evidence before we reach a conclusion about it, so that we are able to see the whole situation clearly. Finally, with the contradictions, emotions, and fallacies removed, we'll be able to explain *how* we arrived at our conclusion—the truth—regardless of how we may feel on the matter.

Temple Worship

Prof. Bartholomew Dean of the University of Kansas at Lawrence, who studied under Richard Evans Schultes at Harvard, claimed in a recent conversation that, aside from the Wasson library, there is a temple at Harvard dedicated to Wasson. Dean said that he was once taken there and requested to sign a guest list, which he says he refused to do. No doubt such a guest list would be revealing. It's a list I'd love to get my hands on.

It is fitting that there is a temple dedicated to Wasson at Harvard, because, as I'll show, we are, in fact, dealing with "a story that is … of such character as to serve to explain some … belief, institution, or natural phenomenon…" Webster further defines the word *legend* as:

> **c:** a popular myth usually of current or recent origin… **d:** one around whom such stories and traditions have grown up; one having a special status as a result of possessing or being held to possess extraordinary qualities that are usually partly real and partly mythical.

As told by Gordon Wasson in the May 13, 1957, edition of *Life* magazine, this myth begins:

> It was a walk in the woods, many years ago, that launched my wife and me on our quest of the mysterious mushroom. We were married in London in 1926, she being Russian, born and brought up in Moscow. She had lately qualified as a physician at the University of London. I am from Great Falls, Montana, of Anglo-Saxon origins. In the late summer of 1927, recently married, we spent our holiday in the Catskill Mountains in New York State. In the afternoon of the first day we went strolling along a lovely mountain path, through woods crisscrossed by the slanting rays of a descending sun. We were young, carefree and

> in love. Suddenly my bride abandoned my side. She had spied wild mushrooms in the forest, and racing over the carpet of dried leaves in the woods, she knelt in poses of adoration before first one cluster and then another of these growths. In ecstasy she called each kind by an endearing Russian name. She caressed the toadstools, savored their earthy perfume. Like all good Anglo-Saxons, I knew nothing about the fungal world and felt that the less I knew about those putrid, treacherous excrescences the better. For her they were things of grace, infinitely inviting to the perceptive mind. She insisted on gathering them, laughing at my protests, mocking my horror. She brought a skirtful back to the lodge. She cleaned and cooked them. That evening she ate them, alone. Not long married, I thought to wake up the next morning a widower.
>
> These dramatic circumstances, puzzling and painful for me, made a lasting impression on us both. From that day on we sought an explanation for this strange cultural cleavage separating us in a minor area of our lives.... (Wasson 1957).

I say it's a myth because even Wasson's own daughter, Masha, found it to be questionable:

> *As much as I respected my father's integrity, I recall that for years I did not believe him* when he said his interest in mushrooms began on his honeymoon in 1927. Such an explanation seemed to me like a Hollywood soap opera, something out of character for my father. *Eventually, however, I concluded that the story was true, for he told it sincerely and consistently* (Masha Britten in Riedlinger 1990/1997: 33ff; emphasis mine).

But notice how Masha threw in that added caveat for good measure:

> Eventually, however, I concluded that the story was true, for he told it sincerely and consistently.

Also notice how she starts out the paragraph with an assertion of her respect for her father's integrity, almost as if to say that she doesn't respect his integrity: "As much as I respected my father's integrity, I recall that for years I did not believe him." Often when someone has to assert their belief in something, it's because they're actually questioning it, or they wouldn't mention it at all. And when we understand that Wasson's wife, Valentina Pavlovna, was from the Russian intelligentsia, or Russian elite (Wasson and Wasson 1957: 4ff), Wasson's story of her acting the role of a Russian peasant woman in the woods on a mushroom hunt seems even more absurd—"like a Hollywood soap opera." One might question whether a member of the Russian elite would have as much understanding of mushrooms as the common peasant folk, and be so familiar with all of the mushroom names from childhood, as Valentina claimed (Wasson and Wasson 1957: 4ff).

The more I contemplate this story the more absurd it seems, and the more justifiable Masha's doubt becomes. With this in mind, it seems that Masha, intentionally or not, left us a breadcrumb of skepticism. And though he missed the underlying implications, Andy Letcher in *Shroom* picked up on this same issue, also identifying it as a myth:

> It must be said that while this hoary old story has become something of a foundational myth for modern mushroom enthusiasts, it was repeated by Wasson ad infinitum and grew ever taller in the telling. Its growing resemblance to a Hollywood movie script made Wasson's own daughter, Masha, question whether it had any substance at all, but eventually she conceded that the incident had genuinely occurred, however embroidered the story had become over the years. This is itself telling for, as we shall see, Wasson had a knack of overworking dry empirical facts in the interests of a good story (Letcher 2007: 81).

It's less widely known that Valentina did her own write-up on their mushroom experiences in Oaxaca, Mexico, and her article was also timed for publication the same week as Wasson's article that was published in *Life* on May 13, 1957. Valentina's article was published in *This Week* magazine on May 19, 1957, which went out to approximately twelve million newspaper subscribers.[2] We'll return to this topic in a moment.

But some might ask: why should we dwell on such minor, insignificant contradictions? Or are they minor and insignificant? Is it possible that such clues lead us to places that tell a very different story? Is Masha using a fallacy to dismiss it? Essentially, what is being said here is that if someone repeats a lie often enough, then, based on an appeal to sincerity and consistency, we can accept it as fact.

Rather than allowing fallacies to determine our conclusion for us, what would be the process of proper investigation to find out if Masha's doubt regarding her father was valid? What would it take? Do we need to go to Wasson's Harvard archive to find out?

Well, if we could, Harvard might be a good place to start. But I suppose that I should provide a little preamble to this issue here.

I've been working on this investigation since 2006, and I knew, and had heard from others, that I might get banned from the Wasson archive at Harvard's Herbaria if I approached them directly and honestly, as in fact I did (below). However, in the interim years I went through many university archives and searched out all sorts of things on Wasson and acquired thousands of pages of material on him, nearly all of which I didn't find listed any place in the Harvard University Herbaria website index. This led me to the conclusion that the Harvard collection is an extremely selective assortment, a facade of specific items that further the Wassonian legends and myths. In other words, early on I realized that every conversation has two sides, and that Wasson's archive at Harvard would only have his side of any collection of the letters. By going to other university archives I was able to reconstruct much of the information simply by following the leads of the names of the wealthy elite and intelligence members with whom Wasson was associated, and who also happened to maintain their own archives at other universities. This way I reverse-engineered everything I needed through these other archives at other universities. And before I ever sent my inquiry to Harvard I was already certain that what they hold there is only a carefully selected presentation, mostly only pertaining to Wasson's ethnomycology work, which furthers the Wassonian myth and leaves out most of what might lead researchers to question not only the very foundations of the field, but its so-called founder as well.

But unfortunately Masha Wasson Britten, Wasson's adopted daughter, oversees the Wasson archive at Harvard herself and doesn't allow anyone in without first getting them to tell her what they want to see and what they're going to say about it—before they've even seen it! This of course is a logical impossibility and requires a bit of argumentum ad ignorantium, or even worse, just plain lying and bullshitting.

Here is Harvard's response after sending them my initial inquiry:

> Your request was forwarded to me. Are you interested in setting up an appointment to use these materials? If so I need a formal proposal submitted. Nothing too long, just a few sentences about your scholarly affiliation (if any), your purpose (book, article, dissertation, etc.), and what point you are making about Wasson. The heirs are very involved with the use of this collection and any request to publish must be approved by them (Lisa DeCesare, Head of Archives and Public Services, Botany Libraries, Harvard University Herbaria, June 15, 2011.).

My reply to Lisa at Harvard, from January 20, 2012:

> Dear Lisa,
>
> Thank you for your reply. My apologies for such a long delay in getting back to you.
>
> I'm an independent scholar, though my work in this field is stored permanently at Purdue. I'm affiliated via research with many dozens of professors and scholars in the field.
>
> I'm writing a biography on Gordon Wasson titled: The Secret History of Magic Mushrooms: Magic Mushrooms, the CIA, and the Legend of R. Gordon Wasson.

(Part of) the point I'm making about Wasson is in regard to his ties to the intelligence establishment—esp. Allen Dulles and John Foster Dulles, the Council on Foreign Relations—he acted as chairman, the Century Club and Pilgrim Society, MK-ULTRA, public relations, George de Mohrenschildt, and the various Russia funds that they ran together for J. P. Morgan. I'm also interested in why his daughter, Masha, felt that his story about his walk through the woods was "like a Hollywood soap opera." I think I have the answer to her reservation on the matter but there are documents that I'd like to verify and go through in context.

I'm especially interested in missives that would show Wasson to have intentionally created the psychedelic movement via his ties to Luce through the CFR (Council on Foreign Relations) and Century and the head of the CIA—Dulles. As well as any documents showing his side of the conversation regarding such actions or ties to intelligence and/or media establishment, including George Kennan, Edward Bernays, and many, many others. I know that he and Kennan and Bernays were all close.

I would need to see what the missives actually say before I could possibly know exactly what I'd write about them, else I commit the fallacy of argumentum ad ignorantium. I think that's a fairly impossible request to ask what one is going to write about something before they've actually seen it. But I'd be happy to share my work and findings with Wasson's family.

Of course much of my biography will also cover the more mundane aspects of his life, so I'd like to see what I can in that regard as well.

Those that I've listed below are from months ago and I have many others that I'd like to request once access is granted.

Thank you for your time. I look forward to meeting you and viewing the archives.

Sincerely,
Jan Irvin

Lisa's response of February 3, 2012:

> Jan,
>
> I am sorry to report that at this point your request to access the collection has been denied.
>
> Lisa D.

I replied on February 3, 2012:

> Hi Lisa, was there any reason stated as to why?

To which she replied, February 3, 2012:

> No, sorry, there wasn't.
>
> Lisa D.

Of course this was the response I was expecting. I and several professors interested in investigating this matter had discussed this topic and how I should proceed. If I were granted access to the archives, then great, I'd be able to verify a handful of the other, less important materials. If, on the other hand, I were denied access, then I'd just publish their refusal to grant access and bring attention to the issue. In fact, publishing their notice of refusal to grant access is almost better than giving me access, as it shows a probability that there is a concerted effort to keep people out of the Wasson archives if they aren't likely to perpetuate the Wassonian legends and myths.

I proceeded with the truth, letting the Harvard Herbaria know exactly my intention for the book, and, as has happened to others who intended to do honest research on Wasson, my request was denied by Masha herself, the Guardian of the Wassonian Legends and Myths.

No other archive at any other university, or any place for that matter, that I've ever come across, has ever made such a requirement in connection with acquiring documents. I've filed CIA FOIA

(Freedom of Information Act) requests, I've been through CFR archives, Yale, Stanford, Princeton, Columbia, and on and on, and none has ever made such an absurd request, nor has any one of them ever failed to provide a document—until now.

Others, such as Robert Forte, have also been blocked from the Wasson archive at the Harvard Herbaria. Forte claims he was blocked from the archive for merely asserting during a public lecture in New York in 2008 that Wasson was associated with the inner circle of American fascism. To paraphrase Forte's lecture:

> Scholars of the psychedelics have frequently commented on the synchronicity of Hofmann's discoveries with the discovery and propagation of nuclear weapons. The effect of LSD was discovered just six months after the atom was split. Huxley might have been the first to call LSD the atom bomb of the soul, and Frank Barron wondered if nature was keeping itself in balance by slipping these sacraments into society at the time they were most needed. Since man now had this savage power of nuclear weaponry it better have a corresponding leap in consciousness. Not only was this synchronous in time, but recently I've learned that psychedelics came into America through individuals associated with this dark, destructive, and anti-democratic forces. Gordon Wasson, it is well known, was a Wall Street Banker. I've learned that, not only was he employed on Wall Street by Morgan, but he was actually on the inner most circle of American fascism.... (Forte 2008)

Due to space constraints on this essay I must reserve much of this story for my upcoming book and video on this subject, *The Secret History of Magic Mushrooms,* though I will provide here some of the best discoveries I've made over recent years.

Soma

Returning to our doubt regarding the myth of Wasson and Valentina's walk through the woods in 1927, we come to what may have been, at least in part, the inspiration for Wasson's studies of mushrooms as soma, as well as his original interest in the Mexican mushroom practices.

A comparison of the effects of soma with those of the *Amanita muscaria* and cannabis was first proposed in the book *Scatalogic* [sic] *Rites of All Nations* by John G. Bourke, 1891. The author dedicated more than thirty pages (pp. 65–99) to the study of the ritualistic use of mushrooms, including the Siberian *Amanita muscaria* urine–drinking custom, and Mexican mushroom practices. This is probably where Wasson first learned of the ritualistic use of mushrooms, urine consumption, and Soma. On page ninety-eight is a letter to Bourke by a Dr. J. W. Kingsley:

> I remember being shown this fungus by an Englishman who was returning … from Siberia. He fully confirmed all that I had heard on the subject, having seen the orgy [mushroom rituals] himself.… Nothing religious in this, you may say; but look at the question a little closer and you will see that these "intoxicants" … were at first looked upon as media able to raise the mere man up to a level with his gods, and enable him to communicate with them, as was certainly the case with the "soma" of the Hindu ecstatics and the hashich [sic] I have seen used by some tribes of Arabs.

Most scholars claim that Wasson was the progenitor of these ideas, but this is not wholly accurate. It appears that Wasson may have "borrowed" several key ideas from Bourke's research and expanded upon them throughout his career, subsequently creating the field of ethnomycology. Thereafter it appears that Bourke was relegated mostly to rare catalogue and bibliographical entries published by Wasson and a few other scholars of his ilk.[3] However, Bourke is not to be found, as one should expect him to be, given the extent of his studies on the subject, in the main body of text in most of the books published on the subject for the last half century.

The coincidences don't stop there. J. P. Morgan, Jr. was also involved in mushroom research, and, as Donald H. Pfister points out in *Mycologia*, Morgan appears to have funded Harvard's Herbaria:

> In 1928, Wasson entered the banking world and joined the Guaranty Trust Company of New York. He spent extended periods of time in Argentina and London. In 1934, he joined the staff of J. P. Morgan and Co. (which merged with Guaranty Trust to become Morgan Guaranty Trust) and remained with the firm until 1963, from 1943 as a vice president. The Morgan connection is an interesting one upon which I will digress for a moment. J. P. Morgan, Jr. (Harvard, class of 1889) took courses with Farlow and wrote an undergraduate thesis under his direction. He was a student while Roland Thaxter was a graduate student. If Harvard tradition represents the situation correctly, Morgan was devoted to mycology. His generosity was important, particularly to Thaxter, during the period of the establishment of the Farlow Reference Library and Herbarium as a separately endowed unit. In a letter to Farlow upon that man's 70th birthday, Morgan thanked Farlow for allowing him to work under "your inspiring presence." Certainly something mycological lived on at Morgan Guaranty Trust with Wasson as a vice president (Pfister 1998: 11–13).

In a future essay or book, I'll also show that J. P. Morgan, Sr. was also interested in collecting mushroom art in relation to Shakespeare from as early as the 1850s.

> I wondered if his Morgan bank employers had expressed reservations when told he was about to reveal to the world that he had partaken of the magic mushrooms.
>
> "Not at all," Gordon said. "I suspect that *only* Morgan would have tolerated what I did" (Riedlinger 1990/1997: 209; italics from original).

J. P. Morgan Bank and Skull and Bones Created Time-Life Inc.

Wasson's direct boss at J. P. Morgan was Henry P. Davison Jr. Davison was a senior partner and generally regarded as Morgan's personal emissary (Mullins 1993: 1). As it turns out, it was Henry P. Davison who essentially created (or at least funded) the *Time-Life* magazines for J. P. Morgan in 1923. After a row with Henry Luce for publishing an article against the war for Britain in *Life,* Davison "became the company's first investor in *Time* magazine and a company director" (Chernow 2001: 466).

Another J. P. Morgan partner, Dwight Morrow, also helped to finance the Time Life start-up. Davison kept Henry Luce in charge of the company as president, as he and Luce were both members of Yale's Skull and Bones secret society, being initiated in 1920. In 1946, Davison and Luce then made C.D. Jackson, former head of U.S. Psychological Warfare, vice president of Time-Life. It seems to me that the entire operation at Time-Life was purely for spreading propaganda to the American public for the purposes of the intelligence community, J. P. Morgan, and the elite. On a side note, Henry P. Davison's brother, Frederick Trubee Davison, was Assistant to the U.S. Secretary of War, and also became Director of Personnel for the CIA. Frederick was also a Skull and Bones man, initiated in 1918. Frederick's son, Daniel P. Davison, also became a banker and a Skull and Bones man, in 1949, and headed United States Trust.

Yet another Skull and Bones man behind the establishment of Time-Life was Briton Hadden, who worked with Davison, Luce, and Morrow in setting up the organization. Hadden was also initiated into Skull and Bones in 1920. The list of Bones men that tie in directly to Wasson and his clique is astounding, and also includes people like Averell Harriman, initiated 1913, who worked with Wasson at the CFR[4] and was a director there.[5] Harriman, a financial backer of the Nazi Party until 1938, as was Prescott Bush, was initiated to Skull and Bones in 1917.

In the *Executive Intelligence Review* of June 25, 2004, Steven P. Meyer and Jeffrey Steinberg explain:

> Luce's personal lawyer, who would come to represent his entire media empire, was his brother-in-law Tex Moore, of Cravath, deGersdorff, Swaine and Wood, the same firm which deployed both *Allen and John Foster Dulles* to facilitate bringing Hitler to power in the early 1930s.
>
> *Luce was an intimate of Britain's Lord Beaverbrook and the Prince of Wales,* who were notoriously pro-Hitler and members of the Cliveden set. He also formed an extremely close relationship with Winston Churchill, himself a promoter of Hitler in the early 1930s [emphasis mine].

Documents also reveal that Luce was a member of the Century Club, an exclusive "art club" that Wasson had much to do with and may have held some position with, and which was filled with members of the intelligence and banking community. Members such as George Kennan, Walter Lippmann, and Frank Altschul appear to have been nominated to the Century Club by Wasson himself.[6] Graham Harvey in *Shamanism* says that Luce and Wasson were friends, and this is how he came to publish in *Life:*

> A New York investment banker, Wasson was well acquainted with the movers and shakers of the Establishment. Therefore, it was natural that he should turn to his friend Henry Luce, publisher of *Life*, when he needed a public forum in which to announce his discoveries (Harvey 2002: 433).

It was Luce, Wasson's friend, who featured Hitler as man of the year for 1938 in the January 2, 1939, issue of *Time*.

However, here's the most common mythical version of the story that we've all been fed—as told by *Time* magazine in 2007:

> Wasson and his buddy's mushroom trip might have been lost to history, but he was so enraptured by the experience that on his return to New York, he kept talking about it to friends. As

> Jay Stevens recalls in his 1987 book *Storming Heaven: LSD and the American Dream,* one day during lunch at the Century Club, an editor at Time Inc. (the parent company of TIME) overheard Wasson's tale of adventure. The editor commissioned a first-person narrative for *Life*.

And being that this article was written in the post–Luce and Jackson age, the author was a little more candid about the Wasson/Luce/J. P. Morgan/psychedelic revolution connections:

> After Wasson's article was published, many people sought out mushrooms and the other big hallucinogen of the day, LSD. (In 1958, Time Inc. cofounder Henry Luce and his wife Clare Booth Luce dropped acid with a psychiatrist. Henry Luce conducted an imaginary symphony during his trip, according to *Storming Heaven.*) The most important person to discover drugs through the *Life* piece was Timothy Leary himself. Leary had never used drugs, but a friend recommended the article to him, and Leary eventually traveled to Mexico to take mushrooms. Within a few years, he had launched his crusade for America to "turn on, tune in, drop out." In other words, you can draw a woozy but vivid line from the sedate offices of J. P. Morgan and Time Inc. in the '50s to Haight-Ashbury in the '60s to a zillion drug-rehab centers in the '70s. Long, strange trip indeed (Cloud 2007).

In *The Sacred Mushroom Seeker,* a third version of this story is told by Allan Richardson:

> Sometime just before or soon after our return from the '56 expedition, Gordon and I were dining at the Century Club in New York. He noticed Ed Thompson, the managing editor of *Life* magazine, alone at a table nearby, and asked him to join us. We talked about the article Gordon was working on to publicize what he'd discovered in Mexico. Thompson said Life might be interested in publishing it, and invited us to make a presentation at his offices (Richardson in Riedlinger 1990/1997: 199).

As we noted above, nowhere do these accounts mention Valentina's own write-up in *This Week* magazine,which was coincidently released that same week (May 19, 1957) to twelve million newspaper subscribers. Also coincidently, *This Week* was published by Joseph P. Knapp, who was a director of Morgan's Guarantee Trust, where Wasson had begun while working for Morgan in 1928.

In light of the above, the idea that Wasson published his "Seeking the Magic Mushroom" article in May 1957, in *Life,* due to a "chance meeting with an editor," seems ridiculous. In fact, Abby Hoffman is quoted as saying that Luce did more to popularize LSD than Timothy Leary (who first learned of mushrooms through Wasson's *Life* article). Luce's own wife, Clare Boothe Luce, who was, interestingly, also a member of the CFR, agreed:

> I've always maintained that Henry Luce did more to popularize acid than Timothy Leary. Years later I met Clare Boothe Luce at the Republican convention in Miami. She did not disagree with this opinion. America's version of the Dragon Lady caressed my arm, fluttered her eyes and cooed, "We wouldn't want everyone doing too much of a good thing" (Hoffman 1980: 73).

Here we see their elitist, secretive philosophy shining through. Due to space constraints we'll have to save the details for another article, but what we see here is a dialectic: both the popularizing and outlawing of psychedelics by the same group of people through propaganda. And the main reason to occult (keep secret) is to be able to use them against others.

Did the editor overhear Wasson? Did Wasson ask him to join them? Why the contradictions? Or, should we follow Graham Harvey's inference that Luce and Wasson were already friends, which seems the most likely?

With the fact that Wasson's boss, Davison, was a director and investor of Time-Life, and that Knapp was a director of Morgan's Guarantee Trust, and that Wasson and Luce were both members of the Century Club (an intelligence community front) and the CFR, where Wasson served as a chairman,[7] and with all of the ties to J. P.

Morgan and Skull and Bones, it's hard to believe that Wasson's article published in *Life* wasdue to a chance meeting. So I must ask: What are the mathematical possibilities of so many coincidences happening, as pertains to the stories, myths, and legends about Wasson? Are we to believe in coincidence theory—that he bumped into the editor at the Century Club? Or are we to look in the direction that the evidence points—using logic and reason—that Wasson worked with and was involved with the intelligence community on many levels, as was Luce, and that the "'Seeking the Magic Mushroom" story was published in *Life* to further some secret agenda for the banking elite? This should now be coming clear. But what was their agenda?

There are several reasons why the psychedelic movement may have been launched, including attempts to distract people from government policy failure; extracting information from people under the influence, such as with MK-ULTRA; making money from the drugs through the pharmaceutical industry; and even pacifying people with a Huxleyan-like soma or with positivist spirituality so that they could be more easily controlled.

Furthermore, documents from Yale reveal that Wasson had been sharing his mushroom research with intelligence officials since at least 1950.[8] Wasson had also sent copies of his book *Mushrooms, Russia and History* to George Kennan[9] and Frank Altschul,[10] among many others, as soon as copies were available. Kennan worked with the OSS (Office of Strategic Services, the precursor of the CIA) in Germany,[11] was the Ambassador to the USSR, and also worked with the CFR. There is more on him and Altschul below. It would be fascinating to see a complete list of exactly who received the 100 copies of *Mushrooms, Russia and History* that Wasson gave away. I have a fairly well supported suspicion that many of the receivers belonged to the Century Club, CFR, or CIA, or a mixture of all three.

Enter Edward Bernays, the Father of Propaganda

And there is one more connection here. Wasson was friends with Edward Bernays, the father of propaganda and spin, who was also a friend of Henry Luce and, as it turns out, was a major influence on Goebbels, the man in charge of Nazi propaganda.

> The conscious and intelligent manipulation of the organized habits and opinions of the masses is an important element in democratic society. *Those who manipulate this unseen mechanism of society constitute an invisible government which is the true ruling power of our country.... We are governed, our minds are molded, our tastes formed, our ideas suggested, largely by men we have never heard of.* This is a logical result of the way in which our democratic society is organized. Vast numbers of human beings must cooperate in this manner if they are to live together as a smoothly functioning society.... In almost every act of our daily lives, whether in the sphere of politics or business, in our social conduct or our ethical thinking, we are dominated by the relatively small number of persons ... who understand the mental processes and social patterns of the masses. It is they who pull the wires which control the public mind (Bernays 1928: 1).

It was based on a hunch alone that I searched out the ties between Wasson and Bernays. The following was the only citation I could find revealing that the two had spent extensive time together, though, no doubt, in some other archive, there is much more yet to be discovered.

In a file located at the US Library of Congress is an odd draft, likely intended to be some form of propaganda or endorsement, wherein Bernays discusses his relationship with Wasson.[12] This letter also reveals that Wasson and Valentina had adopted Masha, and "lived on East End Avenue." Bernays further states:

> Gordon Wasson was one of those newspapermen who consciously or unconsciously recognized the implications of the contacts he made in that capacity. He found these contacts important, outstanding. This led to other places and other things. In the *New York Tribune* financial department he had made contact with the house on the corner, Broad and Wall—J. P. Morgan. Then he had given up newspaper work and become associated with the home (Morgan's "house on the corner"). First he was in the publicity department. When Martin Eagen died, he assumed the function of publicity man with J. Pierpont Morgan. He was highly respected by his own people. He was intelligent, smooth. His mind was a highly, splendidly geared functioning mechanism.... Wasson made it his business and he got pleasure out of it too, of associating with a broad segment of society. This was not unimportant in maintaining contacts for the house on the corner [Broad and Wall—J. P. Morgan], with the rest of the world.
>
> Not until long after I knew him did I find out in [Prof. Raymond] Moley's book "The First Seven Years" [*sic*] published in 1939, a reference to Gordon Wasson. Moley wrote a memo in 1934 and made recommendations for the Stock Exchange Commission membership. Next to Gordon Wasson, whom he recommended, he added, "a resident of New Jersey, handled foreign securities for Guaranty Company, has acted a liaison between Wall Street and Landis, Cohen and Corcoran because his friendship with them was known downtown. Knows security business and the Act thoroughly having helped in its drafting, very well-liked by treasury and commerce, would certainly be recommended by the Guaranty and Stock Exchange and therefore would be acceptable to Wall Street."

Bernays's letter concludes with:

> I saw Wasson very often between 1934 and '44; I never had the slightest inkling he had been thought of for this position. His conversation was bland, never personal, always on the most general subjects.[13]

Though speculation, I've long been of the opinion that Bernays personally trained Wasson during the decade from 1934 to 1944 in the arts of propaganda and public relations spin for J. P. Morgan. I'll provide more evidence of this claim in a moment. I find it interesting, though, that it is from Bernays, the very father of public relations, that we find the most about Wasson's position in PR with Morgan.

Thomas Riedlinger's book *The Sacred Mushroom Seeker,* which may be seen as the official biography on Wasson, only touches on his work in "communications, public relations—that sort of thing":

> DeWitt Peterkin, retired vice president in charge of domestic lending, joined J. P. Morgan & Co. in 1937. Gordon was already there, initially as a credit banker. He soon proved himself "a great person for putting together the background and history" of Morgan's accounts, recalled Peterkin.... In subsequent years, Gordon's role as a credit banker gave way to new responsibilities. Eventually, *as vice president, he would (end) up in charge of "communications, public relations—that sort of thing,"* recalled Peterkin. Personal contact with overseas clients was part of the job.
>
> "Unbeknownst to most people, we for many years were one of the bankers for the Vatican," Peterkin said. "And Gordon used to have private audiences with the Pope." Though *he could not recall which particular Pope,* other sources later told me it had been Pius XII – and that Gordon had not liked him much (Riedlinger 1990/1997: 210; emphasis mine).

And though Riedlinger's quote is vague if he's referring to Peterkin or Wasson, wouldn't it seem rather irregular if Wasson would have private audiences with the pope, and yet not remember which pope?

The Case of Wasson's "Remorse"

On September 26, 1970, Wasson published an article in *TheNew York Times* wherein he is supposedly distraught and expresses remorse regarding the then-recent reports of "hippies, psychopaths and adventurers and pseudo–research workers" descending on Huautla de Jimenez in Oaxaca, Mexico:

> Huautla, when I first knew it as a humble out-of-the-way Indian village, has become a true mecca for hippies, psychopaths, adventurers, pseudo-research workers, the miscellaneous crew of our society's drop-outs. The old ways are dead and I fear that my responsibility is heavy, mine and Maria Sabina's.... As for me, what have I done? I made a cultural discovery of importance. Should I have suppressed it? It has led to further discoveries the reach of which remains to be seen. Should these further discoveries have remained stultified by my unwillingness to reveal the secret of the Indians' hallucinogens?
>
> Yet what I have done gives me nightmares: I have unleashed on lovely Huautla a torrent of commercial exploitation of the vilest kind. Now the mushrooms are exposed for sale everywhere—in every marketplace, in every village doorway. Everyone offers his services as a "priest" of the rite, even the politicos.... The whole of the countryside is agog with the furtive movements of hippies, the comings and goings of the "federalistas," the Dogberries with their blundering efforts to root them out (Wasson 1970: 29).

Here is a very startling conversation between Wasson and Bertram Wolfe that I found in the Bertram Wolfe papers at The Hoover Institute at Stanford, which puts Wasson's *New York Times* article in a whole new light:

> October 8, 1970:
>
> Dear Mr. Wasson:
>
> I was greatly interested in your article in *TheNew York Times* on "The Sacred Mushroom".... I marked your note of sadness near the end and wish to tell you that you have nothing to reproach yourself for. Knowledge will out. If one man doesn't spread it another will. The hippies, peddlers, and Dogberries will in, for

> nature abhors a vacuum. You may have hastened it a little by publishing in Life, rather than in a magazine of anthropologists, but the process was inevitable.[14]
>
> October 13, 1970:
>
> Dear Mr. Wolfe:
>
> Do you remember your last letter to me? I was asking you where Tolstoy had said the printing press was a mighty engine for disseminating ignorance. *This Mazatec affair is a case in point.*
>
> R. Gordon Wasson[15] [emphasis mine]

In other words, what we're dealing with in this essay is this very group of propagandists: "Those who manipulate this unseen mechanism of society constitute an invisible government which is the true ruling power of our country ... men we have never heard of." In fact, many of them we have heard of, two of them being Edward Bernays and R. Gordon Wasson.

The ramifications of Wasson's above statement affects so many things on so many levels that it is disturbing to contemplate: First, in the *New York Times* article, Wasson sheds crocodile tears over his so-called dilemma of releasing the information about the mushrooms, while at the same time disparaging entire groups of people with sweeping generalizations and ad hominem remarks, and relishing his power to create commerce and distraction among the people he despises. Then he casts half the blame on Maria Sabina. He never once addresses his intelligence agendas: that he worked with the CFR and CIA (more on this in a moment). As Maria Sabina relates, had Wasson not gone to the town mayor's office and spoken to Cayetano García Mendoza, who was acting as mayor, Sabina would not have given him the mushrooms. She thought the mayor's visit to her home was official business, so she felt obligated to serve Wasson:

> Cayetano then explained to Doña María that he had told the visitors, "I know a true wise woman." Cayetano asked Doña María

if he could bring the strangers to her home so that she might teach them the true knowledge of the mushrooms. Doña María replied, "If you want to, I can't say no."

> Years later, María Sabina stated that she felt compelled to accept Wasson's request because of Cayetano's official position, and she assumed Cayetano's visit to her humble dwelling that hot summer day was official business.... In 1971, Wasson read an interview with María Sabina which appeared in the European magazine *L'Europe,* published in Milan. It reported that when Cayetano had requested her aid in helping the foreigners, she did so because she felt she had no choice. But she also declared that when she was asked to meet them (Wasson and Richardson) that she "should have said no."[16]

But even more disturbing is what Wasson wrote to Bertram Wolfe: "*Tolstoy had said the printing press was a mighty engine for disseminating ignorance. This Mazatec affair is a case in point.*" Here it's clear that Wasson is a disciple of Edward Bernays and is using PR, or propaganda, to manipulate the public's opinion. He is making himself out to appear remorseful while at the same time furthering his campaign against Huaulta de Jimenez by publishing the article in *The New York Times.* And Wolfe appears gratifyingly dazzled by Wasson's intellect, so Wasson lets him in on the secret of the hidden agenda, while sharing his contempt of the common people at the same time.

Whatever secret consequences Wasson and his friends expected from their exploitation of mushrooms, it had severe and direct consequences for the people who passed on their knowledge to him:

> From the moment when the strangers arrived the "Holy Children" lost their purity. They lost their strength. They were profaned. From now on they will serve no purpose. There is no help for it. Before Wasson I felt that the Holy Children elevated me. I no longer feel so (Estrada 1981: 90–91)…. [T] he divine mushroom no longer belongs to us [the Indians of Mesoamerica]. Its sacred language has been profaned. The

> language has been spoiled and it is indecipherable for us.... Now the mushrooms speak NQUI LE [English]. Yes, it's the tongue that the foreigners speak.... The mushrooms have a divine spirit. They always had it for us, but the foreigners arrived and frightened it away.... (Estrada 1981: 205)

In response to Maria Sabina's words, above, Wasson stated:

> These words make me wince, but I was merely the precursor of the New Day. I arrived in the same decade with the highway, the airplane, the alphabet. The Old Order was in danger of passing with no one to record its passing. The Wisdom of the *Sabia*, genuine though it was, has nothing to give to the world of tomorrow (Wasson 1980: 223).

I couldn't disagree more that the wisdom of the *Sabia* (wise one or wise woman) has nothing for the world of tomorrow—as the last three decades of hindsight have shown us since Wasson wrote that in 1980. And maybe someone without an agenda would have made a more accurate recording. And there is a big difference between being the precursor for the New Day, and being a tool for the elite, and using Sabina and the mushrooms for PR and secret intelligence purposes.

The Hall Carbine Affair

It appears that Wasson was able to gain his position at J. P. Morgan's bank as VP of Public Relations (propaganda) by helping to cover up J. P. Morgan, Sr.'s involvement in the Civil War's Hall Carbine Affair, to which Wasson titled his own book on the matter. Documents uncovered at Yale University in the Andrews archives reveal that Wasson had been telling the Civil War historian Allan Nevins what to write about J. P. Morgan and the carbine affair,[17] and then Wasson would turn and cite Nevins as an appeal to authority in his own arguments on the matter—which is an obvious conflict of interest, not to mention that someone working in PR for Morgan might likewise have a conflict of interest in writing an account of the matter. Furthermore, Wasson had been telling Prof. Charles McLain Andrews about the entire affair,[18] and Andrews had forwarded Wasson's manuscript to Nevins.[19] Here are a few quotes on Nevins from Wasson's *Hall Carbine Affair:*

> In 1939, three books appeared in which, at long last, the Hall Carbine Affair was presented in true perspective. Allan Nevins in his revised life of Fremont told the story accurately, with emphasis on Fremont's part in it.
>
> Shortly afterwards F. S. Crofts & Co. published a *Casebook in American Business History,* by two Harvard professors, N. S. B. Gras, who holds the Straus chair in Business History, and Henrietta M. Larson. In the chapter on Morgan they wrote:
>
> ...The other episode is the Hall carbine affair. The story is too long to recount here, but an extensive search has failed to uncover any contemporary proof that justifies the deductions about Morgan's business character which many writers have drawn from the episode.

Before the end of the year Macmillan brought out Herbert L. Satterlee's life of J. Pierpont Morgan, in which the episode was summarized. In reviewing this work for *The New York Times,* Allan Nevins called special attention to the carbine matter:

> Mr. Satterlee offers a convincing exculpation of Morgan from one of the charges most frequently brought against him: the allegation that in 1861 he assisted one Simon Stevens in operations which defrauded the Federal Government upon a sale of defective Hall carbines to General Fremont's army. The carbines were not really defective, but were a valuable arm. What loss the government suffered was attributed in the main to the carelessness of its own War Department, and Morgan was never a party at interest in the transaction, being merely the person from whom one of those parties borrowed some money (Dec. 17, 1939) (Wasson 1948: 114).

> The Nevins review was only one of many references by critics to the new account of the carbine episode in the Satterlee book. The Associated Press carried the story at some length on November 26, 1939. The reviewer in *Time* raised a question about it in the issue of December 18, which prompted letters of comment from Herbert L. Satterlee, Lewis Corey, and Gordon Roberts in the issues of February 5 and 19, 1940 (Wasson 1948: 115).

Here are a few of the quotes I've found from the Andrews archives at Yale on Wasson and Nevins's behind-the-scenes interaction on the matter. It's clear that Wasson is attempting to make J. P. Morgan, Sr. look innocent—despite his guilt:

> December 15, 1937
>
> I could make a very good use of the copy of my Civil War Carbine monograph that Mr. Nevins has, if he is back from California. My recollection is that he would be returning about this time. I hope it is not too much trouble for you to make sure that he returns it.
>
> I think my name does not appear on the monograph. Do you happen to remember whether you let him know who wrote it? If not, there might be an advantage in leaving him in the dark if we should publish the manuscript through some other medium.
>
> R. Gordon Wasson[20] (emphasis mine)

> August 15, 1939
>
> Dear Mr. Andrews:
>
> I hasten to write you to assure you *that Allen [sic] Nevins treated my manuscript exactly as I would've wished him to do.* He refers and is taxed to a "careful investigation" which "has shown that he must announce transaction and was really prudent and commendable." *In an appendix he summarizes the episode in two or*

three pages. He doesn't identify "the recent investigation," and for this I am very glad. Since his revised Life came out, he and I had an exchange of cordial letters on the subject.

R. Gordon Wasson (emphasis mine)[21]

October 28, 1941

I am most grateful to you for your comments on the Hall Carbine paper, and we shall give earnest consideration to your advice. I have sent a copy of it to Allan Nevins, with whom I have often discussed it, and also to our good friend Steve Benet. We wish to think out carefully our procedure, and, fortunately, we can choose our own time. Perhaps after we let the matter simmer for some months we may bring out a second and larger edition. (emphasis mine)[22]

Here's what historian Charles Morris had to say on the matter in *The Tycoons:*

> For the Hall carbine affair, see R. Gordon Wasson, *The Hall Carbine Affair: A Study in Contemporary Folklore* (New York: Pandick Press, 1948),*although Wasson (and Carosso) would have it that Morgan did not know that the rifles were being resold to the government, which is implausible.*For the muckraker version of the affair, see Mathew Josephson, *The Robber Barons: The Great American Capitalists* (New York: Harcourt, Brace and World 1962), pp. 60–61(Morris 2005: 337; emphasismine).

And historian Matthew Josephson had this to say about the affair in *Robber Barons:*

> A certain Simon Stevens, who had an option for 5,000 Hall carbines, through another dealer named Eastman, came to Morgan with an urgent request for a loan against this war material which he soon hoped to sell to the government at a profit. In advance, he had by telegraph arranged to sell them to General Fremont, who headed the Western Army quartered

> near St. Louis. Stevens, who had long been engaged in obscure transactions with customhouse officials, may or may not have divulged that he needed the sum of $17,486 from Morgan in order to purchase the carbines from the very same government at Washington whose army in the West clamored for guns. This paradoxical situation was caused by the fact that the carbines in question were found by inspection to be so defective that they would shoot off the thumbs of the soldiers using them. The quartermaster at Washington sold them for $3.50 apiece. "The government had sold one day for $17,486 arms which it had agreed the day before to purchase for $109,912," as a Congressional committee later discovered. That young Morgan (then 24) knew of this situation is plain from the fact that after arrival of the consignment of guns at General Fremont's division, he bluntly presented his claim not for the money he had advanced, but for all of the $58,175, half of the shipment having been already paid for in good faith.

Morgan's claim for the full sum of $109,912, where he had loaned only $17,486, may have been an indication to the Congress that his part in the affair was something more than a passive money-lender's. In the ensuing investigation, March 3, 1863, a Committee on Government Contracts, amid such outcry on "pillage, fraud, extortion," had demanded that Morgan disclose the terms upon which he had entered the transaction, though without breaking his obdurate silence. The Congressmen had not been convinced that this large and sullen young man's operations "inured to the benefit of the people," and had seen fit to lecture him. Of him and his fellow their report had said:

> He cannot be looked upon as a good citizen, entitled to favorable consideration of his claim, who seeks to augment the vast burdens, daily increasing, that are to weigh on the future industry of the country, by demands upon the treasury for which nothing entitled to the name of an equivalent has been rendered ...Worse than traitors in arms are the men who pretending loyalty to the flag, feast and fatten on the misfortunes of the nation, while patriot blood is crimsoning the plains of

> the South and bodies of their countrymen are moldering in the dust (Josephson 1962: 61ff).

I wonder if when Morris and Josephson wrote these passages they knew that Wasson was working in PR for J. P. Morgan, and that Wasson had actually sent Nevins his manuscript so that their stories would match up? I highly doubt it, however. Chances are that I'm the first to make this discovery—unfortunately. And while the story has been well evidenced that Morgan did in fact swindle the U.S. government, it couldn't be any more suspicious that a man, Wasson, who worked for J. P. Morgan's Bank in PR, should write such a story and then become Vice President of Public Relations, and also happened to have spent time with Edward Bernays during this book's writing. There are just too many coincidences stacked on top of coincidences for there to be any coincidence!

Securities and Exchange Commission

Professor Raymond Moley's book *After Seven Years*, mentioned by Bernays above, states:

> I had asked the President to talk over these appointments with me because, since the time I had assisted him in formulating his New York State parole system, I had seen so much good legislation for which he fought partly nullified by the appointment of poor administrators. At that very moment he was in process of frittering away his Communications Act in the same familiar way. It was clear that the Securities and Exchange Commission might be transformed into a purely perfunctory body if it fell under the influence of those interests it was supposed to supervise. Or, equally bad, it might fall under the domination of men who had no knowledge of the practical operation of the stock exchange.

The President listened to a recital of these facts good-naturedly and asked for a list of recommendations. This I laid before him early in June, 1934. It read as follows:

Stock Exchange Commission Membership

Memorandum

1. Kennedy The best bet for Chairman because of executive ability, knowledge of habits and customs of business to be regulated and ability to moderate different points of view on Commission.

2. Landis Better as member than as Chairman because he is essentially a representative of strict control and operates best when defending that position against opposition from contrary view.

3. Mathews Familiar with operation of blue sky laws and with present Securities Act. He is a Republican from Wisconsin and failure to take him over would antagonize Republican Progressives in Wisconsin.

4. Ben Cohen He is as able as Landis and more experienced. He has participated to a greater extent tha anyone else in the drafting of both Securities and Stock Exchange Acts. His personality would gain friends as people grew to know him. Enormously well thought of by Judge Mack Frankfurter, etc.

5. Paul Shields Expresses progressive ideas about regulation by law. Strongly recommended by Averell Harriman. Was associated with Dillon, Reed and probably would be strongly recommended by Clarence Dillon.

6. Gordon Wasson A resident of New Jersey. Handled foreign securities for Guaranty Company. Has acted as liaison between Wall Street and Landis, Cohen and Corcoran, because his friendship with them was known downtown. Knows securities business and the act thoroughly, having helped in its drafting.

Very well-liked by Treasury and Commerce. Would certainly be recommended by the Guaranty and the Stock Exchange and therefore would be acceptable to Wall Street.

7. Frank Shaughnessy Hiram Johnson would be an excellent judge of him. He is well thought of by Charles B. Henderson of the R.F.C. who knows him.

8. Judge Healy Could be counted upon to be sound and liberal in his interpretation. However, he would be a better member of the Federal Trade Commission.

Party affiliations: Democrat—Kennedy, Landis, Cohen, Shaughnessy Republican—Wasson, Mathews, Healy (Moley 1971: 287)

And it is here that we discover that Wasson actually helped to draft the Stock Exchange Act. A study of the Stock Exchange Act in light of the current financial crisis would be interesting in view of Wasson's participation in its authoring. And it was also Wasson's boss's father, J. P. Morgan, Sr., the same J. P. Morgan who swindled the government in the carbine affair, above, who secretly established the U.S. Federal Reserve at Jekyll Island (Mullins, 1993). But we also discover here that Wasson was one of eight nominees selected to chair the Securities and Exchange Commission for the U.S. government.

Thomas C. Wasson

Robert Gordon Wasson had a brother: Thomas Campbell Wasson. Jews assassinated Thomas in Jerusalem while he served as the first Consul General of the new state of Israel, a position he had only begun a few weeks before he was assassinated. At 2 p.m. on May 22, 1948, he was shot with a .30 caliber rifle while he was approaching the U.S. Consulate. He died on May 23, 1948—just ten days after the establishment of the State of Israel on *May 13.*

Thomas looked incredibly like R.G. Wasson, almost close enough to be twins. And interestingly, one writer even reported that it was Robert Wasson, and not Thomas Wasson, who had been killed:

> Our American Consul Mr. Robert Wasson was shot by Jews on Friday and died today.[23]
>
> Bertha Spafford Vesta, May 23, 1948

With all of the PR and false information put out by Wasson up to this point, I want to say that there is no evidence, at least at this moment, to show that there was some cover-up with the assassination, other than news reports initially trying to pin it on the Arabs. The confusion between Thomas and Robert seems to be just that—though I admit I've not looked into the matter any further.

Thomas had also served as the U.S. Vice Consul in Melbourne, Australia, as well as in Puerto Cortes, Honduras, and Consul in Lagos, Nigeria.

The main point is that Gordon Wasson had direct ties in his own family to high levels of the U.S. government and international politics—which may provide a lead for possible future research.

The JFK Assassination

And in an even more bizarre twist that is far stranger than fiction, readers may be shocked to discover that all of this ties into the Kennedy assassination. Several names mentioned above are involved, including Henry Luce and C.D. Jackson. C.D. Jackson purchased the Zapruder film of JFK's assassination. Jackson and Henry Luce stored the film away from the public in the vaults at Time-Life for decades—again, a company funded by J. P. Morgan and Wasson's boss. Furthermore, Wasson was close friends with George De Mohrenschildt, with whom he ran the Russian Student Fund for Russian immigrants on behalf of the CIA (below), and he also worked on various Russian programs with George's brother,

Professor Dimitri Von Mohrenschildt.[24] George De Mohrenschildt's wife worked for Abe Zapruder—who, ironically, filmed the assassination. And of course de Mohrenschildt was a close friend of Lee Harvey Oswald, the so-called "lone gunman." De Mohrenschildt apparently committed suicide just minutes before reporters arrived to interview him, and when his body was found there was a phone book in his pocket with Gordon Wasson's name and number, along with others such as George H. W. Bush, the former president and director of the CIA.

CIA agent - George de Mohrenschildt Phonebook 1954-55 Type entries

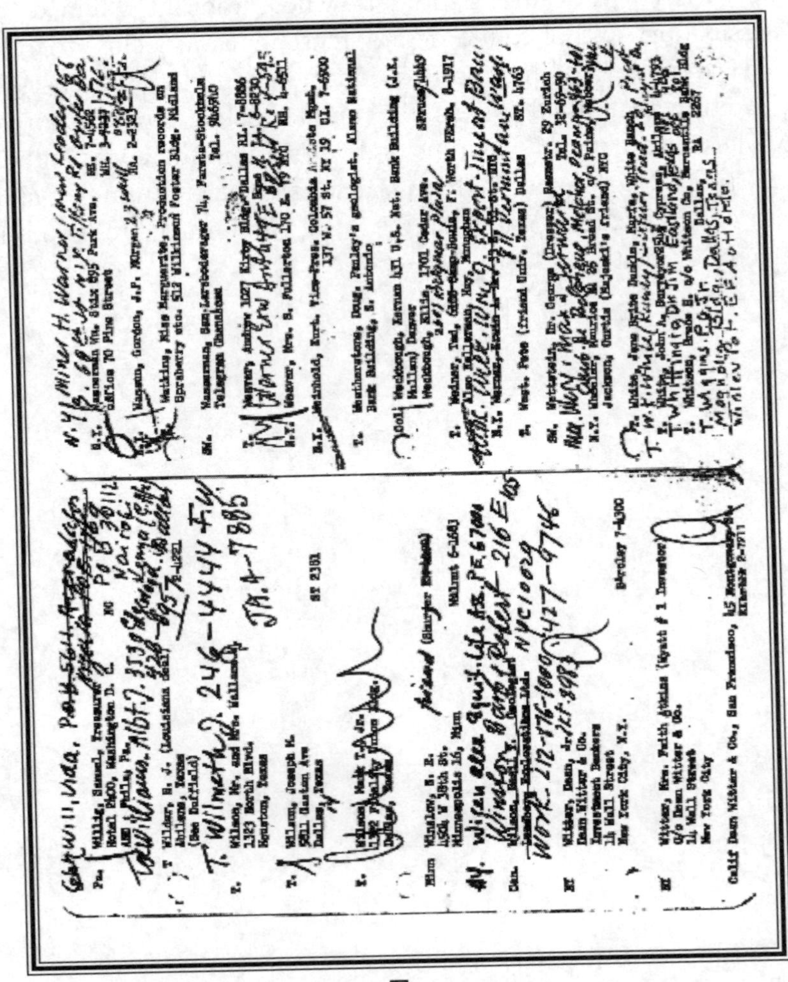

Pa. Willig, Samuel, Treasurer
Hotel 2400, Washington D. C.
Phila, Pa.

T Wilder, H. J. (Louisiana deal)
Abilene, Texas
(See Duffield)

T. Wilson, Mr. and Mrs. Wallace
1323 North Blvd.
Houston, Texas

T. Wilson, Joseph M.
5811 Gaston Ave
Dallas, Texas ST 2381

T. Wilson, Mark T. Jr.
1322 Fidelity Union Bldg.
Dallas, Texas

Minn Winslow, S. E. (Sharjer)
4504 W 38th St.
Minneapolis 16, Minn Walnut 6-1683

Can. Wilson, Basil Y. Geologist
Lundberg Explorations Ltd.

NY Witter, Dean, Jr.
Dean Witter & Co.
Investment Bankers
14 Wall Street
New York City, N.Y. BArclay 7-4300

NY Witter, Mrs. Faith Atkins (Wyatt # 1 Investor)
C/o Dean Witter & Co.
14 Wall Street
New York City

Calif Dean Witter & Co., San Francisco, 45 Montgomery St.
EXbrook 2-7911

N.Y. Wasserman Wm. Stix 695 Park Ave. RE. 7-4562
Office 70 Pine Street WH. 3-4237

N.Y. Wasson, Gordon, J.P. Morgan 23 Wall RA. 2-2323

Watkins, Miss Marguerite, Production records on
Spraberry etc. 512 Wilkinson Foster Bldg. Midland

SW. Wasserman, Sam-Larsbodevager 74, Farsta-Stockholm
Telegram Chansbose Tel. 946940

T. Weaver, Andrew 1027 Kirby Bldg. Dallas RI. 7-8886
6-8230

N.Y. Weaver, Mrs. S. Fullerton 170 E. 79 NYC RH. 4-6511

N.Y. Weinhold, Kurt. Vice-Pres. Colombia Artists Mgmt.
137 W. 57 St. NY 19 CI. 7-6900

T. Weatherstone, Doug. Fanley's geologist. Alamo National
Bank Building, S. Antonio

Col. Weckbough, Kernan 431 U.S. Nat. Bank Building (J.K.
Mullen) Denver
Weckbough, Ellis, 1701 Cedar Ave. SPruce 7-4449

T. Weiner, Ted, F. Worth FErsh. 8-1917
Also Kellerman, Hay, Monaghan

N.Y. Warner, Erwin

T. West. Pete (friend Univ. Texas) Dallas ST. 4763

SW. Wettstein, Dr. George (Dresser) Rennstr. 29 Zurich
Tel. 32-69-90

N.Y. Wheeler, Maurice M 25 Broad St. c/o Paine, Webber
Jackson, Curtis (Hajeski's friend) NYC

T. White, Jane Bribe Dunkin, Marfa, White Ranch

T. White, John A. Surveyor 2514 Cypress, Abilene 4-4793

T. Whitson, Brads S. c/o Whitson Co, Mercantile Bank Bldg
Dallas, RA 2267

Handwritten entries vary after 1955 - published by -Whistleblower Bruce C. Adamson

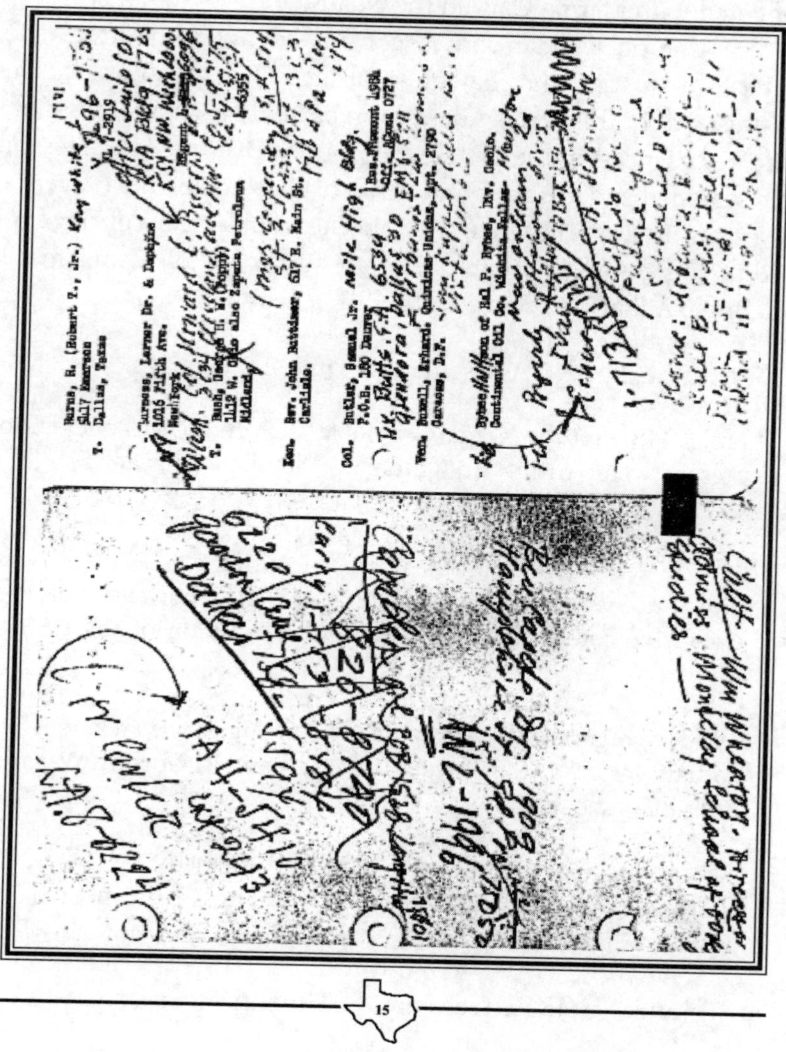

Y. Burns, R. (Hubert F., Jr.) Kay white
5417 Emerson
Dallas, Texas

Burgess, Larmar Dr. & Daphne
1016 Fifth Ave.
New York

T. Bush, George H. W. (Poppy)
1412 W. Ohio also Zapata Petroleum
Midland

Ken. Rev. John Buttdorf, 617 E. Main St.
Carlisle.

Col. Butler, Samuel Jr.
P.O.B. 180 Denver

Vene. Buxell, Erhard. Quimicas-Unidas, Apt. 2790
Caracas, D.F.

Bybee, Hal F. Bybee, Inv. Geolo.
Continental Oil Co. Wichita Falls

15

(*Evidence obtained from the West Palm Beach Sheriff's Office. Acquired by and republished with thanks to Bruce Adamson.*)

Soon after JFK's assassination, Jackson and Luce also successfully negotiated with Marina Oswald the exclusive rights to her story.

Bruce Campbell Adamson is considered a leading researcher on the JFK assassination, having published eleven volumes on his investigation. In this series Adamson repeatedly lists Wasson as one of the key suspects in the plot's organization. Over the last few years I've researched and acquired and verified all of Adamson's references to Wasson. In *every* instance they checked out—many of them are listed in this essay's endnotes. Here are just a few of his references from Bruce Adamson's series on the JFK assassination.

From volume 3a (JKF Assassination Timeline Chart):

> **Jan. 1948: George Kennan** spoke at CFR on Soviet Policy. Also present were Arthur Houghton, Jr., Stephen Duggan, Sr., J.C. Campbell, Henry V. Poor and **R. Gordon Wasson.**
>
> **1952:** Alexander Dallin was associate director; P. Mosely was director of research; **R.G. Wasson** and F. Barghoorn were **on the executive committee of the Research Program of the USSR.** All tied to CIA.
>
> **1953:** George Allen spoke at the CFR on Yugoslavia's relationship with the West. NAR, J.T. Duce, P. Mosely and **R. Gordon Wasson** were in attendance.
>
> George Allen was introduced to Joseph Kennedy by Robert D. Murphy. Alexander Tarsaidze = D.V. Mohr, in the book *Four Myths.*

From volume 3b (JKF Assassination Timeline Chart):

> **1959:** Jan. 15 Anastas I. Mikoyan spoke at CFR. In attendance: HFA (CIA), **Geo. Kennan,** Sig Michelson (CBS), J. Jessup (Luce), Philip Mosely (CIA), K. Roosevelt (CIA), H. Sargeant (CIA), John Gunther, **R. G. Wasson (CIA),** Fred and James Warburg.

1960: Sept. 30 Josip Tito spoke at CFR. In attendance were John Gunther, J.N. Hazard, Arthur A. Houghton, Jr., **H. Luce,** J.J. McCloy, **R.G. Wasson** and Daniel Schoor.

1962: May 8 Philip Mosely presided for Luce's man in Moscow at CFR. Others in attendance: J. Jessup, **R.G. Wasson (CIA).**

Dec. 27 H. Salisbury spoke at CFR; **(CIA agent) R. Gordon Wasson** presided.

1963: Oct. 31 CIA consultant, Philip Mosely spoke at CFR on "Russia Faces East and West." Others in attendance include A. Doak Barnett, R. Blum, J.C. Campbell, **R. Donald [Gordon]**[25]**Wasson (CIA),** (AD), and Professor Frederick Barghoorn was supposed to have been there. Barghoorn was arrested two days later in Moscow.

From Adamson's JFK—volume 4a, p. 22:

Was Salisbury's analysis at the Dallas right wing conspiracy theory directed at H.L. Hunt or the oil depletion allowance? He does not say specifically. We know that Harrison was tied to Dimitri Von Mohrenschildt and also many of the same acquaintances. On December 27, 1962, Harrison E. Salisbury spoke at the CFR on the subject of Implications of the Sino-Soviet Rupture. **R. Gordon Wasson (CIA agent) presided.** Other important members included **Frank Altschul**, Robert Blum, Spruille Braden, Alexander Dallin, George S. Franklin, Jr., and Howland Sargeant. **All except Blum are tied to Dimitri and Dulles**....

While de Mohrenschildt was entertaining Oswald, Salisbury was contending that Communism was not a unitary and monolithic movement....

p. 29: In 1952, while Alex Dallin was Associate Director and Philip E. Mosely (CIA consultant) was **Director of the Research Program on the USSR, R. Gordon Wasson (CIA agent)** and accused CIA agent Frederick C. Barghoorn were on the Executive Committee of the Research Program....

From Adamson's JFK—volume 4b, p. 57:

> **Kennan** spoke in January of 1947 at the Council on Foreign Affairs meeting in New York City. The meeting was on The Soviet Way of Thought and Its Effect on Soviet Foreign policy (53, Princeton, Seely G. Mudd Library, Dulles Papers, Kennan File, Council on Foreign Relations report January 7, 1947).
>
> **Kennan** was the discussion leader and others present who were interconnected with this work included: **Frank Altschul;** Arthur H. Dean; George S. Franklin and Arthur A. Houghton.... Other members of the CFR who were friends with Dimitri Von Mohrenschildt included **John C. Campbell of** *Time-Life;* Stephen Duggan Sr., whose son sat on the editorial board of the *Russian Review;* Henry V. Poor, of Amcomlib **and R. Gordon Wasson, a CIA agent and a Director of the Russian Student Fund**....
>
> **p. 58:** On May 18th 1959, Director of Studies at the CFR, Philip Mosely gave a speech on "The Impressions of Moscow." Frank Altschul presided. Others in attendance were Hamilton Fish Armstrong [husband of Carmen Barnes who was a friend of George de Mohrenschildt's]; Frederick C. Barghoorn [friend of Dimitri's and arrested by KGB in November 1963]; John N. Hazard; **C.D. Jackson (bought Zapruder's film);** Henry V. Poor and Howland Sargeant.... It is important to note that **Wasson was an officer of the Research Program on the USSR,** located at 401 West 118th Street in New York City. Other officers of the program included ... **Philip E. Mosely, Alexander J. Dallin,** Frederick C. Barghoorn **and R. Gordon Wasson.** In 1952 this Research Program was seeking Dimitri's advice for counseling seriously on USSR organization on the role of classics in Soviet culture (57, Hoover Institute, *Russian Review* Papers, Box, 2, Alexander Dallin to D.V. Mohrenschildt April 11, 1952).
>
> In 1950, **Dulles approved George Kennan's membership into the Century Association**, located at 7 West 43rd Street in New York. Apparently Hamilton Fish Armstrong nominated Kennan **and Gordon Wasson (CIA agent) had seconded it.** On November 15, 1950 Dulles said of Kennan that he was one

> of the most capable writers in foreign affairs and "Certainly, he would make a most desirable member of the Century Club" (59, Princeton, Seely G. Mudd Library, Dulles Papers, Kennan File, A. Dulles to the Committee on Admissions, Nov. 15, 1950).

From Adamson's JFK—volume 8a, p. 3:

> On September 30, 1960, Marshal Josip Tito spoke in New York at the CFR meeting on Yugoslav Foreign Policy. Other important people who knew Dimitri Von Mohrenschildt (and) Dulles and who are important for the study of JFK and RFK's assassinations were: John Gunther, John N. Hazard, Arthur A. Houghton, Jr., Henry R. Luce, John J. McCloy, Edward V. Poor, Daniel Schoor and CIA agent R. Gordon Wasson[26] (10, CFR meetings vol. XXXVIII, July 1960–June 1961 (S–Z), Bruce C. Adamson).

James Moore and the Red Herring

As I have considered all of these connections over the years, one question always comes up. What about James Moore? Moore was a CIA agent. He contributed $2,000 to Wasson's trip. Here is how this myth begins:

> Apparently, one of the "various foundations" from which Gordon was hoping to obtain a grant was the Geschickter Fund in Washington, D.C. It had been mentioned to him as a possible source of funding by James Moore, the CIA operative, when he initially contacted Gordon in August 1955. Unknown to Gordon, the Fund was a front for the CIA to channel money secretly. According to John Marks' book *The Search for the "Manchurian Candidate"* (New York: Dell, 1979), it anted up $2,000 to help finance Gordon's expedition in the spring of 1956 (Richardson 1990/97: 203).

"Nervous and paranoid" correctly describes a "short-order chemist" for the CIA, James Moore (Lee & Shlain, 1985; Marks, 1979;

> Stevens, 1987), who secretly infiltrated one of Wasson's small expeditions into the Sierra Mazateca in 1956.
>
> A scientist from the CIA's "Project ARTICHOKE" had traveled to México in search of a so-called "stupid bush" and other plants which might derange the human mind, politically useful to control enemies' minds in war time. Large quantities of morning glory seeds were sent to CIA laboratories for analysis by CIA scientists searching for compounds useful for extracting confessions, locating stolen or lost objects, perhaps even predicting the future. Visionary mushrooms were of special interest in these investigations. According to documents obtained via the Freedom of Information Act, James Moore was an expert in chemical synthesis who worked for the CIA. In 1956, Moore invited himself into one of Wasson's expeditions to México. He offered Wasson a grant for $2,000 dollars from a CIA-front known as the Geschickter Fund for Medical Research, Inc. *In 1955, Wasson had declined to collaborate openly with the CIA.*"
>
> Moore collected specimens for his CIA-sponsored research and returned to Maryland, where he endeavored to isolate for the CIA the active principle of both the mushrooms and morning glory seeds. Unfortunately for Moore he was unable to find the active ingredients in the mushrooms and lucky for the world that he didn't find them since they would have most likely been used as tools of mind war under the direction of the CIA[27] (emphasis mine).

Notice that the above passage does not say that Wasson declined to collaborate with the CIA. It says that, "In 1955, Wasson had declined to collaborate *openly* with the CIA." In other words, if Allen's statement is correct, while Wasson may have refused to collaborate "openly" with the CIA, this does not mean that he declined to collaborate with the CIA—two very different things. Then how would Wasson collaborate? He would need a cover story.

Here's how MK-ULTRA expert Hank Albarelli describes the myth in *A Terrible Mistake:*

Especially significant in the history of LSD and psychotropic drugs is the work of Gordon Wasson and his wife Valentina Pavlovna. The couple traveled the globe in search of exotic and rare psychoactive mushrooms, and they were the first to use the term "ethnomycology." Over a forty year period, the two collected and catalogued the "food of the Gods." In 1977, Wasson commented that throughout his many excursions to Mexico from 1952 through 1962, "I didn't send a single sample to an American mycologist. I didn't get a penny, not a single grant from any government sources. I'm perfectly sure of that."

There is no reason to doubt Wasson, but what he did not know at the time of his excursions was that the United States government was closely monitoring every one of his trips and that each and every one of his collected samples found their way back from Mexico to CIA-funded laboratories. Wasson also sent his samples to Albert Hofmann at Sandoz Labs in Switzerland. Hofmann, according to Wasson, "was doing the key work synthesizing the active ingredients" of the samples. What Wasson again did not realize was that the fruits of all of his and Hofmann's labors were being plucked from the vine by the U.S. Army and CIA both of whom, since at least 1948, had covert operatives working in the Sandoz Laboratories.

Wasson also was unaware of CIA penetration into a number of his Mexico excursions. In 1956, Dr. James Moore of the University of Delaware, under secret contract with the CIA's TSS, traveled to the Oaxaca section of Mexico to collect *rivea corymbosa* samples. Moore, according to Wasson, was collaborating with the Argentine-based mycologist, Dr. Rolf Singer, a Bavarian-born Jew who had fled Nazi Germany in 1933 for Czechoslovakia. Eventually, he traveled to the United States where *he secured a job doing research at Harvard University, and in 1948, he left the U.S. to go to Argentina to study hallucinogenic mushrooms.*

Wasson, in a 1977 interview, implied that Singer had some sort of ties to the CIA through Moore, but the specifics are unclear and it must be stated here that Wasson reportedly did not care much for Singer and considered his work "rushed" and often

> "borrowed" from others. Wasson only traveled once with Moore, in 1956, and the experience was horrible, he said. Said Wasson: "he was an awful ass.... He expected to have a water closet in Mexico. It was laughable."
>
> Wasson also reported that he had once been approached by either the CIA or FBI. "I'm not sure which," he said. They wanted him "to do work for the government." He turned them down, saying he thought the effort "patriotic," but did not want his work being classified secret. "I wanted to publish all my findings," he explained.
>
> In the same interview, Wasson said that Albert Hofmann "work in some way with the CIA" and that Hofmann's "discoveries were imparted in whole by Sandoz to the U.S. government. Sandoz wanted to be on the right side of things." Hofmann's connection to the CIA has never been officially confirmed by the CIA, which maintains a policy of not commenting on or revealing information on foreign citizens who find their way into its employment (Albarelli 2009: 359; emphasis mine).

There seems to be a repeated theme with Wasson disparaging people he actually knows are agents. I brought attention to this in my book *The Holy Mushroom* in regards to Wasson's actions with Dr. Andrija Puharich,[28] and I think he's doing the same here with Moore. Wasson wants to conceal his own identity as a CIA agent or asset, and to make himself look more innocent in the entire affair.

The above accounts seem absurdly impossible in light of all of the information regarding Wasson's own participation in the CFR and CIA and with all of his own connections to all of these people in the CIA and intelligence. I consider the entire James Moore story to be a red herring. A red herring is a fallacy that leads someone from one topic to another. In other words, he's a decoy or a scapegoat. When we consider Moore as a decoy, the contradictions in the storyline disappear. Wasson and Allen Dulles were friends; the CIA had known all along about Wasson's work; Dulles worked with the German conglomerate IG Farben, which was related with Sandoz

AG.[29] It's hard to believe that the CIA needed a field agent when they had Wasson himself. Rather than admitting that the entire project was an elite/CIA/intelligence operation, it was best to slip an agent into the storyline who would serve to lead researchers astray for decades. That way Wasson didn't have to work for the CIA *openly,* and he could still publish his books, which he just published in elite publishing houses—too expensive for anyone to acquire—and delivered many of them to the CIA and CFR himself. It was a slick move, and fooled many hundreds of researchers—but like all lies it was bound to be exposed. If anything, Wasson could likely have been Moore's superior at the CIA, and Dulles himself would have likely approved the $2,000. Surely Dulles and Wasson had already discussed it over dinner at the Century Club. Wasson possibly needed a chemist along for the trip who could also aid in collecting mushroom samples—and could act as a possible future scapegoat should someone uncover their plot.

Masha Wasson Britten

It's also hard to believe that Masha isn't aware of many of these things. Found in the Frank Altschul archives at Columbia University is a hand-written letter from Masha to Altschul thanking him for a weekend they spent together in 1958 after the death of her mother, Valentina, who, as it turns out, was also a friend of Altschul. If Masha and Altschul were lovers it's not clear, though she would have been about twenty-three at the time.

> January 20, 1959
>
> Dear Mr. Altschul,
>
> Please forgive me for not writing sooner. I do wish to thank you for the lovely time I spent with you in the country. I really needed to get away and I cannot think of another place I would have enjoyed as much.

> I had a good rest, something I have not had in a long time. It was also comforting to be with friends since at that time I was just beginning to feel the real impact of what had happened[....]
>
> Again, I thank you for the wonderful weekend and I'm sorry for the delay.
>
> Love,
> Masha[30]

Altschul was not only a banker, but, like Allen Dulles, was a director of the CFR (1944–72)[31], and also served at several of the same CFR meetings that were chaired by Wasson himself—where Luce was also present.[32] Altschul was also a member of the Century Club,[33] and was one of those behind such secret operations as Operation Mockingbird, a CIA "psychological information campaign against the American people."[34]

On February 17, 1951, Wasson gave a lecture on Russian policy to the Practicing Law Institute. He later had 1,000 copies of the lecture published in small book form, titled *Toward a Russian Policy,*[35] which he published anonymously with Frank Altschul's publishing firm, Overbrook Press. Included in Columbia University's Overbrook Press collection is Wasson's personal list of people that he had this book sent to, which include: Allen W. Dulles, John Foster Dulles, General Dwight Eisenhower, C.D. Jackson, Henry Luce, Robert Oppenheimer, David Rockefeller, and Frank Wisner—just to name a few.[36]

> But I should wish you to see the whole talk, which will be appearing shortly in an edition being printed by Frank Altschul's Overbrook Press. Since Frank is in constant touch with Mr. C.D. Jackson, I suggest you call this fact to Mr. Jackson's attention, if he is interested in going ahead with your project.[37]

Frank Altschul's son, Arthur G. Altschul, was also a member of the CFR with Frank and Wasson,[38] and became a partner of the infamous Goldman, Sachs & Co that defrauded the American public for billions of tax dollars in 2008, though Arthur had died in 2002.

Who doesn't have their hands dirty in the world of psychedelics and deep politics?

And so the investigation continues....

Moving Forward

Clearly the study of entheogens in religious myths and practices is a valid one. What is not clear from Wasson's work is how much of his work is a real, honest investigation of mushrooms in religion, and how much concerns his secret elitist agendas. In a court of law, if someone is shown to lie under oath, everything they say is to be dismissed. And while Wasson wasn't under oath, and while much, though not all, of his research appears genuine, it seems clear that we'll need to fact-check every detail of his research, point by point, before we can ever again use him as a credible source in the fields of ethnomycology and ethnobotany.

Those who twist the facts of reality to their own selfish agendas, sacrificing truth and humanity in the process, bring the whole of the world down with them. If what they did was based in integrity, they wouldn't need to act in secrecy, to commit sophistry, to occult the truth at the cost of the many to profit the few.

Conclusion

It's often hard for us to look at our own legends and myths and to question our own beliefs. In fact, many people think it's easier to go on believing a myth than it is to do the research and ground work to discover the truth or the actual history behind such legends and myths.

Some legends and myths are created by those with ill intentions to occult (keep secret) information for their own gain—"a story invented as a veiled explanation of a truth." When information is occulted, those who maintain that secret knowledge have control over those who don't.

We can go through our entire lives believing in all sorts of legends and myths, being misled by those who wish to fool us, to manipulate and control us, and violating natural law, for their own irrational, selfish ends. And as the mushrooms have the power to free our minds, so does the truth. True to its purpose, the study of ethnomycology has revealed more legends and myths, some of the biggest legends and myths thus far discovered to be based around mushrooms: those of R. Gordon Wasson.

At the start of this essay we began with a quote from Wasson that came from the introduction of his book *The Hall Carbine Affair*. Here is the rest of that quote, where Wasson provides us with a page of philosophizing that serves to bring this article full circle:

> Legends are often history processed to point some moral. They are misleading as history, but they help us to understand the people who invent and believe in them. Usually the world recognizes as legends only the outgrown cables of earlier generations. But this is merely because, believing as we do our own legends, we do not recognize them for what they are.
>
> It is proposed in this little essay to dissect sinew by sinew, and nerve by nerve, a living legend, a legend born in our own generation and ... palpitant with the vitality of unchallenged acceptance. This specimen of mis-belief will be tested as real history is tested. In its own right it is only a modest little yarn, but we shall scrutinize it as rigorously as if it made all the difference. Its start is an obscure happening of some three-quarters of a century ago, of no great importance then and of none at all for a long time after, until it was taken hold of, clothed upon, and finished off ... by a school of writers who call themselves historians and serious thinkers.
>
> Starting with nothing, or as good as nothing, these molders of opinion by a very act of creation have built up from it a history, a moral, a warning, an economics, and in reverse a vision of a new and better world. A mouse having labored, a mountain was born. Legends that take hold on the popular imagination are the ones that tell the people what they wish to believe, and

> this legend took hold. Thus fact became fiction, and fiction History: a little incident, released by uncorking the bottle, magically swelled before our very eyes into a Horrible Example, solemnly authenticated as Truth by our college of augurs.
>
> Only a trifle, you may say, to give so much time to. But the history of this legend will point a moral: a moral that the authors of the legend surely never dreamed of! (Wasson 1948: v ff)

Through our own belief in his legends and myths, we had refused to look at, much less acknowledge, the gravitas of the truth. We wanted to believe that we knew him, and that he couldn't have done such a wrong.

And while Maria Sabina said there was no remedy for the damage done, maybe this article is the first step in the right direction. If there is a way, having honesty and integrity and bringing forth the truth about Wasson and the elite's psychedelic agenda may be the first step. Through honesty and integrity we can begin to cure and heal the misdeeds caused by such incredibly blind selfishness, and move forward into the light of truth, free of such malicious deception and agendas that have weighed our field of study down since its inception.

What was the purpose of the Wassons' publishing in *Life* and *This Week* magazines, rather than in an anthropology journal? With the ties to Morgan, Skull and Bones, Edward Bernays, C.D. Jackson, Henry Luce, the CFR and the CIA, it seems that their campaign against Huaulta de Jimenez was intentional, as was the influx of "hippies, psychopaths and adventurers and pseudo-research workers" who descended upon the place. Was it an experiment in economics, to see how the banking elite and CIA could fully corrupt and commercialize a remote, indigenous village, while at the same time launching a positivist psychological warfare campaign?

From spies and intelligence, to propaganda and mind control operations for the elite, to the assassination of presidents, the real story behind R. Gordon Wasson is far more interesting and disturbing than we've ever envisioned.

In the endnotes of this essay I've included dozens of references to major university archives where stores of Wasson documents are held—outside of Masha and Harvard's control. By publishing these sources for the first time I'm providing other researchers the path to work around this blockade and to begin to reassemble the documents necessary to amass the real history behind R. Gordon Wasson and the foundations of ethnomycology—and the launch of the psychedelic movement. This was just the tip of the iceberg.

And now the dyke has broken, and Masha sits there with her finger in a hole, in a fruitless attempt to stop the flood. If I'm wrong, then let her simply open up the Wasson archive at Harvard for all to see that there's nothing there to hide, and to also disprove these citations I've provided herein—and I'll admit that I'm the fool.

But if I'm correct, what are the implications? We've seen a cover-up of a mind control and propaganda campaign regarding mushrooms and the field of ethnomycology that reaches to the highest levels of the U.S. government, intelligence, and banking, and may tie directly into MK-ULTRA. We've also seen a concerted effort to cover up the origins of one of America's wealthiest banking families—the Morgans. We've seen ties to the American fascists. And what's worse, we've uncovered a possible cover-up of a conspiracy to commit the murder of a U.S. president—John F. Kennedy.

In this study of contemporary psychedelic mythology we've dissected, borrowing from Wasson's words, almost sinew by sinew, nerve by nerve, a living legend that lived in our own generation, and a myth that began some three-quarters of a century ago. We've tested the myth's misbelief as real history is tested; peeled the clothes off and scrutinized all that was piled upon it by the college of augurs—as if it made all the difference in the world. Underneath it all we've found a wretched little mouse—a solemn little creature, now unmasked, that we must ironically thank for uncorking the bottle. Indeed, a moral the author surely never dreamed of!

And maybe it's wishful thinking, but may the mushrooms remain forevermore pure, and never again be defiled for the deceitful, irrational agendas of the elite.

This essay is dedicated to the honor, purity, and sanctity of the mushrooms—and to the Mazatec peoples of Oaxaca, Mexico, especially from Huaulta de Jimenez, from which they came, who were also profaned. The Mazatecs had their religion co-opted, their culture infiltrated, their sacrament corrupted and commercialized.

A mouse having labored a mountain was born, but it's the truth that shall set you free.

Bibliography

Allegro, J. 1970. *The Sacred Mushroom and the Cross.* Reprinted 2009, Gnostic Media.

Albarelli, H. 2009. *A Terrible Mistake: The Murder of Frank Olson and the CIA's Secret Cold War Experiments,* Trine Day.

Bernays, E. 1928. *Propaganda.*

Botanical Museum Leaflets, Harvard University, March 10, 1963. Vol. 20, No. 2a.

Bourke, J. 1891. *Scatalogic Rites of All Nations.*

Chernow, R. 2001. *The House of Morgan.*

Cloud, J. 2007. "When the Elites Loved LSD." *Time* Magazine, April 23.

Estrada, A. 1981. *María Sabina: Her Life and Chants.*

Forte, R. 2008. Horizons Conference, New York City, NY: September.

Harvey, G. 2002. *Shamanism.* NY: Routledge

Hoffman, A. 1980. *Soon to be a Major Motion Picture,* New York: G.P. Putnam's Sons.

Irvin, J. 2008. *The Holy Mushroom: Evidence of Mushrooms in Judeo-Christianity.* Gnostic Media.

Josephson, M. 1962. *Robber Barons, The Great American Capitalists,* 1861–1901. 1962.

Letcher, A. 2007. *Shroom.* New York: HarperCollins Publishers.

Moley, R. 1971. *After Seven Years,* University of Nebraska Press.

Morris, C. 2005. *The Tycoons,* 2005.

Mullins, E. 1993. *Secrets of the Federal Reserve.*

Pfister, D. 1988. R. Gordon Wasson 1898–1986. In *Mycologia,* 80(1).

Riedlinger, T. 1990/1997. *The Sacred Mushroom Seeker.*

Wasson, R. 1948. *The Hall Carbine Affair.*

Wasson, R. 1957. "Seeking The Magic Mushroom." *Life* magazine, May 13.

Wasson, R. and Wasson, V. 1957. *Mushrooms, Russia and History.* New York: Pantheon Books.

Wasson, R. 1970. "Drugs: The Sacred Mushroom." *The New York Times,* 26 Sept.

Wasson, R. 1980. *The Wondrous Mushroom.*

Notes

1. *Webster's Third New International Dictionary,* unabridged, Encyclopedia Britannica, 1986.

2. Valentina Pavlovna Wasson, I Ate the Sacred Mushrooms, in *This Week Magazine,* May 19, 1957. p. 8ff; see also Wikipedia's entry for *This Week* magazine's 1957 circulation numbers

3. Botanical Museum Leaflets, Harvard University, March 10, 1963. Vol. 20, No. 2a, p. 39

4. The CFR archives, Princeton University, Mudd Library: MC104, box 451: folder 1—Mikoyan

5. CFR Historical Roster of Directors and Officers—http://www.cfr.org/about/history/cfr/appendix.html

6. Hamilton Fish Armstrong, Wasson Archives, Harvard Botanical Museum. Foreign Affairs (CFR) letterhead, dated November 10, 1950. "Dear Gordon: I have written these Century members to

say that you and I are proposing George Kennan for membership: Boris A. Bakhmeteff, Charles C. Burlingham, Allen Dulles, General Dwight D. Eisenhower, Philip C. Jessup, Geroid Tanquary Robinson, William L. Shirer, Dean G. Acheson, James B. Conant, Edward Mead Earle, Herbert B. Elliston, Joseph C. Grew, William L. Langer, Robert A. Lovett. In addition George gave me some other names: Imrie de Vegh, John Foster Dulles, Thomas S. Lamont, Russell C. Leffingwell, Vannevar Bush, Everett Case [...]

7. The CFR archives, Princeton University, Mudd Library: MC104: Box 451: Folder 1, Folder 6; Box 455: Folder 1; Box 459: Folder 4

8. Paul Charles Blum Papers, Manuscripts and Archives, Yale University Library, MS 900, 2005—M—080, Box 2: folder 26.

9. George F. Kennan papers, Princeton University, Mudd Library, (MC #076), Box 51: folder 2.

10. Frank Altschul archives, Columbia University Rare Book & Manuscripts Library, Box 58, folder 1 and 2.

11. George F. Kennan papers, Princeton University, Mudd Library, (MC #019), Box 35: folder 27.

12. US Library of Congress, Bernays collection: Part I: Book File, 1890—1965, n.d. BOX I:459, Wasson, Gordon

13. Hoover Institute, Stanford University. Bertram D. Wolfe papers. Box: 15, Folder: 72

14. Ibid.

15. John W. Allen, Wasson's First Voyage, http://www.erowid.org/plants/mushrooms/mushrooms_article5.shtml

16. Andrews papers, Manuscripts and Archives, Yale University Library, box 24: folder 287; box 25: folder 296; box 31: folder 355; box 32: folder 370; box 37: folder 418, 419, 420; box 40: folder 441; box 42: folder 456, 460; box 43: folder 465; box 46: folder 500, 507; box 47: folder 512.

17. Ibid.

18. Andrews archive, Manuscripts and Archives, Yale University Library, Box 40: folder 441.

19. Ibid., Box 37: folder 419.

20. Ibid., Box 40: folder 441.

21. Ibid., Box 42: folder 460.

22. "Our Jerusalem. An American Family in the Holy City 1881—1949." p. 379. Published by the Middle East Export Press.INC. Printed in Lebanon. Copyright, 1950 Bertha Spafford Vesta and Evelyn Wells.

23. Russian Review records, Hoover Institute, Box 2: folder 1952.

24. "Donald is a type o. I remember most of the sources came from the CFR while I was in New York in 1995." – Bruce Adamson

25. Republished with permission and thanks to Bruce Adamson. For all of Adamson's research on the JFK assassination, please see http://www.ciajfk.com/jfkbooks.html.

26. John W. Allen, Wasson's First Voyage (from Mushroom Pioneers) http://www.erowid.org/plants/mushrooms/mushrooms_article5.shtml

27. Jan Irvin, *The Holy Mushroom:Evidence of Mushrooms in Judeo-Christianity,* Gnostic Media, 2008, p. 24.

28. See the Allen Dulles entry on WikiPedia, and see also Encyclopedia Britannica's entry on Novartis AG: http://www.britannica.com/EBchecked/topic/421043/Novartis-AG.

29. Frank Altschul archives, Columbia University Rare Book & Manuscript Library, Box 58: folder 1 and 2.

30. CFR Historical Roster of Directors and Officers. http://www.cfr.org/about/history/cfr/appendix.html.

31. The CFR archives, Princeton University, Mudd Library: MC104: Box 451: Folder 1, Folder 6; Box 455: Folder 1; Box 459: Folder 4

32. Frank Altschul archives, Columbia University Rare Book & Manuscript Library, Box 58: folder 1 and 2.

33. Peter Phillips, Lew Brown, and Bridget Thornton, US Electromagnetic Weapons and Human Rights, Sonoma State University, Project Censored Media Freedom Foundation, 2006. http://globalresearch.ca/articles/ElectromagWeapons.pdf.

34. Alexander Kazem-Bek papers, Columbia University Rare Book & Manuscript Library, Box 9: folder 13.

35. Overbrook Press collection, Columbia University Rare Book & Manuscript Library, Box 9: folder 287.

36. Dwight MacDonald Papers, Manuscripts and Archives, Yale University Library, Box 55: folder 346

37. The CFR archives, Princeton University, Mudd Library: MC104, box 451: folder 1—Mikoyan

Index

5-HT receptors – 35-36

A

abortion – 168

absinthe – 152, 217

absinthol – 217

abstinence – 96, 101, 130-131, 144, 545

Achilles – 402, 443

Acrisius – 429-430

Actaeon – 428

active imagination – 523-524, 532-533, 535, 546, 550, 554

Adam and Eve – 108, 142, 146, 177, 196, 215, 409, 490, 503-504

adaptation – 25-26, 29-30, 32-33, 37, 39, 43-44, 529

addiction – 12, 28-29

Adelheid of Sommerschenburg – 112, 116-117, 139, 170-171, 201

adolescence – 120, 127

Aegeus – 351

Aeneas – 17, 388-395, 398-401, 404-406, 411-415, 426, 429-430, 432-433, 439

Aeneid – 17, 391, 400, 415, 432

Aeschylus – 403

Agamemnon – 430

Agaricus muscarius – 490

agave – 422, 428, 494

Agni – 214, 250, 540

Agnus dei – 182

Agora – 355

Aissawa – 222-223, 257-258

Al Biruni – 239, 272

Al Khidr – 221

alchemy – 95, 100-101, 114, 168, 416-417, 520, 522, 524-525

Alcibiades – 353, 356

Alcmaeonids – 353, 356, 359

Alexander the Great – 221, 262, 276, 367, 407-408, 430

Alexandra – 392, 406, 437, 439

Algeria – 232, 488, 503, 511

alkaloids – 40-41, 145, 147-149, 167, 223, 502, 539, 545

Allecto – 430

Allegro, J. – 87, 102, 162, 188, 280, 333, 565, 567

altered states of consciousness – 12, 23, 26, 31, 39, 43, 45, 214, 364

Amalthea (Goat) – 243, 274-275

Amanita caesarea – 409, 503

Amanita muscaria – 10, 16, 19, 64, 93, 105, 135, 140, 144, 155-157, 160-161, 163-164, 166, 177, 179, 181, 189, 199, 215, 223, 239-240, 279-306, 308-310, 316-317, 333, 340, 358, 368, 371, 405, 408, 410, 421, 425, 453, 462, 465-466, 468-470, 472, 476-477, 486-487, 489-493, 499, 502-504, 508, 510, 577

Amanita pantherina – 153, 155-156, 161

Amanita regalis – 161

amanuensis – 101, 113-114, 117, 137, 113-115, 117, 143

Amata – 429-433, 538

ambivalence – 101, 128, 132

ambrosia – 165, 243, 339-340, 358, 408, 538

Amon – 430

Amphion – 422

Amphipolis – 368

amrita – 243, 538, 540

Anadenanthera colubrina – 329

Anatolian – 367, 404, 406, 411, 423

Anatolian goddess – 367, 423

ancestor worship – 3

Anchises – 388-389, 392, 398, 411, 413

ancient aliens – 10

angel – 166, 187, 195, 200, 220, 237, 239, 334

Anicia Juliana – 99, 150

Anna – 133, 155, 178-179, 188-191, 197, 201

annulus – 178, 190, 425

anointing oil – 14, 16, 52-55, 61-63, 67-69, 75, 148

Anthesteria – 359, 361, 374

Anthony, M. – 433

anthropomorphic figures – 473, 489, 501

anthroposophy – 520, 537

antibiotics – 155

Antiope – 422

aphrodisiac – 59, 123, 129, 132, 145-146

Aphrodite – 60, 370, 411

Apicius – 409, 445

apipíltzin – 498

apocalypse – 66, 138, 445

Apollinian drive – 526, 528, 534, 538

Apollo – 379, 388, 411, 426, 445

apostles – 102, 200

arbutus – 357

Arbutus unedo – 357

arc of the covenant – 99

Arcadia – 413, 429

Archbishop Henry of Mainz – 107, 111

archon – 351, 353, 374

arginine vasopressin receptor (AVPR1a) – 39

Argonauts – 344, 400, 428
Argus – 433
Ariadne – 361
Aristeo Matías – 498, 508
aristocracy – 352, 356, 363, 367
Aristophanes – 345-348, 351, 355, 359, 367, 372, 375, 377-379, 384, 428
Aristotle – 344, 520
Artaxerxes II – 218, 262
Artemisia – 152, 217, 232-233, 254
Artemis – 266, 374
Arthurian romance – 523
Ascanius – 414
ascetic – 93, 101, 112, 130, 132, 170, 173
ass' ears – 185, 200
Assyrian – 58-60, 216
astral projection – 184
astro(theo)logy – 137
astrology – 367
Athenaeus – 345
Athens – 16, 332, 344, 351, 353-356, 359-361, 367, 372, 374, 376, 379, 383, 426-427, 502
atman – 521, 532, 536
Atropa belladonna – 149, 153, 235
atropine – 145, 147, 261
Attis – 337, 406
Augustine of Hippo – 414, 431, 521
Augustus – 393, 395, 409-410, 413-414, 416, 433
aureole – 160-161 176, 181, 185, 193, 335
autonomous control – 92, 118
Avalokitesvara – 279, 336
avatar – 338, 342, 462, 464-465, 472-473
Avesta/Avestan – 63-64, 227, 254, 262, 264, 271, 291, 301
ayahuasca – 147, 279, 309, 329-330,
Aztec – 6, 18, 165, 285, 296, 454-456, 462, 464-467, 471, 473-474, 491-492, 496-497

B

B-endorphin – 26-27, 30
Bacchae – 221, 360-361, 366, 383, 423-424
Bacchantes – 222, 226, 245
Bacchus – 221, 230, 265, 399, 421, 436, 375, 398
bacteria – 89, 155, 158-159
Bactrian-Margiana Archaeological complex (BMAC) – 56
Bali – 507
ballgame – 452, 470, 478
balsam – 227-228, 233, 263
Barbarossa – 110-111, 126, 174, 126, 132, 136, 174
Bardo – 341-342
barley – 213, 228, 263, 409, 502
barsom – 227-229, 261-263
Bdelykleon – 345
Beaker People – 412
beating (ritual) – 227, 230-231, 266
bee – x

beech (tree) – 146, 154-155, 157-158, 160, 189, 489

beer – 144, 148, 159, 163, 233, 228, 272

belladonna – 149, 153, 235,

Bellerophon – 429

Benedict of Nursia – 96

Benedictine – 86, 90, 93, 95-98, 101, 106, 108, 111, 128, 132, 138, 144

Benghazi, Libya – x

Bering Strait – 163-164, 490

Bernard of Clervaux – 107, 112, 172-174, 198

Bernays, E. – 574, 584-586, 588-589, 595, 613

Berserker – 298-299, 301, 303, 368

Bertault, R. – 488

Bes – 404

besom – 227, 261, 263

besom/broom/barsom – 229, 233-234, 231

bier – 94

big bang – 88

bile – 137, 169, 418

bipedalism – 39

birch – 95, 153-154, 156, 158, 160, 189, 229-230, 235, 263-265, 281, 302

bird – 144, 185, 216, 233-234, 269, 275, 326, 348-401, 405, 417, 428, 454, 460-461, 464, 468, 472-473, 522, 610

blood/blood letting – 108, 115, 129, 137, 162, 165, 169, 177, 182, 190-191, 196, 215, 221, 223, 241, 250, 283, 290, 307, 324, 347, 373, 402, 416-417, 425-426, 434, 457, 461, 464, 466-467, 469-470, 498, 533, 540, 594

Blood Council – 172

blood of Christ – 115, 217, 177, 182, 190-191, 215, 540

blue – 99, 135, 165, 175, 179-181, 183, 195, 367, 408, 430, 466, 522, 596

bluing – 180, 488

Boas, F. – 474

Boddhisattva – 336

body of Christ – 171, 176, 182, 190-191, 540

Boeotia – 275, 358, 360, 365, 403, 406, 419, 426, 428

bolets – 486-488, 505, 508-510

Boletus (species) – 505-506

B. kumaeus – 506

B. manicus – 506

B. nigerrimus - 506

B. nigroviolaceous – 506

B. reayi – 506

Bolivia – 502

Boötes – 361

Boreas – 400-401, 406

Bosch, H. – 338

Bosporos – 406

brainwashing – 6

Brasidas – 368-369

bread – 16, 18, 65, 155, 160, 163, 167, 211, 276, 333-334, 367, 393-394, 397-399, 405, 408-409, 431, 436, 503, 571

brides of Christ – 112, 170, 173

broom – 153-154, 162, 227, 231, 233-234, 260-261

brujo – 498, 507

Buddhism – 214, 521

Bufo – 490

bufotenin – 162, 490

Bujlud – 230-232

bull – 53, 185, 232, 244-246, 266, 276, 298, 337, 347, 359, 362-363, 366-367, 374, 405, 419, 424, 489

burning bush – 177

butterfly – 407

C

C. G. Jung Institute – 523-524

cactus – 16, 320, 324, 326, 329, 331, 492

Cacus – 429

Cadmus – 275, 403, 410-411, 418-419, 420-424, 426-428

caduceus – 166, 183, 196

Caesar – 395, 409, 413-414, 433, 503

Calais – 400

calamus – 54, 63, 238

Calchas – 416

calotte – 177-178

Calypso – 421

camauro – 178

Cambyses – 403

Camilla, G. – 503

Campania – 411, 420, 427

Canada – 19, 51, 62, 164, 490, 508, 510, 519, 549

Canis Minoris – 361

cannabis – 12, 14, 16, 51-53, 55-56, 60-65, 67, 69, 70-76, 83, 87, 144, 147, 150, 57-59, 149, 201, 203, 219, 228, 238, 242, 249, 256, 261, 263, 384, 577

canonization – 91, 98, 174-175

Capacha Culture – 491, 493

Capture of Miletos – 349

Caral – 320, 322-323

carved stone – 265, 229, 320, 323, 326-329, 344, 391, 407, 459-460, 463, 466, 491, 500, 503

Cassandra – 392, 406, 413

Castalian Spring – 421

Castor and Pollux – 164, 404

Çatal Hüyük – 419

Cathar – 97, 172-173

Catherine of Genoa – 135, 198

cattle – 157, 164, 170, 229, 235, 238, 390, 429, 509

Cattle of the Sun – 397-398, 429

Caucasus – 61, 220, 249, 254-255, 412

Causae et Curae – 86, 114, 137, 142

cave – 220, 242, 274, 324, 401, 425-426, 428, 461, 465, 470, 488

Cecrops – 344

cedar – 154-156, 160, 189, 215, 217, 234, 242, 252-253

Celaeno – 388-389, 392, 398

celery – 393

Celestial Bull – 337

Celts – 189, 237, 245, 246, 276, 296, 307

Central America – 18-19, 341, 461, 476, 485-486, 500, 509-510

Century Club – 574, 580-583, 605, 609-610

CFR (Council on Foreign Relations) – 574, 576, 579, 582-583, 588, 602-605, 608-610, 613, 618

Chac – 461, 467, 470

chakra – 165-166, 185

chalice – 87, 115, 160, 176, 182, 190-191, 194, 196-197, 213, 335, 541

Charet, F. – 520

Chavín de Huantar – 16, 319-321, 324-325, 327-332

cheese – 87, 143, 160, 182, 267

Chernow, R. – 579

Chiapas – 458-459, 492

Chichimecs – 471

chimera – 429

chimpanzee – 2, 13, 32-36

China – xi, 10-11, 250, 320, 358, 486, 488, 505

Chionides – 363

Christian art/artists – 87, 333

Christian, born again – 191

Christian of Buch – 126, 171

Christian sects/Christianity – 2, 14, 16, 18, 51, 74, 87, 126, 145, 162, 171, 175, 191, 198, 197, 212-215, 239-240, 252, 261, 345, 407, 431, 499-500, 503, 510, 521-522, 534, 537, 540, 554, 565

Christian cemeteries – 407

Christian Eucharist – 212

Christian sacraments – 541

Christian self-sacrifice – 537

Christmas – 162, 169, 183, 225-227, 259

Chukchee tribe – 306

Chukotka – 487

church music – 44, 86-87, 97, 117, 121, 138, 140-141, 175, 194, 230, 346, 365

Churchill, W. – 581

CIA (Central Intelligence Agency) – 583, 588, 606, 608-609

Cilicia – 419, 426

cinnamon – 53-54, 73, 151

Circe – 275, 406, 433

circle of life – 135

city Dionysia – 359-360, 363, 375

civilization – ix, 20, 320-323, 458, 474, 486, 505, 509

Clashing Rocks – 269, 406, 408

Claudius – 409, 412, 532

Clavaria – 487

Claviceps purpurea – 167, 396, 502-503, 510

Clement of Alexandria – 345

Cleon – 345, 428
Cleopatra – 433
clitoris – 184, 195, 370
Cliveden – 581
cloud – 103-104, 118, 130, 135, 141, 194, 236-237, 337, 351
cluster headache – 89, 92, 117, 122, 147, 151
cocaine – 25, 35, 544
Codex Aureus – 195
Codex Borgia – 286, 317
Codex Dresden – 463
Codex Florentine – 454
Codex Galindo – 191
Codex Madrid – 316, 469
Codex Magliabechiano – 496-496
Codex Rupertsberg – 136, 194-195
Codex Vienna – 473
Codex Vindobonensis – 472-473, 493
cognitive development/functioning – 27, 31-32, 34-36, 38, 42-44, 88, 92, 118, 528
cognitive deficits – 30
cognitive dissonance – 132
Colima – 493, 491
collusion – 121
Colombia – 329, 486, 501, 510
comedy – 345, 347-349, 351, 362-363, 365-366, 374-375
conception – 129, 132, 137, 169, 187-188, 190, 200, 237, 233, 338, 528, 531, 537, 549
Congo – 259
Conocybe – 487
consciousness – 11-14, 23-26, 28-30, 32, 34-35, 37-38, 40-45, 92, 118-121, 123, 151, 153, 188, 258, 321, 324, 330-332, 338, 472, 522, 529-531-533-535-538, 541-542, 546-547, 576
constellation – 169, 183, 361
consubstantiality – 191
contemplation – 185, 528
Copelandia – 487, 507
Cordyceps capitata – 487
Corona Borealis – 361
corona de Cristo – 498-499
corybant/corybantic – 265, 406
Corycian crocus – 425
Corycian Cave – 421, 425-426, 428
cosmic center – 471
cosmic consciousness – 41
Cosmic Egg – 88, 102, 114, 133, 160, 168, 174, 176, 182, 189-191, 194, 197
cosmic enlightenment – 106
cosmic passage/plane/path – 423, 421, 474
Cosmic Tree (of Knowledge) – 176, 187
cosmology – 137, 144, 169, 198, 235, 302, 328
Council of Reims – 172
cow – 91, 231, 235-238, 246, 405, 419, 424, 429, 433
cow-maiden – 429, 433
crab/crab dance – 345, 348-351, 359, 370, 375, 378, 440

crab lice – 349

creativity – 27-28

crescent moon – 183-184, 190-191, 195

Cretan – 275, 406, 411

Creatan Rhea – 404

Crete – 366, 401, 412, 419

crocus – 425-426

cross – 18, 161, 170, 176, 178, 181, 190, 194, 196, 215, 234, 268, 295, 394, 522, 537, 541, 565, 567

cross-cultural – 23, 324

crown/crowning – 100, 102, 113, 126, 136, 170, 174, 176, 184, 192, 200, 218, 239, 269, 327, 341, 361, 392, 487, 498

crown chakra – 184

crusade – 581

cumin – 168, 122

curandera – 496

curandero – 316, 329, 507

Curetes – 412

Cybele – 365-366, 404, 406, 432

Cyclops – 404

Cylon – 353

CYP2D6 gene – 33

cypress – 156, 189, 215, 217, 250, 268

cytochrome P450 – 33

D

Dacians – 368

dactyls – 406

Danaids – 434

dance/dancer – 6, 39, 43-44, 126, 217, 224, 240, 245, 330, 344-346, 348-350, 358, 363, 375, 377-378, 384, 406, 493

Dardanus – 412-414, 429

Dark Ages – ix

darnel – 396-397, 435

Datura – 86, 134, 144, 147-149, 153, 178-180, 186, 255, 264, 268, 276, 410, 421

Demeter – 167, 213, 249, 340, 355, 364, 372, 404, 503

decapitation – 296-297, 452, 462, 464, 466-470, 478

deer – 159, 162, 185, 223, 240-241, 247, 273, 294, 433, 489, 536

delirium – 92, 123, 145, 147, 217, 281

Delphi – 99, 139, 156, 165, 176, 186, 265, 356, 379, 398, 419, 421, 424, 426

delusion/delusional – 34, 93, 95, 123, 126, 146-147, 396

demagogue – 355, 372, 375, 428, 363, 368, 371

Demeter – 167, 213, 249, 340, 355, 364, 372, 404, 503

democracy – 17, 343-344, 348, 351-353, 355, 359-360, 372

depression – 13, 30, 117, 123, 168, 335

detoxification – 310

Deucalion – 344, 351

devil/devilish – 87, 108, 130, 140, 146, 148, 152, 154, 171, 173, 180, 185-186, 200, 224, 234, 268, 456-457, 494, 497, 511

diabolic – 136, 152
diarrhea – 282, 284, 287
Dictyophora – 487
Dido – 391, 395, 432-433
Dietrich of Echternach – 89
Dikaiopolis – 359
dildo – 355, 428
Dionysia in the City – 360
Dionysian – 221-223, 226, 230, 241, 244, 275, 343, 358-360, 362-363, 373, 375, 420, 526, 528, 537-539, 541
Dionysius of Halicarnassus – 393, 429, 449
Dioscorides – 254, 345, 376
Dioskouroi – 404
Dirke – 421
Disibodenberg – 86, 93-94, 96-97, 100-101, 107, 109-111, 113-114, 131, 140-141, 143, 170
disinhibition – 42
displays – 30, 40, 97-100, 120, 123, 125, 171, 175, 184, 200, 225, 231, 259, 344, 349, 363, 371, 375, 429, 328, 416, 460, 492, 550
dithyramb – 344, 375
DMT (dimethyltryptamine) – 16, 41, 321, 329, 330, 332
DMT snuff – 329
Dodona – 400, 395
doksaal – 191-192
donkey ears – 180, 185
dopamine/dopaminergic systems – 13, 25-28, 30-32, 34-36, 43-44
Dorian – 351, 356, 372
dote/dowry – 94, 111
double snakeheads – 196
double standards – 121, 130, 132
dove – 185, 408
dragon – 185, 296, 420, 582
drugs – xi, 23-26, 29-30, 33, 35-36, 43, 45, 51-52, 71, 73-74, 121, 165, 211-212, 220, 224, 226, 231, 244, 247, 249, 275, 293, 319, 321, 324, 331, 509, 525, 543, 553-554, 548-549, 566, 581, 583, 607
Druid/Druidism – 156, 162, 244-247, 276, 395
Dulles, A. – 574, 580, 603-604, 608-610, 617
Dulles, J. F. – 574, 580, 604, 610, 617
dung – 159, 156, 164, 349-350, 489, 495
dung-mushroom – 156, 340, 495
dwarf/dwarfish – 235, 268, 283, 290, 349, 305-307, 338, 403-406, 408, 411, 425, 427, 461
dynorphins – 26

E

eagles – 472
Earth goddess – 476
Echidna – 425, 428
Echion – 422, 423
Eckhart, M. – 342
ecstasy – 9, 40, 65, 102-103, 185, 238, 293, 340, 361, 397, 488, 491, 539, 570

ectomycorrhizal – 155, 157, 189, 160

Edda, The Prose – 163, 212, 243

Eden, Garden of – 215, 185-186, 431, 490, 503

Eden Tree – 157, 186, 215, 490, 503

Edoni – 368

Egg of the Universe – 87, 128, 160, 168, 189

Egypt/Egyptian – 11, 54, 56-57, 59-61, 70, 145, 275, 320, 376, 391, 402, 411, 419, 428, 430, 345, 403

Ehecatl – 285-286, 317, 461, 473

Eibingen – 113

Eisner, B. – 552-553

Ekholm, G. – 475, 480

elfin eddy (fairy wind) – 401

El Niño – 322

El Salvador – 459, 500

Elaphomyces – 159, 487

Eleusinian Mysteries – 16, 212-213, 237, 332, 343, 362, 364, 372, 374, 387, 542

Eleusis – 16, 19, 213, 256, 275, 332, 340, 353, 355, 374, 502

Eleutherai – 360

elfin eddy – 401

Elijah – 220, 221

Elisabeth of Schönau – 132, 144, 174, 198

emotional development – 36, 42, 93, 118, 120-121, 124

Emperor Frederick Barbarossa – 110-111, 126, 132, 136, 174

enculturation – 6

enema – 471

encephalins – 25-26

enlightenment – 86, 98, 105-106, 134, 166, 176, 184, 191, 194, 336

Enodia – 244, 248, 275

entheogen/entheogenic – x-xi, 1, 14, 18, 85-86, 88, 92-93, 101-102, 104, 109, 112-115, 122, 127, 134-136, 138-139, 141, 143, 146, 150, 157, 165-166, 173, 179, 182, 184, 189, 192-193, 200, 211, 223, 229, 245, 258, 261, 265, 268, 280-281, 329, 343, 373, 387, 402, 420-421, 423, 453, 458, 565

entoptics – 185, 201

ephedra – 56, 64, 242, 254

ephod – 99

Epigenes of Sicyon – 345

epiphany – 96, 101-102, 105-106, 109, 134, 147, 192, 200-201

ergonovine – 502

ergot – 19, 36, 122, 133, 166-168, 362, 364, 374, 396-397, 486, 502-503, 508, 510

Erigone – 360-361

Eros – 370

estrus – 433

Eteocles – 424

ethereal oils – 136, 144, 425

Ethiopia – 54, 167, 215, 224, 238-239, 401, 403

ethnomycology – 20, 565-568, 573, 577, 607, 611-612, 614

Etruscan – 340, 403, 405-406, 409-412, 413-417, 418, 429, 443

Eucharist – 212-213, 356, 431, 456

euphoria 30, 147, 150, 338, 147

Euripides – 213, 221, 351, 361, 372, 383, 423

Europa – 418

Evander – 429

evangeliar – 99, 195-196

Evening Star – 236, 461-462, 465, 470, 474, 570

evolution – 4, 11, 13, 23-25, 27-31, 32-35, 37, 39-40, 43-45, 75, 423, 536, 581

existential anxiety – 92, 119-120

Exodus – 14, 53, 61-62, 67-68, 73, 75, 335

extraversion – 525-531, 535

extrovert – 527

eye sockets – 427, 493, 501

eye winking – 193

eyeballs – 285, 317, 369, 384, 473, 493

eyes (wide) open – 193

eyes closed – 185, 330, 253

Ezekiel – 55, 70-72, 74, 106, 261

F

fairy/fairy lore/fairy food – 86, 401, 407-409, 415, 440

fairy table – 407-409

Farben, IG – 608

fasces – 229, 264-265

fate(s)/fateful/fatalis – 120, 244, 388, 391, 407, 415, 424, 456

Fäulnispilz – 87

Fertile Crescent – 55-56

fig/fig gesture – 217-218, 345, 357, 370-371

fingers – 170, 368, 371

fireball – 177

fire/fire-breathing – 16, 64-66, 102, 104, 106, 133-134, 137, 169, 177, 184, 191-192, 214, 219, 229-230, 250, 252, 255, 265, 267, 277, 298, 322, 325, 335, 362, 371, 374, 397, 417, 424, 436, 457, 464, 478, 539-540

fire, libido – 540

fire of passion – 539

fire pits – 322

fire sacrifice – 214, 250

fire of the Holly Ghost – 191-192

fire walk – 382

fire water/rain – 540

flame – 66, 101-102, 104-105, 118, 135-136, 141, 176-178, 191-192, 200, 213, 219, 372, 400

Fleck, K. – 533

Fliegenpilz – 157

fleur-de-lis – x, 1 47, 176, 186

Flor et Blancheflor – 533-534

fly – 433

fly agaric/*Amanita muscaria* – 64, 86-87, 92-93, 95, 99, 102, 115, 133, 135-136, 139, 141-142, 146, 156-157, 159, 161-164, 166, 177, 181, 183, 191-193, 197-199, 215, 227, 234, 239-241, 261, 268, 293, 306, 308, 334-336, 339, 408, 490 flying/flying ointment – 62-63, 105, 128, 130-131, 134, 148-149, 145, 153-154, 160, 168-169, 178-181, 189-190, 194, 222, 270, 333, 337, 400, 501

flying virgins – 401

FOIA (Freedom of Information Act) – 575

forge – 404, 425

forgery – 345, 405, 411

Forte, R. – 576

foundation stories – 375, 411, 415, 418-419, 421, 571, 614

France – 167, 173-174, 217, 490, 504, 511

Frazer, J. – 216-217, 253

Freemasons/Masons – 522

Freidel, D. – 465, 471

fresco – 195

fumigant/fumigation – 58, 214, 220-221, 231-232, 239-241, 269

fungi – 3, 4-5, 8, 11-14, 37, 85-86, 88-89, 95, 101, 109, 140, 142-143, 146, 155-157, 159-160, 164, 166-168, 181, 189-190, 407, 455, 486-487, 497, 500, 502, 511

fungicides – 155, 167

fungilore – 162

Furies (Erinyes) – 426

G

gadfly (oistros) – 433

gall – 418, 443

Gallic – 218

gangrene – 122, 167-168

Ganoderma – 158, 499-500

Ganymedes – 370

gastrointestinal distress – 489-490, 492

gemstones – 112, 133, 168, 173

Genius/genius – 34, 125-126, 175, 236, 416

Georgics – 409

Germany – 87, 89, 96, 108, 132, 134, 158, 167, 188, 195, 198-199, 174, 266, 405, 583, 607

Geryon – 429

Gilgamesh – 160-161, 216, 541

gills – 176, 181, 190, 425

Ginzburg, C. – 225-226

glossolalia – 102

Glover, E. – 544

glyphs/petroglyphs – 19, 459, 464, 469, 487

goat – 212, 219, 221-224, 226, 231, 233, 235, 238, 240-243, 244, 247, 249, 254, 267, 271, 273-274, 339, 344, 346, 351, 375, 390, 399

goat-man – 223, 231, 362, 370

goatskin – 221, 360

Golden Apples – 402, 408

Golden Fleece – 161, 176-177, 190, 344

golden nuggets – 160, 176-177, 182

Gomphus – 487

goose – 348, 370

Gorgon – 351, 401-402, 405, 408, 418, 427, 429-430, 432-434, 448

Gorilla – 224, 259

Gras, N. – 591

Great Dionysia – 360, 362-363

Great Lakes – 490

Greece – 19, 99, 139, 148, 174, 244, 249, 262, 268, 340, 367, 382-383, 395, 407, 410, 413, 502, 508, 510

Greeks – 6, 137, 145, 216, 219, 262, 275, 344, 355, 373, 413, 426, 428, 430, 502

Green Man – 252

Green One – 221

Gregory the Great, St. – 131, 521

Guadalajara – 491

Guatemala – 19, 285, 291, 452-453, 459, 461, 465, 472, 477, 487, 491-492, 496, 500, 501, 510

guilt – xi, 97, 129, 132, 229, 592

H

Hadden, B. – 579

Hajj – 332

Hall Carbine Affair – 590-591, 593, 612

hallucination – 44, 63, 92-93, 89, 102, 105-106, 122-123, 135, 139, 145-146, 148, 150-151, 157, 161, 165, 167, 192-193, 217-218, 256, 259, 281, 300, 305, 340

Hanegraaff, W. – 520

Hannibal – 432

haoma – 63-66, 212-214, 228-229, 231-235, 237-238, 243, 246, 250, 254, 261-262, 266-267, 274, 367-368, 476, 538

haomavarga – 368

Harding, E. – 541

Harmonia – 422-424, 426

Harpies – 389-391, 393, 397-398, 400-402, 406, 437

Harriman, A. – 579, 596

Haruspicy – 416

Harvard Divinity School – 37

Harvard University – 494-495, 569, 572-573, 575, 607, 614

Harvey, G. – 580, 582

hashish (hashich) – 57-58, 62, 70, 75, 228, 271

head – 62, 102, 122, 127, 135-136, 325, 147, 150, 152, 155, 159, 162, 164, 177, 180-181, 184, 190, 193-194, 215, 229, 231, 248, 252, 276, 284, 295-297, 299, 304, 324, 328-329, 341, 367, 374, 399, 406, 408, 410, 415, 418, 448, 452, 465-466, 468, 470, 473-474, 476, 478, 487, 491, 498, 500-501

headache – 89, 92, 117, 122, 151

headdress – 330, 460, 466, 469, 474, 476

head louse – 351

Hecate – 275, 397

Hector – 411

Heiðrun (Goat) – 211-212, 243

Heimiella anguiformis – 506

Helen – 423

hellebore – 59, 243, 346
henbane – 86, 134, 143-144, 148-149, 153, 180, 186, 222
hepatoscopy – 416
Hephaestus – 403-404, 424, 438
Hera – 366, 419
Heracles/Herakles – 402, 429
herb/herbal/herbalist – 1, 5, 59, 74, 87, 95, 100, 110, 122, 137, 140, 142-143, 146, 149, 153, 155-156, 158, 175, 217-218, 226, 228-229, 264-265, 288, 335, 361, 364, 372, 397, 401, 414, 420-421, 433
heretic – 172-173, 431
Hermes – 99, 197, 385, 400, 407
Herodotus – 60-61, 219-220, 244, 411
Hesperides – 402, 408
hetaera – 346
High Expressed Emotion – 124
high priest/priestess – 85-87, 99-100, 112-113, 126-127, 139, 156, 162, 170, 173, 185, 192, 200
High Times – 51
Hildesheim – 195-196, 504
Hindu Kush – 214, 218, 224, 240, 250, 253-254, 256, 274
Hinduism – 51, 531
Hipparchos – 354
Hippias – 354, 356
hippocampal-septal system – 40
hippocampus – 26
Hippolytus – 247, 415
Hitler, A. – 580
Hollywood Hospital – 549
Holy Grail – 99, 115, 160, 176, 190, 523
Holy Mushroom – 16, 135, 146
holy soma – 296
Holy Spirit/Ghost – 69, 98, 102, 104-106, 133-134, 136
Holy Virgin – 100, 141
Homer/Homeric – 17, 57, 213, 344, 354, 414, 416, 419, 429
hominids – 31-32
homosexual – 130, 132, 428
Honduras – 507, 598
honey – 16, 59, 71, 143, 152, 212-213, 221, 237, 242, 283, 248-249, 256, 263, 274, 276, 290, 306, 320, 335-336, 395, 455, 471
honeymoon – 570
hood – 97, 100, 132, 445
Hoover Institute – 587, 604
Horace – 345, 396
horse – 157, 163-164, 238-239, 261, 283, 302, 339, 352, 367, 402
host – 192
Houston, J. – 552
Huautla de Jiménez – 494, 496, 499, 507, 587
Hubbard, A. – 549-551, 553
human CYP2D6 gene – 33
human sacrifice – 5, 420, 432, 455, 466, 478

humor – 137, 150-151, 157, 169, 226, 418
Hunahpu – 470
hymn – 213, 141, 163, 236, 274, 286, 307, 419, 476-477
hyoscyamine – 145, 148
Hyperboreans – 401
hypnogogia – 123
hypnopompia – 123
hysterical – 120-122, 126, 129

I

Iacchus - 362
ibotenic acid – 161, 281-282, 289, 293-295, 490
Ice Age – 490
icon – 57, 128, 196, 320, 337, 403, 451, 457, 463, 473
iconoclastic fury – 188, 199
Ikarios – 360
Ilium (Troy) – 414
illusion – 89-90, 93, 121-122, 153, 471, 520
immaculate conception – 188, 190
immortality – 216, 221, 237, 239, 266, 272, 280, 340, 463-464, 533, 538, 540-544, 547, 540
incarnation – 104, 138, 224, 226, 274-275, 521
incense – 55, 59, 62-63, 72, 75, 213-214, 219-220-221, 254-255, 266, 269, 277, 316, 466
inclusorium – 90, 92-95, 97, 99, 127-129, 153
Indians – 349, 453-454, 456, 464, 477, 490-501, 507-508, 510-511, 587, 589
individuation – 530, 534, 536, 553
indolic substances – 490, 494, 502, 505, 511
indoles/indolic – 36, 41, 259, 490, 494, 502, 505, 511
Indonesia – 507
Indra – 214, 251, 287, 292-293, 299, 296
inferiority complex – 101, 119
inner vision – 16, 40, 96, 115, 126, 135, 138, 184-185, 331
Inquisition – 15, 149, 165, 172, 499, 511, 565
instincts – 526
intoxication – 16, 71-72, 216, 219, 232, 245, 282, 292, 331, 235, 251, 287, 303, 364, 398, 403, 432, 454, 538, 541, 545
introvert/extrovert – 38, 91, 527-529, 531-532, 537, 546
Iran, Iranians – 67, 214, 218-219, 221, 229, 235, 237, 242, 246, 249, 254-255, 272, 276, 288, 477
Isaiah – 53, 55
Isenheim altar – 334-335
Ishtar – 59
Isis – 419
Islam – 13-15, 51, 211, 213-214, 221, 248, 251, 254, 257, 262, 264
Ismene – 421
Italus, King – 413

Italy – 96, 174, 388, 395, 406, 409, 413, 429, 432-433, 504
Iulus – 388, 395, 398, 414
ivy – 253, 339, 362, 364, 368, 373, 383, 421
Ixion – 340, 410

J

Jabir ibn Hayyan – 523
Jackson, C. – 579, 581, 598, 602, 604, 610, 613
Jacob's ladder – 187
jaguar – 319-320, 326, 328, 332, 454, 460-461, 464, 466-469, 473-474
Janus-faced deity – 474
Japan – 288-290, 306, 485-486, 507
Jason – 258, 344, 403, 406, 424-425, 428
Jeremiah – 55
Joachim – 133, 188-190
Jocasta – 427
Josephson, M. – 593, 595
Julius Caesar – 414, 433
juniper – 156, 214-215, 217-218, 224-225, 232-234, 239-242, 250, 253-254, 267-268, 273
Jutta of Sponheim – 86, 90, 93-94, 143, 114-115
Juxtlahuaca cave – 461

K

K'awil – 461, 465
kaalkopjes - 164
Kaballah – 97
Kabeiroi – 365, 403-404, 406, 411-413, 419, 423, 427, 430
Kadmilos – 403
Kahlköpfe – 157, 164
Kalash – 214-215, 218, 222, 224-225, 233, 239, 250-251
Kaminaljuyu – 472
Karkínos – 347-349-350, 377
Kaulomyketes – 422, 425, 445
Kennan, G. – 574, 580, 583, 602, 604, 617
Kennedy, J. – 21, 596-598, 602, 614
Kenya – 509
khat – 238, 271-272
Khidr – 221
kingship – 340, 344, 351-352
Kingsley, J. – 577
Kithairon – 260-261
kiva – 331
Kleisthenes – 359, 353
Knapp, J. – 582
Knights – 347, 355, 428
Knights Templar – 174
knucklebone – 370
komos – 363
Konon – 393
koobl tourroum – 505
Koryak tribe – 240, 283-285, 297-299
korybantes – 365-366
krater – 420
Kreousa – 426

Kukulcan – 461, 466
kundalini – 166
Kuno of Disibodenberg – 107, 109
Kuretes – 366
kykeon – 167, 213, 332

L

La Venta – 460
labia majora/minora – 136, 184
ladder – 187, 239
Lake Copais – 426
Lake Titicaca – 501
Lamb of God – 177, 182
lamellae – 160, 190
lamp – 326, 369-371
lantern – 369, 371
Lares – 404
Latinus – 426, 429-430
Lavinia – 426, 429
Lavinium – 405
Leary, T. – 581-582
legend/legendary – 20, 59, 63, 65-66, 126, 221, 224, 238, 283, 304, 333, 337, 410-412, 415, 418, 459-460, 464, 466-467, 473, 492, 498, 539, 541, 544, 565-567, 569, 572-573, 575, 583, 611-614
Lamachos – 359, 378
Lemnos – 365, 403-404, 412
Lenaia – 361-363
lesbian – 130-131
levirate – 131
libation – 213-214, 229, 239, 250, 267, 406
Liber Scivias – 86, 101, 107, 132, 136-137, 166, 174, 196-197
Liberal Arts – 97
Liberty Cap – 140, 164-165, 179, 181-183, 197
libido – 525-528, 530, 532, 539-540, 544, 546
Lienzo de Zacatepec – 498
lightning and thunder/legends – 234, 405-492
lily – 147, 178, 410, 421, 533-535, 537, 546, 554
limbic system – 25-28, 31, 35, 41-42, 44,
Ling Zhi – 158
lingua ignota – 113, 138-139
Linnaeus – 161, 357, 490
Lippmann, W. – 580
literae ignotae – 138-139
little men/people/soldiers – 403, 404, 406, 454, 488
liver – 15, 416-418
living water – 105, 135, 144, 161-163, 176, 182, 184, 193-194
Livy – 432
locoweeds – 235
Logos – 168, 520, 540,
loincloth – 178, 190
Lolium temulentum – 396-397
Lophophora williamsii – 492
Louvre Museum – 403
Loxicha (San Agustín) – 498
Loyola, St. Ignatius – 542

LSD (Lysergic acid dimethylamide) – 13, 20, 34-36, 63, 122, 149, 167, 502, 547, 552, 576, 581-582, 607
Lübeck (Germany) – 179, 188, 191
Luce, C. – 579-584, 602-603
Luce, H. – 574, 598, 603, 605, 610, 613
Lull, R. – 531
lunar – 190, 367, 419, 463
lunatic – 184, 541
Luther, M. – 189
Lycoperdon – 487, 495
Lycophron – 392, 406, 435
Lycurgus – 340, 368
Lysandra – 407-408
Lysandra tombstone – 408
lysergic acid – 167, 502

M

Macbeth – 420
Macedonia – 244, 262, 264, 271, 366-367
macrocosm – 86, 169, 200
macrofungi – 155
macropsia – 489-491, 493, 503-504
macropsy – 105
madness – 167, 217-218, 244-245, 248, 346, 361, 430, 454, 505-506, 541
Maecenas – 409, 414
maenads – 337, 339-341, 358, 361-362, 368
Magi/magi – 114, 160, 164, 168, 213, 247
magic brew – 148
magical thinking – 6, 14, 92, 118
Maimonides, M. – 523
mandrake – 86, 134, 144-146, 148-149, 153-154, 180, 222, 234, 265, 268
Manikin Scepter god – 461
María Sabina – 308, 496, 507-508, 587-590, 613
Marmor Parium – 344
Masatec Indians – 340-341
masturbation – 96, 128, 130-132
materialism – 551
Matias, A. – 498, 508
Maya/Mayan/Mayan mushroom stones – 18, 284-285, 304, 451-453, 456-457, 459-472, 478, 492, 495-496, 500-501
Mazatecs – 615
mead/Mead of Inspiration – 15, 165, 212, 239, 243, 283-284, 290, 296, 300, 305-307, 540
Mecca – 332
Medea – 351, 402, 424-425, 428
median raphe nuclei – 36
Medusa – 351, 402, 408, 418, 427-429, 448
Megacles – 353-354
megalomania – 126, 192
Melampes/Melampus – 243
Melusina – x
mescaline – 16, 41, 292-293, 320-321, 494, 552-553, 547-551

Mesoamerica – 18, 280, 285, 291, 296, 309, 451-454, 457-458, 460-461, 463-465, 470-478, 489, 492-493, 589

mesocortical – 31

mesolimbic – 26-28, 31, 42

Mesopotamia – 59, 216, 320, 323, 416

metaphysics – 19, 98, 554

Mexico – 19, 286, 290-291, 294-295, 304-305, 308-309, 316, 320, 341, 452, 454, 458-459, 461, 463, 465, 471, 476-477, 485-487, 491-493, 495-497, 499, 501-502, 506-511, 571, 581, 587, 607-608, 615

mescal – 494

Mice (Múes) – 347-348

microcosm – 169, 416-417

Midas – 185

Middle Ages – 19, 87, 98, 109, 122, 128, 130, 143, 148-149, 155-156, 158, 169-169, 177, 225-226, 338, 490, 499, 502-503, 510

midwife – 130, 133

migraine – 89, 92, 122, 126, 167-168

Milan – 589

milk – 15, 108, 143, 159, 161, 182, 211-213, 217-219, 221, 223, 229, 231-233, 235-237, 239, 241-244, 246-248, 254, 267, 274-275, 287, 358, 436

mimesis – 39, 44, 362, 370, 398

minerals – 168

Minos – 419

mirror – 128, 184, 233, 340, 370, 410, 416

mistletoe – 234-235, 240, 246, 264, 268-269, 368

Mithen Model – 7-9

Mithra(s)/Mithraic/Mithraism – 18, 229, 254, 237, 337, 365, 367, 394

MK-ULTRA – 20, 574, 583, 606, 614

monastic enclosure – 92, 94-95, 100, 111, 127

moon – 103, 169, 176, 183-184, 191, 195, 321, 419, 470, 462, 541, 570

Morgan, J. – 21, 283, 299, 574, 576-579, 581-583, 585-586, 590-591-595, 597-598, 613-614

Morning Star/Venus – 461-463, 465-467, 470, 472, 474

Morocco – 222, 266, 488, 503

mosaics, mushrooms – 503

Moses – 53, 73-74, 215

Moses Maimonides – 523

mother goddess – 404, 411, 476, 406

mold – 155

Mount Ida – 429

Mount Penteli – 345

mucus – 156, 158, 162, 169, 325, 329-330, 371-372

Muhammad – 13, 15

murals – 19, 457, 487-489

muscarine – 161, 281-282, 284-285, 287, 293, 295, 490

muscazone – 490

muscimol – 105, 135, 161, 193, 281-282, 289, 295, 451, 490

mushroom-bull – 359

mushroom stones – 459, 500

mushroom tree – 302

mushroom warriors – 422

mushroom-Venus religion – 462

Musquitias Indians – 507

mycelium – 154, 189, 397

Mycenae – 341, 379, 402, 418, 429-430, 433

mycophobia – 87, 157, 201, 499

Myrrh (*Cammiphora myrrha*) – 53-54, 73

mystical play – 86, 113, 127, 140

N

Nairobi – 509

Nána – 406

nanacatépetl glyph – 498

Napoleon – x

narcissism – 124

narcotic fungi – 487

narthex (thyrsus) – 230, 373, 417, 420-421

nasal mucus – 330, 371

National Geographic – xi

nausea – 105, 122, 147, 149, 151, 161-162, 240, 282, 290, 293, 330, 397, 472

Nazi Party – 584, 579, 607

nectar – 256, 339-340, 358, 538, 540

Neleids – 353, 356

Neleus – 238, 353

Neoplatonic – 521, 531, 537-537, 539

Nepal – 486

nepenthe – 57

Nero – 394

Nestor – 352-354

neuraxis – 41

neurognostic – 45

neurohormone – 32

neuropeptide – 33

neurotheology – 38

neurotransmitters – 25, 28, 31-32, 37-38

neurotropic fungi – 37, 487

Nevado de Colima – 491, 493

New York Times – 586-589, 591

New York Tribune – 585

Nietzsche, F. – 526, 528, 534, 540, 544

nightshades – 144, 149

NLP (Neuro-Linguistic Programming) – 8-9

nocturnal ceremonies – 494, 496, 507

nonda – 505

Nordic regions – 368, 490

nose – 216, 252, 261, 306, 325, 329, 368, 371-372, 470-471, 491

nostril – 330, 346-347, 350, 359, 371

nucleus accumbens – 26

nutmeg – 151

O

Oaxaca – 286, 295, 305, 341, 494, 571, 587, 607, 615

Odilia Clementia – 112

Odysseus – 356, 390, 406, 411, 421

Oedipus Rex – 398

Ogygia – 421, 426-427

Oil of Mercy – 215

ointment/flying ointment – 62-63, 67, 86, 98, 110, 122, 128, 130-131, 136, 139, 143-145, 147-150, 153-155, 162-163, 169, 179-180, 194, 222, 261

Ojibwa Indians – 490, 510

oksaal/doksaal – 191-192

oligarchy – 352, 372

Olmec – 18, 458-461, 464, 466-467, 476-478

Olympia/Olympian – 335, 352, 373, 423, 428

Olympias – 430

omnipotence – 119, 125

Omphagia – 222-223, 241, 247

Onan – 131

one eye – 404, 427

one foot – 427

one-leg – 465-466, 422

Operation Mockingbird – 610

Ophites – 431

opioid cis-regulation – 33

Opus Dei – 96

oracle – 99, 139,148, 156, 162, 244, 296, 320, 327, 389, 426

Orcus – 401

ordeal – 214, 229-230, 254-255, 265-266, 325, 330, 332, 428

Oreithyia – 401

Orestes – 374

orgasm – 128-129, 132, 154

original sin – 188

Osmond, H. – 547, 549

OSS (Office of Strategic Services) – 549, 583

Ossetes – 219

Ouranos – 426

Ouroboros – 135, 185

out-of-body experience – 28, 105, 184

out orbit eyes – 501

Ovid – 397, 424

P

PACAP (pituitary cyclase-activating polypeptide precursor) – 32-33

Panaeolus sphinctrinus – 487, 494-495

pagan – 85, 98-99, 145, 154, 157, 162, 154, 172, 565

Pahnke, W. – 37

Paleolithic – xi, 3, 14, 21, 324, 412, 475-477, 487

paleomammalian brain – 41-42, 45

Pallas – 351, 433-434

palm tree/ leave – 156, 185

Pan – 370, 420

Panama – 501
Panathenaean Festival – 354-355
Panther (feline) – 337
Papaver – 150-151
Papua New Guinea – 486, 488, 504-506, 509-510
Paracelsus – 521
paradoxical intention – 121
paralysis – 121, 129, 258
paraments (liturgical) – 175, 177, 179, 196
Parian Chronicle – 344
Parnassus – 421, 428
parsley – 393
Pátzcuaro – 491
pea crab (Pinnotheres pisum) – 350
Peace – 348-349
pearl and oyster (shell) – 183-184
Pediculosis capitis – 351
Peisistratos – 353-356, 359
Pelasgian – 353-354, 403, 406, 423, 431, 351
Peleus – 423
Penates – 405-406, 412-413
penicillium – 155
penis – 129, 147, 347-350, 366, 369-372, 405, 408, 415, 425, 427, 467, 470
penitence – 101
pennyroyal – 213
Pentecost – 86, 102, 104-105, 177
Pentheus – 361, 368, 423-424, 428
Pericles – 344, 353, 355-356, 368
Persephone – 167, 343, 372, 387, 404, 409, 503
Perseus – 341, 367, 402, 409, 418, 423, 429-430
Persia – 58, 63-67, 70, 74, 213, 218, 227, 238, 247, 262, 272, 347-349, 356, 362, 366, 376, 394, 401, 403, 476, 478, 523
personality development – 86, 88, 93, 118, 121, 123-124, 192, 550
personality disorder – 34, 121, 123-125, 168, 192
Peru/Peruvian – 16, 319-321, 323, 328-329, 500-501
petroglyphs – 19, 487
peyote (*Lophophora williamsii*) – 279, 294, 309, 320, 471, 492
phallic/ithyphallic – 265, 373, 403, 405, 408, 415, 425, 500
phallic amulet – 265
phallic digits – 422
phallic dwarfs – 403, 406
phallic man-root – 265
phallic mushrooms – 425, 500
phallic pillar – 373
phallic satyrs – 373
phallic stones – x
Phanes – 366
pharmacratic inquisition – 565
pharmakos – 230
phenylalkylamine – 41
Philip – 174, 367, 430
Philokleon – 345, 348-349, 363, 366, 368, 370, 377

philosopher's stone – 102, 114, 133, 160, 168, 542, 549, 553
Phineus – 400-403, 406,408
Phoenician – 403, 410-411, 418-419, 438
Phrixus – 428
Phrygian cap – 164, 183, 327, 367, 410, 415, 427
Phrynichos – 347-349, 377
Phthirus pubis – 349
Physica – 86-87, 95, 100, 114, 136-137, 142-143, 158
pigmentarius – 110, 133, 136
pileolus – 177
pileus (hat, mushroom) – 164-165, 179-180, 182-183, 201, 337, 421, 468
Pilgrim Society – 323, 574
Pilsintecuhtli – 473
pine – 160, 201, 213, 215, 217, 222, 232-234, 242, 268, 281, 399, 489, 498
pinna guard crab (*Pinnotheres pisum*) – 351
Pinna nobilis – 350
piss/pissed – 162, 292, 371-372
piule – 498-499
Plaincourault mural – 504
Plaincourt, France – 490
plait/plaited – 112, 170
Plato/platonic – 115, 129-130, 194, 356, 364-365, 539
Pliny – 54-55, 243, 246-247, 371, 396
Plotinus – 539-540
Plutarch – 218, 254, 356
Poland – 238, 266, 333
political correctness – ix, xi, 14, 19
Polyaenus – 244-245
Polyneices – 424
polypeptide – 32
Pompey – 275, 394
Pope Benedict XVI – 134, 174
Pope Clement XIV – 415
Pope Eugene III – 112, 134, 174
Pope Innocent III – 172
Pope Innocent IV – 134
Pope Lucius III – 172
Popocatépetl – 497-498
Popol Vuh – 284-285, 297, 464, 468, 470
poppy (*Papaver rhoeas*) – 56, 64, 150-151, 242, 264
Portulaca oleracea – 357-358, 590,
Postclassic – 466, 473
PR (propaganda) – 20, 579, 582, 584, 586, 589, 613-614
Preclassic – 291, 340, 460, 466, 471
pre-Hispanic times – 460, 493, 510
prehistoric murals – 486-489, 510
Priam – 411
primordium – 133, 160, 168, 178, 189-190
prodynorphin – 33
Prohibition – 549
Prometheus – 417, 425
prophecy – 12-13, 15, 17-18, 21, 68, 91, 388-390, 392-394, 398, 400, 406, 424

prophet(s) – 13, 16, 69, 74, 88, 93, 102. 106, 128, 162, 175, 212-213, 220, 239, 243, 333, 408

prophetess – 95, 127, 139, 171, 188, 252, 392

prophetessa teutonia – 134, 174

prophetic – 93, 95, 107, 133, 135, 187, 275, 301, 340, 395, 415-416

Psalms – 334, 335

Psathyrella – 487

pseudo-Dionysius the Areopagite – 521

pseudologica fantastica – 193

psilocybin – 14, 25, 34-35, 37-38, 41, 43, 140, 157, 165, 179, 180, 182, 462, 466, 470, 472, 474, 486, 492-493, 500, 502, 510

Psilocybe aztecorum

P. caerulescens – 497

P. campanulatus – 486, 494-495

P. coprophila – 504

P. cubensis – 166, 486-487, 495, 497, 507, 509

P. hispanica – 486

P. hoogshagenii – 486-487, 499

P. mairei – 486, 488, 503

P. mexicana – 166, 487, 493, 495

P. moseri – 487, 501

P. muliercula – 487, 498

P. semilanceata – 504

P. subcubensis – 487, 507, 509

P. yungensis – 487, 502

P. zapotecorum – 487, 492-493, 497-499, 501

Psyche – 407

psychedelics – 24, 34-38, 41-42, 45, 211-212, 248, 256, 308-309, 329, 330, 334, 453, 473, 503, 523, 525, 529, 547, 551-554, 565-568, 574, 576, 581-583, 611, 613-614

psychointegrators – 41-42

psychopathology – 86, 194, 550

psychosis – 20, 168, 334, 546, 552

Ptah – 403

puberty – 120-121, 127-128, 365

Puccara Culture – 501

Puebla – 286, 497, 499

punk – 371-372

Purepecha Indian – 491

pygmy – 403

Pyrenees – 489

Python – 421

Q

qat/ghat/khat – 238-239, 271-272

Quetzalcóatl – 285-286, 493-494, 511

Quiche Maya – 284, 304, 456, 462, 464-465, 470

Quimbaya culture – 501

quincunx – 471

Qumran – 156

R

Russula. kirinea – 506

R. maenadum – 506

R. nondorbingi – 506

R. pseudomaenadum – 506

R. wahgiensis – 506

Raimundi stela – 330

rain – 142, 287, 321, 370-371, 405, 462, 465, 467, 478, 540

rainbow – 400

rain god (Tlaloc) – 461

rainmaking – 216

raven/raven's bread – 16, 297, 333-334, 347, 405

recipe – 59, 61, 72, 109, 113, 136, 139, 143, 340, 395, 409

recluse – 95, 102

red-white-green – 179, 201

Reg Veda – 214, 280, 288, 296

Regional Museum, Guadalajara – 491

reindeer – 162, 223, 240-241, 294

Reko – 494-495

resurrection – 18, 179, 191, 374, 461-462, 466-467, 470, 472, 474

revelation – 66, 75-76, 86, 102, 126, 134, 137, 169, 192-193, 199, 251, 338, 341, 542

rhapsodist – 344

Rhea – 274, 366, 383, 404

rhododendron – 220, 251, 256

Richardis of Stade – 86, 93, 96-97, 100-101, 112-117, 120-121, 125-126, 128-130, 135, 137, 139, 143, 170-171, 184-185, 192-194, 199

Robigalia – 397

Romanticism, German – 536, 554

rood screen – 191

rootlets – 146, 189

roots – 29, 140, 145-146, 154-155, 164, 179-180, 189-191, 227, 229, 258-259, 262, 302, 305, 393-394, 425, 464, 475

rose – 100, 177-178, 245, 256, 353, 522, 533-535, 537

Rosicrucian – 522, 533, 537, 546, 553-554

Rules of Pamiers – 172

Rupertsberg – 86, 100, 108-109, 111-117, 125, 127-129, 136-140, 170-171, 194-195, 199-200

Rural Dionysia – 358-360, 362-363, 373

Russian Orthodox – 163-164, 196

Russula agglutinata – 506

russulas – 486, 505, 508, 110

rye – 155, 502

S

Sabazios – 347, 356, 366-368, 404, 407, 411, 423-424, 431

Sabina, M. – 308, 496, 507-508, 587-590, 613

sacrament – 17, 37, 67, 94, 171, 192, 199, 211-213, 227, 244-245, 250, 261, 276, 284, 303, 307, 309, 331, 343, 387, 390, 394, 402-403, 406, 423, 431-432, 502, 541, 576, 615

Sacred Mushroom – 95, 102, 104, 105, 154, 162-164, 177, 181, 188-190, 193, 198, 283, 302,

307, 338, 341, 368, 463, 470, 472-473, 485-486, 492-498, 501-502, 507-510, 565, 567-568, 587

Sacrificial Lamb – 177, 182

Sahagun, B. – 454-455, 471, 494, 497

Sahara Desert – 487-488, 510

Sami of Lapland – 162-163

Sami nissati – 58

Samothrace – 365, 367, 380, 403, 412-413, 419, 423, 429

Samothracian – 406, 423

San Agustín Loxicha – 498

San Lorenzo, Mexico – 458-459

San Pedro (Trichocereus spp.) – 16, 320, 324, 326, 329-331

Sandoz – 547, 607-608

Santa Claus – 162, 224

santonin – 217-218, 268

saprotrophic – 157

Sargon – 216

Saskatchewan – 547, 549

Satan – 130

satyr – 339-340, 362, 373, 375, 403, 420

scapegoat – 244, 230, 608-609

Scivias – 86,101, 104, 106-107, 132, 136-137, 174, 194, 197-198

sclerotia – 166-167, 502-503

scopolamine – 145, 147-148, 261

scrotum – 129, 371

Scythians – 59-61, 63, 66, 67, 219,

Sechin – 323-325, 330

seer – 275, 416-418, 531

self-fulfilling prophecy – 108, 127, 193, 398

sensory deprivation – 123

separation anxiety – 117, 120

serotonin – 13, 25-26, 32-34, 39, 41-43, 165

serpent – 275, 285, 302, 341, 344, 367, 405, 407, 416, 418-422, 424, 428, 430-431, 433, 445, 455, 460-461, 464, 467-468, 504

Servius – 395

set and setting – 549

Seth – 215, 234, 252, 431

sexual intercourse – 191

sexuality – xi, 97, 101, 127, 129, 132, 524, 546

shade-foot – 422

Shakespeare – 371, 420, 578

shaman/shamanism – x-xi, 3, 5, 8, 19, 23-24, 28, 37-39, 43-45, 51, 74-75, 85, 87, 106, 133, 156-157, 162-164, 166, 177, 194, 214-215, 218, 224-226, 230, 232, 240, 225, 246, 250, 256, 276, 300-303, 324, 306, 308, 328-329, 357-358, 402, 406, 408, 410, 416-418, 420-421, 423, 459, 462, 470, 472, 476-477, 487-489, 496, 498, 507-509, 565

shame – xi, 125, 238, 268, 348

shape-shifting – 246, 325, 328

Siberia/Siberian – 16, 33, 154, 161-164, 223, 239, 256, 272, 283-284, 289, 291-295, 298-302, 306, 308-309, 453, 477, 486-490, 492, 495, 508, 510

Sina-Sina – 505

Siva-linga – x, 445, 479, 491, 579, 583, 613

skull – 215, 445, 470, 491, 579, 583

Skull and Bones – 583, 613

snails – 240, 240

snake/snakeheads – 144, 166, 185, 196, 222, 242, 274, 326, 328, 424, 426, 431, 448, 454, 493

Snakeroot – 235

snot – 369, 371

snuff – 16, 321, 329-330, 369, 371-372

snuffing tubes – 331

social isolation – 89, 122-123

Socrates – 351

sodomy – 131

solanine – 149

solar disk – 160, 176, 181, 183

solitary confinement – 123, 326

Solon – 356-357

soma – 19, 166, 212, 214, 228, 231, 236-237, 243, 246, 249, 251, 262, 269, 280, 286-294, 296, 299, 301, 305, 307, 309, 474, 476-477, 490, 519, 521, 523, 525, 538-545, 547, 549, 554, 576-577, 583

Sophocles – 398

soul – 28, 35, 43, 90, 101, 103, 106, 115-116, 130-131, 140, 144, 184-185, 187, 189-190, 274, 276, 296, 336, 338, 358, 407, 418, 430, 467, 520-521, 533-531, 537-540, 576

South America – 19, 54, 458, 485-486, 493, 496, 500, 509-510

Spain – 19, 454, 486-487, 489, 510

Spartoi – 422

spelt (*Triticum spelta*)/spelt cakes – 263, 393-394-395, 397

Sphinx – 424, 427-428

Spielrein, S. – 527

spirit-abductors – 401

sponge – 371, 405

spruce – 133, 155-156, 160-161

spruce cone – 190

Srophades – 400

St. George – 185, 200

St. Paul – 16, 106, 334, 541

Staircase to Heaven – 154

Star Wars – 171

stipe – 282, 407, 420, 421, 425, 465, 468

stone urns – 409

Strabo – 55, 213, 275, 393

strawberry tree – 357-358

Strophades – 400-401

Stropharia cubenisi – 496

substrate – 24-25, 37, 44, 182

Suidas – 345

Sumerian – 58

sun – 18, 103-104, 106, 118, 142, 160, 176, 183-184, 225, 261,

337, 373, 390, 397-398, 429, 456-457, 461-465, 467, 474, 541, 569

suntiama – 507

symbiotic – 95, 117, 121, 140, 153-156, 160-161, 189, 281, 302-303

Symplegades – 406

synod of Trier – 107, 109, 125

Syrian Orthodox – 196

T

Tabernathe iboga – 258

table – 17, 194, 334-335, 367, 374, 387-388-390-393-395, 398, 402, 405-406, 407-409, 428, 433, 488, 501

taboo – 18, 289, 291, 340, 347, 390, 397, 399, 402, 405-406, 408-409

Tages – 414-416, 418

tarbfeis – 245-246

Tarchon – 415-416, 418

Tarim mummies – xi

Tassili caves (Sahara Desert) – 19, 488

Telemachus – 354

Tellegren Absorption Scale – 39

Tengswich of Andernach – 112-113, 170

Tenochtitlán – 497

teonanácatl – 487, 492, 494, 496-497, 516

Teotihuacan – 470

teotlacuilnanácatl – 500

terpene – 216, 218, 226, 240, 252

testes/testicles – 129, 349, 351, 369, 407

Tetela del Volcán – 497

The Tycoons – 593

Theater of Dionysus – 344, 362, 366

Thebes (Greece) – 334, 365, 379, 403, 410, 418-419, 421-424, 426-427

Theophrastus – 357

theory of humors – 137

Theosophical Society – 520

theosophy – 520, 537, 553

Theseus – 351, 379

Thespis – 344-346, 356-357, 359-360, 375, 377, 381

Thetis – 423

This Week magazine – 572, 582, 613

Thrace – 365-368, 380, 389, 400, 403, 407

three-tiered cosmos – 478

Thucydides – 355

thujone – 216-217

thunder/thunderstruck – 234, 405, 492

Thunderbolt legend – 492

Thuya – 216-217, 268

thyrsus/narthex – 213, 226, 261, 362, 373, 420, 445

Tiber – 405

Time-Life magazine – 579-582, 598, 604

tinder – 157-158, 264, 371

tithe – 94

tlacuiles – 497-498

Tlaloc – 341, 461, 464-465, 467, 471-473

Tlatilco – 459, 471

toad – 162, 185, 341, 420, 458-459, 490

toad bones – 458

toadstool – 160, 201, 307, 334, 337, 341, 407- 408, 420, 440, 570

tobacco – 145, 220, 255, 523

Tollan – 459, 461

Toltec – 455, 459, 462, 464, 466, 471

tonsure – 96, 102, 106, 135, 141, 143, 155, 159

toxins – 25, 29-30, 33, 256, 291, 364, 396-397, 417-418, 545-546, 554

tragedy (Greek) – 17, 115, 226, 344-349, 366, 375

Trajan – 368

trance – xi, 6, 65, 141, 153, 163, 184, 191, 222, 245-246, 250, 251, 253, 257, 366, 401, 454

trans-oceanic/transpacific contact – 475-476

transitional object – 118-119,

transubstantiation – 190

trauma/traumatic – 86, 94, 117, 120, 124, 192, 545

Tree of Jesse – 11, 179, 188-189, 191

Tree of Knowledge – 176, 187

Tree of Life – 11, 156, 189

tree roots – 140, 154-155, 179, 189-191, 227, 302, 393-394, 425

trinity – 188, 191, 474

Trivium – 97

Trojans – 392, 411-412

trophy trumpet – 176

Troy – 356, 404, 411-414, 424, 430

truffles – 166, 409

Trugaeus – 350

Tula – 459, 461

Tunisia – 503

turd – 349, 369, 374

Turnus – 415, 426, 429-430, 432-434, 449

turpentine – 216-218, 262

Typhon – 425, 428

Tyrrhenus – 414, 429, 433

U

UFOs – 525

underworld – 284, 297, 307, 327, 389, 401, 426, 455, 461-462, 464-470, 472-474, 478

unicorn – 185

United States Trust – 579

University of California, Los Angeles – 552

University of Kansas – 569

urine – 105, 135, 159, 161-162, 193, 223, 280, 284, 292-295, 417, 489, 577

US Psychological Warfare – 579, 613

Ussher, J. – ix

uterotonic – 503

V

vagina – 128, 137, 147, 153-154, 184, 194
Valley of Mexico – 471
van Gogh, V. – 217
Vancouver – 51, 549
Vascellum – 487, 495
vasopressin – 39, 43
velum universale – 160, 178
venom – 242, 274, 418, 420, 429-430, 445
Venus – 18, 433, 436, 465, 461-465, 467, 469-475, 477
Veracruz – 459, 477
vesica pisces – 184, 195, 197
Vienna Dioscurides – 99, 150
Virgil – 17, 387, 390-393, 395-396, 400, 402, 408-409, 411, 417, 432-433
Virola tree – 329
Visio – 89, 91, 93, 122, 135, 199
visio-theory – 98
Vision Serpent – 461
visions – 40, 42, 65-66, 86-88, 90, 92-93, 95-96, 98, 102, 106-109, 122-123, 126-127, 134-135, 137-139, 141, 143-145, 157, 167, 169, 192-193, 195, 197-199, 255, 301, 306, 330, 332, 338, 340-341, 346, 362, 365-366, 397, 402, 454-455, 486, 488-490, 494, 502, 505, 508, 521, 533, 550
volcano – 318, 497-498
Volmar – 86, 90, 95-97, 100-102, 106, 111, 113, 115, 120, 133, 135, 138-140, 171, 181, 184, 192-193, 199
Volvariella – 503
vomit/vomiting – 5, 148, 240, 248, 282, 287, 289-290, 293, 330, 472
von Franz, Marie-Louise – 524
Vulcan – 405
vultures – 472
vulva – 128, 147, 184, 194, 196-197, 358, 370-371, 421

W

Wall Street – 576, 585, 596-597
warlocks – 510-511
Wasps – 345, 347-351, 359, 363, 365-369, 377-378
wax plate – 104, 106, 193, 200
werewolf – 368
Weyburn Hospital – 547
Wiccan – 154, 162
Wilbert of Gembloux – 90
wild boar – 185, 224, 259
Wildman – 225, 227, 230-231
wine – 57, 66, 72, 108, 143, 145, 152, 159, 177, 190, 192, 211-213, 218-221, 261, 276, 296, 339, 345-347, 356-364, 368, 374, 376, 403, 413, 416, 420-421, 427, 443, 541-542
wine press of God's wrath – 108
wing – 90, 184, 195, 239, 326, 349, 407, 415-416, 427-428, 501
witches/witchcraft – 133, 149, 154, 162, 167, 261, 397, 402, 504
witches' besom – 227

witches' brew – 98, 143, 162
witches' brooms – 233-234
witches' cauldron – 420
witches' flying ointment – 62, 77, 86, 98, 128, 130-131, 136, 135, 148, 153, 169, 179-180, 222
witches' Sabbath – 154
wolf – 144, 185, 433
wolfsbane – 222
wool/woolen – 130, 182, 225, 288-289, 476
world axis – 187
world soul – 534, 539-540
world spirit – 533, 537
world tree – 235, 242-243, 269, 302-303, 307
wormwood – 152, 217, 232-233, 242, 254

X

Xanthias – 345, 349, 367
Xbalanque – 470
xenobiotic metabolizing genes – 33
Xenokles – 348-349
Xerxes – 218, 367
Xibalba/Xibalbans – 284, 297, 470
xibalbaj okox – 469
Xochipala – 471
Xochipil – 473
Xolotl – 465, 470

Y

Yahweh – 14, 68, 367, 404
Yale University – 321
Yanomami – 329
Yemen – 238-239, 272
yoga – 531-533, 535, 546
yoni – 87, 128, 136-137, 183-184, 196
Yurimagua Indians – 501

Z

Zagros Mountains – 219
Zalmoxis – 368
Zapotec Indians – 477, 498-499
Zapruder film – 598-599
Zetes – 400
Zethos – 422
Zeus – 242-243, 274, 355, 366-368, 370, 373, 395, 404, 408, 411, 418, 423-426, 428, 430
zizania – 397
zodiac – 169, 183
Zoroaster – 63, 65-66, 233-234, 237-238, 301
zucchetto – 178
Zurich Psychology Club – 524

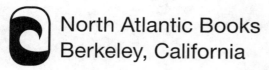